OXFORD WORLD'S CLASSICS

PAST AND PRESENT

THOMAS CARLYLE was born in 1795 in Ecclefechan, a small market
village in Dumfriesshire. He studied for the ministry, enrolled in law
classes, and taught briefly before deciding on a career as a writer.
During the 1820s, his essays and translations helped to introduce
German literature and thought to a British audience. *Sartor Resartus*,
his one full-scale work of imaginative fiction, was first published
periodically in 1833–4. In 1826 Carlyle married Jane Welsh. In 1834
they moved from Scotland to London and settled at Cheyne Row,
Chelsea. It was here that Carlyle wrote the works that confirmed his
position as the most influential of the Victorian cultural leaders: *The
French Revolution* (1837), *On Heroes and Hero-Worship* (1841), *Past
and Present* (1843), *Latter-Day Pamphlets* (1850), and the six-volume
history of *Frederick the Great* (1858–65). His *Reminiscences* were
published shortly after his death, in 1881.

DAVID R. SORENSEN is Professor of English at Saint Joseph's
University, Philadelphia. He has published extensively on Thomas
Carlyle and is a senior editor of the Duke-Edinburgh *Collected
Letters of Thomas and Jane Welsh Carlyle* (1970–). His most recent
publications include the Oxford Scholarly Edition of Carlyle's *The
French Revolution* (2020) and the Oxford World's Classics edition of
the same work (2019). He is also co-editor of *Carlyle Studies Annual*
(2006–).

BRENT E. KINSER is Professor of English at Western Carolina
University. He is an editor of the Duke-Edinburgh *Collected Letters
of Thomas and Jane Welsh Carlyle* (1970–) and managing editor of
Carlyle Letters Online. His most recent work is the Oxford Scholarly
Edition of Carlyle's *The French Revolution* (2020) and the Oxford
World's Classics edition of the same work (2019). He is also co-editor
of *Carlyle Studies Annual* (2006–).

OXFORD WORLD'S CLASSICS

For over 100 years Oxford World's Classics have brought
readers closer to the world's great literature. Now with over 700
titles—from the 4,000-year-old myths of Mesopotamia to the
twentieth century's greatest novels—the series makes available
lesser-known as well as celebrated writing.

The pocket-sized hardbacks of the early years contained
introductions by Virginia Woolf, T. S. Eliot, Graham Greene,
and other literary figures which enriched the experience of reading.
Today the series is recognized for its fine scholarship and
reliability in texts that span world literature, drama and poetry,
religion, philosophy, and politics. Each edition includes perceptive
commentary and essential background information to meet the
changing needs of readers.

OXFORD WORLD'S CLASSICS

THOMAS CARLYLE

Past and Present

Introduction by
DAVID R. SORENSEN

Text Edited with Notes by
DAVID R. SORENSEN
and
BRENT E. KINSER

OXFORD
UNIVERSITY PRESS

OXFORD
UNIVERSITY PRESS

Great Clarendon Street, Oxford, OX2 6DP,
United Kingdom

Oxford University Press is a department of the University of Oxford.
It furthers the University's objective of excellence in research, scholarship,
and education by publishing worldwide. Oxford is a registered trade mark of
Oxford University Press in the UK and in certain other countries

Editorial material © David R. Sorensen and Brent E. Kinser 2023

The moral rights of the authors have been asserted

First Edition published in 2023

Published in the United States of America by Oxford University Press
198 Madison Avenue, New York, NY 10016, United States of America

British Library Cataloguing in Publication Data
Data available

Library of Congress Control Number: 2022948021

ISBN 978-0-19-884108-1

Printed and bound in the UK by
Clays Ltd, Elcograf S.p.A.

CONTENTS

CONTENTS

INTRODUCTION

'Not Yesterday but Today': The Genesis of Past and Present

CARLYLE'S fourth major work *Past and Present* was published in April 1843, two years after *On Heroes and Hero-Worship* (1841), which had been based on series of popular lectures that he delivered in London in 1840.[1] The 'fashionable classes'[2] attending these sessions acclaimed him as a 'Prophet', but he was privately offended that they seemed more impressed by his eccentric Scottish mannerisms and fierce apocalyptic invective than his talents as a historian. The tragic fate of his friend Edward Irving, a Church of Scotland prelate who achieved fame as a charismatic sage and was subsequently deposed from the ministry, sharpened Carlyle's disdain for 'respectable' opinion. In a eulogy he wrote for Irving in 1835, he remarks bitterly: 'By a fatal chance, Fashion cast her eye on him, as on some impersonations of Novel-Cameronianism, some wild product of Nature from the wild mountains; Fashion crowded round him, with her meteor lights, and Bacchic dances; breathed her foul incense on him; intoxicating, poisoning.'[3] In *Reminiscences* (1881), Carlyle recalled his last meeting with the disgraced preacher, whose health was declining: '[Irving] expressed to me his satisfaction at my having taken to "writing History" . . .; study of History, he seemed to intimate, was the study of things real, practical, and actual, and would bring me closer upon all reality whatsoever'.[4]

Carlyle's smouldering resentment against literary 'Fashion' carried over into *Past and Present*. On the one hand, he deliberately designed the work as a response to the 'Condition of England Question' that he

---

[1] See Owen Dudley Edwards, ' "The Tone of the Preacher": Carlyle as Public Lecturer in *On Heroes, Hero-Worship, and the Heroic in History*', in David R. Sorensen and Brent E. Kinser (eds.), *On Heroes, Hero-Worship, and the Heroic in History* (New Haven: Yale University Press, 2013), 199–208.

[2] *The Collected Letters of Thomas and Jane Welsh Carlyle* (hereafter *CL*), ed. Ian Campbell, Aileen Christianson, David R. Sorensen, Jane Roberts, Liz Sutherland, Katherine Inglis, and Brent E. Kinser, 49 vols. (Durham, NC: Duke UP, 1970–), xii. 141.

[3] 'Death of Edward Irving', in *Critical and Miscellaneous Essays* (hereafter *CME*), iii. 321, in *Works*, ed. H. D. Traill, 30 vols. (London: Chapman and Hall, 1896–9).

[4] *Reminiscences* (hereafter *Rem.*), ed. K. J. Fielding and Ian Campbell (Oxford: Oxford World's Classics, 1997), 346.

had posed in his pamphlet *Chartism* (1839), 'What means this bitter discontent of the Working Classes?' (*CME* iv. 119). On the other, he aspired to be more than a celebrity controversialist. In his correspondence, he sends mixed signals of his intentions. He frequently refers to the angry didacticism of this new work as '*A Chartism*, Part Second'. It is a 'Tract for the Times', 'a most questionable, redhot, indignant thing' that 'tells lumps of the truth, in a franker manner than I have ever done hitherto'. He considers the piece as 'one of the most outspoken writings that has ever come from me'. Yet elsewhere, he cryptically vows to handle this 'grand . . . Question' in a 'somewhat unexpected way' in order to fathom its 'moral, political, [and] historical' repercussions (*CL* xvi. 53, 76, 38, 56, 131).

During the period in which he composed this 'indignant thing', he strove assiduously to expand and enrich its rhetorical and thematic boundaries. The manuscripts of the First Draft and Printer's Copy reveal the fruitful tensions in his outlook between representing the past as past and representing the past as present.[5] His narrative bristles with nervous intensity as he repeatedly shifts his tone, from abrasive and provocative to discursive and meditative. Part of this friction was due to the circumstances of the book's creation. *Past and Present* originated in the wake of Carlyle's failure to write a history of Oliver Cromwell's life and times, a project that he pursued 'in earnest from at least 1838'.[6] He admits to Ralph Waldo Emerson on 28 March 1842, 'I had begun to write some Book on Cromwell: I have often begun, but know not how to set about it; the most unutterable of all subjects I ever felt much meaning to lie in it. There is risk yet that, with the loss of still farther labour, I may have to abandon it' (*CL* xvi. 102). With increasing exasperation, Carlyle realized that his methods of history were inextricably connected to his role as a public *provocateur*. He could not write about the past without being embroiled in the controversies of the present.

Though he distrusted and mocked political activism, including his own, he felt compelled to engage imaginatively with entrenched and

---

[5] See Grace Calder, *The Writing of* Past and Present: *A Study of Carlyle's Manuscripts* (New Haven: Yale University Press, 1949), 11 (hereafter Calder). Commenting on Carlyle's hybrid perspective, Lord Acton described Book II of *Past and Present* as 'the most remarkable piece of historical thinking in the language'; see *Lectures on the French Revolution* (London: Macmillan, 1920), 358.

[6] Dale J. Trela, *A History of Carlyle's Oliver Cromwell's Letters and Speeches* (Lampeter: Mellen Press, 1992), 1.

conflicting 'points of vision'.[7] He counsels Emerson on 19 July 1842, 'There is no use in writing of things past, unless they can be made in fact things present: not yesterday at all, but simply today and what it holds of fulfilment and promises is *ours*' (*CL* xv. 229). The stimulus that he received from debate emboldened him to recreate history from the vantage point of the various factions. But the Cromwell material that he had studied thus far was a miasma of 'jumbling, drowsy, endless stupidities' (*CL* xii. 305). In the summer of 1842, Carlyle wallowed in a quagmire of 'Dryasdust' antiquarianism, 'ashamed' of his silence in the face of a public crisis. On 18 July, colliers in Hanley, Staffordshire went on strike and pledged not to resume work until wages and conditions improved. Riots and stoppages soon spread to other towns in the Potteries. By mid-August, Chartists were deeply involved in the unrest, lending their support to the workers' demand that 'all labour cease until the People's Charter become the law of the land'.[8]

On 11 August, a demoralized Carlyle impulsively agreed to join his friend Stephen Spring-Rice, a customs commissioner, for a four-day boat journey to Margate, Ostend, Bruges, and Ghent. Not for the first time in his career, contact with European cultural currents opened his eyes to the insularity of English life. In a written account of the tour, he is typically scathing about the Catholic rituals he witnesses at Bruges, where he entertains a desire to kick the 'fat priests . . . into the canals'. But he asks, 'what would follow were they gone?' His reply looks ahead to *Past and Present*: 'Atheistic Benthamism, French editorial "Rights of Man" and <u>grande nation</u>, that is a far worse thing, a far <u>untruer</u> thing.' Prone to resist Arnoldian 'sweetness and light',[9] Carlyle is nonetheless touched by the sacred relics and artwork

---

[7] Thomas Carlyle, *The French Revolution: A History in Three Volumes* (hereafter *FR*), ed. Mark Cumming, David R. Sorensen, Mark Engel, and Brent E. Kinser (Oxford: Oxford University Press, 2020), i. 165, iii. 237 and n. See also Philip Rosenberg, *The Seventh Hero: Thomas Carlyle and the Theory of Radical Activism* (Cambridge, MA: Harvard University Press, 1974) and Gertrude Himmelfarb, 'Radical History', *Commentary* 58/3 (Sept. 1974), 96–7.

[8] Dorothy Thompson, *The Chartists: Popular Politics in the Industrial Revolution* (1984; London: Breviary, 2013), 205, quoting the Chartist activist Thomas Cooper. See also Robert Fyson, 'The Crisis of 1842: Chartism, the Colliers' Strike and the Outbreak in the Potteries', in James Epstein and Dorothy Thompson (eds.), *The Chartist Experience: Studies in Working-Class Radicalism and Culture* (London: Macmillan, 1982), 194–220.

[9] Matthew Arnold, *Culture and Anarchy* (1869), ed. Jane Garnett (Oxford: Oxford World's Classics, 2009), 9.

that he encounters. In the Church of Our Lady at Bruges, he rhapsodizes about the 'marble mother-and-child by Michel Angelo' and the Virgin's 'air of sorrow [and] infinite earnestness'.[10]

This brief tour may have quietly refreshed his deep spiritual instincts, but the insurgency sweeping through the industrial districts in the north of England continued to unsettle him. In a postscript to his travel narrative he exclaims, 'Alas, while I scribble down these things, all Lancashire is risen in Chartist insurrection. Can a thinking Englishman, in these hours, find nothing suitabler to write!'[11] In another letter to Emerson on 29 August, Carlyle admits that 'the one hope of help' for 'my own poor generation' lay in 'the possibility of new Cromwells, and new Puritans'. But he was hamstrung by his lacklustre research material and daunted by his protean conception of history. 'I cannot write *two Books at once*,' he complains; 'cannot be in the seventeenth century and in the nineteenth century at one and the same moment.' He fretted that if he subsumed the past into the noisy disputes of the 'strange new Today' (p. 22), it might evaporate. The seventeenth century is '*worthless*', he declares, 'except precisely in so far as it can be made the *nineteenth*; and yet let anybody *try* that enterprise!' (*CL* xv. 57). Consumed by disquietude, he appeared to forget that he had already 'tried' a similar 'enterprise' with respect to eighteenth-century France.

Carlyle as a historian was always fascinated by the mysterious ways in which the past perpetually encroached upon the present, imposing itself haphazardly 'through perpetual metamorphoses'.[12] The 'meanest Day', he often mused, is composed of a 'conflux of two Eternities' (*FR* i. 103). In *The French Revolution* (1837), he deliberately conceived 'a Scotch peasant rebellion translated into Parisian Sansculottism'.[13]

---

[10] Thomas Carlyle, 'The Shortest Tour on Record', *Carlyle Studies Annual* 29 (2013), 58–9. See also Brent E. Kinser, 'Thomas Carlyle's Journey to the Netherlands and the Genesis of *Past and Present*', *Carlyle Studies Annual* 29 (2013), 25–38.

[11] 'The Shortest Tour on Record', 80.

[12] *Sartor Resartus*, ed. Rodger L. Tarr (Berkeley and Los Angeles: University of California Press, 2000), 174. As Mark Salber Phillips notes, 'The truth is that every one of Carlyle's histories entailed writing "two books at once".' See *On Historical Distance* (New Haven: Yale University Press, 2013), 122. See also Billie Melman, *The Culture of History: English Uses of the Past 1800–1953* (Oxford: Oxford University Press, 2006), 66–91, and Oliver Goldstein, 'Thomas Carlyle's "radical conservatism in prose"', *Carlyle Studies Annual* 34 (2021–2), 215–43.

[13] Patrick Brantlinger, *The Spirit of Reform: British Literature and Politics, 1832–1867* (Cambridge, MA: Harvard University Press, 1977), 74.

Simultaneously, he recast the revolutionary cataclysm as an admonition to England's governing classes of the terrible cost of apathy and indifference.[14] In his 'FLAME-PICTURE' he likens the predicament of France before the Revolution to Ireland in the 1830s, a 'Sanspotato' nation, 'the third soul of whom had not for thirty weeks each year as many third-rate potatoes as would sustain him' (*FR* iii. 184, 237; *CME* iv. 136). In the autumn of 1842, he re-enacted a familiar pattern in his career and searched for historical figures through whom he could 'express his own convictions about the present'.[15] To release his combative energies, he needed biographical precedents. His rescue from his slough of equivocation was provoked by a series of opportune coincidences.

Still drawn to his fascination with the seventeenth century, Carlyle took a three-day 'pilgrimage to Cromwell land' (*CL* xv. 67) from 6 to 8 September, during which he visited the Protector's birthplace in Huntingdon, house in Ely, and farm in St Ives. He also toured two medieval landmarks, the Abbey of Bury St Edmunds and Ely Cathedral. In *Past and Present*, he recalls a scene that disturbed the tranquillity of his peregrinations. Riding from Huntingdon to St Ives 'where Oliver first took to farming' (*CL* xv. 75), he is shocked by the sight of a group of unemployed labourers, crowding around 'the Workhouse . . . sitting on wooden benches, in front of their Bastille . . . some half-hundred or more of these men. Tall robust figures, young mostly or of middle age; of honest countenance, many of them thoughtful and even intelligent looking men. They sat there, near by one another; but in a kind of torpor, especially in a silence, which was very striking.' Their spiritual deprivation is as notable as their haggard physical state. Their souls are cankered and in their 'manifold inarticulate distress and weariness', they evoke the idea of 'Dante's Hell' (p. 18.).

This grim image of Victorian indigence contrasts sharply with Carlyle's favourable impressions of Bury St Edmunds, 'a prosperous brisk Town . . . with its clear brick houses [and] ancient clean streets' (p. 55), where he is met by John William Donaldson, headmaster of

[14] See Rodger L. Tarr, 'Thomas Carlyle's Growing Radicalism: The Social Context of *The French Revolution*', *Costerus*, 1 (1974), 113–26.
[15] K. J. Fielding, 'A Preface by Carlyle by the Editors', in K. J. Fielding and Rodger L. Tarr (eds.), *Carlyle Past and Present: A Collection of New Essays* (London: Vision Press, 1976), 21.

the local King Edward's School and author of a treatise on Greek tragic drama. Jane Welsh Carlyle, who detested Donaldson, sarcastic-ally mentions to her cousin Jeannie Welsh on 2 September that Carlyle 'was most *abundantly* welcomed to Bury' by the tuft-hunting native of Haddington (*CL* xv. 65). Donaldson may have introduced his guest to local dignitaries and helped organize his itinerary. Though mocking his role as a 'picturesque tourist'—an expression popular-ized by the Edinburgh publishers Adam Black and Charles Black, who included it in the title of their bestselling guide to the Scottish highlands—Carlyle meticulously drew maps for himself and con-ducted a detailed study of his surroundings.

In *Past and Present*, he characterizes the 'long, black and massive . . . monastic ruins' of Bury St Edmunds as 'properly the Funeral Monument of Saint or Landlord Edmund' (pp. 55, 63). He is par-ticularly struck by the sight of three seventeenth-century houses built into the ruins of the west front of the abbey church, which dramatize the interpenetration of the past into the present. A fourth and larger residence at No. 1, The Churchyard ('Abbey Ruins'), belongs to John Greene, 'the present respectable Mayor of Bury',[16] who is a magis-trate and son of the founder of the local Greene King brewery. Carlyle drolly compares him to a Muslim religious mendicant, who has his 'dwelling in the extensive, many-sculptured Tombstone of St. Edmund; in one of the brick niches thereof' (p. 63). The sight of these curious structures prompts Carlyle to reflect that 'Certain Times do crystal-lise themselves in a magnificent manner' (p. 63).[17] He is far less taken with the published plan of the Bury churchwardens to rebuild the Norman Tower, which once served as the ceremonial entrance to the abbey where the monks received 'The Lord Abbot' after his election on Palm Sunday, 11 March 1182.

---

[16] In a further Carlylean twist to historical analogy, John Greene's house was central to a ghost story written by his daughter Margaretta in 1862 about a 'Grey Lady' whose spirit haunted the Abbey Ruins. The book provoked a 'near riot' in 1862 'when people keen to see the ghost of its heroine . . . packed into the town's Great Churchyard'. See *The Secret Disclosed: A Legend of St. Edmund's Abbey*, introd. Francis Young (St Edmunds: St Jurmin Press, 2019), vi.

[17] William Baker has conjectured that another Carlyle MS fragment in the Walpole Collection, King's School, Canterbury was written 'late in 1842 or early 1843'. In the piece, Carlyle describes a visit to the Cistercian 'New Abbey' near Dumfries. The piece seems to be 'an anticipation of *Past and Present*, rather than a stale repetition'. See Baker, 'The Wisdom of Our Ancestors and Daniel Hipps', *Carlyle Newsletter* 3 (1982), 2.

Parodying the logic of restoration in *Past and Present*, Carlyle urges visitors to 'see here the ancient massive Gateway, of architecture interesting to the eye of Dilettantism; and farther on, that other ancient Gateway, now about to tumble, unless Dilettantism, in these very months, can subscribe money to cramp and prop it!' (p. 55). He applies the word 'Dilettantism'—'a lover of art and architecture, a member of the Society of Dilettanti'[18]—with withering accuracy. Tellingly, the churchwardens pitched their funding request on aesthetic rather than spiritual grounds. As *The Bury and Norwich Post* solemnly proclaims on 14 December 1842, 'There is no one at all acquainted with this Tower . . . but must take a deep interest in its fate; and the more intimate their knowledge of the history of art, and the peculiar beauties of which this Tower has been the faithful enduring record, the more anxious will be their desire for its preservation.'[19] For Carlyle, this 'sham-reverence' stands out in stark opposition to Abbot Samson's pious and munificent renovation of the altar supporting the shrine of St Edmund, which had been damaged by fire in 1198. In contrast to the 'Dilettante' scheme of the Bury churchwardens, the abbot's plan to preserve the 'martyred Body of Edmund landlord' is prompted by a 'noble awe' for 'the memory of him, symbol and promoter of many other right noble things' (p. 118).

In a letter to John Sterling on 6 September, Carlyle recounts his 'two hour' visit to Ely Cathedral, which conjures up for him a stirring vision of spiritual reconciliation. He recalls that in this same building, Cromwell once chastised a refractory priest: 'Tonight, as the heaving bellows [of the organ] blew, and the yellow sunshine streamed in thro' those high windows, . . . I looked aloft, and my eyes filled with very tears to look at all this, and remember beside it . . . Oliver Cromwell's, "Cease your fooling, and come out, sir!" In these two antagonisms lie what volumes of meaning!' (*CL* xv. 68). Carlyle's epiphany anticipates the controlling religious argument of *Past and Present*. Until the eighteenth century, England and Scotland were united by a loosely Protestant and theocratic 'Mythus', the roots of which could be traced to the medieval era. In rejecting God, the 'United' Kingdom abandoned a common moral and spiritual heritage that was rooted in

[18] See J. A. W. Bennett, 'Carlyle and the Medieval Past', *Reading Medieval Studies* 4 (1978), 4.

[19] 'The Norman Tower', *The Bury and Norwich Post* (14 Dec. 1842), 2.

a holistic vision of society as a divinely sanctioned and interdependent partnership. Enamoured with material progress, laissez-faire, and 'mammon-worship', the leaders of the country repudiated its national history and traditions, and in consequence, its unique identity.

The 'Magical Pick-Lock': Carlyle and the Chronica Jocelini

The topography of Bury St Edmunds was still fresh in Carlyle's mind when on 12 October he borrowed a copy of John Gage Rokewode's Camden Society edition of *Chronica Jocelini de Brakelonda* (1842) from the London Library. Given his detestation of the 'Dryasdust Printing Societies' (*CME* iv. 347) such as the Camden, Carlyle's praise for Rokewode's edition was unusual.[20] He considered the work both expertly edited and 'most entertaining' (*CL* xv. 129) and soon recognized that the monograph could serve as the *Springwürzel*—the 'magical picklock'[21]—to his embryonic 'moral, political, [and] historical' project. In manuscript jottings written in this period, he abruptly refers to 'Jocelin of St. Edmundsbury', the recto side of which continues a long summary of Cromwell's career (*CL* xv. 129 and n.). He remarks tersely, 'This present book . . . the private chronicle of an old St. Edmundsbury monk, now seven centuries old, is very far removed from us in many ways. . . . And the ideas and ways of life of worthy Jocelin, covered deeper than Pompeii and the lavaashes and inarticulate wreck of seven hundred years—!'[22]

To Carlyle's surprise, the remoteness of Rokewode's text diminished as he probed its contents. Sifting through Jocelin's chronicle, as well as other medieval texts, Victorian travel guides, parliamentary reports, biographies, dictionaries, encyclopaedia entries, and newspapers, he

---

[20] See K. J. Fielding and Heather Henderson, 'Carlyle and the Book Clubs', *Publishing History* 6 (1979), 37–62.

[21] TC, 'Biography' (1832), in *Essays on Literature* (hereafter *EOL*), ed. Fleming McClelland, Brent E. Kinser, and Chris R. Vanden Bossche (Berkeley and Los Angeles: University of California Press, 2020), 135.

[22] Written between 7 September 1841 and 27 November 1843, these jottings were originally miscatalogued in the Forster Collection at the Victoria and Albert Museum (now the National Art Library) as ' "Statesman of the Commonwealth." (1840). MS and Proofs, Letters, etc.: including Fragment of and Materials for a new life of Strafford. Also notes by Mr. Carlyle', Forster Collection (FC 48. e. 36), fo. 56v. Transcription of the MS courtesy of the late Professor K. J. Fielding. (Hereafter abbreviated as Forster Collection.)

pieced together 'a mosaic of allusion':[23] an amorphous patchwork of history, memoir, anecdote, legend, satire, and invective. At an early stage, he labels the work 'Samson of St. Edmundsbury: or Past and Present: (a Historical Essay?)' (Calder, 1), but as his query implies, he remained undecided as to whether he was writing an essay, a pamphlet, or a book. His letters between November 1842 and January 1843 record intermittent progress. On 13 November 1842, he reports to his brother Alexander that 'my writing, after a terrible haggle, does begin to move a little, tho' a very little: I have to be thankful for the day of small things; I must beat lustily while the metal is redhot' (*CL* xv. 179). Three days later he tells his brother John that 'I cannot tell you what this thing I am writing is; I myself do not know' (*CL* xv. 202). Towards the end of December, he expects 'before long to have *something* ready for printing,—tho' not the *thing* I was chiefly meaning' (*CL* xv. 252).

Only Jane Welsh Carlyle, who read the manuscript, was privy to his true intentions. On 21 December 1842, she confides to her cousin Jeannie Welsh that 'Carlyle has . . . a considerable bundle of M.S. *not* about Cromwell at all!—but about that old Abbot of St Edmonds Bury!!—which he "rather wishes me to read and give him my views about" ' (*CL* xv. 246). On 8 January 1843, she divulges the whole 'secret', but warns her cousin, 'see that you keep it to yourself—Carlyle is no more writing about *Oliver Cromwell* than you and I are! . . . I know he has such a way of tacking on extraneous discussions to his subject—but when I found at last a long biography of *that Abbot Samson!* then indeed—I asked what on earth *has* all this to do with Cromwell—and learned that Cromwell was not begun . . . . Nevertheless for I know not what Reason he lets everybody go on questioning him of his Cromwell and answers so as to leave them in the persuasion he is busy with that and nothing else' (*CL* xvi. 14–15). With characteristic shrewdness, Jane supported Thomas's diversionary tactics.

Fending off enquiries, Carlyle wrote with the quiet confidence that he had located his pivotal historical source in Jocelin's 'private Boswellean Notebook' (p. 50). Like the ancient arches that served as a foundation for the houses in the abbey church, the *Chronica Jocelini* sustained his harangue against his times, 'which the horrible aspect of

[23] Stanley Williams, 'Carlyle's Past and Present: A Prophecy', *South Atlantic Quarterly* 21/1 (Jan. 1922), 32.

things here has forced from me' (*CL* xvi. 76). The narrator of the chronicle becomes a familiar figure to him, 'like a next-door neighbour', acting as his guide and confidant (p. 53). In the pages of his manuscript, Jocelin converts 'a mutilated black ruin amid green botanic expanses' into a 'real-phantasmagory' of 'Monks, Abbot, Hero-worship, Government, Obedience, Cœur-de-Lion and St. Edmund's Shrine' (p. 120). Of equal importance, he illuminates the medieval past of St Edmundsbury without idealizing its institutions or inhabitants. The world he occupies, 'England of the Year 1200', is 'no chimerical vacuity or dreamland, peopled with mere vaporous Fantasms' (p. 53). Through the lens of Jocelin, Carlyle affirms his vision of the present as a 'conflux of two Eternities' (*FR* i. 103).

In *Past and Present*, Carlyle refers to the monk as 'a kind of born *Boswell*, though an infinitesimally small one', and in 'spite of his beautiful childlike character, is but an altogether imperfect "mirror" of these old-world things'. He is 'weak and garrulous . . . but human' (pp. 50, 53, 57). Like Boswell, Jocelin's lack of philosophical depth benefits his narrative, which yields radiant vignettes of the hardships, pleasures, and absurdities of everyday life in the medieval world. The monk catches the 'Conversation' ('Biography', in *EOL*, 132)[24] of Bury St Edmunds in a way that 'Chartularies [and] Doctrines of the Constitution' cannot. The voices of the 'thieves at the Abbot's judgment bar' can be heard as they 'deny; claim wager of battle; fight, are beaten, and *then* hanged' (pp. 57, 69). Like Jonathan Swift, whom Carlyle revered for his keen talents of observation, Jocelin exhibits a 'thingy'[25] connection to his environment. With abundant delight, Carlyle revels in his descriptions, spotted through 'fitful apertures', of 'looms dimly going, dye-vats . . . old women spinning yarn', and ' "dungheaps" lying quiet at most doors (*ante foras*, says the incidental Jocelin) for the Town has yet not improved police' (p. 69). For Carlyle, Jocelin's *Chronica* opens up the personal domain of a 'foreign Time' (p. 59), and enables him to gauge its interior condition of life against that of the present.[26]

[24] See also David R. Sorensen, 'Carlyle, Boswell's *Life of Johnson* and the "Conversation of History"', *Prose Studies* 16 (Aug. 1993), 27–40.

[25] Dennis Donoghue, *Jonathan Swift: A Critical Introduction* (Cambridge: Cambridge University Press, 1969), 142.

[26] As Simon Heffer pertinently remarks, 'What gives [*Past and Present*] its force . . . is his use of history to tell the story'; see *Moral Desperado: A Life of Thomas Carlyle* (London: Weidenfeld and Nicolson, 1997), 228.

The Catholic priest and historian David Knowles succinctly summarizes the historical value of Jocelin's pedestrian views: 'None of the
conversation preserved by [him] deserves to live in virtue of any
intrinsic excellence; it is merely the ephemeral stuff that passes in any
group of men; its only value is that it shows us in photographic detail
what otherwise could be reconstructed but vaguely in the imagination, and presents us with a glimpse of the daily life that is elsewhere
concealed behind the conventional language of the typical letter-
writers and chroniclers.'[27] In 'the gossip of one poor monk' (p. 123),
Carlyle encounters a precious artefact free of theological varnish that
shone a clear but flickering light on 'an extinct species' (p. 52). With
his eye fixed firmly on practical matters, Jocelin is ideally suited to
write the biography of Abbot Samson, a man whose faith never
inclines him to retreat from worldly responsibility.

The monk's laconic manner is important to Carlyle for rhetorical,
as well as historical, reasons. In *Past and Present*, he is acutely sensi-
tive to the fact that a wide variety of writers have already used the
Middle Ages as a means to condemn the iniquities of industrialism,
including William Cobbett, Samuel Taylor Coleridge, Benjamin
Disraeli, Robert Southey, Augustus Welby Pugin, and Sir Walter
Scott. In the House of Commons, the 'Young Englanders' advanced
a political programme founded on an idealized notion of feudal
England. Led by Alexander Baillie Cochrane, Lord John Manners,
and George Augustus Smythe, the movement gained notoriety with
its advocacy of paternalism, guilds, and agrarian communalism.
Though he shared Young England's hostility to laissez-faire, Carlyle
distanced himself from their 'shovel-hat' nostalgia for an aristocratic
and bucolic idyll (*CL* xvii. 312). The *Chronica Jocelini*, he ascertains,
is an effective antidote to their 'sentimental and other cobwebberies'
(p. 191).

Jocelin's 'descendental' portrayal of 'Brother Samson' awakens
deep emotions in Carlyle. It is no coincidence that in Book II of *Past
and Present*, the abbot's character coalesces in his imagination with
that of his father, a stonemason, builder, and farmer, whom he eulo-
gized in an 1832 memoir that was included in *Reminiscences*. In his

---

[27] Knowles, *The Monastic Order in England: A History of Its Development from the
Times of St Dunstan to the Fourth Lateran Council 940–1216* (hereafter Knowles),
2nd edn. (Cambridge: Cambridge University Press, 1966), 307.

opening reference to the *Chronica Jocelini*, Carlyle mentions that 'often, in the portrait of early grandfathers, this and the other enigmatic feature of the newest grandson shall disclose itself, to mutual elucidation' (p. 49). Abbot Samson and James Carlyle manifest a moral and spiritual strength that is apparent in their philosophy, disposition, language, and religion. Contemptuous of 'the clamours or the murmurs of Public Opinion', Carlyle senior stoically applies 'the great maxim of his philosophy . . . that man was created to work, not to speculate, or feel, or dream'. His 'toil and patient and perennial endurance' are emblems of his faith (*Rem.*, 7, 8, 17).

In 1795, the year of Thomas's birth, James Carlyle was roughly the same age as Abbot Samson in 1173, when he became 'Master' to the novice Jocelin. From his earliest days, Thomas was 'ever more or less awed and chilled before [his father]' (*Rem.*, 14). James Carlyle was 'a natural man; singularly free from all manner of affectation . . . fearing God and diligently working in God's Earth with contentment, hope and unwearied resolution'. 'He was irascible, choleric, and we all dreaded his wrath,' Carlyle recollects, 'yet passion never mastered him, or maddened him; it rather inspired him with new vehemence of insight, and more piercing emphasis of wisdom.' When angered, 'his words were like sharp arrows that smote into the very heart'. James Carlyle belonged to a world of 'Substance and Solidity', and was 'among the last of the true men, which Scotland (on the old system) produced, or can produce'. He is a 'half developed' version of Abbot Samson, lacking any formal learning, but though denied an education, he spent from his 'small hard-earned funds' to send his son to university. Carlyle hypothesizes that 'perhaps among Scotch peasants [he was] what Samuel Johnson was among English Authors'. At the centre of his life was his religion, the 'pole-star' of his life that 'made him and kept him, "in all points a man"' (*Rem.*, 7, 9, 6, 8, 7, 13, 5, 10, 13). With rapt concentration, the son read Jocelin's account of Abbot Samson through the lens of another upright and strict 'Master'.

In *Past and Present*, Carlyle emphasizes Abbot Samson's spiritual ancestry not only with his father but also with the two dominant 'lineal children' (p. 49) of English and Scottish history, John Knox and Oliver Cromwell. The abbot stands at the fountainhead of Carlyle's genealogy of morals: he is the forefather of Knox, whom he describes in *On Heroes* as 'a good honest intellectual talent, no transcendent one' and Cromwell, as 'a sober industrious farmer . . . a true devout

man'.[28] For Carlyle, Rokeby's edition of the *Chronica Jocelini* symbolically fills in a gaping typological elision in Scottish history. In *On
Heroes*, he observes that until the emergence of Knox in the sixteenth
century, Scotland was a 'poor barren country, full of continual broils,
dissensions . . . a people in the last state of rudeness and destitution,
little better than Ireland at this day'. Knox's renown is of 'world-
interest'. According to Carlyle, he is 'the Chief Priest and Founder . . .
of the Faith that became Scotland's, New England's, Oliver Cromwell's',
and the progenitor of 'Scotch Literature and Thought, Scotch
Industry; James Watt, David Hume, Walter Scott, Robert Burns'
(*Heroes*, 122–4).[29]

The *Chronica Jocelini* offers Carlyle the missing first chapter of this
national epic, with Abbot Samson incarnating the 'religiosity' that
later incited the Scottish Reformation and Puritan Revolution.[30]
Their common bond is the silent credo that 'man was created to
work'. Carlyle sees no difference between 'Palace-building' and
'Kingdom-founding': each task calls for individual renunciation in
a greater service to God and society. At the core of the Scottish-
English character is the precept that 'food and all else were simply
and solely there as a means of *doing work*' (*Rem.* 6, 16). Personally,
Carlyle's Abbot Samson exhibits the same 'Faithfulness, Veracity, real
Worth' (p. 135) that associates him with Knox's Scotland, Cromwell's
England, and his father's 'old system'. The abbot is a 'stout-made'
individual of 'grave taciturn ways' who is a 'thoughtful, firm-standing
man; much loved by some, not loved by all; his clear eyes flashing
into you, in an almost inconvenient way!' (p. 173–4). Religion is the
'pole-star' of his life as well, and his 'worship was like his daily bread

[28] Carlyle, *On Heroes, Hero-Worship, and the Heroic in History* (hereafter *Heroes*), ed.
Michael K. Goldberg, Joel J. Brattin, and Mark Engel (Berkeley and Los Angeles:
University of California Press, 1993), 127, 183.

[29] Carlyle used the same argument to reject the liberal idea that the Declaration of
Arbroath, signed in 1320, represented the birth of democracy and Scottish independ-
ence. See David R. Sorensen, ' "Old Round O": Carlyle, Knox, and the Declaration of
Arbroath', in Klaus Peter Müller (ed.), *Scotland and Arbroath 1320–2020* (Berlin: Peter
Lang, 2020), 289–306.

[30] The *Chronica Jocelini* helped to reinforce Carlyle's conception of the 'Puritan
Revolution' as a religious, rather than a political, phenomenon. As Blair Worden notes,
'In the Eighteenth Century Whigs and biographers of Cromwell had been embarrassed
by the "enthusiasm" of the Roundhead cause. Carlyle made its "enthusiasm" a merit.'
See 'Thomas Carlyle and Oliver Cromwell', *Proceedings of the British Academy* 105
(2000), 138.

. . . which he ate at stated intervals, and lived and did his work upon!' For Carlyle, Abbot Samson's Catholicism is essentially Scottish: 'This is [his] Catholicism of the Twelfth Century—something like the *Ism* of all true men in all true centuries' (p. 113).

With evident satisfaction, Carlyle repeats Samson's anecdote about disguising himself as a Scotsman on his first trip to Rome to avoid being imprisoned by the supporters of the antipope, Victor IV (Cardinal Ottaviano), to whom the Scots were loyal. The abbot recounts 'putting on the garb of a Scotchman, and taking the gesture of one, . . . and when anybody mocked at me, I would brandish my staff in the manner of that weapon they call gaveloc, uttering comminatory words after the way of the Scotch'. In a footnote, Carlyle proudly points out that '*Gaveloc* is still the Scotch name for crowbar' (p. 75). From his perspective, Samson's disguise is redundant. In Jocelin's text, the abbot evinces a steely temperament, which combines 'rigorous stoicism and Calvinism which is Hyper-Stoicism . . . suffer, abstain; thou art there to abstain and endure' (TC to John Gibson Lockhart, 5 April 1842; *CL* xiv. 122). He is a man 'whom no severity would break to complain, and no kindness soften into smiles or thanks' (p. 76).

The abbot's ascent from 'poor mendicant' to '*Dominus Abbas*' convinces Carlyle that '[h]e that cannot be servant of many, will never be master, true guide and deliverer of many' (p. 89–90). Like the 'irascible and choleric' James Carlyle, Samson can 'rage like a wolf', but represses his anger to conserve it 'as noble central heat, fruitful, strong, beneficent; not . . . as wasteful volcanoism to scorch and consume!' (p. 92). As a leader, he is a 'skilful man; full of cunning insight, lively interests; always discerning the road to his object, be it circuit, be it short-cut, and victoriously travelling forward thereon' (p. 111). To the charge that Jocelin portrays the abbot as 'too secular for a devout man', Carlyle cites the example of Samson returning to the abbey after a 'dusty pilgrimage', and sitting silently 'at the foot of St. Edmund's Shrine' (p. 111). On two occasions, Carlyle reinforces the idea of the abbot's Scottish piety by rendering Jocelin's Latin translations from the Greek Vulgate in the English of the Scottish Metrical Psalter (1650). In one memorable instance, he sternly rebukes 'the lazy Monks' for giving the abbot 'the most trouble'. His harsh verdict, borrowed from the Psalter, is applicable to nineteenth-century Scotland as well as twelfth-century Bury St Edmunds: 'We have become a laughing stock to mankind' (p. 98–9).

The source of Abbot Samson's strength is his flinty spirituality. Carlyle is drawn to the monk because Samson emerges from obscurity to become 'a man of power, and not simply within his region, where he acted as the king's vice-gerent'. The monastery of Bury St Edmunds is 'not a withdrawn community, secluded and segregated from ordinary life . . . but a centre of political power and influence'.[31] Moreover, when the abbot assumes his new position, the convent is in a state of moral, economic, and spiritual 'dilapidation'. The parlous fiscal state of the abbey reflects the moral bankruptcy of its administrators: 'rain beating through it, material rain and metaphorical, from all quarters of the compass. . . . Our Prior is remiss; our Cellarers, officials are remiss, our Monks are remiss: what man is not remiss?' (p. 88). Amidst this upheaval, Carlyle apprehends a civic ideal that is absent from his own century: the organic conception of society as a hierarchical body that tied individual free will to the higher duties of labour, learning, cooperation, and worship. In restoring the fiscal health of the Bury St Edmunds monastery, Abbot Samson also revitalizes the feudal dream of society as an aggregation of mutually responsible citizens of God.

Samson's 'right good apprenticeship', like those of Knox and Cromwell, consists in applying the lesson that 'to learn obeying is the art of governing' (p. 89). In Carlyle's mind, the abbot's training foreshadows certain stages of the *Bildung* ('self-development') doctrine of Goethe, 'the first of the moderns' (*Rem.*, 321), who teaches the wisdom of self-renunciation (*Entsagen*) and the 'harmonious development of being, the first and last object of all true culture' (*CME* i. 20).[32] The Weimar 'Genius' infused Carlyle with a reverence for a Pietist 'religious life that relied on meditation, inwardness and the aspiration towards moral goodness'.[33] Carlyle notices an analogous process unfolding in the life of Abbot Samson. Prior to his election, he undergoes a rigorous training of moral, intellectual, and spiritual purification, and teaches himself to be a skilled linguist, jurist, and preacher. Like Goethe's Wilhelm Meister, he acquires the 'talent of silence' (p. 96), with the knowledge that the 'best is not to be explained by

[31] Diana Greenway and Jane Sayers, introduction to *Chronicle of the Abbey of Bury St Edmunds* (Oxford: Oxford World's Classics, 2008), p. ix.

[32] See John Lamb, ' "Spiritual Enfranchisement": *Sartor Resartus* and the Politics of *Bildung*', *Studies in Philology* 107/2 (2010), 259–82.

[33] Jeremy Adler, *Johann Wolfgang von Goethe* (London: Reaktion Books, 2020), 42.

words. The spirit in which we act is the highest matter' (*Works*, xxiv. 76). But Carlyle refuses to idealize Samson. He values him for his skills as 'an able administrator, a firm and just governor, and an upright, God-fearing man, and such have not been wanting to any profession or in any age' (Knowles, 306–7). For Carlyle, the 'want' of such governors in early Victorian England is the urgent imperative of the age, which buttresses his own attempts to 'revive' the 'faint image' of 'a man fearing God, and fearing nothing else; of whom as First Lord of the Treasury, as King, Chief Editor, High Priest, we could be so glad and proud' (p. 123).

'Horrid Enchantment': England in the Industrial Age

In a diary entry of May 1843, Emerson analyzed the 'independent' manner in which Carlyle formulated his 'masterly criticism on the times' in *Past and Present*. Comparing him to 'Gulliver among the Lilliputians', Emerson defines Carlyle's main purpose in the book: 'The poet is here for this, to dwarf and destroy all merely temporary circumstance, and to glorify the perpetual circumstance of men, e. g. dwarf British Debt and raise Nature and social life.' Here is the secret to the creation of 'Carlyle's . . . immortal newspaper'.[34] The Swiftian reversal of time and proportion that Emerson notes is germane to Carlyle's strategy in the three 'redhot' books that enclose the biography of 'The Ancient Monk': 'Proem', 'The Modern Worker', and 'Horoscope'. Emerson could not have known the extent to which his friend forefronted quotidian detail in his narrative. Though he was hesitant to admit the fact, Carlyle was a vigilant and avid reader of newspapers, regularly combing the columns of *The Examiner*, edited by his friend 'the philosophic radical' Albany Fonblanque, and often consulting the more conservative *Times*, edited by John Delane. In addition, family members routinely sent him him articles from the northern and Scottish papers. In *Past and Present*, he exploits these assets exhaustively to convey an electric impression of the 'inane Chimera' of public life in the industrial age.

Carlyle configures his text as a 'Tailor's Hell' (p. 238), a storage area under a tailor's table into which scraps and shreds of excess cloth are

---

[34] *The Correspondence of Thomas Carlyle and Ralph Waldo Emerson, 1834–1872*, ed. Charles Eliot Norton, 2 vols. (Boston: Osgood, 1883), ii. 35.

thrown. His aim is to show that the vaunted 'Force of Public Opinion' (p. 40), the arbiter of correct judgement in politics and morality, is little more than a repository of vapid platitudes. Fittingly, Carlyle 'raises' the past and 'dwarfs' the present by attacking the sycophants of 'Dilettantism and 'Mammonism' in their own language. He jeers at their inflated sense of importance and uses repetition and inverted commas to ridicule their bluster. The literary critic John Rosenberg aptly delineates the result as 'a kind of estranged or inverted elegy, in which the past usurps the present, and the present appears phantasmal or unreal'.[35] In *Past and Present*, every sphere of nineteenth-century life—cultural, economic, philosophical, political, scientific, and theological—possesses a hallucinatory quality.

This 'horrid enchantment' arises as a result of the displacement of divinity in the eighteenth century: 'To speak in the ancient dialect, we "have forgotten God;"'—in the most modern dialect and very truth of the matter, we have taken up the Fact of this Universe as it *is not*' (p. 129). Carlyle himself is uneasily poised between the two 'dialects', venerating the stringent certitudes of Abbot Samson, James Carlyle, John Knox, and Oliver Cromwell, without believing in 'historical Christianity' or the 'facts alleged in the Apostles' creed'.[36] But he is still confident that the Bible offers a symbolic and poetic version of the truth (a 'Proem') that can spur noble and heroic thoughts and actions. He steadfastly espouses the belief that all things in the universe are beholden to and judged by divine 'Truth'.[37] During the 'Reign of No-God' (*Cromwell, Works*, vi. 1), which began in the sceptical eighteenth century and carried over into the nineteenth, England's leaders 'have forgotten the right Inner True, and taken up with the Outer Sham-true' (p. 22). They operate with the assurance that all ethical issues can be settled by the litmus tests of Benthamite 'Enlightened Selfishness', the 'cash nexus', and the 'Greatest Happiness Principle'. This trinity comprises the 'Social Gangrene' (p. 129) of Utilitarianism, which infects all classes and ranks, and creates a fractured society that is the moral and spiritual antithesis of twelfth-century Bury St Edmunds.

[35] Rosenberg, *Elegy for an Age: The Presence of the Past in Victorian Literature* (London: Anthem Press, 2005), 17.

[36] James Anthony Froude, *Thomas Carlyle: A History of the First Forty Years of His Life, 1795–1835*, 2 vols. (London: Longmans and Green, 1882), ii. 260.

[37] See Ruth apRoberts, *The Ancient Dialect: Thomas Carlyle and Comparative Religion* (Berkeley and Los Angeles: University of California Press, 1988), 66–7.

In Book I of *Past and Present*, Carlyle organizes a montage of phrases and images that captures the 'fatal paralysis' of a nineteenth-century governing authority that has become a 'deceptive Simulacrum' (pp. 21, 260). The manners and morals of the leaders betray their crude literalism and imperviousness to the divine. They mistake 'jargon' for clear speech, 'sham-heroes' for heroes, 'Nature' for 'Redtape', and 'Fact' for 'Semblance'. Their legitimacy is bolstered by a phalanx of civil servants, specialists, journalists, political economists, and pamphleteers who cater to their infatuation with 'Quack' panaceas. Carlyle deftly employs the myths of Midas and the Sphinx to exhibit the limits of this 'Enlightened' system. The first myth presents the anomalous spectacle of a country 'full of wealth . . . dying of inanition'; the second, of its leaders failing to answer the Sphinx's question, 'What is to be done?' (pp. 17, 37).

While its present-day governing classes vacillate, Carlyle thunders, 'this rich English Nation has sunk or is fast sinking into a state, to which . . . there was literally never any parallel' (p. 19). In a letter to the Scottish political economist and professor of theology Thomas Chalmers on 11 October 1841, he cites 'the late trial at Stockport, in Cheshire, of a human father and human mother, for poisoning three of their children to gain successively some £3, 8s. from a Burial Society for each of them'. The murder case of Ann and Robert Sandys was shocking, but probably not exceptional. Carlyle imparts to Chalmers that a 'barrister of my acquaintance' has told him 'that the official people durst not go farther into this business; that this case was by no means a solitary one there; that, on the whole, they thought it good to close up the matter swiftly again from the light of day, and investigate it no deeper' (*CL xiii.* 275). His informant was Bryan Waller Procter, who travelled in the northern circuit as a metropolitan commissioner of lunacy. Adopting the pen name 'Barry Cornwall', Procter contributed poetry to many journals and wrote 'The Burial Club, 1839' about the Sandys scandal.[38]

Procter's conjecture was substantiated by the Poor Law reformer Edwin Chadwick, who published an *Inquiry into the Practice of Interment in Towns* in 1843. In his report, he quotes from a letter written by Henry Coppock, town clerk of Stockport, dated 25 January

---

[38] See Coventry Patmore (ed.), *Bryan Waller Procter: An Autobiographical Fragment and Biographical Notes*, ed. Coventry Patmore (Boston: Roberts, 1877), 226–7.

1843: 'I have no doubt that infanticide to a considerable extent has been committed in the borough of Stockport'. Chadwick adds that Robert Sandys's death sentence was 'commuted to transportation for life . . . without any communication to the parties prosecuting'.[39] Once more contemplating the houses built into the ruins of the abbey church, Carlyle devises an evocative metaphor of a hidden landscape concealed beneath familiar geographical forms to represent 'an incident worth lingering on': 'In the British land a human Mother and Father, of white skin and professing the Christian religion, had done this thing. . . . Such instances are like the highest mountain apex emerged into view; under which lies a whole mountain region and land, not yet emerged' (p. 19). The Sandys family belongs to a geographical and cultural region that is far more 'foreign' to the 'British land' than Jocelin's ancient abbey of Bury St Edmunds.

For Carlyle, no event displays the myopia of the governing classes, or their political opponents, more conspicuously than the Manchester Insurrection of July and August 1842. The quelling of the riots in the industrial districts in September generates a predictable chorus of reactions, all of which seem 'spectral'. Only the workers themselves, in their fearless call for 'A fair day's-wages for a fair-day's work', articulate a clear and direct policy that is based on the principles of 'eternal Justice'. But their assertion of this 'everlasting right of man' is soon muffled by a cacophony of competing views from 'Landlord interests, Manufacturing interests, Tory–Whig interests, and who knows what other interests' (pp. 30–1).

Whig and Liberal opinion, adhering to the verities of 'political economy', blames the riots on the Corn Law tariffs, which violate the law of 'Supply-and-demand, law of Laissez-faire, and other idle Laws and Un-laws' (p. 33); Tories console themselves that, in the words of a *Times* editorial, 'the character of this movement' has 'none of those elements which make a really popular movement formidable'.[40] Meanwhile, members of the radical 'Continental Democratic Movement', some of whom Carlyle knew personally, accuse the English insurrectionists of displaying 'a want of the proper animal

[39] *Report on the Sanitary Conditions of the Labouring Population of Great Britain: A Supplementary Report on the Results of a Special Inquiry into the Practice of Interment in Towns* (London: Clowes, 1843), 235, 237.
[40] *The Times* (17 Aug. 1842), 4.

courage indispensable in these ages' (p. 28). Contrary to the political consensus, he affirms that the Manchester Insurrection is a profoundly heroic and constructive accomplishment, the reverberations of which can be detected throughout society.

Like 'Truth' and 'Justice', work for Carlyle constitutes one of the primordial bonds between God and humanity, and without it, nothing of 'Substance and Solidity' can exist for long. The degeneration of workers and work forms the core of the 'Condition of England Question', and starkly contradicts Victorian truisms about 'Progress', 'Freedom', and 'Democracy'. In 'a manner audible to every reflective soul in this kingdom', the Manchester operatives boldly and courageously raise the question that has 'become *our* Sphinx-riddle': ' "What do you mean to do with us?" ' It is one that excites 'deep pity in all good men, deep anxiety in all men whatever; and no conflagration or outburst of madness came to cloud that feeling anywhere, but everywhere it operates unclouded' (p. 30).

In Book I, their question stands out as a palpable 'Fact' amidst the 'entanglements' of 'clouded' theories and 'Formulas' being touted by politicians and political economists. As Carlyle nimbly suggests in Book II, 'Monk Samson' grapples with a similar question following his election as abbot in 1182. The problem of 'what do do' with his monks and the abbey engrosses his faculties for the remainder of his life. But unlike the governing classes of Victorian England, he regards himself as a 'servant' of his flock, suffering 'from them, and for them', and leading them 'out of weakness into strength, out of defeat into victory'. Jocelin's final view of Abbot Samson depicts him immersed in a flurry of activity, 'bustling and . . . justling till the still Night come'. 'Across the chasm of Seven Centuries', Carlyle mercurially substitutes this fading image of purposeful and devoted industry with a harrowing profile of the 'Modern Worker', mired in hunger, bewilderment, and unemployment (pp. 91, 119–20, 57).

'The Stupidest in Speech, The Wisest in Action': Work, Leadership, Democracy, and the Future of Industrial Society

In the final two books of *Past and Present*, Carlyle explores ways that the spiritual malaise of the modern world—'man has lost the *soul* out of him' (p. 129)—has vitiated every layer of its social order and has created an elaborate network of mutually reinforcing '*Un*veracities'.

In 'senate-houses, spouting-clubs, leading-articles, pulpits and platforms', pundits laud the merits of laissez-faire and industrialists defer to the ineluctable laws of 'Supply-and-demand, . . . Free-trade, [and] Competition'. Relations between masters and workers are restricted to '*Cash-payment*', which 'absolves and liquidates all engagements of man' (pp. 170, 137). The eclipse of 'God's absolute laws' by this new 'Gospel' robs work of its sacred element. Driven by the need for greater efficiency, industrialists categorize their employees as units of production, subdivide their tasks ('the division of labour'), and separate them from the final result of their labour. In turn, this Benthamite splintering of work for the sake of greater productivity undermines creativity, initiative, and self-worth. As a result, Carlyle insists, the spiritual health of workers deteriorates as the 'cash-nexus' numbs their interest in anything other than physical survival.[41]

For Carlyle, the 'Phantasm' of modern life extends to material goods themselves, the intrinsic value of which exists in inverse proportion to the 'Puffery' expended on them through the medium of advertising. He muses that the cheapness and shabbiness of existence are embodied by 'the very Paper I now write on . . . made, it seems, partly of plaster-lime well-smoothed, and obstructs my writing!' In the present arrangements, 'You are lucky if you can find now any good Paper,—any work really *done*; search where you will, from highest Phantasm apex to lowest Enchanted basis' (p. 133). He knows from bitter experience that the words he writes are subject to the same codes that oblige him to use this inferior paper. His position as an author, subject to the 'present laws of copyright' (pp. 46–7), leads him to sympathize with those who suffer at the mercy of these same 'nomadic' economic principles that require all people to be left to fend for themselves.

To the chagrin of Tories, Whigs, and Radicals, Carlyle refuses to endorse any of their political aims. In *Past and Present* he declares, 'We write no Chapter on the Corn-Laws, in this place' (p. 165). He was reiterating sentiments that he expressed in a letter of 24 January 1840 to the Manchester editor Thomas Ballantyne, who asked why he

---

[41] Frank Lea has argued that for Karl Marx, as for Carlyle, the division of labour was the enemy of 'all-round development': 'No matter how preoccupied with Wages, Prices and Profits Marx may be, he never loses sight of that Goethean ideal'; see *The Ethics of Reason: An Essay in Moral Philosophy* (London: Brentham Press, 1975), 189. See also Gareth Stedman Jones, *Karl Marx: Greatness and Illusion* (Cambridge, MA: Harvard University Press, 2016), 43–4, 72–3.

had not included a section in his pamphlet *Chartism* (1839) on 'the abrogation of the Corn-Laws'. Carlyle omits the topic, he explains, because it is 'the Cause of the Middle-Classes and manufacturing Capitalists still *more* than it is that of the Lower Classes'. Instead, he prefers to lend his voice to a 'great[er] cause': 'The soul of all justifiable Radicalism as I think, and of which this other is but an outpost and preliminary, continues *dumb*, able to express itself only in groans and convulsions, and does need a spokesman' (*CL* xii. 23). The abolition of the Corn Laws will remove a barrier to trade, but it will not ease the burdens of the working poor for long: 'If our Trade in twenty years, "flourishing" as never Trade flourished, could double itself; yet then also, by the old Laissez-faire method, our Population is doubled: we shall then be as we are, only twice as many of us, twice and ten times as unmanageable!' (p. 169). In Carlyle's view, the arguments of the Corn Law repealers in the name of laissez-faire are no more relevant to the working classes than the defence of the status quo offered by members of the idle 'Game-preserving Aristocracy' (p. 260).

In *Past and Present*, Carlyle reserves his harshest vituperation for members of the idle nobility and their supporters among the Oxbridge establishment. He exposes the collusion between them in his handling of a 'jocose' remark uttered by Dr Robert Bullock Marsham, warden of Merton College, Oxford and an opponent of the repeal of the tariffs, at a meeting of Buckinghamshire Conservatives on 24 January 1843. In a speech reported in *The Times*, Marsham dismisses the claim that England does not produce sufficient food for its population, and disputes the figure used by Chartists and Anti-Corn Law League activists that 10,000,000 people were starving: 'They forget that 5,000,000 live on oatmeal and more than 5,000,000 rejoice in potatoes. Put these together, and it will be found, *communibus annis*, that the kingdom does in fact support its population, and without much distress.'[42] Carlyle seizes on the comment as a clear illustration of the complacency with which educational leaders encourage the 'insolent Donothingism' of the aristocracy. Their mutual indifference to the Dantean spectacle of the '5,000,000' living on potatoes jeopardizes the prospects for peaceful political reform. More ominously, Carlyle fears, aristocratic cynicism and snobbery will kindle the 'Berserkir-rage' of the English working classes: 'When two millions

[42] *The Times* (26 Jan. 1843), 4.

of one's brother-men sit in Workhouses, and five millions, as is insolently said, "rejoice in potatoes," there are various things that must be
begun, let them end where they can' (pp. 140, 151, 153).

In vowing to speak for the silent working classes, Carlyle distinguishes between their 'grim inarticulate veracity' (p. 155) and the
political aims they uphold as Chartists. The true cause of their misery
lies in the 'dumb' regions of their 'souls', beyond the 'fish-oil transparencies' of the 'People's Petition' (p. 30). '*Laissez-faire*' has crushed
their aspirations for social harmony, political consensus, and moral
equilibrium. The world they inhabit is a spiritual void: they are ener-
vated by dispiriting poverty, robbed of any curiosity or wonder about
the natural world, and cut off from both the past and the future.
Carlyle's attitude to their political aspirations is double-edged. He
applauds the Chartist goal of individual reform as a prerequisite
to political change, which coincides with his own commitment to
Goethe's ideal of *Bildung*, but doubts whether such noble objectives
can ever be attained through the ignoble vehicle of the 'ballot box'.

Deceived by the 'Morrison's Pill' of popular sovereignty, the working classes fail to grasp how the political system functions to weaken
them individually and collectively. In *Chartism*, Carlyle argues that
'Democracy' is 'the consummation of No-government and *Laissez-
faire*' (*CME* iv. 159). In *Past and Present*, he enlarges the list to include
'No Society'. 'We call it a Society,' he laments, 'and go about professing openly the totalest separation, isolation' (p. 137). In theory,
parliamentary democracy caters to the interests of all people, but in
practice, 'the National Palaver' is 'a vested interest' of the wealthy
and privileged that is rife with bribery and corruption. It provides the
veneer of consensus to an arena of 'mutual hostility', 'cloaked under
due Laws-of-war named "fair competition"'' (pp. 196, 137). Since the
passage of the Reform Bill in 1832, the tendency of politicians to regard
society as a 'Body-politic', rather than a 'Soul-politic' (*CME* ii. 67)
has accelerated. Not coincidentally, the Act signalled the ascendancy
of 'Plugson of Undershot,' the champion of 'Manchester Commercial
Philosophy' (*CL* xlvi. 11) and 'Bobus Higgins, Sausage-maker,' the
worshipper of 'power, cash, [and] celebrity' (p. 41), at the same time
as it left the working classes vulnerable to the inconstant laws of supply and demand.

In Book IV of *Past and Present*, Carlyle devises his own idiosyncratic
version of a 'Horoscope', by substituting the birth of democracy for

an individual, and by assessing the disposition of the 'godly centuries' rather than the planets. Having documented the fiery 'Death-Birth' (*FR* i. 64) of 'Democracy' in *The French Revolution*, Carlyle concedes in Book III that it 'is everywhere the inexorable demand of these ages, swiftly fulfilling itself' (p. 193). He then positions himself adroitly in relation to Alexis de Tocqueville, whose *Democracy in America* (1835, 1840) recently received an appreciative reception in the English press.[43] After reading the first two volumes, Carlyle informs Mill that 'Tocqueville . . . suits you a little better than he did me' (7 Oct. 1840; *CL* xii. 278), but he discreetly takes note of the French author's reservations about the political culture of the new republic.

Reviewing Tocqueville's first volume in 1835, Mill discussed the Frenchman's prognosis that under democratic rule, 'all individuality of character, and independence of thought and sentiment, [will] be prostrated under the despotic yoke of public opinion'. He then cites Tocqueville's disparaging opinion that 'I am acquainted with no country in which there reigns, in general, less independence of mind, and real freedom of discussion, than in America'.[44] In *Past and Present*, Carlyle receives their testimony as a confirmation that democracy is inimical to the Goethean ideal of self-cultivation, which he prefigures in the 'rigorous stoicism' of Abbot Samson, John Knox, Oliver Cromwell, and James Carlyle. Self-restraint is impossible to nurture in a setting where individuals are at the mercy of 'Free-trade, Competition, and Devil take the hindmost' (p. 156). '[T]hought, reflection, articulate utterance and understanding' (p. 234), the bedrock of true 'liberty', are eroded by this squalid and unremitting fight for a decent wage. In such circumstances, 'Democracy' means 'despair of finding any Heroes to govern you' (p. 193).[45]

---

[43] See e.g. *The Times* (9 June 1835), 5; *The Examiner* (8 Nov. 1835), 713; *The Sun* (20 Oct. 1835), 3; and *The Morning Post* (24 Oct. 1835), 2. See also Joanna Innes, Mark Philp, and Robert Saunders, 'The Rise of Democratic Discourse in the Reform Era: Britain in the 1830s and 1840s', in Joanna Innes and Mark Philp (eds.), *Re-imagining Democracy in the Age of Revolutions: America, France, Britain, Ireland 1750–1850* (Oxford: Oxford University Press, 2013), 114–28.

[44] 'De Tocqueville on Democracy in America', *The London Review* 30.3 (July-Jan., 1835–6), 119. For Mill on Tocqueville, see Frank Prochaska, *Eminent Victorians on Victorian Democracy: The View from Albion* (Oxford: Oxford University Press, 2012), 23–46.

[45] See George Currie, 'Alexis de Tocqueville, John Stuart Mill and Thomas Carlyle on Democracy', PhD thesis, Queen Mary College, University of London (2016) and Joel A. Johnson, *Beyond Practical Virtue: A Defence of Liberal Democracy Through Literature* (Columbia: University of Missouri Press, 2007), 33–4.

Consistent with his attack against 'this actual England', Carlyle proposes remedies that show the imprint of his Scottish background. In 1835 he privately outlined a plan for a national system of education that was designed after Knox and Cromwell's republican visions of 'a *believing* nation', in which 'the meanest man becomes not a Citizen only, but a Member of Christ's visible Church; a veritable Hero, if he prove a man!' (*Heroes*, 124).[46] In *Past and Present*, he revives this proposal for a national curriculum that enshrines the 'infinite nature of Duty' and the 'Protestant form of reading this message as the glory of these late ages' (*CL* viii. 36). He even hopes that this blueprint will be incorporated into an 'Emigration' and 'Teaching Service' to impel residents of the British Empire to participate in a 'Conquest over Chaos'. To his frustration, doctrinal disputes between Protestants, Roman Catholics, and Dissenters continue to scupper his hopes for state-funded primary education designed on the principle that 'all light and science . . . is of God' (p. 235). If England is not yet ready for learning purged of theological 'Speciosities', then the 'Gospel of Work' should be invoked as an alternative means of instruction and discipline. The English working classes might be 'stupidest in speech', but their 'unspoken sense, [and] inner silent feeling of what is true' mark them out as the 'wisest in action' (pp. 85, 149, 148).

For Carlyle, work is the purest form of learning, a divinely ordained activity that harmonizes thinking and doing, bridges the divide between abstract theory and 'unspoken' habit, and serves as a catalyst to a wider knowledge of the world. In *Past and Present*, he entrusts the task of rejuvenating this ideal to the 'Master-Workers', who are 'England's hope at present'. These 'Captains of Industry' are ideally placed to interpret the motto of 'the old Monks, "*Laborare est Orare*, Work is Worship"' (186, 181). Like Abbot Samson, who rose from the ranks of the monks to become their leader, the 'Masters' have inherited a clear conception of their civic responsibilities: 'For these his thousand men [the Master-Worker] has to provide raw-material, machinery, arrangement, houseroom; and ever at the week's end, wages by due sale' (p. 187). An early exponent of Saint-Simon's

---

[46] See J. H. S. Burleigh, *A Church History of Scotland* (Oxford: Oxford University Press, 1960), 166–74 and C. H. Firth, *Oliver Cromwell and the Rule of the Puritans in England* (London: Knickerbocker Press, 1900), 357.

cooperative 'Organization of Labour', Carlyle foresees the creation of a new social hierarchy, to be presided over by meritorious leaders who understand the primacy of duty and obedience. Though as yet 'only half-alive, spell-bound amid money-bags and ledgers', this 'virtual Industrial Aristocracy' (p. 240) possesses the capacity to redefine the relationship between capital and labour as a collaborative rather than a competitive venture. They are the harbingers of a peaceful revolution in industrial society.

In this new arrangement, 'nomadic' ties are superseded by 'permanent contracts' in a 'joint enterprise'. In 'some ulterior, perhaps not far-distant stage of this "Chivalry of Labour,"' the 'Master-Worker' might find it 'possible, and needful, to grant his Workers permanent *interest* in his enterprise and theirs' (p. 247). Though he advocates for profit-sharing and cooperative industry, Carlyle is neither a liberal nor a socialist. Whereas liberalism delivers the promise of 'No-Guidance' and a world that is 'alien [and] not a home at all', socialism trumpets the slightly less invidious 'False-Guidance' of the 'oppression of man by his Mock-Superiors'. But this dream of 'Sisterhood [and] brotherhood' runs contrary to nature, merit, and 'finding Government by your Real-Superiors' (pp. 241, 197, 189). Recalling the career of Abbot Samson, Carlyle submits that '[d]espotism is essential in most enterprises' (p. 248). The one 'Freedom' worth having, that which grows from the enrichment of the 'Soul', can only be attained through a 'despotism' that is made '*just*'. For Carlyle, the establishment of an 'Aristocracy of Talent'—or in twentieth-century language, a 'meritocracy'—is predicated on the necessity of a disciplined, obedient, and regimented social organism.

Carlyle's hope in *Past and Present* that 'Captains of Industry' might form the vanguard of a movement to transfigure work stemmed from his contacts with the Marshall family of Leeds. John Marshall, whom Carlyle met at his mansion in Grosvenor Street, London, in May 1838, was the son of a linen draper who amassed a fortune from mechanizing flax spinning at factories in Shrewsbury and Leeds, and served as MP for Yorkshire from 1826 to 1830 (*CL* x. 95). He was active in educational circles, and supported a number of Benthamite causes, including the setting-up of University College London. In *Reminiscences*, Carlyle remembers him as a 'modest, yet dignified looking person, full of respect for intellect, wisdom and worth . . . with a definite and mildly *imperativeness* to his subalterns'. Marshall's house is 'resplendent, not *gaudy* or offensive, with wealth and its fruits and furnishings' (*Rem.*, 143).

In 1840, Marshall opened a large factory, Temple Mill in Holbeck, Leeds, which Carlyle cites as an exemplar in *Past and Present*. He also corresponded with Marshall's third son, James Garth, who was active in the Anti-Corn Law League and one of the founders of the Leeds Parliamentary Reform Association. Like his father, James Garth Marshall regards education as a crucial means of advancement for the working classes, and he erects a school in Holbeck together with a library 'for reading and acquiring useful knowledge, without which mere school education is very imperfect'.[47] Writing on 27 October 1841, Carlyle exhorts Marshall to 'preach and prophesy in all ways that Labor is honorable, that Labor alone is honorable'. On 7 December he advises Marshall to abandon his project to reform the 'Suffrage' and proselytize on behalf of a refurbished nobility: 'We must have industrial *barons*, of a quite new suitable sort; workers *loyally* related to their taskmasters,—related in God (as we may well say); not related in Mammon alone! This will be the real aristocracy, in place of the sham one' (*CL* xiii. 289, 317).

It took Carlyle less than a decade to accept that his expectations for the creation of this new ruling elite had been disappointed. The 'black eccentricities and consuming fires' (*Rem.*, 149) of *Latter-Day Pamphlets* (1850) were partly the result of his belated awareness that in *Past and Present*, he had misread his times. Contrary to what he wished, England was not ripe for the revival of fundamentalist 'religiosity'.[48] Carlyle also perceived that he had underestimated the fidelity of the 'Captains of Industry' to the laws of supply and demand, and to the stereotype of 'John Bull' as a self-interested *homo economicus*. From the 1830s onwards, Manchester cotton manufacturers waged a national campaign to thwart legislation that promised more power to trade unions. Though they were imbued with 'a pervasive sense of the duties of wealth', they were also driven by self-interest,

---

[47] *Factories Inquiry Commission, Supplementary Report of the Central Board, Part I* (London: House of Commons, 25 Mar. 1834), 113.

[48] See Hector Macpherson, *Thomas Carlyle* (Edinburgh: Oliphant, Anderson, and Ferrier, 1896), 'There was surely something pathetically absurd in the spectacle of [Carlyle] endeavouring to cure social and political diseases by preaching the resuscitation of Puritanism at a time when the intellect of the day was parting company with theocratic conceptions' (p. 144).

which was 'never far below the surface'.[49] Many of them interpreted Carlyle's 'gospel of work' as a homily against 'idleness' and 'frivolity', rather than as a radical prescription for the wholehearted reform of industrial relations.[50]

By denying the working classes any political avenue for effectuating '*Laborare est Orare*', Carlyle in *Past and Present* leaves final responsibility for 'the organisation of labour' with the 'Captains of Industry' and their political allies. The career of James Garth Marshall illustrates the pitfalls of relying upon the 'Masters' to reform themselves. W. G. Rimmer, the biographer of the Marshall family, attributes the demise of the firm to the 'fatalism and paralysis' of John Marshall's successors, particularly James Garth Marshall: 'Like his brothers he sensed a growing gulf between himself and those he employed. All the partners felt uneasy, even guilty at times, about the contrast between their wealth and the condition of the hands.'[51] The spectre of Abbot Samson haunted the Marshalls, long after they abandoned his principles.

Postscript: 'Expanded, Almost Transformed': The Discordant Legacy of *Past and Present*

For an eclectic array of nineteenth-century scientists, writers, artists, activists, revolutionaries, and politicians struggling with issues of faith and ideology, Carlyle's spiritual and political unorthodoxy in *Past and Present* was magnetic. In a series of letters that he wrote to the mathematician Thomas Hirst between 1847 and 1849, the Irish physicist John Tyndall enthused about the originality of the author's approach. When Hirst questions him about Carlyle's religion, Tyndall demurs: '[T]o deduce [his] ideas of religion from the work is impossible—he purposely avoids touching upon religious theories, and insists on the general principles of earnestness of soul and energy

---

[49] See Anthony Howe, *The Cotton Masters, 1830–1860* (Oxford: Oxford University Press, 1984), 302–3, 305.

[50] See e.g. W. R. Greg, '*Literary and Social Judgments* (London: Trübner, 1868), 136. Greg, who (unsuccessfully) managed his father's cotton mill at Hudcar Mill, near Bury, was a strident opponent of factory legislation; see Mary B. Rose, *The Gregs of Quarry Bank Hill: The Rise and Decline of a Family Firm, 1750–1914* (Cambridge: Cambridge University Press, 1986).

[51] *Marshalls of Leeds Flax-Spinners 1788–1886* (Cambridge: Cambridge University Press, 1960), 270.

of action'. Paraphrasing Fichte, Tyndall asserts that Carlyle's religion is 'not a <u>persuasion</u>, [but] a life'. The 'leading idea' of *Past and Present*, he concludes, is 'the application of the principles handled in Heroes & Hero Worship to politics, its aims rather at elevating the whole system of politics than at obtaining any single measure or series of measures, we have no Morrison's pill for social maladies'.[52] Dickens interpreted the book in an equally supple way, surveying Carlyle's 'gospel of work' from a wide variety of angles in *A Christmas Carol* (1843), *David Copperfield* (1850), *Bleak House* (1853), *Hard Times* (1854), and *Little Dorrit* (1857).[53]

John Ruskin, who defined himself as both a 'violent Tory of the old school' and 'a Communist of the old school', espied a route in *Past and Present* that circuitously led him from art and architecture to social and political reform.[54] His discipleship to Carlyle was fraught with insecurity, doubt, and confusion, but in his mentor's dramatic contrast between medieval integrity and modern shallowness, he identified an enduring set of critical touchstones.[55] Late in his life Ruskin informs his friend Alfred Macfee that he is sending him a copy of the book 'which I read no more because it has become a part of myself, and my old marks in it are now useless, because in my heart I mark it all'.[56] Ruskin's literary output confirmed the validity of this statement. Carlyle's incidental commentary on builders and buildings in the work anticipated the various stages of Ruskin's career as an art and social critic: his disavowal of historical conservation in *The Seven Lamps of Architecture* (1849), exposure of the dehumanization of industrial work and the mechanical uniformity of its products in *The Stones of Venice* (1851–3), condemnation of laissez-faire in *Unto this Last* (1860), reinvention of work in *Crown of Wild Olive* (1866),

---

[52] John Tyndall, *Correspondence 1843–1849*, ed. Melinda Baldwin and Janet Browne (London: Pickering and Chatto, 2015), ii. 241 (Tyndall to Hirst, 29 May 1847); ii. 298 (Tyndall to Hirst, 21 Nov. 1848).

[53] See Martin Danahay, 'Work', in Sally Ledger and Holly Furneaux (eds.), *Charles Dickens in Context* (Cambridge: Cambridge University Press, 2011), 194–202.

[54] Ruskin, *Praeterita*, ed. Francis O'Gorman (Oxford: Oxford World's Classics, 2012), 7 and *Fors Clavigera*, in *Complete Works*, ed. E. T. Cook and Alexander Wedderburn (London: George Allen, 1903–12), xxvii. 116.

[55] See David R. Sorensen, 'Ruskin and Carlyle', in Francis O'Gorman (ed.), *The Cambridge Companion to John Ruskin* (Cambridge: Cambridge University Press, 2015), 189–209.

[56] Ruskin, *Complete Works*, ed. Cook and Wedderburn, xxvii. 179 and n.

founding of the Guild of St George (1871)[57] as a response to 'Carlyle's grander exhortation to the English landholders in *Past and Present*',[58] and embrace of cooperative agrarian communities in *Fors Clavigera* (1871–84).

Women too were attracted to the book as an outlet for reflection and dissent. In her novels *Mary Barton* (1848) and *North and South* (1854), Elizabeth Gaskell's treatment of the 'Condition of England Question' was decisively shaped by her reading of *Past and Present*. In the preface to her first industrial novel, she echoes Carlyle in lending a voice to the working classes 'to give some utterance to the agony which, from time to time, convulses this dumb people'.[59] In *North and South*, Gaskell subtly deviates from Carlyle's teachings and represents the economic failure of Mr Thornton, a 'Captain of Industry', as a necessary step towards his moral redemption. At the conclusion of the novel, he is no longer 'a master', but hopes to find a managerial position that will allow him the 'opportunity of cultivating some intercourse with the hands beyond the mere "cash nexus" '.[60] But Thornton only arrives at this summit through the intervention of Margaret Hale, who 'proves her sisterhood' (p. 139) by persuading the 'stiff and rigid' industrialist to see the limitations of Carlylean 'wise despotism'.[61] Other noteworthy female activists—Vera Brittain, Octavia Hill, and Beatrice Webb among them—followed Gaskell in regarding the author of *Past and Present* as both a feminist inspiration and scourge.[62]

Carlyle's 'gospel of work' was treated by number of Victorian painters, including James Sharples in *The Forge* (1849), Ford Madox

---

[57] See James Dearden, *John Ruskin's Guild of St. George* (Sheffield: Guild of St George, 2010) and Mark Frost, *The Lost Companions and John Ruskin's Guild of St. George* (London: Anthem Press, 2014).

[58] Ruskin, *Complete Works*, ed. Cook and Wedderburn, xxx. 95.

[59] Gaskell, *Mary Barton*, ed. Shirley Foster (Oxford: Oxford World's Classics, 2006), 3.

[60] Gaskell, *North and South*, ed. Angus Easson (Oxford: Oxford World's Classics, 1998), 431; see also the introd. by Sally Shuttleworth, pp. ix–xxxiv.

[61] *North and South*, ed. Easson, 113, 120.

[62] See Vera Brittain, *Testament of Youth: An Autobiographical Study of the Years, 1900–1925* (New York: Penguin, 1989), 646; *Life of Octavia Hill as Told in her Letters*, ed. C. Edmund Maurice (London: Macmillan, 1913), vii. 313–14; Beatrice Webb, *My Apprenticeship* (1926), introd. Norman Mackenzie (Cambridge: Cambridge University Press, 1979), 180–1. For examples of 'working-class women [who] found a feminist in Carlyle', see Jonathan Rose, *The Intellectual Life of the British Working Classes* (New Haven: Yale University Press, 2001), 44–5.

Brown in his magnum opus *Work* (1852–63), and William Bell Scott in *Iron and Coal* (1861).[63] The designer, socialist, and author William Morris investigated the radical possibilities of Carlyle's 'gospel of work' in a variety of literary, aesthetic, and political contexts.[64] *Past and Present* even drew the attention of the composer Richard Wagner when he was revising the score and libretto of his opera *Parsifal* (1882) between 1877 and 1882. In an entry to her diaries dated 14 May 1879, Cosima Wagner reports her husband's pleasure in reading 'Carlyle's history of the Abbey of St. Edmundsbury; very gripping. R. very taken with Henry II (in his judgment on the newly elected Abbot Samson). He is also highly amused by the monks' Latin.' Four days later, she records that Wagner 'comes to me around noon to tell me about what he has just been reading in Carlyle (about religion, the Pope, the London hatter) and has so much enjoyed'. On 19 May, she recounts, 'In the evening we finish Carlyle's story of the abbey, which moves us greatly, particularly the exhumation scene. . . . The end of the day is rendered particularly significant for me by Novalis's remark about the body, quoted by Carlyle ["We touch Heaven when we lay our hand on a human Body"]. The poet expresses what the loving heart performs.'[65] Wagner was undoubtedly intrigued by the parallels between Abbot Samson, with his antique heart, 'like a child's in its simplicity,' and Parsifal, 'the innocent fool . . . enlightened through compassion'.[66] Similar too were their challenges, with both Samson and Parsifal striving to restore moral and spiritual purity in their kingdoms. In Book II of *Past and Present*, Wagner also received a clear exposition of his belief that 'where Religion becomes artificial, it is for Art to save the spirit of Religion'.[67]

[63] See Tim Barringer, *Men at Work: Art and Labour in Victorian Britain* (New Haven: Yale University Press, 2005); Gregory Dart, 'The Reworking of "Work"', *Victorian Literature and Culture* 27/1 (1999), 69–96; and Gerard Curtis, 'Ford Madox Brown's *Work*: An Iconographic Analysis', *Art Bulletin* 74/4 (Dec. 1992), 623–66.

[64] See Rob Breton, 'William Morris and the Gospel of Work', *Utopian Studies* 13/1 (2002), 43–56; Rob Knowles, 'Carlyle, Ruskin, and Morris: Work Across the "River of Fire"', *History of Economics Review* 34.1 (2001): 127–45; and William Glasnier, *William Morris and the Early Days of the Socialist Movement* (London: Longmans, Green, 1921).

[65] *Cosima Wagner's Diaries*, ii. *1878–1883*, ed. Martin Gregor-Dellin and Dietrich Mack, trans. Geoffrey Skelton (New York: Harcourt Brace Jovanovich, 1978), 310.

[66] *Parsifal*, trans. Lionel Salter (London: Overture, 1986), 115.

[67] 'Religion and Art' (1880), in *Richard Wagner's Prose Works*, trans. William Ashton Ellis (London: Kegan Paul, Trench, Trübner, 1897), p. vi.

In *Past and Present* Carlyle proclaimed that his goal was to redeem 'noble Conservatism' as the ingrained political creed of the English working classes. 'Bull is a born Conservative,' he declares, 'all great peoples are Conservative' (p. 150). Tory party supporters of the Corn Law tariffs—'ignoble Conservatives'—tarnished their principles for the sake of political expediency and wrongly equated the word with the defence of aristocratic privilege. For Carlyle, 'true Conservatism' described a mental complexion, rather than a political or class affiliation. It signified a reverence for the efforts of previous generations, and an unstated belief in work as a symbolic act of historical solidarity. In the Forster Collection manuscript, he applies the term to his own literary exertions: 'He is a <u>conservative</u> . . . who brings back the Past visible into the Present living Time. . . . Shew me . . . the life of the past, ye shew me the worth of the Past; how I, had I lived then, would have been a zealous citizen of it, and worked and striven and fought for it . . . how for the spirit and real meaning of it, I may still in these present days work and strive.'

Carlyle differentiates his historical philosophy from that of the Whigs and Benthamites—the 'true Revolutionists'—who 'would cut us off sheer asunder from whatsoever went before; representing all that went before as lifeless ashes, as a thing one blesses God one has no farther trade with' (Forster Collection, fo. 110r). But paradoxically, his definition of 'Conservatism' as the preservation and conservation of 'Truth and Justice' remained more pertinent to radicals and socialists than members of the Tory party. Friedrich Engels, the son of a wealthy German 'Captain of Industry' who owned textile mills in Barmen and Salford, visited England in 1842 and immediately acknowledged Carlyle's importance to the creation of a distinctively British brand of socialist thought. Radicalized while studying at the University of Berlin the previous year, Engels admired the Scotsman's prickly refusal to align himself with any particular political party or faction.

In a review of *Past and Present* published in Karl Marx's *Rheinische Zeitung* in 1844, Engels commended Carlyle for his independence of thought. 'Of all the fat books and thin pamphlets which have appeared in England in the past year for the entertainment or edification of "educated society",' he declares, 'Carlyle's book is the only one which strikes a human chord, presents human relations and shows traces of a human point of view.'[68] The same judgement was applicable to Engels's most Carlylean work, *The Condition of the Working Class in England* (1844), which was not translated into English until 1887. In this study, written to comprehend 'the present state of the English proletariat', he too strikes a personal 'chord' by subordinating his doctrinaire and protoscientific philosophy of history to 'a human point of view'. In an 1845 preface to the book, addressed 'To the Working Classes of Britain', Engels divulges the extent to which Carlyle's Boswellian sensibility helped to shape his own techniques. 'I wanted more than a mere *abstract* knowledge of my subject,' he confesses; 'I wanted to see you in your own homes, to observe you in your everyday life, to chat with you on your condition and grievances.'[69]

In 1897, the prominent American sociologist Charles Zueblin corroborated Engels's assessment of Carlyle's impact on British left-wing opinion. In his essay 'A Sketch of Socialistic Thought in England,' Zueblin maintained that between 1848 and 1864, the 'place of honor [among British Socialists] in this period undoubtedly belongs to Carlyle': 'While his teachings have had to be made positive, expanded, almost transformed by his followers, before they could contribute to the collectivist ideal, they . . . aided indirectly every progressive social movement by weakening the faith in the existing order. If Carlyle was not a socialist he was the most powerful anti-individualist of the century.'[70] Christian Socialists, Chartist 'ultra Radicals', and the disciples of the Welsh cotton spinner and reformer Robert Owen each hailed *Past and Present* as a figurative manifesto of their respective political agendas.[71] In the June issue of *Tait's Edinburgh Magazine*, John Stuart Blackie characterizes Carlyle as 'a preacher out of the

[68] 'Past and Present by Thomas Carlyle', trans. Christopher Upward, in *Marx and Engels: Collected Works, 1843–1844* (London: Lawrence and Wishart, 1975), iii. 444. In a letter to Engels of 9 April 1863, Marx praised *The Condition of the English Working Classes* for its 'human warmth and . . . humour that makes our later writings—where "black and white" have become "grey and grey"— seem positively distasteful'; see Marx and Engels, *Werke* (Berlin: Dietz-Verlag, 1957), xxx. 343.

[69] *The Condition of the English Working Classes*, ed. David McLellan (Oxford: Oxford World's Classics, 1993), 9.

[70] Zueblin, 'A Sketch of Socialistic Thought in England', *American Journal of Sociology* 2/5 (Mar. 1897), 648.

[71] See Mark Allison, 'The Mustard Seed of British Socialism: Carlyle, Robert Owen, and "Infallible Influence"', in Paul E. Kerry, Albert D. Pionke, and Megan Dent (eds.), *Thomas Carlyle and the Idea of Influence* (Madison: Fairleigh Dickinson University Press, 2018), 279–92.

pulpit,—a prophet perhaps; . . . a thinker of power and originality,
a soul burdened with moral message to its fellow souls—a heart
from the fiery centre of Nature shot direct . . . literally "raging
with humanity" '.[72] British socialists were eager to emulate his tone
and spirit.

One of his most vociferous adherents was Isaac Ironside, a Chartist,
Owenite socialist, and founding director of the Sheffield Working
Men's Association in 1837. He was roused by Carlyle's attacks against
the 'Paralytic Radicalism' (*CME* iv. 191) of the Anti-Corn Law
League and supported his call for national education and a centralized programme of public works for the unemployed. In his estimate,
the Chelsea seer was the 'mastermind of the age'.[73] On 29 December
1843, Ironside disrupted a meeting organized to raise funds for the
imprisoned factory reformer Richard Oastler. In a dramatic speech,
he assailed the Corn Law repealers for their 'pretence of regard for
the poor' and support of free trade. He then 'read an extract from
"Carlyle's Past and Present" on the subject of competition', and
reminded his audience that this is 'a book read by the rich, and written in consequence of Rd. Oastler'. His speech was greeted by both
'Loud cheers, and hisses'.[74] It was exactly the kind of chaotic reception that would have satisfied Carlyle.

Ironside's allegiance to *Past and Present* was not an isolated phenomenon in British Radical circles. Unlike too many 'respectable'
social reformers claiming to speak for the dispossessed, Carlyle conveyed a natural sense of camaraderie with them. As the Selkirk-born
anthropologist, classicist, and historian Andrew Lang insisted,
Carlyle's sympathy was an atavistic reflex: '[He] inherited the *religion*
of the Border, the legacy of the persecuted remnant, the wild hill-folk

---

[72] [John Stuart Blackie], 'Thomas Carlyle's Past and Present', *Tait's Edinburgh
Magazine* 10 (June 1843), 341. See also J. F. C. Harrison, *Quest for the Moral World:
Robert Owen and the Owenites in Britain and America* (New York: Scribner's, 1969) and
Gregory Claeys, *Citizens and Saints: Politics and Anti-Politics in Early British Socialism*
(Cambridge: Cambridge University Press, 1989).

[73] Ironside, quoted in the *Sheffield and Rotheram Independent* (12 Feb. 1848), 2. For
Carlyle and Ironside, see Alexander Jordan, ' "A condition hideous to all good citizens":
A Newly Discovered Letter from Isaac Ironside to Thomas Carlyle', *Carlyle Studies
Annual* 34 (2021–2), 17–26.

[74] 'The Liberation of Mr. Oastler', *Sheffield and Rotheram Independent* (30 Dec. 1843),
5. See also John Salt, 'Isaac Ironside 1808–1870: The Motivation of a Radical
Educationist', *British Journal of Educational Studies* 19/2 (June 1971), 183–201.

who fought at Drumclog, and who left their bones in the bed of the Hettlar Burn, where the dragoons fired down from the heights on the praying multitude. . . . His own people had no part or lot [in the romance of the past] but sorrow. . . . He was all his life on the side of the poor.'[75] Carlyle's dour compassion attracted notable converts such as Charles Kingsley, a Church of England clergyman, Chartist, Christian socialist, and in 1860, Regius Professor of Modern History at Cambridge. In his autobiographical novel *Alton Locke* (1850), Kingsley includes a radical bookseller named Sandy Mackaye, modelled on Carlyle, whom the latter considered 'nearly perfect' (*CL* xxv. 268).[76]

Other progressive figures were more measured in their praise. In *The History of Co-operation in England* (1875–9), the free-thinker George Jacob Holyoake credits Carlyle with restoring respect for workers among the industrialists: 'To his manly and contagious indignation has been greatly owing the improved regard . . . shown for craftsman. Thoughtfulness for the workman might be manifested as an act of patronage, but not as an act of duty.'[77] Yet Holyoake has no illusions about Carlyle's reactionary tendencies: he is 'at once brutal, contemptuous, and tender—unjust, yet loving justice—reverencing right in man, yet exhorting them to despotism'. 'In politics', Holyoake declares, Carlyle's 'influence has been wholly disastrous. On industry, his teachings have been less malign. His theory of the Organization of Labour has given us State Socialists. . . . But it seemed never to occur to him that there can be no general pride in labour, no dignity in it, until it is endowed with the right of profit in its performance.'[78]

Nonetheless, politicians associated with the labour movement were strongly taken with Carlyle's attacks against laissez-faire in *Past and Present*. In 1906 William Thomas Stead, pioneering journalist and editor of the *Review of Reviews*, examined the reading habits of forty-five Labour Party members recently elected to the House of

---

[75] Lang, 'Mr. Carlyle's Reminiscences', *Fraser's Magazine* 23 (Apr. 1881), 516–17.

[76] See Lucas Kwong, 'Killing Alton: The Politics of Spiritual Autobiography in *Alton Locke*', *Religion & Literature* 47/1 (Spring 2015), 123–42 and Alan Rauch, 'The Tailor Transformed: Kingsley's *Alton Locke* and the Notion of Change', *Studies in the Novel* 25/2 (Summer 1993), 196–213.

[77] Holyoake, *The History of Co-operation in England: Its Literature and Advocates*, 2 vols. (London: Trübner, 1875–9), i. 17–18.

[78] Holyoake, 'Thomas Carlyle the Thinker' (1843), in *Sixty Years of an Agitator's Life*, 2 vols. (London: Unwin, 1892), ii. 302, i. 191–2.

Commons. Asked to name the authors and books 'which they had found most helpful in their early struggle with adverse circumstances', thirteen cited Carlyle, behind John Ruskin (seventeen), Charles Dickens (sixteen), and the Bible (fourteen). In his preface, Stead points out that not one of these elected representatives 'profited by the rich endowments of Oxford and Cambridge', and 'what culture they have, they obtained from the chapel, from that popular university the public library, or still more frequently from the small collection of books found in the homes of the poor'.[79] Carlyle's corrosive attacks against the moral failures of capitalism, together with his emphasis on self-cultivation, played a major role in their education. Still, most tacitly accepted that it 'was not easy to be in harmony with Mr. Carlyle'[80] and none of them heeded his injunctions to spurn the 'False Guidance' of political agitation.

Carlyle's 'theocratic conception' in *Past and Present* may have looked obsolete in the twentieth century, but his moral fervour was contagious. In his introduction to the Oxford World's Classics edition of the book in 1909, the Anglo-Catholic G. K. Chesterton shrewdly remarked that the puritanical impulse common to Abbot Samson, Knox, and Cromwell was also inherent in the psychology of socialists: '[Carlyle] is already the first prophet of the Socialists and great voice against the social wrong. He has, indeed, almost all the qualities of the Socialists, their strenuousness, their steady protest, their single eye, also something of their Puritanism and their unconscious but instinctive dislike of democracy. Carlyle was the first who called in political inequality to remedy economic inequality, but he will not be the last.'[81] Chesterton's comment proved to be accurate. Socialism as it developed in England owed more to Carlyle's idea of the working classes guided by a morally and spiritually rejuvenated class of 'Master Workers' than it did to Marx and Engels's theory of class

---

[79] [W. T. Stead], 'The Labour Party and the Books that Helped to Make It', *Review of Reviews* 33 (1906), 568.

[80] Lang, 'Mr. Carlyle's Reminiscences', 517.

[81] Introduction to Carlyle, *Past and Present* (London: Oxford World's Classics, 1909), p. xi. See Lowell Frye, 'G. K. Chesterton and the "Shaggy Old Malcontent": Rereading Thomas Carlyle on the Threshold of the Twentieth Century', in Paul E. Kerry, Albert D. Pionke, and Megan Dent (eds.), *Thomas Carlyle and the Idea of Influence* (Madison: Fairleigh Dickinson University Press, 2018), 305–18 and Owen Dudley Edwards, 'Carlyle and Catholicism, Part II: G. K. Chesterton and *Past and Present*', *Carlyle Studies Annual* 24 (2008), 37–62.

conflict creating the scenario for violent revolution, the overthrow of the bourgeoisie, and the triumph of the proletariat.

The version of radical social change propagated by the Independent Labour Party (ILP) relied on a very different set of claims.[82] Keir Hardie, the Welsh founder of the ILP, held that Carlyle changed the future direction of British socialism by emphasizing 'the spiritual side of man's being; showing how all material things are but useful in so far as they serve to aid in developing character'.[83] In his pamphlet *The New Religion* (1895), the socialist journalist and author Robert Blatchford echoed this view. He singled out Carlyle's description 'half a century ago' in *Past and Present* of the 'inarticulate . . . dumb, altogether unconscious, want' of the Manchester manual workers. Blatchford surmises that this 'want' is now being addressed by the ILP, 'and, which is of more value and significance than the exist-ence of any party, there is blazing or smouldering amongst our densely-populated districts, a new enthusiasm; almost a new reli-gion'. The propagators of this faith are 'indebted to the idol-breaking of Carlyle, to the ideal-making of Ruskin, and to the trumpet-tongued proclamation by the titanic Whitman of the great message of true Democracy'.[84]

Other writers questioned the sincerity of Carlyle's commitment to the 'religion of humanity'.[85] At the end of the nineteenth century, Joseph Conrad inaugurated a critical trend in his novella *Heart of Darkness* (1899) that culminated in George Orwell's vilification of Carlyle in the 1940s as a pioneer of twentieth-century totalitarianism. Pointedly, the Polish exile did not distinguish *Past and Present* from Carlyle's later reactionary writings.[86] He detected in the Victorian sage's cruel gibes against Roman Catholics, the Irish, Jews, and Africans, a streak of hubris that allied him with the 'strong, lusty, red-eyed devils' who in 1885 administered King Leopold's murderous

[82] For Carlyle, Marx, and the ILP, see Jonathan Mendilow, 'Carlyle, Marx, & the Independent Labor Party: Alternative Routes to Socialism', *Polity* 17/2 (Winter 1984), 225–47.

[83] *Labour Leader* (Jan. 1893); quoted in Mendilow, 'Carlyle, Marx, & the Independent Labor Party', 225.

[84] *The New Religion*, Pass-On Pamphlets No. 9 (London: Clarion Press, 1909), 2, 4.

[85] See Kenneth J. Fielding, 'A Skeptical Elegy as in Auchtertool Kirkyard', in *Literature and Belief*, ed. Paul E. Kerry and Jessie S. Calder, 25/1–2 (2005), 255.

[86] See Alison L. Hopgood, 'Carlyle and Conrad: *Past and Present* and 'Heart of Darkness', *Review of English Studies* 90 (May 1972), 162–72.

reign of terror in the Belgian Congo. In his paean to the 'Captains of Industry' in Book IV of *Past and Present*, Carlyle envisages a future generation of leaders abrogating 'all laws of the bucaniers' and radiating 'pity, nobleness and manly valour' in their quest to achieve God's 'Justice' (p. 242). In *Heart of Darkness*, the 'Workers, with a capital,' contrary to being 'emissar[ies] of light', behave as 'sordid buccaneers'. These agents from the 'sepulchral city' (London) mercilessly plunder Africa and brutally enslave its inhabitants as an act of homage to the 'strange witchcraft' of imperialism. Their unbridled hero Kurtz presides over a campaign of violence and mayhem, while deluding himself that he is educating the natives in the true meaning of 'Work' through Carlylean 'permission, persuasion, and even compulsion' (p. 190). The British and European sponsors of this exploitation justify their barbarism by appealing to the wisdom of the Chelsea seer, who is an accomplice to their 'flabby, pretending, weak-eyed devil of a rapacious and pitiless folly'.[87]

Conrad's excoriating critique of Carlyle, however one-sided, resonated with many twentieth-century critics who implicated him in Kaiser Wilhelm II's militarism, and later, in Adolf Hitler's genocidal ethnonationalism.[88] Among them, Carlyle's most hostile and influential detractor was Orwell. In his essay 'The English People' (written 1943; published 1947), Orwell blames Carlyle for subverting a notion that was especially dear to the 'English common people'.[89] What differentiates them from the upper classes, as well as from the European working classes, Orwell contends, is 'their non-acceptance of the modern cult of power worship'. Motivated by a vague Christian instinct, which has less to do with theology than sociology, the English proletariat clings tenaciously to the adage 'that might is not right'.[90]

[87] Joseph Conrad, *Heart of Darkness and Other Tales*, ed. Cedric Watts (Oxford: Oxford World's Classics, 2002), 117, 113, 133, 127, 140, 117.

[88] See e.g. Eric Bentley, 'The Premature Death of Thomas Carlyle (1795–1945), An Obituary and a Footnote', *American Scholar* 15/1 (Winter 1945–6), 69–76. For a historical perspective, see David R. Sorensen, 'A Failure of Faith: Herbert Grierson, Thomas Carlyle, and the British Academy "Master Mind" Lecture of 1940', *British Academy Review* 21 (Jan. 2013), 39–43 and '"The Great Pioneer of National Socialist Philosophy?": Carlyle and Twentieth-Century Totalitarianism', in *Thomas Carlyle & the Totalitarian Temptation*, ed. Tom Toremans and Tamara Gosta, special issue, *Studies in the Literary Imagination* 45/1 (Spring 2012), 43–66.

[89] George Orwell, *The Collected Essays, Journalism, and Letters, 1920–1950*, ed. Sonia Orwell and Ian Angus, 4 vols. (Harmondsworth: Penguin Books, 1984), iii. 22.

[90] Orwell, *Essays*, iii. 22.

For Orwell, no one bears heavier responsibility for this fatal breach in England between 'the intelligentsia and the common people' than the author of *Past and Present*. 'From Carlyle onwards,' he argues, 'the British intelligentsia have tended to take their ideas from Europe and have been infected by habits of thought that derive ultimately from Machiavelli. All the cults that have been fashionable in the last dozen years . . . are in the last analysis forms of power worship.'[91] Two years later in 'Notes on Nationalism' (1945), Orwell brands Carlyle 'one of the intellectual fathers of Fascism'.[92] His harsh judgement deflected scrutiny from the selective affinities that linked him to the author of *Past and Present*, who characterized the English working classes in similar terms. According to Carlyle, they are a 'Reforming People' who are suspicious of political 'Formulas' and 'Practical Solecisms'. To them, ' "death," compared with falsehoods and injustices, is light'. They are also a people who cherish their history, and revere their 'Cromwells, Hampdens, their Pyms and Bradshaws' (p. 151). In his last published novel, the dystopian *Nineteen Eighty-Four* (1949), Orwell imagines a ruthlessly mechanistic totalitarian society that is governed by the slogan, 'Who controls the past controls the future: who controls the present controls the past.'[93] In the society of 'Big Brother', the obliteration of memory is the first step towards the annihilation of human identity. Ironically, but for his own pre-occupation with 'power worship', Orwell would have discovered a similarly prescient and humane warning against the abuse of history in *Past and Present*, where Carlyle resurrects a 'godlike Reality' that 'gross Atheis[ts]' 'sacrilegiously mishandled; effaced, and what is worse, defaced!' (pp. 213, 85).

---

[91] Orwell, *Essays*, iii. 22.   [92] Orwell, *Essays*, iii. 425.
[93] Orwell, *Nineteen Eighty-Four*, ed. John Bowen (Oxford: Oxford World's Classics, 2021), 192.

A NOTE ON THE TEXT

THE present text is based on the first English edition of *Past and Present*, published in London by Chapman and Hall on 24 April 1843. For a detailed textual history, see Calder's study; Tarr's *Bibliography*, A13, pp. 98–107; and *P&P Strouse*, pp. lxxviii–lxxxiv. The 'Summary' of *Past and Present* included on pp. 3–15 was prepared under TC's supervision for the Uniform Edition of his collected works (volume v, 1858) and was included in all subsequent lifetime versions. The text is in its original state, with page references renumbered to coordinate with the present edition.

SELECT BIBLIOGRAPHY

Primary Sources

Abstract of the Population Census of 1841 (London: Fullarton, 1845).

Adair, James, *The History of the American Indians* (London: Dilly, 1775).

Addison, Joseph, 'The Vision of Mirna', *The Spectator*, No. 159 (1 Sept. 1711), 317–18

Aiken, Peter Freeland, *A Comparative View of the Constitutions of Great Britain and the United States of America in Six Lectures* (London: Longman et al., 1842).

[Al-Hariri], *Die verwandlungen des Ebu Seid von Serug; oder Die Makamen des Hariri*, trans. Friedrich Rückert (Stuttgart: Cotta, 1826).

Alison, William Pulteney, *Observations on the Management of the Poor in Scotland, and its Effects on the Health of the Great Towns* (Edinburgh: Blackwood, 1840).

'Architecture.—Norman Tower at Bury', *Gentleman's Magazine* 18 (Sept. 1842), 302–3.

Ashworth, Henry, 'Statistics of the Present Depression Trade at Bolton; showing the mode in which it affects the different Classes of Manufacturing Population', *Journal of the Statistical Society of London* 5 (Apr. 1842), 74–81.

Austin, Sarah (trans.), *Characteristics of Goethe: From the German of Falk, Von Müller &c.*, 3 vols. (London: Wilson, 1833).

Babbage, Charles, *On the Economy of Machinery and Manufacturers*, 4th edn. (London: Knight, 1835).

Bacon, Francis, *Essays*, ed. Clark Sutherland Northup (Boston: Houghton Mifflin, 1908).

Baines, Jr., Edward, *The Social, Educational, and Religious State of the Manufacturing Districts*, 3rd edn. (London: Simpkin, Marshall, 1843).

Baker, Richard, *A Chronicle of the Kings of England: From the Time of the Romans Government, unto the Death of King James* (London: Sawbridge, Tooke, Sawbridge, 1684).

Balbo, Cesare, *Vita di Dante*, 2 vols. (Turin: Pomba, 1839).

Barclay, Robert, *An Apology for the True Christian Divinity, as the same is held forth, and preached by the People called, in Scorn, Quakers* ([London?]: n.p., 1678).

Baxter, G. R. Wythen, *The Book of the Bastiles; or, The History of the Working of the New Poor Law* (London: Stephens, 1841).

Beames, Thomas, *The Rookeries of London: Past, Present, and Prospective* (London: Bosworth, 1850).

Bentham, Jeremy, *A Comment on the Commentaries and A Fragment of Government*, ed. J. H. Burns and H. L. A. Hart (Oxford: Clarendon Press, 1977).

Bentham, Jeremy, *The Constitutional Code*, vol. ix of *Works*, ed. John Bowring (Edinburgh: Tait, 1841).

Biden, Christopher, *Naval Discipline: Subordination Contrasted with Insub-ordination; or, a View of the Necessity of Passing a Law Establishing an Efficient Naval Discipline on Board Ships in the Merchant-Service* (London: Richardson, 1830).

Black's Picturesque Tourist of Scotland: With an accurate travelling map; engraved charts and views of scenery; plans of Edinburgh and Glasgow; and a copious itinerary (Edinburgh: Adam and Charles Black, 1838).

Blanc, Louis, *Organisation du travail* (Paris: Administration de Librairie 1841).

Bolingbroke, Henry St John, Lord Viscount, *Letters on the Study and Use of History*, 2 vols. (London: Millar, 1752).

Bowyer, George, *The English Constitution: A Popular Commentary on the Constitutional Law of England* (London: Burns, 1841).

Britton, John, and Edward Wedlake Brayley, *The Beauties of England and Wales*, 18 vols. (London: Maiden et al., 1801–15).

Brooke, James Williamson, *The Democrats of Marylebone* (London: Cleaver, 1839).

Burnet, Gilbert, *The History of the Reformation of the Church of England: The First Part, of the Progress Made in it during the Reign of Henry VIII* (London: Chiswell, 1679).

Butler, H. E. (trans. and ed.), *The Chronicle of Jocelin of Brakelond* (London: Nelson, 1949).

Buxton, Sir Thomas Fowell, *The African Slave Trade and Its Remedy* (London: Murray, 1840).

[Carlyle, John Aitken], 'Medical Quackery and Mr. St. John Long', *Fraser's Magazine* 1 (1830), 451–56.

'Carlyle's Chartism', *Tait's Edinburgh Review* 7 (Feb. 1840), 115–20.

[Chadwick, Edwin], *Report on the Sanitary Conditions of the Labouring Population of Great Britain: A Supplementary Report on the Results of a Special Inquiry into the Practice of Interment in Towns* (London: Clowes, 1843).

[Chadwick, Edwin], *Report to Her Majesty's principal Secretary of State for the Home Department, from the Poor Law Commissioners, on an Inquiry into the Sanitary Condition of the Labouring Population of Great Britain* (London: Clowes, 1842).

[Chadwick, Edwin], *Report to the Secretary of State for the Home Department, from the Poor Law Commissioners, on the Training of Pauper Children; with Appendices* (London: Clowes, 1841).

[Chadwick, Edwin, and William Nassau Senior], *Poor Law Commissioners' Report of 1834* (London: Darling, 1905).

Chalmers, George, *Caledonia: or, An Account Historical and Topographic, of North Britain from the Most Ancient to the Present Times with a Dictionary of Places, Chronological and Philological*, vol. i (London: Cadell and Davies, 1807).

Chalmers, Thomas, *On Political Economy in Connexion with the Moral State and Moral Prospects of Society*, 2nd edn. (Glasgow: Collins, 1832).

Clarke, Sir Ernest (ed.), *The Chronicle of Jocelin of Brakelond* (London: Murray, 1907).

Clarke, Samuel, *Works*, 4 vols. (London: Knapton, 1738).

Coke, Edwin, *The First Part of the Institutes of the Lawes of England, or a Commentarie upon Littleton* (London: Islip, 1628).

Cromwelliana: A Chronological Detail of Events in which Oliver Cromwell was Engaged from the Year 1642 to his Death 1658 (London: Machell Stace, 1810).

Croxall, Samuel (trans.), *The Fables of Aesop; with Instructive Applications* (Halifax: Milner, 1843).

[Cruickshank, George], *The Gallery of 140 Comicalities, which has appeared from time to time, in that most Popular Sporting Paper', Bell's Life in London'* (London: Goodger, 1831).

Davis, John Francis, *The Chinese: A General Description of the Empire of China and its Inhabitants*, 2 vols. (London: Knight, 1836).

Davis, John Francis, *The Fortunate Union, A Romance, Translated from the Chinese Original, to which is added, a Chinese Tragedy*, 2 vols. (London: Oriental Translation Fund, 1829).

Deck, J[ohn], *A Guide to the Town, Abbey and Antiquities of Bury St. Edmunds* (Ipswich: Deck; London: Longman, 1821).

Deck, J[ohn], *A Guide to the Town, Abbey and Antiquities of Bury St. Edmunds*, 2nd edn. (Bury: Jackson, 1836).

De Quincey, Thomas, 'Homer and the Homeridæ', *Blackwood's Edinburgh Magazine* 50 (Oct. 1841), 411–27.

'Diary of a Dilettante', *Ainsworth's Magazine: A Monthly Miscellany of Romance, General Literature, and Art*, ed. William Harrison Ainsworth, 4 (May 1842), 229–32.

Dickens, Charles, *American Notes: For General Circulation*, 2 vols. (London: Chapman and Hall, 1842).

Dickens, Charles, *The Letters of Charles Dickens*, ed. Madeline House, Graham Storey, Kathleen Tillotson, et al., 12 vols. (Oxford: Clarendon Press, 1965–2002).

'Disinterment of Hampden', *Annual Register* 70 (July 1828), 93–95.

'Disinterment of Hampden', *Gentleman's Magazine* 98 (Aug. 1828), 125–7.

'Domestic Servants', *Journal of Civilization* 20 (18 Sept. 1841), 326–31.

Donovan, Jeremiah, *Rome, Ancient and Modern and Its Environs*, 4 vols. (Rome: Puccinelli, 1842–1844).

Dryden, John, *The Spanish Fryar, or The Double Discovery. Acted at the Duke's Theatre* (London: Richard and Jacob Tonson, 1681).

Du Cange, Sieur Charles de Fresne, *Glossarium ad Scriptores Mediæ et Infamæ Græcitatis*, 2 vols. (Lugduni, 1688).

Du Cange, Sieur Charles de Fresne, *Glossarium ad Scriptores Mediæ et Infamæ Latinitatis*, 3 vols. (Paris: Billaine, 1678).

Du Chesne, André, Ordericus Vitdalis, Gulielmus Pictaviensis, and Francis Maseres, *Historiæ anglicanæ circà tempus conquestûs Angliæ à Gulielmo Notho, Normannorum duce, selecta monumenta* (London: White, 1807).

Dugdale, William, *Monasticon anglicanum*, 6 vols. (London: Longman, 1817–30).

Engels, Friedrich. 'The Internal Crises', *Rheinische Zeitung* 344 (10 Dec. 1844); pub. in Marx and Engels, *Collected Works* (1975–2004), vol. ii.

'England and her Colonies in the West', *Fraser's Magazine* 4 (Nov. 1831), 436–46.

[Everett, Edward], *The Prospect of Reform in Europe: From the North American Review, Published at Boston, M. A. July 1, 1831* (London: Rich, 1831).

First Report of the Church Commission, as Finally Settled, March 17 [1835]. [n.p.]

First Report of the Commissioners—Mines (London: William Clowes, 1842).

Fox, George, *A Journal or Historical Account of the Life, Travels, Sufferings, Christian Experiences and Labour of Love in the Work of the Ministry*, vol. i (London: Northcott, 1694).

Gaskell, Peter, *The Manufacturing Population of England* (London: Baldwin and Craddock, 1833).

Gibbon, Edward, *The Decline and Fall of the Roman Empire*, ed. Betty Radice, 8 vols. (London: Folio Society, 1983).

Giles, J. A., *The Works of Gildas and Nennius* (London: Bohn, 1841).

Gillingwater, Edmund, *An Historical and Descriptive Account of St. Edmund's Bury in the County of Suffolk* (St Edmund's Bury: Rackham, 1804).

[Glasse, Hannah], *The Art of Cookery Made Plain and Easy* (London: Ashburn's, 1747).

Goethe, Johann Wolfgang von, *Sprüche in Prosa: Maximen und Reflexionen*, ed. Herman Krüger-Westend (Leipzig: Verlag, 1908).

Goethe, Johann Wolfgang von, *Werke*, 54 vols. (Stuttgart: Cotta, 1828–33).

Gorton, John, *A Topographical Dictionary of Great Britain and Ireland*, 3 vols. (London: Chapman and Hall, 1833).

Grimm, Jacob (ed.), *Deutsche Sagen*, 2 vols. (Berlin: Nicholaische Buchandlung, 1818).

Hallam, Henry, *Constitutional History from the Accession of Henry VII to the Death of George II*, 4th edn., 2 vols. (London: John Murray, 1842).

Hamilton, Revd James, 'Parish of New Abbey', in *New Statistical Account of Scotland* (Edinburgh: Blackwood, 1845), iv. 244–55.

Hansard's Parliamentary Debates . . . from the Year 1803 to the Present Time, 361 vols. (London: Baldwin and Craddock et al., 1829–91).

Harland, John, *Mamecestre: Being Chapters from the Early Recorded History of the Barony; the Lordship of Manor; The Vill, Borough, or Town, of Manchester*, 3 vols. (Chetham: Chetham Society, 1861–2).

Harmer, Anthony [Henry Wharton], *A Specimen of Some Errors and Defects in the History of the Reformation of the Church of England; Wrote by Gilbert Burnet, D.D., now Lord Bishop of Sarum* (London: Taylor, 1693).

Head, Sir George. *A Home Tour of the Manufacturing Districts of England in the Summer of 1835* (London: Murray, 1835).

Henry, Robert, *The History of Great Britain from the First Invasion of It by the Romans Under Julius Caesar*, 2nd edn., 6 vols. (Dublin: Byrne, Jones, 1789–94).

Hervey, Lord Francis (trans.), *Corolla Sancti Eadmundi: The Garland of Saint Edmund, King and Martyr* by Abbo de Fleury (New York: Dutton, 1907).

Hordynski, Joseph, *History of the Late Polish Revolution, and the Events of the Campaign* (Boston: Carter and Hendee, 1832).

Hume, David, *A Treatise of Human Nature*, ed. L. A. Selby-Bigge, 2nd edn., rev. P. H. Nidditch (1978; Oxford: Oxford University Press, 1985).

Hume, David, *The History of England from the Invasion of Julius Caesar to the Revolution of 1688*, foreword by William B. Todd, 6 vols. (Indianapolis: Liberty Fund, 1983).

Irving, Washington, *A History of the Life and Voyages of Christopher Columbus*, 4 vols. (London: Murray, 1828).

Johnson, Captain Charles, *A General History of the Pyrates from their First Rise and Settlement in the Island of Providence, to the Present Time* (London: Warner, 1724).

Johnson, Samuel, *Prayers and Meditations*, ed. George Strahan, 2nd edn. (London: Cadell, 1785).

Joinville, Jean, Sire de, *Mémoires* (1819), vol. ii of Claude Bernard Petitot, Alexandre Petitot, and L. J. N. Monmerqué (eds.), *Collection complète des mémoires relatifs à l'histoire de France depuis le règne de Philippe-Auguste jusqu'au commencement du dix- septième siècle*, 130 vols. (Paris: Foucault, 1819–29).

Kippis, Andrew (ed.), *Biographica Britannica, or the lives of the most eminent persons who have flourished in Great Britain and Ireland, from the earliest ages down to the present time*, 2nd edn., 5 vols. (London: Strahan et al., 1778–93).

Knight, Charles (ed.), *London*, 6 vols. (London: Bohn, 1841).

Knight, Charles (ed.), *The Pictorial Edition of the Works of Shakespere*, 8 vols. (London: Knight; Clowes, 1838–43).

Laing, Samuel (trans.), *The Heimskringla; or, Chronicle of the Kings of Norway*, 3 vols. (London: Longman, Brown, Green, and Longmans, 1844).

Lanthenas, François-Xavier, *Écrits et discours composés pour la Convention nationale*, 2 vols. (Paris: De l'imprimerie du Cercle sociale, 1793, 1795).

Lemoinne, John, 'De la législation anglaise sur les céréales', *Revue des deux mondes* 32 (1 Oct. 1842), 97–121.

Leroux, Pierre, *De la mutilation d'un écrit posthume de Théodore Jouffroy* (Paris: Saint-Pères, 1843).

Lockhart, John Gibson, *Life of Robert Burns* (Edinburgh: Constable; London: Hurst, Chance, 1828).

Lockhart, John Gibson, *Memoirs of the Life of Sir Walter Scott, Bart*, 7 vols. (Edinburgh: Cadell, 1837–8).

Lockhart, John Gibson, 'On the Cockney School of Poetry', *Blackwood's Edinburgh Magazine* 2 (Oct. 1817), 38–41.

Lyttelton, George, Lord, *The History of the Life of King Henry the Second*, 3rd edn., 6 vols. (London: Dodsley, 1769–73).

Macaulay, Thomas Babington, 'Hallam's Constitutional History', *The Edinburgh Review* 48 (Sept. 1828), 96–169.

Macaulay, Thomas Babington, 'John Dryden', *The Edinburgh Review* 47 (Jan. 1828), 4–36.

McCulloch, John Ramsay, *A Dictionary, Critical, Geographical, Statistical and Historical*, 2 vols. (London: Longman, Brown, Green, and Longmans, 1846).

'Mackenzie's Haiti and Bayley's Four Years in the West Indies', *Fraser's Magazine* 2 (Aug. 1830), 61–6.

Madden, Frederic (ed.), *Matthæi Parisiensis, monachi Sancti Albani, Historia Anglorum, sive, ut vulgo dicitur, Historia minor. Item, ejusdem Abbreviatio Chronicorum Angliæ*, 3 vols. (London: Longmans et al., 1866–9).

Malthus, Thomas, *An Essay on the Principle of Population, as it Affects the Future Improvement of Society with Remarks on the Speculations of Mr. Godwin, M. Condorcet, and Other Writers* (London: Johnson, 1798).

Marx, Karl, and Friedrich Engels, *Collected Works*, 50 vols. (London: Lawrence and Wishart, 1975–2004).

Mascou (Mascov), Johann Jacob. *The History of the Ancient Germans*, trans. Thomas Lediard (London: Mechell, 1738).

Maslen, Thomas John, *Suggestions for the Improvement of our Towns and Houses* (London: Smith, Elder, 1843).

Mayhew, Henry, *London Labour and the London Poor*, 4 vols. (London: Griffin, Bohn, 1861–2).

Mill, James, 'Aristocracy', *London and Westminster Review* 30 (Jan. 1836), 283–306.

Mill, John Stuart, 'Tocqueville's Democracy in America', *The Edinburgh Review* 72 (Oct. 1840), 1–47.

Milton, John, *Prose Works*, ed. Charles Symmons, 7 vols. (London: Johnson, 1806).

[Moir, George], *Fragments from the History of John Bull*, chs. V–VII, *Blackwood's Edinburgh Magazine* 34 (Dec. 1833), 890–901.

Monypenny, David, *Proposed Alteration of the Scottish Poor Laws* (Edinburgh: Whyte, 1840).

'Movements in the Church', *Fraser's Magazine* 26 (Dec. 1842), 715–29.

Muratori, Ludovico Antonio (ed.), *Rerum Italicarum Scriptores ab anno æræ Christianæ 500 ad annum 1500*, 28 vols. (Milan: Società Palatina, 1723–51).

[Neaves, Charles], 'The Late George Moir', *Blackwood's Edinburgh Magazine* 109 (Jan. 1871), 109–17.

Nennius, *Historia Britonum*, Ad fidem codicum manuscriptorum recensuit Josephus Stevenson (London: English Historical Society, 1838).

'New South Wales', *Quarterly Review* 37 (Jan., 1828), 1–32.

Nicholson, William, 'Narrative and Explanations of the Appearance of Phantoms and Other Figures in the Exhibition of the Phantasmagoria', *Journal of Natural Philosophy, Chemistry, and the Arts* 1 (Feb. 1802), 147–50.

Ninth Annual Report of the Poor Law Commissioners with Appendices (London: Knight, 1843).

Oastler, Richard, *The Fleet Papers: Being letters to Thomas Thornhill, esq. of Riddlesworth, in the County of Norfolk; from Richard Oastler, his prisoner in the Fleet*, 4 vols. (London: Pavey, 1841–4).

Oldys, William, and Thomas Park (eds.), *The Harleian Miscellany: A Collection of Scarce, Curious, and Entertaining Pamphlets and Tracts, As well in Manuscript as in Print. Selected from the Library of Edward Harley, second earl of Oxford*, 10 vols. (London: White, Murray, Harding, 1808–13).

Palmerston, Viscount, *Speech of the Right Hon. Viscount Palmerston, in the House of Commons, on Wednesday, the 16th of February 1842, on Lord John Russell's Motion Against the Sliding Scale of Duties on the Importation of Foreign Corn* (London: Ridgeway, 1842).

Park, Mungo, *Travels in the Interior Districts of Africa: Performed Under the Direction and Patronage of the African Association, in the Years 1795, 1796, and 1797* (London: Bulmer, Nicol, 1799).

Plutarch's Lives, trans. John and William Langhorne, 6 vols. (London: Robinson et al., 1823).

Prossner, G. F., *Antiquities of Hampshire Illustrated in the Ruins of Ancient Buildings* (Guildford: Kohler, 1842).

Raphael's Prophetic Almanac Being the Prophetic Messenger, Weather Guide, and Ephemeris for 1843 (London: William Charlton Wright, 1842).

Rapin de Thoyras, Paul de, *The History of England*, trans. N. Tindal, 2nd edn., 2 vols. (London: Knapton, 1732–3).

Ready Reckoner; or, Trader's Sure Guide, new edn. (Edinburgh: Darling, 1788).

Reports from Commissioners: Condition of the Hand-Loom Weavers, Session 26 January–22 June 1841, vol. x (London: Clowes, 1841), 1–136.

Report from the Select Committee of the House of Commons on Improvement of Health of Towns (Interment of Bodies), in *The Seasonal Papers Printed by Order of the House of Lords . . . Session 1842* (London: HM Printing Office, 1842), 1–159.

Report from the Select Committee on the Health of Towns; together with Minutes of Evidence Taken Before Them (London: House of Commons, 1840).

Report from the Select Committee on Agriculture . . . 2 August 1833 (London: House of Commons, 1833).

'Review.—Chronica Jocelini de Brakelonda', *Gentleman's Magazine* 15 (Feb., 1841), 172–5.

Richardson, G. F., *Geology for Beginners* (London: Ballière, 1842).

Ritson, Joseph, *Robin Hood: A Collection of All the Ancient Poems, Songs, and Ballads Now Extant Related to that Celebrated English Outlaw*, 2 vols. (London: Egerton, 1795).

Robertson, William, *The History of the Reign of the Emperor Charles V*, 3 vols. (London: Strahan, 1769).

Robin Hood's Garland: Being a Compleat History of All the Notable and Merry Exploits by Him and his Men on divers Occasions (Leeds: Printing Office, 1775).

[Rokewode], John Gage, 'Historical Notices of the Great Bell Tower of the Abbey Church of St. Edmundsbury', *Archaeologia* 23 (1831), 327–33.

Roscoe, Henry, *Life of William Roscoe*, 2 vols. (London: Cadell, 1833).

Ruskin, John, *Works*, ed. E. T. Cook and Alexander Wedderburn, Library Edn., 39 vols. (London: George Allen, 1903).

Rymer, Thomas, *Fœdera: Conventiones, literæ, et cujuscunque generis acta publica, inter reges Angliæ, et alios quosvis imperatores, reges, pontifices, principes, vel communitates, ab ineunte sæculo duodecimo, viz. ab anno 1101, ad nostra usque tempora, habita aut tractata*, 20 vols. (London: Churchill, 1704–35).

[Sacy, Antoine Isaac Silvestre de Sacy, and Henri d'Audiffret], 'Mahomet', in *Biographie universelle, ancienne et moderne*, vol. xxvi (Paris: Michaud, 1820).

[Saint-Simon, Henri, comte de], *Nouveau Christianisme, dialogues entre un conservateur et un novateur* (Paris: Bossange, 1825).

Sale, George (trans.), *The Koran, Commonly Called the Alcoran of Mohammed . . . to which is Prefixed A Preliminary Discourse*, 2 pts. (London: Ackers, Wilcox, 1734).

Scott, Walter, *Redgauntlet: A Tale of the Eighteenth Century*, 3 vols. (Edinburgh: Constable; London: Hurst, Robinson, 1824).

Scott, Walter, *Rokeby; A Poem* (Edinburgh: Ballantyne; London: Longman, Hurst, Rees, Orme and Brown, 1813).

Selden, John (ed.), *Eadmeri Monachi Cantuariensis Historiæ Nouorum, siue, sui sæculi Libri VI* (London: Stanesbeij, Meighen, and Dew, 1623).

Sheppard, Charles, *An Historical Account of the Island of St. Vincent* (London: Ridgway; Liverpool: Robinson; and Glasgow: Smith, 1831).

'Shilling', in vol. xix of *Encyclopædia Britannica: or, a Dictionary of Arts, Sciences, and Miscellaneous Literature*, 6th edn. (Edinburgh: Constable, 1823), 241.

Shuttleworth, James Phillips Kay, 'Observations and Experiments Concerning Molecular Irritation of the Lungs as One Source of Tubercular Consumption; and on Spinners' Phthisis', *North of England Surgical and Medical Journal* (Feb. 1831), 348–63.

'Sir Christopher Wren', in *Lives of Eminent Persons* (London: Baldwin and Craddock, 1833), 1–32.

Smedley, Edward, Hugh James Rose, and Henry John Rose (eds.), *Encyclopædia Metropolitana, or Universal Dictionary of Knowledge*, 29 vols. (London: Fellowes, Rivington, et al., 1817–45).

Smith, Adam, *An Inquiry into the Nature and Causes of the Wealth of Nations* (1776), 4 vols. (London: Charles Knight, 1835–9).

Southey, Robert, *A Vision of Judgement* (London: Longman, Hurst, Rees, Orme, and Brown, 1821).

Southey, Robert, *The Life of Wesley and the Rise and Progress of Methodism*, 2 vols. (London: Longman, Hurst, Rees, Orme, and Brown, 1820).

Spelman, Sir Henry, *Archaeologus in Modum Glossarii* (London: Beale, 1626).

Sproule, John, *A Treatise on Agriculture Suited to the Soil and Climate of Ireland* (Dublin: Curry and Jun, 1839).

Stow, John, *A Survey of London . . . Reprinted from the Text of 1603*, introd. Charles Lethbridge Kingsford, 2 vols. (Oxford: Clarendon Press, 1980).

Sturleson, Snorri, *The Heimskringla; or Chronicles of the Kings of Norway*, trans. Samuel Laing, 3 vols. (London: Longman, Brown, Green, and Longmans, 1844).

Sterne, Laurence, *The Life and Opinions of Tristram Shandy, Gentleman*, ed. Ian Campbell Ross (Oxford: Oxford World's Classics Edition, 2009).

Taylor, William Cooke, *Notes of a Tour in the Manufacturing Districts of Lancashire; in a series of Letters to His Grace, the Archbishop of Dublin* (London: Duncan and Malcolm, 1842).

Tennyson, Alfred, *Poems*, 2 vols. (London: Moxon, 1842).

'The Chronicle of Jocelin de Brakelond', *British and Foreign Review* 15 (April 1843), 54–79.

The Condition and Treatment of the Children Employed in the Mines and Collieries of the United Kingdom (London: Strange, 1842).

The Finance Accounts I.–VIII. of the United Kingdom for the Year 1842, Ended Fifth January 1843 (London: House of Commons, 1843).

The Lyre: A Collection of the Most Approved English, Irish, and Scottish Songs, 3 vols. (Edinburgh: Rollo, 1824).

The Popular Encyclopedia; being a general dictionary of arts, sciences, literature, biography, ethics, and political economy, ed. A. Whitelaw, 7 vols. (Glasgow: Blackie, 1835–41).

The Small Edition of the Post Office London Directory 1843 (London: Kelly, 1843).

'The Manufacture of Linen Yarn (1842)', in *The Useful Arts and Manufacture of Great Britain*, No. 7 (London: Society for the Promoting Christian Knowledge, 1848).

Thierry, Augustin, *Histoire de la conquête de l'Angleterre par les Normands*, 3 vols. (Paris: Didot, 1825).

Thomas, John Wesley, Revd. (ed.), *Lyra Britannica, or, Select Beauties of Modern English Poetry* (London: Stephens, 1830).

Thompson, William, *An Inquiry into the Principles of the Distribution of Wealth Most Conducive to Human Happiness; Applied to the Newly Proposed System of Voluntary Equality of Wealth* (London: Longman et al., 1824).

Tocqueville, Alexis de, *De la démocratie en Amerique*, 4 vols. (Paris: Gosselin, 1835, 1840).

Tocqueville, Alexis de, *Democracy in America*, trans. Henry Reeve, 4 vols. (London: Saunders and Otley, 1835, 1840).

Torrens, R., *A Letter to Sir Robert Peel, Bart., on the Condition of England* (London: Smith, Elder & Co., 1843).

Tymms, Samuel, *A Handbook of Bury St. Edmunds, in the County of Suffolk*, with additions by J. R. Thompson, 5th edn. (London: Simpkin, Marshall, 1885).

Vaughan, Robert, *The Age of Great Cities: Or, Modern Society Viewed in its Relation to Intelligence, Morals, and Religion* (London, 1843).

[Voltaire, François Marie Arouet], *Histoire de l'empire de Russie sous Pierre le Grand*, 2 vols. (n.p.: 1759–63).

Voltaire, François Marie Arouet, *Œuvres complètes de Voltaire*, 97 vols. (Paris: Baudouin Frères, 1825–34).

Wallez, Jean Baptiste Guislan, *Précis historique des négociations entre la France et Saint-Domingue* (Paris: Ponthieu, Peytieux, and Treuttel and Wurtz, 1826).

Wilkinson, John Gardner, *Manners and Customs of the Ancient Egyptians*, 3 vols. (London: Murray, 1837).

Wilson, John, 'The Factory System', *Blackwood's Edinburgh Magazine* 33 (April 1833), 419–50.

Yates, Richard, *An Illustration of the Monastic Life and Antiquities of the Town and Abbey of St. Edmunds Bury* (London: Nichols, 1805).

Yates, Richard, *History and Antiquities of the Abbey of St. Edmund's Bury*, 2nd edn. (London: Nichols, 1843).

Select Bibliography: Secondary Sources

Altick, Richard D., 'Past and Present: Topicality as Technique', in John Clubbe (ed.), *Carlyle and His Contemporaries: Essays in Honor of Charles Richard Sanders* (Durham, NC: Duke University Press, 1976), 112–28.

Altick, Richard D., *The Shows of London* (Cambridge, MA: Harvard University Press, 1978).

Andrews, Corey E., *The Genius of Scotland: The Cultural Production of Robert Burns, 1785–1834* (Leiden: Brill, 2015).

Baker, William, 'The London Library Borrowings of Thomas Carlyle, 1841–1844', *Library Review* 30 (Summer 1981), 89–95.

Bale, Anthony P., '"House Devil, Town Saint": Anti-Semitism and Hagiography in Medieval Suffolk', in Sheila Delany (ed.), *Chaucer and the Jews: Sources, Contexts, Meanings* (London: Routledge, 2002), 185–210.

Barczewski, Stephanie, *Myth and National Identity in Nineteenth Century Britain: The Legends of King Arthur and Robin Hood* (Oxford: Oxford University Press, 2000).

Basdeo, Stephen, 'Reading *Robin Hood's Garland* in the Eighteenth Century', *Bulletin for the International Association for Robin Hood Studies* 2 (2018), 1–16.

Baumgarten, Murray, 'Picturesque Tourist in the Victorian Industrial City: Carlyle, the Stereoscope, and the Social Text', *Carlyle Studies Annual* 17 (1997), 61–72.

Bell, Daniel, *The End of Ideology: On the Exhaustion of Political Ideas in the Fifties* (Glencoe: Free Press, 1959).

Benham, Allan Rogers, and Henry Greenleaf Pearson (eds.), *The Voice of Carlyle: An Abridgment of Past and Present* (Boston: Atlantic Monthly Press, c.1924).

Besoni, Daniele, 'The Periodicity of Crises: A Survey of the Literature Before 1850', *Journal of the History of Economic Thought* 32/1 (2010), 85–132.

Bezucha, Robert, *The Lyons Uprising of 1834: Social and Political Conflict in the Early July Monarchy* (Cambridge, MA: Harvard University Press, 1974).

Blake, Kathleen, *Pleasures of Benthamism: Victorian Literature, Utility, Political Economy* (Oxford: Oxford University Press, 2009).

Brattin, Joel J., 'New Manuscript Evidence about the Origin of *Past and Present*', *Nineteenth-Century Prose* 23/1 (1996), 13–24.

Breton, Rob, *Gospels and Grit: Work and Labour in Carlyle, Conrad, and Orwell* (Toronto: University of Toronto Press, 2005).

Breton, Rob, 'Utopia and Thomas Carlyle's "Ancient Monk"', *English Language Notes* 51/1 (Spring/Summer 2013), 211–22.

Brock, Peter, 'Polish Democrats and English Radicals 1832–1862: A Chapter in the History of Anglo-Polish Relations', *Journal of Modern History* 25/2 (1953), 139–56.

Buckler, William E., '*Past and Present* as Literary Experience: An Essay in the Epistemological Imagination', *Prose Studies* 1 (1978), 4–23.

Cameron, Rondo E., 'Papal Finance and the Temporal Power, 1815–1871', *Church History* 26/2 (June 1957), 132–42.

Campbell, Ian, 'Carlyle and Education', in Paul Kerry and Marylu Hill (eds.), *Thomas Carlyle Resartus: Reappraising Carlyle's Contribution to the Philosophy of History, Political Theory, and Cultural Criticism* (Madison: Fairleigh Dickinson University Press, 2010), 49–61.

Castle, Terry, 'Phantasmagoria: Spectral Technology and the Metaphorics of Modern Reverie', *Critical Inquiry* 15/1 (Autumn 1988), 26–81.

Chadwick, Owen, *A History of the Popes 1830–1914* (Oxford: Oxford University Press, 1998).

Chase, Malcolm, *Chartism: A New History* (Manchester: Manchester University Press, 2007).

Church, R. A., 'Profit Sharing and Labour Relations in England in the Nineteenth Century', *International Review of Social History* 16/1 (1971), 2–16.

Cumming, Mark (ed.), *The Carlyle Encyclopedia* (Madison: Fairleigh Dickinson University Press, 2004).

Cunningham, John, 'Lord Wallscourt of Ardfry (1747–1849), An Early Irish Socialist', *Journal of the Galway Archæological and Historical Society* 57 (2005), 90–112.

Curry, Patrick, *A Confusion of Prophets: Victorian and Edwardian Astrology* (London: Collins and Brown, 1992).

Davies, Norman, *God's Playground: A History of Poland*, 2 vols. (New York: Columbia University Press, 1982).

Davies, Owen, *Magic and Culture 1736–1951* (Manchester: Manchester University Press,

Dimsdale, Nicholas, and Anthony Hotson (eds.), *British Financial Crises Since 1825* (Oxford: Oxford University Press, 2015).

Drewett, Peter L., and I. W. Stuart, 'Excavations in the Norman Gate Tower of Bury St. Edmunds Abbey', *Proceedings of the Suffolk Institute of Archæology* 33 (1975), 241–52.

Dunstan, William, 'The Real Jarndyce versus Jarndyce', *The Dickensian* 93 (Spring 1997), 27–33.

Dyer, Isaac W., 'Carlyle Reconsidered', *Sewanee Review* 41/2 (1933), 141–51.

Dyos, H. J., and Michael Wolf, *The Victorian City: Images and Realities*, 2 vols. (London: Routledge and Kegan Paul, 1973).

Edwards, Owen Dudley, 'Carlyle versus Macaulay: A Study in History', *Carlyle Studies Annual* 27 (2011), 177–206.

Edwards, Owen Dudley, '"True Thomas": Carlyle and the Legacy of Millennialism', in David R. Sorensen and Rodger L. Tarr (eds.), *The Carlyles at Home and Abroad* (Aldershot: Ashgate, 2004), 60–76.

Edwards, Owen Dudley, 'Victorian Historical Consciousness—Carlyle, Macaulay, Froude, and Lecky: A Review Essay', *Carlyle Studies Annual* 29 (2013), 115–36.

Edwards, Owen Dudley, '"Of No Moment to Me": The Critical Reception of Carlyle's *Historical Sketches*', *Carlyle Studies Annual* 34 (2021–2022), 27–55.

Elton, Oliver (trans.), *The First Nine Books of the Danish History of Saxo Grammaticus* (London: Nutt, 1894).

Fielding, K. J., 'Carlyle and Cromwell: The Writing of History and "Dryasdust" ', in Jerry D. James and Rita B. Bottoms (eds.), *The Norman & Charlotte Strouse Lectures on Carlyle & His Era*, vol. ii (Santa Cruz: The University Library, 1985), 45–67.

Fielding, K. J., 'Carlyle and the Saint Simonians (1830–1832), New Considerations', in John Clubbe (ed.), *Carlyle and His Contemporaries: Essays in Honor of Charles Richard Sanders* (Durham, NC: Duke University Press, 1976), 35–59.

Fielding, K. J., 'Carlyle and the Speddings: New Letters', *Carlyle Newsletter* 7 (1986), 12–20.

Fielding, K. J., 'Ireland, John Mitchel and His "Sarcastic Friend" Thomas Carlyle', in J. Schwend, S. Hageman, and H. Volkel (eds.), *Literatur im Kontext / Literature in Context: Festschrift for Horst W. Drescher* (Frankfurt: Peter Lang, 1992), 131–43.

Finer, S. E., *The Life and Times of Sir Edwin Chadwick* (London: Methuen 1952).

Finlayson, Geoffrey B. A. M., *The Seventh Earl of Shaftesbury 1801–1885* (London: Eyre Methuen, 1981).

FitzGerald, Edward, *Letters, 1830–1883*, ed. Alfred McKinley Terhune and Annabelle Burdick Terhune, 4 vols. (Princeton: Princeton University Press, 1980).

Flanders, Judith, *The Victorian City: Everyday Life in Dickens's London* (London: Atlantic, 2012).

Fox Bourne, H. R., *English Newspapers: Chapters in the History of Journalism*, 2 vols. (London: Chatto and Windus, 1887).

Frye, Lowell, 'Romancing the Past: Walter Scott and Thomas Carlyle', *Carlyle Studies Annual* 16 (1996), 37–49.

Gasquet, Francis Aidan, *English Monastic Life* (London: Methuen, 1904).

Georgianna, Linda, 'Carlyle and Jocelin of Brakelond: A Chronicle Revisited', *Browning Institute Studies* 8 (1980), 103–27.

Gerrard, Daniel, 'Jocelin of Brakelond and the Power of of Abbot Samson', *Journal of Medieval History* 40/1 (2014), 1–23.

Goss, Erin M., 'Midas-Eared England: The Production of Meaning in Thomas Carlyle's *Past and Present*', *Prose Studies* 30/3 (2008), 266–85.

Goss, Erin M., 'Reading Cant, Transforming the Nation: Carlyle's *Past and Present*', in Bianca Tredennick (ed.), *Victorian Transformations: Genre, Nationalism and Desire in Nineteenth-Century Literature* (Oxford: Routledge, 2011), 95–114.

Halévy, Élie, *A History of the English People in 1815*, introd. Graham Wallis (New York: Harcourt, Brace, 1924).

Harper, Malcom M'L., *Rambles in Galloway* (Dalbeattie: Fraser, 1896).

Haury, David A., *The Origins of the Liberal Party and Liberal Imperialism: The Career of Charles Buller, 1806–1848* (New York: Garland, 1987).

Helfand, William H., 'James Morrison and His Pills', *Transactions of the British Society for the History of Pharmacy* 1/3 (1974), 101–35.

Helm, Elijah, *Chapters in the History of the Manchester Chamber of Commerce and An Address by Lord Rosebery, K.G., K.T., on the occasion of the Centenary Celebration* (London: Simpkin, Marshall, Hamilton, Kent, [1902]).

Heyrendt-Sherman, Catherine, 'From Social Reformer to Political Conservative: Thomas Carlyle and the Practicalities of French and Victorian Politics', *Carlyle Studies Annual* 34 (2021–22), 167–88.

Hill, Marylu, 'The "Magical Speculum": Vision and Truth in Carlyle's Early Histories', in David R. Sorensen and Rodger L. Tarr (eds.), *The Carlyles at Home and Abroad* (Aldershot: Ashgate, 2004), 83–90.

Hilles, Frederick W., 'The Hero as Revolutionary: Godefroy Cavaignac', in John Clubbe (ed.), *Carlyle and His Contemporaries: Essays in Honor of Charles Richard Sanders* (Durham, NC: Duke University Press, 1976), 74–90.

Hilton, Boyd, *A Mad, Bad, & Dangerous People?: England 1783–1846* (Oxford: Clarendon Press, 2006).

Himmelfarb, Gertrude, *The Idea of Poverty: England in the Industrial Age* (New York: Knopf, 1984).

Hirsch, Gordon, 'History Writing in *Past and Present*', *Prose Studies* 7/3 (1984), 225–31.

Hitchens, Fred H., *The Colonial Land and Emigration Commission* (Philadelphia: University of Pennsylvania Press, 1931).

Hosler, John D., 'Chivalric Carnage?: Fighting, Capturing and Killing at the Battles of Dol and Farnham in 1173', in Craig M. Nakashian and Daniel P. Franke (eds.), *Prowess, Piety, and Public Order in Medieval Society: Studies in Honor of Richard W. Kaeuper* (Leiden: Brill, 2017), 36–61.

Illustrated Memorial Volume of the Carlyle's House Purchase Fund Committee, with Catalgoue of Carlyle's Books, Manuscripts, Pictures and Furniture Exhibited Therein (London: Carlyle House Memorial Trust, [1896]).

Jackson, Lee, *Dirty Old London: The Victorian Fight Against Filth* (New Haven: Yale University Press, 2014).

Jann, Rosemary, 'Democratic Myths in Victorian Medievalism', *Browning Institute Studies* 8 (1980), 129–40.

Jenkins, Mick, *The General Strike of 1842* (London: Lawrence and Wishart, 1980).

John, Brian, *Supreme Fictions: Studies in the Work of William Blake, Thomas Carlyle, W. B. Yeats, and D. H. Lawrence* (Montreal and London: McGill-Queen's University Press, 1974.

Jordan, Alexander, 'Carlyle and Political Economy: "The Dismal Science" in Context', *English Historical Review* 132 (Apr. 2017), 286–317.

Jordan, Alexander, '"Noble Just Industrialism": Saint-Simonism in the Political Thought of Thomas Carlyle', PhD diss. European University Institute, 2015.

Jordan, Alexander, 'Thomas Carlyle and Stoicism', *Classical Reception Journal* 13/2 (2021), 212–33.

Kennedy, Meegan, '"Throes and struggles . . . witnessed with painful distinctness": The Oxy-Hydrogen Microscope, Performing Science, and the Projection of the Moving Image', *Victorian Studies* 62/1 (2019), 85–118.

Kerry, Paul E., and Laura Judd, 'Temporality and Spatial Relations in *Past and Present: New Insights into Carlyle's Philosophy of History*', in Paul Kerry and Marylu Hill (eds.), *Thomas Carlyle Resartus: Reappraising Carlyle's Contribution to the Philosophy of History, Political Theory, and Cultural Criticism* (Madison: Fairleigh Dickinson University Press, 2010), 148–69.

Kutolawski, John F., 'Victorian Historians on Poland', *Polish Review* 49/3 (2004), 968–89.

Larkin, Henry, *Carlyle and the Open Secret of His Life* (London: Kegan Paul, Trench, 1886).

Lattek, Christine, *Revolutionary Refugees: German Socialism in Britain, 1840–1860* (London: Routledge, 2006).

Le Pichon, Alain (ed.), *China Trade and Empire: Jardine, Matheson & Co. and the Origins of British Rule in Hong Kong 1827–1843* (Oxford: Oxford University Press, 2006).

Liberman, Anatoly, 'Berserks in History and Legend', *Russian History* 32/3–4 (Fall–Winter 2005), 401–11.

Liddell, Henry George, and Robert Scott, *Greek–English Lexicon*, 7th edn. (New York: Harper, 1883).

McAleer, John Philip, 'The West-Facade Complex at the Abbey Church of Bury St. Edmunds: A Description of the Evidence for Its Reconstruction', *Proceedings of the Suffolk Institute of Archaelogy and History* 39/2 (1998), 127–50.

McDonagh, Josephine, *Child Murder & British Culture, 1740–1900* (Cambridge: Cambridge University Press, 2003).

McParland, Robert, *Charles Dickens's American Audience* (New York: Lexington Books, 2010).

Monaco, C. S., *The Rise of Modern Jewish Politics: Extraordinary Movement* (London: Routledge, 2013).

Morrow, John, 'Carlyle and the "Condition of Ireland Question"', *Historical Journal* 51/3 (2008), 643–67.

Morrow, John, 'The Paradox of Peel as Carlylean Hero', *Historical Journal* 40/1 (1997), 97–110.

Morrow, John, *Thomas Carlyle* (London: Hambledon, 2006).

Munsche, P. B., *Gentlemen and Poachers: The English Game Laws, 1671–1831* (Cambridge: Cambridge University Press, 1981).

Neill, Elizabeth, 'Hume's Moral Sublime', *British Journal of Aesthetics* 37/3 (July 1997), 246–58.

Nixon, Jude, 'Thomas Carlyle's Igdrasil', *Carlyle Studies Annual* 25 (2009), 49–60.

O'Gorman, Francis, and Katherine Turner (eds.), *The Victorians and the Eighteenth Century* (2004; London: Routledge, 2017).

Park, T. Peter, 'Thomas Carlyle and the Jews', *Journal of European Studies* 20 (1990), 1–21.

Paz, Denis G., *The Politics of Working-Class Education in Britain 1830–1850* (Manchester: Manchester University Press, 1980).

Pellegrino Sutcliffe, Marcella, *Victorian Radicals and Italian Democrats* (Woodbridge: Boydell Press, 2014).

Pilbeam, Pamela M., *The 1830 Revolution in France* (London: Routledge, 1991).

Pinner, Rebecca, *The Cult of St. Edmund in Medieval East Anglia* (Woodbridge: Boydell Press, 2015).

Polden, Patrick, 'Stranger than Fiction? The Jennens Inheritance in Fact and Fiction. Part 1: The Jennens Fortune in the Courts', *Common Law World Review* 32 (2003), 211–47.

Polden, Patrick, 'Stranger than Fiction? The Jennens Inheritance in Fact and Fiction, Part 2: The Business of Fortune Hunting', *Common Law World Review* 32 (2003), 338–67.

Pollard, John, *Money and the Rise of the Modern Papacy: Financing the Vatican, 1850–1950* (Cambridge: Cambridge University Press, 2005).

Power, Rondo E., 'Papal Finance and Temporal Power (1815–1871)', *Church History* 26/2 (1957), 132–42.

Pratt, Branwen Bailey, 'Carlyle and Dickens: Heroes and Hero-Worshippers', *Dickens Studies Annual* 12 (1983), 233–46.

Prothero, Iorwerth, *Radical Artisans in England and France 1830–1870* (Cambridge: Cambridge University Press, 1997).

Rackham, Oliver, 'The Abbey Woods', in Antonia Gransden (ed.), *Bury St. Edmunds: Medieval Art, Architecture, Archaeology and Economy* (London: British Archaeological Association, Conference Transactions XX, 1998), 139–60.

Raven, J. J., *The Bells of England* (New York: Dutton, 1906).

Rees Jones, Sarah, and Sethina Watson, *Christians and Jews in Angevin England: The York Massacre of 1190, Narratives and Contexts* (Woodbridge: Boydell & Brewer, 2013).

Reid, T. Wemyss, *The Life, Letters, and Friendships of Richard Monckton Milnes, First Lord Houghton*, 3rd edn., 2 vols. (London: Cassell, 1891).

Richards, Bernard, 'William Fox Talbot and Thomas Carlyle: Connections', *Carlyle Studies Annual* 31 (2015–16), 85–108.

Rigby, Anne, *Imperfect Histories: The Elusive Past and the Legacy of Romantic Historicism* (Ithaca, NY: Cornell University Press, 2001).

Roberts, David, *Paternalism in Early Victorian England* (New Brunswick, NJ: Rutgers University Press, 1979).

Roberts, Phillip, 'Philip Carpenter and the Convergence of Science and Entertainment in the Early Nineteenth-Century Instrument Trade', *Science Museum Group Journal* 7 (Spring 2017); doi: dx.doi.org/10.15180. 170707.

Rosenberg, John D., *Carlyle and the Burden of History* (Oxford: Clarendon Press, 1985).

Rowell, Geoffrey, *The Vision Glorious: Themes and Personalities of the Catholic Revival in Anglicanism* (Oxford: Oxford University Press, 1991).

Rude, Fernand, *La Révolte des Canuts (1831–1834)* (Paris: Découverte, 1982).

St Clair, William, and Annika Bautz, 'Imperial Decadence: The Making of the Myths in Bulwer-Lyttton's *The Last Days of Pompeii*', *Victorian Literature and Culture* 40 (2012), 359–96.

Schiell, Annette, *Fundraising, Flirtation and Fancywork: Charity Bazaars in Nineteenth Century Australia* (Newcastle: Cambridge Scholars, 2012).

Schoch, Richard W., 'We Do Nothing but Enact History', *Nineteenth Century Literature* 54/1 (1999), 27–52.

Seigel, Jules, 'Carlyle and Peel: The Prophet's Search for a Heroic Politician and an Unpublished Fragment', *Victorian Studies* 26/2 (1983), 181–95.

Silberling, Norman J., 'Financial and Monetary Policy of Great Britain During the Napoleonic Wars', *Quarterly Journal of Economics* 38/2 (1924), 214–33.

Simmons, Claire A., *Reversing the Conquest: History and Myth in Nineteenth-Century British Literature* (New Brunswick, NJ: Rutgers University Press, 1990).

Smelser, Neil J., *Social Paralysis and Social Change: British Working-Class Education in the Nineteenth Century* (Berkeley and Los Angeles: University of California Press, 1991).

Sorensen, David R., '"A Very Strange Plant": Carlyle, John Mitchel, and the Political Legacy of Swift', in William Baker and Michael Lister (eds.), *David Daiches: A Celebration of His Life and Work* (Brighton: Sussex Academic Press, 2008), 172–9.

Sorensen, David R., 'Carlyle, Gibbon, and the "Miraculous Thing" of History', *Carlyle Annual* 12 (1991), 33–43.

Sorensen, David R., '"Une religion plus digne de la Divinité": A New Source for Carlyle's Essay on Mahomet', *Carlyle Studies Annual* 23 (2007), 13–77.

Sorensen, David R., and Brent E. Kinser (eds.), *On Heroes, Hero-Worship, and the Heroic in History* (New Haven: Yale University Press, 2013).

Spencer, David, *The Political Economy of Work* (London: Routledge, 2009).

Stein, Richard L., 'Midas and the Bell-Jar: Carlyle's Poetics of History', *Victorian Newsletter* 58 (1980), 5–9.

Tarr, Rodger L., *Thomas Carlyle: A Descriptive Bibliography* (Pittsburgh: University of Pittsburgh Press, 1989).

Tennyson, G. B., 'Unnoted Encyclopaedia Articles by Carlyle', *ELN* 1 (1963), 108–12.

The Baronial and Ecclesiastical Antiquities of Scotland, illustrated by Robert William Billings, Historical Description by John Hill Burton, 4 vols. (Edinburgh: Oliver and Boyd, 1901).

Thompson, Dorothy, *The Chartists: Popular Politics in the Industrial Revolution* (1984; London: Breviary, 2013).

Turnbull, Richard, *Shaftesbury: The Great Reformer* (London: Lion Turnbull, 2010).

Ulrich, John, '"A Labor of Death and A Labor Against Death": Translating the Corpse of History in Carlyle's *Past and Present*', *Carlyle Studies Annual* 15 (1995), 33–47.

Ulrich, John, *Signs of Their Times: History, Labor, and the Body in Cobbett, Carlyle, and Disraeli* (Athens: Ohio University Press, 2002).

Ulrich, John, 'The Reinscription of Labor in Carlyle's *Past and Present*', *Criticism* 37/3 (1995), 443–68.

Ulrich, John, 'Thomas Carlyle, Richard Owen, and the Paleontological Articulation of the Past', *Journal of Victorian Culture* 11/1 (2006), 30–58.

Vanden Bossche, Chris R., 'Chartism, Class Discourse, and the Captain of Industry: Social Agency in *Past and Present*', in Paul Kerry and Marylu Hill (eds.), *Thomas Carlyle Resartus: Reappraising Carlyle's Contribution to the Philosophy of History, Political Theory, and Cultural Criticism* (Madison: Fairleigh Dickinson University Press, 2010). 30–48.

Vanden Bossche, Chris R., 'Cedric the Saxon and the Haiti Duke of Marmalade: Race in *Past and Present*', in David R. Sorensen and Rodger L. Tarr (eds.), *The Carlyles at Home and Abroad* (Aldershot: Ashgate, 2004), 137–50.

Waithe, Marcus, 'The Pen and the Hammer: Thomas Carlyle, Ebenezer Elliot, and the "active poet"', in Kirstie Blair and Mina Gorji (eds.), *Class and the Canon: Constructing Labouring Class Poetry and Poetics, 1780–1900* (Basingstoke: Macmillan, 2013), 116–35.

Wang, Sonlin, 'Thomas Carlyle and Chinese Matters', *Carlyle Society, Occasional Papers* 28 (2015–16), 37–63.

Ward Fay, Peter, *The Opium War, 1840–1842: Barbarians in the Celestial Empire in the Early Part of the Nineteenth Century and the War by which They Forced Her Gates Ajar* (Chapel Hill: North Carolina University Press, 1997).

Webster, Paul, 'The Cult of St. Edmund, King and Martyr, and the Medieval Kings of England', *History* 105 (Oct. 2020), 636–51.

Wells, Kentwood D., 'Fleas the Size of Elephants: The Wonders of the Oxyhydrogen Microscope', *Magic Lantern Gazette* 29/2–3 (2017), 3–34.

Widner, Michael, 'Samson's Touch and a Thin Red Line: Reading the Bodies of Saints and Jews in Bury St. Edmunds', *Journal of English and Germanic Philology* 111/3 (July 2012), 339–59.

Wise, Sarah, *The Blackest Streets: The Life and Death of a Victorian Slum* (New York: Random House, 2013).

Worden, Blair, 'The Victorians and Oliver Cromwell', in Stefan Collini, Richard Whatmore, and Brian Young (eds.), *History, Religion, and Culture 1750–1950* (Cambridge: Cambridge University Press, 2000), 112–35.

Worden, Blair, 'Thomas Carlyle and Oliver Cromwell', *Proceedings of the British Academy* 105 (2000), 131–70.

Young, Brian, *The Victorian Eighteenth Century: An Intellectual History* (Oxford: Oxford University Press, 2007).

Further Reading in Oxford World's Classics

Boswell, James, *Life of Johnson*, ed. R. W. Chapman, introd. Pat Rogers.

Carlyle, Thomas, *Sartor Resartus*, ed. Kerry McSweeney and Peter Sabor.

Carlyle, Thomas, *The French Revolution*, ed. David R. Sorensen and Brent E. Kinser.

Conrad, Joseph, *Heart of Darkness and Other Tales*, ed. Cedric Watts.

Dickens, Charles, *A Christmas Carol and Other Christmas Books*, ed. Robert Douglas-Fairhurst.

Dickens, Charles, *Bleak House*, ed. Stephen Gill.

Dickens, Charles, *David Copperfield*, ed. Nina Burgis.

Dickens, Charles, *Dombey and Son*, ed. Alan Horsman.

Dickens, Charles, *Hard Times*, ed. Paul Schlicke.

Dickens, Charles, *Little Dorrit*, ed. Harvey Peter Sucksmith.

Disraeli, Benjamin, *Sybil: or the Two Nations*, ed. Nicholas Shrimpton.

Engels, Friedrich, *The Condition of the Working Classes in England*, ed. David McLellan.

Gaskell, Elizabeth, *Mary Barton*, ed. Shirley Foster.

Gaskell, Elizabeth, *North and South*, ed. Angus Easson.

Mayhew, Henry, *London Labour and the London Poor*, ed. Robert Douglas-Fairhurst.

Orwell, George, *Nineteen Eighty-Four*, ed. John Bowen.

Ruskin, John, *Praeterita*, ed. Francis O'Gorman.

Ruskin, John, *Selected Writings*, ed. Dinah Birch.

Scott, Walter, *Ivanhoe*, ed. Ian Duncan.

Scott, Walter, *Redgauntlet*, ed. Kathryn Sutherland.

A CHRONOLOGY OF THOMAS
AND JANE WELSH CARLYLE

1795 (4 Dec.) Thomas Carlyle born at Ecclefechan; Napoleon suppresses royalist uprising in Paris, Directory established.

1796 (21 July) Death of Robert Burns.

1801 (14 July) Jane Baillie Welsh born at Haddington, Scotland.

1806 TC attends Annan Academy.

1809 TC attends Edinburgh University, returns to Annan Academy as mathematic teacher in 1814.

1815 (15 Oct.) Napoleon defeated at Waterloo.

1816–18. TC teaching at Kirkcaldy Burgh School, forms friendship with Edward Irving

1818 TC moves to Edinburgh, begins learning German.

1819 (16 Aug.) Peterloo Massacre; Walter Scott publishes *Ivanhoe*.

1821 TC meets Jane Baillie Welsh in Haddington.

1823 'Life of Schiller', *London Magazine*.

1824 Translation of Legendre's *Elements of Geometry*, death of Byron.

1825 *Life of Schiller.*

1826 (17 Oct.) TC marries Jane Welsh; TC and JWC move to 21 Comely Bank, Edinburgh.

1827 *German Romance*, 'Jean Paul Friedrich Richter'.

1828 'Burns' and 'Goethe'; TC and JWC move to Craigenputtoch.

1829 'Voltaire' and 'Signs of the Times'; TC begins *Sartor Resartus*; Catholic Emancipation Act, allowing Catholics to serve in Parliament.

1830 July Revolution in France; armed uprising by Polish cadets in Warsaw.

1831 'Characteristics', MS of *Sartor* finished; revolt in Lyons, France, for higher wages; Game Law Act establishes licensure and seasons for hunting.

1832 Reform Act abolishes rotten boroughs, expands suffrage; deaths of Carlyle's father James (22 Jan.), Goethe (22 Mar.), Walter Scott (21 Sept.).

1833 *Sartor Resartus* serialized in *Fraser's Magazine*; Factory Act restricts workday in textile mills to twelve hours for persons aged 13–17 and to eight hours for those 9–12.

1834   New Poor Law Act enacted; Carlyles move to 5 Cheyne Row, Chelsea, and TC witnesses the burning of St Stephen's Chapel, Westminster Palace, seat of the House of Commons since 1295; (7 Dec.) death of Edward Irving.

1835   Translation of vol. i of Tocqueville's *Democracy in America* by Henry Reeve; TC publishes 'Death of Edward Irving' in January issue of *Fraser's Magazine*.

1836   *Sartor Resartus* published in Boston as a book.

1837   *The French Revolution*; seven public lectures on German literature.

1838   *Sartor Resartus* published in London; twelve public lectures on European literature; People's Charter established.

1839   TC, *Chartism*; first British edition of *Critical and Miscellaneous Essays*; six public lectures on modern revolution in Europe; TC launches initiative to found the London Library (1841); first Opium War begins (–1842); Anti-Corn-Law League established; petition to the House of Commons in support of Thomas Noon Talfourd's Copyright Act (passed in 1842).

1840   (5–22 May) Six public lectures etc. Six public lectures on Heroes; (30 Mar.) death of 'Beau' Brummell, Regency dandy and socialite; translation of vol. ii of Tocqueville's *Democracy in America* by Henry Reeve.

1841   *On Heroes, Hero-Worship, and the Heroic in History*; Niger Expedition; Robert Peel begins second term as Tory prime minister; riots against the government of Louis-Philippe in Paris.

1842   (25 Feb.) Death of JWC's mother, Grace Welsh; (July) colliers strike in Hanley, Staffordshire leading to a general uprising and work stoppages throughout England; (11–15 Aug.) TC takes a four-day trip to the Netherlands; (Sept.) TC visits St Edmundsbury, Ely, Cambridge, and Workhouse of St Ives, Huntingdon; (12 Oct.) borrows *Chronica Jocelini de Brakelonda* from the London Library

1843   (Feb.–Mar.) TC finishes MS printer's copy, and proofreading; (11 Apr.) *Past and Present* published; (July) 'Dr. Francia' published in *Foreign Quarterly Review*. *Historical Sketches* (1898) composed.

1844   Engels reviews 'Past and Present', *Rheinische Zeitung*; (18 Sept.) death of John Sterling.

1845   TC, *Cromwell's Letters and Speeches*; Peel tries to resign after failing to repeal the Corn Laws, but following the collapse of Russell's government, he is reinstated; Irish potato crop. fails; New Poor Law Act passed for Scotland; Engels publishes a German edition of *The Condition of the Working Class in England*; Gaskell, *Mary Barton*.

1846 Corn Laws repealed, tariffs to be gradually reduced; (5–10 Sept.) TC's first visit to Ireland, meets Young Irelanders and hears speech by Daniel O'Connell.

1848 Revolution in Europe; (Apr.) Chartist demonstration at Kennington Common; Chartism disbanded as an organized movement; (21 Feb.) Marx and Engels publish *The Communist Manifesto*.

1849 (3 July–6 Aug.) TC's second visit to Ireland; writes *Reminiscences of My Irish Journey* (pub. 1882); (Dec.) publishes 'Occasional Discourse on the Negro Question' in *Fraser's Magazine*; Corn Laws abolished. Ruskin, *The Seven Lamps of Architecture*; James Sharples, *The Forge*.

1850 TC, *Latter-Day Pamphlets*; (2 July) death of Robert Peel; Kingsley, *Alton Locke;* Dickens, *David Copperfield*.

1851 TC, *Life of Sterling*; (4–7 Oct.) TC visits Paris, writes 'Excursion to Paris', later published in *Last Words* (1892); Great Exhibition opened by Queen Victoria at the Crystal Palace, Hyde Park; Ruskin, *The Stones of Venice*.

1852 TC visits Germany, begins biography of Frederick the Great; death of the Duke of Wellington; Ford Madox Brown, *Work*.

1853 (25 Dec.) Death of TC's mother, Margaret Aitken Carlyle; Crimean War begins (–1856); Dickens, *Bleak House*.

1854 Gaskell, *North and South*; Dickens, *Hard Times*.

1857 Indian Mutiny; Dickens, *Little Dorrit*.

1858 TC's second visit to Germany; vols. i and ii of TC's *History of Friedrich II. of Prussia: Called Frederick the Great* published; British East India Company dissolved.

1860 Ruskin, *Unto this Last*.

1861 William Bell Scott, *Iron and Coal*.

1862 Vol. iii of *Frederick* published.

1864 Vol. iv of *Frederick* published.

1865 Vols. v and vi of *Frederick* published.

1866 (2 Apr.) TC delivers inaugural address as Rector of Edinburgh University; (21 Apr.) death of JWC; TC begins memoir of JWC (finished 18 July); Ruskin, *The Crown of Wild Olive*.

1867 TC, *Shooting Niagara*; John Stuart Mill's proposal to allow women the vote defeated in Parliament; Disraeli's Reform Act grants vote to all householders and lodgers paying £10 or more per year.

1871 Ruskin, *Fors Clavigera* and founding of the Guild of St George.

1872–3 Emerson visits TC; Mary Carlyle Aitken cares for her uncle at Cheyne Row.

1875   *Early Kings of Norway* and *An Essay on the Portraits of John Knox*.

1879   (15 Sept.) Death of TC's brother John.

1881   (5 Feb.) Death of TC; (Mar.) Froude's edition of *Reminiscences* published.

A TIMELINE OF CHRONICA
JOCELINI DE BRAKELOND

869 Edmund, king of the East Angles, defeated and slain in battle.

925 Æthelstan (d. 939), king of the Anglo-Saxons, establishes a religious house to preserve St Edmund's bodily remains.

c.985–7 Abbo of Fleury writes *Passio Sancti Eadmundi*.

1020 King Cnut provides grant for the construction of the first stone church at Bury; his charter enshrines rights over the jurisdiction of the developing town of Bury.

1032 Church consecrated on 18 October.

1044 Visit of King Edward the Confessor (d. 1066) to the shrine of St Edmund; royal charter extends the abbey's jurisdiction of lands in the county of Suffolk.

1071 Abbot Baldwin opposes the plans of Herfast (d. 1084), bishop of Thetford, to remove his episcopal seat to St Edmund's.

1081 Royal council in London resolves dispute in favour of Baldwin.

1095 Completion of abbey choir, translation of the relics by Abbot Baldwin to the new shrine at St Edmunds.

c.1100 *De miraculis sancti Eadmundi*, attributed to Hermann, monk and hagiographer.

1135 Birth of Samson of Tottington; accession of King Stephen.

1154 Death of King Stephen; accession of King Henry II.

c.1155 Birth of Jocelin of Brakelond.

1157 Hugh I, prior of Westminister, elected abbot.

1159–63 Journey of Samson to Rome on the matter of the church of Woolpit. Imprisonment of Samson at Castle Acre.

1163 Henry of Essex's duel with Robert de Montfort.

1165 Samson becomes a monk at Bury St Edmunds.

1170 Murder of Thomas à Becket in Canterbury Cathedral.

1172 Abbot Hugh obtains exemption from legatine authority.

1173 (17 Oct.) Battle of Fornham. Deposition of Prior Hugh; appointment of Prior Robert. Jocelin de Brakelond becomes a monk at Bury.

1174–5 Visitation of Archbishop Richard of Canterbury to the abbey.

1175   (21 Apr.) Pope Alexander III exempts Bury from any visitation by a papal legatée.

1180   Death of Abbot Hugh; abbot's estates taken into royal custody.

1180–2 Prior Robert rules the house, while Robert de Cokefield and Robert de Flamvill serve as wards of the abbey's lands. Samson, appointed sub-sacristan, constructs buildings and undertakes repairs.

1181   (10 June) Martyrdom of St Robert of Bury, allegedly murdered by the Jews. Residence of the archbishop of Norway in the abbey.

1182   The delegates of the monastery appear before Henry II to choose a new abbot.

       (21 Feb.) Election of Samson as abbot; (28 Feb.) receives the benediction; (21 Mar.) arrives at the monastery of St Edmund's; appointed judge in ecclesiastical causes.

1186–7 Dispute with monks of Canterbury over jurisdiction in Monks Eleigh.

1187   Jerusalem captured by Saladin; launch of the Third Crusade.

1188   King Henry II visits Bury.

1189   Death of Henry II, accession of Richard I.

1190   Expulsion of Jews from Bury.

1192   Richard I captured and imprisoned in Germany.

1193   Abbot Samson visits Richard I in Germany.

1194   Release and return of Richard I.

1195   Illegal tournament held near Bury.

1196–7 Abbot Samson settles dispute with Knights over castle defence and appoints clerk as cellarer.

1197–8 Abbot Samson visits Normandy, Coventry, and Oxford.

1198   Election of Pope Innocent III; fire at St Edmund's shrine; Abbot Samson exhumes and views the body of St Edmund.

1199   Death of Richard I and accession of King John, who visits Bury.

1201   Cokefield case heard before king's court; death of Prior Robert and appointment of Herbert; monks of Ely establish market at Lakenheath.

1201–2 Abbot Samson disputes with bishop of Ely over jurisdiction, and with monks of Bury over the liberties of the court and cellarer.

*c.*1202 Death of Jocelin of Brakelond.

1212   (30 Dec.) Death of Abbot Samson.

1216   Death of King John, accession of Henry III.

1539   Dissolution of the monastery of St Edmund.

SUMMARY OF PAST AND PRESENT

BOOK I.—PROEM.

CHAP. I. *Midas.*

THE condition of England one of the most ominous ever seen in this world: Full of wealth in every kind, yet dying of inanition. Workhouses, in which no work can be done. Destitution of Scotland. Stockport Assizes. (p. 19).—England's unprofitable success: Human faces glooming discordantly on one another. Midas longed for gold, and the gods gave it him. (21).

CHAP. II. *The Sphinx.*

The grand unnameable Sphinx-riddle, which each man is called upon to solve. Notions of the foolish concerning justice and judgment. Courts of Westminister, and the general High Court of the Universe. The one strong thing, the just thing, the true thing. (p. 25).—A noble Conservatism, as well as an ignoble. In all battles of men each fighter, in the end, prospers according to his right: Wallace of Scotland. (26).—Fact and Semblance. What is Justice? As many men as there are in a Nation who can *see* Heaven's Justice, so many are there who stand between it and perdition. (27).

CHAP. III. *Manchester Insurrection.*

Peterloo not an unsuccessful Insurrection. Governors who wait for Insurrection to instruct them, getting into the fatallest courses. Unspeakable County Yeomanry. Poor Manchester operatives, and their huge inarticulate question: Unhappy Workers, unhappier Idlers, of this actual England! (p. 30).—Fair day's-wages for fair day's-work: Milton's 'wages;' Cromwell's. Pay to each man what he has earned and done and deserved; what more have we to ask?—Some not insupportable approximation indispensable and inevitable. (31).

CHAP. IV. *Morrison's Pill.*

A state of mind worth reflecting on. No Morrison's Pill for curing the maladies of Society. Universal alteration of regimen and way of life: Vain jargon giving place to some genuine Speech again. (p. 36).—If we walk according to the Law of this Universe, the Law-Maker will befriend us: if not, not. Quacks, sham heroes, the one bane of the world. Quack and Dupe, upper side and under of the selfsame substance. (37).

CHAP. V. *Aristocracy of Talent.*

All misery the fruit of unwisdom: Neither with individuals nor with Nations is it fundamentally otherwise. Nature in late centuries universally supposed to be dead, but now everywhere asserting herself to be alive and miraculous. The guidance of this country not sufficiently wise. (p. 39).—Aristocracy of Talent, or government by the Wisest, a dreadfully difficult affair to get started. The true *eye* for talent; and the flunkey eye for respectability, warm garnitures and larders dropping fatness: Bobus and Bobissimus. (41).

CHAP. VI. *Hero-Worship.*

Enlightened Egoism, never so luminous, not the rule by which man's life can be led: a *soul*, different from a stomach in any sense of the world. Hero-worship, done differently in every epoch of the world. Reform, like Charity, must begin at home. 'Arrestment of the knaves and dastards,' beginning by arresting our own poor selves out of that fraternity. (p. 45).—The present Editor's purpose to himself full of hope. A Loadstar in the eternal sky: A glimmering of light, for here and there a human soul. (46).

BOOK II.—THE ANCIENT MONK.

CHAP. I. *Jocelin of Brakelond.*

How the Centuries stand lineally related to each other. The one Book not permissible, the kind that has nothing in it. Jocelin's 'Chronicle,' a private Boswellean Notebook, now seven centuries old. How Jocelin, from under his monk's cowl, looked out on that narrow section of the world in a really *human* manner: A wise simplicity in him; a veracity that goes deeper than words. Jocelin's Monk-Latin; and Mr. Rokewood's editorial helpfulness and fidelity. (p. 50).— A veritable Monk of old Bury St. Edmunds worth attending to. This England of ours, of the year 1200: Cœur-de-Lion: King Lackland, and his thirteenpenny mass. The poorest historical Fact, and the grandest imaginative Fiction. (54).

CHAP. II. *St. Edmundsbury.*

St. Edmund's Bury, a prosperous brisk Town: Extensive ruins of the Abbey still visible. Assiduous Pedantry, and its rubbish-heaps called 'History.' Another world it was, when those black ruins first saw the sun as walls. At lowest, O dilettante friend, let us know always that it *was* a world. No easy matter to get across the chasm of Seven Centuries: Of all helps, a Boswell, even a small Boswell, the welcomest. (p. 57).

CHAP. III. *Landlord Edmund.*

'Battle of Fornham,' a fact, though a forgotten one. Edmund, Landlord of the Eastern Counties: A very singular kind of 'landlord.' How he came to be 'sainted.' Seen and felt to have done verily a man's part in this life-pilgrimage of his. How they took up the slain body of their Edmund, and reverently embalmed it. (p. 62).—Pious munificence, every growing by new pious gifts. Certain Times do crystallise themselves in a magnificent manner; others in a rather shabby one. (63).

CHAP. IV. *Abbot Hugo.*

All things have two faces, a light one and a dark: The Ideal has to grow in the Real, and to seek its bed and board there, often in a very sorry manner. Abbot Hugo, grown old and feeble. Jew debts, and Jew creditors. How approximate justice strives to accomplish itself. (p. 65).—In the old monastic Books, almost no mention whatever of 'personal religion.' A poor Lord Abbot, all stuck-over with horse-leeches: A 'royal commmission of inquiry,' to no purpose. A monk's first duty, obedience. Magister Samson, Teacher of the Novices. The Abbot's providential death. (67).

CHAP. V. *Twelfth Century.*

Inspectors or Custodiars; the King not in any breathless haste to appoint a new Abbot. Dim and very strange looks that monk-life to us. Our venerable ancient spinning grandmothers, shrieking, and rushing out with their distaffs. Lakenheath eels, too slippery to be caught. (p. 70).—How much is alive in England, in that Twelfth Century; how much not yet come into life. Feudal Aristocracy; Wilhelmus Conquestor: Not a steeple-chimney yet got on end from sea to sea. (71).

CHAP. VI. *Monk Samson.*

Monk-Life and Monk-Religion. A great heaven-high Unquestionability, encompassing, interpenetrating all human Duties. Our modern Arkwright Joe-Manton ages: All human dues and reciprocities changed into one great due of 'cash-payment.' The old monks but a limited class of creatures, with a somewhat dull life of it. (p. 72).—One Monk of a taciturn nature distinguishes himself among those babbling ones. A Son of poor Norfolk parents. Little Samson's awful dream: His poor mother dedicates him to St. Edmund. He grows to be a learned man, of devout grave nature. Sent to Rome on business; and returns *too* successful: Method of travelling thither in those days. His tribulations at home: Strange conditions under which Wisdom has sometimes to struggle with Folly. (77).

CHAP. VII. *The Canvassing.*

A new Abbot to be elected. Even gossip, seven centuries off, has significance. The Prior with Twelve Monks, to wait on his Majesty at Waltham. An 'election' the one important social act: Given the Man a People choose, the worth and worthlessness of the People itself is given. (79).

CHAP. VIII. The Election.

Electoral methods and manipulations. Brother Samson ready oftenest with some question, some suggestion, that has wisdom in it. The Thirteen off to Waltham, to choose their Abbot: In the solitude of the Convent, Destiny thus big and in her birthtime, what gossiping, babbling, dreaming of dreams! (p. 81).—King Henry II. in his high Presence-chamber. Samson chosen Abbot: The King's royal acceptation. (84).—

St. Edmundsbury Monks, without express ballot-box or other winnowing machine. In every Nation and Community, there is at all times, *a fittest*, wisest, bravest, best. Human worth and human Worthlessness. (p. 85).

Chap. IX. *Abbot Samson.*

The Lord Abbot's arrival at St. Edmundsbury: The selfsame Samson, yesterday a poor mendicant, this day finds himself a *Dominus Abbas* and mitred Peer of Parliament. (p. 86).—Depth and opulence of true social vitality in those old barbarous ages. True Governors go about under all manner of disguises now as then. Genius, Poet; what these words mean. George the Third, head charioteer of England; and Robert Burns, gauger of ale in Dumfries. (87).—How Abbot Samson found a Convent all in dilapidation. His life-long harsh apprenticeship to governing, namely obeying. First get your Man; all is got. Danger of blockheads. (90).

Chap. X. *Government.*

Beautiful, how the chrysalis governing-soul, shaking off its dusty slough and prison, starts forth winged, a true royal soul!—One first labour, to institute a strenuous review and radical reform of his economics. Wheresoever Disorder may stand or lie, let it have a care; here is a man that has declared war with it. (p. 92).—In less than four years the Convent Debts are all liquidated; and the harpy Jews banished from St. Edmundsbury. New life springs beneficent everywhere: Spiritual rubbish as little tolerated as material. (93).

Chap. XI. *The Abbot's Ways.*

Reproaches, open and secret, of ingratitude, unsociability: Except for 'fit men' in all kinds, hard to say for whom Abbot Samson had much favour. Remembrance of benefits. (p. 94).—An eloquent man, but intent more on substance than on ornament. A just clear heart the basis of all true talent. One of the justest of judges: His invaluable 'talent of silence.' The kind of people he liked worst. Hospitality and stoicism. (95).—The country, in those days, still dark with noble wood and umbrage: How the old trees gradually died out, no man heeding it. Monachism itself, so rich and fruitful once, now all rotted into *peat*. Devastations of four-footed cattle and Henry-the-Eighths. (98).

CHAP. XII. *The Abbot's Troubles.*

The troubles of Abbot Samson, more than tongue can tell. Not the spoil of victory, only the glorious toil of battle, can be theirs who really govern. An insurrection of the Monks: Behave better, ye remiss Monks, and thank Heaven for such an Abbot. (p. 100).— Worn down with incessant toil and tribulation: Gleams of hilarity too; little snatches of encouragement granted even to a Governor. How my Lord of Clare, coming to claim his undue 'debt,' gets a Rowland for his Oliver. A Life of Literature; noble and ignoble. (102).

CHAP. XIII. *In Parliament.*

Confused days of Lackland's usurpation, while Cœur-de-Lion was away: Our brave Abbot took helmet himself, excommunicating all who should favour Lackland. King Richard a captive in Germany. (p. 103).—St. Edmund's Shrine not meddled with: A Heavenly Awe overshadowed and encompassed, as it still ought and must, all earthly Business whatsoever. (104).

CHAP. XIV. Henry of Essex.

How St. Edmund punished terribly, yet with mercy: A Narrative, significant of the Time. Henry Earl of Essex, a standard-bearer of England: No right reverence for the Heavenly in Man. A traitor or a coward. Solemn Duel, by the King's appointment. An evil Conscience doth make cowards of us all. (106–7).

CHAP. XV. *Practical-Devotional.*

A Tournament proclaimed and held in the Abbot's domain, in spite of him. Roystering young dogs brought to reason. The Abbot a man that generally remains master at last: The importunate Bishop of Ely is outwitted. A man that dare abide King Richard's anger, with justice on his side. Thou brave Richard, thou brave Samson! (p. 111).—The basis of Abbot Samson's life, truly religion. His zealous interest in the Crusades. The great antique heart, like a child's in its simplicity, like a man's in its earnest solemnity and depth. His comparative silence as to religion, precisely the healthiest sign of him and it. Methodism, Dilettantism, Puseyism. (113).

Chap. XVI. *St. Edmund.*

Abbot Samson built many useful, many pious edifices: All ruinous, incomplete things, an eye-sorrow to him. Rebuilding the great Altar: A glimpse of the glorious Martyr's very Body. What a scene; how far vanished from us, in these unworshiping ages of ours! The manner of men's Hero-worship, verily the innermost fact of their existence, determining all the rest. (p. 118).—On the whole, who knows how to reverence the Body of Man?—Abbot Samson, at the culminating point of his existence: Our real-phantasmagory of St. Edmundsbury plunges into the bosom of the Twelfth Century again, and all is over. (120).

Chap. XVII. *The Beginnings.*

Formulas, the very skin and muscular tissue of a Man's Life: Living Formulas, and dead. Habit the deepest law of human nature. A pathway through the pathless. Nationalities. Pulpy infancy, kneaded, baked into any form you choose: The Man of Business; the hard-handed Labourer, the genus Dandy. No mortal out of the depths of Bedlam, but lives by Formulas. (p. 123).—The hosts and generations of brave men. Oblivion has swallowed: Their crumbled dust, the soil of our life-fruit grows on. Invention of Speech; Forms of Worship; Methods of Justice. This English Land, here and now, the summary of what was wise, and noble, and accordant with God's Truth, in all the generations of English Men. The thing called 'Fame.' (126).

BOOK III.—THE MODERN WORKER.

Chap. I. *Phenomena.*

How men have 'forgotten God;' taken the Fact of this Universe as it *is not*; God's Laws, become a Greatest-Happiness Principle, a Parliamentary Expediency. Man has lost the *soul* out of him, and begins to find the want of it. (p. 129).—The old Pope of Rome, with his stuffed dummy to do the kneeling for him. Few men that worship by the rotatory Calabash, do it in half so great, frank or effectual a way. (132).—Our Aristocracy, no longer able to *do* its work; and not in the least conscious that it has any work to do. The Champion of England 'lifted into his saddle.' The Hatter in the Strand, mounting a huge lath-and-plaster Hat. Our noble ancestors have fashioned for us, in how many thousand senses, a 'life-road;' and we their sons, are madly, literally enough, 'consuming the way.' (135).

CHAP. II. *Gospel of Mammonism.*

Heaven and Hell, often as the words are on our tongue, got to be fabulous or semi-fabulous for most of us. The real 'Hell' of the English. Cash-payment, *not* the sole or even the chief relation of human beings. Practical Atheism, and its despicable fruits. (p. 138).— One of Dr. Alison's melancholy facts: A poor Irish Widow in the Lanes of Edinburgh, *proving* her sisterhood. Until we get a human *soul* within us, all things are *im*possible. Infatuated geese, with feathers and without. (140).

CHAP. III. *Gospel of Dilettantism.*

Mammonism at least works; but 'Go gracefully idle in Mayfair,' what does or can that mean?—Impotent, insolent Donothingism in Practice, and Saynothingism in Speech. No man now speaks a plain word: Insincere Speech, the prime material of insincere Action. (p. 141).— Moslem parable of Moses and the Dwellers by the Dead Sea: The Universe *become* a Humbug, to the Apes that thought it one. (142).

CHAP. IV. *Happy.*

All work, noble; and every noble crown a crown of thorns. Man's pitiful pretension to be what he calls 'happy:' His Greatest-Happiness Principle fast becoming a rather unhappy one. Byron's large audience. A philosophical Doctor: A disconsolate Meat-jack, gnarring and creaking with rust and work. (pp. 144–5).—The only 'happiness' a brave man ever troubled himself much about, the happiness to get his work done. (145).

CHAP. V. *The English.*

With all thy theoretic platitudes, what a depth of practical sense in thee, great England! A dumb people, who can do great acts, but not describe them. The noble Warhorse, and the Dog of Knowledge: The freest utterances not by any means the best. (p. 146).—The done Work, much more than the spoken Word, an epitome of the man.

The Man of Practice, and the Man of Theory: Ineloquent Brindley. The English, of all Nations, the stupidest in speech, the wisest in action: Sadness and seriousness: Unconsciously this great Universe is great to them. The Silent Romans. John Bull's admirable insensibility to Logic. (p. 150).—All great Peoples conservative. The English Ready-Reckoner a Solecism in East-Cheap. Berserkir-rage. Truth and Justice alone *capable* of being 'conserved.' Bitter indignation engendered by the Corn-Laws in every just English heart. (152-3).

CHAP. VI. *Two Centuries.*

The 'Settlement' of the year 1660, one of the mournfullest that ever took place in this land of ours. The true end of Government, to guide men in the way that they should go. The true good of this life, the portal of infinite good in the life to come. Oliver Cromwell's body hung on the Tyburn-gallows; the type of Puritanism found futile, inexecutable, execrable. The Spiritualism of England, for two godless centuries, utterly forgettable: Her practical Material Work alone memorable. (p. 155).—Bewildering obscurations and impediments: Valiant Sons of Toil enchanted, by the million, in their Poor-Law Bastille. Giant Labour, yet to be the King of this Earth. (156).

CHAP. VII. *Over-Production.*

An idle Governing Class addressing its Workers with an indictment of 'Over-Production.' Duty of justly apportioning the Wages of Work done. A game-preserving Aristocracy, guiltless of producing or apportioning anything. Owning the soil of England. (p. 163).—The Working Aristocracy, steeped in ignoble Mammonism: The Idle Aristocracy, with its yellow parchments and pretentious futilities. (158-9).

CHAP. VIII. *Unworking Aristocracy.*

Our Land the *Mother* of us all: No true Aristocracy but must possess the Land. Men talk of 'selling' Land: Whom it belongs to. Our much-*consuming* Aristocracy: By the law of their position bound to furnish guidance and governance. Mad and miserable Corn-Laws. (p. 162).—The Working Aristocracy, and its terrible New-Work:

The Idle Aristocracy, and its horoscope of despair. (163).—A High Class without duties to do, like a tree planted on precipices. In a valiant suffering for others, not in a slothful making others suffer for us, did nobleness ever lie. The Pagan Hercules; the Czar of Russia. (165).—Parchments, venerable and not venerable. Benedict the Jew, and his usuries. No CHAPTER on the Corn-Laws: The Corn-Laws too mad to have a CHAPTER. (165).

CHAP. IX. *Working Aristocracy.*

Many things for the Working Aristocracy, in their extreme need, to consider. A National Existence supposed to depend on 'selling cheaper' than any other People. Let inventive men try to invent a little how cotton at its present cheapness could be somewhat justlier divided. Many 'impossibles' will have to become possible. (168).—Supply-and-demand: For what noble work was there ever yet any audible 'demand' in that poor sense? (169).

CHAP. X. *Plugson of Undershot.*

Man's philosophies usually the 'supplement of his practice:' Symptoms of social death. Cash-Payment: The Plugson Ledger, and the Tablets of Heaven's Chancery, discrepant exceedingly. (p. 172).— All human things do require to have an Ideal in them. How murderous Fighting became a 'glorious Chivalry'. Noble devout-hearted Chevaliers. Ignoble Bucaniers and Chactaw Indians: Howel Davies. Napoleon flung out, at last, to St. Helena; the latter end of him sternly compensating for the beginning. (174).—The indomitable Plugson, as yet a Bucanier and Chactaw. William Conqueror and his Norman followers. Organisation of Labour: Courage, there are yet many brave men in England! (177).

CHAP. XI. *Labour.*

A perennial nobleness, and even sacredness in Work. Significance of the Potter's Wheel. Blessed is he who has found his Work; let him ask no other blessedness. (p. 178).—A brave Sir Christopher, and his Paul's Cathedral: Every noble work, at first 'impossible.' Columbus, royallest Sea-king of all: A depth of Silence, deeper than the Sea; a Silence unsoundable; known to God only. (180).

Chap. XII. *Reward.*

Work is Worship: Labour, wide as the Earth, has its summit in Heaven. One monster there is in the world, the idle man. (p. 181).— 'Fair day's-wages for a fair day's-work,' the most unrefusable demand. The 'wages' of every noble Work, in Heaven or else Nowhere: The brave man has to *give* his Life away. He that works, bodies forth the form of Things Unseen. Strange mystic affinity of Wisdom and Insanity: All Work, in its degree, a making of Madness sane. (185).—Labour not a devil, even when encased in Mammonism: The unredeemed ugliness, a slothful People. The vulgarest Plugson of a Master-Worker, not a man to strangle by Corn-Laws and Shotbelts. (186).

Chap. XIII. *Democracy.*

Man must actually have his debts and earnings a little better paid by man. At no time was the lot of the dumb millions of toilers so entirely unbearable as now. Sisterhood, brotherhood, often forgotten; but never before so expressly denied. Mungo Park and his poor Black Benefactress. (pp. 189–90).—Gurth born thrall of Cedric the Saxon: Liberty, a Divine thing; but 'liberty to die by starvation' not so divine. Nature's Aristocracies. William Conqueror, a resident House-Surgeon provided by Nature for her beloved English People. (192).—Democracy, the despair of finding Heroes to govern us, and contented putting up with the want of them. The very Tailor unconsciously symbolising the reign of Equality. Wherever ranks do actually exist, strict division of costumes will also be enforced. (194).—Freedom from oppression, an indispensable yet most insignificant portion of Human Liberty. A *best path* does exist for every man; a thing which, here and now, it were of all things *wisest* for him to do. Mock Superiors and Real Superiors. (196–7).

Chap. XIV. *Sir Jabesh Windbag.*

Oliver Cromwell, the remarkablest Governor we have had for the last five centuries or so: No volunteer in Public Life, but plainly a balloted soldier: The Government of England put into his hands. (p. 198).— Windbag, weak in the faith of a God; strong only in the faith that Paragraphs and Plausibilities bring votes. Five years of popularity or unpopularity; and *after* those five years, an Eternity. Oliver has to appear before the Most High Judge: Windbag, appealing to 'Posterity.' (200).

CHAP. XV. *Morrison Again.*

New Religions: This new stage of progress, proceeding 'to invent God,' a very strange one indeed. (p. 202).—Religion, the Inner Light or Moral Conscience of a man's soul. Infinite difference between a Good man and a Bad. The great Soul of the World, just and not unjust: Faithful, unspoken, but not ineffectual 'prayer.' Penalties: The French Revolution; cruellest Portent that has risen into created Space these ten centuries. Man needs no 'New Religion;' nor is like to get it: Spiritual Dastardism, and sick folly. (206).—One Liturgy which does remain forever unexceptionable, that of *Praying by Working.* Sauerteig on the symbolic influences of Washing. Chinese Pontiff-Emperor and his significant 'punctualities.' (208).—Goethe and German Literature. The great event for the world, now as always, the arrival in it of a new Wise Man. Goethe's *Mason-Lodge.* (210).

BOOK IV. — HOROSCOPE.

CHAP. I. *Aristocracies.*

To predict the Future, to manage the Present, would not be so impossible, had not the Past been so sacrilegiously mishandled: A godless century, looking back to centuries that were godly. (p. 213).—A new real Aristocracy and Priesthood. The noble Priest always a noble *Aristos* to begin with, and something more to end with. Modern Preachers, and the *real* Satanas that now is. Abbot-Samson and William-Conqueror times. The mission of a Land Aristocracy, a *sacred* one, in both senses of that old word. Truly a 'Splendour of God' did dwell in those old rude veracious ages. Old Anselm travelling to Rome, to appeal against King Rufus. Their quarrel at bottom a great quarrel. (219).—The boundless Future, predestined, nay already extant though unseen. Our Epic, not *Arms and the Man*, but *Tools and the Man*; an infinitely wider kind of Epic. Important that our grand Reformation were begun. (223).

Chap. II. *Bribery Committee.*

Our theory, perfect purity of Tenpound Franchise; our practice, irremediable bribery. Bribery, indicative not only of length of purse, but of brazen dishonesty: Proposed improvements. A Parliament, starting with a lie in its mouth, promulgates strange horoscopes of itself. (p. 225).—Respect paid to those worthy of no respect: Pandarus Dogdraught. The indigent discerning Freeman; and the kind of men he is called upon to vote for. (226).

Chap. III. *The One Institution.*

The 'Organisation of Labour,' if well understood, the Problem of the whole Future. Governments of various degrees of utility. Kilkenny Cats; Spinning-Dervishes; Parliamentary Eloquence. A Prime-Minister who would dare believe the heavenly omens. (p. 230).—Who can despair of Governments, that passes a Soldier's Guard-house?—Incalculable what, by arranging, commanding and regimenting, can be made of men. Organisms enough in the dim huge Future; and 'United Services' quite other than the red-coat one. (233)—Legislative interference between Workers and Master-Workers increasingly indispensable. Sanitary Reform: People's Parks: A right Education Bill, and effective Teaching Service. Free bridge for Emigrants: England's sure markets, among her Colonies. London, the *All-Saxon-Home*, rendezvous of all the 'Children of the Harz Rock.' (236).—The English essentially conservative: Always the invincible instinct to hold fast by the Old, to admit the *minimum* of New. Yet new epochs do actually come; and with them new peremptory necessities. A certain Editor's stipulated work. (237).

Chap. IV. *Captains of Industry.*

Government can do much, but it can in nowise do all. Fall of Mammon: To be a noble Master among noble Workers, will again be the first ambition with some few. (239).—The Leaders of Industry, virtually the Captains of the World: Doggeries and Chivalries. Isolation, the sum-total of wretchedness to man. All social growth in this world have required organising; and Work, the grandest of human interests, does now require it. (242).

Chap. V. *Permanence.*

The 'tendency to persevere,' to persist in spite of hindrances, discouragements and 'impossibilities,' that which distinguishes the Species Man from the Genus Ape. Month-long contracts, and Exeter-Hall purblindness. A practical manufacturing Quaker's care for his workmen. (p. 245).—Blessing of Permanent Contract: Permanence in all things, at the earliest possible moment, and to the latest possible. Vagrant Sam-Slicks. The wealth of a man the number of things he loves and blesses, which he is loved and blessed by. (247).—The Worker's *interest* in the enterprise with which he is connected. How to reconcile Despotism with Freedom. (248).

Chap. VI. *The Landed.*

A man with fifty, with five hundred, with a thousand pounds a day, given him freely, without condition at all, might be a rather strong Worker: The sad reality, very ominous to look at. Will he awaken, be alive again; or is this death-fit very death?—Goethe's Duke of Weimar. Doom of Idleness. (p. 250).—To sit idle aloft, like absurd Epicurus'-gods, a poor life for a man. Independence, 'lord of the lion-heart and eagle-eye:' Rejection of sham Superiors, the needful preparation for obedience to *real* Superiors. (252).

Chap. VII. *The Gifted.*

Tumultuous anarchy, calmed by noble effort into fruitful sovereignty. Mammon like Fire, the usefullest of servants, if the frightfullest of masters. Souls to whom the omnipotent guinea is, on the whole, an impotent guinea: Not a May-game in this man's life; but a battle and stern pilgrimage: God's justice, human Nobleness, Veracity and Mercy, the essence of his very being. (p. 255).—What a man of Genius is. The Highest 'Man of Genius.' Genius the clearer presence of God Most High in a man. Of intrinsic Valetisms you cannot, with whole Parliaments to help you, make a Heroism. (257).

Chap. VIII. *The Didactic.*

One preacher who does preach with effect, and gradually persuade all persons. Repentant Captains of Industry: A Chactaw Fighter, become a Christian Fighter. (p. 258).—Doomsday in the afternoon. The 'Christianity' that cannot get on without a minimum of Four-thousand-five-hundred, will give place to something better that can. Beautiful to see the brutish empire of Mammon cracking everywhere. A strange, chill, almost ghastly dayspring in Yankeeland itself. Here as there, Light is coming into the world. Whoso believes, let him begin to fulfil: 'Impossible,' where Truth and Mercy and the everlasting Voice of Nature order, can have no place in the brave man's dictionary. (259).—Not on Ilion's or Latium's plains; on far other plains and places henceforth can noble deeds be done. The last Partridge of England shot and ended: Aristocracies with beards on their chins. O, it is great, and there is no other greatness: To make some nook of God's Creation a little fruitfuller; to make some human hearts a little wiser, manfuller, happier: It is work for a God! (260).

BOOK I.

PROEM.

CHAPTER I.

MIDAS.*

THE condition of England,* on which many pamphlets are now in
the course of publication, and many thoughts unpublished are going
on in every reflective head, is justly regarded as one of the most ominous, and withal one of the strangest, ever seen in this world. England
is full of wealth, of multifarious produce, supply for human want in
every kind; yet England is dying of inanition. With unabated bounty
the land of England blooms and grows; waving with yellow harvests;
thick-studded with workshops, industrial implements, with fifteen
millions of workers understood to be the strongest, the cunningest
and the willingest our Earth ever had; these men are here; the work
they have done, the fruit they have realised is here, abundant, exuberant on every hand of us: and behold, some baleful fiat as of Enchantment
has gone forth, saying, "Touch it not, ye workers, ye master-workers,
ye master-idlers; none of you can touch it, no man of you shall be the
better for it; this is enchanted fruit!" On the poor workers such fiat
falls first, in its rudest shape; but on the rich master-workers too it
falls; neither can the rich master-idlers, nor any richest or highest
man escape, but all are like to be brought low with it, and made 'poor'
enough, in the money-sense or a far fatailer one.

Of these successful skilful workers some two millions, it is now
counted, sit in Workhouses, Poor-law Prisons; or have 'out-door
relief'* flung over the wall to them,—the workhouse Bastille being filled
to bursting,* and the strong Poor-law broken asunder by a stronger.[1]
They sit there, these many months now; their hope of deliverance as yet
small. In workhouses, pleasantly so named, because work cannot be

---

[1] The Return of Paupers for England and Wales, at Ladyday, 1842, is, 'In-door
221,687, Out-door 1,207,402, Total 1,429,089.'—(*Official Report.*)*

done in them. Twelve hundred thousand workers in England alone; their cunning right-hand lamed, lying idle in their sorrowful bosom; their hopes, outlooks, share of this fair world, shut in by narrow walls. They sit there, pent up, as in a kind of horrid enchantment; glad to be imprisoned and enchanted, that they may not perish starved. The picturesque Tourist,* in a sunny autumn day, through this bounteous realm of England, descries the Union Workhouse on his path. 'Passing by the Workhouse of St. Ives in Huntingdonshire,* on a bright day last autumn,' says the picturesque Tourist, 'I saw sitting on wooden benches, in front of their Bastille and within their ring-wall and its railings, some half-hundred or more of these men. Tall robust figures, young mostly or of middle age; of honest countenance, many of them thoughtful and even intelligent-looking men. They sat there, near by one another; but in a kind of torpor, especially in a silence, which was very striking. In silence: for, alas, what word was to be said? An Earth all lying round, crying, Come and till me, come and reap me;—yet we here sit enchanted! In the eyes and brows of these men hung the gloomiest expression, not of anger, but of grief and shame and manifold inarticulate distress and weariness; they returned my glance with a glance that seemed to say, "Do not look at us. We sit enchanted here, we know not why. The Sun shines and the Earth calls; and, by the governing Powers and Impotences of this England, we are forbidden to obey. It is impossible, they tell us!"* There was something that reminded me of Dante's Hell in the look of all this; and I rode swiftly away.'

So many hundred thousands sit in workhouses: and other hundred thousands have not yet got even workhouses; and in thrifty Scotland itself, in Glasgow or Edinburgh City, in their dark lanes, hidden from all but the eye of God, and of rare Benevolence the minister of God, there are scenes of woe and destitution and desolation, such as, one may hope, the Sun never saw before in the most barbarous regions where men dwelt. Competent witnesses, the brave and humane Dr. Alison, who speaks what he knows,* whose noble Healing Art in his charitable hands becomes once more a truly sacred one, report these things for us: these things are not of this year, or of last year, have no reference to our present state of commercial stagnation, but only to the common state. Not in sharp fever-fits, but in chronic gangrene of this kind is Scotland suffering. A Poor-law, any and every Poor-law, it may be observed, is but a temporary measure; an anodyne, not a remedy: Rich and Poor, when once the naked facts of their condition have come into collision, cannot long subsist together on a mere Poor-law True enough:—and yet human beings cannot be left to die! Scotland too, till something better come, must have a Poor-law,* if Scotland is not to be a byword among the nations. O, what a waste is there; of noble and thrice-noble national virtues; peasant Stoicisms, Heroisms; valiant manful habits, soul of a Nation's worth,—which all the metal of Potosi* cannot purchase back; to which the metal of Potosi, and all you can buy with *it*, is dross and dust!

Why dwell on this aspect of the matter? It is too indisputable, not doubtful now to any one. Descend where you will into the lower class, in Town or Country, by what avenue you will, by Factory Inquiries, Agricultural Inquiries, by Revenue Returns, by Mining-Labourer Committees,* by opening your own eyes and looking, the same sorrowful result discloses itself: you have to admit that the working body of this rich English Nation has sunk or is fast sinking into a state, to which, all sides of it considered, there was literally never any parallel. At Stockport Assizes,—and this too has no reference to the present state of trade, being of date prior to that,—a Mother and a Father are arraigned* and found guilty of poisoning three of their children, to defraud a 'burial-society' of some 3*l*. 8*s*. due on the death of each child: they are arraigned, found guilty; and the official authorities, it is whispered, hint that perhaps the case is not solitary, that perhaps you had better not probe farther into that department of things.* This is in the autumn of 1841;* the crime itself is of the previous year or season. "Brutal savages, degraded Irish,"* mutters the idle reader of Newspapers; hardly lingering on this incident. Yet it is an incident worth lingering on; the depravity, savagery and degraded Irishism being never so well admitted. In the British land a human Mother and Father, of white skin and professing the Christian religion, had done this thing; they, with their Irishism and necessity and savagery, had been driven to do it. Such instances are like the highest mountain apex emerged into view; under which lies a whole mountain region and land, not yet emerged. A human Mother and Father had said to themselves, What shall we do to escape starvation? We are deep sunk here, in our dark cellar;* and help is far.—Yes, in the Ugolino Hunger-tower, stern things happen; best-loved little Gaddo fallen dead on his Father's knees!*—The Stockport Mother and Father think and hint: Our poor little starveling Tom, who cries all day for victuals, who will see only evil and not good in this world: if he were out of misery at once; he well dead, and the rest of us perhaps kept alive? It is thought, and hinted; at last it is done. And now Tom being killed, and all spent and eaten, Is it poor little starveling Jack that must go, or poor little starveling Will?—What an inquiry of ways and means!*

In starved sieged cities, in the uttermost doomed ruin of old Jerusalem fallen under the wrath of God, it was prophesied and said, 'The hands of the pitiful women have sodden their own children.'* The stern Hebrew imagination could conceive no blacker gulf of wretchedness; that was the ultimatum of degraded god-punished man. And we here, in modern England, exuberant with supply of all kinds, besieged by nothing if it be not by invisible Enchantments, are we reaching that?——How come these things?* Wherefore are they, wherefore should they be?

Nor are they of the St. Ives workhouses, of the Glasgow lanes,* and Stockport cellars, the only unblessed among us. This successful industry of England, with its plethoric wealth, has as yet made nobody rich; it is an enchanted wealth, and belongs yet to nobody. We might ask, Which of us has it enriched? We can spend thousands where we once spent hundreds; but can purchase nothing good with them. In Poor and Rich, instead of noble thrift and plenty, there is idle luxury alternating with mean scarcity and inability. We have sumptuous garnitures for our Life, but have forgotten to *live* in the middle of them. It is an enchanted wealth; no man of us can yet touch it. The class of men who feel that they are truly better off by means of it, let them give us their name!

Many men eat finer cookery, drink dearer liquors,—with what advantage they can report, and their Doctors can: but in the heart of them, if we go out of the dyspeptic stomach, what increase of blessedness is there? Are they better, beautifuller, stronger, braver? Are they even what they call 'happier?'* Do they look with satisfaction on more things and human faces in this God's-Earth; do more things and human faces look with satisfaction on them? Not so. Human faces gloom discordantly, disloyally on one another. Things, if it be not mere cotton and iron things, are growing disobedient to man. The Master Worker is enchanted, for the present, like his Workhouse Workman; clamours, in vain hitherto, for a very simple sort of 'Liberty:' the liberty 'to buy where he finds it cheapest, to sell where he finds it dearest.'* With guineas jingling in every pocket, he was no whit richer; but now, the very guineas threatening to vanish, he feels that he is poor indeed. Poor Master Worker! And the Master Unworker, is not he in a still fataller situation? Pausing amid his game-preserves, with awful eye,*—as he well may! Coercing fifty-pound tenants;* coercing, bribing, cajoling; doing what he likes with his own.* His mouth full of loud futilities, and arguments to prove the excellence of his Corn-law; and in his heart the blackest misgiving, a desperate half-consciousness that his excellent Corn-law is *in*defensible,* that his loud arguments for it are of a kind to strike men too literally *dumb*.

To whom, then, is this wealth of England wealth? Who is it that it blesses; makes happier, wiser, beautifuller, in any way better? Who has got hold of it, to make it fetch and carry for him, like a true servant, not like a false mock-servant; to do him any real service whatsoever? As yet no one. We have more riches than any Nation ever had before; we have less good of them than any Nation ever had before. Our successful industry is hitherto unsuccessful; a strange success, if we stop here! In the midst of plethoric plenty, the people perish;* with gold walls, and full barns, no man feels himself safe or satisfied. Workers, Master Workers, Unworkers, all men, come to a pause; stand fixed, and cannot farther. Fatal paralysis spreading inwards, from the extremities, in St. Ives workhouses, in Stockport cellars,* through all limbs, as if towards the heart itself. Have we actually got enchanted then; accursed by some god?—

Midas longed for gold, and insulted the Olympians.* He got gold, so that whatsoever he touched became gold,—and he, with his long ears, was little the better for it. Midas had misjudged the celestial music-tones; Midas had insulted Apollo and the gods: the gods gave him his wish, and a pair of long ears, which also were a good appendage to it. What a truth in these old Fables!

CHAPTER II.

THE SPHINX.

How true, for example, is that other old Fable of the Sphinx,* who sat by the wayside, propounding her riddle to the passengers, which if they could not answer she destroyed them! Such a Sphinx is this Life of ours, to all men and societies of men. Nature, like the Sphinx, is of womanly celestial loveliness and tenderness; the face and bosom of a goddess, but ending in claws and the body of a lioness. There is in her a celestial beauty,—which means celestial order, pliancy to wisdom; but there is also a darkness, a ferocity, fatality, which are infernal. She is a goddess, but one not yet disimprisoned; one still half-imprisoned,—the inarticulate, lovely still encased in the inarticulate, chaotic. How true! And does she not propound her riddles to us? Of each man she asks daily, in mild voice, yet with a terrible significance, "Knowest thou the meaning of this Day? What thou canst do Today; wisely attempt to do?" Nature, Universe, Destiny, Existence, howsoever we name this grand unnameable Fact in the midst of which we live and struggle,* is as a heavenly bride and conquest to the wise and brave, to them who can discern her behests and do them; a destroying fiend to them who cannot. Answer her riddle, it is well with thee. Answer it not, pass on regarding it not, it will answer itself; the solution for thee is a thing of teeth and claws; Nature is a dumb lioness, deaf to thy pleadings, fiercely devouring. Thou art not now her victorious bridegroom;* thou art her mangled victim, scattered on the precipices, as a slave found treacherous, recreant, ought to be and must.

With Nations it is as with individuals: Can they rede the riddle of Destiny?* This English Nation, will it get to know the meaning of *its* strange new Today? Is there sense enough extant, discoverable anywhere or anyhow, in our united twenty-seven million heads* to discern the same; valour enough in our twenty-seven million hearts to dare and do the bidding thereof? It will be seen!—

The secret of gold Midas, which he with his long ears never could discover, was, That he had offended the Supreme Powers;—that he had parted company with the eternal inner Facts of this Universe, and followed the transient outer Appearances thereof; and so was arrived *here*. Properly it is the secret of all unhappy men and unhappy nations. Had they known Nature's right truth, Nature's right truth would have made them free. They have become enchanted; stagger spell-bound, reeling on the brink of huge peril, because they were not wise enough. They have forgotten the right Inner True, and taken up with the Outer Sham-true. They answer the Sphinx's question *wrong*. Foolish men cannot answer it aright! Foolish men mistake transitory semblance for eternal fact, and go astray more and more.

Foolish men imagine that because judgment for an evil thing is delayed, there is no justice, but an accidental one, here below. Judgment for an evil thing is many times delayed some day or two, some century or two, but it is sure as life, it is sure as death! In the centre of the world-whirlwind,* verily now as in the oldest days, dwells and speaks a God. The great soul of the world is *just*. O brother, can it be needful now, at this late epoch of experience, after eighteen centuries of Christian preaching for one thing, to remind thee of such a fact; which all manner of Mahometans, old Pagan Romans, Jews, Scythians and heathen Greeks,* and indeed more or less all men that God made, have managed at one time to see into; nay which thou thyself, till 'redtape' strangled the inner life of thee,* hadst once some inkling of: That there *is* justice here below; and even, at bottom, that there is nothing else but justice! Forget that, thou hast forgotten all. Success will never more attend thee: how can it now? Thou hast the whole Universe against thee. No more success: mere sham-success, for a day and days; rising ever higher,—towards its Tarpeian Rock.* Alas, how, in thy soft-hung Longacre vehicle,* of polished leather to the bodily eye, of redtape philosophy, of expediencies, clubroom moralities, Parliamentary majorities to the mind's eye, thou beautifully rollest: but knowest thou whitherward? It is towards the *road's end*. Old use-and-wont; established methods, habitudes, *once* true and wise; man's noblest tendency, his perseverance, and man's ignoblest, his inertia; whatsoever of noble and ignoble Conservatism there is in men and Nations, strongest always in the strongest men and Nations: all this is as a road to thee, paved smooth through the abyss,—till all this *end*. Till men's bitter necessities can endure thee no more. Till Nature's patience with thee is done; and there is no road or footing any farther, and the abyss yawns sheer!—

Parliament and the Courts of Westminster* are venerable to me; how venerable; grey with a thousand years of honourable age! For a thousand years and more, Wisdom and faithful Valour, struggling amid much Folly and greedy Baseness, not without most sad distortions in the struggle, have built them up; and they are as we see. For a thousand years, this English Nation has found them useful or supportable; they have served this English Nation's want; *been* a road to it through the abyss of Time. They are venerable, they are great and strong. And yet it is good to remember always that they are not the venerablest, nor the greatest nor the strongest! Acts of Parliament are venerable; but if they correspond not with the writing on the 'Adamant Tablet,'* what are they? Properly their one element of venerableness,

of strength or greatness, is, that they at all times correspond therewith as near as by human possibility they can. They are cherishing
destruction in their bosom every hour that they continue otherwise.

Alas, how many causes that can plead well for themselves in the
Courts of Westminster; and yet in the general Court of the Universe,
and free Soul of Man, have no word to utter! Honourable Gentlemen
may find this worth considering, in times like ours. And truly, the
din of triumphant Law-logic, and all shaking of horse-hair wigs and
learned-sergeant* gowns having comfortably ended, we shall do well
to ask ourselves withal, What says that high and highest Court to the
verdict? For it is the Court of Courts, that same; where the universal
soul of Fact and very Truth sits President;—and thitherward, more
and more swiftly, with a really terrible increase of swiftness, all causes
do in these days crowd for revisal,—for confirmation, for modifica-
tion, for reversal with costs. Dost thou know that Court; hast thou
had any Law-practice there? What, didst thou never enter; never file
any petition of redress, reclaimer,* disclaimer or demurrer, written as
in thy heart's blood, for thy own behoof or another's; and silently
await the issue? Thou knowest not such a Court? Hast merely heard
of it by faint tradition as a thing that was or had been? Of thee, I think,
we shall get little benefit.

For the gowns of learned-sergeants are good: parchment records,
fixed forms, and poor terrestrial Justice, with or without horse-hair,
what sane man will not reverence these? And yet, behold, the man is
not sane but insane, who considers these alone as venerable. Oceans
of horse-hair, continents of parchment, and learned-sergeant eloquence, were it continued till the learned tongue wore itself small in
the indefatigable learned mouth, cannot make unjust just. The grand
question still remains, Was the judgment just? If unjust, it will not
and cannot get harbour for itself, or continue to have footing in this
Universe, which was made by other than One Unjust. Enforce it by
never such statuting, three readings, royal assents;* blow it to the four
winds with all manner of quilted trumpeters and pursuivants, in the
rear of them never so many gibbets and hangmen, it will not stand, it
cannot stand. From all souls of men, from all ends of Nature, from
the Throne of God above, there are voices bidding it: Away, away!
Does it take no warning; does it stand, strong in its three readings, in
its gibbets and artillery-parks? The more woe is to it, the frightfuller
woe. It will continue standing, for its day, for its year, for its century,

doing evil all the while; but it has One enemy who is Almighty: dissolution, explosion, and the everlasting Laws of Nature incessantly advance towards it; and the deeper its rooting, more obstinate its continuing, the deeper also and huger will its ruin and overturn be.

In this God's-world, with its wild-whirling eddies and mad foam-oceans, where men and nations perish as if without law, and judgment for an unjust thing is sternly delayed, dost thou think that there is therefore no justice? It is what the fool hath said in his heart.* It is what the wise, in all times, were wise because they denied, and knew forever not to be. I tell thee again, there is nothing else but justice. One strong thing I find here below: the just thing, the true thing. My friend, if thou hadst all the artillery of Woolwich* trundling at thy back in support of an unjust thing; and infinite bonfires visibly waiting ahead of thee, to blaze centuries long for thy victory on behalf of it,—I would advise thee to call halt, to fling down thy baton, and say, "In God's name, No!" Thy 'success?' Poor devil, what will thy success amount to? If the thing is unjust, thou hast not succeeded; no, not though bonfires blazed from North to South, and bells rang, and editors wrote leading-articles, and the just thing lay trampled out of sight, to all mortal eyes an abolished and annihilated thing. Success? In few years, thou wilt be dead and dark,—all cold, eyeless, deaf; no blaze of bonfires, ding-dong of bells or leading-articles visible or audible to thee again at all forever: What kind of success is that!—

It is true all goes by approximation in this world; with any not insupportable approximation we must be patient. There is a noble Conservatism as well as an ignoble.* Would to Heaven, for the sake of Conservatism itself, the noble alone were left, and the ignoble, by some kind severe hand, were ruthlessly lopped away, forbidden ever more to shew itself! For it is the right and noble alone that will have victory in this struggle; the rest is wholly an obstruction, a postponement and fearful imperilment of the victory. Towards an eternal centre of right and nobleness, and of that only, is all this confusion tending. We already know whither it is all tending; what will have victory, what will have none! The Heaviest will reach the centre. The Heaviest, sinking through complex fluctuating media and vortices, has its deflexions, its obstructions, nay at times its resiliences, its reboundings; whereupon some blockhead shall be heard jubilating, "See, your Heaviest ascends!"—but at all moments it is moving centreward, fast as is convenient for it; sinking, sinking; and, by laws older than the World, old as the Maker's first Plan of the World, it has to arrive there.

Await the issue. In all battles, if you await the issue, each fighter has prospered according to his right. His right and his might,* at the close of the account, were one and the same. He has fought with all his might, and in exact proportion to all his right he has prevailed. His very death is no victory over him. He dies indeed; but his work lives, very truly lives. A heroic Wallace, quartered on the scaffold, cannot hinder that his Scotland become, one day, a part of England:* but he does hinder that it become, on tyrannous unfair terms, a part of it; commands still, as with a god's voice, from his old Valhalla and Temple of the Brave,* that there be a just real union as of brother and brother, not a false and merely semblant* one as of slave and master. If the union with England be in fact one of Scotland's chief blessings, we thank Wallace withal that it was not the chief curse. Scotland is not Ireland:* no, because brave men rose there, and said, "Behold, ye must not tread us down like slaves; and ye shall not,—and cannot!" Fight on, thou brave true heart, and falter not, through dark fortune and through bright. The cause thou fightest for, so far as it is true, no farther, yet precisely so far, is very sure of victory. The falsehood alone of it will be conquered, will be abolished, as it ought to be: but the truth of it is part of Nature's own Laws, cooperates with the World's eternal Tendencies, and cannot be conquered.

The *dust* of controversy, what is it but the *falsehood* flying off from all manner of conflicting true forces, and making such a loud dust-whirlwind,—that so the truths alone may remain, and embrace brotherlike in some true resulting-force! It is ever so. Savage fighting Heptarchies:* their fighting is an ascertainment, who has the right to rule over whom; that out of such waste-bickering* Saxondom a peace fully cooperating England may arise. Seek through this Universe; if with other than owl's eyes, thou wilt find nothing nourished there, nothing kept in life, but what has right to nourishment and life. The rest, look at it with other than owl's eyes, is not living; is all dying, all as good as dead! Justice was ordained from the foundations of the world; and will last with the world and longer.

From which I infer that the inner sphere of Fact, in this present England as elsewhere, differs infinitely from the outer sphere and spheres of Semblance. That the Temporary, here as elsewhere, is too apt to carry it over the Eternal. That he who dwells in the temporary Semblances and does not penetrate into the eternal Substance will *not* answer the Sphinx-riddle of Today, or of any Day. For the substance alone is substantial; that *is* the law of Fact: if you discover not that, Fact, who already knows it, will let you also know it by and by!

What is Justice? that, on the whole, is the question of the Sphinx to us. The law of Fact is, that Justice must and will be done. The sooner the better; for the Time grows stringent, frightfully pressing! "What is Justice?" ask many, to whom cruel Fact alone will be able to prove responsive. It is like jesting Pilate asking, What is Truth?* Jesting Pilate had not the smallest chance to ascertain what was Truth. He could not have known it, had a god shewn it to him. Thick serene opacity, thicker than amaurosis,* veiled those smiling eyes of his to Truth; the inner *retina* of them was gone paralytic, dead. He looked at Truth; and discerned her not, there where she stood. "What is Justice?" The clothed embodied Justice that sits in Westminster Hall,* with penalties, parchments, tipstaves,* is very visible. But the *un*embodied Justice, whereof that other is either an emblem, or else is a fearful indescribability, is not so visible! For the unembodied Justice is of Heaven; a Spirit, and Divinity of Heaven,—*in*visible to all but the noble and pure of soul. The impure ignoble gaze with eyes, and she is not there. They will prove it to you by logic, by endless Hansard Debatings,* by bursts of Parliamentary eloquence.* It is not consolatory to behold! For properly, as many men as there are in a Nation who *can* withal see Heaven's invisible Justice, and know it to be on Earth also omnipotent, so many men are there who stand between a Nation and perdition. So many, and no more. Heavy-laden England, how many hast thou in this hour? The Supreme Power sends new and ever new, all *born* at least with hearts of flesh and not of stone;—and heavy Misery itself, once heavy enough, will prove didactic!—

CHAPTER III.

MANCHESTER INSURRECTION.*

BLUSTEROWSKI, Colacorde, and other Editorial prophets* of the Continental Democratic Movement, have in their leading-articles shewn themselves disposed to vilipend* the late Manchester Insurrection, as evincing in the rioters an extreme backwardness to battle; nay as betokening in the English People itself, perhaps a want of the proper animal-courage indispensable in these ages. A million hungry operative men started up, in utmost paroxysm of desperate protest against their lot; and, ask Colacorde and company, How many shots were fired? Very few in comparison! Certain hundreds of drilled soldiers sufficed to suppress this million-headed hydra,* and tread it down, without the smallest appeasement or hope of such, into its subterranean settlements again, there to reconsider itself. Compared with our revolts in Lyons, in Warsaw and elsewhere, to say nothing of incomparable Paris City past or present,* what a lamblike Insurrection!—

The present Editor is not here, with his readers, to vindicate the character of Insurrections; nor does it matter to us whether Blusterowski and the rest may think the English a courageous people or not courageous. In passing, however, let us mention that, to our view, this was not an unsuccessful Insurrection; that as Insurrections go, we have not heard lately of any that succeeded so well.

A million of hungry operative men, as Blusterowski says, rose all up, came all out into the streets, and—stood there. What other could they do? Their wrongs and griefs were bitter, insupportable, their rage against the same was just: but who are they that cause these wrongs, who that will honestly make effort to redress them? Our enemies are we know not who or what; our friends are we know not where!* How shall we attack any one, shoot or be shot by any one? O, if the accursed invisible Nightmare, that is crushing out the life of us and ours, would take a shape; approach us like the Hyrcanian tiger,* the Behemoth of Chaos,* the Archfiend himself; in any shape that we could see, and fasten on!—A man can have himself shot with cheerfulness; but it needs first that he see clearly for what. Shew him the divine face of Justice, then the diabolic monster which is eclipsing that: he will fly at the throat of such monster, never so monstrous, and need no bidding to do it. Woolwich grapeshot will sweep clear all streets,* blast into invisibility so many thousand men: but if your Woolwich grapeshot be but eclipsing Divine Justice, and the God's-radiance itself gleam recognisable athwart such grapeshot,—then, yes then is the time come for fighting and attacking. All artillery-parks have become weak, and are about to dissipate: in the God's-thunder, their poor thunder slackens, ceases; finding that it is, in all senses of the term, a *brute* one!—

That the Manchester Insurrection stood still, on the streets, with an indisposition to fire and bloodshed, was wisdom for it even as an Insurrection. Insurrection, never so necessary, is a most sad necessity; and governors who wait for that to instruct them, are surely getting into the fatallest courses,—proving themselves Sons of Nox and Chaos,* of blind Cowardice, not of seeing Valour! How can there be any remedy in insurrection? It is a mere announcement of the disease,—visible now even to Sons of Night. Insurrection usually 'gains' little; usually wastes how much! One of its worst kinds of waste, to say nothing of the rest, is that of irritating and exasperating men against each other, by violence done; which is always sure to be injustice done, for violence does even justice unjustly.

Who shall compute the waste and loss, the obstruction of every sort, that was produced in the Manchester region by Peterloo alone! Some thirteen unarmed men and women cut down,—the number of the slain and maimed is very countable:* but the treasury of rage, burning hidden or visible in all hearts ever since, more or less perverting the effort and aim of all hearts ever since, is of unknown extent. "How ye came among us, in your cruel armed blindness, ye unspeakable County Yeomanry, sabres flourishing, hoofs prancing, and slashed us down at your brute pleasure; deaf, blind to all *our* claims and woes and wrongs; of quick sight and sense to your own claims only! There lie poor sallow workworn weavers, and complain no more now; women themselves are slashed and sabred, howling terror fills the air; and ye ride prosperous, very victorious,—ye unspeakable: give *us* sabres too, and then come-on a little!" Such are Peterloos. In all hearts that witnessed Peterloo, stands written, as in fire-characters, or smoke-characters prompt to become fire again, a legible balance-account of grim vengeance; very unjustly balanced, much exaggerated, as is the way with such accounts; but payable readily at sight, in full with compound interest! Such things should be avoided as the very pestilence. For men's hearts ought not to be set against one another; but set *with* one another, and all against the Evil Thing only. Men's souls ought to be left to see clearly; not jaundiced, blinded, twisted all awry, by revenge, mutual abhorrence, and the like. An Insurrection that can announce the disease, and then retire with no such balance-account opened anywhere, has attained the highest success possible for it.

And this was what these poor Manchester operatives, with all the darkness that was in them and round them, did manage to perform.

They put their huge inarticulate question, "What do you mean to do with us?" in a manner audible to every reflective soul in this kingdom; exciting deep pity in all good men, deep anxiety in all men whatever; and no conflagration or outburst of madness came to cloud that feeling anywhere, but everywhere it operates unclouded. All England heard the question: it is the first practical form of *our* Sphinx-riddle. England will answer it; or, on the whole, England will perish;—one does not yet expect the latter result!

For the rest, that the Manchester Insurrection could yet discern no radiance of Heaven on any side of its horizon; but feared that all lights, of the O'Connor* or other sorts, hitherto kindled, were but deceptive fish-oil transparencies,* or bog will-o'-wisp lights, and no dayspring from on high:* for this also we will honour the poor Manchester Insurrection, and augur well of it. A deep unspoken sense lies in these strong men,—inconsiderable, almost stupid, as all they can articulate of it is. Amid all violent stupidity of speech, a right noble instinct of what is doable and what is not doable never forsakes them: the strong inarticulate men and workers, whom *Fact* patronises; of whom, in all difficulty and work whatsoever, there is good augury! This work too is to be done: Governors and Governing Classes that *can* articulate and utter, in any measure, what the law of Fact and Justice is, may calculate that here is a Governed Class who will listen.

And truly this first practical form of the Sphinx-question, inarticulately and so audibly put there, is one of the most impressive ever asked in the world. "Behold us here, so many thousands, millions, and increasing at the rate of fifty every hour. We are right willing and able to work; and on the Planet Earth is plenty of work and wages for a million times as many. We ask, If you mean to lead us towards work; to try to lead us,—by ways new, never yet heard of till this new unheard-of Time? Or if you declare that you cannot lead us? And expect that we are to remain quietly unled, and in a composed manner perish of starvation? What is it you expect of us? What is it you mean to do with us?" This question, I say, has been put in the hearing of all Britain; and will be again put, and ever again, till some answer be given it.

Unhappy Workers, unhappier Idlers, unhappy men and women of this actual England! We are yet very far from an answer, and there will be no existence for us without finding one. "A fair day's-wages for a fair day's-work:"* it is as just a demand as Governed men ever made of Governing.* It is the everlasting right of man. Indisputable as Gospels, as arithmetical multiplication-tables: it must and will have itself fulfilled;—and yet, in these times of ours, with what enormous difficulty, next-door to impossibility! For the times are really strange; of a complexity intricate with all the new width of the ever-widening world; times here of half-frantic velocity of impetus, there of the deadest-looking stillness and paralysis; times definable as shewing two qualities, Dilettantism and Mammonism;—most intricate obstructed times! Nay, if there were not a Heaven's radiance of Justice, prophetic, clearly of Heaven, discernible behind all these confused world-wide entanglements, of Landlord interests, Manufacturing interests, Tory-Whig interests, and who knows what other interests, expediencies, vested interests, established possessions, inveterate Dilettantisms, Midas-eared Mammonisms,*—it would seem to every one a flat impossibility, which all wise men might as well at once abandon. If you do not know eternal Justice from momentary Expediency, and understand in your heart of hearts how Justice, radiant, beneficent, as the all-victorious Light-element, is also in essence, if need be, an all-victorious *Fire*-element,* and melts all manner of vested interests, and the hardest iron cannon, as if they were soft wax, and does ever in the long-run rule and reign, and allows nothing else to rule and reign,—you also would talk of impossibility! But it is only difficult, it is not impossible. Possible? It is, with whatever difficulty, very clearly inevitable.

Fair day's-wages for fair day's-work! exclaims a sarcastic man: alas, in what corner of this Planet, since Adam first awoke on it, was that ever realised? The day's-wages of John Milton's day's-work, named *Paradise Lost* and *Milton's Works*, were Ten Pounds paid by instalments, and a rather close escape from death on the gallows.* Consider that: it is no rhetorical flourish; it is an authentic, altogether quiet fact,—emblematic, quietly documentary of a whole world of such, ever since human history began. Oliver Cromwell quitted his farming; undertook a Hercules' Labour* and lifelong wrestle with that Lernean Hydra-coil, wide as England, hissing heaven-high through its thousand crowned, coroneted, shovel-hatted quack-heads;* and he did wrestle with it, the truest and terriblest wrestle I have heard of; and he wrestled it, and mowed and cut it down a good many stages, so that its hissing is ever since pitiful in comparison, and one can walk abroad in comparative peace from it;—and his wages, as I understand, were burial under the gallows-tree near Tyburn Turnpike, with his head on the gable of Westminster Hall,* and two centuries now of mixed cursing and ridicule* from all manner of men. His dust lies under the Edgeware Road, near Tyburn Turnpike, at this hour; and his memory is—Nay, what matters what his memory is? His memory, at bottom, is or yet shall be as that of a god: a terror and horror to all quacks and cowards and insincere persons; an everlasting encouragement, new memento, battleword, and pledge of victory to all the brave. It is the natural course and history of the Godlike, in every place, in every time. What god ever carried it with the Tenpound Franchisers; in Open Vestry, or with any Sanhedrim of considerable standing?* When was a god found 'agreeable' to everybody? The regular way is to hang, kill, crucify your gods, and execrate and trample them under your stupid hoofs for a century or two; till you discover that they are gods,—and then take to braying over them, still in a very long-eared manner!—So speaks the sarcastic man; in his wild way, very mournful truths.

Day's-wages for day's-work? continues he: The Progress of Human Society consists even in this same, The better and better apportioning of wages to work. Give me this, you have given me all. Pay to every man accurately what he has worked for, what he has earned and done and deserved,—to this man broad lands and honours, to that man high gibbets and treadmills:* what more have I to ask? Heaven's Kingdom, which we daily pray for, *has* come; God's will is done on Earth even as it is in Heaven!* This *is* the radiance of celestial Justice; in the light or in the fire of which all impediments, vested interests, and iron cannon, are more and more melting like wax, and disappearing from the pathways of men. A thing ever struggling forward; irrepressible, advancing inevitable; perfecting itself, all days, more and more,—never to be *perfect* till that general Doomsday, the ultimate Consummation, and Last of earthly Days.

True, as to 'perfection' and so forth, answer we; true enough! And yet withal we have to remark, that imperfect Human Society holds itself together, and finds place under the Sun, in virtue simply of some *approximation* to perfection being actually made and put in practice. We remark farther, that there are supportable approximations, and then likewise insupportable. With some, almost with any, supportable approximation men are apt, perhaps too apt, to rest indolently patient, and say, It will do. Thus these poor Manchester manual workers mean only, by day's-wages for day's-work, certain coins of money adequate to keep them living;—in return for their work, such modicum of food, clothes and fuel as will enable them to continue their work itself! They as yet clamour for no more; the rest, still inarticulate, cannot yet shape itself into a demand at all, and only lies in them as a dumb wish; perhaps only, still more inarticulate, as a dumb, altogether unconscious want.* *This* is the supportable approximation they would rest patient with, That by their work they might be kept alive to work more!—*This* once grown unattainable, I think, your approximation may consider itself to have reached the *in*supportable stage; and may prepare, with whatever difficulty, reluctance and astonishment, for one of two things, for changing or perishing! With the millions no longer able to live, how can the units keep living? It is too clear the Nation itself is on the way to suicidal death.

Shall we say then, The world has retrograded in its talent of apportioning wages to work, in late days? The world had always a talent of that sort, better or worse. Time was when the mere *hand*worker needed not announce his claim to the world by Manchester Insurrections!— The world, with its Wealth of Nations, Supply-and-demand and such like,* has of late days been terribly inattentive to that question of work and wages. We will not say the poor world has retrograded even here: we will say rather, the world has been rushing on with such fiery animation to get work and ever more work done, it has had no time to think of dividing the wages; and has merely left them to be scrambled for by the Law of the Stronger, law of Supply-and-demand, law of Laissez-faire, and other idle Laws and Un-laws, saying, in its dire haste to get the work done, That is well enough!

And now the world will have to pause a little, and take up that other side of the problem, and in right earnest strive for some solution of that. For it has become pressing. What is the use of your spun shirts? They hang there by the million unsaleable; and here, by the million, are diligent bare backs that can get no hold of them. Shirts are useful for covering human backs; useless otherwise, an unbearable mockery otherwise. You have fallen terribly behind with that side of the problem! Manchester Insurrections, French Revolutions, and thousandfold phenomena great and small, announce loudly that you must bring it forward a little again. Never till now, in the history of an Earth which to this hour nowhere refuses to grow corn if you will plough it, to yield shirts if you will spin and weave in it, did the mere manual two-handed worker (however it might fare with other workers) cry in vain for such 'wages' as *he* means by 'fair wages,' namely food and warmth! The Godlike could not and cannot be paid; but the Earthly always could. Gurth, a mere swineherd, born thrall of Cedric the Saxon, tended pigs in the wood, and did get some parings of the pork.* Why, the four-footed worker has already *got* all that this two-handed one is clamouring for! How often must I remind you? There is not a horse in England, able and willing to work, but *has* due food and lodging;* and goes about sleek-coated, satisfied in heart. And you say, It is impossible. Brothers, I answer, if for you it be impossible, what is to become of you? It is impossible for us to believe it to be impossible. The human brain, looking at these sleek English horses, refuses to believe in such impossibility for English men. Do you depart quickly; clear the ways soon, lest worse befal. We for our share do purpose, with full view of the enormous difficulty, with total disbelief in the impossibility, to endeavour while life is in us, and to die endeavouring, we and our sons, till we attain it or have all died and ended.

Such a Platitude* of a World, in which all working horses could be well fed, and innumerable working men should die starved, were it not best to end it; to have done with it, and restore it once for all to the *Jötuns,* Mud-giants, Frost-giants and Chaotic Brute-gods of the Beginning?* For the old Anarchic Brute-gods it may be well enough; but it is a Platitude which Men should be above countenancing by their presence in it. We pray you, let the word *impossible* disappear from your vocabulary in this matter. It is of awful omen; to all of us, and to yourselves first of all.

CHAPTER IV.

MORRISON'S PILL.*

WHAT is to be done, what would you have us do?* asks many a one, with a tone of impatience, almost of reproach; and then, if you mention some one thing, some two things, twenty things that might be done, turns round with a satirical tehee, and, "These are your remedies!" The state of mind indicated by such question, and such rejoinder, is worth reflecting on.

It seems to be taken for granted, by these interrogative philosophers, that there is some 'thing,' or handful of 'things,' which could be done; some Act of Parliament, 'remedial measure' or the like,* which could be passed, whereby the social malady were fairly fronted, conquered, put an end to; so that, with your remedial measure in your pocket, you could then go on triumphant, and be troubled no farther. "You tell us the evil," cry such persons, as if justly aggrieved, "and do not tell us how it is to be cured!"

How it is to be cured? Brothers, I am sorry I have got no Morrison's Pill for curing the maladies of Society. It were infinitely handier if we had a Morrison's Pill, Act of Parliament, or remedial measure, which men could swallow, one good time, and then go on in their old courses, cleared from all miseries and mischiefs! Unluckily we have none such; unluckily the Heavens themselves, in their rich pharmacopœia, contain none such. There will no 'thing' be done that will cure you. There will a radical universal alteration of your regimen and way of life take place; there will a most agonising divorce between you and your chimeras, luxuries and falsities, take place; a most toilsome, all but 'impossible' return to Nature, and her veracities, and her integrities, take place: that so the inner fountains of life may again begin, like eternal Light-fountains, to irradiate and purify your bloated, swollen, foul existence, drawing nigh, as at present, to nameless death! Either death or else all this will take place. Judge if, with such diagnosis, any Morrison's Pill is like to be discoverable!

But the Life-fountain within you once again set flowing,* what innumerable 'things,' whole sets and classes and continents of 'things,' year after year, and decade after decade, and century after century, will then be doable and done! Not Emigration, Education, Corn-Law Abrogation, Sanitary Regulation, Land Property-Tax;* not these alone, nor a thousand times as much as these. Good Heavens, there will then be light in the inner heart of here and there a man, to discern what is just, what is commanded by the Most High God, what *must* be done, were it never so 'impossible.' Vain jargon in favour of the palpably unjust will then abridge itself within limits. Vain jargon, on Hustings,* in Parliaments or wherever else, when here and there a man has vision for the essential God's-Truth of the things jargoned of, will become very vain indeed. The silence of here and there such a man, how eloquent in answer to such jargon! Such jargon, frightened at its own gaunt echo, will unspeakably abate; nay, for a while, may almost in a manner disappear,—the wise answering it in silence, and even the simple taking cue from them to hoot it down wherever heard. It will be a blessed time; and many 'things' will become doable,—and when the brains are out, an absurdity will die!* Not easily again shall a Corn-Law argue ten years for itself; and still talk and argue, when impartial persons have to say with a sigh that, for so long back, they have heard no 'argument' advanced for it but such as might make the angels and almost the very jackasses weep!*—

Wholly a blessed time: when jargon might abate, and here and there some genuine speech begin. When to the noble opened heart, as to such heart they alone do, all noble things began to grow visible; and the difference between just and unjust, between true and false, between work and sham-work, between speech and jargon, was once more, what to our happier Fathers it used to be, *infinite*,—as between a Heavenly thing and an Infernal: the one a thing which you were *not* to do, which you were wise not to attempt doing; which it were better for you to have a millstone tied round your neck, and be cast into the sea,* than concern yourself with doing!—Brothers, it will not be a Morrison's Pill, or remedial measure, that will bring all this about for us.

And yet, very literally, till, in some shape or other, it be brought about, we remain cureless; till it begin to be brought about, the cure does not begin. For Nature and Fact, not Redtape and Semblance, are to this hour the basis of man's life; and on those, through never such strata of these, man and his life and all his interests do, sooner or later, infallibly come to rest,—and to be supported or be swallowed according as they agree with those. The question is asked of them, not, How do you agree with Downing-street and accredited Semblance? but, How do you agree with God's Universe and the actual Reality of things? This Universe *has* its Laws. If we walk according to the Law, the Law-Maker will befriend us; if not, not. Alas, by no Reform Bill, Ballot-box, Five-point Charter,* by no boxes or bills or charters, can you perform this alchemy: 'Given a world of Knaves to produce an Honesty from their united action!'* It is a distillation, once for all, not possible. You pass it through alembic after alembic,* it comes out still a Dishonesty, with a new dress on it, a new colour to it. 'While we ourselves continue valets, how *can* any hero come to govern us?'* We are governed, very infallibly, by the 'sham-hero,'—whose name is

Quack, whose work and governance is Plausibility, and also is Falsity and Fatuity; to which Nature says, and must say when it comes to *her* to speak, eternally No! Nations cease to be befriended of the Law-Maker, when they walk *not* according to the Law. The Sphinx-question remains unsolved by them, becomes ever more insoluble.

If thou ask again, therefore, on the Morrison's-Pill hypothesis, What is to be done? allow me to reply: By thee, for the present, almost nothing. Thou there, the thing for thee to do is, if possible, to cease to be a hollow sounding-shell of hearsays, egoisms, purblind dilettant-isms; and become, were it on the infinitely small scale, a faithful dis-cerning soul. Thou shalt descend into thy inner man, and see if there be any traces of a *soul* there; till then there can be nothing done! O brother, we must if possible resuscitate some soul and conscience in us, exchange our dilettantisms for sincerities, our dead hearts of stone for living hearts of flesh.* Then shall we discern, not one thing, but, in clearer or dimmer sequence, a whole endless host of things that can be done. *Do* the first of these; do it; the second will already have become clearer, doabler; the second, third and three-thousandth will then have begun to be possible for us. Not any universal Morrison's Pill shall we then, either as swallowers or as venders, ask after at all; but a far different sort of remedies: Quacks shall no more have domin-ion over us, but true Heroes and Healers!

Will not that be a thing worthy of 'doing;' to deliver ourselves from quacks, sham-heroes; to deliver the whole world more and more from such? They are the one bane of the world. Once clear the world of them, it ceases to be a Devil's-world, in all fibres of it wretched, accursed; and begins to be a God's-world, blessed, and working hourly towards blessedness. Thou for one wilt not again vote for any quack, do honour to any edge-gilt vacuity in man's shape:* cant shall be known to thee by the sound of it;—thou wilt fly from cant with a shudder never felt before; as from the opened litany of Sorcerers' Sabbaths,*—the true Devil-worship of this age, more horrible than any other blasphemy, profanity or genuine blackguard-ism elsewhere audible among men. It is alarming to witness,—in its present completed state! And Quack and Dupe, as we must ever keep in mind, are upper-side and under of the selfsame substance; con-vertible personages: turn up your dupe into the proper fostering element, and he himself can become a quack; there is in him the due prurient insincerity, open voracity for profit, and closed sense for truth, whereof quacks too, in all their kinds, are made.

Alas, it is not to the hero, it is to the sham-hero that, of right and necessity, the valet-world belongs. 'What is to be done?' The reader sees whether it is like to be the seeking and swallowing of some 'remedial measure!'

CHAPTER V.

ARISTOCRACY OF TALENT.

WHEN an individual is miserable, what does it most of all behove him to do? To complain of this man or of that, of this thing or of that? To fill the world and the street with lamentation, objurgation? Not so at all; the reverse of so. All moralists advise him not to complain of any person or of any thing, but of himself only. He is to know of a truth that being miserable he has been unwise, he. Had he faithfully followed Nature and her Laws, Nature, ever true to her Laws, would have yielded fruit and increase and felicity to him: but he has followed other than Nature's Laws; and now Nature, her patience with him being ended, leaves him desolate; answers with very emphatic significance to him: No. Not by this road, my son; by another road shalt thou attain well-being: this, thou perceivest is the road to ill-being; quit this!—So do all moralists advise: that the man penitently say to himself first of all, Behold I was not wise enough; I quitted the laws of Fact, which are also called the Laws of God, and mistook for them the laws of Sham and Semblance, which are called the Devil's Laws; therefore am I here!

Neither with Nations that become miserable is it fundamentally otherwise. The ancient guides of Nations, Prophets, Priests or whatever their name, were well aware of this; and, down to a late epoch, impressively taught and inculcated it. The modern guides of Nations, who also go under a great variety of names, Journalists, Political Economists, Politicians, Pamphleteers, have entirely forgotten this, and are ready to deny this. But it nevertheless remains eternally undeniable: nor is there any doubt but we shall all be taught it yet, and made again to confess it: we shall all be striped and scourged till we do learn it; and shall at last either get to know it, or be striped to death in the process. For it is undeniable! When a Nation is unhappy, the old Prophet was right and not wrong in saying to it: Ye have forgotten God, ye have quitted the ways of God, or ye would not have been unhappy.* It is not according to the laws of Fact that ye have lived and guided yourselves, but according to the laws of Delusion, Imposture, and wilful and unwilful *Mistake* of Fact; behold therefore the Unveracity is worn out; Nature's long-suffering with you is exhausted; and ye are here!

Surely there is nothing very inconceivable in this, even to the Journalist, to the Political Economist, Modern Pamphleteer, or any two-legged animal without feathers!* If a country finds itself wretched, sure enough that country has been *mis*guided: it is with the wretched Twenty-seven Millions, fallen wretched, as with the Unit fallen wretched: they as he have quitted the course prescribed by Nature and the Supreme Powers, and so are fallen into scarcity, disaster, infelicity; and pausing to consider themselves, have to lament and say, Alas, we were not wise enough. We took transient superficial Semblance for everlasting central Substance; we have departed far away from the *Laws* of this Universe, and behold now lawless Chaos and inane Chimera* is ready to devour us!—'Nature in late centuries,' says Sauerteig,* 'was universally supposed to be dead; an old eight-day clock, made many thousand years ago, and still ticking, but dead as brass,—which the Maker, at most, sat looking at,* in a distant, singular, and indeed incredible manner: but now I am happy to observe, she is everywhere asserting herself to be not dead and brass at all, but alive and miraculous, celestial-infernal, with an emphasis that will again penetrate the thickest head of this Planet by and by!' ——

Indisputable enough to all mortals now, the guidance of this country has not been sufficiently wise: men too foolish have been set to the guiding and governing of it, and have guided it *hither;* we must find wiser,—wiser, or else we perish! To this length of insight all England has now advanced; but as yet no farther. All England stands wringing its hands, asking itself, nigh desperate, What farther? Reform Bill proves to be a failure; Benthamee Radicalism, the gospel of 'Enlightened Selfishness,'* dies out, or dwindles into Five-point Chartism, amid the tears and hootings of men: what next are we to hope or try? Five-point Charter, Free-trade; Church-extension,* Sliding-scale;* what, in Heaven's name, are we next to attempt, that we sink not in inane Chimera, and be devoured of Chaos?—The case is pressing, and one of the most complicated in the world. A God's-message never came to thicker-skinned people; never had a God's-message to pierce through thicker integuments, into heavier ears. It is Fact, speaking once more, in miraculous thunder-voice, from out of the centre of the world;—how unknown its language to the deaf and foolish many; how distinct, undeniable, terrible and yet beneficent, to the hearing few: Behold, ye shall grow wiser, or ye shall die! Truer to Nature's Fact, or inane Chimera will swallow you; in whirlwinds of fire, you and your Mammonisms, Dilettantisms, your Midas-eared philosophies, double-barrelled Aristocracies,* shall disappear!—Such is the God's-message to *us*, once more, in these modern days.

We must have more Wisdom to govern us, we must be governed by the Wisest, we must have an Aristocracy of Talent! cry many. True, most true; but how to get it? The following extract from our young friend of the *Houndsditch Indicator** is worth perusing: 'At this time,' says he, 'while there is a cry everywhere, articulate or inarticulate, for an "Aristocracy of Talent,"* a Governing Class namely which did govern, not merely which took the wages of governing, and could not with all our industry be kept from misgoverning, corn-lawing, and playing the very deuce with us,—it may not be altogether useless to remind some of the greener-headed sort what a dreadfully difficult affair the getting of such an Aristocracy is! Do you expect, my friends, that your indispensable Aristocracy of Talent is to be enlisted straight-way, by some sort of recruitment aforethought, out of the general population; arranged in supreme regimental order; and set to rule over us? That it will be got sifted, like wheat out of chaff, from the Twenty-seven Million British subjects; that any Ballot-box, Reform Bill, or other Political Machine, with Force of Public Opinion never so active on it, is likely to perform said process of sifting? Would to Heaven that we had a sieve; that we could so much as fancy any kind of sieve, wind-fanners, or ne-plus-ultra of machinery, devisable by man, that would do it!

'Done nevertheless, sure enough, it must be; it shall and will be. We are rushing swiftly on the road to destruction; every hour bring-ing us nearer, until it be, in some measure, done. The doing of it is not doubtful; only the method and the costs! Nay I will even mention to you an infallible sifting-process whereby he that has ability will be sifted out to rule among us, and that same blessed Aristocracy of

Talent be verily, in an approximate degree, vouchsafed us by and by: an infallible sifting-process; to which, however, no soul can help his neighbour, but each must, with devout prayer to Heaven, endeavour to help himself. It is, O friends, that all of us, that many of us, should acquire the true *eye* for talent, which is dreadfully wanting at present! The true eye for talent presupposes the true reverence for it,—O Heavens, presupposes so many things!

'For example, you Bobus Higgins,* Sausage-maker on the great scale, who are raising such a clamour for this Aristocracy of Talent, what is it that you do, in that big heart of yours, chiefly in very fact pay reverence to? Is it to talent, intrinsic manly worth of any kind, you unfortunate Bobus? The manliest man that you saw going in a ragged coat, did you ever reverence him; did you so much as know that he was a manly man at all, till his coat grew better? Talent! I understand you to be able to worship the fame of talent, the power, cash, celebrity or other success of talent; but the talent itself is a thing you never saw with eyes. Nay what is it in yourself that you are proudest of, that you take most pleasure in surveying meditatively in thoughtful moments? Speak now, is it the bare Bobus stript of his very name and shirt, and turned loose upon society, that you admire and thank Heaven for; or Bobus with his cash-accounts and larders dropping fatness,* with his respectabilities, warm garnitures, and pony-chaise, admirable in some measure to certain of the flunkey species? Your own degree of worth and talent, is it of *infinite* value to you; or only of finite,—measurable by the degree of currency, and conquest of praise or pudding, it has brought you to? Bobus, you are in a vicious circle, rounder than one of your own sausages; and will never vote for or promote any talent, except what talent or sham-talent has already *got* itself voted for!'—We here cut short the *Indicator;* all readers perceiving whither he now tends.

'More Wisdom' indeed: but where to find more Wisdom? We have already a Collective Wisdom,* after its kind,—though 'class-legislation,' and another thing or two, affect it somewhat! On the whole, as they say: Like people like priest;* so we may say: Like people like king. The man gets himself appointed and elected who is ablest—to be appointed and elected. What can the incorrupti-blest *Bobuses* elect, if it be not some *Bobissimus*,* should they find such?

Or, again, perhaps there is not in the whole Nation, Wisdom enough, 'collect' it as we may, to make an adequate Collective! That too is a case which may befal: a ruined man staggers down to ruin because there was not wisdom enough in him; so, clearly also, may Twenty-seven Million collective men!—But indeed one of the infalliblest fruits of Unwisdom in a Nation is that it cannot get the use of what Wisdom is actually in it; that it is not governed by the wisest it has, who alone have a divine right* to govern in all Nations; but by the sham-wisest, or even by the openly not-so-wise if they are handiest otherwise! This is the infalliblest result of Unwisdom; and also the balefullest, immeasurablest,—not so much what we can call a poison-*fruit*, as a universal death-disease, and poisoning, of the whole tree. For hereby are fostered, fed into gigantic bulk, all manner of Unwisdoms, poison-fruits; till, as we say, the life-tree everywhere is made a upas-tree,* deadly Unwisdom overshadowing all things; and there is done what lies in human skill to stifle all Wisdom everywhere in the birth, to smite our poor world barren of Wisdom,—and make your utmost Collective Wisdom, were it collected and elected by Rhadamanthus, Æacus and Minos,* not to speak of drunken Tenpound Franchisers with their ballot-boxes, an inadequate Collective! The Wisdom is not now there: how will you 'collect' it? As well wash Thames mud, by improved methods, to find more gold in it.*

Truly, the first condition is indispensable, That Wisdom be there: but the second is like unto it,* is properly one with it: these two conditions act and react through every fibre of them, and go inseparably together. If you have much Wisdom in your Nation, you will get it faithfully collected; for the wise love Wisdom, and will search for it as for life and salvation. If you have little Wisdom, you will get even that little ill-collected, trampled under foot, reduced as near as possible to annihilation; for fools do not love Wisdom; they are foolish, first of all, because they have never loved Wisdom,—but have loved their own appetites, ambitions, their coroneted coaches, tankards of heavy-wet.* Thus is your candle lighted at both ends, and the progress towards consummation is swift. Thus is fulfilled that saying in the Gospel: To him that hath shall be given; and from him that hath not, shall be taken away even that which he hath.* Very literally, in a very fatal manner, that saying is here fulfilled.

Our 'Aristocracy of Talent' seems at a considerable distance yet; does it not, O Bobus?

CHAPTER VI.

HERO-WORSHIP.

To the present Editor, not less than to Bobus, a Government of the Wisest, what Bobus calls an Aristocracy of Talent, seems the one healing remedy: but he is not so sanguine as Bobus with respect to the means of realising it. He thinks that we have at once missed realising it, and come to need it so pressingly, by departing far from the inner eternal Laws, and taking up with the temporary outer semblances of Laws. He thinks that 'enlightened Egoism,' never so luminous, is not the rule by which man's life can be led. That 'Laissez-faire,' 'Supply-and-demand,' 'Cash-payment for the sole nexus,'* and so forth, were not, are not, and will never be, a practicable Law of Union for a Society of Men. That Poor and Rich, that Governed and Governing, cannot long live together on any such Law of Union. Alas, he thinks that man has a soul in him, *different* from the stomach in any sense of this word; that if said soul be asphyxied, and lie quietly forgotten, the man and his affairs are in a bad way. He thinks that said soul will have to be resuscitated from its asphyxia; that if it prove irresuscitable, the man is not long for this world. In brief, that Midas-eared Mammonism, double-barrelled Dilettantism, and their thousand adjuncts and corollaries, are *not* the Law by which God Almighty has appointed this his Universe to go. That, once for all, these are not the Law: and then farther that we shall have to return to what *is* the Law,—not by smooth flowery paths, it is like, and with 'tremendous cheers' in our throat; but over steep untrodden places, through stormclad chasms, waste oceans, and the bosom of tornadoes; thank Heaven, if not through very Chaos and the Abyss! The resuscitating of a soul that has gone to asphyxia is no momentary or pleasant process, but a long and terrible one.*

To the present Editor, 'Hero-worship,' as he has elsewhere named it, means much more than an elected Parliament, or stated Aristocracy, of the Wisest; for, in his dialect, it is the summary, ultimate essence, and supreme practical perfection of all manner of 'worship,' and true worships* and noblenesses whatsoever. Such blessed Parliament and, were it once in perfection, blessed Aristocracy of the Wisest, god-honoured and man-honoured, he does look for, more and more perfected,—as the topmost blessed practical apex of a whole world reformed from sham-worship, informed anew with worship, with truth and blessedness! He thinks that Hero-worship, done differently in every different epoch of the world, is the soul of all social business among men; that the doing of it well, or the doing of it ill, measures accurately what degree of well-being or of ill-being there is in the world's affairs. He thinks that we, on the whole, do our Hero-worship worse than any Nation in this world ever did it before: that the Burns an Exciseman, the Byron a Literary Lion,* are intrinsically, all things considered, a baser and falser phenomenon than the Odin a God, the Mahomet a Prophet of God.* It is this Editor's clear opinion, accordingly, that we must learn to do our Hero-worship better; that to do it better and better, means the awakening of the Nation's soul from its asphyxia, and the return of blessed life to us,—Heaven's blessed life, not Mammon's galvanic accursed one.* To resuscitate the Asphyxied, apparently now moribund, and in the last agony if not resuscitated: such and no other seems the consummation.

'Hero-worship,' if you will,—yes, friends; but, first of all, by being ourselves of heroic mind. A whole world of Heroes; a world not of Flunkeys, where no Hero-King *can* reign: that is what we aim at! We, for our share, will put away all Flunkeyism, Baseness, Unveracity from us; we shall then hope to have Noblenesses and Veracities set over us; never till then. Let Bobus and Company sneer, "That is your Reform!" Yes, Bobus, that is our Reform; and except in that, and what will follow out of that, we have no hope at all. Reform, like Charity, O Bobus, must begin at home. Once well at home, how will it radiate outwards, irrepressible, into all that we touch and handle, speak and work; kindling ever new light, by incalculable contagion, spreading in geometric ratio, far and wide,—doing good only, wheresoever it spreads, and not evil.

By Reform Bills, Anti-Corn-Law Bills, and thousand other bills and methods, we will demand of our Governors, with emphasis, and for the first time not without effect, that they cease to be quacks, or else depart; that they set no quackeries and blockheadisms anywhere to rule over us, that they utter or act no cant to us,—that it will be better if they do not. For we shall now know quacks when we see them; cant, when we hear it, shall be horrible to us! We will say, with the poor Frenchman at the Bar of the Convention, though in wiser style than he, and 'for the space' not 'of an hour' but of a lifetime:

*"Je demande l'arrestation des coquins et des lâches."** 'Arrestment of the knaves and dastards:' ah, we know what a work that is; how long it will be before *they* are all or mostly got 'arrested:'—but here is one; arrest him, in God's name; it is one fewer! We will, in all practicable ways, by word and silence, by act and refusal to act, energetically demand that arrestment,—*"je demande cette arrestation-là!"*—and by degrees infallibly attain it. Infallibly: for light spreads; all human souls, never so bedarkened, love light; light once kindled spreads, till all is luminous;—till the cry, *"Arrest* your knaves and dastards" rises imperative from millions of hearts, and rings and reigns from sea to sea. Nay, how many of them may we not 'arrest' with our own hands, even now; we! Do not countenance them, thou there: turn away from their lackered sumptuosities, their belauded sophistries, their serpent graciosities, their spoken and acted cant, with a sacred horror, with an *Apage Satanas.**—Bobus and Company, and all men will gradually join us. We demand arrestment of the knaves and dastards, and begin by arresting our own poor selves out of that fraternity. There is no other reform conceivable. Thou and I, my friend, can, in the most flunkey world, make, each of us, *one* non-flunkey, one hero, if we like: that will be two heroes to begin with:—Courage! even that is a whole world of heroes to end with, or what we poor Two can do in furtherance thereof!

Yes, friends: Hero-kings, and a whole world not unheroic,—there lies the port and happy haven, towards which, through all these storm-tost seas,* French Revolutions, Chartisms, Manchester Insurrections, that make the heart sick in these bad days, the Supreme Powers are driving us. On the whole, blessed be the Supreme Powers, stern as they are! Towards that haven will we, O friends; let all true men, with what of faculty is in them, bend valiantly, incessantly, with thousand-fold endeavour, thither, thither! There, or else in the Ocean-abysses, it is very clear to me, we shall arrive.

Well; here truly is no answer to the Sphinx-question; not the answer a disconsolate Public, inquiring at the College of Health,* was in hopes of! A total change of regimen, change of constitution and existence from the very centre of it; a new body to be got, with resuscitated soul,—not without convulsive travail-throes; as all birth and new-birth presupposes travail! This is sad news to a disconsolate discerning Public, hoping to have got off by some Morrison's Pill, some Saint-John's corrosive mixture and perhaps a little blistery friction on the back!*—We were prepared to part with our Corn-Law, with various Laws and Unlaws: but this, what is this?

Nor has the Editor forgotten how it fares with your ill-boding Cassandras in Sieges of Troy.* Imminent perdition is not usually driven away by words of warning. Didactic Destiny has other methods in store; or these would fail always. Such words should, nevertheless, be uttered, when they dwell truly in the soul of any man. Words are hard, are importunate; but how much harder the importunate events they foreshadow! Here and there a human soul may listen to the words,—who knows how many human souls?—whereby the importunate events, if not diverted and prevented, will be rendered *less* hard. The present Editor's purpose is to himself full of hope.

For though fierce travails, though wide seas and roaring gulfs lie before us, is it not something if a Loadstar,* in the eternal sky, do once more disclose itself; an everlasting light, shining through all cloud-tempests and roaring billows, ever as we emerge from the trough of the sea: the blessed beacon, far off on the edge of far horizons, towards which we are to steer incessantly for life? Is it not something; O Heavens, is it not all? There lies the Heroic Promised Land; under that Heaven's-light, my brethren, bloom the Happy Isles,*—there, O there! Thither will we;

'There dwells the great Achilles whom we knew.'[1]*

There dwell all Heroes, and will dwell: thither, all ye heroic-minded!—The Heaven's Loadstar once clearly in our eye, how will each true man stand truly to *his* work in the ship; how, with undying hope, will all things be fronted, all be conquered. Nay, with the ship's prow once turned in that direction, is not all, as it were, already well? Sick wasting misery has become noble manful effort with a goal in our eye. 'The choking Nightmare chokes us no longer; for we *stir* under it; the Nightmare has already fled.'*—

Certainly, could the present Editor instruct men how to know Wisdom, Heroism, when they see it, that they might do reverence to *it* only, and loyally make it ruler over them,—yes, he were the living epitome of all Editors, Teachers, Prophets, that now teach and prophesy; he were an *Apollo*-Morrison, a Trismegistus* and *effective* Cassandra! Let no Able Editor hope such things. It is to be expected

---

[1] Tennyson's Poems (*Ulysses*).

the present laws of copyright,* rate of reward per sheet, and other considerations, will save him from that peril. Let no Editor hope such things: no;— and yet let all Editors aim towards such things, and even towards such alone! One knows not what the meaning of editing and writing is, if even this be not it.

Enough, to the present Editor it has seemed possible some glimmering of light, for here and there a human soul, might lie in these confused Paper-Masses now intrusted to him;* wherefore he determines to edit the same. Out of old Books, new Writings, and much Meditation not of yesterday, he will endeavour to select a thing or two; and from the Past, in a circuitous way, illustrate the Present and the Future. The Past is a dim indubitable fact: the Future too is one, only dimmer; nay properly it is the *same* fact in new dress and development. For the Present holds in it both the whole Past and the whole Future;—as the LIFE-TREE IGDRASIL,* wide-waving, many-toned, has its roots down deep in the Death-kingdoms, among the oldest dead dust of men, and with its boughs reaches always beyond the stars; and in all times and places is one and the same Life-tree!

BOOK II.

THE ANCIENT MONK.

CHAPTER I.

JOCELIN OF BRAKELOND.*

WE will, in this Second Portion of our Work, strive to penetrate a little, by means of certain confused Papers, printed and other,* into a somewhat remote Century; and to look face to face on it, in hope of perhaps illustrating our own poor Century thereby. It seems a circuitous way; but it may prove a way nevertheless. For man has ever been a striving, struggling, and, in spite of wide-spread calumnies to the contrary, a veracious creature: the Centuries too are all lineal children of one another; and often, in the portrait of early grandfathers, this and the other enigmatic feature of the newest grandson shall disclose itself, to mutual elucidation. This Editor will venture on such a thing.

Besides, in Editors' Books, and indeed everywhere else in the world of Today, a certain latitude of movement grows more and more becoming for the practical man. Salvation lies not in tight lacing, in these times;—how far from that, in any province whatsoever! Readers and men generally are getting into strange habits of asking all persons and things, from poor Editors' Books up to Church Bishops and State Potentates, not, By what designation art thou called; in what wig and black triangle* dost thou walk abroad? Heavens, I know thy designation and black triangle well enough! But, in God's name, what art thou? Not Nothing, sayest thou! Then if not, How much and what? This is the thing I would know; and even *must* soon know, such a pass am I come to! —— What weather-symptoms,—not for the poor Editor of Books alone!

The Editor of Books may understand withal that if, as is said, 'many kinds are permissible,' there is one kind not permissible, 'the kind that has nothing in it, *le genre ennuyeux*;'* and go on his way accordingly. —

A certain Jocelinus de Brakelonda, a natural-born Englishman, has left us an extremely foreign Book,[1]* which the labours of the Camden Society have brought to light in these days.* Jocelin's Book, the 'Chronicle,' or private Boswellean Notebook,* of Jocelin, a certain old St. Edmundsbury Monk and Boswell, now seven centuries old, how remote is it from us; exotic, extraneous; in all ways, coming from far abroad! The language of it is not foreign only but dead: Monk-Latin lies across not the British Channel, but the ninefold Stygian Marshes, Stream of Lethe,* and one knows not where! Roman Latin itself, still alive for us in the Elysian Fields of Memory,* is domestic in comparison. And then the ideas, life-furniture, whole workings and ways of this worthy Jocelin; covered deeper than Pompeii* with the lava-ashes and inarticulate wreck of seven hundred years!

Jocelin of Brakelond cannot be called a conspicuous literary character; indeed few mortals that have left so visible a work, or footmark, behind them can be more obscure. One other of those vanished Existences,* whose work has not yet vanished;—almost a pathetic phenomenon, were not the whole world full of such! The builders of Stonehenge,* for example:—or alas, what say we, Stonehenge and builders? The writers of the *Universal Review* and *Homer's Iliad;** the paviers of London streets;—sooner or later, the entire Posterity of Adam! It is a pathetic phenomenon; but an irremediable, nay, if well meditated, a consoling one.

By his dialect of Monk-Latin, and indeed by his name, this Jocelin seems to have been a Norman Englishman; the surname *de Brakelonda* indicates a native of St. Edmundsbury itself, *Brakelond* being the known old name of a street or quarter in that venerable Town.* Then farther, sure enough, our Jocelin was a Monk of St. Edmundsbury Convent; held some '*obedientia*,'* subaltern officiality there, or rather, in succession several; was, for one thing, 'chaplain to my Lord Abbot,* living beside him night and day for the space of six years;'*—which last, indeed, is the grand fact of Jocelin's existence, and properly the origin of this present Book, and of the chief meaning it has for us now. He was, as we have hinted, a kind of born *Boswell*, though an infinitesimally small one; neither did he altogether want his *Johnson* even

---

there and then. Johnsons are rare; yet, as has been asserted, Boswells perhaps still rarer,*—the more is the pity on both sides! This Jocelin, as we can discern well, was an ingenious and ingenuous, a cheery-hearted, innocent, yet withal shrewd, noticing, quick-witted man; and from under his monk's cowl, has looked out on that narrow section of the world in a really *human* manner; not in any *simial*, canine, ovine, or otherwise *in*human manner,—afflictive to all that have humanity! The man is of patient, peaceable, loving, clear-smiling nature; open for this and that. A wise simplicity is in him; much natural sense; a *veracity* that goes deeper than words. Veracity: it is the basis of all; and, some say, means genius itself; the prime essence of all genius whatsoever!* Our Jocelin, for the rest, has read his classical manuscripts, his Virgilius, his Flaccus, Ovidius Naso;* of course still more, his Homilies and Breviaries,* and if not the Bible, considerable extracts of the Bible. Then also he has a pleasant wit; and loves a timely joke, though in mild subdued manner: very amiable to see. A learned grown man, yet with the heart as of a good child; whose whole life indeed has been that of a child,—St. Edmundsbury Monastery a larger kind of cradle for him, in which his whole prescribed duty was to *sleep* kindly, and love his mother well! This is the Biography of Jocelin; 'a man of excellent religion,' says one of his contemporary Brother Monks, '*eximiæ religionis, potens sermone et opere*.'*

For one thing, he had learned to write a kind of Monk or Dog-Latin,* still readable to mankind; and, by good luck for us, had bethought him of noting down thereby what things seemed notablest to him. Hence gradually resulted a *Chronica Jocelini;* new Manuscript in the *Liber Albus* of St. Edmundsbury.* Which Chronicle, once written in its childlike transparency, in its innocent good-humour, not without touches of ready pleasant wit and many kinds of worth, other men liked naturally to read: whereby it failed not to be copied, to be multiplied, to be inserted in the *Liber Albus*; and so surviving Henry the Eighth, Putney Cromwell, the Dissolution of Monasteries,* and all accidents of malice and neglect for six centuries or so, it got into the *Harleian Collection*,*—and has now therefrom, by Mr. Rokewood of the Camden Society, been deciphered into clear print; and lies before us, a dainty thin quarto, to interest for a few minutes whomsoever it can.

Here too it will behove a just Historian gratefully to say that Mr. Rokewood, Jocelin's Editor, has done his editorial function well.

Not only has he deciphered his crabbed Manuscript into clear print; but he has attended, what his fellow editors are not always in the habit of doing, to the important truth that the Manuscript so deciphered ought to have a meaning for the reader. Standing faithfully by his text, and printing its very errors in spelling, in grammar or otherwise, he has taken care by some note to indicate that they are errors, and what the correction of them ought to be.* Jocelin's Monk-Latin is generally transparent, as shallow limpid water. But at any stop that may occur, of which there are a few, and only a very few, we have the comfortable assurance that a meaning does lie in the passage, and may by industry be got at; that a faithful editor's industry had already got at it before passing on. A compendious useful Glossary is given; nearly adequate to help the uninitiated through: sometimes one wishes it had been a trifle larger;* but, with a Spelman and Ducange at your elbow,* how easy to have made it far too large! Notes are added, generally brief; sufficiently explanatory of most points. Lastly, a copious correct Index; which no such Book should want, and which unluckily very few possess. And so, in a word, the *Chronicle of Jocelin* is, as it professes to be, unwrapped from its thick cerements, and fairly brought forth into the common daylight, so that he who runs, and has a smattering of grammar, may read.*

We have heard so much of Monks; everywhere, in real and fictitious History, from Muratori Annals to Radcliffe Romances,* these singular two-legged animals, with their rosaries and breviaries, with their shaven crowns, hair-cilices,* and vows of poverty, masquerade so strangely through our fancy; and they are in fact so very strange an extinct species of the human family,—a veritable Monk of Bury St. Edmunds is worth attending to, if by chance made visible and audible. Here he is; and in his hand a magical speculum,* much gone to rust indeed, yet in fragments still clear; wherein the marvellous image of his existence does still shadow itself, though fitfully, and as with an intermittent light! Will not the reader peep with us into this singular *camera lucida,* where an extinct species, though fitfully, can still be seen alive? Extinct species, we say; for the live specimens which still go about under that character are too evidently to be classed as spurious in Natural History: the Gospel of Richard Arkwright once promulgated,* no Monk of the old sort is any longer possible in this world. But fancy a deep-buried Mastodon, some fossil Megatherion,

Ichthyosaurus,* were to begin to *speak* from amid its rock-swathings, never so indistinctly! The most extinct fossil species of Men or Monks can do, and does, this miracle,—thanks to the Letters of the Alphabet, good for so many things.

Jocelin, we said, was somewhat of a Boswell; but unfortunately, by Nature, he is none of the largest, and distance has now dwarfed him to an extreme degree. His light is most feeble, intermittent, and requires the intensest kindest inspection; otherwise it will disclose mere vacant haze. It must be owned, the good Jocelin, spite of his beautiful childlike character, is but an altogether imperfect 'mirror' of these old-world things! The good man, he looks on us so clear and cheery, and in his neighbourly soft-smiling eyes we see so well our *own* shadow,—we have a longing always to cross-question him, to force from him an explanation of much. But no; Jocelin, though he talks with such clear familiarity, like a next-door neighbour, will not answer any question: that is the peculiarity of him, dead these six hundred and fifty years, and quite deaf to us, though still so audible! The good man, he cannot help it, nor can we.

But truly it is a strange consideration this simple one, as we go on with him, or indeed with any lucid simple-hearted soul like him: Behold therefore, this England of the Year 1200 was no chimerical vacuity or dreamland, peopled with mere vaporous Fantasms, Rymer's Fœdera,* and Doctrines of the Constitution;* but a green solid place, that grew corn and several other things. The Sun shone on it; the vicissitude of seasons and human fortunes. Cloth was woven and worn; ditches were dug, furrow-fields ploughed, and houses built. Day by day all men and cattle rose to labour, and night by night returned home weary to their several lairs. In wondrous Dualism, then as now, lived nations of breathing men; alternating, in all ways, between Light and Dark: between joy and sorrow, between rest and toil,—between hope, hope reaching high as Heaven, and fear deep as very Hell. Not vapour Fantasms, Rymer's Fœdera at all! Cœur-de-Lion was not a theatrical popinjay with greaves and steel-cap on it,* but a man living upon victuals,—*not* imported by Peel's Tariff.* Cœur-de-Lion came palpably athwart this Jocelin at St. Edmundsbury; and had almost peeled the sacred gold '*Feretrum*,'* or St. Edmund Shrine itself, to ransom him out of the Danube Jail.*

These clear eyes of neighbour Jocelin looked on the bodily presence of King John; the very John *Sansterre* or Lackland, who signed

Magna Charta afterwards in Runnymead.* Lackland, with a great
retinue, boarded once, for the matter of a fortnight, in St. Edmundsbury Convent; daily in the very eyesight, palpable to the very fingers
of our Jocelin: O Jocelin, what did he say, what did he do; how looked
he, lived he;—at the very lowest, what coat or breeches had he on?
Jocelin is obstinately silent. Jocelin marks down what interests *him*;
entirely deaf to *us*. With Jocelin's eyes we discern almost nothing of
John Lackland. As through a glass darkly,* we with our own eyes
and appliances, intensely looking, discern at most: A blustering,
dissipated, human figure, with a kind of blackguard quality air, in
cramoisy* velvet, or other uncertain texture, uncertain cut, with
much plumage and fringing; amid numerous other human figures of
the like; riding abroad with hawks; talking noisy nonsense;—tearing
out the bowels of St. Edmundsbury Convent (its larders namely and
cellars) in the most ruinous way, by living at rack and manger* there.
Jocelin notes only, with a slight subacidity of manner, that the King's
Majesty, *Dominus Rex*, did leave, as gift for our St. Edmund Shrine,
a handsome enough silk cloak,—or rather pretended to leave, for one
of his retinue borrowed it of us, and *we* never got sight of it again;
and, on the whole, that the *Dominus Rex*, at departing, gave us 'thirteen *sterlingii*,'* one shilling and one penny, to say a mass for him; and so
departed,—like a shabby Lackland as he was! 'Thirteen pence sterling,'
this was what the Convent got from Lackland, for all the victuals he
and his had made away with. We of course said our mass for him,
having covenanted to do it,—but let impartial posterity judge with
what degree of fervour!

And in this manner vanishes King Lackland; traverses swiftly our
strange intermittent magic-mirror, jingling the shabby thirteen pence
merely; and rides with his hawks into Egyptian night again.* It is
Jocelin's manner with all things; and it is men's manner and men's
necessity. How intermittent is our good Jocelin; marking down, without eye to *us*, what *he* finds interesting! How much in Jocelin, as in all
History, and indeed in all Nature, is at once inscrutable and certain;
so dim, yet so indubitable; exciting us to endless considerations. For
King Lackland *was* there, verily he; and did leave these *tredecim sterlingii* if nothing more, and did live and look in one way or the other,
and a whole world was living and looking along with him! There, we
say, is the grand peculiarity;* the immeasurable one; distinguishing,
to a really infinite degree, the poorest historical Fact from all Fiction

whatsoever. Fiction, 'Imagination,' 'Imaginative Poetry,' &c. &c., except as the vehicle for truth, or *fact* of some sort,—which surely a man should first try various other ways of vehiculating, and conveying safe,—what is it? Let the Minerva* and other Presses respond!—

But it is time we were in St. Edmundsbury Monastery, and Seven good Centuries off. If indeed it be possible, by any aid of Jocelin, by any human art, to get thither, with a reader or two still following us?

CHAPTER II.

ST. EDMUNDSBURY.

THE *Burg*, Bury, or 'Berry' as they call it, of St. Edmund* is still a prosperous brisk Town; beautifully diversifying, with its clear brick houses, ancient clean streets, and twenty or fifteen thousand busy souls,* the general grassy face of Suffolk; looking out right pleasantly, from its hill-slope, towards the rising Sun: and on the eastern edge of it, still runs, long, black and massive, a range of monastic ruins;* into the wide internal spaces of which the stranger is admitted on payment of one shilling.* Internal spaces laid out, at present, as a botanic garden.* Here stranger or townsman, sauntering at his leisure amid these vast grim venerable ruins, may persuade himself that an Abbey of St. Edmundsbury did once exist; nay there is no doubt of it: see here the ancient massive Gateway,* of architecture interesting to the eye of Dilettantism; and farther on, that other ancient Gateway, now about to tumble,* unless Dilettantism, in these very months, can subscribe money to cramp it and prop it!*

Here, sure enough, is an Abbey; beautiful in the eye of Dilettantism. Giant Pedantry also will step in, with its huge *Dugdale* and other enormous *Monasticons* under its arm, and cheerfully apprise you, That this was a very great Abbey,* owner and indeed creator of St. Edmund's Town itself, owner of wide lands and revenues; nay that its lands were once a county of themselves; that indeed King Canute or Knut was very kind to it, and gave St. Edmund his own gold crown* off his head, on one occasion; for the rest, that the Monks were of such and such a genus, such and such a number;* that they had so many carucates* of land in this hundred, and so many in that; and then farther that the large Tower or Belfry was built by such a one, and the smaller Belfry* was built by &c. &c.—Till human nature can stand no more of it; till human nature desperately take refuge in forgetfulness, almost in flat disbelief of the whole business, Monks, Monastery, Belfries, Carucates and all! Alas, what mountains of dead ashes, wreck and burnt bones, does assiduous Pedantry dig up from the Past Time, and name it History, and Philosophy of History;* till, as we say, the human soul sinks wearied and bewildered; till the Past Time seems all one infinite incredible grey void, without sun, stars, hearth-fires, or candle-light; dim offensive dust-whirlwinds filling universal Nature; and over your Historical Library, it is as if all the Titans* had written for themselves: DRY RUBBISH SHOT HERE!*

And yet these grim old walls are not a dilettantism and dubiety; they are an earnest fact. It was a most real and serious purpose they were built for! Yes, another world it was, when these black ruins, white in their new mortar and fresh chiselling, first saw the sun as walls, long ago. Gauge not, with thy dilettante compasses, with that placid dilettante simper, the Heaven's-Watchtower of our Fathers, the fallen God's-Houses, the Golgotha* of true Souls departed!

Their architecture, belfries, land-carucates? Yes,—and that is but a small item of the matter. Does it never give thee pause, this other strange item of it, that men then had a *soul*,—not by hearsay alone, and as a figure of speech; but as a truth that they *knew*, and practically went upon! Verily it was another world then. Their Missals have become incredible, a sheer platitude, sayest thou? Yes, a most poor platitude; and even, if thou wilt, an idolatry and blasphemy, should any one persuade *thee* to believe them, to pretend praying by them. But yet it is pity we had lost tidings of our souls:—actually we shall have to go in quest of them again, or worse in all ways will befal! A certain degree of soul, as Ben Jonson reminds us, is indispensable to keep the very body from destruction of the frightfullest sort; to 'save us,' says he, 'the expense of *salt*.'* Ben has known men who had soul enough to keep their body and five senses from becoming carrion, and save salt:—men, and also Nations. You may look in Manchester Hunger-mobs and Corn-law Commons Houses, and various other quarters, and say whether either soul or else salt is not somewhat wanted at present!—

Another world, truly: and this present poor distressed world might get some profit by looking wisely into it, instead of foolishly. But at lowest, O dilettante friend, let us know always that it *was* a world, and not a void infinite of grey haze with fantasms swimming in it. These old St. Edmundsbury walls, I say, were not peopled with fantasms; but with men of flesh and blood, made altogether as we are. Had thou and I then been, who knows but we ourselves had taken refuge from an evil Time, and fled to dwell here, and meditate on an Eternity, in such fashion as we could? Alas, how like an old osseous fragment, a broken blackened shin-bone of the old dead Ages,* this black ruin looks out, not yet covered by the soil; still indicating what a once gigantic Life lies buried there! It is dead now, and dumb; but was alive once, and spake. For twenty generations,* here was the earthly arena where painful living men worked out their life-wrestle,—looked at by Earth, by Heaven and Hell. Bells tolled to prayers; and men, of many humours,* various thoughts, chanted vespers, matins;—and round the little islet of their life rolled forever (as round ours still rolls, though we are blind and deaf) the illimitable Ocean, tinting all things with *its* eternal hues and reflexes; making strange prophetic music! How silent now; all departed, clean gone. The World-Dramaturgist* has written: *Exeunt.* The devouring Time-Demons have made away with it all: and in its stead, there is either nothing; or what is worse, offensive universal dustclouds, and grey eclipse of Earth and Heaven, from 'dry rubbish shot here!'—

Truly, it is no easy matter to get across the chasm of Seven Centuries, filled with such material. But here, of all helps, is not a Boswell the welcomest; even a small Boswell? Veracity, true simplicity of heart, how valuable are these always! He that speaks what *is* really in him, will find men to listen, though under never such impediments. Even gossip, springing free and cheery from a human heart, this too is a kind of veracity and *speech*;—much preferable to pedantry and inane grey haze! Jocelin is weak and garrulous, but he is human. Through the thin watery gossip of our Jocelin, we do get some glimpses of that deep-buried Time; discern veritably, though in a fitful intermittent manner, these antique figures and their life-method, face to face! Beautifully, in our earnest loving glance, the old centuries melt from opaque to partially translucent, transparent here and there; and the void black Night, one finds, is but the summing up of innumerable peopled luminous *Days*. Not parchment Chartularies,* Doctrines of the Constitution, O Dryasdust;* not altogether, my erudite friend!—

Readers who please to go along with us into this poor *Jocelini Chronica* shall wander inconveniently enough, as in wintry twilight, through some poor stript hazel-grove, rustling with foolish noises, and perpetually hindering the eyesight; but across which, here and there, some real human figure is seen moving: very strange; whom we could hail if he would answer;—and we look into a pair of eyes deep as our own, *imaging* our own, but all unconscious of us; to whom we for the time are become as spirits and invisible!

CHAPTER III.

LANDLORD EDMUND.

SOME three centuries or so had elapsed since *Beodric's-worth*[1]* became St. Edmund's *Stow*, St. Edmund's *Town* and Monastery, before Jocelin entered himself a Novice there. 'It was,' says he, 'the year after the Flemings were defeated at Fornham St. Genevieve.'*

Much passes away into oblivion: this glorious victory over the Flemings at Fornham has, at the present date, greatly dimmed itself out of the minds of men. A victory and battle nevertheless it was, in its time: some thrice-renowned Earl of Leicester, not of the De Montfort breed,* (as may be read in Philosophical and other Histories, could any human memory retain such things,) had quarrelled with his sovereign, Henry Second of the name; had been worsted, it is like, and maltreated, and obliged to fly to foreign parts; but had rallied there into new vigour; and so, in the year 1173, returns across the German Sea with a vengeful army of Flemings. Returns, to the coast

---

[1] Dryasdust puzzles and pokes for some biography of this Beodric; and repugns to consider him a mere East-Anglian Person of Condition, not in need of a biography,—whose peonð, *weorth* or *worth*, that is to say, *Growth*, Increase, or as we should now name it, *Estate*,* that same Hamlet and wood Mansion, now St. Edmund's Bury, originally was. For, adds our erudite Friend, the Saxon peonðan, equivalent to the German *werden*, means to *grow*, to *become*;* traces of which old vocable are still found in the North-country dialects, as, 'What is *word* of him?' meaning 'What is *become* of him?' and the like. Nay we in modern English still say, 'Wo *worth* the hour'* (Wo *befal* the hour), and speak of the '*Weird* Sisters;' not to mention the innumerable other names of places still ending in *weorth* or *worth*. And indeed, our common noun *worth*, in the sense of *value*, does not this mean simply, What a thing has *grown* to, What a man has *grown* to, How much he amounts to,—by the Threadneedle-street* standard or another!

of Suffolk; to Framlingham Castle, where he is welcomed; westward towards St. Edmundsbury and Fornham Church,* where he is met by the constituted authorities with *posse comitatus;* and swiftly cut in pieces, he and his, or laid by the heels; on the right bank of the obscure river Lark,—as traces still existing will verify.

For the river Lark, though not very discoverably, still runs or stagnates in that country; and the battle-ground is there; serving at present as a pleasure-ground to his Grace of Newcastle.* Copper pennies of Henry II.* are still found there;—rotted out from the pouches of poor slain soldiers, who had not had *time* to buy liquor with them. In the river Lark itself was fished up, within man's memory, an antique gold ring; which fond Dilettantism can almost believe may have been the very ring Countess Leicester threw away, in her flight, into that same Lark river or ditch.[1]* Nay, few years ago, in tearing out an enormous superannuated ash-tree, now grown quite corpulent, bursten, superfluous, but long a fixture in the soil, and not to be dislodged without revolution,—there was laid bare, under its roots, 'a circular mound of skeletons wonderfully complete,'* all radiating from a centre, faces upwards, feet inwards; a 'radiation' not of Light, but of the Nether Darkness rather; and evidently the fruit of battle; for 'many of the heads were cleft, or had arrow-holes in them.' The Battle of Fornham, therefore, is a fact, though a forgotten one; no less obscure than undeniable,—like so many other facts.

Like the St. Edmund's Monastery itself! Who can doubt, after what we have said, that there was a Monastery here at one time? No doubt at all there was a Monastery here; no doubt, some three centuries prior to this Fornham Battle, there dwelt a man in these parts, of the name of Edmund, King, Landlord, Duke or whatever his title was, of the Eastern Counties;—and a very singular man and landlord he must have been.

For his tenants, it would appear, did not complain of him in the least; his labourers did not think of burning his wheatstacks, breaking into his game-preserves; very far the reverse of all that. Clear evidence, satisfactory even to my friend Dryasdust, exists that, on the contrary, they honoured, loved, admired this ancient Landlord to a quite astonishing degree,*—and indeed at last to an immeasurable

---

[1] Lyttelton's History of Henry II. (2nd Edition), v. 169, &c.

and inexpressible degree; for, finding no limits or utterable words for their sense of his worth, they took to beatifying and adoring him! 'Infinite admiration,' we are taught, 'means worship.'

Very singular,—could we discover it! What Edmund's specific duties were; above all, what his method of discharging them with such results was, would surely be interesting to know; but are *not* very discoverable now. His Life has become a poetic, nay a religious *Mythus*; though, undeniably enough, it was once a prose Fact, as our poor lives are; and even a very rugged unmanageable one. This land-lord Edmund did go about in leather shoes, with *femoralia** and body-coat of some sort on him; and daily had his breakfast to procure; and daily had contradictory speeches, and most contradictory facts not a few, to reconcile with himself. No man becomes a Saint in his sleep. Edmund, for instance, instead of *reconciling* those same contradictory facts and speeches to himself; which means *subduing*, and, in a manlike and godlike manner, conquering them to himself,— might have merely thrown new contention into them, new unwis-dom into them, and so been conquered *by* them; much the commoner case! In that way he had proved no 'Saint,' or Divine-looking Man, but a mere Sinner, and unfortunate, blameable, more or less Diabolic-looking man! No landlord Edmund becomes infinitely admirable in his sleep.

With what degree of wholesome rigour his rents were collected we hear not. Still less by what methods he preserved his game, whether by 'bushing' or how,*—and if the partridge seasons were 'excellent,' or were indifferent. Neither do we ascertain what kind of Corn-bill he passed, or wisely-adjusted Sliding-scale:—but indeed there were few spinners in those days; and the nuisance of spinning, and other dusty labour, was not yet so glaring a one.

How then, it may be asked, did this Edmund rise into favour; become to such astonishing extent a recognised Farmer's Friend?* Really, except it were by doing justly and loving mercy, to an unpre-cedented extent, one does not know.* The man, it would seem, 'had walked,' as they say, 'humbly with God;'* humbly and valiantly with God; struggling to make the Earth heavenly, as he could: instead of walking sumptuously and pridefully with Mammon, leaving the Earth to grow hellish as it liked. Not sumptuously with Mammon? How then could he 'encourage trade,'—cause Howel and James,* and many wine-merchants to bless him, and the tailor's heart (though in

a very shortsighted manner) to sing for joy? Much in this Edmund's
Life is mysterious.

That he could, on occasion, do what he liked with his own is,
meanwhile, evident enough. Certain Heathen Physical-Force Ultra-
Chartists, 'Danes' as they were then called,* coming into his territory with their 'five points,' or rather with their five-and-twenty
thousand *points* and edges too, of pikes namely and battle-axes; and
proposing mere Heathenism, confiscation, spoliation, and fire and
sword,—Edmund answered that he would oppose to the utmost
such savagery. They took him prisoner; again required his sanction
to said proposals. Edmund again refused. Cannot we kill you? cried
they.—Cannot I die? answered he. My life, I think, is my own to do
what I like with!* And he died, under barbarous tortures, refusing to
the last breath;* and the Ultra-Chartist Danes *lost* their propositions;—
and went with their 'points' and other apparatus, as is supposed, to
the Devil, the Father of them. Some say, indeed, these Danes were
not Ultra-Chartists, but Ultra-Tories, demanding to reap where
they had not sown, and live in this world without working, though
all the world should starve for it; which likewise seems a possible
hypothesis. Be what they might, they went, as we say, to the Devil;
and Edmund doing what he liked with his own, the Earth was got
cleared of them.

Another version is, that Edmund on this and the like occasions
stood by his order;* the oldest, and indeed only true order of Nobility
known under the stars, that of Just Men and Sons of God, in opposition to Unjust and Sons of Belial,*—which latter indeed are
second-oldest, but yet a very unvenerable order. This, truly, seems the
likeliest hypothesis of all. Names and appearances alter so strangely, in
some half-score centuries; and all fluctuates chameleon-like, taking
now this hue, now that. Thus much is very plain, and does not change
hue: Landlord Edmund was seen and felt by all men to have done
verily a man's part in this life-pilgrimage of his; and benedictions, and
outflowing love and admiration from the universal heart, were his
meed. Well-done! Well-done! cried the hearts of all men. They raised
his slain and martyred body; washed its wounds with fast-flowing universal tears;* tears of endless pity, and yet of a sacred joy and triumph.
The beautifullest kind of tears,—indeed perhaps the beautifullest
kind of thing: like a sky all flashing diamonds and prismatic radiance;
all weeping, yet shone on by the everlasting Sun:—and *this* is not a sky,

it is a Soul and living Face! Nothing liker the *Temple of the Highest*,* bright with some real effulgence of the Highest, is seen in this world.

O, if all Yankee-land follow a small good 'Schnüspel the distinguished Novelist'* with blazing torches, dinner-invitations, universal hep-hep-hurrah, feeling that he, though small, *is* something; how might all Angle-land once follow a hero-martyr and great true Son of Heaven! It is the very joy of man's heart to admire, where he can; nothing so lifts him from all his mean imprisonments, were it but for moments, as true admiration. Thus it has been said, 'all men, especially all women, are born worshippers;'* and will worship, if it be but possible. Possible to worship a Something, even a small one; not so possible a mere loud-blaring Nothing! What sight is more pathetic than that of poor multitudes of persons met to gaze at Kings' Progresses, Lord Mayors' Shews,* and other gilt-gingerbread phenomena of the worshipful sort, in these times; each so eager to worship; each, with a dim fatal sense of disappointment, finding that he cannot rightly here! These be thy gods, O Israel?* And thou art so *willing* to worship,—poor Israel!

In this manner, however, did the men of the Eastern Counties take up the slain body of their Edmund, where it lay cast forth in the village of Hoxne; seek out the severed head, and reverently reunite the same.* They embalmed him with myrrh and sweet spices, with love, pity, and all high and awful thoughts; consecrating him with a very storm of melodious adoring admiration, and sun-dyed showers of tears;—joyfully, yet with awe (as all deep joy has something of the awful in it), commemorating his noble deeds and godlike walk and conversation while on Earth. Till, at length, the very Pope and Cardinals at Rome were forced to hear of it;* and they, summing up as correctly as they well could, with *Advocatus-Diaboli** pleadings and their other forms of process, the general verdict of mankind, declared: That he had, in very fact, led a hero's life in this world; and being now *gone*, was gone as they conceived to God above, and reaping his reward *there*. Such, they said, was the best judgment they could form of the case;—and truly not a bad judgment. Acquiesced in, zealously adopted, with full assent of 'private judgment,'* by all mortals.

The rest of St. Edmund's history, for the reader sees he has now become a *Saint*, is easily conceivable. Pious munificence provided him a *loculus*,* a *feretrum* or shrine; built for him a wooden chapel, a stone temple,* ever widening and growing by new pious gifts;—such the overflowing heart feels it a blessedness to solace itself by giving. St. Edmund's Shrine glitters now with diamond flowerages, with a plating of wrought gold. The wooden chapel, as we say, has become a stone temple. Stately masonries, long-drawn arches, cloisters, sounding aisles buttress it, begirdle it far and wide. Regimented companies of men, of whom our Jocelin is one, devote themselves, in every generation, to meditate here on man's Nobleness and Awfulness, and celebrate and shew forth the same, as they best can,—thinking they will do it better here, in presence of God the Maker, and of the so Awful and so Noble made by Him. In one word, St. Edmund's Body has raised a Monastery round it. To such length, in such manner, has the Spirit of the Time visibly taken body, and crystallised itself here. New gifts, houses, farms, *katalla*[1]—come ever in. King Knut, whom men call Canute, whom the Ocean-tide would not be forbidden to wet,*—we heard already of this wise King, with his crown and gifts; but of many others, Kings, Queens, wise men and noble loyal women, let Dryasdust and divine Silence be the record! Beodric's-worth has become St. Edmund's *Bury;*—and lasts visible to this hour. All this that thou now seest, and namest Bury Town, is properly the Funeral Monument of Saint or Landlord Edmund. The present respectable Mayor of Bury may be said, like a Fakeer (little as he thinks of it), to have his dwelling in the extensive, many-sculptured Tombstone of St. Edmund; in one of the brick niches thereof* dwells the present respectable Mayor of Bury.

Certain Times do crystallise themselves in a magnificent manner; and others, perhaps, are like to do it in rather a shabby one!—But Richard Arkwright too will have his Monument, a thousand years hence: all Lancashire and Yorkshire, and how many other shires and countries, with their machineries and industries, for his monument! A true *pyr*amid or '*flame*-mountain,'* flaming with steam fires and useful labour over wide continents, usefully towards the Stars, to a certain height;—how much grander than your foolish Cheops Pyramids or Sakhara clay ones!* Let us withal be hopeful, be content or patient.

---

[1] Goods, properties; what we now call *chattels*, and still more singularly *cattle*, says my erudite friend!*

CHAPTER IV.

ABBOT HUGO.*

IT is true, all things have two faces, a light one and a dark. It is true,
in three centuries, much imperfection accumulates; many an Ideal,
monastic or other, shooting forth into practice as it can, grows to
a strange enough Reality; and we have to ask with amazement, Is this
your Ideal! For, alas, the Ideal always has to grow in the Real, and to
seek out its bed and board there, often in a very sorry way. No beautifullest Poet is a Bird-of-Paradise, living on perfumes; sleeping in the
æther with outspread wings.* The Heroic, *independent* of bed and
board, is found in Drury-lane Theatre* only; to avoid disappoint-
ments, let us bear this in mind.

By the law of Nature, too, all manner of Ideals have their fatal
limits and lot; their appointed periods, of youth, of maturity or perfection, of decline, degradation, and final death and disappearance.
There is nothing born but has to die. Ideal monasteries, once grown
real, do seek bed and board in this world; do find it more and more
successfully; do get at length too intent on finding it, exclusively
intent on that. They are then like diseased corpulent bodies fallen
idiotic, which merely eat and sleep; *ready* for 'dissolution,' by a Henry
the Eighth or some other. Jocelin's St. Edmundsbury is still far from
this last dreadful state: but here too the reader will prepare himself to
see an Ideal not sleeping in the æther like a bird-of-paradise, but
roosting as the common woodfowl do, in an imperfect, uncomfortable, more or less contemptible manner!—

Abbot Hugo, as Jocelin, breaking at once into the heart of the business, apprises us, had in those days grown old, grown rather blind,
and his eyes were somewhat darkened, *aliquantulum caligaverunt oculi
ejus.** He dwelt apart very much, in his *Talamus* or peculiar Chamber;
got into the hands of flatterers, a set of mealy-mouthed persons who
strove to make the passing hour easy for him,—for him easy, and for
themselves profitable; accumulating in the distance mere mountains
of confusion. Old Dominus Hugo sat inaccessible in this way, far in
the interior, wrapt in his warm flannels and delusions; inaccessible to
all voice of Fact; and bad grew ever worse with us. Not that our worthy
old *Dominus Abbas** was inattentive to the divine offices, or to the

maintenance of a devout spirit in us or in himself; but the Account-Books of the Convent fell into the frightfullest state, and Hugo's annual Budget grew yearly emptier, or filled with futile expectations, fatal deficit, wind and debts!

His one worldly care was to raise ready money;* sufficient for the day is the evil thereof.* And how he raised it: From usurious insatiable Jews;* every fresh Jew sticking on him like a fresh horseleech,* sucking his and our life out; crying continually, Give, Give!* Take one example instead of scores. Our *Camera* having fallen into ruin, William the Sacristan* received charge to repair it; strict charge, but no money; Abbot Hugo would, and indeed could, give him no fraction of money. The *Camera* in ruins, and Hugo penniless and inaccessible, Willelmus Sacrista borrowed Forty Marcs (some Seven-and-twenty Pounds) of Benedict the Jew,* and patched up our Camera again. But the means of repaying him? There were no means. Hardly could *Sacrista, Cellerarius* or any public officer,* get ends to meet, on the indispensablest scale, with their shrunk allowances: ready money had vanished.

Benedict's Twenty-seven pounds grew rapidly at compound-interest,* and at length, when it had amounted to One hundred pounds, he, on a day of settlement, presents the account to Hugo himself! Hugo already owed him another One hundred of his own; and so here it has become Two hundred! Hugo, in a fine frenzy, threatens to depose the Sacristan, to do this and do that; but, in the mean while, How to quiet your insatiable Jew? Hugo, for this couple of hundreds, grants the Jew his bond for Four hundred payable at the end of four years. At the end of four years there is, of course, still no money; and the Jew now gets a bond for Eight hundred and eighty pounds, to be paid by instalments, Four-score pounds every year. Here was a way of doing business!

Neither yet is this insatiable Jew satisfied or settled with: he had papers against us of 'small debts fourteen years old;' his modest claim amounts finally to 'Twelve hundred pounds besides interest;'*—and one hopes he never got satisfied in this world; one almost hopes he was one of those beleaguered Jews who hanged themselves in York Castle shortly afterwards,* and had his usances and quittances and horse-leech papers summarily set fire to!* For approximate justice will strive to accomplish itself; if not in one way, then in another. Jews, and also Christians and Heathens, who accumulate in this manner, though furnished with never so many parchments, do, at times, 'get their grinder-teeth successively pulled out of their head,* each day a new grinder,' till they consent to disgorge again. A sad fact,—worth reflecting on.

Jocelin, we see, is not without secularity: Our *Dominus Abbas* was intent enough on the divine offices; but then his Account-Books—?— One of the things that strike us most, throughout, in Jocelin's *Chronicle*, and indeed in Eadmer's *Anselm*,* and other old monastic Books, written evidently by pious men, is this, That there is almost no mention whatever of 'personal religion'* in them; that the whole gist of their thinking and speculation seems to be the 'privileges of our order,' 'strict exaction of our dues,' 'God's honour' (meaning the honour of our Saint), and so forth. Is not this singular? A body of men, set apart for perfecting and purifying their own souls, do not seem disturbed about that in any measure: the 'Ideal' says nothing about its idea; says much about finding bed and board for itself! How is this?

Why, for one thing, bed and board are a matter very apt to come to speech: it is much easier to *speak* of them than of ideas; and they are sometimes much more pressing with some! Nay, for another thing, may not this religious reticence, in these devout good souls, be perhaps a merit, and sign of health in them? Jocelin, Eadmer, and such religious men, have as yet nothing of 'Methodism;'* no Doubt or even root of Doubt. Religion is not a diseased self-introspection, an agonising inquiry: their duties are clear to them, the way of supreme good plain, indisputable, and they are travelling on it. Religion lies over them like an all-embracing heavenly canopy, like an atmosphere and life-element, which is not spoken of, which in all things is presupposed without speech. Is not serene or complete Religion the highest aspect of human nature; as serene Cant, or complete No-religion, is the lowest and miserablest? Between which two, all manner of earnest Methodisms, introspections, agonising inquiries, never so morbid, shall play their respective parts, not without approbation.

But let any reader fancy himself one of the Brethren in St. Edmundsbury Monastery under such circumstances! How can a Lord Abbot, all stuck over with horseleeches of this nature, front the world? He is fast losing his life-blood, and the Convent will be as one of Pharaoh's lean kine.* Old monks of experience draw their hoods deeper down; careful what they say: the monk's first duty is obedience. Our Lord the King, hearing of such work, sends down his Almoner to make investigations: but what boots it? Abbot Hugo assembles us in Chapter;* asks, "If there is any complaint?"* Not a soul of us dare answer, "Yes, thousands!" but we all stand silent, and the Prior even says that things are in a very comfortable condition. Whereupon old Abbot Hugo, turning to the royal messenger, says, "You see!"—and the business terminates in that way. I, as a brisk-eyed, noticing youth and novice, could not help asking of the elders, asking of Magister Samson in particular: Why he, well-instructed and a knowing man, had not spoken out, and brought matters to a bearing? Magister Samson was Teacher of the Novices, appointed to breed us up to the rules, and I loved him well. "*Fili mi*,"* answered Samson, "the burnt child shuns the fire. Dost thou not know, our Lord the Abbot sent me once to Acre in Norfolk, to solitary confinement and bread and water, already? The Hinghams, Hugo and Robert,* have just got home from banishment for speaking. This is the hour of darkness; the hour when flatterers rule and are believed. *Videat Dominus*, let the Lord see, and judge."

In very truth, what could poor old Abbot Hugo do?* A frail old man; and the Philistines were upon him,—that is to say, the Hebrews. He had nothing for it but to shrink away from them; get back into his warm flannels, into his warm delusions again. Happily, before it was quite too late, he bethought him of pilgriming to St. Thomas of Canterbury.* He set out, with a fit train, in the autumn days of the year 1180; near Rochester City, his mule threw him, dislocated his poor kneepan, raised incurable inflammatory fever; and the poor old man got his dismissal from the whole coil at once. St. Thomas à Becket, though in a circuitous way, had *brought* deliverance! Neither Jew usurers, nor grumbling monks, nor other importunate despicability of men or mud-elements afflicted Abbot Hugo any more; but he dropt his rosaries, closed his account-books, closed his old eyes, and lay down into the long Sleep. Heavy-laden hoary old Dominus Hugo, fare thee well.

One thing we cannot mention without a due thrill of horror:* namely, that, in the empty exchequer of Dominus Hugo, there was not found one penny to distribute to the Poor that they might pray for his soul! By a kind of godsend, Fifty shillings did, in the very nick of time, fall due, or seem to fall due, from one of his Farmers (the *Firmarius* de Palegrava), and he paid it, and the Poor had it; though, alas, this too only *seemed* to fall due, and we had it to pay again afterwards. Dominus Hugo's apartments were plundered by his servants, to the last portable stool, in a few minutes after the breath was out of his body. Forlorn old Hugo, fare thee well forever.

CHAPTER V.

TWELFTH CENTURY.

OUR Abbot being dead, the *Dominus Rex*, Henry II., or Ranulf de Glanvill *Justiciarius* of England for him,* set Inspectors or Custodiars over us;—not in any breathless haste to appoint a new Abbot, our revenues coming into his own *Scaccarium*, or royal Exchequer, in the meanwhile. They proceeded with some rigour, these Custodiars; took written inventories, clapt-on seals, exacted everywhere strict tale and measure: but wherefore should a living monk complain? The living monk has to do his devotional drill-exercise; consume his allotted *pitantia*, what we call *pittance*, or ration of victual; and possess his soul in patience.

Dim, as through a long vista of Seven Centuries, dim and very strange looks that monk-life to us; the ever-surprising circumstance this, That it is a *fact* and no dream, that we see it there, and gaze into the very eyes of it! Smoke rises daily from those culinary chimney-throats; there are living human beings there, who chant, loud-braying, their matins, nones, vespers; awakening *echoes*, not to the bodily ear alone. St. Edmund's Shrine, perpetually illuminated, glows ruddy through the Night, and through the Night of Centuries withal; St. Edmundsbury Town paying yearly Forty pounds for that express end.* Bells clang out; on great occasions, all the bells. We have Processions, Preachings, Festivals, Christmas Plays, *Mysteries* shewn in the Churchyard, at which latter the Townsfolk sometimes quarrel.* Time was, Time is, as Friar Bacon's Brass Head* remarked; and withal Time will be. There are three Tenses, *Tempora*, or Times; and there is one Eternity; and as for us,

We are such stuff as Dreams are made of!*

Indisputable, though very dim to modern vision, rests on its hill-slope that same *Bury*, *Stow*, or Town of St. Edmund; already a considerable place, not without traffic, nay manufactures, would Jocelin only tell us what. Jocelin is totally careless of telling: but, through dim fitful apertures, we can see *Fullones*, 'Fullers,'* see cloth-making; looms dimly going, dye-vats, and old women spinning yarn. We have Fairs too, *Nundinæ*,* in due course; and the Londoners give us much trouble, pretending that they, as a metropolitan people, are exempt from toll.* Besides there is Field-husbandry, with perplexed settlement of Convent rents: corn-ricks pile themselves within burgh, in their season; and cattle depart and enter; and even the poor weaver has his cow;—'dungheaps' lying quiet at most doors (*ante foras*, says the incidental Jocelin), for the Town has yet no improved police.* Watch and ward nevertheless we do keep, and have Gates,— as what Town must not; thieves so abounding; war, *werra*, such a frequent thing! Our thieves, at the Abbot's judgment bar, deny; claim wager of battle;* fight, are beaten, and *then* hanged. 'Ketel, the thief,' took this course; and it did nothing for him,*—merely brought us, and indeed himself, new trouble!

Every way a most foreign Time. What difficulty, for example, has our *Cellerarius* to collect the *repselver*,* 'reaping silver,' or penny, which each householder is by law bound to pay for cutting down the Convent grain! Richer people pretend that it is commuted, that it is this and the other; that, in short, they will not pay it. Our *Cellerarius* gives up calling on the rich. In the houses of the poor, our *Cellerarius* finding, in like manner, neither penny nor good promise, snatches, without ceremony, what *vadium* (pledge, *wad*) he can come at: a jointstool, kettle, nay the very house-door, '*hostium;*' and old women, thus exposed to the unfeeling gaze of the public, rush out after him with their distaffs and the angriest shrieks: '*vetulæ exibant cum colis suis*,' says Jocelin, '*minantes et exprobrantes*.'*

What a historical picture, glowing visible, as St. Edmund's Shrine by night, after Seven long Centuries or so! *Vetulæ cum colis*: My venerable ancient spinning grandmothers,—ah, and ye too have to shriek, and rush out with your distaffs;* and become Female Chartists, and scold all evening with void doorway,—and in old Saxon, as we in modern, would fain demand some Five-point Charter,* could it be fallen in with, the Earth being too tyrannous!—Wise Lord Abbots, hearing of such phenomena, did in time abolish or commute the reappenny, and one nuisance was abated. But the image of these justly offended old women, in their old wool costumes, with their angry features, and spindles brandished, lives forever in the historical memory. Thanks to thee, Jocelin Boswell. Jerusalem was taken by the Crusaders, and again lost by them;* and Richard Cœur-de-Lion 'veiled his face'* as he passed in sight of it: but how many other things went on, the while!

Thus, too, our trouble with the Lakenheath eels* is very great. King Knut, namely, or rather his Queen* who also did herself honour by honouring St. Edmund, decreed by authentic deed yet extant on parchment, that the Holders of the Town Fields, once Beodric's, should, for one thing, go yearly and catch us four thousand eels in the marsh-pools of Lakenheath. Well, they went, they continued to go; but, in later times, got into the way of returning with a most short account of eels. Not the due six-score apiece; no, Here are two-score, Here are twenty, ten,—sometimes, Here are none at all; Heaven help us, we *could* catch no more, they were not there! What is a distressed *Cellerarius* to do? We agree that each Holder of so many acres shall pay one penny yearly, and let go the eels as too slippery. But alas, neither is this quite effectual: the Fields, in my time, have got divided among so many hands, there is no catching of *them* either; I have known our Cellarer get seven and twenty pence formerly, and now it is much if he get ten pence farthing (*vix decem denarios et obolum**). And then their sheep, which they are bound to fold nightly in our pens, for the manure's sake; and, I fear, do not always fold: and their *aver-pennies*, and their *avragiums*, and their *fodercorns*,* and mill-and-market dues! Thus, in its undeniable but dim manner, does old St. Edmundsbury spin and till, and laboriously keep its pot boiling, and St. Edmund's Shrine lighted, under such conditions and averages as it can.*

How much is still alive in England; how much has not yet come into life! A Feudal Aristocracy is still alive, in the prime of life; superintending the cultivation of the land, and less consciously the distribution of the produce of the land, the adjustment of the quarrels of the land; judging, soldiering, adjusting; everywhere governing the people,—so that even a Gurth born thrall of Cedric* lacks not his due parings of the pigs he tends. Governing;—and, alas, also game-preserving, so that a Robert Hood, a William Scarlet and others have, in these days, put on Lincoln coats, and taken to living, in some universal-suffrage manner,* under the greenwood tree!*

How silent, on the other hand, lie all Cotton-trades and such like; not a steeple-chimney yet got on end from sea to sea! North of the Humber, a stern Willelmus Conquestor burnt the Country,* finding it unruly, into very stern repose. Wild fowl scream in those ancient silences, wild cattle roam in those ancient solitudes; the scanty sulky Norse-bred population all coerced into silence,—feeling that under these new Norman Governors their history has probably as good as *ended.* Men and Northumbrian Norse populations know little what has ended, what is but beginning! The Ribble and the Aire roll down, as yet unpolluted by dyers' chemistry;* tenanted by merry trouts and piscatory otters; the sunbeam and the vacant wind's-blast alone traversing those moors. Side by side sleep the coal-strata and the iron-strata for so many ages; no Steam-Demon has yet risen smoking into being. Saint Mungo rules in Glasgow;* James Watt* still slumbering in the deep of Time. *Mancunium,* Manceaster, what we now call Manchester, spins no cotton,—if it be not *wool* 'cottons,' clipped from the backs of mountain sheep. The Creek of the Mersey gurgles, twice in the four-and-twenty hours, with eddying brine, clangorous with sea-fowl; and is a *Lither*-Pool,* a *lazy* or sullen Pool, no monstrous pitchy City, and Seahaven of the world! The Centuries are big; and the birth-hour is coming, not yet come. *Tempus ferax, tempus edax rerum.**

CHAPTER VI.

MONK SAMSON.

WITHIN doors, down at the hill-foot, in our Convent here, we are a peculiar people,—hardly conceivable in the Arkwright Corn-Law ages, of mere Spinning-Mills and Joe-Mantons!* There is yet no Methodism among us, and we speak much of Secularities: no Methodism; our Religion is not yet a horrible restless Doubt, still less a far horribler composed Cant; but a great heaven-high Unquestionability, encompassing, interpenetrating the whole of Life. Imperfect as we may be, we are here, with our litanies, shaven crowns, vows of poverty, to testify incessantly and indisputably to every heart, That this Earthly Life and *its* riches and possessions, and good and evil hap, are not intrinsically a reality at all, but *are* a shadow of realities eternal,* infinite; that this Time-world, as an air-image, fearfully *emblematic*, plays and flickers in the grand still mirror of Eternity; and man's little Life has Duties that are great, that are alone great, and go up to Heaven and down to Hell. This, with our poor litanies, we testify and struggle to testify.

Which, testified or not, remembered by all men, or forgotten by all men, does verily remain the fact, even in Arkwright Joe-Manton ages! But it is incalculable, when litanies have grown obsolete; when *fodercorns, avragiums*, and all human dues and reciprocities have been fully changed into one great due of *cash payment;* and man's duty to man reduces itself to handing him certain metal coins, or covenanted money-wages, and then shoving him out of doors; and man's duty to God becomes a cant, a doubt, a dim inanity, a 'pleasure of virtue'* or such like; and the thing a man does infinitely fear (the real *Hell* of a man) is 'that he do not make money and advance himself,'—I say, it is incalculable what a change has introduced itself everywhere into human affairs! How human affairs shall now circulate everywhere not healthy life-blood in them, but, as it were, a detestable copperas banker's ink;* and all is grown acrid, divisive, threatening dissolution; and the huge tumultuous Life of Society is galvanic, devil-ridden, too truly possessed by a devil! For, in short, Mammon *is* not a god at all; but a devil,* and even a very despicable devil. Follow the Devil faithfully, you are sure enough to *go* to the Devil: whither else *can* you go?—In such situations, men look back with a kind of mournful recognition even on poor limited Monk-figures, with their poor litanies; and reflect, with Ben Jonson, that soul is indispensable,* some degree of soul, even to save you the expense of salt!—

For the rest, it must be owned, we Monks of St. Edmundsbury are but a limited class of creatures, and seem to have a somewhat dull life of it. Much given to idle gossip; having indeed no other work, when our chanting is over. Listless gossip, for most part, and a mitigated slander; the fruit of idleness, not of spleen. We are dull, insipid men, many of us; easy-minded; whom prayer and digestion of food will avail for a life. We have to receive all strangers in our Convent, and lodge them gratis;* such and such sorts go by rule to the Lord Abbot and his special revenues; such and such to us and our poor Cellarer, however straitened. Jews themselves send their wives and little ones hither in war-time, into our *Pitanceria*; where they abide safe, with due *pittances*,*—for a consideration. We have the fairest chances for

collecting news. Some of us have a turn for reading Books; for meditation, silence; at times we even write Books. Some of us can preach,
in English-Saxon, in Norman French, and even in Monk-Latin;*
others cannot in any language or jargon, being stupid.

Failing all else, what gossip about one another! This is a perennial
resource. How one hooded head applies itself to the ear of another,
and whispers—*tacenda*. Willelmus Sacrista, for instance, what does
he nightly over in that Sacristy of his? Frequent bibations, '*frequentes
bibationes et quædam tacenda*,'*—eheu! We have '*tempora minutionis*,'*
stated seasons of blood-letting, when we are all let blood together; and
then there is a general free-conference, a sanhedrim of clatter. For all
our vow of poverty, we can by rule amass to the extent of 'two shillings;'* but it is to be given to our necessitous kindred, or in charity.
Poor Monks! Thus too a certain Canterbury Monk was in the habit of
'slipping, *clanculo* from his sleeve,'* five shillings into the hand of his
mother, when she came to see him, at the divine offices, every two
months. Once, slipping the money clandestinely, just in the act of
taking leave, he slipt it not into her hand but on the floor, and another
had it; whereupon the poor Monk, coming to know it, looked mere
despair for some days; till Lanfranc the noble Archbishop,* questioning his secret from him, nobly made the sum *seven* shillings,[1] and said,
Never mind!

One Monk of a taciturn nature distinguishes himself among these
babbling ones: the name of him Samson; he that answered Jocelin,
"*Fili mi*, a burnt child shuns the fire."* They call him 'Norfolk
Barrator,' or litigious person;* for indeed, being of grave taciturn
ways, he is not universally a favourite; he has been in trouble more
than once. The reader is desired to mark this Monk. A personable
man of seven-and-forty; stout-made, stands erect as a pillar; with
bushy eyebrows, the eyes of him beaming into you in a really strange
way; the face massive, grave, with 'a very eminent nose;' his head
almost bald, its auburn remnants of hair, and the copious ruddy
beard, getting slightly streaked with grey.* This is Brother Samson;
a man worth looking at.

He is from Norfolk, as the nickname indicates; from Tottington in
Norfolk,* as we guess; the son of poor parents there. He has told me,

---

[1] Eadmeri Hist. 8.

Jocelin, for I loved him much, That once in his ninth year he had an alarming dream;*—as indeed we are all somewhat given to dreaming here. Little Samson, lying uneasily in his crib at Tottington, dreamed that he saw the Arch Enemy in person, just alighted in front of some grand building, with outspread bat-wings, and stretching forth detestable clawed hands to grip him, little Samson, and fly off with him: whereupon the little dreamer shrieked desperate to St. Edmund for help, shrieked and again shrieked; and St. Edmund, a reverend heavenly figure, did come,—and indeed poor little Samson's mother, awakened by his shrieking, did come; and the Devil and the Dream both fled away fruitless. On the morrow, his mother, pondering such an awful dream, thought it were good to take him over to St. Edmund's own Shrine, and pray with him there. See, said little Samson at sight of the Abbey-Gate; see, mother, this is the building I dreamed of! His poor mother dedicated him to St. Edmund,—left him there with prayers and tears: what better could she do? The exposition of the dream, Brother Samson used to say, was this: *Diabolus* with outspread bat-wings shadowed forth the pleasures of this world, *voluptates hujus sæculi*, which were about to snatch and fly away with me, had not St. Edmund flung his arms round me, that is to say, made me a monk of his. A monk, accordingly, Brother Samson is; and here to this day where his mother left him. A learned man, of devout grave nature; has studied at Paris,* has taught in the Town Schools here,* and done much else; can preach in three languages, and, like Dr. Caius, 'has had losses'* in his time. A thoughtful, firm-standing man; much loved by some, not loved by all; his clear eyes flashing into you, in an almost inconvenient way!

Abbot Hugo, as we said, had his own difficulties with him; Abbot Hugo had him in prison once, to teach him what authority was, and how to dread the fire in future. For Brother Samson, in the time of the Antipopes,* had been sent to Rome on business; and, returning successful, was too late,—the business had all misgone in the interim! As tours to Rome are still frequent with us English, perhaps the reader will not grudge to look at the method of travelling thither in those remote ages. We happily have, in small compass, a personal narrative of it. Through the clear eyes and memory of Brother Samson, one peeps direct into the very bosom of that Twelfth Century, and finds it rather curious. The actual *Papa*, Father, or universal President of Christendom, as yet not grown chimerical,* sat there; think of that only! Brother Samson went to Rome as to the real Light-fountain of this lower world; we now—!—But let us hear Brother Samson, as to his mode of travelling:

'You know what trouble I had for that Church of Woolpit; how I was despatched to Rome in the time of the Schism between Pope Alexander and Octavian; and passed through Italy at that season, when all clergy carrying letters for our Lord Pope Alexander were laid hold of, and some were clapt in prison, some hanged; and some, with nose and lips cut off, were sent for ward to our Lord the Pope, for the disgrace and confusion of him (*in dedecus et confusionem ejus*). I, however, pretended to be Scotch,* and putting on the garb of a Scotchman, and taking the gesture of one, walked along; and when anybody mocked at me, I would brandish my staff in the manner of that weapon they call *gaveloc*,[1] uttering comminatory words after the way of the Scotch. To those that met and questioned me who I was, I made no answer but: *Ride, ride Rome; turne Cantwereberei.*[2]* Thus did I, to conceal myself and my errand, and get safer to Rome under the guise of a Scotchman.

'Having at last obtained a Letter from our Lord the Pope according to my wishes, I turned homewards again. I had to pass through a certain strong town on my road; and lo, the soldiers thereof surrounded me, seizing me, and saying: "This vagabond (*iste solivagus*), who pretends to be Scotch, is either a spy, or has Letters from the false Pope Alexander." And whilst they examined every stitch and rag of me, my leggings (*caligas*), breeches, and even the old shoes that I carried over my shoulder in the way of the Scotch,—I put my hand into the leather scrip I wore, wherein our Lord the Pope's Letter lay, close by a little jug (*ciffus*) I had for drinking out of; and the Lord God so pleasing, and St. Edmund, I got out both the Letter and the jug together; in such a way that, extending my arm aloft, I held the Letter hidden between jug and hand: they saw the jug, but the Letter they saw not. And thus I escaped out of their hands in the name of the Lord. Whatever money I had they took from me; wherefore I had to beg from door to door, without any payment (*sine omni expensa*) till

---

[1] Javelin, missile pike. *Gaveloc* is still the Scotch name for *crowbar*.

[2] Does this mean, "Rome forever; Canterbury *not*" (which claims an unjust Supremacy over us)! Mr. Rokewood is silent. Dryasdust would perhaps explain it,—in the course of a week or two of talking; did one dare to question him!

I came to England again. But hearing that the Woolpit Church was already given to Geoffry Ridell,* my soul was struck with sorrow because I had laboured in vain. Coming home, therefore, I sat me down secretly under the Shrine of St. Edmund, fearing lest our Lord Abbot should seize and imprison me, though I had done no mischief; nor was there a monk who durst speak to me, nor a laic who durst bring me food except by stealth.'¹*

Such resting and welcoming found Brother Samson, with his worn soles, and strong heart! He sits silent, revolving many thoughts, at the foot of St. Edmund's Shrine. In the wide Earth, if it be not Saint Edmund, what friend or refuge has he? Our Lord Abbot, hearing of him, sent the proper officer to lead him down to prison, clap 'foot-gyves on him' there. Another poor official furtively brought him a cup of wine; bade him "be comforted in the Lord." Samson utters no complaint; obeys in silence. 'Our Lord Abbot, taking counsel of it, banished me to Acre, and there I had to stay long.'*

Our Lord Abbot next tried Samson with promotions; made him Subsacristan, made him Librarian,* which he liked best of all, being passionately fond of Books: Samson, with many thoughts in him, again obeyed in silence; discharged his offices to perfection, but never thanked our Lord Abbot,—seemed rather as if looking into him, with those clear eyes of his. Whereupon Abbot Hugo said, *Se nunquam vidisse*,* he had never seen such a man; whom no severity would break to complain, and no kindness soften into smiles or thanks:—a questionable kind of man!

In this way, not without troubles, but still in an erect clear-standing manner, has Brother Samson reached his forty-seventh year; and his ruddy beard is getting slightly grizzled. He is endeavouring, in these days, to have various broken things thatched in; nay perhaps to have the Choir itself completed, for he can bear nothing ruinous. He has gathered 'heaps of lime and sand;' has masons, slaters working, he and *Warinus monachus noster*, who are joint keepers of the Shrine; paying out the money duly,—furnished by charitable burghers of St. Edmundsbury, they say. Charitable burghers of St. Edmundsbury? To me Jocelin it seems rather, Samson and Warinus, whom he leads, have privily hoarded the oblations at the Shrine itself, in these late

¹ Jocelini Chronica, p. 36.

years of indolent dilapidation, while Abbot Hugo sat wrapt inaccessible; and are struggling, in this prudent way, to have the rain kept out![1]—Under what conditions, sometimes, has Wisdom to struggle with Folly; get Folly persuaded to so much as thatch out the rain from itself! For indeed if the Infant govern the Nurse, what dexterous practice on the Nurse's part will not be necessary!*

It is a new regret to us that, in these circumstances, our Lord the King's Custodiars, interfering, prohibited all building or thatching from whatever source; and no Choir shall be completed, and Rain and Time, for the present, shall have their way. Willelmus Sacrista, he of 'the frequent bibations and some things not to be spoken of;' he, with his red nose, I am of opinion, had made complaint to the Custodiars; wishing to do Samson an ill turn:—Samson his *Sub*-sacristan, with those clear eyes, could not be a prime favourite of his! Samson again obeys in silence.*

CHAPTER VII.

THE CANVASSING.

Now, however, come great news to St. Edmundsbury:* That there is to be an Abbot elected; that our interlunar obscuration is to cease; St. Edmund's Convent no more to be a doleful widow, but joyous and once again a bride! Often in our widowed state had we prayed to the Lord and St. Edmund, singing weekly a matter of 'one-and-twenty penitential Psalms, on our knees in the Choir,'* that a fit Pastor might be vouchsafed us. And, says Jocelin, had some known what Abbot we were to get, they had not been so devout, I believe!—Bozzy Jocelin opens to mankind the floodgates of authentic Convent gossip; we listen, as in a Dionysius' Ear,* to the inanest hubbub, like the voices at Virgil's Horn-Gate of Dreams.* Even gossip, seven centuries off, has significance.* List, list, how like men are to one another in all centuries:

'*Dixit quidam de quodam*, A certain person said of a certain person, "He, that *Frater*, is a good monk, *probabilis persona*; knows much of the order and customs of the church; and though not so perfect

a philosopher as some others, would make a very good Abbot. Old
Abbot Ording, still famed among us, knew little of letters. Besides, as
we read in Fables, it is better to choose a log for king, than a serpent,
never so wise, that will venomously hiss and bite his subjects."—
"Impossible!" answered the other: "How can such a man make a sermon in the chapter, or to the people on festival days, when he is
without letters? How can he have the skill to bind and to loose, he who
does not understand the Scriptures? How—?"'

And then 'another said of another, *alius de alio*, "That *Frater* is
a *homo literatus*, eloquent, sagacious; vigorous in discipline; loves the
Convent much, has suffered much for its sake." To which a third
party answers, "From all your great clerks good Lord deliver us!
From Norfolk barrators, and surly persons, That it would please thee
to preserve us, We beseech thee to hear us, good Lord!"' Then
'another *quidam* said of another *quodam*, "That *Frater* is a good man-
ager (*husebondus*);" but was swiftly answered, "God forbid that a man
who can neither read nor chant, nor celebrate the divine offices, an
unjust person withal, and grinder of the faces of the poor, should ever
be Abbot!"' One man, it appears, is nice in his victuals. Another is
indeed wise; but apt to slight inferiors; hardly at the pains to answer,
if they argue with him too foolishly. And so each *aliquis* concerning
his *aliquo*,—through whole pages of electioneering babble. 'For,' says
Jocelin, 'So many men, as many minds.' Our Monks 'at time of blood-
letting, *tempore minutionis*,' holding their sanhedrim of babble, would
talk in this manner: Brother Samson, I remarked, never said anything; sat silent, sometimes smiling; but he took good note of what
others said, and would bring it up, on occasion, twenty years after. As
for me Jocelin, I was of opinion that 'some skill in Dialectics, to distinguish true from false,' would be good in an Abbot. I spake, as a rash
Novice in those days, some conscientious words of a certain benefac-
tor of mine; 'and behold, one of those sons of Belial' ran and reported
them to him, so that he never after looked at me with the same face
again!* Poor Bozzy!—

Such is the buzz and frothy simmering ferment of the general
mind and no-mind; struggling to 'make itself up,' as the phrase is, or
ascertain what *it* does really want: no easy matter, in most cases.
St. Edmundsbury, in that Candlemas season of the year 1182,* is
a busily fermenting place. The very clothmakers sit meditative at
their looms; asking, Who shall be Abbot?* The *sochemanni* speak of

it,* driving their ox-teams afield; the old women with their spindles: and none yet knows what the days will bring forth.

The Prior, however, as our interim chief, must proceed to work; get ready 'Twelve Monks,' and set off with them to his Majesty at Waltham,* there shall the election be made. An election, whether managed directly by ballot-box on public hustings, or indirectly by force of public opinion, or were it even by open alehouses, landlords' coercion, popular club-law, or whatever electoral methods, is always an interesting phenomenon. A mountain tumbling in great travail, throwing up dustclouds and absurd noises, is visibly there; uncertain yet what mouse or monster it will give birth to.

Besides it is a most important social act; nay, at bottom, the one important social act. Given the men a People choose, the People itself, in its exact worth and worthlessness, is given. A heroic people chooses heroes, and is happy;* a valet or flunkey people chooses sham-heroes, what are called quacks, thinking them heroes, and is not happy. The grand summary of a man's spiritual condition, what brings out all his herohood and insight, or all his flunkeyhood and horn-eyed dimness, is this question put to him, What man dost thou honour? Which is thy ideal of a man; or nearest that? So too of a People: for a People too, every People, *speaks* its choice,—were it only by silently obeying, and not revolting,—in the course of a century or so. Nor are electoral methods, Reform Bills and such like, unimportant. A People's electoral methods are, in the long-run, the express image of its electoral *talent;* tending and gravitating perpetually, irresistibly, to a conformity with that: and are, at all stages, very significant of the People. Judicious readers, of these times, are not disinclined to see how Monks elect their Abbot in the Twelfth Century: how the St. Edmundsbury mountain manages its midwifery; and what mouse or man the outcome is.*

CHAPTER VIII.

THE ELECTION.

Accordingly our Prior assembles us in Chapter; and, we adjuring him before God to do justly, nominates, not by our selection, yet with our assent, Twelve Monks, moderately satisfactory. Of whom are Hugo Third-Prior, Brother Dennis a venerable man, Walter the *Medicus*, Samson *Subsacrista*, and other esteemed characters,—though Willelmus *Sacrista*, of the red nose, too is one. These shall proceed straightway to Waltham; and there elect the Abbot as they may and can. Monks are sworn to obedience; must not speak too loud, under penalty of foot-gyves, limbo, and bread and water: yet monks too would know what it is they are obeying. The St. Edmundsbury Community has no hustings, ballot-box, indeed no open voting: yet by various vague manipulations, pulse-feelings, we struggle to ascertain what its virtual aim is, and succeed better or worse.*

This question, however, rises, alas a quite preliminary question: Will the *Dominus Rex* allow us to choose freely?* It is to be hoped! Well, if so, we agree to choose one of our own Convent. If not, if the *Dominus Rex* will force a stranger on us, we decide on demurring, the Prior and his Twelve shall demur: we can appeal, plead, remonstrate; appeal even to the Pope, but trust it will not be necessary. Then there is this other question, raised by Brother Samson: What if the Thirteen should not themselves be able to agree? Brother Samson *Subsacrista*, one remarks, is ready oftenest with some question, some suggestion, that has wisdom in it. Though a servant of servants, and saying little, his words all tell, having sense in them; it seems by his light mainly that we steer ourselves in this great dimness.

What if the Thirteen should not themselves be able to agree? Speak, Samson, and advise.—Could not, hints Samson, Six of our venerablest elders be chosen by us, a kind of electoral committee, here and now: of these, 'with their hand on the Gospels, with their eye on the *Sacrosancta*,' we take oath that they will do faithfully; let these, in secret and as before God, agree on Three whom they reckon fittest; write their names in a Paper, and deliver the same sealed, forthwith, to the Thirteen: one of these Three the Thirteen shall fix on, if permitted. If not permitted, that is to say, if the *Dominus Rex* force us to demur,—the Paper shall be brought back unopened, and publicly burned, that no man's secret bring him into trouble.*

So Samson advises, so we act; wisely, in this and in other crises of the business. Our electoral committee, its eye on the *Sacrosancta* is soon named, soon sworn; and we striking up the Fifth Psalm, '*Verba mea,*

'Give ear unto my words, O Lord,
My meditation weigh,'

march out chanting, and leave the Six to their work in the Chapter
here. Their work, before long, they announce as finished: they, with
their eye on the Sacrosancta, imprecating the Lord to weigh and witness their meditation, have fixed on Three Names, and written them
in this Sealed Paper. Let Samson Subsacrista, general servant of the
party, take charge of it. On the morrow morning, our Prior and his
Twelve will be ready to get under way.*

This then is the ballot-box and electoral winnowing-machine they
have at St. Edmundsbury:* a mind fixed on the Thrice Holy, an
appeal to God on high to witness their meditation: by far the best, and
indeed the only good electoral winnowing-machine,—if men have
souls in them. Totally worthless, it is true, and even hideous and poisonous, if men have no souls. But without soul, alas what winnowing-
machine in human elections, can be of avail? We cannot get along
without soul; we stick fast, the mournfullest spectacle; and salt itself
will not save us!*

On the morrow morning, accordingly, our Thirteen set forth; or
rather our Prior and Eleven; for Samson, as general servant of the
party, has to linger, settling many things. At length he too gets upon
the road; and, 'carrying the sealed Paper in a leather pouch hung
round his neck; and *froccum bajulans in ulnis*' (thanks to thee Bozzy
Jocelin), 'his frock-skirt, looped over his elbows,'* shewing substantial stern-works, tramps stoutly along. Away across the Heath, not yet
of Newmarket and horse-jockeying; across your Fleam-dike and
Devil's-dike, no longer useful as a Mercian East-Anglian boundary or
bulwark:* continually towards Waltham, and the Bishop of Winchester's
House there, for his Majesty is in that. Brother Samson, as purse-
bearer, has the reckoning always, when there is one, to pay; 'delays are
numerous,' progress none of the swiftest.

But, in the solitude of the Convent, Destiny thus big and in her
birthtime, what gossiping, what babbling, what dreaming of dreams!
The secret of the Three our electoral Elders alone know: some Abbot
we shall have to govern us; but which Abbot, O which! One Monk
discerns in a vision of the night-watches, that we shall get an Abbot of
our own body, without needing to demur: a prophet appeared to him
clad all in white, and said, "Ye shall have one of yours, and he will rage

among you like a wolf, *sæviet ut lupus.*"* Verily!—then which of ours?
Another Monk now dreams: he has seen clearly which; a certain
Figure taller by head and shoulders than the other two, dressed in alb
and *pallium*, and with the attitude of one about to fight;*—which tall
Figure a wise Editor would rather not name at this stage of the business! Enough that the vision is true: that Saint Edmund himself, pale
and awful, seemed to rise from his Shrine, with naked feet, and say
audibly, "He, *ille*, shall veil my feet;" which part of the vision also
proves true. Such guessing, visioning, dim perscrutation of the
momentous future: the very clothmakers, old women, all townsfolk
speak of it, 'and more than once it is reported in St. Edmundsbury,
This one is elected; and then, This one and That other.' Who knows?

But now, sure enough, at Waltham 'on the Second Sunday of
Quadragesima,' which Dryasdust declares to mean the 22d day of
February, year 1182, Thirteen St. Edmundsbury Monks are, at last,
seen processioning towards the Winchester Manorhouse; and in some
high Presence-chamber, and Hall of State, get access to Henry II. in
all his glory. What a Hall,—not imaginary in the least, but entirely
real and indisputable, though so extremely dim to us; sunk in the
deep distances of Night! The Winchester Manorhouse has fled bodily, like a Dream of the old Night; not Dryasdust himself can shew
a wreck of it. House and people, royal and episcopal, lords and varlets, where are they? Why *there*, I say, Seven Centuries off; sunk *so* far
in the Night, there they *are;* peep through the blankets of the old
Night, and thou wilt see! King Henry himself is visibly there, a vivid,
noble-looking man, with grizzled beard, in glittering uncertain costume; with earls round him, and bishops and dignitaries, in the like.
The Hall is large, and has for one thing an altar near it,—chapel and
altar adjoining it; but what gilt seats, carved tables, carpeting of rush-
cloth, what arras-hangings, and a huge fire of logs:—alas, it has
Human Life in it; and is not that the grand miracle, in what hangings
or costume soever?*—

The *Dominus Rex*, benignantly receiving our Thirteen with their
obeisance, and graciously declaring that he will strive to act for God's
honour, and the Church's good, commands, 'by the Bishop of Winchester
and Geoffrey the Chancellor,'—*Galfridus Cancellarius*, Henry's and
the Fair Rosamond's authentic Son present here!—commands,
"That they, the said Thirteen, do now withdraw, and fix upon Three

from their own Monastery." A work soon done; the Three hanging ready round Samson's neck, in that leather pouch of his. Breaking the seal, we find the names,—what think *ye* of it, ye higher dignitaries, thou indolent Prior, thou Willelmus *Sacrista* with the red bottle-nose?—the names, in this order: of Samson *Subsacrista*, of Roger the distressed Cellarer, of Hugo *Tertius-Prior.**

The higher dignitaries, all omitted here, 'flush suddenly red in the face:' but have nothing to say. One curious fact and question certainly is, How Hugo Third-Prior, who was of the electoral committee, came to nominate *himself* as one of the Three? A curious fact which Hugo Third-Prior has never yet entirely explained, that I know of!—However, we return, and report to the King our Three names; merely altering the order; putting Samson last, as lowest of all. The King, at recitation of our Three, asks us: "Who are they? Were they born in my domain? Totally unknown to me! You must nominate three others." Whereupon Willelmus Sacrista says, "Our Prior must be named, *quia caput nostrum est*, being already our head." And the Prior responds, "Willelmus Sacrista is a fit man, *bonus vir est*,"—for all his red nose. Tickle me Toby and I'll tickle thee! Venerable Dennis too is named; none in his conscience can say nay. There are now Six on our List. "Well," said the King, "they have done it swiftly, they! *Deus est cum eis.*" The Monks withdraw again; and Majesty revolves, for a little, with his *Pares* and *Episcopi*, Lords or '*Law-wards*' and Soul-Overseers, the thoughts of the royal breast. The Monks wait silent in an outer room.*

In short while, they are next ordered, To add yet another three; but not from their own Convent; from other Convents, "for the honour of my kingdom." Here,—what is to be done here? We will demur, if need be! We do name three, however, for the nonce: the Prior of St. Faith's, a good Monk of St. Neot's, a good Monk of St. Alban's; good men all; all made abbots and dignitaries since, at this hour. There are now Nine upon our List. What the thoughts of the Dominus Rex may be farther? The Dominus Rex, thanking graciously, sends out word that we shall now strike off three. The three strangers are instantly struck off. Willelmus Sacrista adds that he will of his own accord decline,—a touch of grace and respect for the *Sacrosancta*, even in Willelmus! The King then orders us to strike off a couple more; then yet one more: Hugo Third-Prior goes, and Roger *Cellerarius*, and venerable Monk Dennis;—and now there remain on our List two only, Samson Subsacrista and the Prior.*

Which of these two? It were hard to say,—by Monks who may get themselves foot-gyved and thrown into limbo, for speaking! We humbly request that the Bishop of Winchester and Geoffrey the Chancellor may again enter, and help us to decide. "Which do you want?" asks the Bishop. Venerable Dennis made a speech, 'commending the persons of the Prior and Samson; but always in the corner of his discourse, *in angulo sui sermonis*, brought Samson in.' "I see!" said the Bishop: "We are to understand that your Prior is somewhat remiss; that you want to have him you call Samson for Abbot." "Either of them is good," said venerable Dennis, almost trembling; "but we would have the better, if it pleased God." "Which of the two *do* you want?" inquires the Bishop pointedly. "Samson!" answered Dennis; "Samson!" echoed all of the rest that durst speak or echo anything; and Samson is reported to the King accordingly. His Majesty, advising of it for a moment, orders that Samson be brought in with the other Twelve.*

The King's Majesty, looking at us somewhat sternly, then says: "You present to me Samson; I do not know him: had it been your Prior, whom I do know, I should have accepted him: however, I will now do as you wish. But have a care of yourselves. By the true eyes of God, *per veros oculos Dei*, if you manage badly, I will be upon you!" Samson, therefore, steps, forward, kisses the King's feet; but swiftly rises erect again, swiftly turns towards the altar, uplifting with the other Twelve, in clear tenor-note, the Fifty-first Psalm, '*Miserere mei Deus*,

> 'After thy loving-kindness, Lord,
> Have mercy upon *me*;'

with firm voice, firm step and head, no change in his countenance whatever. "By God's eyes," said the King, "that one, I think, will govern the Abbey well." By the same oath (charged to your Majesty's account), I too am precisely of that opinion! It is some while since I fell in with a likelier man anywhere than this new Abbot Samson. Long life to him, and may the Lord *have* mercy on him as Abbot!*

Thus, then, have the St. Edmundsbury Monks, without express ballot-box or other good winnowing-machine, contrived to accomplish the most important social feat a body of men can do, to winnow out the man that is to govern them: and truly one sees not that, by any winnowing-machine whatever, they could have done it better. O ye kind Heavens, there is in every Nation and Community *a fittest*, a wisest, bravest, best; whom could we find and make King over us, all were in very truth well;—the best that God and Nature had permitted *us* to make it! By what art discover him? Will the Heavens in their pity teach us no art; for our need of him is great!

Ballot-boxes, Reform Bills, winnowing-machines: all these are good, or are not so good;—alas, brethren, how *can* these, I say, be other than inadequate, be other than failures, melancholy to behold? Dim all souls of men to the divine, the high and awful meaning of Human Worth and Truth, we shall never, by all the machinery in Birmingham, discover the True and Worthy. It is written, 'if we are ourselves valets, there shall exist no hero for us; we shall not know the hero when we see him;'*—we shall take the quack for a hero; and cry, audibly through all ballot-boxes and machinery whatsoever, Thou art he; be thou King over us!

What boots it? Seek only deceitful Speciosity,* money with gilt carriages, 'fame' with newspaper-paragraphs, whatever name it bear, you will find only deceitful Speciosity; godlike Reality will be forever far from you. The Quack shall be legitimate inevitable King of you; no earthly machinery able to exclude the Quack. Ye shall be born thralls of the Quack, and suffer under him, till your hearts are near broken, and no French Revolution or Manchester Insurrection, or partial or universal volcanic combustions and explosions, never so many, can do more than 'change the *figure* of your Quack;'* the essence of him remaining, for a time and times.—"How long, O Prophet?" say some, with a rather melancholy sneer. Alas, ye *un*prophetic, ever till this come about: Till deep misery, if nothing softer will, have driven you out of your Speciosities *into* your Sincerities; and you find that there either is a Godlike in the world, or else ye are an unintelligible madness; that there is a God, as well as a Mammon and a Devil, and a Genius of Luxuries and canting Dilettantisms and Vain Shows! How long that will be, compute for yourselves. My unhappy brothers!—

CHAPTER IX.

ABBOT SAMSON.

So then the bells of St. Edmundsbury clang out one and all, and in church and chapel the organs go: Convent and Town, and all the west

side of Suffolk, are in gala; knights, viscounts, weavers, spinners, the
entire population, male and female, young and old, the very sockmen
with their chubby infants,—out to have a holiday, and see the Lord
Abbot arrive! And there is 'stripping barefoot' of the Lord Abbot at
the Gate, and solemn leading of him in to the High Altar and Shrine;
with sudden 'silence of all the bells and organs,' as we kneel in deep
prayer there; and again with outburst of all the bells and organs, and
loud *Te Deum* from the general human windpipe; and speeches by the
leading viscount, and giving of the kiss of brotherhood; the whole
wound up with popular games, and dinner within doors of more than
a thousand strong, *plus quam mille comedentibus in gaudio magno.**

In such manner is the selfsame Samson once again returning to us,
welcomed on *this* occasion. He that went away with his frock-skirts
looped over his arm, comes back riding high; suddenly made one of
the dignitaries of this world. Reflective readers will admit that here
was a trial for a man. Yesterday a poor mendicant, allowed to possess
not above two shillings of money, and without authority to bid a dog
run for him, this man today finds himself a *Dominus Abbas*, mitred
Peer of Parliament, Lord of manorhouses, farms, manors, and wide
lands; a man with 'Fifty Knights under him,'* and dependent swiftly
obedient multitudes of men. It is a change greater than Napoleon's;*
so sudden withal. As if one of the Chandos day-drudges* had, on
awakening some morning, found that *he* overnight was become Duke!
Let Samson with his clear-beaming eyes see into that, and discern it
if he can. We shall now get the measure of him by a new scale of inches,
considerably more rigorous than the former was. For if a noble soul is
rendered tenfold beautifuller by victory and prosperity, springing now
radiant as into his own due element and sun-throne; an ignoble one is
rendered tenfold and hundredfold uglier, pitifuller. Whatsoever vices,
whatsoever weaknesses were in the man, the parvenu will shew us
them enlarged, as in the solar microscope,* into frightful distortion.
Nay, how many mere seminal principles of vice, hitherto all whole-
somely kept latent, may we now see unfolded, as in the solar hot-
house, into growth, into huge universally-conspicuous luxuriance
and development!

But is not this, at any rate, a singular aspect of what political and
social capabilities, nay let us say what depth and opulence of true
social vitality, lay in those old barbarous ages, That the fit Governor

could be met with under such disguises, could be recognised and laid hold of under such? Here he is discovered with a maximum of two shillings in his pocket, and a leather scrip round his neck; trudging along the highway, his frock-skirts looped over his arm. They think this is he nevertheless, the true Governor; and he proves to be so. Brethren, have we no need of discovering true Governors, but will sham ones forever do for us? These were absurd superstitious block-heads of Monks; and we are enlightened Tenpound Franchisers, without taxes on knowledge!* Where, I say, are our superior, are our similar or at all comparable discoveries? We also have eyes, or ought to have; we have hustings, telescopes; we have lights, link-lights and rush-lights of an enlightened free Press, burning and dancing every-where, as in a universal torch-dance; singeing your whiskers as you traverse the public thoroughfares in town and country. Great souls, true Governors, go about under all manner of disguises now as then. Such telescopes, such enlightenment,*—and such discovery! How comes it, I say; how comes it? Is it not lamentable; is it not even, in some sense amazing?

Alas, the defect, as we must often urge and again urge, is less a defect of telescopes than of some eyesight. Those superstitious blockheads of the Twelfth Century had no telescopes, but they had still an eye: not ballot-boxes; only reverence for Worth, abhorrence of Unworth. It is the way with all barbarians. Thus Mr. Sale informs me, the old Arab Tribes would gather in liveliest *gaudeamus*,* and sing, and kindle bonfires, and wreath crowns of honour, and solemnly thank the gods that, in their Tribe too, a Poet had shewn himself. As indeed they well might; for what usefuller, I say not nobler and heav-enlier thing could the gods, doing their very kindest, send to any Tribe or Nation in any time or circumstances? I declare to thee, my afflicted quack-ridden brother, in spite of thy astonishment, it is very lamentable! We English find a Poet, as brave a man as has been made for a hundred years or so anywhere under the Sun; and do we kindle bonfires, or thank the gods? Not at all. We, taking due counsel of it, set the man to gauge ale-barrels in the Burgh of Dumfries;* and pique ourselves on our 'patronage of genius.'*

Genius, Poet: do we know what these words mean? An inspired Soul once more vouchsafed us, direct from Nature's own great fire-heart, to see the Truth, and speak it, and do it; Nature's own sacred voice heard once more athwart the dreary boundless element of hearsaying and canting, of twaddle and poltroonery, in which the bewildered Earth, nigh perishing, has *lost its way*. Hear once more, ye bewildered benighted mortals; listen once again to a voice from the inner Light-sea and Flame-sea, Nature's and Truth's own heart; know the Fact of your Existence what it is, put away the Cant of it which it is *not;* and knowing, do, and let it be well with you!——

George the Third is Defender of something we call 'the Faith'* in those years; George the Third is head charioteer of the Destinies of England, to guide them through the gulf of French Revolutions, American Independences; and Robert Burns is Gauger of ale in Dumfries. It is an Iliad in a nutshell.* The physiognomy of a world now verging towards dissolution, reduced now to spasms and death-throes, lies pictured in that one fact,—which astonishes nobody, except at me for being astonished at it. The fruit of long ages of confirmed Valethood, entirely confirmed as into a Law of Nature; cloth-worship and quack-worship: entirely *confirmed* Valethood,*— which will have to *un*confirm itself again; God knows, with difficulty enough!——

Abbot Samson had found a Convent all in dilapidation; rain beating through it, material rain and metaphorical, from all quarters of the compass. Willelmus Sacrista sits drinking nightly, and doing mere *tacenda*. Our larders are reduced to leanness, Jew Harpies and unclean creatures our purveyors; in our basket is no bread. Old women with their distaffs rush out on a distressed Cellarer in shrill Chartism. 'You cannot stir abroad but Jews and Christians pounce upon you with unsettled bonds;' debts boundless seemingly as the National Debt of England. For four years our new Lord Abbot never went abroad but Jew creditors and Christian, and all manner of creditors, were about him; driving him to very despair. Our Prior is remiss; our Cellarers, officials are remiss, our Monks are remiss: what man is not remiss? Front this, Samson, thou alone art there to front it; it is thy task to front and fight this, and to die or kill it. May the Lord have mercy on thee!*

To our antiquarian interest in poor Jocelin and his Convent, where the whole aspect of existence, the whole dialect, of thought, of speech, of activity, is so obsolete, strange, long-vanished, there now super-adds itself a mild glow of human interest for Abbot Samson; a real pleasure, as at sight of man's work, especially of governing, which is man's highest work, done *well*. Abbot Samson had no experience in governing; had served no apprenticeship to the trade of governing,— alas, only the hardest apprenticeship to that of obeying. He had never in any court given *vadium* or *plegium*,* says Jocelin; hardly ever seen a court, when he was set to preside in one. But it is astonishing, continues Jocelin, how soon he learned the ways of business; and, in all sorts of affairs, became expert beyond others. Of the many persons offering him their service 'he retained one Knight skilled in taking *vadia* and *plegia;*' and within the year was himself well skilled. Nay, by and by, the Pope appoints him Justiciary in certain causes; the King one of his new Circuit Judges: official Osbert is heard saying, "That Abbot is one of your shrewd ones, *disputator est;* if he go on as he begins, he will cut out every lawyer of us!"[1]*

Why not? What is to hinder this Samson from governing? There is in him what far transcends all apprenticeships; in the man himself there exists a model of governing, something to govern by! There exists in him a heart-abhorrence of whatever is incoherent, pusillanimous, unveracious,—that is to say, chaotic, *un*governed; of the Devil, not of God. A man of this kind cannot help governing! He has the living ideal of a governor in him; and the incessant necessity of struggling to unfold the same out of him. Not the Devil or Chaos, for any wages, will he serve; no, this man is the born servant of Another than them. Alas, how little avail all apprenticeships, when there is in your governor himself what we may well call *nothing* to govern by: nothing;—a general grey twilight, looming with shapes of expediencies, parliamentary traditions, division-lists,* election-funds, leading-articles; this, with what of vulpine alertness and adroitness soever, is not much!

But indeed what say we, apprenticeship? Had not this Samson served, in his way, a right good apprenticeship to governing; namely, the harshest slave-apprenticeship to obeying! Walk this world with no friend in it but God and St. Edmund, you will either fall into the ditch, or learn a good many things. To learn obeying is the fundamental art of governing. How much would many a Serene Highness have learned, had he travelled through the world with water-jug and empty wallet, *sine omni expensa;* and, at his victorious return, sat down not to newspaper-paragraphs and city-illuminations, but at the foot of St. Edmund's Shrine to shackles and bread and water! He that cannot be

---

[1] Jocelini Chronica, p. 25.

servant of many, will never be master, true guide and deliverer of many;—that is the meaning of true mastership. Had not the Monk-life extraordinary 'political capabilities' in it; if not imitable by us, yet enviable? Heavens, had a Duke of Logwood, now rolling sumptuously to his place in the Collective Wisdom,* but himself happened to plough daily, at one time, on seven-and-sixpence a week,* with no out-door relief,—what a light, unquenchable by logic and statistic and arithmetic, would it have thrown on several things for him!

In all cases, therefore, we will agree with the judicious Mrs. Glass: 'First catch your hare!'* First get your man; all is got: he can learn to do all things, from making boots, to decreeing judgments, governing communities; and will do them like a man. Catch your no-man,—alas, have you not caught the terriblest Tartar in the world! Perhaps all the terribler, the quieter and gentler he looks. For the mischief that one blockhead, that every blockhead does, in a world so feracious, teeming with endless results as ours, no ciphering will sum up. The quack bootmaker is considerable; as corn-cutters can testify, and desperate men reduced to buckskin and list-shoes.* But the quack priest, quack high-priest, the quack king! Why do not all just citizens rush, half-frantic, to stop him, as they would a conflagration? Surely a just citizen *is* admonished by God and his own Soul, by all silent and articulate voices of this Universe, to do what in *him* lies towards relief of this poor blockhead-quack, and of a world that groans under him. Run swiftly; relieve him,—were it even by extinguishing him! For all things have grown so old, tinder-dry, combustible; and he is more ruinous than conflagration. Sweep him *down*, at least; keep him strictly within the hearth: he will then cease to be conflagration; he will then become useful, more or less, as culinary fire. Fire is the best of servants; but what a master! This poor blockhead too is born for uses: why, elevating him to mastership, will you make a conflagration,* a parish-curse or world-curse of him?

CHAPTER X.

GOVERNMENT.

How Abbot Samson, giving his new subjects seriatim the kiss of fatherhood in the St. Edmundsbury chapterhouse, proceeded with cautious energy to set about reforming their disjointed distracted way of life; how he managed with his Fifty rough *Milites* (Feudal Knights), with his lazy Farmers, remiss refractory Monks, with Pope's Legates,* Viscounts, Bishops, Kings; how on all sides he laid about him like a man, and putting consequence on premiss, and everywhere the saddle on the right horse, struggled incessantly to educe organic method out of lazily fermenting wreck,—the careful reader will discern, not without true interest, in these pages of Jocelin Boswell. In most antiquarian quaint costume, not of garments alone, but of thought, word, action, outlook and position, the substantial figure of a man with eminent nose, bushy brows and clear-flashing eyes, his russet beard growing daily greyer, is visible, engaged in true governing of men. It is beautiful how the chrysalis governing-soul, shaking off its dusty slough and prison, starts forth winged, a true royal soul! Our new Abbot has a right honest unconscious feeling, without insolence as without fear or flutter, of what he is and what others are. A courage to quell the proudest, an honest pity to encourage the humblest. Withal there is a noble reticence in this Lord Abbot: much vain unreason he hears; lays up without response. He is not there to expect reason and nobleness of others; he is there to give them of his own reason and nobleness. Is he not their servant, as we said, who can suffer from them, and for them; bear the burden their poor spindle-limbs totter and stagger under; and in virtue *thereof* govern them, lead them out of weakness into strength, out of defeat into victory!

One of the first Herculean Labours Abbot Samson undertook, or the very first, was to institute a strenuous review and radical reform of his economics. It is the first labour of every governing man, from *Paterfamilias** to *Dominus Rex*. To get the rain thatched out from you is the preliminary of whatever farther, in the way of speculation or of action, you may mean to do. Old Abbot Hugo's budget, as we saw, had become empty, filled with deficit and wind. To see his account-books clear, be delivered from those ravening flights of Jew and Christian creditors, pouncing on him like obscene harpies wherever he shewed face, was a necessity for Abbot Samson.

On the morrow after his instalment, he brings in a load of money-bonds, all duly stamped, sealed with this or the other Convent Seal: frightful, unmanageable, a bottomless confusion of Convent finance. There they are;—but there at least they all are; all that shall be of them. Our Lord Abbot demands that all the official seals in use among us be now produced and delivered to him. Three-and-thirty seals turn up; are straightway broken, and shall seal no more: the Abbot only, and those duly authorised by him shall seal any bond.* There are but two ways of paying debt: increase of industry in raising income, increase of thrift in laying it out. With iron energy, in slow but steady undeviating perseverance, Abbot Samson sets to work in both directions. His troubles are manifold: cunning *milites*, unjust bailiffs, lazy sockmen, he an inexperienced Abbot; relaxed lazy monks, not disinclined to mutiny in mass: but continued vigilance, rigorous method, what we call 'the eye of the master,'* work wonders. The clear-beaming eyesight of Abbot Samson, steadfast, severe, all-penetrating,—it is like *Fiat lux** in that inorganic waste whirlpool; penetrates gradually to all nooks, and of the chaos makes a *kosmos* or ordered world!

He arranges everywhere, struggles unweariedly to arrange, and place on some intelligible footing, the 'affairs and dues, *res ac redditus*,'* of his dominion. The Lakenheath eels* cease to breed squabbles between human beings; the penny of *reap-silver* to explode into the streets the Female Chartism of St. Edmundsbury.* These and innumerable greater things. Wheresoever Disorder may stand or lie, let it have a care; here is the man that has declared war with it, that never will make peace with it. Man is the Missionary of Order;* he is the servant not of the Devil and Chaos, but of God and the Universe! Let all sluggards and cowards, remiss, false-spoken, unjust, and otherwise diabolic persons have a care: this is a dangerous man for them. He has a mild grave face; a thoughtful sternness, a sorrowful pity: but there is a terrible flash of anger in him too; lazy monks often have to murmur, "*Sævit ut lupus*, He rages like a wolf; was not our Dream true!"* 'To repress and hold-in such sudden anger he was continually careful,' and succeeded well:*—right, Samson; that it may become in thee as noble central heat, fruitful, strong, beneficent; not blaze out, or the seldomest possible blaze out, as wasteful volcanoism to scorch and consume!

"We must first creep, and gradually learn to walk,"* had Abbot Samson said of himself, at starting. In four years he has become a great walker; striding prosperously along; driving much before him. In less than four years, says Jocelin, the Convent Debts were all liquidated: the harpy Jews not only settled with, but banished, bag and baggage,* out of the *Bannaleuca* (Liberties, *Banlieue*)* of St. Edmundsbury,—so has the King's Majesty been persuaded to permit. Farewell to *you*, at any rate; let us, in no extremity, apply again to you! Armed men march them over the borders, dismiss them under stern penalties,—sentence of excommunication* on all that shall again harbour them here: there were many dry eyes at their departure.

New life enters everywhere, springs up beneficent, the Incubus of Debt once rolled away. Samson hastes not; but neither does he pause to rest.* This of the Finance is a life-long business with him;—Jocelin's anecdotes are filled to weariness with it. As indeed to Jocelin it was of very primary interest.

But we have to record also, with a lively satisfaction, that spiritual rubbish is as little tolerated in Samson's Monastery as material. With due rigour, Willelmus Sacrista, and his bibations and *tacenda* are, at the earliest opportunity, softly, yet irrevocably put an end to.* The bibations, namely, had to end; even the building where they used to be carried on was razed from the soil of St. Edmundsbury, and 'on its place grow rows of beans:'* Willelmus himself, deposed from the Sacristy and all offices, retires into obscurity, into absolute taciturnity unbroken thenceforth to this hour. Whether the poor Willelmus did not still, by secret channels, occasionally get some slight wetting of vinous or alcoholic liquor,—now grown, in a manner, indispensable to the poor man? Jocelin hints not; one knows not how to hope, what to hope! But if he did, it was in silence and darkness; with an ever-present feeling that teetotalism was his only true course.* Drunken dissolute Monks are a class of persons who had better keep out of Abbot Samson's way. *Sævit ut lupus;** was not the Dream true! murmured many a Monk. Nay Ranulf de Glanvill, Justiciary in Chief, took umbrage at him,* seeing these strict ways; and watched farther with suspicion: but discerned gradually that there was nothing wrong, that there was much the opposite of wrong.

CHAPTER XI.

THE ABBOT'S WAYS.

ABBOT SAMSON shewed no extraordinary favour to the Monks who had been his familiars of old; did not promote them to offices,—*nisi* *essent idonei,* unless they chanced to be fit men! Whence great discontent among certain of these, who had contributed to make him Abbot: reproaches, open and secret, of his being 'ungrateful, hard-tempered, unsocial, a Norfolk *barrator* and *paltenerius.*'*

Indeed, except it were for *idonei,* 'fit men,'* in all kinds, it was hard to say for whom Abbot Samson had much favour. He loved his kindred well, and tenderly enough acknowledged the poor part of them; with the rich part, who in old days had never acknowledged him, he totally refused to have any business. But even the former he did not promote into offices; finding none of them *idonei.* 'Some whom he thought suitable he put into situations in his own household, or made keepers of his country places: if they behaved ill, he dismissed them without hope of return.' In his promotions, nay almost in his benefits, you would have said there was a certain impartiality. 'The official person who had, by Abbot Hugo's order, put the fetters on him at his return from Italy, was now supported with food and clothes to the end of his days at Abbot Samson's expense.'*

Yet he did not forget benefits; far the reverse, when an opportunity occurred of paying them at his own cost. How pay them at the public cost;—how, above all, by *setting fire* to the public, as we said; clapping 'conflagrations' on the public,* which the services of blockheads, *non-idonei,* intrinsically are! He was right willing to remember friends, when it could be done. Take these instances: 'A certain chaplain who had maintained him at the Schools of Paris by the sale of holy water, *quæstu aquæ benedictæ;*—to this good chaplain he did give a vicarage, adequate to the comfortable sustenance of him.' 'The Son of Elias, too, that is, of old Abbot Hugo's Cupbearer, coming to do homage for his Father's land, our Lord Abbot said to him in full court: "I have, for these seven years, put off taking thy homage for the land which Abbot Hugo gave thy Father, because that gift was to the damage of Elmswell, and a questionable one: but now I must profess myself overcome; mindful of the kindness thy Father did me when I was in bonds; because he sent me a cup of the very wine his master had been drinking, and bade me be comforted in God."'

'To Magister Walter, son of Magister William de Dice, who wanted the vicarage of Chevington, he answered: "Thy Father was Master of the Schools; and when I was an indigent *clericus,* he granted me freely and in charity an entrance to his School, and opportunity of learning; wherefore I now, for the sake of God, grant to thee what thou askest."'

Or lastly, take this good instance,—and a glimpse, along with it, into long-obsolete times: 'Two *Milites* of Risby, Willelm and Norman, being adjudged in Court to come under his mercy, *in misericordia ejus,*' for a certain very considerable fine of twenty shillings, 'he thus addressed them publicly on the spot: "When I was a Cloister-monk, I was once sent to Durham on business of our church; and coming home again, the dark night caught me at Risby, and I had to beg a lodging there. I went to Dominus Norman's, and he gave me a flat refusal. Going then to Dominus Willelm's, and begging hospitality, I was by him honourably received. The twenty shillings therefore of *mercy*, I, without mercy, will exact from Dominus Norman; to Dominus Willelm, on the other hand I, with thanks, will wholly remit the said sum." '* Men know not always to whom they refuse lodgings; men have lodged Angels unawares!*—

It is clear Abbot Samson had a talent; he had learned to judge better than Lawyers, to manage better than bred Bailiffs:—a talent shining out indisputable, on whatever side you took him. 'An eloquent man he was,' says Jocelin, 'both in French and Latin; but intent more on the substance and method of what was to be said, than on the ornamental way of saying it. He could read English Manuscripts very elegantly, *elegantissime:* he was wont to preach to the people in the English tongue, though according to the dialect of Norfolk, where he had been brought up; wherefore indeed he had caused a Pulpit to be erected in our church both for ornament of the same, and for the use of his audiences.'* There preached he, according to the dialect of Norfolk: a man worth going to hear.

That he was a just clear-hearted man, this, as the basis of all true talent, is presupposed. How can a man, without clear vision in his heart first of all, have any clear vision in the head? It is impossible! Abbot Samson was one of the justest of judges; insisted on understanding the case to the bottom, and then swiftly decided without feud or favour. For which reason, indeed, the Dominus Rex, searching for such men, as for hidden treasure and healing to his distressed realm, had made him one of the new Itinerant Judges,*—such as continue to this day. "My curse on that Abbot's court," a suitor was heard imprecating, "*Maledicta sit curia istius Abbatis*, where neither gold nor silver can help me to confound my enemy!"* And old friendships and all connexions forgotten, when you go to seek an office from him! "A kinless loon," as the Scotch said of Cromwell's new judges,*—intent on mere indifferent fair-play!

Eloquence in three languages is good; but it is not the best. To us, as already hinted, the Lord Abbot's eloquence is less admirable than his *in*eloquence, his great invaluable 'talent of silence!'* ' *"Deus, Deus,"* said the Lord Abbot to me once, when he heard the Convent were murmuring at some act of his, "I have much need to remember that Dream they had of me, that I was to rage among them like a wolf. Above all earthly things I dread their driving me to do it. How much do I hold in, and wink at; raging and shuddering in my own secret mind, and not outwardly at all!" He would boast to me at other times: "This and that I have seen, this and that I have heard; yet patiently stood it."* He had this way, too, which I have never seen in any other man, that he affectionately loved many persons to whom he never or hardly ever shewed a countenance of love.* Once on my venturing to expostulate with him on the subject, he reminded me of Solomon: "Many sons I have; it is not fit that I should smile on them."* He would suffer faults, damage from his servants,* and know what he suffered, and not speak of it; but I think the reason was, he waited a good time for speaking of it, and in a wise way amending it. He intimated, openly in chapter to us all, that he would have no eaves-dropping: "Let none," said he, "come to me secretly accusing another, unless he will publicly stand to the same; if he come otherwise, I will openly proclaim the name of him. I wish, too, that every Monk of you have free access to me, to speak of your needs or grievances when you will." '*

The kinds of people Abbot Samson liked worst were these three: '*Mendaces, ebriosi, verbosi*, Liars, drunkards, and wordy or windy persons;'—not good kinds, any of them! He also much condemned 'persons given to murmur at their meat or drink, especially Monks of that disposition.' We remark, from the very first, his strict anxious order to his servants to provide handsomely for hospitality, to guard 'above all things that there be no shabbiness in the matter of meat and drink, no look of mean parsimony *in novitate mea*, at the beginning of my Abbotship;' and to the last he maintains a due opulence of table and equipment for others: but he is himself in the highest degree indifferent to all such things.*

'Sweet milk, honey, and other naturally sweet kinds of food, were what he preferred to eat: but he had this virtue,' says Jocelin, 'he never changed the dish (*ferculum*) you set before him, be what it might. Once when I, still a novice, happened to be waiting table in the refectory, it came into my head' (rogue that I was!) 'to try if this were true; and I thought I would place before him a *ferculum* that would have displeased any other person, the very platter being black and broken. But he, seeing it, was as one that saw it not: and now some little delay taking place, my heart smote me that I had done this; and so, snatching up the platter (*discus*), I changed both it and its contents for a better, and put down that instead; which emendation he was angry at, and rebuked me for,'*—the stoical monastic man! 'For the first seven years he had commonly four sorts of dishes on his table; afterwards only three, except it might be presents, or venison from his own parks, or fishes from his ponds. And if, at any time, he had guests living in his house at the request of some great person, or of some friend, or had public messengers, or had harpers (*citharœdos*), or any one of that sort, he took the first opportunity of shifting to another of his Manor-houses, and so got rid of such superfluous individuals,'[1]*—very prudently, I think.

As to his parks, of these, in the general repair of buildings, general improvement and adornment of the St. Edmund Domains, 'he had laid out several, and stocked them with animals, retaining a proper huntsman with hounds: and, if any guest of great quality were there, our Lord Abbot with his Monks would sit in some opening of the woods, and see the dogs run; but he himself never meddled with hunting, that I saw.'[2]*

'In an opening of the woods;'—for the country was still dark with wood in those days; and Scotland itself still rustled shaggy and leafy like a damp black American Forest, with cleared spots and spaces here and there. Dryasdust advances several absurd hypotheses as to the insensible but almost total disappearance of these woods;* the thick wreck of which now lies as *peat*, sometimes with huge heart-of-oak timberlogs imbedded in it, on many a height and hollow. The simplest reason doubtless is that by increase of husbandry, there was increase of cattle; increase of hunger for green spring food; and so more and

[1] Jocelini Chronica, p. 31.   [2] Jocelini Chronica, p. 21.

more the new seedlings got yearly eaten out in April; and the old trees, having only a certain length of life in them, died gradually, no man heeding it, and disappeared into *peat*.

A sorrowful waste of noble wood and umbrage! Yes,—but a very common one; the course of most things in this world. Monachism itself, so rich and fruitful once, is now all rotted into *peat*; lies sleek and buried,—and a most feeble bog-grass of Dilettantism, all the crop we reap from it! That also was frightful waste; perhaps among the saddest our England ever saw. Why will men destroy noble Forests, even when in part a nuisance, in such reckless manner; turning loose four-footed cattle and Henry-the-Eighths into them!* The fifth part of our English soil,* Dryasdust computes, lay consecrated to 'spiritual uses,' better or worse:* solemnly set apart to foster spiritual growth and culture of the soul, by the methods then known: and now—it too, like the four-fifths, fosters what? Gentle shepherd, tell me what!*—

CHAPTER XII.

THE ABBOT'S TROUBLES.

THE troubles of Abbot Samson, as he went along in this abstemious, reticent, rigorous way, were more than tongue can tell. The Abbot's mitre once set on his head, he knew rest no more. Double, double, toil and trouble;* that is the life of all governors that really govern: not the spoil of victory, only the glorious toil of battle can be theirs. Abbot Samson found all men more or less headstrong, irrational, prone to disorder; continually threatening to prove *un*governable.

His lazy Monks gave him most trouble. 'My heart is tortured,' said he, 'till we get out of debt, *cor meum cruciatum est.*'* Your heart, indeed;—but not altogether ours! By no deviseable method, or none of three or four that he devised, could Abbot Samson get these Monks of his to keep their accounts straight; but always, do as he might, the Cellerarius at the end of the term is in a coil, in a flat deficit,— verging again towards debt and Jews. The Lord Abbot at last declares sternly he will keep our accounts too himself; will appoint an officer of his own to see our Cellerarius keep them.* Murmurs thereupon among us: Was the like ever heard? Our Cellerarius a cipher; the very

Townsfolk know it: *subsannatio et derisio sumus*, we have become a laughing stock to mankind.* The Norfolk barrator and paltener!—

And consider, if the Abbot found such difficulty in the mere economic department, how much in more complex ones, in spiritual ones perhaps! He wears a stern calm face; raging and gnashing teeth, *fremens* and *frendens*, many times, in the secret of his mind. Withal, however, there is a noble slow perseverance in him; a strength of 'subdued rage'* calculated to subdue most things: always, in the long-run, he contrives to gain his point.

Murmurs from the Monks, meanwhile, cannot fail; ever deeper murmurs, new grudges accumulating. At one time, on slight cause, some drop making the cup run over, they burst into open mutiny: the Cellarer will not obey, prefers arrest on bread and water to obeying; the Monks thereupon strike work; refuse to do the regular chanting of the day, at least the younger part of them with loud clamour and uproar refuse:—Abbot Samson has withdrawn to another residence, acting only by messengers: the awful report circulates through St. Edmundsbury that the Abbot is in danger of being murdered by the Monks with their knives! How wilt thou appease this, Abbot Samson? Return; for the Monastery seems near catching fire!*

Abbot Samson returns; sits in his *Thalamus* or inner room, hurls out a bolt or two of excommunication: lo, one disobedient Monk sits in limbo, excommunicated, with foot-shackles on him, all day; and three more our Abbot has gyved 'with the lesser sentence, to strike fear into the others!' Let the others think with whom they have to do. The others think; and fear enters into them. 'On the morrow morning we decide on humbling ourselves before the Abbot, by word and gesture, in order to mitigate his mind. And so accordingly was done. He, on the other side, replying with much humility, yet always alleging his own justice and turning the blame on us, when he saw that we were conquered, became himself conquered. And bursting into tears, *perfusus lachrymis*, he swore that he had never grieved so much for anything in the world as for this, first on his own account, and then secondly and chiefly for the public scandal which had gone abroad, that St. Edmund's Monks were going to kill their Abbot. And when he had narrated how he went away on purpose till his anger should cool, repeating this word of the philosopher, "I would have taken vengeance on thee, had not I been angry," he arose weeping, and embraced each and all of us with the kiss of peace. He wept; we all wept:'[1]*—what a picture! Behave better ye remiss Monks, and thank Heaven for such an Abbot; or know at least that ye must and shall obey him.

Worn down in this manner, with incessant toil and tribulation, Abbot Samson had a sore time of it; his grizzled hair and beard grew daily greyer. Those Jews, in the first four years, had 'visibly emaciated him:'* Time, Jews, and the task of Governing, will make a man's beard very grey! 'In twelve years,' says Jocelin, 'our Lord Abbot had grown wholly white as snow, *totus efficitur albus sicut nix.*'* White, atop, like the granite mountains:—but his clear-beaming eyes still look out, in their stern clearness, in their sorrow and pity; the heart within him remains unconquered.

Nay sometimes there are gleams of hilarity too; little snatches of encouragement granted even to a Governor. 'Once my Lord Abbot and I, coming down from London through the Forest, I inquired of an old woman whom we came up to, Whose wood this was, and of what manor, who the master, who the keeper?'—All this I knew very well beforehand, and my Lord Abbot too, Bozzy that I was! But 'the old woman answered, The wood belonged to the new Abbot of St. Edmund's, was of the manor of Harlow, and the keeper of it was one Arnald. How did he behave to the people of the manor? I asked farther. She answered that he used to be a devil incarnate, *dæmon vivus*, an enemy of God, and flayer of the peasants' skins,'—skinning them like live eels, as the manner of some is: 'but that now he dreads the new Abbot, knowing him to be a wise and sharp man, and so treats the people reasonably, *tractat homines pacifice.*' Whereat the Lord Abbot *factus est hilaris,*—could not but take a triumphant laugh for himself; and determines to leave that Harlow manor yet unmeddled with, for a while.[2]*

A brave man, strenuously fighting, fails not of a little triumph, now and then, to keep him in heart. Everywhere we try at least to give the adversary as good as he brings; and, with swift force or slow watchful manœuvre, extinguish this and the other solecism, leave one solecism less in God's Creation; and so *proceed* with our battle, not slacken or

---

[1] Jocelini Chronica, p. 85.   [2] Jocelini Chronica, p. 24.

surrender in it! The Fifty feudal Knights, for example, were of unjust greedy temper, and cheated us, in the Installation-day, of ten knights'-fees;—but they know now whether that has profited them aught, and I Jocelin know. Our Lord Abbot for the moment had to endure it, and say nothing; but he watched his time.*

Look also how my Lord of Clare,* coming to claim his *un*due 'debt' in the Court at Witham, with barons and apparatus, gets a Rowland for his Oliver!* Jocelin shall report: 'The Earl, crowded round (*constipatus*) with many barons and men at arms, Earl Alberic and others standing by him, said, "That his bailiffs had given him to understand they were wont annually to receive for his behoof, from the Hundred of Risebridge and the bailiffs thereof, a sum of five shillings, which sum was now unjustly held back;"—and he alleged farther that his predecessors had been infeft, at the Conquest, in the lands of Alfric son of Wisgar, who was Lord of that Hundred, as may be read in Domesday Book by all persons.—The Abbot, reflecting for a moment, without stirring from his place, made answer: "A wonderful deficit, my Lord Earl, this that thou mentionest! King Edward gave to St. Edmund that entire Hundred, and confirmed the same with his Charter; nor is there any mention there of those five shillings. It will behove thee to say, for what service, or on what ground, thou exactest those five shillings." Whereupon the Earl, consulting with his followers, replied, That he had to carry the Banner of St. Edmund* in wartime, and for this duty the five shillings were his. To which the Abbot: "Certainly, it seems inglorious, if so great a man, Earl of Clare no less, receive so small a gift for such a service. To the Abbot of St. Edmund's it is no unbearable burden to give five shillings. But Roger Earl Bigot holds himself duly seised, and asserts that he by such seisin has the office of carrying St. Edmund's Banner; and he did carry it when the Earl of Leicester and his Flemings were beaten at Fornham. Then again Thomas de Mendham says that the right is his. When you have made out with one another, that this right is thine, come then and claim the five shillings, and I will promptly pay them!" Whereupon the Earl said, He would speak with Earl Roger his relative; and so the matter *cepit dilationem*,' and lies undecided to the end of the world.* Abbot Samson answers by word or act, in this or the like pregnant manner, having justice on his side, innumerable persons: Pope's Legates, King's Viscounts, Canterbury Archbishops, Cellarers, *Sochemanni*;—and leaves many a solecism extinguished.

On the whole, however, it is and remains sore work. 'One time, during my chaplaincy, I ventured to say to him: "*Domine*, I heard thee, this night after matins, wakeful, and sighing deeply, *valde suspirantem*, contrary to thy usual wont." He answered: "No wonder. Thou, son Jocelin, sharest in my good things, in food and drink, in riding and such like; but thou little thinkest concerning the management of House and Family, the various and arduous businesses of the Pastoral Care, which harrass me, and make my soul to sigh and be anxious." Whereto I, lifting up my hands to Heaven: "From such anxiety, Omnipotent Merciful Lord deliver me!"—I have heard the Abbot say, If he had been as he was before he became a Monk, and could have anywhere got five or six marcs of income,' some three pound ten of yearly revenue, 'whereby to support himself in the schools, he would never have been Monk nor Abbot. Another time he said with an oath, If he had known what a business it was to govern the Abbey, he would rather have been Almoner, how much rather Keeper of the Books, than Abbot and Lord. That latter office he said he had always longed for beyond any other. *Quis talia crederet*,' concludes Jocelin, 'Who can believe such things?'*

Three pound ten, and a life of Literature, especially of quiet Literature, without copyright, or world-celebrity of literary-gazettes,—yes, thou brave Abbot Samson, for thyself it had been better, easier, perhaps also nobler! But then, for thy disobedient Monks, unjust Viscounts; for a Domain of St. Edmund overgrown with Solecisms, human and other, it had not been so well. Nay neither could *thy* Literature, never so quiet, have been easy. Literature, when noble, is not easy; but only when ignoble. Literature too is a quarrel, and internecine duel, with the whole World of Darkness that lies without one and within one;—rather a hard fight at times, even with the three pound ten secure. Thou, there where thou art, wrestle and duel along, cheerfully to the end; and make no remarks!

CHAPTER XIII.

IN PARLIAMENT.

OF Abbot Samson's public business we say little, though that also was great. He had to judge the people as Justice Errant, to decide in weighty arbitrations and public controversies; to equip his *milites*, send them duly in war-time to the King;—strive every way that the Commonweal, in his quarter of it, take no damage.

Once, in the confused days of Lackland's usurpation, while Cœur-de-Lion was away, our brave Abbot took helmet himself, having first excommunicated all that should favour Lackland; and led his men in person to the siege of *Windleshora*, what we now call Windsor; where Lackland had entrenched himself, the centre of infinite confusions; some Reform Bill, then as now, being greatly needed. There did Abbot Samson 'fight the battle of reform,'—with other ammunition one hopes, than 'tremendous cheering' and such like! For these things he was called 'the magnanimous Abbot.'*

He also attended duly in his place in Parliament *de arduis regni;* attended especially, as in *arduissimo*, when 'the news reached London that King Richard was captive in Germany.' Here 'while all the barons sat to consult,' and many of them looked blank enough, 'the Abbot started forth, *prosiliit coram omnibus*, in his place in Parliament, and said, That *he* was ready to go and seek his Lord the King, either clandestinely by subterfuge (*in tapinagio*), or by any other method; and search till he found him, and got certain notice of him; he for one! By which word,' says Jocelin, 'he acquired great praise for himself,'*— unfeigned commendation from the Able Editors of that age.

By which word;—and also by which *deed:* for the Abbot actually went, 'with rich gifts to the King in Germany;'[1]* Usurper Lackland being first rooted out from Windsor, and the King's peace somewhat settled.

As to these 'rich gifts,' however, we have to note one thing: In all England, as appeared to the Collective Wisdom, there was not like to be treasure enough for ransoming King Richard; in which extremity certain Lords of the Treasury, *Justiciarii ad Scaccarium*,* suggested that St. Edmund's Shrine, covered with thick gold, was still untouched. Could not it, in this extremity be peeled off, at least in part; under condition, of course, of its being replaced, when times mended? The Abbot, starting plumb up, *se erigens*, answered: "Know ye for certain, that I will in no wise do this thing; nor is there any man who could force me to consent thereto. But I will open the doors of

---

[1] Jocelini Chronica, pp. 39, 40.

the Church: Let him that likes enter; let him that dares come forward!" Emphatic words, which created a sensation round the woolsack. For the Justiciaries of the *Scaccarium* answered, 'with oaths, each for himself: "I won't come forward, for my share; nor will I, nor I! The distant and absent who offended him, Saint Edmund has been known to punish fearfully; much more will he those close by, who lay violent hands on his coat, and would strip it off!" These things being said, the Shrine was not meddled with, nor any ransom levied for it.'[1]*

For Lords of the Treasury have in all times their impassable limits, be it by 'force of public opinion'* or otherwise; and, in those days a heavenly Awe overshadowed and encompassed, as it still ought and must, all earthly Business whatsoever.

CHAPTER XIV.

HENRY OF ESSEX.

OF St. Edmund's fearful avengements have they not the remarkablest instance still before their eyes? He that will go to Reading Monastery may find there, now tonsured into a mournful penitent Monk, the once proud Henry Earl of Essex; and discern how St. Edmund punishes terribly, yet with mercy! This Narrative is too significant to be omitted as a document of the Time. Our Lord Abbot, once on a visit at Reading, heard the particulars from Henry's own mouth; and thereupon charged one of his Monks to write it down,—as accordingly the Monk has done, in ambitious rhetorical Latin; inserting the same, as episode, among Jocelin's garrulous leaves. Read it here; with ancient yet with modern eyes.*

Henry Earl of Essex, Standard-bearer of England, had high places and emoluments;* had a haughty high soul, yet with various flaws, or rather with one many-branched flaw and crack, running through the texture of it. For example, did he not treat Gilbert de Cereville in the most shocking manner? He cast Gilbert into prison; and with chains and slow torments, wore the life out of him there.* And Gilbert's

---

[1] Jocelini Chronica, p. 71.

crime was understood to be only that of innocent Joseph: the Lady Essex was a Potiphar's Wife,* and had accused poor Gilbert! Other cracks, and branches of that widespread flaw in the Standard-bearer's soul we could point out: but indeed the main stem and trunk of all is too visible in this, That he had no right reverence for the Heavenly in Man,—that far from shewing due reverence to St. Edmund, he did not even shew him common justice. While others in the Eastern Counties were adorning and enlarging with rich gifts St. Edmund's resting-place, which had become a city of refuge for many things, this Earl of Essex flatly defrauded him, by violence or quirk of law, of five shillings yearly, and converted said sum to his own poor uses! Nay, in another case of litigation, the unjust Standard-bearer, for his own profit, asserting that the cause belonged not to St. Edmund's Court, but to *his* in Lailand Hundred, 'involved us in travellings and innumerable expenses, vexing the servants of St. Edmund for a long tract of time.' In short, he is without reverence for the Heavenly, this Standard-bearer; reveres only the Earthly, Gold-coined; and has a most morbid lamentable flaw in the texture of him.* It cannot come to good.

Accordingly, the same flaw, or St.-Vitus *tic*, manifests itself ere long in another way. In the year 1157, he went with his Standard to attend King Henry, our blessed Sovereign (whom *we* saw afterwards at Waltham), in his War with the Welsh. A somewhat disastrous War; in which while King Henry and his force were struggling to retreat Parthian-like, endless clouds of exasperated Welshmen hemming them in, and now we had come to the 'difficult pass of Coleshill,' and as it were to the nick of destruction,—Henry Earl of Essex shrieks out on a sudden (blinded doubtless by his inner flaw, or 'evil genius' as some name it), That King Henry is killed, That all is lost,—and flings down his Standard to shift for itself there! And, certainly enough, all *had* been lost, had all men been as he;—had not brave men, without such miserable jerking *tic-douloureux* in the souls of them, come dashing up, with blazing swords and looks, and asserted That nothing was lost yet, that all must be regained yet. In this manner King Henry and his force got safely retreated, Parthian-like, from the pass of Coleshill and the Welsh War.[1] But, once home again, Earl Robert de Montfort, a kinsman of this Standard-bearer's, rises up in

[1] See Lyttelton's Henry II., ii. 384.

the King's Assembly to declare openly that such a man is unfit for bearing English Standards, being in fact either a special traitor, or something almost worse, a coward namely, or universal traitor. Wager of Battle in consequence; solemn Duel, by the King's appointment, 'in a certain Island of the Thames-stream at Reading, *apud Radingas*, short way from the Abbey there.' King, Peers, and an immense multitude of people, on such scaffoldings and heights as they can come at, are gathered round, to see what issue the business will take. The business takes this bad issue, in our Monk's own words faithfully rendered:

'And it came to pass, while Robert de Montfort thundered on him manfully (*viriliter intonâsset*) with hard and frequent strokes, and a valiant beginning promised the fruit of victory, Henry of Essex, rather giving way, glanced round on all sides; and lo, at the rim of the horizon, on the confines of the River and land, he discerned the glorious King and Martyr Edmund, in shining armour, and as if hovering in the air; looking towards him with severe countenance, nodding his head with a mien and motion of austere anger. At St. Edmund's hand there stood also another Knight, Gilbert de Cereville, whose armour was not so splendid, whose stature was less gigantic; casting vengeful looks at him. This he seeing with his eyes, remembered that old crime brings new shame. And now wholly desperate, and changing reason into violence, he took the part of one blindly attacking, not skilfully defending. Who while he struck fiercely was more fiercely struck; and so, in short, fell down vanquished, and it was thought, slain. As he lay there for dead, his kinsmen, Magnates of England, besought the King, that the Monks of Reading might have leave to bury him. However, he proved not to be dead, but got well again among them; and now, with recovered health, assuming the Regular Habit, he strove to wipe out the stain of his former life, to cleanse the long week of his dissolute history by at least a purifying sabbath, and cultivate the studies of Virtue into fruits of eternal Felicity.'[1]*

Thus does the Conscience of man project itself athwart whatsoever of knowledge or surmise, of imagination, understanding, faculty, acquirement, or natural disposition he has in him; and, like light through coloured glass,* paint strange pictures 'on the rim of the

[1] Jocelini Chronica, p. 52.

horizon'* and elsewhere! Truly, this same 'sense of the Infinite nature of Duty'* is the central part of all with us; a ray as of Eternity and Immortality, immured in dusky many-coloured Time, and its deaths and births. Your 'coloured glass' varies so much from century to century;—and, in certain money-making, game-preserving centuries, it gets so terribly opaque! Not a Heaven with cherubim surrounds you then, but a kind of vacant leaden-coloured Hell. One day it will again cease to be *opaque*, this 'coloured glass.' Nay, may it not become at once translucent and *un*coloured? Painting no Pictures more for us, but only the everlasting Azure itself? That will be a right glorious consummation!—

Saint Edmund from the horizon's edge, in shining armour, threatening the misdoer in his hour of extreme need: it is beautiful, it is great and true. So old, yet so modern, actual; true yet for every one of us, as for Henry the Earl and Monk! A glimpse as of the Deepest in Man's Destiny, which is the same for all times and ages. Yes, Henry my brother, there in thy extreme need, thy soul is *lamed;* and behold thou canst not so much as fight! For Justice and Reverence *are* the everlasting central Law of this Universe; and to forget them, and have all the Universe against one, God and one's own Self for enemies, and only the Devil and the Dragons for friends, is not that a 'lameness' like few? That some shining armed St. Edmund hang minatory on thy horizon, that infinite sulphur-lakes hang minatory, or do not now hang,—this alters no whit the eternal fact of the thing. I say, thy soul is lamed, and the God and all Godlike in it marred: lamed, paralytic, tending towards baleful eternal death, whether thou know it or not;—nay hadst thou never known it, that surely had been worst of all!—

Thus, at any rate, by the heavenly Awe that overshadows earthly Business, does Samson, readily in those days, save St. Edmund's Shrine, and innumerable still more precious things.

CHAPTER XV.

PRACTICAL-DEVOTIONAL.*

HERE indeed, perhaps, by rule of antagonisms, may be the place to mention that, after King Richard's return, there was a liberty of tourneying given to the fighting men of England: that a Tournament was proclaimed in the Abbot's domain, 'between Thetford and St. Edmundsbury,'—perhaps in the Euston region, on Fakenham Heights, midway between these two localities: that it was publicly prohibited by our Lord Abbot; and nevertheless was held in spite of him,—and by the parties, as would seem, considered 'a gentle and free passage of arms.'*

Nay, next year, there came to the same spot four-and-twenty young men, sons of Nobles, for another passage of arms; who, having completed the same, all rode into St. Edmundsbury to lodge for the night. Here is modesty! Our Lord Abbot, being instructed of it, ordered the Gates to be closed; the whole party shut in. The morrow was the Vigil of the Apostles Peter and Paul; no outgate on the morrow. Giving their promise not to depart without permission, those four-and-twenty young bloods dieted all that day (*manducaverunt*) with the Lord Abbot, waiting for trial on the morrow. 'But after dinner,'—mark it, posterity!—'the Lord Abbot retiring into his *Thalamus*, they all started up, and began carolling and singing (*carolare et cantare*); sending into the Town for wine; drinking, and afterwards howling (*ululantes*);—totally depriving the Abbot and Convent of their afternoon's nap; doing all this in derision of the Lord Abbot, and spending in such fashion the whole day till evening, nor would they desist at the Lord Abbot's order! Night coming on, they broke the bolts of the Town-Gates, and went off by violence!'[1] Was the like ever heard of? The roysterous young dogs; carolling, howling, breaking the Lord Abbot's sleep,—after that sinful chivalry cock-fight of theirs! They too are a feature of distant centuries, as of near ones. St. Edmund on the edge of your horizon, or whatever else there, young scamps, in the dandy state, whether cased in iron or in whalebone, begin to caper and carol on the green Earth! Our Lord Abbot excommunicated most of them; and they gradually came in for repentance.*

Excommunication is a great recipe with our Lord Abbot; the prevailing purifier in those ages. Thus when the Townsfolk and Monkmenials quarrelled once at the Christmas Mysteries in St. Edmund's Churchyard, and 'from words it came to cuffs, and from cuffs to cuttings and the effusion of blood,'—our Lord Abbot excommunicates sixty of the rioters, with bell, book and candle (*accensis candelis*), at

---

[1] Jocelini Chronica, p. 40.

one stroke.[1] Whereupon they all come suppliant, indeed nearly naked, 'nothing on but their breeches, *omnino nudi præter femoralia*, and prostrate themselves at the Church-door.'* Figure that!

In fact, by excommunication or persuasion, by impetuosity of driving or adroitness in leading, this Abbot, it is now becoming plain everywhere, is a man that generally remains master at last. He tempers his medicine to the malady, now hot, now cool; prudent though fiery, an eminently practical man. Nay sometimes in his adroit practice there are swift turns almost of a surprising nature! Once, for example, it chanced that Geoffrey Riddell Bishop of Ely, a Prelate rather troublesome to our Abbot, made a request of him for timber from his woods towards certain edifices going on at Glemsford. The Abbot, a great builder himself, disliked the request; could not however give it a negative. While he lay, therefore, at his Manorhouse of Melford not long after, there comes to him one of the Lord Bishop's men or monks, with a message from his Lordship, "That he now begged permission to cut down the requisite trees in Elmswell Wood,"—so said the monk: Elms*well*, where there are no trees but scrubs and shrubs, instead of Elm*set*, our true *nemus*, and high-towering oak-wood, here on Melford Manor! Elmswell? The Lord Abbot, in surprise, inquires privily of Richard his Forester; Richard answers that my Lord of Ely has already had his *carpentarii* in Elm*set*, and marked out for his own use all the best trees in the compass of it. Abbot Samson thereupon answers the monk: "Elmswell? Yes surely, be it as my Lord Bishop wishes." The successful monk, on the morrow morning, hastens home to Ely; but, on the morrow morning, 'directly after mass,' Abbot Samson too was busy! The successful monk, arriving at Ely, is rated for a goose and an owl; is ordered back to say that Elmset was the place meant. Alas, on arriving at Elmset, he finds the Bishop's trees, they 'and a hundred more,' all felled and piled, and the stamp of St. Edmund's Monastery burnt into them,—for roofing of the great tower we are building there! Your importunate Bishop must seek wood for Glemsford edifices in some other *nemus* than this.* A practical Abbot!

We said withal there was a terrible flash of anger in him: witness his address to old Herbert the Dean, who in a too thrifty manner has erected a wind-mill for himself on his glebe-lands at Haberdon. On

[1] Ibid. p. 68.

the morrow, after mass, our Lord Abbot orders the Cellerarius to
send off his carpenters to demolish the said structure *brevi manu*, and
lay up the wood in safe keeping. Old Dean Herbert, hearing what was
toward, comes tottering along hither, to plead humbly for himself and
his mill. The Abbot answers: "I am obliged to thee as if thou hadst cut
off both my feet! By God's face, *per os Dei*, I will not eat bread till that
fabric be torn in pieces. Thou art an old man, and shouldst have
known that neither the King nor his Justiciary dare change aught
within the Liberties, without consent of Abbot and Convent: and thou
hast presumed on such a thing? I tell thee, it will *not* be without damage to my mills; for the Townsfolk will go to thy mill, and grind their
corn (*bladum suum*) at their own good pleasure; nor can I hinder them,
since they are free men. I will allow no new mills on such principle.
Away, away; before thou gettest home again, thou wilt see what thy
mill has grown to!"[1]—The very reverend, the old Dean totters home
again in all haste; tears the mill in pieces by his own *carpentarii*, to
save at least the timber; and Abbot Samson's workmen, coming up,
find the ground already clear of it.*

Easy to bully down poor old rural Deans, and blow their wind-
mills away: but who is the man that dare abide King Richard's
anger; cross the Lion in his path, and take him by the whiskers!
Abbot Samson too; he is that man, with justice on his side. The case
was this. Adam de Cokefield, one of the chief feudatories of
St. Edmund, and a principal man in the Eastern Counties, died, leaving
large possessions, and for heiress a daughter of three months; who
by clear law, as all men know, became thus Abbot Samson's ward;
whom accordingly he proceeded to dispose of to such person as
seemed fittest. But now King Richard has another person in view, to
whom the little ward and her great possessions were a suitable thing.
He, by letter, requests that Abbot Samson will have the goodness to
give her to this person. Abbot Samson, with deep humility, replies
that she is already given. New letters from Richard, of severer tenor;
answered with new deep humilities, with gifts and entreaties, with
no promise of obedience. King Richard's ire is kindled; messengers
arrive at St. Edmundsbury, with emphatic message to obey or tremble! Abbot Samson, wisely silent as to the King's threats, makes

---

[1] Jocelini Chronica, p. 43.

answer: "The King can send if he will, and seize the ward: force and power he has to do his pleasure, and abolish the whole Abbey. I never can be bent to wish this that he seeks, nor shall it by me be ever done. For there is danger lest such things be made a precedent of, to the prejudice of my successors. *Videat Altissimus*, Let the Most High look on it. Whatsoever thing shall befal I will patiently endure."*

Such was Abbot Samson's deliberate decision. Why not? Cœur-de-Lion is very dreadful, but not the dreadfulest. *Videat Altissimus.* I reverence Cœur-de-Lion to the marrow of my bones, and will in all right things be *homo suus;* but it is not, properly speaking, with terror, with any fear at all. On the whole, have I not looked on the face of 'Satan with outspread wings;'* steadily into Hellfire these seven-and-forty years;—and was not melted into terror even at that, such the Lord's goodness to me? Cœur-de-Lion!

Richard swore tornado oaths, worse than our armies in Flanders,* To be revenged on that proud Priest. But in the end he discovered that the Priest was right; and forgave him, and even loved him. 'King Richard wrote, soon after, to Abbot Samson, That he wanted one or two of the St. Edmundsbury dogs, which he heard were good.' Abbot Samson sent him dogs of the best; Richard replied by the present of a ring, which Pope Innocent the Third had given him.* Thou brave Richard, thou brave Samson! Richard too, I suppose, 'loved a man,' and knew one when he saw him.

No one will accuse our Lord Abbot of wanting worldly wisdom, due interest in worldly things. A skilful man; full of cunning insight, lively interests; always discerning the road to his object, be it circuit, be it short-cut, and victoriously travelling forward thereon. Nay rather it might seem, from Jocelin's Narrative, as if he had his eye all but exclusively directed on terrestrial matters,* and was much too secular for a devout man. But this too, if we examine it, was right. For it is *in* the world that a man, devout or other, has his life to lead, his work waiting to be done. The basis of Abbot Samson's, we shall discover, was truly religion, after all. Returning from his dusty pilgrimage, with such welcome as we saw, 'he sat down at the foot of St. Edmund's Shrine.'* Not a talking theory that; no, a silent practice: Thou St. Edmund with what lies in thee, thou now must help me, or none will!

This also is a significant fact: the zealous interest our Abbot took in the Crusades. To all noble Christian hearts of that era, what earthly enterprise so noble? 'When Henry II., having taken the cross, came to St. Edmund's, to pay his devotions before setting out, the Abbot secretly made for himself a cross of linen cloth, and, holding this in one hand and a threaded needle in the other, asked leave of the King to assume it!' The King could not spare Samson out of England;—the King himself indeed never went.* But the Abbot's eye was set on the Holy Sepulchre, as on the spot of this Earth where the true cause of Heaven was deciding itself. 'At the retaking of Jerusalem by the Pagans, Abbot Samson put on a cilice and hair-shirt, and wore undergarments of hair-cloth ever after; he abstained also from flesh and flesh-meats (*carne et carneis*) thenceforth to the end of his life.'* Like a dark cloud eclipsing the hopes of Christendom, those tidings cast their shadow over St. Edmundsbury too: Shall Samson Abbas take pleasure while Christ's Tomb is in the hands of the Infidel? Samson, in pain of body, shall daily be reminded of it, admonished to grieve for it.

The great antique heart: how like a child's in its simplicity, like a man's in its earnest solemnity and depth! Heaven lies over him wheresoever he goes or stands on the Earth; making all the Earth a mystic Temple to him, the Earth's business all a kind of worship. Glimpses of bright creatures flash in the common sunlight; angels yet hover doing God's messages among men: that rainbow was set in the clouds by the hand of God! Wonder, miracle encompass the man; he lives in an element of miracle; Heaven's splendour over his head, Hell's darkness under his feet. A great Law of Duty, high as these two Infinitudes, dwarfing all else, annihilating all else,—making royal Richard as small as peasant Samson, smaller if need be!—The 'imaginative faculties?' 'Rude poetic ages?' The 'primeval poetic element?'* O for God's sake, good reader, talk no more of all that! It was not a Dilettantism this of Abbot Samson. It was a Reality, and it is one. The garment only of it is dead;* the essence of it lives through all Time and all Eternity!—

And truly, as we said above, is not this comparative silence of Abbot Samson as to his religion, precisely the healthiest sign of him and of it? 'The Unconscious is the alone Complete.'* Abbot Samson all along a busy working man, as all men are bound to be, his religion, his worship was like his daily bread to him;—which he did not take the trouble to talk much about; which he merely ate at stated intervals, and lived and did his work upon! This is Abbot Samson's Catholicism of the Twelfth Century;—something like the *Ism* of all true men in all true centuries, I fancy! Alas, compared with any of the *Isms* current in these poor days, what a thing! Compared with the respectablest, morbid, struggling Methodism, never so earnest; with the respectablest, ghastly, dead or galvanised Dilettantism, never so spasmodic!

Methodism with its eye forever turned on its own navel;* asking itself with torturing anxiety of Hope and Fear, "Am I right, am I wrong? Shall I be saved, shall I not be damned?"—what is this, at bottom, but a new phasis of *Egoism*, stretched out into the Infinite; not always the heavenlier for its infinitude! Brother, so soon as possible, endeavour to rise above all that. "Thou *art* wrong; thou art like to be damned:" consider that as the fact, reconcile thyself even to that, if thou be a man;—then first is the devouring Universe subdued under thee, and from the black murk of midnight and noise of greedy Acheron,* dawn as of an everlasting morning, how far above all Hope and all Fear, springs for thee, enlightening thy steep path, awakening in thy heart celestial Memnon's music!*

But of our Dilettantisms, and galvanised Dilettantisms; of Puseyism—O Heavens, what shall we say of Puseyism,* in comparison to Twelfth-Century Catholicism? Little or nothing; for indeed it is a matter to strike one dumb.

> The Builder of this Universe was wise,
> He plann'd all souls, all systems, planets, particles:
> The Plan He shap'd all Worlds and Æons by
> Was——Heavens!—Was thy small Nine-and-thirty Articles?*

That certain human souls, living on this practical Earth, should think to save themselves and a ruined world by noisy theoretic demonstrations and laudations of *the* Church, instead of some unnoisy, unconscious, but *practical*, total, heart-and-soul demonstration of *a* Church: this, in the circle of revolving ages, this also was a thing we were to see. A kind of penultimate thing, precursor of very strange consummations; last thing but one? If there is no atmosphere, what will it serve a man to demonstrate the excellence of lungs? How much profitabler when you can, like Abbot Samson, breathe; and go along your way!

CHAPTER XVI.

ST. EDMUND.

ABBOT SAMSON built many useful, many pious edifices;* human dwellings, churches, church-steeples, barns;—all fallen now and vanished, but useful while they stood. He built and endowed 'the Hospital of Babwell;'* built 'fit houses for the St. Edmundsbury Schools.'* Many are the roofs once 'thatched with reeds' which he 'caused to be covered with tiles;' or if they were churches, probably 'with lead.'* For all ruinous incomplete things, buildings or other, were an eye-sorrow to the man. We saw his 'great tower of St. Edmund's;'* or at least the roof-timbers of it lying cut and stamped in Elmset Wood. To change combustible decaying reed-thatch into tile or lead, and material, still more, moral wreck into raintight order, what a comfort to Samson!

One of the things he could not in any wise but rebuild was the great Altar,* aloft on which stood the Shrine itself; the great Altar, which had been damaged by fire, by the careless rubbish and careless candle of two somnolent Monks, one night,—the Shrine escaping almost as if by miracle! Abbot Samson read his Monks a severe lecture: "A Dream one of us had, that he saw St. Edmund naked and in lamentable plight. Know ye the interpretation of that Dream? St. Edmund proclaims himself naked, because ye defraud the naked Poor of your old clothes, and give with reluctance what ye are bound to give them of meat and drink: the idleness moreover and negligence of the Sacristan and his people is too evident from the late misfortune by fire. Well might our Holy Martyr seem to lie cast out from his Shrine, and say with groans that he was stript of his garments, and wasted with hunger and thirst!"*

This is Abbot Samson's interpretation of the Dream;—diametrically the reverse of that given by the Monks themselves, who scruple not to say privily, "It is *we* that are the naked and famished limbs of the Martyr;* we whom the Abbot curtails of all our privileges, setting his own official to control our very Cellarer!" Abbot Samson adds, that this judgment by fire has fallen upon them for murmuring about their meat and drink.

Clearly enough, meanwhile, the Altar, whatever the burning of it mean or foreshadow, must needs be reedified. Abbot Samson reedifies it, all of polished marble; with the highest stretch of art and sumptuosity, reembellishes the Shrine for which it is to serve as pediment.* Nay farther, as had ever been among his prayers, he enjoys, he sinner, a glimpse of the glorious Martyr's very Body in the process; having solemnly opened the *Loculus*, Chest or sacred Coffin, for that purpose. It is the culminating moment of Abbot Samson's life. Bozzy Jocelin himself rises into a kind of Psalmist solemnity on this occasion; the laziest monk 'weeps' warm tears, as *Te Deum* is sung.*

Very strange;—how far vanished from us in these unworshipping ages of ours! The Patriot Hampden, best beatified man we have, had lain in like manner some two centuries in his narrow home, when certain dignitaries of us, 'and twelve grave-diggers with pulleys,' raised him also up,* under cloud of night; cut off his arm with penknives, pulled the scalp off his head,—and otherwise worshipped our Hero Saint in the most amazing manner![1] Let the modern eye look earnestly on that old midnight hour in St. Edmundsbury Church, shining yet on us, ruddy-bright, through the depths of seven hundred years; and consider mournfully what our Hero-worship once was, and what it now is! We translate with all the fidelity we can:

'The Festival of St. Edmund now approaching, the marble blocks are polished, and all things are in readiness for lifting of the Shrine to its new place. A fast of three days was held by all the people, the cause and meaning thereof being publicly set forth to them. The Abbot announces to the Convent that all must prepare themselves for transferring of the Shrine, and appoints time and way for the work. Coming therefore that night to matins, we found the great Shrine (*feretrum magnum*) raised upon the Altar, but empty; covered all over with white doeskin leather, fixed to the wood with silver nails; but one pannel of the Shrine was left down below, and resting thereon, beside its old column of the Church, the Loculus with the Sacred Body yet lay where it was wont. Praises being sung, we all proceeded to commence our disciplines (*ad disciplinas suscipiendas*). These finished, the Abbot and certain with him are clothed in their albs; and, approaching reverently, set about uncovering the Loculus. There was an outer cloth of linen, enwrapping the Loculus and all; this we found tied on the upper side with strings of its own: within this was a cloth of silk, and then another linen cloth, and then a third; and so at last the Loculus

---

[1] Annual Register (year 1828, Chronicle, p. 93), Gentleman's Magazine, &c. &c.

was uncovered, and seen resting on a little tray of wood, that the bottom of it might not be injured by the stone. Over the breast of the Martyr, there lay, fixed to the surface of the Loculus, a Golden Angel about the length of a human foot; holding in one hand a golden sword, and in the other a banner: under this there was a hole in the lid of the Loculus, on which the ancient servants of the Martyr had been wont to lay their hands for touching the Sacred Body. And over the figure of the Angel was this verse inscribed:

Mar tiris ecce zoma servat Michaelis agalma.[1]

At the head and foot of the Loculus were iron rings whereby it could be lifted.

'Lifting the Loculus and Body, therefore, they carried it to the Altar; and I put-to my sinful hand to help in carrying, though the Abbot had commanded that none should approach except called. And the Loculus was placed in the Shrine; and the pannel it had stood on was put in its place, and the Shrine for the present closed. We all thought that the Abbot would shew the Loculus to the people; and bring out the Sacred Body again, at a certain period of the Festival. But in this we were wofully mistaken, as the sequel shews.

'For in the fourth holiday of the Festival, while the Convent were all singing *Completorium*, our Lord Abbot spoke privily with the Sacristan and Walter the Medicus; and order was taken that twelve of the Brethren should be appointed against midnight, who were strong for carrying the pannel-planks of the Shrine, and skilful in unfixing them, and putting them together again. The Abbot then said that it was among his prayers to look once upon the Body of his Patron; and that he wished the Sacristan and Walter the Medicus to be with him. The Twelve appointed Brethren were these: The Abbot's two Chaplains, the two Keepers of the Shrine, the two Masters of the Vestry; and six more, namely, the Sacristan Hugo, Walter the Medicus, Augustin, William of Dice, Robert, and Richard. I, alas, was not of the number.

'The Convent therefore being all asleep, these Twelve, clothed in their albs, with the Abbot, assembled at the Altar; and opening a pannel of the Shrine, they took out the Loculus; laid it on a table, near where the Shrine used to be; and made ready for unfastening the lid,

---

[1] This is the Martyr's Garment, which Michael's Image guards.

which was joined and fixed to the Loculus with sixteen very long nails. Which when, with difficulty, they had done, all except the two forenamed associates are ordered to draw back. The Abbot and they two were alone privileged to look in. The Loculus was so filled with the Sacred Body that you could scarcely put a needle between the head and the wood, or between the feet and the wood: the head lay united to the body, a little raised with a small pillow. But the Abbot, looking close, found now a silk cloth veiling the whole Body, and then a linen cloth of wondrous whiteness; and upon the head was spread a small linen cloth, and then another small and most fine silk cloth, as if it were the veil of a nun. These coverings being lifted off, they found now the Sacred Body all wrapt in linen; and so at length the lineaments of the same appeared. But here the Abbot stopped; saying he durst not proceed farther, or look at the sacred flesh naked. Taking the head between his hands, he thus spake groaning: "Glorious Martyr, holy Edmund, blessed be the hour when thou wert born. Glorious Martyr, turn it not to my perdition that I have so dared to touch thee, I miserable and sinful; thou knowest my devout love, and the intention of my mind." And proceeding, he touched the eyes; and the nose, which was very massive and prominent (*valde grossum et valde eminentem*); and then he touched the breast and arms and raising the left arm he touched the fingers, and placed his own fingers between the sacred fingers. And proceeding he found the feet standing stiff up, like the feet of a man dead yesterday; and he touched the toes, and counted them (*tangendo numeravit*).

'And now it was agreed that the other Brethren should be called forward to see the miracles; and accordingly those ten now advanced, and along with them six others who had stolen in without the Abbot's assent, namely, Walter of St. Alban's, Hugh the Infirmirarius, Gilbert brother of the Prior, Richard of Henham, Jocellus our Cellarer, and Turstan the Little; and all these saw the Sacred Body, but Turstan alone of them put forth his hand, and touched the Saint's knees and feet. And that there might be abundance of witnesses, one of our Brethren, John of Dice, sitting on the roof of the Church, with the servants of the Vestry, and looking through, clearly saw all these things.'*

What a scene; shining luminous effulgent, as the lamps of St. Edmund do, through the dark Night; John of Dice, with vestry-men, clambering on the roof to look through; the Convent all asleep,

and the Earth all asleep,—and since then, Seven Centuries of Time
mostly gone to sleep! Yes, there, sure enough, is the martyred Body of
Edmund landlord of the Eastern Counties, who, nobly doing what he
liked with his own, was slain three hundred years ago: and a noble awe
surrounds the memory of him, symbol and promoter of many other
right noble things.

But have not we now advanced to strange new stages of Hero-
worship, now in the little Church of Hampden, with our penknives
out, and twelve grave-diggers with pulleys? The manner of men's
Hero-worship, verily it is the innermost fact of their existence, and
determines all the rest,—at public hustings, in private drawing-
rooms, in church, in market, and wherever else. Have true reverence,
and what indeed is inseparable therefrom, reverence the right man,
all is well;* have sham-reverence, and what also follows, greet with it
the wrong man, then all is ill, and there is nothing well. Alas, if Hero-
worship become Dilettantism, and all except Mammonism be a vain
grimace, how much, in this most earnest Earth, has gone and is evermore going to fatal destruction, and lies wasting in quiet lazy ruin, no
man regarding it! Till at length no heavenly *Ism* any longer coming
down upon us, *Isms* from the other quarter have to mount up. For the
Earth, I say, is an earnest place; Life is no grimace, but a most serious
fact. And so, under universal Dilettantism much having been stript
bare, not the souls of men only, but their very bodies and bread-
cupboards having been stript bare, and life now no longer possible,—all is reduced to desperation, to the iron law of Necessity and
very Fact again; and to temper Dilettantism, and astonish it, and burn
it up with infernal fire, arises Chartism, *Bare-back-ism*, Sansculottism
so-called!* May the gods, and what of unworshipped heroes still
remain among us, avert the omen.—

But however this may be, St. Edmund's Loculus, we find, has the
veils of silk and linen reverently replaced, the lid fastened down again
with its sixteen ancient nails; is wrapt in a new costly covering of silk,
the gift of Hubert Archbishop of Canterbury: and through the sky-
window John of Dice sees it lifted to its place in the Shrine, the pan-
nels of this latter duly refixed, fit parchment documents being
introduced withal;—and now John and his vestrymen can slide down
from the roof, for all is over, and the Convent wholly awakens to matins.
'When we assembled to sing matins,' says Jocelin, 'and understood

what had been done, grief took hold of all that had not seen these things, each saying to himself, "Alas, I was deceived." Matins over, the Abbot called the Convent to the great Altar; and briefly recounting the matter, alleged that it had not been in his power, nor was it permissible or fit, to invite us all to the sight of such things. At hearing of which, we all wept, and with tears sang *Te Deum laudamus;* and hastened to toll the bells in the Choir.'*

Stupid blockheads, to reverence their St. Edmund's dead Body in this manner? Yes, brother;—and yet, on the whole, who knows how to reverence the Body of a Man? It is the most reverend phenomenon under this Sun. For the Highest God dwells visible in that mystic unfathomable Visibility, which calls itself "I" on the Earth. 'Bending before men,' says Novalis, 'is a reverence done to this Revelation in the Flesh. We touch Heaven when we lay our hand on a human Body.'* And the Body of one Dead;—a temple where the Hero-soul once was and now is not: Oh, all mystery, all pity, all mute *awe* and wonder; *Super*naturalism brought home to the very dullest;* Eternity laid open, and the nether Darkness and the upper Light-Kingdoms;—do conjoin there, or exist nowhere! Sauerteig used to say to me, in his peculiar way: "A Chancery Lawsuit; justice, nay justice in mere money, denied a man, for all his pleading, till twenty, till forty years of his Life are gone seeking it:* and a Cockney Funeral,* Death reverenced by hatchments,* horsehair, brass-lacker, and unconcerned bipeds carrying long poles and bags of black silk:—are not these two reverences, this reverence for Death and that reverence for Life, a notable pair of reverences among you English?"

Abbot Samson, at this culminating point of his existence, may, and indeed must, be left to vanish with his Life-scenery from the eyes of modern men. He had to run into France, to settle with King Richard for the military service there of his St. Edmundsbury Knights; and with great labour got it done.* He had to decide on the dilapidated Coventry Monks; and with great labour, and much pleading and journeying, got them reinstated; dined with them all, and with the 'Masters of the Schools of Oxneford,'—the veritable Oxford *Caput* sitting there at dinner, in a dim but undeniable manner, in the City of Peeping Tom!* He had, not without labour, to controvert the intrusive Bishop of Ely,* the intrusive Abbot of Cluny.* Magnanimous Samson, his life is but a labour and a journey; a bustling and a justling, till the still Night come. He is sent for again, over sea, to advise King Richard touching certain Peers of England, who had taken the Cross, but never followed it to Palestine; whom the Pope is inquiring after. The magnanimous Abbot makes preparation for departure; departs, and —— And Jocelin's Boswellean Narrative, suddenly shorn through by the scissors of Destiny, *ends*.* There are no words more; but a black line, and leaves of blank paper. Irremediable: the miraculous hand that held all this theatric-machinery suddenly quits hold; impenetrable Time-Curtains* rush down; in the mind's eye all is again dark, void; with loud dinning in the mind's ear, our real-phantasmagory* of St. Edmundsbury plunges into the bosom of the Twelfth Century again, and all is over. Monks, Abbot, Hero-worship, Government, Obedience, Cœur-de-Lion and St. Edmund's Shrine, vanish like Mirza's Vision;* and there is nothing left but a mutilated black Ruin amid green botanic expanses, and oxen, sheep and dilettanti pasturing in their places.

CHAPTER XVII.

THE BEGINNINGS.

WHAT a singular shape of a Man, shape of a Time, have we in this Abbot Samson and his history; how strangely do modes, creeds, for-mularies, and the date and place of a man's birth, modify the figure of the man!

Formulas too, as we call them, have a *reality* in Human Life. They are real as the very *skin* and *muscular tissue* of a Man's Life; and a most blessed indispensable thing, so long as they have *vitality* withal, and are a *living* skin and tissue to him! No man, or man's life, can go abroad and do business in the world without skin and tissues. No; first of all these have to fashion themselves,—as indeed they spontan-eously and inevitably do. Foam itself, and this is worth thinking of, can harden into oyster-shell; all living objects do by necessity form to themselves a skin.

And yet, again, when a man's Formulas become *dead;** as all Formulas, in the progress of living growth, are very sure to do! When the poor man's integuments, no longer nourished from within, become dead skin, mere adscititious leather and callosity, wearing thicker and thicker, uglier and uglier; till no *heart* any longer can be felt beating through them, so thick, callous, calcified are they; and all over it has now grown mere calcified oyster-shell, or were it polished mother-of-pearl, inwards almost to the very heart of the poor man:—yes then, you may say, his usefulness once more is quite obstructed; once more, he cannot go abroad and do business in the world; it is time that *he* take to bed, and prepare for departure, which cannot now be distant!

*Ubi homines sunt modi sunt.** Habit is the deepest law of human nature. It is our supreme strength; if also, in certain circumstances, our miserablest weakness.—From Stoke to Stowe is as yet a field, all pathless, untrodden: from Stoke where I live, to Stowe where I have to make my merchandises, perform my businesses, consult my heavenly oracles, there is as yet no path or human footprint; and I, impelled by such necessities, must nevertheless undertake the journey. Let me go once, scanning my way with any earnestness of outlook, and successfully arriving, my footprints are an invitation to me a second time to go by the same way. It is easier than any other way: the industry of 'scanning' lies already invested in it for me; I can go this time with less of scanning, or without scanning at all. Nay the very sight of my footprints, what a comfort for me; and in a degree for all my brethren of mankind! The footprints are trodden and retrodden; the path wears ever broader, smoother, into a broad highway where even wheels can run; and many travel it;—till—till the Town of Stowe disappear from that locality (as towns have been known to do), or no merchandising, heavenly oracle, or real business any longer exist for one there: then why should anybody travel the way?—Habit is our primal, fundamental law;* Habit and Imitation, there is nothing more perennial in us than these two. They are the source of all Working and all Apprenticeship, of all Practice and all Learning, in this world.

Yes, the wise man too speaks, and acts, in Formulas; all men do so. In general the more completely cased with Formulas a man may be, the safer, happier is it for him. Thou who, in an All of rotten Formulas, seemest to stand nigh bare, having indignantly shaken off the superannuated rags and unsound callosities of Formulas,— consider how thou too art still clothed! This English Nationality, whatsoever from uncounted ages is genuine and a fact among thy native People, in their words and ways: all this, has it not made for thee a skin or second-skin, adhesive actually as thy natural skin? This thou hast not stript off, this thou wilt never strip off: the humour that thy mother gave thee* has to shew itself through this. A common, or it may be an uncommon Englishman thou art: but good Heavens, what sort of Arab, Chinaman, Jew-Clothesman, Turk, Hindoo, African Mandingo,* wouldst thou have been, *thou* with those mother-qualities of thine!

It strikes me dumb to look over the long series of faces, such as any full Church, Courthouse, London-Tavern Meeting,* or miscellany of men will shew them. Some score or two of years ago, all these were little red-coloured pulpy infants; each of them capable of being kneaded, baked into any social form you chose: yet see now how they are fixed and hardened,—into artisans, artists, clergy, gentry, learned serjeants, unlearned dandies, and can and shall now be nothing else henceforth!

Mark on that nose the colour left by too copious port and viands; to which the profuse cravat with exorbitant breastpin, and the fixed, forward, and as it were menacing glance of the eyes correspond. That is a 'Man of Business;' prosperous manufacturer, house-contractor, engineer, law-manager; his eye, nose, cravat have, in such work and fortune, got such a character: deny him not thy praise, thy pity. Pity him too, the Hard-handed, with bony brow, rudely combed hair, eyes looking out as in labour, in difficulty and uncertainty; rude mouth, the lips coarse, loose, as in hard toil and lifelong fatigue they have got the habit of hanging:—hast thou seen aught more touching than the rude intelligence, so cramped, yet energetic, unsubduable, true, which looks out of that marred visage? Alas, and his poor wife, with her own hands, washed that cotton neckcloth for him, buttoned that coarse shirt, sent him forth cred-itably trimmed as she could. In such imprisonment lives he, for his part; man cannot now deliver him: the red pulpy infant has been baked and fashioned *so*.

Or what kind of baking was it that this other brother-mortal got, which has baked him into the genus Dandy?* Elegant Vacuum; serenely looking down upon all Plenums and Entities, as low and poor to his serene Chimeraship and *Non*entity laboriously attained! Heroic Vacuum; inexpugnable—while purse and present condition of Society hold out; curable by no hellebore. The doom of Fate was, Be thou a Dandy! Have thy eye-glasses, opera-glasses, thy Long-Acre cabs with white-breeched tiger,* thy yawning impassivities, pococu-rantisms;* *fix* thyself in Dandyhood, undeliverable; it is thy doom.——

And all these, we say, were red-coloured infants; of the same pulp and stuff, few years ago; now irretrievably shaped and kneaded as we see! Formulas? There is no mortal extant, out of the depths of Bedlam,* but lives all skinned, thatched, covered over with Formulas; and is, as it were, held in from delirium and the Inane by his Formulas! They are withal the most beneficent, indispensable of human equip-ments: blessed he who has a skin and tissues, so it be a living one, and the heart-pulse everywhere discernible through it. Monachism, Feudalism, with a real King Plantagenet,* with real Abbots Samson, and their other living realities, how blessed!——

Not without a mournful interest have we surveyed that authentic image of a Time now wholly swallowed. Mournful reflections crowd on us; and yet consolatory. How many brave men have lived before Agamemnon!* Here is a brave governor Samson, a man fearing God, and fearing nothing else; of whom as First Lord of the Treasury, as King, Chief Editor, High Priest, we could be so glad and proud; of whom nevertheless Fame has altogether forgotten to make mention! The faint image of him, revived in this hour, is found in the gossip of one poor Monk, and in Nature nowhere else. Oblivion had so nigh swallowed him altogether, even to the echo of his ever having existed. What regiments and hosts and generations of such has Oblivion already swallowed! Their crumbled dust makes up the soil our life-fruit grows on. Said I not, as my old Norse Fathers taught me, The Life-tree Igdrasil,* which waves round thee in this hour, whereof thou in this hour art portion, has its roots down deep in the oldest Death-Kingdoms; and grows; the Three Nornas, or *Times*, Past, Present, Future, watering it from the Sacred Well!

For example, who taught thee to *speak*? From the day when two hairy-naked or fig-leaved Human Figures began, as uncomfortable dummies, anxious no longer to be dumb, but to impart themselves to one another; and endeavoured, with gaspings, gesturings, with unsyl-labled cries, with painful pantomime and interjections, in a very unsuccessful manner,—up to the writing of this present copyright Book, which also is not very successful! Between that day and this, I say, there has been a pretty space of time; a pretty spell of work, which *somebody* has done! Thinkest thou there were no Poets till Dan Chaucer?* No heart burning with a thought, which it could not hold, and had no word for; and needed to shape and coin a word for,—what thou callest metaphor, trope, or the like? For every word we have, there was such a man and poet. The coldest word was once a glowing new metaphor, and bold questionable originality. 'Thy very ATTENTION, does it not mean an *attentio*, a STRETCHING-TO?'* Fancy that act of the mind, which all were conscious of, which none had yet named,—when this new 'poet' first felt bound and driven to name it! His questionable originality, and new glowing metaphor, was found adoptable, intelligible; and remains our name for it to this day.

Literature:—and look at Paul's Cathedral, and the Masonries and Worships and Quasi-Worships that are there; not to speak of Westminster Hall and its wigs! Men had not a hammer to begin with, not a syllabled articulation: they had it all to make;—and they have made it. What thousand thousand articulate, semi-articulate, earnest-stammering *Prayers* ascending up to Heaven, from hut and cell, in many lands, in many centuries, from the fervent kindled souls of innumerable men, each struggling to pour itself forth incompletely as it might, before the incompletest *Liturgy* could be compiled! The Liturgy, or adoptable and generally adopted Set of Prayers and Prayer-Method, was what we can call the Select Adoptabilities, 'Select Beauties'* well-edited (by Œcumenic Councils and other Useful-Knowledge Societies)* from that wide waste imbroglio of Prayers already extant and accumulated, good and bad. The good were found adoptable by men; were gradually got together, well-edited, accredited: the bad, found inappropriate, unadoptable, were gradually forgotten, disused and burnt. It is the way with human things. The first man who, looking with opened soul on this august Heaven and Earth, this Beautiful and Awful, which we name Nature, Universe and such like, the essence of which remains forever UNNAMEABLE;* he who first, gazing into this, fell on his knees awestruck, in silence as is likeliest,—he, driven by inner necessity, the 'audacious original' that he was, had done a thing, too, which all thoughtful hearts saw straightway to be an expressive, altogether adoptable thing! To bow the knee was ever since the attitude of supplication. Earlier than any spoken Prayers, *Litanias*, or *Leitourgias;** the beginning of all Worship,—which needed but a beginning, so rational was it. What a poet he! Yes, this bold original was a successful one withal. The wellhead this one, hidden in the primeval dusks and distances, from whom as from a Nile-source all *Forms of Worship* flow:*—such a Nile-river (somewhat muddy and malarious now!) of Forms of Worship sprang there, and flowed, and flows, down to Puseyism, Rotatory Calabash,* Archbishop Laud at St. Catherine Creed's,* and perhaps lower!

Things rise, I say, in that way. The *Iliad* Poem, and indeed most other poetic, especially epic things, have risen as the Liturgy did.* The great *Iliad* in Greece, and the small *Robin Hood's Garland* in England,* are each, as I understand, the well-edited 'Select Beauties' of an immeasurable waste imbroglio of Heroic Ballads in their respective centuries and countries. Think what strumming of the seven-stringed heroic lyre, torturing of the less heroic fiddle-catgut, in Hellenic Kings' Courts and English wayside Public Houses; and beating of the studious Poetic brain, and gasping here too in the semi-articulate windpipe of Poetic men, before the Wrath of a Divine Achilles, the Prowess of a Will Scarlet or Wakefield Pinder,* could be adequately sung! Honour to you, ye nameless great and greatest ones, ye long-forgotten brave!

Nor was the Statute *De Tallagio non concedendo*,* nor any Statute, Law-method, Lawyer's-wig, much less were the Statute-Book and Four Courts,* with Coke upon Lyttleton and Three Estates of Parliament* in the rear of them, got together without human labour,—mostly forgotten now! From the time of Cain's slaying Abel* by swift head-breakage, to this time of killing your man in Chancery by inches, and slow heart-break for forty years,*—there too is an interval! Venerable Justice herself began by Wild-Justice;* all Law is as a tamed furrowfield, slowly worked out, and rendered arable, from the waste jungle of Club-Law. Valiant Wisdom tilling and draining; escorted by owl-eyed Pedantry, by owlish and vulturish and many other forms of Folly;—the valiant husbandman assiduously tilling; the blind greedy enemy *too* assiduously sowing tares!* It is because there is yet in venerable wigged Justice some wisdom, amid such mountains of wiggeries and folly, that men have not cast her into the River; that she still sits there, like Dryden's Head in the *Battle of the Books*,*—a huge helmet, a huge mountain of greased parchment, of unclean horsehair, first striking the eye, and then in the innermost corner, visible at last, in size as a hazelnut, a real fraction of God's Justice, perhaps not yet unattainable to some, surely still indispensable to all;—and men know not what to do with her! Lawyers were not all pedants, voluminous voracious persons; Lawyers too were poets, were heroes,—or their Law had been past the Nore* long before this time. Their Owlisms, Vulturisms, to an incredible extent, will disappear by and by, their Heroisms only remaining, and the helmet be reduced to something like the size of the head, we hope!—

It is all work and forgotten work, this peopled, clothed, articulate-speaking, high-towered, wide-acred World. The hands of forgotten brave men have made it a World for us; they,—honour to them; they, in *spite* of the idle and the dastard. This English Land, here and now, is the summary of what was found of wise, and noble, and accordant with God's Truth, in all the generations of English Men. Our English Speech is speakable because there were Hero-Poets of our blood and lineage; speakable in proportion to the number of these. This Land of England has its conquerors, possessors, which change from epoch to epoch, from day to day; but its real conquerors, creators, and eternal proprietors are these following, and their representatives if you can find them: all the Heroic Souls that ever were in England, each in their degree; all the men that ever cut a thistle, drained a puddle out of England, contrived a wise scheme in England, did or said a true and valiant thing in England. I tell thee, they had not a hammer to begin with; and yet Wren built St. Paul's:* not an articulated syllable; and yet there have come English Literatures, Elizabethan Literatures, Satanic-School, Cockney-School* and other Literatures;—once more, as in the old time of the *Leitourgia*, a most waste imbroglio and world-wide jungle and jumble; waiting terribly to be 'well-edited,' and 'well-burnt!' Arachne started with forefinger and thumb, and had not even a distaff;* yet thou seest Manchester, and Cotton Cloth, which will shelter naked backs, at twopence an ell.

Work? The quantity of done and forgotten work that lies silent under my feet in this world, and escorts and attends me, and supports and keeps me alive, wheresoever I walk or stand, whatsoever I think or do, gives rise to reflections! Is it not enough, at any rate, to strike the thing called 'Fame' into total silence for a wise man? For fools and unreflective persons, she is and will be very noisy, this 'Fame,' and talks of her 'immortals' and so forth: but if you will consider it, what is she? Abbot Samson was not nothing because nobody *said* anything of him. Or thinkest thou, the Right Honourable Sir Jabesh Windbag* can be made something by Parliamentary Majorities and Leading Articles? Her 'immortals!' Scarcely two hundred years back can Fame recollect articulately at all; and there she but maunders and mumbles. She manages to recollect a Shakspeare or so;* and prates, considerably like a goose, about him;—and in the rear of that, onwards to the birth of Theuth,* to Hengst's Invasion,* and the bosom of Eternity, it was all blank; and the respectable Teutonic Languages, Teutonic Practices, Existences all came of their own accord,* as the grass springs, as the trees grow; no Poet, no work from the inspired heart of a Man needed there; and Fame has not an articulate word to say about it! Or ask her, What, with all conceivable appliances and mnemonics, including apotheosis and human sacrifices among the number, she carries in her head with regard to a Wodan,* even a Moses, or other such? She begins to be uncertain as to what they were, whether spirits or men of mould,—gods, charlatans; begins sometimes to have a misgiving that they were mere symbols, ideas of the mind; perhaps nonentities, and Letters of the Alphabet! She is the noisiest, inarticulately babbling, hissing, screaming, foolishest unmusicalest of fowls that fly; and needs no 'trumpet,' I think, but her own enormous goose-throat,—measuring several degrees of celestial latitude, so to speak. Her 'wings,' in these days, have grown far swifter than ever; but her goose-throat hitherto seems only larger, louder and foolisher than ever. *She* is transitory, futile, a goose-goddess:—if she were not transitory, what would become of us! It is a chief comfort that she forgets us all; all, even to the very Wodans; and grows to consider us, at last, as probably nonentities and Letters of the Alphabet.

Yes, a noble Abbot Samson resigns himself to Oblivion too, feels *it* no hardship, but a comfort; counts it as a still resting-place, from much sick fret and fever and stupidity, which in the night-watches often made his strong heart sigh. Your most sweet voices, making one enormous goose-voice, O Bobus and Company, how can they be a guidance for any Son of Adam? In *silence* of you and the like of you, the 'small still voices'* will speak to him better; in which does lie guidance.

My friend, all speech and rumour is shortlived, foolish, untrue. Genuine WORK alone, what thou workest faithfully, that is eternal, as

the Almighty Founder and World-Builder himself. Stand thou by
that; and let 'Fame' and the rest of it go prating.

> 'Heard are the Voices,
> Heard are the Sages,
> The Worlds and the Ages:
> "Choose well, your choice is
> Brief and yet endless;
>
> Here eyes do regard you,
> In Eternity's stilness;
> Here is all fulness,
> Ye brave, to reward you;
> Work, and despair not." '[1]*

[1] Goethe.

BOOK III.

THE MODERN WORKER.

CHAPTER I.

PHENOMENA.

But, it is said, our religion is gone: we no longer believe in St. Edmund, no longer see the figure of him 'on the rim of the sky,'* minatory or confirmatory! God's absolute Laws, sanctioned by an eternal Heaven and an eternal Hell, have become Moral Philosophies, sanctioned by able computations of Profit and Loss, by weak considerations of Pleasures of Virtue and the Moral Sublime.*

It is even so. To speak in the ancient dialect, we 'have forgotten God;'*—in the most modern dialect and very truth of the matter, we have taken up the Fact of this Universe as it *is not*. We have quietly closed our eyes to the eternal Substance of things, and opened them only to the Shews and Shams of things. We quietly believe this Universe to be intrinsically a great unintelligible Perhaps;* extrinsically, clear enough, it is a great, most extensive Cattlefold and Workhouse, with most extensive Kitchen-ranges, Dining-tables,—whereat he is wise who can find a place! All the Truth of this Universe is uncertain; only the profit and loss of it, the pudding and praise of it, are and remain very visible to the practical man.

There is no longer any God for us! God's Laws are become a Greatest-Happiness Principle,* a Parliamentary Expediency: the Heavens overarch us only as an Astronomical Time-keeper; a butt for Herschel-telescopes* to shoot science at, to shoot sentimentalities at:—in our and old Jonson's dialect, man has lost the *soul* out of him;* and now, after the due period,—begins to find the want of it! This is verily the plague-spot; centre of the universal Social Gangrene,* threatening all modern things with frightful death. To him that will consider it, here is the stem, with its roots and taproot, with its world-wide upas-boughs* and accursed poison-exudations, under which the world lies writhing in atrophy and agony. You touch the focal-centre

of all our disease, of our frightful nosology of diseases,* when you lay
your hand on this. There is no religion; there is no God; man has lost
his soul, and vainly seeks antiseptic salt. Vainly: in killing Kings, in
passing Reform Bills, in French Revolutions, Manchester Insurrections,
is found no remedy. The foul elephantine leprosy,* alleviated for an
hour, reappears in new force and desperateness next hour.

For actually this is *not* the real fact of the world; the world is not
made so, but otherwise!—Truly, any Society setting out from this No-
God hypothesis, will arrive at a result or two. The *Un*veracities,
escorted, each Unveracity of them by its corresponding Misery and
Penalty; the Phantasms, and Fatuities, and ten-years Corn-Law
Debatings, that shall walk the Earth at noonday,—must needs be
numerous! The Universe *being* intrinsically a Perhaps, being too probably an 'infinite Humbug,' why should any minor Humbug astonish us?
It is all according to the order of Nature; and Phantasms riding with
huge clatter along the streets, from end to end of our existence, astonish
nobody. Enchanted St. Ives' Workhouses and Joe-Manton Aristocracies;
giant working Mammonism near strangled in the partridge-nets of
giant-looking Idle Dilettantism,—this, in all its branches, in its thousand thousand modes and figures, is a sight familiar to us.

The Popish Religion, we are told, flourishes extremely in these years;
and is the most vivacious-looking religion to be met with at present.
"*Elle a trois cents ans dans le ventre,*" counts M. Jouffroy; "*c'est pourquoi
je la respecte!*"*—The old Pope of Rome, finding it laborious to kneel so
long while they cart him through the streets to bless the people on
Corpus-Christi Day,* complains of rheumatism; whereupon his Cardinals
consult;—construct him, after some study, a stuffed cloaked figure, of
iron and wood, with wool or baked hair; and place it in a kneeling pos-
ture. Stuffed figure, or rump of a figure; to this stuffed rump he, sitting
at his ease on a lower level, joins, by the aid of cloaks and drapery, his
living head and outspread hands: the rump with its cloaks kneels, the
Pope looks, and holds his hands spread; and so the two in concert bless
the Roman population on *Corpus-Christi* Day, as well as they can.

I have considered this amphibious Pope, with the wool-and-iron
back, with the flesh head and hands; and endeavoured to calculate his
horoscope. I reckon him the remarkablest Pontiff that has darkened
God's daylight, or painted himself in the human retina, for these
several thousand years. Nay, since Chaos first shivered, and 'sneezed,'

at the Arabs say,* with the first shaft of sunlight shot through it, what stranger product was there of Nature and Art working together? Here is a Supreme Priest who believes God to be—What in the name of God *does* he believe God to be?—and discerns that all worship of God is a scenic phantasmagory of wax-candles, organ-blasts, Gregorian Chants, mass-brayings, purple monsignori, wool-and-iron rumps, artistically spread out,—to save the ignorant from worse.

O reader, I say not who are Belial's elect. This poor amphibious Pope too gives loaves to the Poor; has in him more good latent than he is himself aware of. His poor Jesuits, in the late Italian Cholera, were, with a few German Doctors, the only creatures whom dastard terror had not driven mad: they descended fearless into all gulphs and bedlams; watched over the pillow of the dying, with help, with counsel and hope; shone as luminous fixed stars, when all else had gone out in chaotic night:* honour to them! This poor Pope,—who knows what good is in him? In a Time otherwise too prone to forget, he keeps up the mournfulest ghastly memorial of the Highest, Blessedest, which once was; which, in new fit forms, will again partly have to be. Is he not as a perpetual death's-head and cross-bones, with their *Resurgam*,* on the grave of a Universal Heroism,—grave of a Christianity? Such Noblenesses, purchased by the world's best heart's-blood, must not be lost; we cannot afford to lose them, in what confusions soever. To all of us the day will come, to a few of us it has already come, when no mortal, with his heart yearning for a 'Divine Humility,' or other 'Highest form of Valour,'* will need to look for it in death's-heads, but will see it round him in here and there a beautiful living head.

Besides there is in this poor Pope, and his practice of the Scenic Theory of Worship, a frankness which I rather honour. Not half and half, but with undivided heart does *he* set about worshipping by stage-machinery; as if there were now, and could again be, in Nature no other. He will ask you, What other? Under this my Gregorian Chant, and beautiful wax-light Phantasmagory, kindly hidden from you is an Abyss, of black Doubt, Scepticism, nay Sansculottic Jacobinism;* an Orcus that has no bottom. Think of that. 'Groby Pool* *is* thatched with pancakes,'—as Jeannie Deans's Innkeeper defied it to be! The Bottomless of Scepticism, Atheism, Jacobinism, behold, it is thatched over, hidden from your despair, by stage-properties judiciously arranged. This stuffed rump of mine saves not me only from rheumatism, but you also from what other *isms*! In this your Life-pilgrimage Nowhither, a fine Squallacci marching-music,* and Gregorian Chant, accompanies you, and the hollow Night of Orcus is well hid!

Yes truly, few men that worship by the rotatory Calabash of the Calmucks* do it in half so great, frank or effectual a way. Drury-lane, it is said, and that is saying much, might learn from him in the dressing of parts, in the arrangement of lights and shadows. He is the greatest Play-actor that at present draws salary in this world. Poor Pope; and I am told he is fast growing bankrupt too;* and will, in a measurable term of years (a great way *within* the 'three hundred'*), not have a penny to make his pot boil!* His old rheumatic back will then get to rest; and himself and his stage-properties sleep well in Chaos forevermore.

Or, alas, why go to Rome for Phantasms walking the streets? Phantasms, ghosts, in this midnight hour, hold jubilee, and screech and jabber; and the question rather were, What high Reality any-where is yet awake? Aristocracy has become Phantasm-Aristocracy,* no longer able to *do* its work, not in the least conscious that it has any work longer to do. Unable, totally careless to *do* its work; careful only to clamour for the *wages* of doing its work,—nay for higher, and *palpably* undue wages, and Corn-Laws and *increase* of rents; the old rate of wages not being adequate now! In hydra-wrestle, giant '*Millo*-cracy' so-called,* a real giant, though as yet a blind one and but half-awake, wrestles and wrings in choking nightmare, 'like to be strangled in the partridge-nets of Phantasm-Aristocracy,' as we said, which fancies itself still to be a giant. Wrestles, as under nightmare, till it do awaken; and gasps and struggles thousandfold, we may say, in a truly painful manner, through all fibres of our English Existence, in these hours and years! Is our poor English Existence wholly becoming a Nightmare; full of mere Phantasms?—

The Champion of England, cased in iron or tin, rides into West-minster Hall, 'being lifted into his saddle with little assistance,'* and there asks, If in the four quarters of the world, under the cope of Heaven, is any man or demon that dare question the right of this King? Under the cope of Heaven no man makes intelligible answer,—as several men ought already to have done. Does not this Champion too know the world; that it is a huge Imposture, and bottomless Inanity, thatched over with bright cloth and other ingenious tissues? Him let us leave there, questioning all men and demons.

Him we have left to his destiny; but whom else have we found? From this the highest apex of things, downwards through all strata and breadths, how many fully awakened Realities have we fallen in with:—alas, on the contrary, what troops and populations of Phantasms, not God-Veracities but Devil-Falsities, down to the very lowest stratum,—which now, by such superincumbent weight of Unveracities, lies enchanted in St. Ives' Workhouses, broad enough, helpless enough! You will walk in no public thoroughfare or remotest byway of English Existence but you will meet a man, an interest of men, that has given up hope in the Everlasting, True,* and placed its hope in the Temporary, half or wholly False. The Honourable Member complains unmusically that there is 'devil's-dust' in Yorkshire cloth.* Yorkshire cloth,—why, the very Paper I now write on is made, it seems, partly of plaster-lime well-smoothed, and obstructs my writing!* You are lucky if you can find now any good Paper,—any work really *done*; search where you will, from highest Phantasm apex to lowest Enchanted basis!

Consider, for example, that great Hat seven-feet high, which now perambulates London Streets;* which my Friend Sauerteig regarded justly as one of our English notabilities; "the topmost point as yet," said he, "would it were your culminating and returning point, to which English Puffery* has been observed to reach!"—The Hatter in the Strand of London, instead of making better felt-hats than another, mounts a huge lath-and-plaster Hat, seven-feet high, upon wheels; sends a man to drive it through the streets; hoping to be saved *thereby*. He has not attempted to *make* better hats, as he was appointed by the Universe to do, and as with this ingenuity of his he could very probably have done; but his whole industry is turned to *persuade* us that he has made such! He too knows that the Quack has become God. Laugh not at him, O reader; or do not laugh only. He has ceased to be comic; he is fast becoming tragic. To me this all-deafening blast of Puffery, of poor Falsehood grown necessitous, of poor Heart-Atheism fallen now into Enchanted Workhouses, sounds too surely like a Doom's-blast! I have to say to myself in old dialect: "God's blessing is not written on all this; His curse is written on all this!" Unless perhaps the Universe *be* a chimera;—some old totally deranged eightday clock,* dead as brass; which the Maker, if there ever was any Maker, has long ceased to meddle with?—To my Friend Sauerteig this poor seven-feet Hat-manufacturer, as the topstone of English Puffery, was very notable.

Alas, that we natives note him little, that we view him as a thing of course, is the very burden of the misery.* We take it for granted, the most rigorous of us, that all men who have made anything are expected and entitled to make the loudest possible proclamation of it; call on a discerning public to reward them for it. Every man his own trumpeter; that is, to a really alarming extent, the accepted rule. Make loudest possible proclamation of your Hat: true proclamation if that will do; if that will not do, then false proclamation,—to such extent of falsity as will serve your purpose; as will not seem too false to be credible!—I answer, once for all, that the fact is not so. Nature requires no man to make proclamation of his doings and hat-makings; Nature forbids all men to make such. There is not a man or hat-maker born into the world but feels, at first, that he is degrading himself if he speak of his excellencies and prowesses, and supremacy in his craft: his inmost heart says to him, "Leave thy friends to speak of these; if possible, thy enemies to speak of these; but at all events, thy friends!" He feels that he is already a poor braggart; fast hastening to be a falsity and speaker of the Untruth.

Nature's Laws, I must repeat, are eternal: her small still voice, speaking from the inmost heart of us, shall not, under terrible penalties, be disregarded. No one man can depart from the truth without damage to himself; no one million of men; no Twenty-seven Millions of men. Shew me a Nation fallen everywhere into this course, so that each expects it, permits it to others and himself, I will shew you a Nation travelling with one assent on the broad way.* The broad way, however many Banks of England, Cotton-mills and Duke's Palaces it may have! Not at happy Elysian fields, and everlasting crowns of victory, earned by silent Valour, will this Nation arrive; but at precipices, devouring gulphs, if it pause not. Nature has appointed happy fields, victorious laurel-crowns; but only to the brave and true: *Un*nature, what we call Chaos, holds nothing in it but vacuities, devouring gulfs. What are Twenty-seven Millions, and their unanimity? Believe them not: the Worlds and the Ages, God and Nature and All Men say otherwise.

'Rhetoric all this?' No, my brother, very singular to say, it is Fact all this. Cocker's Arithmetic* is not truer. Forgotten in these days, it is old as the foundations of the Universe, and will endure till the Universe cease. It is forgotten now; and the first mention of it puckers thy sweet countenance into a sneer: but it will be brought to mind again,—unless indeed the Law of Gravitation chance to cease, and men find that they *can* walk on vacancy. Unanimity of the Twenty-seven Millions will do nothing: walk not thou with them; fly from them as for thy life. Twenty-seven Millions travelling on such courses, with gold jingling in every pocket, with vivats heaven-high, are incessantly advancing, let me again remind thee, towards the *firm-land's end*,—towards the end and extinction of what Faithfulness, Veracity, real Worth, was in their way of life. Their noble ancestors have fashioned for them a 'life-road;'—in how many thousand senses, this! There is not an old wise Proverb on their tongue, an honest Principle articulated in their hearts into utterance, a wise true method of doing and despatching any work or commerce of men, but helps yet to carry them forward. Life is still possible to them, because all is not yet Puffery, Falsity, Mammon-worship and Unnature; because somewhat is yet Faithfulness, Veracity and Valour. With a certain very considerable finite quantity of Unveracity and Phantasm, social life is still possible; not with an infinite quantity! Exceed your certain quantity, the seven-feet Hat, and all things upwards to the very Champion cased in tin, begin to reel and flounder,—in Manchester Insurrections, Chartisms, Sliding-scales; the Law of Gravitation not forgetting to act. You advance incessantly towards the land's end; you are, literally enough, 'consuming the way.'* Step after step, Twenty-seven Million unconscious men;—till you are *at* the land's end; till there is not Faithfulness enough among you any more: and the next step now is lifted *not* over land, but into air, over ocean deeps and roaring abysses:—unless perhaps the Law of Gravitation have forgotten to act?

O, it is frightful when a whole Nation, as our Fathers used to say, has 'forgotten God;'* has remembered only Mammon, and what Mammon leads to! When your self-trumpeting Hatmaker is the emblem of almost all makers, and workers, and men, that make anything,—from soul-overseerships, body-overseerships, epic poems, acts of parliament, to hats and shoe-blacking! Not one false man but does uncountable mischief: how much, in a generation or two, will Twenty-seven Millions, mostly false, manage to accumulate? The sum of it, visible in every street, market-place, senate-house, circulating-library, cathedral, cotton-mill, and union-workhouse, fills one *not* with a comic feeling!

CHAPTER II.

GOSPEL OF MAMMONISM.

READER, even Christian Reader as thy title goes, hast thou any notion of Heaven and Hell? I rather apprehend, not. Often as the words are on our tongue, they have got a fabulous or semi-fabulous character for most of us, and pass on like a kind of transient similitude, like a sound signifying little.*

Yet it is well worth while for us to know, once and always, that they are not a similitude, nor a fable nor semi-fable; that they are an everlasting highest fact! "No Lake of Sicilian or other sulphur burns now anywhere in these ages,"* sayest thou? Well, and if there did not! Believe that there does not; believe it if thou wilt, nay hold by it as a real increase, a rise to higher stages, to wider horizons and empires. All this has vanished, or has not vanished; believe as thou wilt as to all this. But that an Infinite of Practical Importance, speaking with strict arithmetical exactness, an *Infinite*, has vanished or can vanish from the Life of any Man: this thou shalt not believe! O brother, the Infinite of Terror, of Hope, of Pity, did it not at any moment disclose itself to thee, indubitable, unnameable? Came it never, like the gleam of *preter*natural eternal Oceans, like the voice of old Eternities, farsounding through thy heart of hearts? Never? Alas, it was not thy Liberalism then; it was thy Animalism!* The Infinite is more sure than any other fact. But only men can discern it; mere building beavers, spinning arachnes, much more the predatory vulturous and vulpine species, do not discern it well!—

'The word Hell,' says Sauerteig, 'is still frequently in use among the English People: but I could not without difficulty ascertain what they meant by it. Hell generally signifies the Infinite Terror, the thing a man *is* infinitely afraid of, and shudders and shrinks from, struggling with his whole soul to escape from it. There is a Hell therefore, if you will consider, which accompanies man, in all stages of his history, and religious or other development: but the Hells of men and Peoples differ notably. With Christians it is the infinite terror of being found guilty before the Just Judge. With old Romans, I conjecture, it was the terror not of Pluto,* for whom probably they cared little, but of doing unworthily, doing unvirtuously, which was their word for un*man*fully. And now what is it, if you pierce through his Cants, his oft-repeated Hearsays, what he calls his Worships and so forth,—what is it that the modern English soul does in very truth dread infinitely, and contemplate with entire despair? What *is* his Hell; after all these reputable, oft-repeated Hearsays, what is it? With hesitation, with astonishment, I pronounce it to be: The terror of "Not succeeding;"* of not making money, fame, or some other figure in the world,—chiefly of not making money! Is not that a somewhat singular Hell?'

Yes, O Sauerteig, it is very singular. If we do not 'succeed,' where is the use of us? We had better never have been born. "Tremble intensely," as our friend the Emperor of China says:* *there* is the black Bottomless of Terror; what Sauerteig calls the 'Hell of the English!'— But indeed this Hell belongs naturally to the Gospel of Mammonism, which also has its corresponding Heaven. For there *is* one Reality among so many Phantasms; about one thing we are entirely in earnest: The making of money. Working Mammonism does divide the world with idle game-preserving Dilettantism;—thank Heaven that there is even a Mammonism, *any*thing we are in earnest about! Idleness is worst, Idleness alone is without hope: work earnestly at anything, you will by degrees learn to work at almost all things. There is endless hope in work, were it even work at making money.

True, it must be owned, we for the present, with our Mammon-Gospel, have come to strange conclusions. We call it a Society; and go about professing openly the totalest separation, isolation. Our life is not a mutual helpfulness; but rather, cloaked under due Laws-of-war, named 'fair-competition' and so forth, it is a mutual hostility. We have profoundly forgotten everywhere that *Cash-payment* is not the sole relation of human beings;* we think, nothing doubting, that *it* absolves and liquidates all engagements of man. "My starving workers?" answers the rich Mill-owner: "Did not I hire them fairly in the market? Did I not pay them, to the last sixpence, the sum covenanted for? What have I to do with them more?"—Verily Mammon-worship is a melancholy creed. When Cain, for his own behoof, had killed Abel, and was questioned, "Where is thy brother?" he too made answer, "Am I my brother's keeper?"* Did I not pay my brother *his* wages, the thing he had merited from me?

O sumptuous Merchant-Prince, illustrious game-preserving Duke, is there no way of 'killing' thy brother but Cain's rude way! 'A good man by the very look of him, by his very presence with us as a fellow wayfarer in this Life-pilgrimage, *promises* so much:'* wo to him if he forget all such promises, if he never know that they were given! To a deadened soul, seared with the brute Idolatry of Sense, to whom going to Hell is equivalent to not making money, all 'promises,' and moral duties, that cannot be pleaded for in Courts of Requests,* address themselves in vain. Money he can be ordered to pay, but nothing more. I have not heard in all Past History, and expect not to hear in all Future History, of any Society anywhere under God's Heaven supporting itself on such Philosophy. The Universe is not made so; it is made otherwise than so. The man or nation of men that thinks it is made so, marches forward nothing doubting, step after step; but marches—whither we know! In these last two centuries of Atheistic Government* (near two centuries now, since the blessed restoration of his Sacred Majesty and Defender of the Faith, Charles Second), I reckon that we have pretty well exhausted what of 'firm earth' there was for us to march on;—and are now, very ominously, shuddering, reeling, and let us hope trying to recoil, on the cliff's edge!—

For out of this that we call Atheism come so many other *isms* and falsities, each falsity with its misery at its heels!—A SOUL is not like wind (*spiritus*, or breath) contained within a capsule; the ALMIGHTY MAKER is not like a Clockmaker that once, in old immemorial ages, having *made* his Horologe of a Universe, sits ever since and sees it go! Not at all. Hence comes Atheism; come, as we say many other *isms;* and as the sum of all, comes Valetism, the *reverse* of Heroism; sad root of all woes whatsoever. For indeed, as no man ever saw the above-said wind-element enclosed within its capsule, and finds it at bottom more deniable than conceivable; so too he finds, in spite of Bridgewater Bequests,* your Clockmaker Almighty an entirely questionable affair, a deniable affair;—and accordingly denies it, and along with it so much else. Alas, one knows not what and how much else! For the faith in an Invisible, Unnameable, Godlike, present everywhere in all that we see and work and suffer, is the essence of all faith whatsoever; and that once denied, or still worse, asserted with lips only, and out of bound prayerbooks only, what other thing remains believable? That Cant well-ordered is marketable Cant; that Heroism means gas-lighted Histrionism; that seen with 'clear eyes' (as they call Valet-eyes), no man is a Hero, or ever was a Hero, but all men are Valets and Varlets.* The accursed practical quintessence of all sorts of Unbelief! For if there be now no Hero, and the Histrio himself begin to be seen into, what hope is there for the seed of Adam here below? We are the doomed everlasting prey of the Quack; who, now in this guise, now in that, is to filch us, to pluck and eat us, by such modes as are convenient for him. For the modes and guises I care little. The Quack once inevitable, let him come swiftly, let him pluck and eat me;—swiftly, that I may at least have done with him; for in his Quack-world I can have no wish to linger. Though he slay me, yet will I despise him.* Though he conquer nations, and have all the Flunkeys of the Universe shouting at his heels, yet will I know well that *he* is an Inanity; that for him and his there is no continuance appointed, save only in Gehenna and the Pool.* Alas, the Atheist world, from its utmost summits of Heaven and Westminster Hall, downwards through poor seven-feet Hats and 'Unveracities fallen hungry,' down to the lowest cellars and neglected hunger-dens of it, is very wretched.

One of Dr. Alison's Scotch facts struck us much.[1] A poor Irish Widow, her husband having died in one of the Lanes of Edinburgh, went forth with her three children, bare of all resource, to solicit help from the Charitable Establishments of that City. At this Charitable Establishment and then at that, she was refused; referred from one to the other, helped by none;—till she had exhausted them all; till her strength and heart failed her: she sank down in typhus-fever; died, and infected her Lane with fever, so that 'seventeen other persons' died of fever there in consequence.* The humane Physician asks thereupon, as with a heart too full for speaking, Would it not have been *economy* to help this poor Widow? She took typhus-fever, and killed seventeen of you!—Very curious. The forlorn Irish Widow applies to her fellow-creatures, as if saying, "Behold I am sinking, bare of help: ye must help me! I am your sister, bone of your bone; one God made us: ye must help me!" They answer, "No; impossible: thou art no sister of ours." But she proves her sisterhood; her typhus-fever kills *them*: they actually were her brothers, though denying it! Had human creature ever to go lower for a proof?

For, as indeed was very natural in such case, all government of the Poor by the Rich has long ago been given over to Supply-and-demand, Laissez-faire and such like, and universally declared to be 'impossible.' "You are no sister of ours; what shadow of proof is there? Here are

[1] Observations on the Management of the Poor in Scotland: By William Pulteney Alison M.D. (Edinburgh, 1840).

our parchments, our padlocks, proving indisputably our money-safes to be *ours*, and you to have no business with them. Depart! It is impossible!"—Nay, what wouldst thou thyself have us do? cry indignant readers. Nothing, my friends,—till you have got a soul for yourselves again. Till then all things are 'impossible.' Till then I cannot even bid you buy, as the old Spartans would have done, two-pence worth of powder and lead, and compendiously shoot to death this poor Irish Widow:* even that is 'impossible' for you. Nothing is left but that she prove her sisterhood by dying, and infecting you with typhus. Seventeen of you lying dead will not deny such proof that she *was* flesh of your flesh; and perhaps some of the living may lay it to heart.

'Impossible:' of a certain two-legged animal with feathers, it is said if you draw a distinct chalk-circle round him, he sits imprisoned, as if girt with the iron ring of Fate; and will die there, though within sight of victuals,—or sit in sick misery there, and be fatted to death. The name of this poor two-legged animal is—Goose; and they make of him, when well fattened, *Pâté de foie gras*, much prized by some!*

CHAPTER III.

GOSPEL OF DILETTANTISM.

BUT after all, the Gospel of Dilettantism,* producing a Governing Class who do not govern, nor understand in the least that they are bound or expected to govern, is still mournfuller than that of Mammonism. Mammonism, as we said, at least works; this goes idle. Mammonism has seized some portion of the message of Nature to man; and seizing that, and following it, will seize and appropriate more and more of Nature's message: but Dilettantism has missed it wholly. 'Make money:' that will mean withal, 'Do work in order to make money.' But, 'Go gracefully idle in Mayfair,'* what does or can that mean? An idle, game-preserving and even corn-lawing Aristocracy, in such an England as ours: has the world, if we take thought of it, ever seen such a phenomenon till very lately? Can it long continue to see such?

Accordingly the impotent, insolent Donothingism in Practice, and Saynothingism in Speech, which we have to witness on that side of our affairs, is altogether amazing. A Corn-Law demonstrating itself openly, for ten years or more, with 'arguments' to make the angels, and some other classes of creatures, weep! For men are not ashamed to rise in Parliament and elsewhere, and speak the thing they do *not* think. 'Expediency,' 'Necessities of Party,' &c. &c.! It is not known that the Tongue of Man is a sacred organ; that Man himself is definable in Philosophy as an 'Incarnate *Word;*'*—the Word not there, you have no Man there either, but a Phantasm instead! In this way it is that Absurdities may live long enough,—still walking and talking for themselves, years and decades after the brains are quite out!* How are 'the knaves and dastards'* ever to be got 'arrested' at that rate?—

"No man in this fashionable London of yours," friend Sauerteig would say, "speaks a plain word to me. Every man feels bound to be something more than plain; to be pungent withal, witty, ornamental. His poor fraction of sense has to be perked into some epigrammatic shape, that it may prick into me;—perhaps (this is the commonest) to be topsyturvied, left standing on its head, that I may remember it the better! Such grinning inanity is very sad to the soul of man. Human faces should not grin on one like masks; they should look on one like faces! I love honest laughter, as I do sunlight; but not dishonest: most kinds of dancing too; but the St.-Vitus kind not at all! A fashionable wit, *ach Himmel*, if you ask, Which, he or a Death's-head, will be the cheerier company for me, pray send *not* him!"

Insincere Speech, truly, is the prime material of insincere Action. Action hangs, as it were, *dissolved* in Speech, in Thought whereof Speech is the shadow; and precipitates itself therefrom. The kind of Speech in a man betokens the kind of Action you will get from him. Our Speech, in these modern days, has become amazing. Johnson complained, "Nobody speaks in earnest, Sir; there is no serious conversation."* To us all serious speech of men, as that of Seventeenth-Century Puritans, Twelfth-Century Catholics, German Poets of this Century, has become jargon, more or less insane. Cromwell was mad and a quack; Anselm, Becket, Goethe, *ditto ditto*.

Perhaps few narratives in History or Mythology are more significant than that Moslem one, of Moses and the Dwellers by the Dead Sea.* A tribe of men dwelt on the shores of that same Asphaltic Lake;* and having forgotten, as we are all too prone to do, the inner facts of Nature, and taken up with the falsities and outer semblances of it, were fallen into sad conditions,—verging indeed towards a certain far deeper Lake.

Whereupon it pleased kind Heaven to send them the Prophet Moses, with an instructive word of warning, out of which might have sprung 'remedial measures' not a few. But no: the men of the Dead Sea discerned, as the valet-species always does in heroes or prophets, no comeliness in Moses; listened with real tedium to Moses, with light grinning, or with splenetic sniffs and sneers, affecting even to yawn; and signified, in short, that they found him a humbug, and even a bore. Such was the candid theory these men of the Asphalt Lake formed to themselves of Moses, That probably he was a humbug, that certainly he was a bore.

Moses withdrew; but Nature and her rigorous veracities did not withdraw. The men of the Dead Sea, when we next went to visit them, were all 'changed into Apes;'[1] sitting on the trees there, grinning now in the most *un*affected manner; gibbering and chattering *complete* nonsense; finding the whole Universe now a most indisputable Humbug! The Universe has *become* a Humbug to these Apes who thought it one! There they sit and chatter, to this hour: only, I think, every Sabbath there returns to them a bewildered half-consciousness, half-reminiscence; and they sit, with their wizzened smoke-dried visages, and such an air of supreme tragicality as Apes may; looking out, through those blinking smoke-bleared eyes of theirs, into the wonderfulest universal smoky Twilight and undecipherable disordered Dusk of Things; wholly an Uncertainty, Unintelligibility, they and it; and for commentary thereon, here and there an unmusical chatter or mew:—truest, tragicalest Humbug conceivable by the mind of man or ape!* They made no use of their souls; and *so* have lost them. Their worship on the Sabbath now is to roost there, with unmusical screeches, and half-remember that they had souls.

Didst thou never, O Traveller, fall in with parties of this tribe? Meseems they are grown somewhat numerous in our day.

CHAPTER IV.

HAPPY.

ALL work, even cotton-spinning, is noble; work is alone noble: be that here said and asserted once more. And in like manner too all

---

[1] Sale's Koran (*Introduction*).

dignity is painful; a life of ease is not for any man, nor for any god. The life of all gods figures itself to us as a Sublime Sadness,—earnestness of Infinite Battle against Infinite Labour. Our highest religion is named the 'Worship of Sorrow.'* For the son of man there is no noble crown, well worn, or even ill worn, but is a Crown of Thorns!*— These things, in spoken words, or still better, in felt instincts alive in every heart, were once well known.

Does not the whole wretchedness, the whole *Atheism* as I call it, of man's ways, in these generations, shadow itself for us in that unspeakable Life-philosophy of his: The pretension to be what he calls 'happy?' Every pitifulest whipster* that walks within a skin has his head filled with the notion that he is, shall be, or by all human and divine laws ought to be, 'happy.' His wishes, the pitifulest whipster's, are to be fulfilled for him; his days, the pitifulest whipster's, are to flow on in ever-gentle current of enjoyment, impossible even for the gods. The prophets preach to us, Thou shalt be happy; thou shalt love pleasant things, and find them. The people clamour, Why have we not found pleasant things?

We construct our theory of Human Duties, not on any Greatest-Nobleness Principle, never so mistaken; no, but on a Greatest-Happiness Principle. 'The word *Soul* with us, as in some Slavonic dialects, seems to be synonymous with *Stomach*.'* We plead and speak, in our Parliaments and elsewhere, not as from the Soul, but from the Stomach;—wherefore, indeed, our pleadings are so slow to profit. We plead not for God's Justice; we are not ashamed to stand clamouring and pleading for our own 'interests,' our own rents and trade-profits; we say, They are the 'interests' of so many; there is such an intense desire for them in us! We demand Free-Trade, with much just vociferation and benevolence, That the poorer classes, who are terribly ill-off at present, may have cheaper New-Orleans bacon.* Men ask on Free-trade platforms, How can the indomitable spirit of Englishmen be kept up without plenty of bacon? We shall become a ruined Nation!—Surely, my friends, plenty of bacon is good and indispensable: but, I doubt, you will never get even bacon by aiming only at that. You are men, not animals of prey,—well-used or ill-used! Your Greatest-Happiness Principle seems to me fast becoming a rather unhappy one.—What if we should cease babbling about 'happiness,' and leave *it* resting on its own basis, as it used to do!—

A gifted Byron rises in his wrath;*—and feeling too surely that he for his part is not 'happy,' declares the same in very violent language, as a piece of news that may be interesting. It evidently has surprised him much. One dislikes to see a man and poet reduced to proclaim on the streets such tidings: but on the whole, as matters go, that is not the most dislikable. Byron speaks the *truth* in this matter; Byron's large audience indicates how true it is felt to be.

'Happy,' my brother? First of all, what difference is it whether thou art happy or not! Today becomes Yesterday so fast, all Tomorrows become Yesterdays; and then there is no question whatever of the 'happiness,' but quite another question. Nay, thou hast such a sacred pity left at least for thyself, thy very pains once gone over into Yesterday become joys to thee. Besides, thou knowest not what heavenly blessedness and indispensable sanative virtue was in them; thou shalt only know it after many days, when thou art wiser!—A benevolent old Surgeon sat once in our company, with a Patient fallen sick by gourmandising, whom he had just, too briefly in the Patient's judgment, been examining. The foolish Patient still at intervals continued to break in on our discourse, which rather promised to take a philosophic turn: "But I have lost my appetite," said he, objurgatively, with a tone of irritated pathos; "I have no appetite; I can't eat!"—"My dear fellow," answered the Doctor in mildest tone, "it isn't of the slightest consequence;"*—and continued his philosophical discoursings with us!

Or does the reader not know the history of that Scottish Iron Misanthrope? The inmates of some town-mansion, in those Northern parts, were thrown into the fearfulest alarm by indubitable symptoms of a ghost inhabiting the next house, or perhaps even the partition-wall! Ever at a certain hour, with preternatural gnarring, growling and screeching, which attended as running bass, there began, in a horrid, semi-articulate, unearthly voice, this song: "Once I was hap-hap-happy, but now I'm *mees*-erable!* Clack-clack-clack, gnarr-r-r, whuz-z: Once I was hap-hap-happy, but now I'm *mees*-erable!"—Rest, rest, perturbed spirit;*—or indeed, as the good old Doctor said: My dear fellow, it isn't of the slightest consequence! But no; the perturbed spirit could not rest; and to the neighbours, fretted, affrighted, or at least insufferably bored by him, it *was* of such consequence that they had to go and examine in his haunted chamber. In his haunted chamber, they find that the perturbed spirit is an unfortunate—Imitator of Byron? No, is an unfortunate rusty

Meat-jack,* gnarring and creaking with rust and work; and this, in Scottish dialect, is *its* Byronian musical Life-philosophy, sung according to ability!

Truly, I think the man who goes about pothering* and uproaring for his 'happiness,'—pothering, and were it ballot-boxing, poem-making, or in what way soever fussing and exerting himself,—he is not the man that will help us to get our 'knaves and dastards arrested!' No; he rather is on the way to increase the number,—by at least one unit and *his* tail! Observe too that this is all a modern affair; belongs not to the old heroic times, but to these dastard new times. 'Happiness our being's end and aim'* is at bottom, if we will count well, not yet two centuries old in the world.

The only happiness a brave man ever troubled himself with asking much about was, happiness enough to get his work done. Not "I can't eat!" but "I can't work!" that was the burden of all wise complaining among men. It is, after all, the one unhappiness of a man. That he cannot work; that he cannot get his destiny as a man fulfilled. Behold, the day is passing swiftly over, our life is passing swiftly over; and the night cometh wherein no man can work.* The night once come, our happiness, our unhappiness,—it is all abolished; vanished, clean gone; a thing that has been: 'not of the slightest consequence' whether we were happy as eupeptic Curtis,* as the fattest pig of Epicurus,* or unhappy as Job with potsherds,* as musical Byron with Giaours* and sensibilities of the heart; as the unmusical Meat-jack with hard labour and rust! But our work,—behold that is not abolished, that has not vanished: our work, behold, it remains, or the want of it remains;—for endless Times and Eternities, remains; and that is now the sole question with us forevermore! Brief brawling Day, with its noisy phantasms, its poor paper-crowns tinsel-gilt, is gone; and divine everlasting Night, with her star-diadems, with her silences and her veracities, is come! What hast thou done, and how? Happiness, unhappiness: all that was but the *wages* thou hadst; thou hast spent all that in sustaining thyself hitherward; not a coin of it remains with thee, it is all spent, eaten: and now thy work, where is thy work? Swift, out with it, let us see thy work!

Of a truth, if man were not a poor hungry dastard, and even much of a blockhead withal, he would cease criticising his victuals to such extent; and criticise himself rather, what he does with his victuals!

CHAPTER V.

THE ENGLISH.

AND yet, with all thy theoretic platitudes, what a depth of practical sense in thee, great England! A depth of sense, of justice, and courage; in which, under all emergencies and world-bewilderments, and under this most complex of emergencies we now live in, there is still hope, there is still assurance!

The English are a dumb people.* They can do great acts, but not describe them. Like the old Romans, and some few others, *their* Epic Poem is written on the Earth's surface: England her Mark! It is complained that they have no artists: one Shakspeare indeed; but for Raphael only a Reynolds; for Mozart nothing but a Mr. Bishop:* not a picture, not a song. And yet they did produce one Shakspeare: consider how the element of Shakspearean melody does lie imprisoned in their nature; reduced to unfold itself in mere Cotton-mills, Constitutional Governments, and such like;—all the more interesting when it does become visible, as even in such unexpected shapes it succeeds in doing! Goethe spoke of the Horse,* how impressive, almost affecting it was that an animal of such qualities should stand obstructed so; its speech nothing but an inarticulate neighing, its handiness mere *hoof*-iness, the fingers all constricted, tied together, the finger-nails coagulated into a mere hoof, shod with iron. The more significant, thinks he, are those eye-flashings of the generous noble quadruped; those prancings, curvings of the neck clothed with thunder.*

A Dog of Knowledge has *free* utterance; but the Warhorse is almost mute, very far from free! It is even so. Truly, your freest utterances are not by any means always the best: they are the worst rather; the feeblest, trivialest; their meaning prompt, but small, ephemeral. Commend me to the silent English, to the silent Romans. Nay, the silent Russians too I believe to be worth something: are they not even now drilling, under much obloquy, an immense semi-barbarous half-world from Finland to Kamtschatka, into rule, subordination, civilisation,—really in an old Roman fashion, speaking no word about it; quietly hearing all manner of vituperative Able Editors speak! While your ever-talking, ever-gesticulating French,* for example, what are they at this moment drilling?—Nay, of all animals, the freest of utterance, I should judge, is the genus *Simia:* go into the Indian woods, say all

Travellers, and look what a brisk, adroit, unresting Ape-population it is!

The spoken Word, the written Poem, is said to be an epitome of the man; how much more the done Work. Whatsoever of morality and of intelligence; what of patience, perseverance, faithfulness, of method, insight, ingenuity, energy; in a word, whatsoever of Strength the man had in him will lie written in the work he does. To work: why, it is to try himself against Nature, and her everlasting unerring Laws; these will tell a true verdict as to the man. So much of virtue and of faculty did *we* find in him; so much and no more! He had such capacity of harmonising himself with *me* and my unalterable ever-veracious Laws; of cooperating and working as *I* bade him;—and has prospered, and has not prospered, as you see!—Working as great Nature bade him: does not that mean virtue of a kind; nay, of all kinds? Cotton can be spun and sold, Lancashire operatives can be got to spin it, and at length one has the woven webs and sells them, by following Nature's regulations in that matter: by not following Nature's regulations, you have them not. You have them not;—there is no Cotton-web to sell: Nature finds a bill against you;* your 'Strength' is not Strength, but Futility! Let faculty be honoured, so far as it is faculty. A man that can succeed in working is to me always a man.

How one loves to see the burly figure of him, this thick-skinned, seemingly opaque, perhaps sulky, almost stupid Man of Practice, pitted against some light adroit Man of Theory, all equipt with clear logic, and able anywhere to give you Why for Wherefore! The adroit Man of Theory, so light of movement, clear of utterance, with his bow full-bent and quiver full of arrow-arguments,—surely he will strike down the game, transfix everywhere the heart of the matter; triumph everywhere as he proves that he shall and must do? To your astonishment, it turns out oftenest No. The cloudy-browed, thick-soled, opaque Practicality, with no logic-utterance, in silence mainly, with here and there a low grunt or growl, has in him what transcends all logic-utterance: a Congruity with the Unuttered! The Speakable, which lies atop, as a superficial film, or outer skin, is his or is not his: but the Doable, which reaches down to the World's centre, you find him there!

The rugged Brindley* has little to say for himself; the rugged Brindley, when difficulties accumulate on him, retires silent, 'generally

to his bed;' retires 'sometimes for three days together to his bed, that
he may be in perfect privacy there,' and ascertain in his rough head
how the difficulties can be overcome. The ineloquent Brindley, behold
he *has* chained seas together; his ships do visibly float over valleys,
invisibly through the hearts of mountains; the Mersey and the Thames,
the Humber and the Severn have shaken hands: Nature most audibly
answers, Yea! The man of Theory twangs his full-bent bow:* Nature's
Fact ought to fall stricken, but does not: his logic-arrow glances from
it, as from a scaly dragon, and the obstinate Fact keeps walking its
way. How singular! At bottom, you will have to grapple closer with
the dragon; take it home to you, by real faculty, not by seeming
faculty; try whether you are stronger or it is stronger. Close with it,
wrestle it: sheer obstinate toughness of muscle; but much more, what
we call toughness of heart, which will mean persistance hopeful and
even desperate, unsubduable patience, composed candid openness,
clearness of mind: all this shall be 'strength' in wrestling your dragon;
the whole man's real strength is in this work, we shall get the measure
of him here.

Of all the Nations in the world at present we English are the stupidest in speech, the wisest in action. As good as a 'dumb' Nation,
I say, who cannot speak, and have never yet spoken,—spite of the
Shakspeares and Miltons who shew us what possibilities there are!—
O Mr. Bull,* I look in that surly face of thine with a mixture of pity
and laughter, yet also with wonder and veneration. Thou complainest
not, my illustrious friend; and yet I believe the heart of thee is full of
sorrow, of unspoken sadness, seriousness,—profound melancholy (as
some have said) the basis of thy being.* Unconsciously, for thou speakest
of nothing, this great Universe is great to thee. Not by levity of floating, but by stubborn force of swimming, shalt thou make thy way. The
Fates sing of thee that thou shalt many times be thought an ass and
a dull ox, and shalt with a godlike indifference believe it. My friend,—and
it is all untrue, nothing ever falser in point of fact! Thou art of those
great ones whose greatness the small passer-by does not discern. Thy
very stupidity is wiser than their wisdom. A grand *vis inertiæ** is in
thee; how many grand qualities unknown to small men! Nature alone
knows thee, acknowledges the bulk and strength of thee: thy Epic, unsung
in words, is written in huge characters on the face of this Planet,—
sea-moles, cotton-trades, railways, fleets and cities; Indian Empires,
Americas, New-Hollands,*—legible throughout the Solar System!

But the dumb Russians too, as I said, they, drilling all wild Asia and wild Europe into military rank and file, a terrible yet hitherto a prospering enterprise, are still dumber. The old Romans also could not *speak*, for many centuries:—not till the world was theirs; and so many speaking Greekdoms, their logic-arrows all spent, had been absorbed and abolished. The logic-arrows, how they glanced futile from obdurate thick-skinned Facts; Facts to be wrestled down only by the real vigour of Roman thews!*—As for me, I honour, in these loud-babbling days, all the Silent rather. A grand Silence that of Romans;—nay the grandest of all is it not that of the gods! Even Triviality, Imbecillity, that can sit silent, how respectable is it in comparison! The 'talent of silence' is our fundamental one. Great honour to him whose Epic is a melodious hexameter Iliad,*—not a jingling Sham-Iliad, nothing true in it but the hexameters and forms merely. But still greater honour, if his Epic be a mighty Empire slowly built together, a mighty Series of Heroic Deeds,—a mighty Conquest over Chaos; *which* Epic the 'Eternal Melodies' have, and must have, informed and dwelt in, as *it* sung itself! There is no mistaking that latter Epic. Deeds are greater than Words. Deeds have such a life, mute but undeniable, and grow as living trees and fruit-trees do; they people the vacuity of Time, and make it green and worthy. Why should the oak prove logically that it ought to grow, and will grow? Plant it, try it; what gifts of diligent judicious assimilation and secretion it has, of progress and resistance, of *force* to grow, will then declare themselves. My much-honoured, illustrious, extremely inarticulate Mr. Bull!—

Ask Bull his spoken opinion of any matter,—oftentimes the force of dulness can no farther go. You stand silent, incredulous, as over a platitude that borders on the Infinite. The man's Churchisms, Dissenterisms, Puseyisms, Benthamisms, College Philosophies,* Fashionable Literatures, are unexampled in this world. Fate's prophecy is fulfilled; you call the man an ox and an ass. But set him once to work,—respectable man! His spoken sense is next to nothing, nine-tenths of it palpable *non*sense: but his unspoken sense, his inner silent feeling of what is true, what does agree with fact, what is doable and what is not doable,—this seeks its fellow in the world. A terrible worker; irresistible against marshes, mountains, impediments, disorder, incivilisation; everywhere vanquishing disorder, leaving it behind him as method and order. He 'retires to his bed three days,' and considers!

Nay withal, stupid as he is, our dear John,—ever, after infinite tumblings, and spoken platitudes innumerable from barrel-heads and parliament-benches, he does settle down somewhere about the just conclusion; you are certain that his jumblings and tumblings will end, after years or centuries, in the stable equilibrium. Stable equilibrium, I say; centre-of-gravity lowest;—not the unstable, with centre-of-gravity highest, as I have known it done by quicker people! For indeed do but jumble and tumble sufficiently, you avoid that worst fault, of settling with your centre-of-gravity highest; your centre-of-gravity is certain to come lowest, and to stay there. If slowness, what we in our impatience call 'stupidity,' be the price of stable equilibrium over unstable, shall we grudge a little slowness? Not the least admirable quality of Bull is, after all, that of remaining insensible to logic; holding out for considerable periods, ten years or more, as in this of the Corn-Laws, after all arguments and shadow of arguments have faded away from him, till the very urchins on the street titter at the arguments he brings. Logic,—Λολική, the 'Art of Speech,'*—does indeed speak so and so; clear enough: nevertheless Bull still shakes his head; will see whether nothing else *illogical*, not yet 'spoken,' not yet able to be 'spoken,' do not lie in the business, as there so often does!—My firm belief is, that, finding himself now enchanted, hand-shackled, foot-shackled, in Poor-Law Bastilles and elsewhere, he will retire three days to his bed, and *arrive* at a conclusion or two! His three-years 'total stagnation of trade,'* alas, is not that a painful enough 'lying in bed to consider himself?' Poor Bull!

Bull is a born Conservative; for this too I inexpressibly honour him. All great Peoples are conservative;* slow to believe in novelties; patient of much error in actualities; deeply and forever certain of the greatness that is in LAW, in Custom once solemnly-established, and now long recognised as just and final.—True, O Radical Reformer, there is no Custom that can, properly speaking, be final; none. And yet thou seest *Customs* which, in all civilised countries, are accounted final;* nay, under the Old-Roman name of *Mores*, are accounted *Morality*, Virtue, Laws of God himself. Such, I assure thee, not a few of them are; such almost all of them once were. And greatly do I respect the solid character,—a blockhead, thou wilt say; yes, but a well-conditioned blockhead, and the best-conditioned,—who esteems all 'Customs once solemnly acknowledged' to be ultimate, divine, and the rule for a man to walk by, nothing doubting, not inquiring farther.

What a time of it had we, were all men's life and trade still, in all parts of it, a problem, a hypothetic seeking, to be settled by painful Logics and Baconian Inductions!* The Clerk in Eastcheap cannot spend the day in verifying his Ready-Reckoner; he must take it as verified, true and indisputable; or his Book-keeping by Double Entry will stand still. "Where is your Posted Ledger?" asks the Master at night.— "Sir," answers the other, "I was verifying my Ready-Reckoner, and find some errors. The Ledger is—!"—Fancy such a thing!

True, all turns on your Ready-Reckoner being moderately correct,— being *not* insupportably incorrect! A Ready-Reckoner which has led to distinct entries in your Ledger such as these: '*Creditor* an English People by fifteen hundred years of good Labour; and *Debtor* to lodging in enchanted Poor-Law Bastilles: *Creditor* by conquering the largest Empire the Sun ever saw; and *Debtor* to Donothingism and "Impossible" written on all departments of the government thereof: *Creditor* by mountains of gold ingots earned; and *Debtor* to No Bread purchasable by them:'—*such* Ready-Reckoner, methinks, is beginning to be suspect; nay is ceasing, and has ceased, to be suspect! Such Ready-Reckoner is a Solecism in Eastcheap;* and must, whatever be the press of business, and will and shall be rectified a little. Business can go on no longer with *it*. The most Conservative English People, thickest-skinned, most patient of Peoples, is driven alike by its Logic and its Unlogic, by things 'spoken,' and by things not yet spoken or very speakable, but only felt and very unendurable, to be wholly a Reforming People.* Their Life as it is has ceased to be longer possible for them.

Urge not this noble silent People; rouse not the Berserkir-rage* that lies in them! Do you know their Cromwells, Hampdens, their Pyms and Bradshaws?* Men very peaceable, but men that can be made very terrible! Men who, like their old Teutsch Fathers in Agrippa's days,* 'have a soul that despises death;' to whom 'death,' compared with falsehoods and injustices, is light;—'in whom there is a rage unconquerable by the immortal gods!'* Before this, the English People have taken very preternatural-looking Spectres by the beard, saying virtually, "And if thou *wert* 'preternatural?' Thou with thy 'divine-rights' grown diabolic wrongs? Thou,—not even 'natural;' decapitable; totally extinguishable!" '— — Yes, just so godlike as this People's patience was, even so godlike will and must its impatience be. Away, ye scandalous Practical Solecisms, children actually of the Prince of

Darkness; ye have near broken our hearts; we can and will endure you no longer! Begone, we say; depart, while the play is good! By the Most High God, whose sons and born missionaries true men are, ye shall not continue here! You and we have become incompatible; can inhabit one house no longer. Either you must go, or we. Are ye ambitious to try *which* it shall be?

O my Conservative friends, who still specially name and struggle to approve yourselves 'Conservative,' would to Heaven I could persuade you of this world-old fact, than which Fate is not surer, That Truth and Justice alone are *capable* of being 'conserved' and preserved! The thing which is unjust, which is *not* according to God's Law, will you, in a God's Universe, try to conserve that? It is so old, say you? Yes, and the hotter haste ought *you*, of all others, to be in to let it grow no older! If but the faintest whisper in your hearts intimate to you that it is not fair,—hasten, for the sake of Conservatism itself, to probe it rigorously, to cast it forth at once and forever if guilty. How will or can you preserve *it*, the thing that is not fair? 'Impossibility' a thousand-fold is marked on that. And ye call yourselves Conservatives, Aristocracies:—ought not honour and nobleness of mind, if they had departed from all the Earth elsewhere, to find their last refuge with you? Ye unfortunate!

The bough that is dead shall be cut away, for the sake of the tree itself. Old? Yes, it is too old. Many a weary winter has it swung and creaked there, and gnawed and fretted, with its dead wood, the organic substance and still living fibre of this good tree; many a long summer has its ugly naked brown defaced the fair green umbrage; every day it has done mischief, and that only: off with it, for the tree's sake, if for nothing more; let the Conservatism that would preserve cut *it* away. Did no wood-forester apprise you that a dead bough with its dead root left sticking there is extraneous, poisonous; is as a dead iron spike, some horrid rusty ploughshare driven into the living substance;—nay is far worse; for in every windstorm ('commercial crisis' or the like), it frets and creaks, jolts itself to and fro, and cannot lie quiet as your dead iron spike would!

If I were the Conservative Party of England (which is another bold figure of speech), I would not for a hundred thousand pounds an hour allow those Corn-Laws to continue! Potosi and Golconda* put together would not purchase my assent to them. Do you count what treasuries of bitter indignation they are laying up for you in

every just English heart? Do you know what questions, not as to
Corn-prices and Sliding-scales alone, they are *forcing* every reflective
Englishman to ask himself? Questions insoluble, or hitherto unsolved;
deeper than any of our Logic-plummets hitherto will sound: questions deep enough,—which it were better that we did not name even
in thought! You are forcing us to think of them, to begin uttering
them. The utterance of them is begun; and where will it be ended,
think you? When two millions of one's brother-men sit in Workhouses,
and five millions, as is insolently said, 'rejoice in potatoes,'* there are
various things that must be begun, let them end where they can.

CHAPTER VI.

TWO CENTURIES.

THE Settlement effected by our 'Healing Parliament'* in the Year of
Grace 1660, though accomplished under universal acclamations from
the four corners of the British Dominions,* turns out to have been
one of the mournfulest that ever took place in this land of ours. It
called and thought itself a Settlement of brightest hope and fulfilment, bright as the blaze of universal tar-barrels and bonfires could
make it: and we find it now, on looking back on it with the insight
which trial has yielded, a Settlement as of despair. Considered well, it
was a Settlement to govern henceforth without God, with only some
decent Pretence of God.

Governing by the Christian Law of God had been found a thing of
battle, convulsion, confusion, an infinitely difficult thing: wherefore
let us now abandon it, and govern only by so much of God's Christian
Law as—as may prove quiet and convenient for us.* What is the end
of Government? To guide men in the way wherein they should go:
towards their true good in this life, the portal of infinite good in a life
to come? To guide men in such way, and ourselves in such way, as the
Maker of men, whose eye is upon us, will sanction at the Great
Day?—Or alas, perhaps at bottom *is* there no Great Day, no sure
outlook of any life to come; but only this poor life, and what of taxes,
felicities, Nell-Gwyns* and entertainments, we can manage to muster
here? In that case, the end of Government will be, To suppress all
noise and disturbance, whether of Puritan preaching, Cameronian

psalm-singing, thieves'-riot, murder, arson, or what noise soever, and—be careful that supplies do not fail! A very notable conclusion, if we will think of it, and not without an abundance of fruits for us. Oliver Cromwell's body hung on the Tyburn-gallows,* as the type of Puritanism found futile, inexecutable, execrable,—yes, that gallows-tree has been a fingerpost into very strange country indeed. Let earnest Puritanism die; let decent Formalism, whatsoever cant it be or grow to, live! We have had a pleasant journey in that direction; and are—arriving at our inn?

To support the Four Pleas of the Crown,* and keep Taxes coming in: in very sad seriousness, has not this been, ever since, even in the best times, almost the one admitted end and aim of Government? Religion, Christian Church, Moral Duty; the fact that man had a soul at all; that in man's life there was any eternal truth or justice at all,—has been as good as left quietly out of sight. Church indeed,—alas, the endless talk and struggle we have had of High-Church, Low-Church, Church-Extension, Church-in-Danger:* we invite the Christian reader to think whether it has not been a too miserable screech-owl phantasm of talk and struggle, as for a 'Church,'—which one had rather not define at present!

But now in these godless two centuries, looking at England and her efforts and doings, if we ask, What of England's doings the Law of Nature had accepted, Nature's King had actually furthered and pronounced to have truth in them,—where is our answer? Neither the 'Church' of Hurd and Warburton,* nor the Anti-Church of Hume and Paine;* not in any shape the Spiritualism of England: all this is already seen, or beginning to be seen, for what it is; a thing that Nature does *not* own. On the one side is dreary Cant, with a *reminiscence* of things noble and divine; on the other is but acrid Candour, with a *prophecy* of things brutal, infernal. Hurd and Warburton are sunk into the sere and yellow leaf;* no considerable body of true-seeing men looks thitherward for healing: the Paine-and-Hume Atheistic theory, of 'things well let alone,'* with Liberty, Equality and the like, is also in these days declaring itself naught, unable to keep the world from taking fire.

The theories and speculations of both these parties, and, we may say, of all intermediate parties and persons, prove to be things which the Eternal Veracity did not accept; things superficial, ephemeral, which already a near Posterity, finding them already dead and brown-leafed, is about to suppress and forget. The Spiritualism of England, for those godless years, is, as it were, all forgettable. Much has been written: but the perennial Scriptures of Mankind have had small accession: from all English Books, in rhyme or prose, in leather binding or in paper wrappage, how many verses have been added to these? Our most melodious Singers have sung as from the throat outwards: from the inner Heart of Man, from the great Heart of Nature,* through no Pope or Philips,* has there come any tone. The Oracles have been dumb.* In brief, the Spoken Word of England has not been true. The Spoken Word of England turns out to have been trivial; of short endurance; not valuable, not available as a Word, except for the passing day. It has been accordant with transitory Semblance; discordant with eternal Fact. It has been unfortunately not a Word, but a Cant; a helpless involuntary Cant, nay too often a cunning voluntary one: either way, a very mournful Cant; the Voice not of Nature and Fact, but of something other than these.

With all its miserable shortcomings, with its wars, controversies, with its trades-unions, famine-insurrections,—it is her Practical Material Work alone that England has to shew for herself! This, and hitherto almost nothing more; yet actually this. The grim inarticulate veracity of the English People, unable to speak its meaning in words, has turned itself silently on things; and the dark powers of Material Nature have answered, Yes, this at least is true, this is not false! So answers Nature. Waste desert-shrubs of the Tropical swamps have become Cotton-trees; and here, under my furtherance, are verily woven shirts,—hanging unsold, undistributed, but capable to be distributed, capable to cover the bare backs of my children of men. Mountains, old as the Creation, I have permitted to be bored through: bituminous fuel-stores, the wreck of forests that were green a million years ago,—I have opened them from my secret rock-chambers, and they are yours, ye English. Your huge fleets, steamships, do sail the sea; huge Indias do obey you; from huge *New* Englands and Antipodal Australias, comes profit and traffic to this Old England of mine! So answers Nature. The Practical Labour of England is *not* a chimerical Triviality: it is a Fact, acknowledged by all the Worlds; which no man and no demon will contradict. It is, very audibly, though very inarticulately as yet, the one God's Voice we have heard in these two atheistic centuries.

And now to observe with what bewildering obscurations and impediments all this as yet stands entangled, and is yet intelligible to no man! How, with our gross Atheism, we hear it not to be the Voice of God to us, but regard it merely as a Voice of earthly Profit-and-Loss. And have a Hell in England,—the Hell of not making money. And coldly see the all-conquering valiant Sons of Toil sit enchanted, by the million, in their Poor-Law Bastille, as if this were Nature's Law;—mumbling to ourselves some vague janglement of Laissez-faire, Supply-and-demand, Cash-payment the one nexus of man to man: Free-trade, Competition, and Devil take the hindmost, our latest Gospel yet preached!

As if, in truth, there were no God of Labour; as if godlike Labour and brutal Mammonism were convertible terms. A serious, most earnest Mammonism grown Midas-eared; an unserious Dilettantism, earnest about nothing, grinning with inarticulate incredulous incredible jargon about all things, as the *enchanted* Dilettanti do by the Dead Sea! It is mournful enough, for the present hour; were there not an endless hope in it withal. Giant LABOUR, truest emblem there is of God the World-Worker, Demiurgus, and Eternal Maker; noble LABOUR, which is yet to be the King of this Earth, and sit on the highest throne,—staggering hitherto like a blind irrational giant, hardly allowed to have his common place on the street-pavements; idle Dilettantism. Dead-Sea Apism, crying out, "Down with him; he is dangerous!"

Labour must become a seeing rational giant, with a *soul* in the body of him, and take his place on the throne of things,—leaving his Mammonism, and several other adjuncts, on the lower steps of said throne.

CHAPTER VII.

OVER-PRODUCTION.

BUT what will reflective readers say of a Governing Class, such as ours, addressing its Workers with an indictment of 'Over-production!'* Over-production: runs it not so? "Ye miscellaneous, ignoble manufacturing individuals, ye have produced too much! We accuse you of making above two-hundred thousand shirts for the bare backs of mankind. Your trousers too, which you have made, of fustian, of cassimere, of Scotch-plaid, of jane, nankeen* and woollen broadcloth, are they not manifold? Of hats for the human head, of shoes for the human foot, of stools to sit on, spoons to eat with—Nay, what say we hats or shoes? You produce gold-watches, jewellries, silver-forks, and epergnes, commodes, chiffoniers, stuffed sofas—Heavens, the Commercial Bazaar* and multitudinous Howel-and-Jameses* cannot contain you. You have produced, produced;—he that seeks your indictment, let him look around.* Millions of shirts, and empty pairs of breeches, hang there in judgment against you.* We accuse you of over-producing: you are criminally guilty of producing shirts, breeches, hats, shoes and commodities, in a frightful overabundance. And now there is a glut, and your operatives cannot be fed!"

Never surely, against an earnest Working Mammonism was there brought, by Game-preserving aristocratic Dilettantism, a stranger accusation, since this world began. My lords and gentlemen,—why, it was *you* that were appointed, by the fact and by the theory of your position on the Earth, to 'make and administer Laws,'—that is to say, in a world such as ours, to guard against 'gluts;' against honest operatives, who had done their work, remaining unfed! I say, *you* were appointed to preside over the Distribution and Apportionment of the Wages of Work done; and to see well that there went no labourer without his hire, were it of money-coins, were it of hemp gallows-ropes: that function was yours, and from immemorial time has been; yours, and as yet no other's. These poor shirt-spinners have forgotten much, which by the virtual unwritten law of their position they should have remembered: but by any written recognised law of their position, what have they forgotten? They were set to make shirts. The Community with all its voices commanded them, saying, "Make shirts;"—and there the shirts are! Too many shirts? Well, that is a novelty, in this intemperate Earth, with its nine-hundred millions of bare backs! But the Community commanded you, saying, "See that the shirts are well apportioned, that our Human Laws be emblem of God's Laws;"—and where is the apportionment? Two million shirtless or ill-shirted workers sit enchanted in Workhouse Bastilles,* five million more (according to some) in Ugolino Hunger-cellars;* and for remedy, you say,—what say you?—"Raise *our* rents!"* I have not in my time heard any stranger speech, not even on the Shores of the Dead Sea.* You continue addressing those poor shirt-spinners and over-producers in really a *too* triumphant manner:

"Will you bandy accusations, will you accuse *us* of over-production? We take the Heavens and the Earth to witness that we have produced nothing at all. Not from us proceeds this frightful overplus of shirts. In the wide domains of created Nature circulates no shirt or thing of our producing. Certain fox-brushes nailed upon our stable-door, the fruit of fair audacity at Melton Mowbray;* these we have produced, and they are openly nailed up there. He that accuses us of producing, let him shew himself, let him name what and when. We are innocent of producing;—ye ungrateful, what mountains of things have we not, on the contrary, had to 'consume,' and make away with!* Mountains of those your heaped manufactures, wheresoever edible or wearable, have they not disappeared before us, as if we had the talent of ostriches, of cormorants, and a kind of divine faculty to eat? Ye ungrateful!—and did you not grow under the shadow of our wings? Are not your filthy mills built on these fields of ours;* on this soil of England, which belongs to—whom think you? And we shall not offer you our own wheat at the price that pleases us, but that partly pleases you? A precious notion! What would become of you, if we chose, at any time, to decide on growing no wheat more?"

Yes, truly, *here* is the ultimate rock-basis of all Corn-Laws; whereon, at the bottom of much arguing, they rest, as securely as they can: What would become of you, if we decided, some day, on growing no more wheat at all? If we chose to grow only partridges henceforth, and a modicum of wheat for our own uses? Cannot we do what we like with our own?*—Yes, indeed! For my share, if I could melt Gneiss Rock,* and create Law of Gravitation; if I could stride out to the Doggerbank,* some morning, and striking down my trident there into the mud-waves, say, "Be land, be fields, meadows, mountains and fresh-rolling streams!" by Heaven, I should incline to have the letting of *that* land in perpetuity, and sell the wheat of it, or burn the wheat of it, according to my own good judgment! My Corn-Lawing friends, you affright me.

To the 'Millo-cracy' so-called, to the Working Aristocracy, steeped too deep in mere ignoble Mammonism, and as yet all unconscious of its noble destinies, as yet but an irrational or semi-rational giant, struggling to awake some soul in itself,—the world will have much to say, reproachfully, reprovingly, admonishingly. But to the Idle Aristocracy, what will the world have to say? Things painful and not pleasant!

To the man who *works*, who attempts, in never so ungracious barbarous a way, to get forward with some work, you will hasten out with furtherances, with encouragements, corrections; you will say to him: "Welcome; thou art ours; our care shall be of thee." To the idler, again, never so gracefully going idle, coming forward with never so many parchments, you will not hasten out; you will sit still, and be disinclined to rise. You will say to him: "Not welcome, O complex Anomaly; would thou hadst staid out of doors: for who of mortals knows what to do with thee? Thy parchments: yes, they are old, of venerable yellowness; and we too honour parchment, old-established settlements, and venerable use and wont. Old parchments in very truth:—yet on the whole, if thou wilt remark, they are young to the Granite Rocks, to the Groundplan of God's Universe! We advise thee to put up thy parchments; to go home to thy place, and make no needless noise whatever. Our heart's wish is to save thee: yet there as thou art, hapless Anomaly, with nothing but thy yellow parchments, noisy futilities, and shotbelts and fox-brushes, who of gods or men can avert dark Fate? Be counselled, ascertain if no work exist for thee on God's Earth; if thou find no commanded-duty there but that of going gracefully idle? Ask, inquire earnestly, with a half-frantic earnestness; for the answer means Existence or Annihilation to thee. We apprise thee of the world-old fact, becoming sternly disclosed again in these days, That he who cannot work in this Universe cannot get existed in it: had he parchments to thatch the face of the world, these, combustible fallible sheepskin, cannot avail him. Home, thou unfortunate; and let us have at least no noise from thee!"

Suppose the unfortunate Idle Aristocracy, as the unfortunate Working one has done, were to 'retire three days to *its* bed,'* and consider itself there, what o'clock it had become?—

How have we to regret not only that men have 'no religion,' but that they have next to no reflection; and go about with heads full of mere extraneous noises, with eyes wide-open but visionless,—for most part, in the somnambulist state!

CHAPTER VIII.

UNWORKING ARISTOCRACY.

IT is well said, 'Land is the right basis of an Aristocracy;'* whoever possesses the Land, he, more emphatically than any other, is the

Governor, Viceking of the people on the Land. It is in these days as it was in those of Henry Plantagenet and Abbot Samson; as it will in all days be. The Land is *Mother* of us all; nourishes, shelters, gladdens, lovingly enriches us all; in how many ways, from our first wakening to our last sleep on her blessed mother-bosom, does she, as with blessed mother-arms, enfold us all!

The Hill I first saw the Sun rise over, when the Sun and I and all things were yet in their auroral hour, who can divorce me from it? Mystic, deep as the world's centre, are the roots I have struck into my Native Soil; no *tree* that grows is rooted so. From noblest Patriotism to humblest industrial Mechanism; from highest dying for your country, to lowest quarrying and coal-boring for it, a Nation's Life depends upon its Land. Again and again we have to say, there can be no true Aristocracy but must possess the Land.

Men talk of 'selling' Land. Land, it is true, like Epic Poems and even higher things, in such a trading world, has to be presented in the market for what it will bring, and as we say be 'sold:' but the notion of 'selling,' for certain bits of metal, the *Iliad* of Homer, how much more the *Land* of the World-Creator, is a ridiculous impossibility! We buy what is saleable of it; nothing more was ever buyable. Who can, or could, sell it to us? Properly speaking, the Land belongs to these two: To the Almighty God; and to all His Children of Men that have ever worked well on it, or that shall ever work well on it. No generation of men can or could, with never such solemnity and effort, sell Land on any other principle: it is not the property of any generation, we say, but that of all the past generations that have worked on it, and of all the future ones that shall work on it.

Again, we hear it said, The soil of England, or of any country, is properly worth nothing, except 'the labour bestowed on it.'* This, speaking even in the language of Eastcheap, is not correct. The rudest space of country equal in extent to England, could a whole English Nation, with all their habitudes, arrangements, skills, with whatso-ever they do carry within the skins of them, and cannot be stript of, suddenly take wing, and alight on it,—would be worth a very consid-erable thing! Swiftly, within year and day, this English Nation, with its multiplex talents of ploughing, spinning, hammering, mining, road-making and trafficking, would bring a handsome value out of such a space of country. On the other hand, fancy what an English Nation, once 'on the wing,' could have done with itself, had there been simply no soil, not even an inarable one, to alight on? Vain all its talents for ploughing, hammering, and whatever else; there is no Earth-room for this Nation with its talents: this Nation will have to *keep* hovering on the wing, dolefully shrieking to and fro; and perish piecemeal; burying itself, down to the last soul of it, in the waste unfirmamented seas. Ah yes, soil, with or without ploughing, is the gift of God.* The soil of all countries belongs evermore, in a very considerable degree, to the Almighty Maker! The last stroke of labour bestowed on it is not the making of its value, but only the increasing thereof.

It is very strange, the degree to which these truisms are forgotten in our days; how, in the ever-whirling chaos of Formulas, we have quietly lost sight of Fact,—which it is so perilous not to keep forever in sight. Fact, if we do not see it, will make us *feel* it by and by!—From much loud controversy and Corn-Law debating there rises, loud though inarticulate, once more in these years, this very question among others, Who made the Land of England? Who made it, this respectable English Land, wheat-growing, metalliferous, carboniferous, which will let readily hand over head for seventy millions or upwards,* as it here lies: who did make it?—"We!" answer the much-*consuming* Aristocracy; "We!" as they ride in, moist with the sweat of Melton Mowbray: "It is we that made it; or are the heirs, assigns and representatives of those who did!"—My brothers, You? Everlasting honour to you, then; and Corn-Laws as many as you will, till your own deep stomachs cry Enough, or some voice of human pity for our famine bids you Hold! Ye are as gods,* that can create soil. Soil-creating gods there is no withstanding. They have the might to sell wheat at what price they list; and the right, to all lengths, and famine-lengths,—if they be pitiless infernal gods! Celestial gods, I think, would stop short of the famine-price; but no infernal nor any kind of god can be bidden stop! ——Infatuated mortals, into what questions are you driving every thinking man in England?

I say, you did *not* make the Land of England; and, by the possession of it, you *are* bound to furnish guidance and governance to England!* That is the law of your position on this God's-Earth; an everlasting act of Heaven's Parliament, not repealable in St. Stephen's* or elsewhere! True government and guidance; not no-government and Laissez-faire; how much less, *mis*-government and Corn-Law! There is not an imprisoned Worker looking out from these Bastilles but appeals, very audibly in Heaven's High Courts, against you, and me, and everyone who is not imprisoned, "Why am I here?"* His appeal is audible in Heaven; and will become audible enough on Earth too, if it remain unheeded here. His appeal is against you, foremost of all; you stand in the front-rank of the accused; you, by the very place you hold, have first of all to answer him and Heaven!

What looks maddest, miserablest in these mad and miserable Corn-Laws is independent altogether of their 'effect on wages,' their effect on 'increase of trade,' or any other such effect: it is the continual maddening proof they protrude into the faces of all men, that our Governing Class, called by God and Nature and the inflexible law of Fact, either to do something towards governing, or to die and be abolished,—have not yet learned even to sit still and do no mischief! For no Anti-Corn-Law League* yet asks more of them than this;— Nature and Fact, very imperatively, asking so much more of them. Anti-Corn-Law League asks not, Do something; but, Cease your destructive misdoing, Do ye nothing!

Nature's message will have itself obeyed: messages of mere Free-Trade, Anti-Corn-Law League and Laissez-faire, will then need small obeying!—Ye fools, in name of Heaven, work, work, at the Ark of Deliverance* for yourselves and us, while hours are still granted you! No: instead of working at the Ark, they say, "We cannot get our hands kept rightly warm;" and *sit obstinately burning the planks*. No madder spectacle at present exhibits itself under this Sun.

The Working Aristocracy; Mill-owners, Manufacturers, Commanders of Working Men: alas, against them also much shall be brought in accusation; much,—and the freest Trade in Corn, total abolition of Tariffs, and uttermost 'Increase of Manufactures' and 'Prosperity of Commerce,' will permanently mend no jot of it. The Working Aristocracy must strike into a new path; must understand that money alone is *not* the representative either of man's success in the world, or of man's duties to man; and reform their own selves from top to bottom, if they wish England reformed. England will not be habitable long, unreformed.

The Working Aristocracy—Yes, but on the threshold of all this, it is again and again to be asked, What of the Idle Aristocracy? Again and again, what shall we say of the Idle Aristocracy, the Owners of the Soil of England; whose recognised function is that of handsomely consuming the rents of England, shooting the partridges of England, and as an agreeable amusement (if the purchase-money and other conveniences serve), dilettante-ing in Parliament and Quarter-Sessions for England? We will say mournfully, in the presence of Heaven and Earth,—that we stand speechless, stupent, and know not what to say! That a class of men entitled to live sumptuously on the marrow of the earth; permitted simply, nay entreated, and as yet entreated in vain, to do nothing at all in return, was never heretofore seen on the face of this Planet. That such a class is transitory, exceptional, and, unless Nature's Laws fall dead, cannot continue. That it has continued now a moderate while; has, for the last fifty years, been rapidly attaining its state of perfection. That it will have to find its duties and do them; or else that it must and will cease to be seen on the face of this Planet, which is a Working one, not an Idle one.

Alas, alas, the Working Aristocracy, admonished by Trades-unions, Chartist conflagrations,* above all by their own shrewd sense kept in perpetual communion with the fact of things, will assuredly reform themselves, and a working world will still be possible:—but the fate of the Idle Aristocracy, as one reads its horoscope hitherto in Corn-Laws and such like, is an abyss that fills one with despair. Yes, my rosy fox-hunting brothers, a terrible *Hippocratic look** reveals itself (God knows, not to my joy) through those fresh buxom countenances of yours. Through your Corn-Law Majorities, Sliding-Scales, Protecting-Duties, Bribery-Elections* and triumphant Kentish-fire,* a thinking eye discerns ghastly images of ruin, too ghastly for words; a handwriting as of MENE, MENE.* Men and brothers, on your Sliding-scale you seem sliding, and to have slid,—you little know whither! Good God! did not a French Donothing Aristocracy, hardly above half a century ago, declare in like manner, and in its featherhead believe in like manner, "We cannot exist, and continue to dress and parade ourselves, on the just rent of the soil of France; but we must have farther payment than rent of the soil, we must be exempted from taxes too,"—we must have a Corn-Law to extend our rent? This was in 1789: in four years more—Did you look into the Tanneries of Meudon,* and the long-naked making for themselves breeches of human skins! May the merciful Heavens avert the omen; may we be wiser, that so we be less wretched.

A High Class without duties to do is like a tree planted on precipices; from the roots of which all the earth has been crumbling.

Nature owns no man who is not a Martyr withal. Is there a man who pretends to live luxuriously housed up; screened from all work, from want, danger, hardship, the victory over which is what we name work;—he himself to sit serene, amid down-bolsters and appliances, and have all his work and battling done by other men? And such man calls himself a *noble*-man? His fathers worked for him, he says; or successfully gambled for him: here *he* sits; professes, not in sorrow but in pride, that he and his have done no work, time out of mind. It is the law of the land, and is thought to be the law of the Universe, that he, alone of recorded men, shall have no task laid on him, except that of eating his cooked victuals, and not flinging himself out of window. Once more I will say, there was no stranger spectacle ever shewn under this Sun. A veritable fact in our England of the Nineteenth Century. His victuals he does eat: but as for keeping in the inside of the window,—have not his friends, like me, enough to do? Truly, looking at his Corn-Laws, Game-Laws,* Chandos-Clauses,* Bribery-Elections and much else, you do shudder over the tumbling and plunging he makes, held back by the lappelles and coatskirts; only a thin fence of window-glass before him,—and in the street mere horrid iron spikes! My sick brother, as in hospital-maladies men do, thou dreamest of Paradises and Eldorados,* which are far from thee. 'Cannot I do what I like with my own?'* Gracious Heaven, my brother, this that thou seest with those sick eyes is no firm Eldorado, and Corn-Law Paradise of Donothings, but a dream of thy own fevered brain. It is a glass-window, I tell thee, so many stories from the street; where are iron spikes and the law of gravitation!

What is the meaning of nobleness, if this be 'noble?' In a valiant suffering for others, not in a slothful making others suffer for us, did nobleness ever lie. The chief of men is he who stands in the van of men; fronting the peril which frightens back all others; which, if it be not vanquished, will devour the others. Every noble crown is, and on Earth will forever be, a crown of thorns. The Pagan Hercules, why was he accounted a hero? Because he had slain Nemean Lions, cleansed Augean Stables,* undergone Twelve Labours only not too heavy for a god. In modern, as in ancient and all societies, the Aristocracy, they that assume the functions of an Aristocracy, doing them or not, have taken the post of honour; which is the post of difficulty, the post of danger,—of death, if the difficulty be not overcome. *Il faut payer de* *sa vie.** Why was our life given us, if not that we should manfully give it? Descend, O Donothing Pomp; quit thy down-cushions; expose thyself to learn what wretches feel,* and how to cure it! The Czar of Russia became a dusty toiling shipwright; worked with his axe in the Docks of Saardam;* and his aim was small to thine. Descend thou: undertake this horrid 'living chaos of Ignorance and Hunger'* weltering round thy feet; say, "I will heal it, or behold I will die foremost in it." Such is verily the law. Everywhere and everywhen a man has to '*pay* with his life;' to do his work, as a soldier does, at the expense of life. In no Piepowder earthly Court* can you sue an Aristocracy to do its work, at this moment: but in the Higher Court, which even *it* calls 'Court of Honour,' and which is the Court of Necessity withal, and the eternal Court of the Universe, in which all Fact comes to plead, and every Human Soul is an apparitor,*—the Aristocracy is answerable, and even now answering, *there*.

Parchments? Parchments are venerable: but they ought at all times to represent, as near as they by possibility can, the writing of the Adamant Tablets; otherwise they are not so venerable! Benedict the Jew in vain pleaded parchments; his usuries were too many. The King said, "Go to, for all thy parchments, thou shalt pay just debt; down with thy dust, or observe this tooth-forceps!" Nature, a far juster Sovereign, has far terribler forceps. Aristocracies, actual and imaginary, reach a time when parchment pleading does not avail them. "Go to, for all thy parchments, thou shalt pay due debt!" shouts the Universe to them, in an emphatic manner. They refuse to pay, confidently pleading parchment: their best grinder-tooth, with horrible agony, goes out of their jaw.* Wilt thou pay now? A second grinder, again in horrible agony, goes: a second, and a third, and if need be, all the teeth and grinders, and the life itself with them;—and *then* there is free payment, and an anatomist-subject* into the bargain!

Reform Bills, Corn-Law Abrogation Bills, and then Land-Tax Bill, Property-Tax Bill,* and still dimmer list of *etceteras;* grinder after grinder:—my lords and gentlemen, it were better for you to arise, and begin doing your work, than sit there and plead parchments!

We write no Chapter on the Corn-Laws,* in this place; the Corn-Laws are too mad to have a Chapter. There is a certain immorality, when there is not a necessity, in speaking about things finished; in chopping into small pieces the already slashed and slain. When the brains are out,* why does not a Solecism die! It is at its own peril if it refuse to die; it ought to make all conceivable haste to die, and get itself buried! The trade of Anti-Corn-Law Lecturer* in these days, still an indispensable, is a highly tragic one.

The Corn-Laws will go, and even soon go: would we were all as sure of the Millennium as they are of going! They go swiftly in these present months; with an increase of velocity, an ever-deepening, ever-widening sweep of momentum, truly notable. It is at the Aristocracy's own damage and peril, still more than at any other's whatsoever, that the Aristocracy maintains them;—at a damage, say only, as above computed, of a 'hundred thousand pounds an hour!'* The Corn-Laws keep all the air hot: fostered by their fever-warmth, much that is evil, but much also, how much that is good and indispensable, is rapidly coming to life among us!

CHAPTER IX.

WORKING ARISTOCRACY.

A POOR Working Mammonism getting itself 'strangled in the partridge-nets of an Unworking Dilettantism,'* and bellowing dreadfully, and already black in the face, is surely a disastrous spectacle! But of a Midas-eared Mammonism, which indeed at bottom all pure Mammonisms are, what better can you expect? No better;—if not this, then something other equally disastrous, if not still more disastrous. Mammonisms, grown asinine, have to become human again, and rational; they have, on the whole, to cease to be Mammonisms, were it even on compulsion, and pressure of the hemp round their neck!—My friends of the Working Aristocracy, there are now a great many things which you also, in your extreme need, will have to consider.

The Continental people, it would seem, are 'exporting our machinery, beginning to spin cotton and manufacture for themselves, to cut us out of this market and then out of that!'* Sad news indeed; but irremediable;—by no means the saddest news. The saddest news is, that we should find our National Existence, as I sometimes hear it said, depend on selling manufactured cotton at a farthing an ell cheaper than any other People. A most narrow stand for a great Nation to base itself on! A stand which, with all the Corn-Law Abrogations conceivable, I do not think will be capable of enduring.

My friends, suppose we quitted that stand; suppose we came honestly down from it, and said: "This is our minimum of cotton-prices. We care not, for the present, to make cotton any cheaper. Do you, if it seem so blessed to you, make cotton cheaper. Fill your lungs with cotton-fuz,* your hearts with copperas-fumes,* with rage and mutiny; become ye the general gnomes of Europe, slaves of the lamp!"*—I admire a Nation which fancies it will die if it do not undersell all other Nations, to the end of the world. Brothers, we will cease to *under*sell them; we will be content to *equal*-sell them; to be happy selling equally with them! I do not see the use of underselling them. Cotton-cloth is already two-pence a yard or lower; and yet bare backs were never more numerous among us. Let inventive men cease to spend their existence incessantly contriving how cotton can be made cheaper; and try to invent, a little, how cotton at its present cheapness could be somewhat justlier divided among us! Let inventive men consider, Whether the Secret of this Universe, and of Man's Life there, does, after all, as we rashly fancy it, consist in making money? There is One God, just, supreme, almighty: but is Mammon the name of him?—With a Hell which means 'Failing to make money,' I do not think there is any Heaven possible that would suit one well; nor so much as an Earth that can be habitable long! In brief, all this Mammon-Gospel, of Supply-and-demand, Competition, Laissez-faire, and Devil take the hindmost, begins to be one of the shabbiest Gospels ever preached on Earth; or altogether the shabbiest. Even with Dilettante partridge-nets, and at a horrible expenditure of pain, who shall regret to see the entirely transient, and at best somewhat despicable life strangled out of *it?* At the best, as we say, a somewhat despicable, unvenerable thing, this same 'Laissez-faire;' and now, at the *worst*, fast growing an altogether detestable one!

"But what is to be done with our manufacturing population, with our agricultural, with our ever-increasing population?" cry many.—Aye, what? Many things can be done with them, a hundred things, and a thousand things,—had we once got a soul, and begun to try. This one thing, of doing for them by 'underselling all people,' and filling our own bursten pockets and appetites by the road; and turning over all care for any 'population,' or human or divine consideration except cash only, to the winds, with a "Laissez-faire" and the rest of it: this is evidently not the thing. 'Farthing cheaper per yard:' no great Nation can stand on the apex of such a pyramid; screwing itself higher and higher; balancing itself on its great-toe! Can England not subsist without being *above* all people in working? England never deliberately purposed such a thing. If England work better than all people, it shall be well. England, like an honest worker, will work as well as she can; and hope the gods may allow her to live on that basis. Laissez-faire and much else being once well dead, how many 'impossibles' will become possible! They are 'impossible,' as cotton-cloth at two-pence an ell was—till men set about making it. The inventive genius of great England will not forever sit patient with mere wheels and pinions, bobbins, straps and billy-rollers* whirring in the head of it. The inventive genius of England is not a Beaver's, or a Spinner's or Spider's genius: it is a *Man's* genius, I hope, with a God over him!

Supply-and-demand? One begins to be weary of such work. Leave all to egoism, to ravenous greed of money, of pleasure, of applause:— it is the Gospel of Despair! Man *is* a Patent-Digester,* then: only give him Free Trade, Free digesting-room; and each of us digest what he can come at, leaving the rest to Fate! My unhappy brethren of the Working Mammonism, my unhappier brethren of the Idle Dilettantism, no world was ever held together in that way for long. A world of mere Patent-Digesters will soon have nothing to digest: such world ends, and by Law of Nature must end, in 'over-population;'* in howling universal famine, 'impossibility,' and suicidal madness, as of endless dog-kennels run rabid. Supply-and-demand shall do its full part, and Free Trade shall be free as air;—thou of the shotbelts, see thou forbid it not, with those paltry, *worse* than 'Mammonish' swindleries and Sliding-scales of thine, which are seen to be swindleries for all thy canting, which in times like ours are very scandalous to see! And Trade never so well freed, and all Tariffs settled or abolished, and Supply-and-demand in full operation,—let us all know that we have yet done nothing; that we have merely cleared the ground for doing.

Yes, were the Corn-Laws ended tomorrow, there is nothing yet ended; there is only room made for all manner of things beginning. The Corn-Laws gone, and Trade made free, it is as good as certain this paralysis of industry will pass away. We shall have another period of commercial enterprise, of victory and prosperity; during which, it is likely, much money will again be made, and all the people may, by the extant methods, still for a space of years, be kept alive and physically fed. The strangling band of Famine will be loosened from our necks; we shall have room again to breathe; time to bethink ourselves, to repent and consider! A precious and thrice-precious space of years; wherein to struggle as for life in reforming our foul ways; in alleviating, instructing, regulating our people; seeking, as for life, that something like spiritual food be imparted them, some real governance and guidance be provided them! It will be a priceless time. For our new period or paroxysm of commercial prosperity will and can, on the old methods of 'Competition and Devil take the hindmost,' prove but a paroxysm: a new paroxysm,—likely enough, if we do not use it better, to be our *last*. In this, of itself, is no salvation. If our Trade in twenty years, 'flourishing' as never Trade flourished, could double itself;* yet then also, by the old Laissez-faire method, our Population is doubled: we shall then be as we are, only twice as many of us, twice and ten times as unmanageable!

All this dire misery, therefore; all this of our poor Workhouse Workmen, of our Chartisms, Trades-strikes, Corn-Laws, Toryisms, and the general downbreak of Laissez-faire in these days,—may we not regard it as a voice from the dumb bosom of Nature, saying to us: Behold! Supply-and-demand is not the one Law of Nature; Cash-payment is not the sole nexus of man with man,—how far from it! Deep, far deeper than Supply-and-demand, are Laws, Obligations sacred as Man's Life itself: these also, if you will continue to do work, you shall now learn and obey. He that will learn them, behold Nature is on his side, he shall yet work and prosper with noble rewards. He that will not learn them, Nature is against him; he shall not be able to do work in Nature's empire,—not in hers. Perpetual mutiny, contention, hatred, isolation, execration shall wait on his footsteps, till all men discern that the thing which he attains, however golden it look or be, is not success, but the want of success.

Supply-and-demand,—alas! For what noble work was there ever yet any audible 'demand' in that poor sense? The man of Macedonia, speaking in vision to an Apostle Paul, "Come over and help us,"* did not specify what rate of wages he would give! Or was the Christian Religion itself accomplished by Prize-Essays, Bridgewater Bequests, and a 'minimum of Four thousand five hundred a year?'* No demand that I heard of was made then, audible in any Labour-market, Manchester Chamber of Commerce,* or other the like emporium and hiring establishment; silent were all these from any whisper of such demand;—powerless were all these to 'supply' it, had the demand been in thunder and earthquake, with gold Eldorados and Mahometan Paradises* for the reward. Ah me, into what waste latitudes, in this Time-Voyage, have we wandered; like adventurous Sindbads;*—where the men go about as if by galvanism, with meaningless glaring eyes, and have no soul, but only a beaver-faculty and stomach! The haggard despair of Cotton-factory, Coal-mine operatives, Chandos Farm-labourers,* in these days, is painful to behold; but not so painful, hideous to the inner sense, as that brutish godforgetting Profit-and-Loss Philosophy and Life-theory, which we hear jangled on all hands of us, in senate-houses, spouting-clubs, leading-articles, pulpits and platforms, everywhere as the Ultimate Gospel and candid Plain-English of Man's Life, from the throats and pens and thoughts of all but all men!—

Enlightened Philosophies, like Molière Doctors, will tell you: "Enthusiasms, Self-sacrifice, Heaven, Hell and such like: yes, all that was true enough for old stupid times; all that used to be true: but we have changed all that, *nous avons changé tout cela!*"* Well; if the heart be got round now into the right side, and the liver to the left; if man have no heroism in him deeper than the wish to eat, and in his soul there dwell now no Infinite of Hope and Awe, and no divine Silence can become imperative because it is not Sinai Thunder,* and no tie will bind if it be not that of Tyburn gallows-ropes,—then verily you have changed all that; and for it, and for you, and for me, behold the Abyss and nameless Annihilation is ready. So scandalous a beggarly Universe deserves indeed nothing else; I cannot say I would save it from Annihilation. Vacuum, and the serene Blue, will be much handsomer; easier too for all of us. I, for one, decline living as a Patent-Digester. Patent-Digester, Spinning-Mule,* Mayfair Clothes-Horse:* many thanks, but your Chaosships will have the goodness to excuse me!

CHAPTER X.

PLUGSON OF UNDERSHOT.

ONE thing I do know: Never, on this Earth, was the relation of man to man long carried on by Cash-payment alone. If, at any time, a philosophy of Laissez-faire, Competition and Supply-and-demand, start up as the exponent of human relations, expect that it will soon end.

Such philosophies will arise: for man's philosophies are usually the 'supplement of his practice;' some ornamental Logic-varnish, some outer skin of Articulate Intelligence, with which he strives to render his dumb Instinctive Doings presentable when they are done. Such philosophies will arise; be preached as Mammon-Gospels, the ultimate Evangel of the World; be believed, with what is called belief, with much superficial bluster, and a kind of shallow satisfaction real in its way:—but they are ominous gospels! They are the sure, and even swift, forerunner of great changes. Expect that the old System of Society is done, is dying and fallen into dotage, when it begins to rave in that fashion. Most Systems that I have watched the death of, for the last three thousand years, have gone just so. The Ideal, the True and Noble that was in them having faded out, and nothing now remaining but naked Egoism, vulturous Greediness, they cannot live; they are bound and inexorably ordained by the oldest Destinies, Mothers of the Universe, to die. Curious enough: they thereupon, as I have pretty generally noticed, devise some light comfortable kind of 'wine-and-walnuts philosophy'* for themselves, this of Supply-and-demand or another; and keep saying, during hours of mastication and rumination, which they call hours of meditation: "Soul, take thy ease;* it is all *well* that thou art a vulture-soul;"—and pangs of dissolution come upon them, oftenest before they are aware!

Cash-payment never was, or could except for a few years be, the union-bond of man to man. Cash never yet paid one man fully his deserts to another; nor could it, nor can it, now or henceforth to the end of the world. I invite his Grace of Castle-Rackrent* to reflect on this;—does he think that a Land Aristocracy when it becomes a Land Auctioneership can have long to live? Or that Sliding-scales will increase the vital stamina of it? The indomitable Plugson too, of the respected Firm of Plugson, Hunks and Company, in St. Dolly Undershot,* is invited to reflect on this; for to him also it will be new, perhaps even newer. Book-keeping by double entry* is admirable, and records several things in an exact manner. But the Mother-Destinies also keep their Tablets; in Heaven's Chancery also there goes on a recording; and things, as my Moslem friends say, are 'written on the iron leaf.'*

Your Grace and Plugson, it is like, go to Church occasionally: did
you never in vacant moments, with perhaps a dull parson droning to
you, glance into your New Testament, and the cash-account stated
four times over, by a kind of quadruple entry,—in the Four Gospels
there? I consider that a cash-account, and balance-statement of work
done and wages paid, worth attending to. Precisely *such*, though on
a smaller scale, go on at all moments under this Sun; and the statement and balance of them in the Plugson Ledgers and on the Tablets
of Heaven's Chancery are discrepant exceedingly;—which ought
really to teach, and to have long since taught, an indomitable common-
sense Plugson of Undershot, much more an unattackable *un*common-
sense Grace of Rackrent, a thing or two!—In brief, we shall have to
dismiss the Cash-Gospel rigorously into its own place: we shall have
to know, on the threshold, that either there is some infinitely deeper
Gospel, subsidiary, explanatory and daily and hourly corrective, to
the Cash one; or else that the Cash one itself and all others are fast
travelling!

For all human things do require to have an Ideal in them; to have
some Soul in them, as we said, were it only to keep the Body unputre-
fied. And wonderful it is to see how the Ideal or Soul, place it in what
ugliest Body you may, will irradiate said Body with its own nobleness;
will gradually, incessantly, mould, modify, new-form or reform said
ugliest Body, and make it at last beautiful, and to a certain degree
divine!—O, if you could dethrone that Brute-god Mammon, and put
a Spirit-god in his place! One way or other, he must and will have to
be dethroned.

Fighting, for example, as I often say to myself, Fighting with steel
murder-tools is surely a much uglier operation than Working, take it
how you will. Yet even of Fighting, in religious Abbot Samson's days,
see what a Feudalism there had grown,—a 'glorious Chivalry,' much
besung down to the present day.* Was not that one of the 'impossiblest' things? Under the sky is no uglier spectacle than two men
with clenched teeth, and hellfire eyes, hacking one another's flesh;
converting precious living bodies, and priceless living souls, into
nameless masses of putrescence, useful only for turnip-manure. How
did a Chivalry ever come out of that; how anything that was not hideous, scandalous, infernal? It will be a question worth considering by
and by.

I remark, for the present, only two things: first, that the Fighting itself was not, as we rashly suppose it, a Fighting without cause, but more or less with cause. Man is created to fight; he is perhaps best of all definable as a born soldier; his life 'a battle and a march,' under the right General. It is forever indispensable for a man to fight: now with Necessity, with Barrenness, Scarcity, with Puddles, Bogs, tangled Forests, unkempt Cotton;—now also with the hallucinations of his poor fellow Men. Hallucinatory visions rise in the head of my poor fellow man; make him claim over me rights which are not his. All Fighting, as we noticed long ago, is the dusty conflict of strengths each thinking itself the strongest, or, in other words, the justest;—of Mights which do in the long-run, and forever will in this just Universe in the long-run, mean Rights.* In conflict the perishable part of them, beaten sufficiently, flies off into dust: this process ended, appears the imperishable, the true and exact.

And now let us remark a second thing: how, in these baleful operations, a noble devout-hearted Chevalier will comfort himself, and an ignoble godless Bucanier and Chactaw Indian.* Victory is the aim of each. But deep in the heart of the noble man it lies forever legible, that, as an Invisible Just God made him, so will and must God's Justice and this only, were it never so invisible, ultimately prosper in all controversies and enterprises and battles whatsoever. What an Influence; ever-present,—like a Soul in the rudest Caliban of a body;* like a ray of Heaven, and illuminative creative *Fiat-Lux*,* in the wastest terrestrial Chaos! Blessed divine Influence, traceable even in the horror of Battlefields and garments rolled in blood:* how it ennobles even the Battlefield; and, in place of a Chactaw Massacre, makes it a Field of Honour! A Battlefield too is great. Considered well, it is a kind of Quintessence of Labour; Labour distilled into its utmost concentration; the significance of years of it compressed into an hour. Here too thou shalt be strong, and not in muscle only, if thou wouldst prevail. Here too thou shalt be strong of heart, noble of soul; thou shalt dread no pain or death, thou shalt not love ease or life; in rage, thou shalt remember mercy, justice;—thou shalt be a Knight and not a Chactaw, if thou wouldst prevail! It is the rule of all battles, against hallucinating fellow Men, against unkempt Cotton, or whatsoever battles they may be, which a man in this world has to fight.

Howel Davies* dyes the West Indian Seas with blood, piles his decks with plunder; approves himself the expertest Seaman, the daringest Seafighter: but he gains no lasting victory, lasting victory is not possible for him. Not, had he fleets larger than the combined British Navy all united with him in bucaniering. He, once for all, cannot prosper in his duel. He strikes down his man: yes; but his man, or his man's representative, has no notion to lie struck down; neither, though slain ten times, will he keep so lying;—nor has the Universe any notion to keep him so lying! On the contrary, the Universe and he have, at all moments, all manner of motives to start up again, and desperately fight again. Your Napoleon is flung out, at last, to St. Helena;* the latter end of him sternly compensating the beginning. The Bucanier strikes down a man, a hundred or a million men: but what profits it? He has one enemy never to be struck down; nay two enemies: Mankind and the Maker of Men. On the great scale or on the small, in fighting of men or fighting of difficulties, I will not embark my venture with Howel Davies: it is not the Bucanier, it is the Hero only that can gain victory, that can do more than *seem* to succeed. These things will deserve meditating; for they apply to all battle and soldiership, all struggle and effort whatsoever in this Fight of Life. It is a poor Gospel, Cash-Gospel or whatever name it have, that does not, with clear tone, uncontradictable, carrying conviction to all hearts, forever keep men in mind of these things.

Unhappily, my indomitable friend Plugson of Undershot has, in a great degree, forgotten them;—as, alas, all the world has; as, alas, our very Dukes and Soul-Overseers have, whose special trade it was to remember them! Hence these tears.*—Plugson, who has indomitably spun Cotton merely to gain thousands of pounds, I have to call as yet a Bucanier and Chactaw; till there come something better, still more indomitable from him. His hundred Thousand-pound Notes, if there be nothing other, are to me but as the hundred Scalps in a Chactaw wigwam. The blind Plugson: he was a Captain of Industry, born member of the Ultimate genuine Aristocracy of this Universe, could he have known it! These thousand men that span and toiled round him, they were a regiment whom he had enlisted, man by man; to make war on a very genuine enemy: Bareness of back, and disobedient Cotton-fibre, which will not, unless forced to it, consent to cover bare backs. Here is a most genuine enemy; over whom all creatures will wish him victory. He enlisted his thousand men; said to them, "Come, brothers, let us have a dash at Cotton!" They follow with cheerful shout; they gain such a victory over Cotton as the Earth has to admire and clap hands at: but, alas, it is yet only of the Bucanier or Chactaw sort,—as good as no victory! Foolish Plugson of St. Dolly Undershot: does he hope to become illustrious by hanging up the scalps in his wigwam, the hundred thousands at his banker's, and saying, Behold my scalps? Why, Plugson, even thy own host is all in mutiny: Cotton is conquered; but the 'bare backs'—are worse covered than ever! Indomitable Plugson, thou must cease to be a Chactaw; thou and others; thou thyself, if no other!

Did William the Norman Bastard,* or any of his Taillefers, *Ironcutters,** manage so? Ironcutter, at the end of the campaign, did not turn off his thousand fighters, but said to them: "Noble fighters, this is the land we have gained; be I Lord in it,—what we will call *Law-ward,** maintainer and *keeper* of Heaven's *Laws*: be I *Law-ward*, or in brief orthoepy *Lord* in it, and be ye Loyal Men around me in it; and we will stand by one another, as soldiers round a captain, for again we shall have need of one another!" Plugson, bucanier-like, says to them: "Noble spinners, this is the Hundred Thousand we have gained, wherein I mean to dwell and plant vineyards; the hundred thousand is mine, the three and sixpence daily was yours: adieu, noble spinners; drink my health with this groat each, which I give you over and above!" The entirely unjust Captain of Industry, say I; not Chevalier, but Bucanier! 'Commercial Law' does indeed acquit him; asks, with wide eyes, What else? So too Howel Davies asks, Was it not according to the strictest Bucanier Custom? Did I depart in any jot or tittle from the Laws of the Bucaniers?

After all, money, as they say, is miraculous. Plugson wanted victory; as Chevaliers and Bucaniers, and all men alike do. He found money recognised, by the whole world with one assent, as the true symbol, exact equivalent and synonym of victory;—and here we have him, a grimbrowed, indomitable Bucanier, coming home to us with a 'victory,' which the whole world is *ceasing* to clap hands at! The whole world, taught somewhat impressively, is beginning to recognise that such victory is but half a victory; and that now, if it please the Powers, we must—have the other half!

Money is miraculous. What miraculous facilities has it yielded, will it yield us; but also what never-imagined confusions, obscurations has it brought in; down almost to total extinction of the moral-sense in large masses of mankind! 'Protection of property,' of what is '*mine*,' means with most men protection of money,—the thing which, had I a thousand padlocks over it, is least of all *mine*; is, in a manner, scarcely worth calling mine! The symbol shall be held sacred, defended everywhere with tipstaves, ropes and gibbets; the thing signified shall be composedly cast to the dogs. A human being who has worked with human beings clears all scores with them, cuts himself with triumphant completeness forever loose from them, by paying down certain shillings and pounds. Was it not the wages I promised you? There they are, to the last sixpence,—according to the Laws of the Bucaniers!— Yes, indeed;—and, at such times, it becomes imperatively necessary to ask all persons, bucaniers and others, Whether these same respectable Laws of the Bucaniers are written on God's eternal Heavens at all, on the inner Heart of Man at all; or on the respectable Bucanier Logbook merely, for the convenience of bucaniering merely? What a question;—whereat Westminster Hall shudders to its driest parchment; and on the dead wigs each particular horsehair stands on end!

The Laws of Laissez-faire, O Westminster, the laws of industrial Captain and industrial Soldier, how much more of idle Captain and industrial Soldier, will need to be remodelled, and modified, and rectified in a hundred and a hundred ways,—and *not* in the Sliding-scale direction, but in the totally opposite one! With two million industrial Soldiers already sitting in Bastilles, and five million pining on potatoes, methinks Westminster* cannot begin too soon!—A man has other obligations laid on him, in God's Universe, than the payment of cash: these also Westminster, if it will continue to exist and have board-wages, must contrive to take some charge of:—by Westminster or by another, they must and will be taken charge of; be, with whatever difficulty, got articulated, got enforced, and to a certain approximate extent, put in practice. And, as I say, it cannot be too soon! For Mammonism, left to itself, has become Midas-eared; and with all its gold mountains, sits starving for want of bread: and Dilettantism with its partridge-nets, in this extremely earnest Universe of ours, is playing somewhat too high a game. 'A man by the very look of him promises so much:'* yes; and by the rent-roll of him does he promise nothing?—

Alas, what a business will this be, which our Continental friends, groping this long while somewhat absurdly about it and about it, call 'Organisation of Labour;'—which must be taken out of the hands of absurd windy persons,* and put into the hands of wise, laborious, modest and valiant men, to begin with it straightway; to proceed with it, and succeed in it more and more, if Europe, at any rate if England, is to continue habitable much longer. Looking at the kind of most noble Corn-Law Dukes or Practical *Duces* we have, and also of right reverend Soul-Overseers, Christian Spiritual *Duces* 'on a minimum of four thousand five hundred,' one's hopes are a little chilled. Courage, nevertheless; there are many brave men in England! My indomitable Plugson,—nay is there not even in thee some hope? Thou art hitherto a Bucanier, as it was written and prescribed for thee by an evil world: but in that grim brow, in that indomitable heart which *can* conquer Cotton, do there not perhaps lie other ten times nobler conquests?

CHAPTER XI.

LABOUR.

FOR there is a perennial nobleness, and even sacredness, in Work. Were he never so benighted, forgetful of his high calling, there is always hope in a man that actually and earnestly works: in Idleness alone is there perpetual despair. Work, never so Mammonish, mean, *is* in communication with Nature; the real desire to get Work done will itself lead one more and more to truth, to Nature's appointments and regulations, which are truth.

The latest Gospel in this world is, Know thy work and do it.* 'Know thyself:' long enough has that poor 'self' of thine tormented thee; thou wilt never get to 'know' it, I believe! Think it not thy business, this of knowing thyself; thou art an unknowable individual: know what thou canst work at; and work at it, like a Hercules! That will be thy better plan.

It has been written, 'an endless significance lies in Work;' a man perfects himself by working. Foul jungles are cleared away, fair seed-fields* rise instead, and stately cities; and withal the man himself first ceases to be a jungle and foul unwholesome desert thereby. Consider how, even, in the meanest sorts of Labour, the whole soul of a man is composed into a kind of real harmony, the instant he sets himself to work! Doubt, Desire, Sorrow, Remorse, Indignation, Despair itself, all these like helldogs lie beleaguering the soul of the poor dayworker, as of every man: but he bends himself with free valour against his task, and all these are stilled, all these shrink murmuring far off into their caves. The man is now a man. The blessed glow of Labour in him, is it not as purifying fire, wherein all poison is burnt up, and of sour smoke itself there is made bright blessed flame!

Destiny, on the whole, has no other way of cultivating us. A formless Chaos, once set it *revolving*, grows round and ever rounder; ranges itself, by mere force of gravity, into strata, spherical courses;* is no longer a Chaos, but a round compacted World. What would become of the Earth, did she cease to revolve? In the poor old Earth, so long as she revolves, all inequalities, irregularities disperse themselves; all irregularities are incessantly becoming regular. Hast thou looked on the Potter's wheel,—one of the venerablest objects; old as the Prophet Ezechiel* and far older? Rude lumps of clay, how they spin themselves up, by mere quick whirling, into beautiful circular dishes. And fancy the most assiduous Potter, but without his wheel; reduced to make dishes, or rather amorphous botches, by mere kneading and baking! Even such a Potter were Destiny, with a human soul that would rest and lie at ease, that would not work and spin! Of an idle unrevolving man the kindest Destiny, like the most assiduous Potter without wheel, can bake and knead nothing other than a botch; let her spend on him what expensive colouring, what gilding and enamelling she will, he is but a botch. Not a dish; no, a bulging, kneaded, crooked, shambling, squint-cornered, amorphous botch,— a mere enamelled vessel of dishonour! Let the idle think of this.

Blessed is he who has found his work; let him ask no other blessedness. He has a work, a life-purpose; he has found it, and will follow it! How, as a free-flowing channel, dug and torn by noble force through the sour mud-swamp of one's existence, like an ever-deepening river there, it runs and flows;—draining off the sour festering water, gradually from the root of the remotest grass-blade; making, instead of pestilential swamp, a green fruitful meadow with its clear-flowing stream. How blessed for the meadow itself, let the stream and *its* value be great or small! Labour is Life: from the inmost heart of the Worker rises his god-given Force, the sacred celestial Life-essence breathed into him by Almighty God; from his inmost heart awakens him to all nobleness,—to all knowledge, 'self-knowledge' and much else, so soon as Work fitly begins. Knowledge? The knowledge that will hold good in working, cleave thou to that; for Nature herself accredits that, says Yea to that. Properly thou hast no other knowledge but what thou hast got by working: the rest is yet all a hypothesis of knowledge; a thing to be argued of in schools, a thing floating in the clouds, in endless logic-vortices, till we try it and fix it. 'Doubt, of whatever kind, can be ended by Action alone.'*

And again, hast thou valued Patience, Courage, Perseverance, Openness to light; readiness to own thyself mistaken, to do better next time? All these, all virtues, in wrestling with the dim brute Powers of Fact, in ordering of thy fellows in such wrestle, there and elsewhere not at all, thou wilt continually learn. Set down a brave Sir Christopher in the middle of black ruined Stoneheaps, of foolish unarchitectural Bishops, redtape Officials, idle Nell-Gwyn Defenders of the Faith; and see whether he will ever raise a Paul's Cathedral out of all that, yea or no! Rough, rude, contradictory are all things and persons, from the mutinous masons and Irish hodmen, up to the idle Nell-Gwyn Defenders, to blustering redtape Officials, foolish unarchitectural Bishops. All these things and persons are there not for Christopher's sake and his Cathedral's; they are there for their own sake mainly!* Christopher will have to conquer and constrain all these,—if he be able. All these are against him. Equitable Nature herself, who carries her mathematics and architectonics not on the face of her, but deep in the hidden heart of her,—Nature herself is but partially for him; will be wholly against him, if he constrain her not! His very money, where is it to come from? The pious munificence of England lies far-scattered, distant, unable to speak, and say, "I am here;"*—must be spoken to before it can speak. Pious munificence, and all help, is so silent, invisible like the gods; impediment, contradictions manifold are so loud and near! O brave Sir Christopher, trust thou in those, notwithstanding, and front all these; understand all these; by valiant patience, noble effort, insight, by man's-strength, vanquish and compel all these,—and, on the whole, strike down victoriously the last topstone of that Paul's Edifice;* thy monument for certain centuries, the stamp 'Great Man' impressed very legibly on Portland-stone there!*—

Yes, all manner of help, and pious response from Men or Nature, is always what we call silent; cannot speak or come to light, till it be seen, till it be spoken to. Every noble work is at first 'impossible.' In very truth, for every noble work the possibilities will lie diffused through Immensity; inarticulate, undiscoverable except to faith. Like

Gideon thou shalt spread out thy fleece at the door of thy tent;* see whether under the wide arch of Heaven there be any bounteous moisture, or none. Thy heart and life-purpose shall be as a miraculous Gideon's fleece, spread out in silent appeal to Heaven; and from the kind Immensities, what from the poor unkind Localities and town and country Parishes there never could, blessed dew-moisture to suffice thee shall have fallen!

Work is of a religious nature:—work is of a *brave* nature; which it is the aim of all religion to be. 'All work of man is as the swimmer's:' a waste ocean threatens to devour him; if he front it not bravely, it will keep its word. By incessant wise defiance of it, lusty rebuke and buffet of it, behold how it loyally supports him, bears him as its conqueror along. 'It is so,' says Goethe, 'with all things that man undertakes in this world.'*

Brave Sea-captain, Norse Sea-king,*—Columbus, my hero, royalest Sea-king of all! it is no friendly environment this of thine, in the waste deep waters;* around thee mutinous discouraged souls, behind thee disgrace and ruin, before thee the unpenetrated veil of Night. Brother, these wild water-mountains, bounding from their deep bases (ten miles deep, I am told), are not entirely there on thy behalf!* Meseems *they* have other work than floating thee forward:—and the huge Winds, that sweep from Ursa Major* to the Tropics and Equators, dancing their giant-waltz through the kingdoms of Chaos and Immensity, they care little about filling rightly or filling wrongly the small shoulder-of-mutton sails in this cockle-skiff of thine!* Thou art not among articulate-speaking friends, my brother; thou art among immeasurable dumb monsters, tumbling, howling wide as the world here.* Secret, far off, invisible to all hearts but thine, there lies a help in them: see how thou wilt get at that. Patiently thou wilt wait till the mad Southwester spend itself, saving thyself by dextrous science of defence, the while: valiantly, with swift decision, wilt thou strike in, when the favouring East,* the Possible, springs up. Mutiny of men thou wilt sternly repress; weakness, despondency, thou wilt cheerily encourage:* thou wilt swallow down complaint, unreason, weariness, weakness of others and thyself;—how much wilt thou swallow down! There shall be a depth of Silence in thee, deeper than this Sea, which is but ten miles deep: a Silence unsoundable; known to God only. Thou shalt be a Great Man. Yes, my World-Soldier, thou of the World Marine-service,—thou wilt have to be *greater* than this tumultuous unmeasured World here round thee is: thou, in thy strong soul, as with wrestler's arms, shalt embrace it, harness it down; and make it bear thee on,—to new Americas, or whither God wills!

CHAPTER XII.

REWARD.

'RELIGION,' I said; for, properly speaking, all true Work is Religion: and whatsoever Religion is not Work may go and dwell among the Brahmins, Antinomians, Spinning Dervishes,* or where it will; with me it shall have no harbour. Admirable was that of the old Monks, '*Laborare est Orare*, Work is Worship.'*

Older than all preached Gospels was this unpreached, inarticulate, but ineradicable, forever-enduring Gospel: Work, and therein have wellbeing. Man, Son of Earth and of Heaven, lies there not, in the innermost heart of thee, a Spirit of active Method, a Force for Work;— and burns like a painfully-smouldering fire, giving thee no rest till thou unfold it, till thou write it down in beneficent Facts around thee! What is immethodic, waste, thou shalt make methodic, regulated, arable; obedient and productive to thee. Wheresoever thou findest Disorder, there is thy eternal enemy; attack him swiftly, subdue him; make Order of him, the subject not of Chaos, but of Intelligence, Divinity and Thee! The thistle that grows in thy path, dig it out, that a blade of useful grass, a drop of nourishing milk, may grow there instead. The waste cotton-shrub, gather its waste white down, spin it, weave it; that, in place of idle litter, there may be folded webs, and the naked skin of man be covered.

But above all, where thou findest Ignorance, Stupidity, Brute-mindedness,—yes, there, with or without Church-tithes and Shovel-hat, with or without Talfourd-Mahon Copyrights,* or were it with mere dungeons and gibbets and crosses, attack it, I say; smite it wisely, unweariedly, and rest not while thou livest and it lives; but smite, smite, in the name of God! The Highest God, as I understand it, does audibly so command thee; still audibly, if thou have ears to hear.* He, even He, with his *un*spoken voice, awfuler than any Sinai thunders* or syllabled speech of Whirlwinds; for the SILENCE of deep Eternities, of Worlds from beyond the morning-stars, does it not speak to thee?

The unborn Ages; the old Graves, with their long-mouldering dust, the very tears that wetted it now all dry,—do not these speak to thee, what ear hath not heard? The deep Death-kingdoms, the Stars in their never-resting courses, all Space and all Time, proclaim it to thee in continual silent admonition. Thou too, if ever man should, shalt work while it is called Today. For the Night cometh, wherein no man can work.*

All true Work is sacred; in all true Work, were it but true hand-labour, there is something of divineness. Labour, wide as the Earth, has its summit in Heaven. Sweat of the brow; and up from that to sweat of the brain, sweat of the heart; which includes all Kepler calculations, Newton meditations,* all Sciences, all spoken Epics, all acted Heroisms, Martyrdoms,—up to that 'Agony of bloody sweat,'* which all men have called divine! O brother, if this is not 'worship,' then I say, the more pity for worship; for this is the noblest thing yet discovered under God's sky. Who art thou that complainest of thy life of toil? Complain not. Look up, my wearied brother; see thy fellow Workmen there, in God's Eternity: surviving there, they alone surviving: sacred Band of the Immortals, celestial Bodyguard of the Empire of Mankind. Even in the weak Human Memory they survive so long, as saints, as heroes, as gods; they alone surviving; peopling, they alone, the unmeasured solitudes of Time! To thee Heaven, though severe, is *not* unkind; Heaven is kind,—as a noble Mother; as that Spartan Mother, saying while she gave her son his shield, "With it, my son, or upon it!"* Thou too shalt return *home* in honour; to thy far-distant Home, in honour; doubt it not,—if in the battle thou keep thy shield! Thou, in the Eternities and deepest Death-kingdoms, art not an alien; thou everywhere art a denizen! Complain not; the very Spartans did not *complain*.

And who art thou that braggest of thy life of Idleness; complacently shewest thy bright gilt equipages; sumptuous cushions; appliances for folding of the hands to mere sleep?* Looking up, looking down, around, behind or before, discernest thou, if it be not in Mayfair alone, any *idle* hero, saint, god, or even devil? Not a vestige of one. In the Heavens, in the Earth, in the Waters under the Earth, is none like unto thee. Thou art an original figure in this Creation; a denizen in Mayfair alone, in this extraordinary Century or Half-Century alone! One monster there is in the world: the idle man. What is his 'Religion?' That Nature is a Phantasm, where cunning beggary or thievery may sometimes find good victual. That God is a lie; and that Man and his Life are a lie.—Alas, alas, who of us *is* there that can say, I have worked? The faithfulest of us are unprofitable servants; the faithfulest of us know that best. The faithfulest of us may say, with sad and true old Samuel, "Much of my life has been trifled away!"* But he that has, and except 'on public occasions' professes to have, no function but that of going idle in a graceful or graceless manner; and of begetting sons to go idle; and to address Chief Spinners and Diggers, who at least *are* spinning and digging, "Ye scandalous persons who produce too much"—My Corn-Law friends, on what imaginary still richer Eldorados, and true iron-spikes with law of gravitation, are ye rushing!

As to the Wages of Work there might innumerable things be said; there will and must yet innumerable things be said and spoken, in St. Stephen's and out of St. Stephen's; and gradually not a few things be ascertained and written, on Law-parchment, concerning this very matter:—'Fair day's-wages for a fair day's-work'* is the most unrefusable demand! Money-wages 'to the extent of keeping your worker alive that he may work more;'* these, unless you mean to dismiss him straightway out of this world, are indispensable alike to the noblest Worker and to the least noble!

One thing only I will say here, in special reference to the former class, the noble and noblest; but throwing light on all the other classes and their arrangements of this difficult matter: The 'wages' of every noble Work do yet lie in Heaven or else Nowhere. Not in Bank-of-England bills, in Owen's Labour-bank,* or any the most improved establishment of banking and money-changing, needest thou, heroic soul, present thy account of earnings. Human banks and labour-banks know thee not; or know thee after generations and centuries have passed away, and thou art clean gone from 'rewarding,'—all manner of bank-drafts, shop-tills, and Downing-street Exchequers lying very invisible, so far from thee! Nay, at bottom, dost thou need any reward? Was it thy aim and life-purpose to be filled with good things for thy heroism; to have a life of pomp and ease, and be what men call 'happy,' in this world, or in any other world? I answer for thee deliberately, No. The whole spiritual secret of the new epoch lies in this, that thou canst answer for thyself, with thy whole clearness of head and heart, deliberately, No!

My brother, the brave man has to give his Life away.* Give it, I advise thee;—thou dost not expect to *sell* thy Life in an adequate manner? What price, for example, would content thee? The just price of thy LIFE to thee,—why, God's entire Creation to thyself, the whole Universe of Space, the whole Eternity of Time, and what they hold: that is the price which would content thee; that, and if thou wilt be candid, nothing short of that! It is thy all; and for it thou wouldst have all. Thou art an unreasonable mortal;—or rather thou art a poor *infinite* mortal, who, in thy narrow clay-prison here, *seemest* so unreasonable! Thou wilt never sell thy Life, or any part of thy Life, in a satisfactory manner. Give it, like a royal heart; let the price be Nothing: thou *hast* then, in a certain sense, got All for it! The heroic man,—and is not every man, God be thanked, a potential hero?—has to do so, in all times and circumstances. In the most heroic age, as in the most unheroic, he will have to say, as Burns said proudly and humbly of his little Scottish Songs, little dewdrops of Celestial Melody in an age when so much was unmelodious: "By Heaven, they shall either be invaluable or of no value; I do not need your guineas for them!"* It is an element which should, and must, enter deeply into all settlements of wages here below. They never will be 'satisfactory' otherwise; they cannot, O Mammon Gospel, they never can! Money for my little piece of work 'to the extent that will allow me to keep working;' yes, this,—unless you mean that I shall go my ways *before* the work is all taken out of me: but as to 'wages'—!—

On the whole, we do entirely agree with those old Monks, *Laborare est Orare*. In a thousand senses, from one end of it to the other, true Work *is* Worship. He that works, whatsoever be his work, he bodies forth the form of Things Unseen;* a small Poet every Worker is. The idea, were it but of his poor Delf Platter,* how much more of his Epic Poem, is as yet 'seen,' half-seen, only by himself; to all others it is a thing unseen, impossible; to Nature herself it is a thing unseen, a thing which never hitherto was;—very 'impossible,' for it is as yet a Nothing! The Unseen Powers had need to watch over such a man; he works in and for the Unseen. Alas, if he look to the Seen Powers only, he may as well quit the business; his No-thing will never rightly issue as a Thing, but as a Deceptivity, a Sham-thing,—which it had better not do!

Thy No-thing of an Intended Poem, O Poet who hast looked merely to reviewers, copyrights, booksellers, popularities, behold it has not yet become a Thing; for the truth is not in it! Though printed, hot-pressed, reviewed, celebrated, sold to the twentieth edition: what is all that? The Thing, in philosophical uncommercial language, is still a No-thing, mostly semblance, and deception of the sight;—benign Oblivion incessantly gnawing at it, impatient till Chaos, to which it belongs, do reabsorb it!—

He who takes not counsel of the Unseen and Silent, from him will never come real visibility and speech. Thou must descend to the *Mothers*, to the *Manes*,* and Hercules-like long suffer* and labour there, wouldst thou emerge with victory into the sunlight. As in battle and the shock of war,—for is not this a battle?—thou too shalt fear no pain or death, shalt love no ease or life; the voice of festive Lubberlands,* the noise of greedy Acheron* shall alike lie silent under thy victorious feet. Thy work, like Dante's, shall 'make thee lean for many years.'* The world and its wages, its criticisms, counsels, helps, impediments, shall be as a waste ocean-flood; the chaos through which thou art to swim and sail. Not the waste waves and their weedy gulf-streams,* shalt thou take for guidance: thy star alone,—'*Se tu segui tua stella!*'* Thy star alone, now clear-beaming over Chaos, nay now by fits gone out, disastrously eclipsed: this only shalt thou strive to follow. O, it is a business, as I fancy, that of weltering your way through Chaos and the murk of Hell! Green-eyed dragons watching you, three-headed Cerberuses,—not without sympathy of *their* sort! "*Eccovi l' uom ch' è stato all' Inferno.*"* For in fine, as Poet Dryden says, you do walk hand in hand with sheer Madness, all the way,*—who is by no means pleasant company! You look fixedly into Madness, and *her* undiscovered, boundless, bottomless Night-empire; that you may extort new Wisdom out of it, as an Eurydice from Tartarus.* The higher the Wisdom, the closer was its neighbourhood and kindred with mere Insanity; literally so;—and thou wilt, with a speechless feeling, observe how highest Wisdom, struggling up into this world, has oftentimes carried such tinctures and adhesions of Insanity still cleaving to it hither!

All Works, each in their degree, are a making of Madness sane;—truly enough a religious operation; which cannot be carried on without religion. You have not work otherwise; you have eye-service, greedy grasping of wages, swift and ever swifter manufacture of semblances to get hold of wages. Instead of better felt-hats to cover your head, you have bigger lath-and-plaster hats set travelling the streets on

wheels. Instead of heavenly and earthly Guidance for the souls of
men, you have 'Black or White Surplice' Controversies,* stuffed
hair-and-leather Popes;—terrestrial *Law-wards*, Lords and Law-
bringers, 'organising Labour' in these years, by passing Corn-Laws.
With all which, alas, this distracted Earth is now full, nigh to bursting. Semblances most smooth to the touch and eye; most accursed,
nevertheless, to body and soul. Semblances, be they of Sham-woven
Cloth or of Dilettante Legislation, which are *not* real wool or substance, but Devil's-dust, accursed of God and man! No man has worked,
or can work, except religiously; not even the poor day-labourer, the
weaver of your coat, the sewer of your shoes. All men, if they work not
as in a Great Taskmaster's eye, will work wrong,* work unhappily for
themselves and you.

Industrial work, still under bondage to Mammon, the rational soul
of it not yet awakened, is a tragic spectacle. Men in the rapidest motion
and self-motion; restless, with convulsive energy, as if driven by
Galvanism, as if possessed by a Devil; tearing asunder mountains,—to
no purpose, for Mammonism is always Midas-eared! This is sad, on the
face of it. Yet courage: the beneficent Destinies, kind in their sternness,
are apprising us that this cannot continue. Labour is not a devil, even
while encased in Mammonism; Labour is ever an imprisoned god,
writhing unconsciously or consciously to escape out of Mammonism!
Plugson of Undershot, like Taillefer of Normandy, wants victory; how
much happier will even Plugson be to have a Chivalrous victory than
a Chactaw one! The unredeemed ugliness is that of a slothful People.
Shew me a People energetically busy; heaving, struggling, all shoulders
at the wheel; their heart pulsing, every muscle swelling, with man's
energy and will;—I shew you a People of whom great good is already
predicable; to whom all manner of good is yet certain, if their energy
endure. By very working, they will learn; they have, Antæus-like,* their
foot on Mother Fact: how can they but learn?

The vulgarest Plugson of a Master-Worker, who can command
Workers, and get work out of them, is already a considerable man.
Blessed and thrice-blessed symptoms I discern of Master-Workers
who are not vulgar men; who are Nobles, and begin to feel that they
must act as such: all speed to these, they are England's hope at present! But in this Plugson himself, conscious of almost no nobleness
whatever, how much is there! Not without man's faculty, insight,

courage, hard energy, is this rugged figure. His words none of the
wisest; but his actings cannot be altogether foolish. Think, how were it,
stoodst thou suddenly in his shoes! He has to command a thousand
men. And not imaginary commanding; no, it is real, incessantly practical.
The evil passions of so many men (with the Devil in them, as in all of
us) he has to vanquish; by manifold force of speech and of silence, to
repress or evade. What a force of silence, to say nothing of the others, is
in Plugson! For these his thousand men he has to provide raw-material,
machinery, arrangement, houseroom; and ever at the week's end, wages
by due sale. No Civil-List,* or Goulburn–Baring Budget* has he to fall
back upon, for paying of his regiment; he has to pick his supplies from
the confused face of the whole Earth and Contemporaneous History,
by his dexterity alone. There will be dry eyes if he fail to do it!——He
exclaims, at present, 'black in the face,' near strangled with Dilettante
Legislation: "Let me have elbow-room, throat-room, and I will not fail!
No, I will spin yet, and conquer like a giant: what 'sinews of war'* lie
in me, untold resources towards the Conquest of this Planet, if instead
of hanging me, you husband them, and help me!"——My indomitable
friend, it is *true*; and thou shalt and must be helped.

This is not a man I would kill and strangle by Corn-Laws, even if
I could! No, I would fling my Corn-Laws and Shotbelts to the Devil;
and try to help this man. I would teach him, by noble precept and
law-precept, by noble example most of all, that Mammonism was not
the essence of his or of my station in God's Universe; but the adscititious excrescence of it; the gross, terrene, godless embodiment of it;
which would have to become, more or less, a godlike one. By noble
real legislation, by true *noble's*-work, by unwearied, valiant, and were
it wageless effort, in my Parliament and in my Parish, I would aid,
constrain, encourage him to effect more or less this blessed change.
I should know that it would have to be effected; that unless it were in
some measure effected, he and I and all of us, I first and soonest of all,
were doomed to perdition!——Effected it will be; unless it were
a Demon that made this Universe; which I, for my own part, do at no
moment, under no form, in the least believe.

May it please your Serene Highnesses, your Majesties, Lordships
and Law-wardships, the proper Epic of this world is not now 'Arms and
the Man;' how much less, 'Shirt-frills and the Man:' no, it is now 'Tools
and the Man:'* that, henceforth to all time, is now our Epic;—and you,
first of all others, I think, were wise to take note of that!

CHAPTER XIII.

DEMOCRACY.

IF the Serene Highnesses and Majesties do not take note of that, then, as I perceive, *that* will take note of itself! The time for levity, insincerity, and idle babble and play-acting, in all kinds, is gone by; it is a serious, grave time. Old long-vexed questions, not yet solved in logical words or parliamentary laws, are fast solving themselves in facts, somewhat unblessed to behold! This largest of questions, this question of Work and Wages, which ought, had we heeded Heaven's voice, to have begun two generations ago or more, cannot be delayed longer without hearing Earth's voice. 'Labour' will verily need to be somewhat 'organised,' as they say,—God knows with what difficulty. Man will actually need to have his debts and earnings a little better paid by man; which, let Parliaments speak of them or be silent of them, are eternally his due from man, and cannot, without penalty and at length not without death-penalty, be withheld. How much ought to cease among us straightway; how much ought to begin straightway, while the hours yet are!

Truly they are strange results to which this of leaving all to 'Cash;' of quietly shutting-up the God's Temple, and gradually opening wide-open the Mammon's Temple, with 'Laissez-faire, and Every man for himself,'—have led us in these days! We have Upper, speaking Classes, who indeed do 'speak' as never man spake before; the withered flimsiness, the godless baseness and barrenness of whose Speech might of itself indicate what kind of Doing and practical Governing went on under it! For Speech is the gaseous element out of which most kinds of Practice and Performance, especially all kinds of moral Performance, condense themselves, and take shape; as the one is, so will the other be. Descending, accordingly, into the Dumb Class in its Stockport Cellars and Poor-Law Bastilles, have we not to announce that they also are hitherto unexampled in the History of Adam's Posterity?

Life was never a May-game for men: in all times the lot of the dumb millions born to toil was defaced with manifold sufferings, injustices, heavy burdens, avoidable and unavoidable; not play at all, but hard work that made the sinews sore and the heart sore. As bond-slaves, *villani, bordarii, sochemanni,** nay indeed as dukes, earls and kings, men were oftentimes made weary of their life; and had to say, in the sweat of their brow and of their soul, Behold, it is not sport, it is grim earnest, and our back can bear no more! Who knows not what massacrings and harryings there have been; grinding, long-continuing, unbearable injustices,—till the heart had to rise in madness, and some "*Eu Sachsen, nimith euer sachses,* You Saxons, out with your gully-knives, then!"* You Saxons, some 'arrestment,' partial 'arrestment of the Knaves and Dastards' has become indispensable!—The page of Dryasdust is heavy with such details.

And yet I will venture to believe that in no time, since the beginnings of Society, was the lot of those same dumb millions of toilers so entirely unbearable as it is even in the days now passing over us. It is not to die, or even to die of hunger, that makes a man wretched; many men have died; all men must die,—the last exit of us all is in a Fire-Chariot of Pain.* But it is to live miserable we know not why; to work sore and yet gain nothing; to be heart-worn, weary, yet isolated, unrelated, girt-in with a cold-universal Laissez-faire: it is to die slowly all our life long, imprisoned in a deaf, dead, Infinite Injustice,* as in the accursed iron belly of a Phalaris' Bull!* This is and remains forever intolerable to all men whom God has made. Do we wonder at French Revolutions, Chartisms, Revolts of Three Days?* The times, if we will consider them, are really unexampled.

Never before did I hear of an Irish Widow reduced to 'prove her sisterhood by dying of typhus-fever and infecting seventeen persons,'*— saying in such undeniable way, "You *see* I was your sister!" Sisterhood, brotherhood, was often forgotten; but not till the rise of these ultimate Mammon and Shotbelt Gospels did I ever see it so expressly denied. If no pious Lord or *Law-ward* would remember it, always some pious Lady ('*Hlaf-dig,*' Benefactress, '*Loaf-giveress,*'* they say she is,— blessings on her beautiful heart!) was there, with mild mother-voice and hand, to remember it; some pious thoughtful *Elder*, what we now call 'Prester,' *Presbyter* or 'Priest,'* was there to put all men in mind of it, in the name of the God who had made all.

Not even in Black Dahomey* was it ever, I think, forgotten to the typhus-fever length. Mungo Park, resourceless, had sunk down to die under the Negro Village-Tree, a horrible White object in the eyes of all. But in the poor Black Woman, and her daughter who stood aghast at him, whose earthly wealth and funded capital consisted of one small calabash of rice, there lived a heart richer than *Laissez-faire*:

they, with a royal munificence, boiled their rice for him; they sang all night to him, spinning assiduous on their cotton distaffs, as he lay to sleep: 'Let us pity the poor white man; no mother has he to fetch him milk, no sister to grind him corn!'* Thou poor black Noble One,—thou *Lady* too: did not a God make thee too; was there not in thee too something of a God!—

Gurth, born thrall of Cedric the Saxon, has been greatly pitied by Dryasdust and others. Gurth, with the brass collar round his neck, tending Cedric's pigs in the glades of the wood, is not what I call an exemplar of human felicity: but Gurth, with the sky above him, with the free air and tinted boscage and umbrage round him, and in him at least the certainty of supper and social lodging when he came home; Gurth to me seems happy, in comparison with many a Lancashire and Buckinghamshire man of these days, not born thrall of anybody! Gurth's brass collar did not gall him: Cedric *deserved* to be his master. The pigs were Cedric's, but Gurth too would get his parings of them. Gurth had the inexpressible satisfaction of feeling himself related indissolubly, though in a rude brass-collar way, to his fellow-mortals in this Earth.* He had superiors, inferiors, equals.—Gurth is now 'emancipated'* long since; has what we call 'Liberty.' Liberty, I am told, is a divine thing.* Liberty when it becomes the 'Liberty to die by starvation' is not so divine!

Liberty? The true liberty of a man, you would say, consisted in his finding out, or being forced to find out the right path, and to walk thereon. To learn, or to be taught, what work he actually was able for; and then by permission, persuasion, and even compulsion, to set about doing of the same! That is his true blessedness, honour, 'liberty' and maximum of wellbeing: if liberty be not that, I for one have small care about liberty. You do not allow a palpable madman to leap over precipices;* you violate his liberty, you that are wise; and keep him, were it in strait-waistcoats, away from the precipices! Every stupid, every cowardly and foolish man is but a less palpable madman: his true liberty were that a wiser man, that any and every wiser man, could, by brass collars, or in whatever milder or sharper way, lay hold of him when he was going wrong, and order and compel him to go a little righter. O, if thou really art my *Senior*, Seigneur, my *Elder*, Presbyter or Priest,—if thou art in very deed my *Wiser*, may a beneficent instinct lead and impel thee to 'conquer' me, to command me! If thou do know better than I what is good and right, I conjure thee in the name of God, force me to do it; were it by never such brass collars, whips and handcuffs, leave me not to walk over precipices! That I have been called, by all the Newspapers, a 'free man' will avail me little, if my pilgrimage have ended in death and wreck. O that the Newspapers had called me slave, coward, fool, or what it pleased their sweet voices to name me, and I had attained not death, but life!—Liberty requires new definitions.

A conscious abhorrence and intolerance of Folly, of Baseness, Stupidity, Poltroonery and all that brood of things, dwells deep in some men: still deeper in others an *un*conscious abhorrence and intolerance, clothed moreover by the beneficent Supreme Powers in what stout appetites, energies, egoisms so-called, are suitable to it;—these latter are your Conquerors, Romans, Normans, Russians, Indo-English; Founders of what we call Aristocracies. Which indeed have they not the most 'divine right' to found;—being themselves very truly Αριστοι, BRAVEST, BEST;* and conquering generally a confused rabble of WORST, or at lowest, clearly enough, of WORSE? I think their divine right, tried, with affirmatory verdict, in the greatest Law-Court known to me, was good! A class of men who are dreadfully exclaimed against by Dryasdust; of whom nevertheless beneficent Nature has oftentimes had need; and may, alas, again have need.

When, across the hundredfold poor scepticisms, trivialisms, and constitutional cobwebberies of Dryasdust, you catch any glimpse of a William the Conqueror, a Tancred of Hauteville* or such like,—do you not discern veritably some rude outline of a true God-made King; whom not the Champion of England cased in tin, but all Nature and the Universe were calling to the throne? It is absolutely necessary that he get thither. Nature does not mean her poor Saxon children to perish, of obesity, stupor or other malady, as yet: a stern Ruler and Line of Rulers therefore is called in,—a stern but most beneficent *Perpetual House-Surgeon* is by Nature herself called in, and even the appropriate *fees* are provided for him! Dryasdust talks lamentably about Hereward and the Fen Counties; fate of Earl Waltheof; Yorkshire and the North reduced to ashes:* all which is undoubtedly lamentable. But even Dryasdust apprises me of one fact: 'A child, in this William's reign, might have carried a purse of gold from end to end of England.'* My erudite friend, it is a fact which outweighs a thousand! Sweep away thy constitutional, sentimental and other cobwebberies; look eye

to eye, if thou still have any eye, in the face of this big burly William
Bastard: thou wilt see a fellow of most flashing discernment, of most
strong lion-heart;—in whom, as it were, within a frame of oak and
iron, the gods have planted the soul of 'a man of genius!' Dost thou
call that nothing? I call it an immense thing!—Rage enough was in
this Willelmus Conquestor, rage enough for his occasions;—and
yet the essential element of him, as of all such men, is not scorching
fire, but shining illuminative *light*. Fire and light are strangely inter-
changeable; nay, at bottom, I have found them different forms of the
same most godlike 'elementary substance' in our world: a thing
worth stating in these days. The essential element of this Conquestor
is, first of all, the most sun-eyed perception of what *is* really what on
this God's-Earth;—which, thou wilt find, does mean at bottom
'Justice,' and 'Virtues' not a few: *Conformity* to what the Maker has
seen good to make; that, I suppose, will mean Justice and a Virtue or
two?—

Dost thou think Willelmus Conquestor would have tolerated ten
years' jargon, one hour's jargon, on the propriety of killing Cotton-
manufactures by partridge Corn-Laws? I fancy, this was not the man
to knock out of his night's-rest with nothing but a noisy bedlamism in
your mouth! "Assist us still better to bush the partridges; strangle
Plugson who spins the shirts?"—"*Par la Splendeur de Dieu!*"*——Dost
thou think Willelmus Conquestor, in this new time, with Steamengine
Captains of Industry on one hand of him, and Joe-Manton Captains
of Idleness on the other, would have doubted which *was* really the
BEST; which did deserve strangling, and which not?

I have a certain indestructible regard for Willelmus Conquestor.
A resident House-Surgeon, provided by Nature for her beloved
English People, and even furnished with the requisite fees, as I said;
for he by no means felt himself doing Nature's work, this Willelmus,
but his own work exclusively! And his own work withal it was;
informed '*par la Splendeur de Dieu*.'—I say, it is necessary to get the
work out of such a man, however harsh that be! When a world, not yet
doomed for death, is rushing down to ever-deeper Baseness and
Confusion, it is a dire necessity of Nature's to bring in her
ARISTOCRACIES, her BEST, even by forcible methods. When their
descendants or representatives cease entirely to *be* the Best, Nature's
poor world will very soon rush down again to Baseness; and it becomes
a dire necessity of Nature's to cast them out. Hence French Revolutions,

Five-point Charters, Democracies, and a mournful list of *Etceteras*, in these our afflicted times.

To what extent Democracy has now reached, how it advances irresistible with ominous, ever-increasing speed, he that will open his eyes on any province of human affairs may discern.* Democracy is everywhere the inexorable demand of these ages, swiftly fulfilling itself. From the thunder of Napoleon battles, to the jabbering of Open-vestry in St. Mary Axe, all things announce Democracy.* A distinguished man, whom some of my readers will hear again with pleasure, thus writes to me what in these days he notes from the Wahngasse of Weissnichtwo,* where our London fashions seem to be in full vogue. Let us hear the Herr Teufelsdröckh again, were it but the smallest word!

'Democracy, which means despair of finding any Heroes to govern you,* and contented putting-up with the want of them,—alas, thou too, *mein Lieber*, seest well how close it is of kin to *Atheism*, and other sad *Isms*: he who discovers no God whatever, how shall he discover Heroes, the visible Temples of God?—Strange enough meanwhile it is, to observe with what thoughtlessness, here in our rigidly Conservative Country, men rush into Democracy with full cry. Beyond doubt, his Excellenz the Titular-Herr Ritter Kauderwälsch von Pferdefuss-Quacksalber,* he our distinguished Conservative Premier himself, and all but the thicker-headed of his Party, discern Democracy to be inevitable as death, and are even desperate of delaying it much!

'You cannot walk the streets without beholding Democracy announce itself: the very Tailor has become, if not properly Sansculottic, which to him would be ruinous, yet a Tailor unconsciously symbolising, and prophesying with his scissors, the reign of Equality. What now is our fashionable coat? A thing of superfinest texture, of deeply meditated cut; with Malines-lace* cuffs; quilted with gold; so that a man can carry, without difficulty, an estate of land on his back? *Keineswegs*, By no manner of means! The Sumptuary Laws* have fallen into such a state of desuetude as was never before seen. Our fashionable coat is an amphibium between barn-sack and drayman's doublet. The cloth of it is studiously coarse; the colour a speckled soot-black or rust-brown grey; the nearest approach to a Peasant's. And for shape,—thou shouldst see it! The last consummation of the year now passing over us is definable as Three Bags; a big bag for the body, two small bags for the arms, and by way of collar a hem! The first Antique Cheruscan who, of felt-cloth or bear's-hide, with bone or metal needle, set about making himself a coat, before Tailors had yet awakened out of Nothing,—did not he make it even so? A loose wide poke for body, with two holes to let out the arms; this was his original coat: to which holes it was soon visible that two small loose pokes, or sleeves, easily appended, would be an improvement.*

'Thus has the Tailor-art, so to speak, overset itself, like most other things; changed its centre-of-gravity; whirled suddenly over from zenith to nadir. Your Stulz, with huge somerset, vaults from his high shop-board down to the depths of primal savagery,*—carrying much along with him! For I will invite thee to reflect that the Tailor, as topmost ultimate froth of Human Society, is indeed swift-passing, evanescent, slippery to decipher; yet significant of much, nay of all. Topmost evanescent froth, he is churned-up from the very lees, and from all intermediate regions of the liquor. The general outcome he, visible to the eye, of what men aimed to do, and were obliged and enabled to do, in this one public department of symbolising themselves to each other by covering of their skins. A smack of all Human Life lies in the Tailor: its wild struggles towards beauty, dignity, freedom, victory; and how, hemmed-in by Sedan and Huddersfield,* by Nescience, Dulness, Prurience, and other sad necessities and laws of Nature, it has attained just to this: Grey Savagery of Three Sacks with a hem!

'When the very Tailor verges towards Sansculottism, is it not ominous? The last Divinity of poor mankind dethroning himself; sinking *his* taper too, flame downmost, like the Genius of Sleep or of Death;* admonitory that Tailor time shall be no more!—For, little as one could advise Sumptuary Laws at the present epoch, yet nothing is clearer than that where ranks do actually exist, strict division of costumes will also be enforced; that if we ever have a new Hierarchy and Aristocracy, acknowledged veritably as such, for which I daily pray Heaven, the Tailor will reawaken; and be, by volunteering and appointment, consciously and unconsciously, a safeguard of that same.'—Certain farther observations, from the same invaluable pen, on our never-ending changes of mode, our 'perpetual nomadic and even ape-like appetite for change and mere change' in all the equipments of our existence, and the 'fatal revolutionary character' thereby manifested, we suppress for the present. It may be admitted that Democracy, in all meanings of the word, is in full career; irresistible by any Ritter Kauderwälsch or other Son of Adam, as times go. 'Liberty' is a thing men are determined to have.

But truly, as I had to remark in the meanwhile, 'the liberty of not being oppressed by your fellow man'* is an indispensable, yet one of the most insignificant fractional parts of Human Liberty. No man oppresses thee, can bid thee fetch or carry, come or go, without reason shewn. True; from all men thou art emancipated: but from Thyself and from the Devil—? No man, wiser, unwiser, can make thee come or go: but thy own futilities, bewilderments, thy false appetites for Money, Windsor Georges* and such like? No man oppresses thee, O free and independent Franchiser: but does not this stupid Porter-pot oppress thee? No Son of Adam can bid thee come or go; but this absurd Pot of Heavy-wet,* this can and does! Thou art the thrall not of Cedric the Saxon, but of thy own brutal appetites, and this scoured dish of liquor. And thou pratest of thy 'liberty?' Thou entire blockhead!

Heavy-wet and gin: alas, these are not the only kinds of thraldom. Thou who walkest in a vain shew,* looking out with ornamental dilettante sniff and serene supremacy at all Life and all Death; and amblest jauntily; perking up thy poor talk into crotchets, thy poor conduct into fatuous somnambulisms;—and *art* as an 'enchanted Ape' under God's sky, where thou mightest have been a man, had proper Schoolmasters and Conquerors, and Constables with cat-o'-nine tails, been vouchsafed thee; dost thou call that 'liberty?' Or your unreposing Mammon-worshipper again, driven, as if by Galvanisms, by Devils and Fixed-Ideas, who rises early and sits late, chasing the impossible; straining every faculty to 'fill himself with the east wind,'*—how merciful were it, could you, by mild persuasion, or by the severest tyranny so-called, check him in his mad path, and turn him into a wiser one! All painful tyranny, in that case again, were but mild 'surgery;' the pain of it cheap, as health and life, instead of galvanism and fixed-idea, are cheap at any price.

Sure enough, of all paths a man could strike into, there *is*, at any given moment, a *best path* for every man; a thing which, here and now, it were of all things *wisest* for him to do;—which could he be but led or driven to do, he were then doing 'like a man,' as we phrase it; all men and gods agreeing with him, the whole Universe virtually exclaiming Well-done to him! His success, in such case, were complete;

his felicity a maximum. This path, to find this path and walk in it, is the one thing needful for him. Whatsoever forwards him in that, let it come to him even in the shape of blows and spurnings, is liberty: whatsoever hinders him, were it wardmotes, open-vestries, poll-booths, tremendous cheers, rivers of heavy-wet, is slavery.

The notion that a man's liberty consists in giving his vote at election-hustings, and saying, "Behold, now I too have my twenty-thousandth part of a Talker in our National Palaver;* will not all the gods be good to me?"—is one of the pleasantest! Nature nevertheless is kind at present; and puts it into the heads of many, almost of all. The liberty especially which has to purchase itself by social isolation, and each man standing separate from the other, having 'no business with him' but a cash-account: this is such a liberty as the Earth seldom saw;—as the Earth will not long put up with, recommend it how you may. This liberty turns out, before it have long continued in action, with all men flinging up their caps round it, to be, for the Working Millions a liberty to die by want of food; for the Idle Thousands and Units, alas, a still more fatal liberty to live in want of work; to have no earnest duty to do in this God's-World any more. What becomes of a man in such predicament? Earth's Laws are silent; and Heaven's speak in a voice which is not heard. No work, and the ineradicable need of work, give rise to new very wondrous life-philosophies, new very wondrous life-practices! Dilettantism, Pococurantism,* Beau-Brummelism,* with perhaps an occasional, half-mad, protesting burst of Byronism, establish themselves: at the end of a certain period,—if you go back to 'the Dead Sea,' there is, say our Moslem friends, a very strange 'Sabbath-day' transacting itself there!*—Brethren, we know but imperfectly yet, after ages of Constitutional Government, what Liberty is and Slavery is.

Democracy, the chase of Liberty in that direction, shall go its full course; unrestrainable by him of Pferdefuss-Quacksalber, or any of *his* household. The Toiling Millions of Mankind, in most vital need and passionate instinctive desire of Guidance, shall cast away False-Guidance; and hope, for an hour, that No-Guidance will suffice them: but it can be for an hour only. The smallest item of human Slavery is the oppression of man by his Mock-Superiors; the palpablest, but I say at bottom the smallest. Let him shake off such oppression, trample it indignantly under his feet; I blame him not, I pity and commend him. But oppression by your Mock-Superiors well shaken off, the grand problem yet remains to solve: That of finding government by your Real-Superiors! Alas, how shall we ever learn the solution of that, benighted, bewildered, sniffing, sneering, godforgetting unfortunates as we are? It is a work for centuries; to be taught us by tribulations, confusions, insurrections, obstructions; who knows if not by conflagration and despair! It is a lesson inclusive of all other lessons; the hardest of all lessons to learn.

One thing I do know: Those Apes, chattering on the branches by the Dead Sea, never got it learned; but chatter there to this day. To them no Moses need come a second time; a thousand Moseses would be but so many painted Phantasms, interesting Fellow-Apes of new strange aspect,—whom they would 'invite to dinner,' be glad to meet with in lion-soirées.* To them the voice of Prophecy, of heavenly monition, is quite ended. They chatter there, all Heaven shut to them, to the end of the world. The unfortunates! O, what is dying of hunger, with honest tools in your hand, with a manful purpose in your heart, and much real labour lying round you done, in comparison? You honestly quit your tools; quit a most muddy confused coil of sore work, short rations, of sorrows, dispiritments and contradictions, having now honestly done with it all;—and await, not entirely in a distracted manner, what the Supreme Powers, and the Silences and the Eternities may have to say to you.

A second thing I know: This lesson will have to be learned,—under penalties! England will either learn it, or England also will cease to exist among Nations. England will either learn to reverence its Heroes, and discriminate them from its Sham-Heroes and Valets and gaslighted Histrios; and to prize them as the audible God's-voice, amid all inane jargons and temporary market-cries, and say to them with heart-loyalty, "Be ye King and Priest, and Gospel and Guidance for us:" or else England will continue to worship new and ever-new forms of Quackhood,—and so, with what resiliences and reboundings matters little, go down to the Father of Quacks! Can I dread such things of England? Wretched, thick-eyed, gross-hearted mortals, why will ye worship lies, and 'Stuffed Clothes-suits created by the ninth-parts of men!'* It is not your purses that suffer; your farm-rents, your commerces, your mill-revenues, loud as ye lament over these; no, it is not these alone, but a far deeper than these: it is your souls that lie dead, crushed down under despicable Nightmares, Atheisms, Brain-fumes; and are not souls at all, but mere succedanea for *salt* to keep your bodies and their appetites from putrefying! Your cotton-spinning and thrice-miraculous mechanism, what is this too, by itself, but a larger kind of Animalism? Spiders can spin, Beavers can build and shew contrivance; the Ant lays-up accumulation of capital, and has, for aught I know, a Bank of Antland. If there is no soul in man higher than all that, did it reach to sailing on the cloud-rack and spinning sea-sand; then I say, man is but an animal, a more cunning kind of brute: he has no soul, but only a succedaneum for salt.* Whereupon, seeing himself to be truly of the beasts that perish, he ought to admit it, I think;—and also straightway universally to kill himself; and so, in a manlike manner at least *end*, and wave these brute-worlds *his* dignified farewell!—

CHAPTER XIV.

SIR JABESH WINDBAG.*

OLIVER CROMWELL, whose body they hung on their Tyburn gallows because he had found the Christian Religion inexecutable in this country, remains to me by far the remarkablest Governor we have had here for the last five centuries or so. For the last five centuries, there has been no Governor among us with anything like similar talent; and for the last two centuries, no Governor, we may say, with the possibility of similar talent,—with an idea in the heart of him capable of inspiring similar talent, capable of co-existing therewith. When you consider that Oliver believed in a God, the difference between Oliver's position and that of any subsequent Governor of this Country becomes, the more you reflect on it, the more immeasurable!

Oliver, no volunteer in Public Life, but plainly a ballotted soldier strictly ordered thither, enters upon Public Life; comports himself there like a man who carried his own life itself in his hand; like a man whose Great Commander's eye was always on him. Not without results. Oliver, well-advanced in years, finds now, by Destiny and his own Deservings, or as he himself better phrased it, by wondrous successive 'Births of Providence,'* the Government of England put into his hands. In senate-house and battle-field, in counsel and in action, in private and in public, this man has proved himself a man: England and the voice of God, through waste awful whirlwinds and environments, speaking to his great heart, summon him to assert formally, in the way of solemn Public Fact and as a new piece of English Law, what informally and by Nature's eternal Law needed no asserting, That he, Oliver, was the Ablest Man of England, the King of England;* that he, Oliver, would undertake governing England. His way of making this same 'assertion,' the one way he had of making it, has given rise to immense criticism: but the assertion itself, in what way soever 'made,' is it not somewhat of a solemn one, somewhat of a tremendous one!

And now do but contrast this Oliver with my right honourable friend Sir Jabesh Windbag, Mr. Facing-both-ways, Viscount Mealymouth, Earl of Windlestraw,* or what other Cagliostro, Cagliostrino, Cagliostraccio,* the course of Fortune and Parliamentary Majorities has constitutionally guided to that dignity, any time during these last sorrowful hundred-and-fifty years! Windbag, weak in the faith of a God, which he believes only at Church on Sundays, if even then; strong only in the faith that Paragraphs and Plausibilities bring votes;* that Force of Public Opinion, as he calls it, is the primal Necessity of Things, and highest God we have:—Windbag, if we will consider him, has a problem set before him which may be ranged in the impossible class. He is a Columbus minded to sail to the indistinct country of NOWHERE, to the indistinct country of WHITHERWARD, by the *friendship* of those same waste-tumbling Water-Alps and howling waltz of All the Winds; not by conquest of them and in spite of them, but by friendship of them, when once *they* have made up their mind! He is the most original Columbus I ever saw. Nay, his problem is not an impossible one: he will infallibly *arrive* at that same country of NOWHERE; his indistinct Whitherward will be a *Thither*ward! In the Ocean Abysses and Locker of Davy Jones,* there certainly enough do he and *his* ship's company, and all their cargo and navigatings, at last find lodgment.

Oliver knew that his America lay THERE,* Westward Ho;—and it was not entirely by *friendship* of the Water-Alps, and yeasty insane Froth-Oceans, that he meant to get thither! He sailed accordingly; had compass-card, and Rules of Navigation,—older and greater than these Froth-Oceans, old as the Eternal God! Or again, do but think of this. Windbag in these his probable five years of office has to prosper and get Paragraphs:* the Paragraphs of these five years must be his salvation, or he is a lost man; redemption nowhere in the Worlds or in the Times discoverable for him.* Oliver too would like his Paragraphs; successes, popularities in these five years are not undesirable to him: but mark, I say, this enormous circumstance: *after* these five years are gone and done, comes an Eternity for Oliver! Oliver has to appear before the Most High Judge: the utmost flow of Paragraphs, the utmost ebb of them, is now, in strictest arithmetic, verily no matter at all; its exact value *zero*; an account altogether erased! Enormous;— which a man, in these days, hardly fancies with an effort! Oliver's Paragraphs are all done, his battles, division-lists, successes all summed: and now in that awful unerring Court of Review, the real question first rises, Whether he has succeeded at all; whether he has not been defeated miserably forevermore? Let him come with world-wide *Io-Pæans*, these avail him not. Let him come covered over with the world's execrations, gashed with ignominious death-wounds, the gallows-rope about his neck: what avails that? The word is, Come thou brave and faithful; the word is, Depart thou quack and accursed!

O Windbag, my right honourable friend, in very truth I pity thee. I say, these Paragraphs, and low or loud votings of thy poor fellow-blockheads of mankind, will never guide thee in any enterprise at all. Govern a country on such guidance? Thou canst not make a pair of shoes, sell a pennyworth of tape, on such. No, thy shoes are vamped up falsely to meet the market; behold, the leather only *seemed* to be tanned; thy shoes melt under me to rubbishy pulp, and are not verit-able mud-defying shoes, but plausible vendible similitudes of shoes,— thou unfortunate, and I! O my right honourable friend, when the Paragraphs flowed in, who was like Sir Jabesh? On the swelling tide he mounted; higher, higher, triumphant, heaven-high. But the Paragraphs again ebbed out, as unwise Paragraphs needs must: Sir Jabesh lies stranded, sunk and forever sinking in ignominious ooze; the Mud-nymphs, and ever-deepening bottomless Oblivion, his portion to eternal time. 'Posterity?' Thou appealest to Posterity, thou?* My right honourable friend, what will Posterity do for thee! The voting of Posterity, were it continued through centuries in thy favour, will be quite inaudible, extra-forensic, without any effect whatever. Posterity can do simply nothing for a man; nor even seem to do much, if the man be not brainsick. Besides, to tell the truth, the bets are a thou-sand to one, Posterity will not hear of thee, my right honourable friend! Posterity, I have found, has generally his own Windbags suffi-ciently trumpeted in all market-places, and no leisure to attend to ours. Posterity, which has made of Norse Odin a similitude, and of Norman William a brute monster, what will or can it make of English Jabesh? O Heavens, 'Posterity!'—

"These poor persecuted Scotch Covenanters," said I to my inquiring Frenchman, in such stinted French as stood at command, *"ils s'en appelaient à"*—*"A la Postérité,"* interrupted he, helping me out.— *"Ah, Monsieur, non, mille fois non!* They appealed to the Eternal God; not to Posterity at all!* *C'était différent."*

CHAPTER XV.

MORRISON AGAIN.

NEVERTHELESS, O Advanced Liberal, one cannot promise thee any 'New Religion,' for some time; to say truth, I do not think we have the smallest chance of any!* Will the candid reader, by way of closing this Book Third, listen to a few transient remarks on that subject?

Candid readers have not lately met with any man who had less notion to interfere with their Thirty-Nine or other Church-Articles; wherewith, very helplessly as is like, they may have struggled to form for themselves some not inconceivable hypothesis about this Universe, and their own Existence there. Superstition, my friend, is far from me; Fanaticism, for any *Fanum** likely to arise soon on this Earth, is far. A man's Church-Articles are surely articles of price to him; and in these times one has to be tolerant of many strange 'Articles,' and of many still stranger 'No-articles,' which go about placarding themselves in a very distracted manner,—the numerous long placard-poles, and questionable infirm paste-pots, interfering with one's peaceable thoroughfare sometimes!

Fancy a man, moreover, recommending his fellow men to believe in God, that so Chartism might abate, and the Manchester Operatives be got to spin peaceably! The idea is more distracted than any placard-pole seen hitherto in a public thoroughfare of men! My friend, if thou ever do come to believe in God, thou wilt find all Chartism, Manchester riot, Parliamentary incompetence, Ministries of Windbag, and the wildest Social Dissolutions, and the burning-up of this entire Planet, a most small matter in comparison. Brother, this Planet, I find, is but an inconsiderable sand-grain in the continents of Being: this Planet's poor temporary interests, thy interests and my interests there, when I look fixedly into that eternal Light-Sea and Flame-Sea with *its* eternal interests, dwindle literally into Nothing; my speech of it is—silence for the while. I will as soon think of making Galaxies and Star-Systems to guide little herring-vessels by, as of preaching Religion that the Constable may continue possible.* O my Advanced-Liberal friend, this new second progress, of proceeding 'to invent God,' is a very strange one!* Jacobinism unfolded into Saint-Simonism* bodes innumerable blessed things; but the thing itself might draw tears from a Stoic!*—As for me, some twelve or thirteen New Religions, heavy Packets, most of them unfranked, having arrived here from various parts of the world,* in a space of six calendar months, I have instructed my invaluable friend the Stamped Postman to introduce no more of them, if the charge exceed one penny.*

Henry of Essex, duelling in that Thames Island, 'near to Reading Abbey,'* had a religion. But was it in virtue of his seeing armed Phantasms of St. Edmund 'on the rim of the horizon,'* looking minatory on him? Had that, intrinsically, anything to do with his religion at all? Henry of Essex's religion was the Inner Light or Moral Conscience* of his own soul; such as is vouchsafed still to all souls of men;—which Inner Light shone here 'through such intellectual and other media' as there were; producing 'Phantasms,' Kircherean Visual-Spectra,* according to circumstances! It is so with all men. The clearer my Inner may shine, through the *less* turbid media, the *fewer* Phantasms it may produce,—the gladder surely shall I be, and not the sorrier! Hast thou reflected, O serious reader, Advanced-Liberal or other, that the one end, essence, use of all religion past, present and to come, was this only: To keep that same Moral Conscience or Inner Light of ours alive and shining;—which certainly the 'Phantasms' and the 'turbid media' were not essential for! All religion was here to remind us, better or worse, of what we already know better or worse, of the quite *infinite* difference there is between a Good man and a Bad; to bid us love infinitely the one, abhor and avoid infinitely the other,—strive infinitely to *be* the one, and not to be the other. 'All religion issues in due Practical Hero-worship.'* He that has a soul unasphyxied will never want a religion; he that has a soul asphyxied, reduced to a succedaneum for salt, will never find any religion, though you rose from the dead to preach him one.

But indeed, when men and reformers ask for 'a religion,' it is analogous to their asking, 'What would you have us to do?' and such like. They fancy that their religion too shall be a kind of Morrison's Pill, which they have only to swallow once, and all will be well. Resolutely once gulp down your Religion, your Morrison's Pill, you have it all plain sailing now: you can follow your affairs, your no-affairs, go along money-hunting, pleasure-hunting, dilettanteing, dangling, and miming and chattering like a Dead-Sea Ape: your Morrison will do your business for you. Men's notions are very strange!—Brother, I say there is not, was not, nor will ever be, in the wide circle of Nature, any Pill or Religion of that character. Man cannot afford thee such; for the very gods it is impossible. I advise thee to renounce Morrison; once for all, quit hope of the Universal Pill. For body, for soul, for individual or society, there has not any such article been made. *Non extat.** In Created Nature it is not, was not, will not be. In the void imbroglios of Chaos only, and realms of Bedlam, does some shadow of it hover, to bewilder and bemock the poor inhabitants *there*.

Rituals, Liturgies, Creeds, Hierarchies: all this is not religion; all this, were it dead as Odinism, as Fetishism,* does not kill religion at all! It is Stupidity alone, with never so many rituals, that kills religion. Is not this still a World? Spinning Cotton under Arkwright and Adam Smith; founding Cities by the Fountain of Juturna, on the Janiculum Mount;* tilling Canaan under Prophet Samuel and Psalmist David,* man is ever man; the missionary of Unseen Powers; and great and victorious, while he continues true to his mission; mean, miserable, foiled, and at last annihilated and trodden out of sight and memory, when he proves untrue. Brother, thou art a Man, I think; thou art not a mere building Beaver, or two-legged Cotton-Spider; thou hast verily a Soul in thee, asphyxied or otherwise! Sooty Manchester,—it too is built on the infinite Abysses; overspanned by the skyey Firmaments; and there is birth in it, and death in it;—and it is every whit as wonderful, as fearful, unimaginable, as the oldest Salem* or Prophetic City. Go or stand, in what time, in what place we will, are there not Immensities, Eternities over us, around us, in us:

'Solemn before us,
Veiled, the dark Portal,
Goal of all mortal:—
Stars silent rest o'er us,
Graves under us silent!'*

Between *these* two great Silences, the hum of all our spinning cylinders, Trades-Unions, Anti-Corn-Law Leagues and Carlton Clubs* goes on. Stupidity itself ought to pause a little and consider that. I tell thee, through all thy Ledgers, Supply-and-demand Philosophies, and daily most modern melancholy Business and Cant, there does shine the presence of a Primeval Unspeakable; and thou wert wise to recognise, not with lips only, that same!

The Maker's Laws, whether they are promulgated in Sinai Thunder, to the ear or imagination, or quite otherwise promulgated, are the Laws of God; transcendant, everlasting, imperatively demanding obedience from all men. This, without any thunder, or with never so much thunder, thou, if there be any soul left in thee, canst know of a truth. The Universe, I say, is made by Law; the great Soul of the World is just and not unjust. Look thou, if thou have eyes or soul left, into this great shoreless Incomprehensible: in the heart of its tumultuous Appearances, Embroilments, and mad Time-vortexes, is there not, silent, eternal, an All-just, an All-beautiful; sole Reality and ultimate controlling Power of the whole? This is not a figure of speech; this is a fact. The fact of Gravitation known to all animals, is not surer than this inner Fact, which may be known to all men. He who knows this, it will sink, silent, awful, unspeakable, into his heart. He will say with Faust:* "Who *dare* name HIM?" Most rituals or 'namings' he will fall in with at present, are like to be 'namings'—which shall be nameless! In silence, in the Eternal Temple,* let him worship, if there be no fit word: Such knowledge, the crown of his whole spiritual being, the life of his life, let him keep and sacredly walk by. He has a religion. Hourly and daily, for himself and for the whole world, a faithful, unspoken, but not ineffectual prayer rises, "Thy will be done."* His whole work on Earth is an emblematic spoken or acted prayer, Be the will of God done on Earth,—not the Devil's will, or any of the Devil's servants' wills! He has a religion, this man; an everlasting Loadstar that beams the brighter in the Heavens, the darker here on Earth grows the night around him. Thou, if thou know not this, what are all rituals, liturgies, mythologies, mass-chantings, turnings of the rotatory calabash? They are as nothing; in a good many respects they are as *less*. Divorced from this, getting half-divorced from this, they are a thing to fill one with a kind of horror; with a sacred inexpressible pity and fear. The most tragical thing a human eye can look on. It was said to the Prophet, "Behold, I will shew thee worse things than these: women weeping to Thammuz."* That was the acme of the Prophet's vision,—then as now.

Rituals, Liturgies, Credos, Sinai Thunder: I know more or less the history of these; the rise, progress, decline and fall of these. Can thunder from all the thirty-two azimuths,* repeated daily for centuries of years, make God's Laws more godlike to me? Brother, No. Perhaps I am grown to be a man now; and do not need the thunder and the terror any longer! Perhaps I am above being frightened; perhaps it is not Fear, but Reverence alone, that shall now lead me!—Revelations, Inspirations? Yes: and thy own god-created Soul; dost thou not call that a 'revelation?' Who made THEE? Where didst Thou come from? The Voice of Eternity, if thou be not a blasphemer and poor asphyxied mute, speaks with that tongue of thine! *Thou* art the latest Birth of Nature; it is 'the Inspiration of the Almighty'* that giveth *thee* understanding! My brother, my brother!—

Under baleful Atheisms, Mammonisms, Joe-Manton Dilettantisms,* with their appropriate Cants and Idolisms, and whatsoever scandalous rubbish obscures and all but extinguishes the soul of man,—religion now is; its Laws, written if not on stone tables, yet on the Azure of Infinitude, in the inner heart of God's Creation, certain as Life, certain as Death! I say the Laws are there, and thou shalt not disobey them. It were better for thee not. Better a hundred deaths than yes. Terrible 'penalties,' withal, if thou still need 'penalties,' are there for disobeying. Dost thou observe, O redtape Politician, that fiery infernal Phenomenon, which men name FRENCH REVOLUTION, sailing, unlooked-for, unbidden; through thy inane Protocol Dominion:— farseen, with splendour, not of Heaven? Ten centuries will see it. There were Tanneries at Meudon* for human skins. And Hell, very truly Hell, had power over God's upper Earth for a season. The cruelest Portent that has risen into created Space these ten centuries: let us hail it, with awestruck repentant hearts, as the voice once more of a God, though of one in wrath. Blessed be the God's-voice; for *it* is true, and Falsehoods have to cease before it! But for that same preternatural quasi-infernal Portent, one could not know what to make of this wretched world, in these days, at all.* The deplorablest quack-ridden, and now hunger-ridden, downtrodden Despicability and *Flebile Ludibrium*,* of redtape Protocols, rotatory Calabashes, Poor-Law Bastilles: who is there that could think of *its* being fated to continue?—

Penalties enough, my brother! This penalty inclusive of all: Eternal Death to thy own hapless Self, if thou heed no other. Eternal Death, I say,—with many meanings old and new, of which let this single one suffice us here: The eternal impossibility for thee to *be* aught but a Chimera, and swift-vanishing deceptive Phantasm, in God's Creation;—swift-vanishing, never to reappear: why should *it* reappear! Thou hadst one chance, thou wilt never have another. Everlasting ages will roll on, and no other be given thee. The foolishest articulate-speaking soul now extant, may not he say to himself: "A whole Eternity I waited to be born; and now I have a whole Eternity waiting to see what I will do when born!"* This is not Theology, this is Arithmetic. And thou but half-discernest this; thou but half-believest it? Alas, on the shores of the Dead Sea on Sabbath, there goes on a Tragedy!—

But we will leave this of 'Religion;' of which, to say truth, it is chiefly profitable in these unspeakable days to keep silence.* Thou needest no 'New Religion;' nor art thou like to get any. Thou hast already more 'religion' than thou makest use of. This day, thou knowest ten commanded duties, seest in thy mind ten things which should be done, for one that thou doest! *Do* one of them; this of itself will shew thee ten others which can and shall be done. "But my future fate?" Yes, thy future fate, indeed! Thy future fate, while thou makest *it* the chief question, seems to me—extremely questionable! I do not think it can be good. Norse Odin, immemorial centuries ago, did not he, though a poor Heathen, in the dawn of Time, teach us that for the Dastard there was, and could be, no good fate; no harbour anywhere, save down with Hela, in the pool of Night!* Dastards, Knaves, are they that lust for Pleasure, that tremble at Pain. For this world and for the next Dastards are a class of creatures made to be 'arrested;' they are good for nothing else, can look for nothing else. A greater than Odin has been here. A greater than Odin has taught us—not a greater Dastardism, I hope! My brother, thou must pray for a *soul;* struggle, as with life-and-death energy, to get back thy soul! Know that; 'religion' is no Morrison's Pill from without, but a reawakening of thy own Self from within:—and, above all, leave me alone of thy 'religions' and 'new religions' here and elsewhere! I am weary of this sick croaking for a Morrison's-Pill religion; for any and for every such. I want none such; and discern all such to be impossible. The resuscitation of old liturgies fallen dead;* much more, the manufacture of

new liturgies that will never be alive:* how hopeless! Stylitisms,*
eremite fanaticisms and fakeerisms; spasmodic agonistic posture-
makings, and narrow, cramped, morbid, if forever noble wrestlings:
all this is not a thing desirable to me. It is a thing the world *has* done
once,—when its beard was not grown as now!

And yet there is, at worst, one Liturgy which does remain forever
unexceptionable: that of *Praying* (as the old Monks did withal) *by
Working*. And indeed the Prayer which accomplished itself in special
chapels at stated hours, and went not with a man, rising up from all
his Work and Action, at all moments sanctifying the same,—what was
it ever good for? 'Work is Worship:' yes, in a highly considerable
sense,—which, in the present state of all 'worship,' who is there that
can unfold! He that understands it well, understands the Prophecy of
the whole Future; the last Evangel, which has included all others. *Its*
cathedral the Dome of Immensity,—hast thou seen it? coped with the
star-galaxies; paved with the green mosaic of land and ocean; and for
altar, verily, the Star-throne of the Eternal! Its litany and psalmody
the noble acts, the heroic work and suffering, and true heart-utterance
of all the Valiant of the Sons of Men. Its choir-music the ancient
Winds and Oceans, and deep-toned, inarticulate, but most speaking
voices of Destiny and History,—supernal ever as of old. Between two
great Silences:

> 'Stars silent rest o'er us,
> Graves under us silent!'

Between which two great Silences, do not, as we said, all human Noises,
in the naturalest times, most *preter*naturally march and roll?—

I will insert this also, in a lower strain, from Sauerteig's *Æsthetische
Springwurzeln*.* 'Worship?' says he: 'Before that inane tumult of
Hearsay filled men's heads, while the world lay yet silent, and the
heart true and open, many things were Worship! To the primeval man
whatsoever good came, descended on him (as, in mere fact, it ever
does) direct from God; whatsoever duty lay visible for him, this
a Supreme God had prescribed. To the present hour I ask thee, Who
else? For the primeval man, in whom dwelt Thought, this Universe
was all a Temple; Life everywhere a Worship.

'What Worship, for example, is there not in mere Washing! Perhaps
one of the most moral things a man, in common cases, has it in his

power to do. Strip thyself, go into the bath, or were it into the limpid pool and running brook, and there wash and be clean; thou wilt step out again a purer and a better man. This consciousness of perfect outer pureness, that to thy skin there now adheres no foreign speck of imperfection, how it radiates in on thee, with cunning symbolic influences, to thy very soul! Thou hast an increase of tendency towards all good things whatsoever. The oldest Eastern Sages, with joy and holy gratitude, had felt it so,—and that it was the Maker's gift and will. Whose else *is* it? It remains a religious duty, from oldest times, in the East.*—Nor could Herr Professor Strauss,* when I put the question, deny that for us at present it is still such here in the West! To that dingy fuliginous Operative, emerging from his soot-mill, what is the first duty I will prescribe, and offer help towards? That he clean the skin of him. *Can* he pray, by any ascertained method? One knows not entirely:—but with soap and a sufficiency of water, he can wash. Even the dull English feel something of this; they have a saying, "Cleanliness is near of kin to Godliness:"*—yet never, in any country, saw I operative men worse washed, and, in a climate drenched with the softest cloudwater, such a scarcity of baths!'—Alas, Sauerteig, our 'operative men' are at present short even of potatoes: what 'duty' can you prescribe to them!

Or let us give a glance at China. Our new friend, the Emperor there, is Pontiff of three hundred million men;* who do all live and work, these many centuries now; authentically patronised by Heaven* so far; and therefore must have some 'religion' of a kind. This Emperor-Pontiff has, in fact, a religious belief of certain Laws of Heaven; observes, with a religious rigour, his 'three thousand punctualities,'* given out by men of insight, some sixty generations since, as a legible transcript of the same,—the Heavens do seem to say, not totally an incorrect one. He has not much of a ritual, this Pontiff-Emperor; believes, it is likest, with the old Monks, that 'Labour is Worship.'* His most public Act of Worship, it appears, is the drawing solemnly at a certain day, on the green bosom of our Mother Earth, when the Heavens, after dead black winter, have again with their vernal radiances awakened her, a distinct red Furrow with the Plough,*—signal that all the Ploughs of China are to begin ploughing and worshipping! It is notable enough. He, in sight of the Seen and Unseen Powers, draws his distinct red Furrow there; saying, and praying, in mute symbolism, so many most eloquent things!

If you ask this Pontiff, "Who made him? What is to become of him and us?" he maintains a dignified reserve; waves his hand and pontiff-eyes over the unfathomable deep of Heaven, the 'Tsien,'* the azure kingdoms of Infinitude; as if asking, "Is it doubtful that we are right *well* made? Can aught that is *wrong* become of us?"—He and his three hundred millions (it is their chief 'punctuality') visit yearly the Tombs of their Fathers; each man the Tomb of his Father and his Mother:* alone there, in silence, with what of 'worship' or of other thought there may be, pauses solemnly each man; the divine Skies all silent over him; the divine Graves, and this divinest Grave, all silent under him; the pulsings of his own soul, if he have any soul, alone audible. Truly it may be a kind of worship! Truly, if a man cannot get some glimpse into the Eternities, looking through this portal,—through what other need he try it?

Our friend the Pontiff-Emperor permits cheerfully, though with contempt, all manner of Buddists, Bonzes, Talapoins and such like, to build brick Temples, on the voluntary principle; to worship with what of chantings, paper-lanterns and tumultuous brayings,* pleases them; and make night hideous,* since they find some comfort in so doing. Cheerfully, though with contempt. He is a wiser Pontiff than many persons think! He is as yet the one Chief Potentate or Priest in this Earth who has made a distinct systematic attempt at what we call the ultimate result of all religion, '*Practical* Hero-worship:' he does incessantly,* with true anxiety, in such way as he can, search and sift (it would appear) his whole enormous population for the Wisest born among them; by which Wisest, as by born Kings, these three hundred million men are governed. The Heavens, to a certain extent, do appear to countenance him. These three hundred millions actually make porcelain, souchong tea,* with innumerable other things; and fight, under Heaven's flag, against Necessity;—and have fewer Seven-Years Wars, Thirty-Years Wars,* French-Revolution Wars, and infernal fightings with each other, than certain millions elsewhere have!

Nay, in our poor distracted Europe itself, in these newest times, have there not religious voices risen,—with a religion new and yet the oldest; entirely indisputable to all hearts of men? Some I do know, who did not call or think themselves 'Prophets,' far enough from that; but who were, in very truth, melodious Voices from the eternal Heart of Nature once again; souls forever venerable to all that have a soul.

A French Revolution is one phenomenon; as complement and spiritual exponent thereof, a Poet Goethe and German Literature is to me another. The old Secular or Practical World, so to speak, having gone up in fire, is not here the prophecy and dawn of a new Spiritual World, parent of far nobler, wider, new Practical Worlds? A Life of Antique devoutness, Antique veracity and heroism, has again become possible,* is again *seen* actual there, for the most modern man. A phenomenon, as quiet as it is, comparable for greatness to no other! 'The great event for the world is, now as always, the arrival in it of a new Wise Man.'* Touches there are, be the Heavens ever thanked, of new Sphere-melody; audible once more, in the infinite jargoning discords and poor scrannel-pipings* of the thing called Literature;—priceless there, as the voice of new Heavenly Psalms! Literature, like the old Prayer-Collections of the first centuries, were it 'well selected from and burnt,'* contains precious things. For Literature, with all its printing-presses, puffing-engines and shoreless deafening triviality, *is* yet 'the Thought of Thinking Souls.'* A sacred 'religion,' if you like the name, does live in the heart of that strange froth-ocean, not wholly froth, which we call Literature; and will more and more disclose itself therefrom;—not now as scorching Fire: the red smoky scorching Fire has purified itself into white sunny Light. Is not Light grander than Fire? It is the same element in a state of purity.

My candid readers, we will march out of this Third Book with a rhythmic word of Goethe's on our lips; a word which perhaps has already sung itself, in dark hours and in bright, through many a heart. To me, finding it devout yet wholly credible and veritable, full of piety yet free of cant; to me, joyfully finding much in it, and joyfully missing so much in it, this little snatch of music, by the greatest German Man, sounds like a stanza in the grand *Road-Song* and *Marching-Song* of our great Teutonic Kindred, wending, wending, valiant and victorious, through the undiscovered Deeps of Time! He calls it *Mason-Lodge*,—not Psalm or Hymn:

> 'The Mason's ways are
> A type of Existence,
> And his persistence
> Is as the days are
> Of men in this world.
>
> The Future hides in it
> Good hap and sorrow;

We press still thorow,
Nought that abides in it
Daunting us,—onward.

And solemn before us,
Veiled, the dark Portal,
Goal of all mortal:—
Stars silent rest o'er us,
Graves under us silent.

While earnest thou gazest,
Comes boding of terror,
Comes phantasm and error,
Perplexes the bravest
With doubt and misgiving.

But heard are the Voices,
Heard are the Sages,
The Worlds and the Ages:
"Choose well, your choice is
Brief and yet endless:

Here eyes do regard you,
In Eternity's stilness;
Here is all fulness,
Ye brave, to reward you;
Work, and despair not." '*

BOOK IV

HOROSCOPE.*

CHAPTER I.

ARISTOCRACIES.

To predict the Future, to manage the Present, would not be so impossible, had not the Past been so sacrilegiously mishandled; effaced, and what is worse, defaced! The Past cannot be seen; the Past, looked at through the medium of 'Philosophical History' in these times,* cannot even be *not* seen: it is misseen; affirmed to have existed,—and to have been a godless Impossibility. Your Norman Conquerors, true royal souls, crowned kings as such, were vulturous irrational tyrants:* your Becket was a noisy egoist and hypocrite;* getting his brains spilt on the floor of Canterbury Cathedral, to secure the main chance,—somewhat uncertain how! "Enthusiasm,"* and even "honest Enthusiasm,"—yes, of course:

'The Dog, to gain his private ends,
Went mad, and bit the Man!'—*

For in truth, the eye sees in all things 'what it brought with it the means of seeing.'* A godless century, looking back on centuries that were godly, produces portraitures more miraculous than any other. All was inane discord in the Past; brute Force bore rule everywhere; Stupidity, savage Unreason, fitter for Bedlam than for a human World! Whereby indeed it becomes sufficiently natural that the like qualities, in new sleeker habiliments, should continue in our time to rule. Millions enchanted in Bastille Workhouses; Irish Widows* proving their relationship by typhus-fever: what would you have? It was ever so, or worse. Man's History, was it not always even this: The cookery and eating-up of imbecile Dupedom by successful Quackhood; the battle, with various weapons, of vulturous Quack and Tyrant against vulturous Tyrant and Quack? No God was in the Past Time; nothing but Mechanisms and Chaotic Brute-Gods:—how

shall the poor 'Philosophic Historian,' to whom his own century is all
godless, see any God in other centuries?

Men believe in Bibles, and disbelieve in them: but of all Bibles the
frightfulest to disbelieve in is this 'Bible of Universal History.'* This
is the Eternal Bible and God's-Book, 'which every born man,' till once
the soul and eyesight are extinguished in him, 'can and must, with his
own eyes, see the God's-Finger writing!' To discredit this, is an *infidelity* like no other. Such infidelity you would punish, if not by fire
and faggot, which are difficult to manage in our times, yet by the most
peremptory order, To hold its peace till it got something wiser to say.
Why should the blessed Silence be broken into noises, to communicate
only the like of this? If the Past have no God's-Reason in it, nothing
but Devil's-Unreason, let the Past be eternally forgotten: mention
it no more;—we whose ancestors were all hanged, why should we
talk of ropes!*

It is, in brief, not true that men ever lived by Delirium, Hypocrisy,
Injustice, or any form of Unreason, since they came to inhabit this
Planet. It is not true that they ever did, or ever will, live except by the
reverse of these. Men will again be taught this. Their acted History
will then again be a Heroism; their written History, what it once was,
an Epic. Nay, forever it is either such, or else it virtually is—Nothing.
Were it written in a thousand volumes, the Unheroic of such volumes
hastens incessantly to be forgotten; the net content of an Alexandrian
Library* of Unheroics is, and will ultimately shew itself to be, *zero*.
What man is interested to remember *it*; have not all men, at all times,
the liveliest interest to forget it?—'Revelations,' if not celestial, then
infernal, will teach us that God is; we shall then, if needful, discern
without difficulty that He has always been! The Dryasdust Philoso-
phisms and enlightened Scepticisms of the Eighteenth Century, historical and other, will have to survive for a while with the Physiologists,*
as a memorable *Nightmare-Dream*. All this haggard epoch, with its
ghastly Doctrines, and death's-head Philosophies 'teaching by example'*
or otherwise, will one day have become, what to our Moslem friends
their godless ages are, 'the Period of Ignorance.'*

If the convulsive struggles of the last Half-Century have taught
poor struggling convulsed Europe any truth, it may perhaps be this as
the essence of innumerable others: That Europe requires a real
Aristocracy, a real Priesthood, or it cannot continue to exist. Huge

French Revolutions, Napoleonisms, then Bourbonisms with their corollary of Three Days, finishing in very unfinal Louis-Philippisms:* all this ought to be didactic! All this may have taught us, That False Aristocracies are insupportable; that No-Aristocracies, Liberty-and-Equalities are impossible; that true Aristocracies are at once indispensable and not easily attained.

Aristocracy and Priesthood, a Governing Class and a Teaching Class: these two, sometimes separate, and endeavouring to harmonise themselves, sometimes conjoined as one, and the King a Pontiff-King:— there did no Society exist without these two vital elements, there will none exist. It lies in the very nature of man: you will visit no remotest village in the most republican country of the world, where virtually or actually you do not find these two powers at work. Man, little as he may suppose it, is necessitated to obey superiors. He is a social being in virtue of this necessity; nay he could not be gregarious otherwise. He obeys those whom he esteems better than himself, wiser, braver; and will forever obey such; and even be ready and delighted to do it.

The Wiser, Braver: these, a Virtual Aristocracy everywhere and everywhen, do in all Societies that reach any articulate shape, develop themselves into a ruling class, an Actual Aristocracy, with settled modes of operating, what are called laws and even *private-laws* or privileges, and so forth; very notable to look upon in this world.— Aristocracy and Priesthood, we say, are sometimes united. For indeed the Wiser and the Braver are properly but one class; no wise man but needed first of all to be a brave man, or he never had been wise. The noble Priest was always a noble *Aristos* to begin with, and something more to end with. Your Luther, your Knox, your Anselm,* Becket, Abbot Samson, Samuel Johnson, if they had not been brave enough, by what possibility could they ever have been wise?—If, from accident or forethought, this your Actual Aristocracy have got discriminated into Two Classes, there can be no doubt but the Priest Class is the more dignified; supreme over the other, as governing head is over active hand. And yet in practice again, it is likeliest the reverse will be found arranged;—a sign that the arrangement is already vitiated; that a split is introduced into it, which will widen and widen till the whole be rent asunder.*

In England, in Europe generally, we may say that these two Virtualities have unfolded themselves into Actualities, in by far the noblest and richest manner any region of the world ever saw. A spiritual Guideship, a practical Governorship, fruit of the grand conscious endeavours, say rather of the immeasurable unconscious instincts and necessities of men, have established themselves; very strange to behold. Everywhere, while so much has been forgotten, you find the King's Palace, and the Viceking's Castle, Mansion, Manorhouse; till there is not an inch of ground from sea to sea but has both its King and Viceking, long due series of Vicekings, its Squire, Earl, Duke or whatever the title of him,—to whom you have given the land, that he may govern you in it.

More touching still, there is not a hamlet where poor peasants congregate, but, by one means and another, a Church-Apparatus has been got together,—roofed edifice, with revenues and belfries; pulpit, reading-desk, with Books and Methods: possibility, in short, and strict prescription, That a man stand there and speak of spiritual things to men. It is beautiful;—even in its great obscuration and decadence, it is among the beautifulest, most touching objects one sees on the Earth. This Speaking Man has indeed, in these times, wandered terribly from the point; has, alas, as it were, totally lost sight of the point: yet, at bottom, whom have we to compare with him? Of all public functionaries boarded and lodged on the Industry of Modern Europe, is there one worthier of the board he has? A man even professing, and never so languidly making still some endeavour, to save the souls of men: contrast him with a man professing to do little but shoot the partridges of men! I wish he could find the point again, this Speaking One; and stick to it with tenacity, with deadly energy: for there is need of him yet! The Speaking Function, this of Truth coming to us with a living voice, nay in a living shape, and as a concrete practical exemplar: this, with all our Writing and Printing Functions, has a perennial place. Could he but find the point again,— take the old spectacles off his nose, and looking up discover, almost in contact with him, what the *real* Satanas, and soul-devouring, world-devouring *Devil*, now is! Original Sin and such like are bad enough, I doubt not: but distilled Gin, dark Ignorance, Stupidity, dark Corn-Law, Bastille and Company, what are they! *Will* he discover our new real Satan, whom he has to fight; or go on droning through his old nose-spectacles about old extinct Satans; and never see the real one, till he *feel* him at his own throat and ours? That is a question, for the world! Let us not intermeddle with it here.

Sorrowful, phantasmal as this same Double Aristocracy of Teachers and Governors now looks, it is worth all men's while to know that the purport of it is and remains noble and most real. Dryasdust, looking merely at the surface, is greatly in error as to those ancient Kings. William Conqueror, William Rufus or Redbeard, Stephen Curthose himself, much more Henry Beauclerc and our brave Plantagenet Henry:* the life of these men was not a vulturous Fighting; it was a valorous Governing,—to which occasionally Fighting did, and alas must yet, though far seldomer now, superadd itself as an accident, a distressing impedimental adjunct. The fighting too was indispensable, for ascertaining who had the might over whom, the right over whom. By much hard fighting, as we once said, 'the unrealities, beaten into dust, flew gradually off;'* and left the plain reality and fact, "Thou stronger than I; thou wiser than I; thou king, and subject I," in a somewhat clearer condition.

Truly we cannot enough admire, in those Abbot-Samson and William-Conqueror times, the arrangement they had made of their Governing Classes. Highly interesting to observe how the sincere insight, on their part, into what did, of primary necessity, behove to be accomplished, had led them to the way of accomplishing it, and in the course of time to get it accomplished! No imaginary Aristocracy would serve their turn; and accordingly they attained a real one. The Bravest men, who, it is ever to be repeated and remembered, are also on the whole the Wisest, Strongest, every way Best, had here, with a respectable degree of accuracy, been got selected; seated each on his piece of territory, which was lent him, then gradually given him, that he might govern it. These Vicekings, each on his portion of the common soil of England, with a Head King over all, were a 'Virtuality perfected into an Actuality' really to an astonishing extent.

For those were rugged stalwart ages; full of earnestness, of a rude God's-truth:—nay, at any rate, their *quilting* was so unspeakably *thinner* than ours; Fact came swiftly on them, if at any time they had yielded to Phantasm! 'The Knaves and Dastards'* had to be 'arrested' in some measure; or the world, almost within year and day, found that it could not live. The Knaves and Dastards accordingly were got arrested. Dastards upon the very throne had to be got arrested, and taken off the throne,—by such methods as there were; by the roughest method, if there chanced to be no smoother one! Doubtless there was much harshness of operation, much severity; as indeed government and surgery are often somewhat severe. Gurth, born thrall of Cedric, it is like, got cuffs as often as pork-parings, if he misdemeaned himself; but Gurth did belong to Cedric:* no human creature then went about connected with nobody; left to go his way into Bastilles or worse, under *Laissez-faire;* reduced to prove his relationship by dying of typhus-fever!—Days come when there is no King in Israel,* but every man is his own king,* doing that which is right in his own eyes;—and tarbarrels are burnt to 'Liberty,' 'Ten-pound Franchise' and the like, with considerable effect in various ways!—

That Feudal Aristocracy, I say, was no imaginary one. To a respectable degree, its *Jarls*, what we now call Earls, were *Strong-Ones** in fact as well as etymology; its Dukes *Leaders*; its Lords *Law-wards*. They did all the Soldiering and Police of the country, all the Judging, Law-making, even the Church-Extension; whatsoever in the way of Governing, of Guiding and Protecting could be done. It was a Land Aristocracy; it managed the Governing of this English People, and had the reaping of the Soil of England in return. It is, in many senses, the Law of Nature, this same Law of Feudalism;—no right Aristocracy but a Land one! The curious are invited to meditate upon it in these days. Soldiering, Police and Judging, Church-Extension, nay real Government and Guidance, all this was actually *done* by the Holders of the Land in return for their Land. How much of it is now done by them; done by anybody? Good Heavens, "Laissez-faire, Do ye nothing, eat your wages and sleep," is everywhere the passionate half-wise cry of this time; and they will not so much as do nothing, but must do mere Corn-Laws! We raise Fifty-two millions, from the general mass of us, to get our Governing done—or, alas, to get ourselves persuaded that it is done: and the 'peculiar burden of the Land' is to pay, not all this, but to pay, as I learn, one twenty-fourth part of all this.* Our first Chartist Parliament,* or Oliver *Redivivus*,* you would say, will know where to lay the new taxes of England!—Or, alas, taxes? If we made the Holders of the Land pay every shilling still of the expense of Governing the Land, what were all that? The Land, by mere hired Governors, cannot be got governed. You cannot hire men to govern the Land: it is by a mission not contracted for in the Stock-Exchange, but felt in their own hearts as coming out of Heaven, that men can govern a Land. The mission of a Land Aristocracy is a *sacred* one, in both the senses of that old word. The footing it stands on, at present, might give rise to thoughts other than of Corn-Laws!—

But truly a 'Splendour of God,' as in William Conqueror's rough oath,* did dwell in those old rude veracious ages; did inform, more and more, with a heavenly nobleness, all departments of their work and life. Phantasms could not yet walk abroad in mere Cloth Tailorage; they were at least Phantasms 'on the rim of the horizon,'* pencilled there by an eternal Light-beam from within. A most 'practical' Hero-worship went on, unconsciously or half-consciously, everywhere. A Monk Samson, with a maximum of two shillings in his pocket, could, without ballot-box, be made a Viceking of, being seen to be worthy. The difference between a good man and a bad man was as yet felt to be, what it forever is, an immeasurable one. Who *durst* have elected a Pandarus Dogdraught,* in those days, to any office, Carlton Club, Senatorship, or place whatsoever? It was felt that the arch Satanas and no other had a clear right of property in Pandarus; that it were better for you to have no hand in Pandarus, to keep out of Pandarus his neighbourhood! Which is, to this hour, the mere fact; though for the present, alas, the forgotten fact. I think they were comparatively blessed times those, in their way! 'Violence,' 'war,' 'disorder:' well, what is war, and death itself, to such a perpetual life-in-death, and 'peace, peace, where there is no peace!'* Unless some Hero-worship, in its new appropriate form, can return, this world does not promise to be very habitable long.

Old Anselm, exiled Archbishop of Canterbury, one of the purest-minded 'men of genius,'* was travelling to make his appeal to Rome* against King Rufus,—a man of rough ways, in whom the 'inner Lightbeam' shone very fitfully. It is beautiful to read, in Monk Eadmer, how the Continental populations welcomed and venerated this Anselm, as no French population now venerates Jean-Jacques* or giant-killing Voltaire; as not even an American population now venerates a Schnüspel the distinguished Novelist!* They had, by phantasy and true insight, the intensest conviction that a God's-Blessing dwelt in this Anselm,—as is my conviction too. They crowded round, with bent knees and enkindled hearts, to receive his blessing, to hear his voice, to see the light of his face.* My blessings on them and on him!—But the notablest was a certain necessitous or covetous Duke of Burgundy,* in straitened circumstances we shall hope,—who reflected that in all likelihood this English Archbishop, going towards Rome to appeal, must have taken store of cash with him to bribe the Cardinals. Wherefore he of Burgundy, for his part, decided to lie in wait and rob him. 'In an open space of a wood,' some 'wood' then green and growing, eight centuries ago, in Burgundian Land,—this fierce Duke, with fierce steel followers, shaggy, savage, as the Russian bear, dashes out on the weak old Anselm; who is riding along there, on his small quiet-going pony; escorted only by Eadmer and another poor Monk on ponies; and, except small modicum of roadmoney, not a gold coin in his possession. The steelclad Russian Bear emerges,* glaring: the old white-bearded man starts not,—paces on unmoved, looking into him with those clear old earnest eyes, with that venerable sorrowful time-worn face; of whom no man or thing need be afraid, and who also is afraid of no created man or thing. The fire-eyes of his Burgundian Grace meet these clear eye-glances, convey them swift to his heart: he bethinks him that probably this feeble, fearless, hoary Figure has in it something of the Most High God;* that probably he shall be damned if he meddle with it,—that, on the whole, he had better not. He plunges, the rough savage, from his war-horse, down to his knees; embraces the feet of old Anselm: he too begs his blessing; orders men to escort him, guard him from being robbed, and under dread penalties see him safe on his way. *Per os Dei*,* as his Majesty was wont to ejaculate!

Neither is this quarrel of Rufus and Anselm, of Henry and Becket, uninstructive to us. It was, at bottom, a great quarrel. For, admitting that Anselm was full of divine blessing, he by no means included in him all forms of divine blessing:—there were far other forms withal, which he little dreamed of; and William Redbeard was unconsciously the representative and spokesman of these. In truth, could your divine Anselm, your divine Pope Gregory* have had their way, the results had been very notable. Our Western World had all become a European Thibet, with one Grand Lama sitting at Rome;* our one honourable business that of singing mass, all day and all night. Which would not in the least have suited us! The Supreme Powers willed it not so.

It was as if King Redbeard unconsciously, addressing Anselm, Becket and the others, had said: "Right Reverend, your Theory of the Universe is indisputable by man or devil. To the core of our heart we feel that this divine thing, which you call Mother Church, does fill the whole world hitherto known, and is and shall be all our salvation and all our desire. And yet—and yet—Behold, though it is an unspoken secret, the world is *wider* than any of us think, Right Reverend!

Behold, there are yet other immeasurable Sacrednesses in this that you call Heathenism, Secularity! On the whole, I, in an obscure but most rooted manner, feel that I cannot comply with you. Western Thibet and perpetual mass-chanting,—No. I am, so to speak, in the family-way; with child, of I know not what,—certainly of something far different from this! I have—*Per os Dei*, I have Manchester Cotton-trades, Bromwicham Iron-trades, American Commonwealths, Indian Empires,* Steam Mechanisms and Shakspeare Dramas, in my belly; and cannot do it, Right Reverend!"—So accordingly it was decided: and Saxon Becket spilt his life in Canterbury Cathedral, as Scottish Wallace did on Tower-hill,* and as generally a noble man and martyr has to do,—not for nothing; no, but for a divine something other than *he* had altogether calculated. We will now quit this of the hard, organic, but limited Feudal Ages; and glance timidly into the immense Industrial Ages, as yet all inorganic, and in a quite pulpy condition, requiring desperately to harden themselves into some organism!

Our Epic having now become *Tools and the Man*,* it is more than usually impossible to prophesy the Future. The boundless Future does lie there, predestined, nay already extant though unseen; hiding, in its Continents of Darkness, 'good hap and sorrow:'* but the supremest intelligence of man cannot prefigure much of it:—the united intelligence and effort of All Men in all coming generations, this alone will gradually prefigure it, and figure and form it into a seen fact! Straining our eyes hitherto, the utmost effort of intelligence sheds but some most glimmering dawn, a little way into its dark enormous Deeps: only huge outlines loom uncertain on the sight; and the ray of prophecy, at a short distance, expires. But may we not say, here as always, Sufficient for the day is the evil thereof!* To shape the whole Future is not our problem;* but only to shape faithfully a small part of it, according to rules already known. It is perhaps possible for each of us, who will with due earnestness inquire, to ascertain clearly what he, for his own part, ought to do: this let him, with true heart, do, and continue doing. The general issue will, as it has always done, rest well with a Higher Intelligence than ours.

One grand 'outline,' or even two, many earnest readers may perhaps, at this stage of the business, be able to prefigure for themselves,—and draw some guidance from. One prediction, or even two, are already possible. For the Life-tree Igdrasil,* in all its new developments, is the selfsame world-old Life-tree: having found an element or elements there, running from the very roots of it in Hela's Realms, in the Well of Mimer and of the Three Nornas or TIMES, up to this present hour of it in our own hearts, we conclude that such will have to continue. A man has, in his own soul, an Eternal; can read something of the Eternal there, if he will look! He already knows what will continue; what cannot, by any means or appliance whatsoever, be made to continue!

One wide and widest 'outline' ought really, in all ways, to be becoming clear to us; this namely: That a 'Splendour of God,' in one form or other, will have to unfold itself from the heart of these our Industrial Ages too; or they will never get themselves 'organised;' but continue chaotic, distressed, distracted evermore, and have to perish in frantic suicidal dissolution. A second 'outline' or prophecy, narrower, but also wide enough, seems not less certain: That there will again *be* a King in Israel; a system of Order and Government; and every man shall, in some measure, see himself constrained to do that which is right in the King's eyes. This too we may call a sure element of the Future; for this too is of the Eternal;—this too is of the Present, though hidden from most; and without it no fibre of the Past ever was. An actual new Sovereignty, Industrial Aristocracy, real not imaginary Aristocracy, is indispensable and indubitable for us.

But what an Aristocracy; on what new, far more complex and cunningly devised conditions than that old Feudal fighting one! For we are to bethink us that the Epic verily is not *Arms and the Man*, but *Tools and the Man*,—an infinitely wider kind of Epic. And again we are to bethink us that men cannot now be bound to men by *brass-collars*,—not at all: that this brass-collar method, in all figures of it, has vanished out of Europe forevermore! Huge Democracy, walking the streets everywhere in its Sack Coat, has asserted so much; irrevocably, brooking no reply! True enough, man *is* forever the 'born thrall' of certain men, born master of certain other men, born equal of certain others, let him acknowledge the fact or not. It is unblessed for him when he cannot acknowledge this fact; he is in the chaotic state, ready to perish, till he do get the fact acknowledged. But no man is, or can henceforth be, the brass-collar thrall of any man; you will have to bind him by other, far nobler and cunninger methods. Once for all, he is to be loose of the brass-collar, to have a scope *as* wide as his faculties now are:—will he not be all the usefuler to you in that new state? Let him go abroad as a trusted one, as a free one; and return home to you with rich earnings at night! Gurth could only tend pigs; this one will build cities, conquer waste worlds.—How, in conjunction with inevitable Democracy, indispensable Sovereignty is to exist:* certainly it is the hugest question ever heretofore propounded to Mankind! The solution of which is work for long years and centuries. Years and centuries, of one knows not what complexion;—blessed or unblessed, according as they shall, with earnest valiant effort, make progress therein, or, in slothful unveracity and dilettantism, only talk of making progress. For either progress therein, or swift and ever swifter progress towards dissolution, is henceforth a necessity.

It is of importance that this grand reformation were begun; that Corn-Law Debatings and other jargon, little less than delirious in such a time, had fled far away, and left us room to begin! For the evil has grown practical, extremely conspicuous; if it be not seen and provided for, the blindest fool will have to feel it ere long. There is much that can wait; but there is something also that cannot wait. With millions of eager Working Men imprisoned in 'Impossibility'* and Poor-Law Bastilles, it is time that some means of dealing with them were trying to become 'possible!' Of the Government of England, of all articulate-speaking functionaries, real and imaginary Aristocracies, of me and of thee, it is imperatively demanded, "How do you mean to manage these men? Where are they to find a supportable existence? What is to become of them,—and of you!"

CHAPTER II.

BRIBERY COMMITTEE.

IN the case of the late Bribery Committee,* it seemed to be the conclusion of the soundest practical minds that Bribery could not be put down;* that Pure Election was a thing we had seen the last of, and must now go on without, as we best could. A conclusion not a little startling; to which it requires a practical mind of some seasoning to reconcile yourself at once! It seems, then, we are henceforth to get ourselves constituted Legislators not according to what merit we may have, or even what merit we may seem to have, but according to the length of our purse, and our frankness, impudence and dexterity in laying out the contents of the same. Our theory, written down in all books and law-books, spouted forth from all barrel-heads, is perfect purity of Tenpound Franchise, absolute sincerity of question put and answer given;—and our practice is irremediable bribery; irremediable, unpunishable, which you will do more harm than good by attempting to punish! Once more, a very startling conclusion indeed; which, whatever the soundest practical minds in Parliament* may think of it, invites all British men to meditations of various kinds.

A Parliament, one would say, which proclaims itself elected and eligible by bribery, tells the Nation that is governed by it a piece of singular news. Bribery: have we reflected what bribery is? Bribery means not only length of purse, which is neither qualification nor the contrary for legislating well; but it means dishonesty, and even impudent dishonesty;—brazen insensibility to lying and to making others lie; total oblivion, and flinging overboard, for the nonce, of any real thing you can call veracity, morality; with dextrous putting on the cast-clothes of that real thing, and strutting about in them! What Legislating can you get out of a man in that fatal situation? None that will profit much, one would think! A Legislator who has left his veracity lying on the door-threshold, he, why verily *he*—ought to be sent out to seek it again!

Heavens, what an improvement, were there once fairly in Downing-street an Election-Office opened, with a tariff of Boroughs! Such and such a population, amount of property-tax, ground-rental, extent of trade; returns two Members, returns one Member, for so much money down: Ipswich so many thousands, Nottingham so many,—as they happened, one by one, to fall into this new Downing-street Schedule A!* An incalculable improvement, in comparison: for now at least you have it fairly by length of purse, and leave the dishonesty, the impudence, the unveracity all handsomely aside. Length of purse and desire to be a Legislator ought to get a man into Parliament, not *with*, but if possible *without* the unveracity, the impudence and the dishonesty! Length of purse and desire, these are, as intrinsic qualifications, correctly equal to zero; but they are not yet *less* than zero,—as the smallest addition of that latter sort will make them!

And is it come to this? And does our venerable Parliament announce itself elected and eligible in this manner? Surely such a Parliament promulgates strange horoscopes of itself. What is to become of

a Parliament elected or eligible in this manner? Unless Belial and
Beelzebub have got possession of the throne of this Universe, such
Parliament is preparing itself for new Reform-bills.* We shall have to
try it by Chartism, or any conceivable *ism*, rather than put up with
this! There is already in England 'religion' enough to get six hundred
and fifty-eight Consulting Men* brought together who do *not* begin
work with a lie in their mouth. Our poor old Parliament, thousands of
years old,* is still good for something, for several things;—though
many are beginning to ask, with ominous anxiety, in these days: For
what thing? But for whatever thing and things Parliament be good,
indisputably it must start with other than a lie in its mouth! On the
whole, a Parliament working with a lie in its mouth, will have to take
itself away. To no Parliament or thing, that one has heard of, did this
Universe ever long yield harbour on that footing. At all hours of the
day and night, some Chartism is advancing, some armed Cromwell is
advancing, to apprise such Parliament: "Ye are no Parliament. In the
name of God,—go!"*

In sad truth, once more, how is our whole existence, in these present days, built on Cant, Speciosity, Falsehood, Dilettantism; with
this one serious Veracity in it: Mammonism! Dig down where you
will, through the Parliament-floor or elsewhere, how infallibly do you,
at spade's depth below the service, come upon this universal *Liars*-
rock substratum! Much else is ornamental; true on barrel-heads, in
pulpits, hustings, Parliamentary benches; but this is forever true and
truest: "Money does bring money's worth; Put money in your
purse."* Here, if nowhere else, is the human soul still in thorough
earnest; sincere with a prophet's sincerity: and 'the Hell of the
English,' as Sauerteig said, 'is the infinite terror of Not getting on,
especially of Not making money.' With results!

To many persons the horoscope of Parliament is more interesting
than to me: but surely all men with souls must admit that sending
members to Parliament by bribery is an infamous solecism; an act
entirely immoral, which no man can have to do with more or less, but
he will soil his fingers more or less. No Carlton Clubs, Reform Clubs,*
nor any sort of clubs or creatures, or of accredited opinions or practices, can make a Lie Truth, can make Bribery a Propriety. The
Parliament should really either punish and put away Bribery, or legalise it by some Office in Downing-street.* As I read the Apocalypses,

a Parliament that can do neither of these things is not in a good way.—And yet, alas, what of Parliaments and their Elections? Parliamentary Elections are but the topmost ultimate outcome of an electioneering which goes on at all hours, in all places, in every meeting of two or more men. It is *we* that vote wrong, and teach the poor ragged Freemen of Boroughs to vote wrong.* We pay respect to those worthy of no respect.

Is not Pandarus Dogdraught a member of select clubs, and admitted into the drawing-rooms of men? Visibly to all persons he is of the offal of Creation; but he carries money in his purse, due lacquer on his dog-visage, and it is believed will not steal spoons. The human species does not with one voice, like the Hebrew Psalmist, 'shun to sit'* with Dogdraught, refuse totally to dine with Dogdraught; men called of honour are willing enough to dine with him, his talk being lively, and his champagne excellent. We say to ourselves, "The man is in good society,"—others have already voted for him; why should not I? We *forget* the indefeasible right of property that Satan has in Dogdraught,—we are not afraid to be near Dogdraught! It is we that vote wrong; blindly, nay with falsity prepense! It is we that no longer know the difference between Human Worth and Human Unworth; or feel that the one is admirable and alone admirable, the other detestable, damnable! How shall *we* find out a Hero and Viceking Samson with a maximum of two shillings in his pocket? We have no chance to do such a thing. We have got out of the Ages of Heroism, deep into the Ages of Flunkeyism,*—and must return or die. What a noble set of mortals are we, who, because there is no Saint Edmund threatening us at the rim of the horizon, are not afraid to be whatever, for the day and hour, is smoothest for us!

And now, in good sooth, why should an indigent discerning Freeman give his vote without bribes? Let us rather honour the poor man that he does discern clearly wherein lies, for him, the true kernel of the matter. What is it to the ragged grimy Freeman of a Tenpound-Franchise Borough, whether Aristides Rigmarole Esq. of the Destructive, or the Hon. Alcides Dolittle of the Conservative Party* be sent to Parliament;—much more, whether the two-thousandth part of them be sent, for that is the amount of his faculty in it? Destructive or Conservative, what will either of them destroy or conserve of vital moment to this Freeman? Has he found either of them care, at bottom, a sixpence for him or his interests, or those of his class or of his cause, or of any class or cause that is of much value to God or to man? Rigmarole and Dolittle have alike cared for themselves hitherto; and for their own clique, and self-conceited crotchets,—their greasy dishonest interests of pudding, or windy dishonest interests of praise; and not very perceptibly for any other interest whatever. Neither Rigmarole nor Dolittle will accomplish any good or any evil for this grimy Freeman, like giving him a five-pound note, or refusing to give it him. It will be smoothest to vote according to value received. That is the veritable fact; and he indigent, like others that are not indigent, acts conformably thereto.

Why, reader, truly, if they asked thee or me, Which way we meant to vote?—were it not our likeliest answer: Neither way! I, as a Tenpound Franchiser, will receive no bribe; but also I will not vote for either of these men. Neither Rigmarole nor Dolittle shall, by furtherance of mine, go and make laws for this country. I will have no hand in such a mission. How dare I! If other men cannot be got in England, a totally other sort of men, different as light is from dark, as star-fire is from street-mud, what is the use of votings, or of Parliaments in England? England ought to resign herself; there is no hope or possibility for England. If England cannot get her Knaves and Dastards 'arrested,' in some degree, but only get them 'elected,' what is to become of England?

I conclude, with all confidence, that England will verily have to put an end to briberies on her Election Hustings and elsewhere, at what cost soever;*—and likewise that we, Electors and Eligibles, one and all of us, for our own behoof and hers, cannot too soon begin, at what cost soever, to put an end to *bribeabilities* in ourselves. The death-leprosy, attacked in this manner, by purifying lotions from without, and by rallying of the vital energies and purities from within, will probably abate somewhat! It has otherwise no chance to abate.

CHAPTER III.

THE ONE INSTITUTION.

WHAT our Government can do in this grand Problem of the Working Classes of England? Yes, supposing the insane Corn-Laws totally abolished, all speech of them ended, and 'from ten to twenty years of new possibility to live and find wages'* conceded us in consequence: What the English Government might be expected to accomplish or attempt towards rendering the existence of our Labouring Millions somewhat less anomalous, somewhat less impossible, in the years that are to follow those 'ten or twenty,' if either 'ten' or 'twenty' there be?

It is the most momentous question. For all this of the Corn-Law Abrogation, and what can follow therefrom, is but as the shadow on King Hezekiah's Dial:* the shadow has gone back twenty years; but will again, in spite of Free-Trades and Abrogations, travel forward its old fated way. With our present system of individual Mammonism, and Government by Laissez-faire, this Nation cannot live. And if, in the priceless interim, some new life and healing be not found, there is no second respite to be counted on. The shadow on the Dial advances thenceforth without pausing. What Government can do? This that they call 'Organising of Labour' is, if well understood, the Problem of the whole Future, for all who will in future pretend to govern men. But our first preliminary stage of it, How to deal with the Actual Labouring Millions of England? this is the imperatively pressing Problem of the Present, pressing with a truly fearful intensity and imminence in these very years and days. No Government can longer neglect it: once more, what can our Government do in it?

Governments are of very various degrees of activity: some, altogether Lazy Governments, in 'free countries' as they are called, seem in these times almost to profess to do, if not nothing, one knows not at first what. To debate in Parliament, and gain majorities; and ascertain who shall be, with a toil hardly second to Ixion's, the Prime Speaker and Spoke-holder, and keep the Ixion's-Wheel* going, if not forward, yet round? Not altogether so:—much, to the experienced eye, is not what it seems! Chancery and certain other Law-Courts seem nothing; yet in fact they are, the worst of them, something: chimneys for the devilry and contention of men to escape by;—a very considerable something! Parliament too has its tasks, if thou wilt look; fit to wearout the lives of toughest men. The celebrated Kilkenny Cats,* through their tumultuous congress, cleaving the ear of Night, could they be said to do nothing? Hadst thou been of them, thou hadst seen! The feline heart laboured, as with steam up—to the bursting point; and death-doing energy nerved every muscle: they had a work there; and did it! On the morrow, two tails were found left, and peaceable annihilation; a neighbourhood *delivered* from despair.

Again, are not Spinning-Dervishes* an eloquent emblem, significant of much? Hast thou noticed him, that solemn-visaged Turk, the eyes shut; dingy wool mantle circularly hiding his figure;— bell-shaped; like a dingy bell set spinning on the *tongue* of it? By centrifugal force the dingy wool mantle heaves itself; spreads more and more, like upturned cup widening into upturned saucer: thus spins he, to the praise of Allah and advantage of mankind, fast and faster, till collapse ensue, and sometimes death!—

A Government such as ours, consisting of from seven to eight hundred Parliamentary Talkers, with their escort of Able Editors and Public Opinion; and for head, certain Lords and Servants of the Treasury, and Chief Secretaries and others, who find themselves at once Chiefs and No-Chiefs, and often commanded rather than commanding,—is doubtless a most complicate entity, and none of the alertest for getting on with business! Clearly enough, if the Chiefs be not self-motive and what we call men, but mere patient lay-figures without self-motive principle, the Government will not move anywhither; it will tumble disastrously, and jumble, round its own axis, as for many years past we have seen it do.—And yet a self-motive man who is not a lay-figure, place him in the heart of what entity you may, will make it move more or less! The absurdest in Nature he will make a little *less* absurd; he. The unwieldiest he will make to move;—that is the use of his existing there. He will at least have the manfulness to depart out of it, if not; to say: "I cannot move in thee, and be a man;* like a wretched drift-log dressed in man's clothes and minister's clothes, doomed to a lot baser than belongs to man, I will not continue with thee, tumbling aimless on the Mother of Dead Dogs* here:—Adieu!"

For, on the whole, it is the lot of Chiefs everywhere, this same. No Chief in the most despotic country but was a Servant withal; at once an absolute commanding General, and a poor Orderly-Sergeant, ordered by the very men in the ranks,—obliged to collect the vote of the ranks too, in some articulate or inarticulate shape, and weigh well the same. The proper name of all Kings is Minister, Servant. In no conceivable Government can a lay-figure get forward! *This* Worker, surely he above all others has to 'spread out his Gideon's Fleece,'* and collect the monitions of Immensity; the poor Localities, as we said, and Parishes of Palace-yard* or elsewhere, having no due monition in them. A Prime Minister, even here in England, who shall dare believe the heavenly omens, and address himself like a man and hero to the great dumb-struggling heart of England; and speak out for it, and act out for it, the God's-Justice it is writhing to get uttered and perishing for want of,—yes, he too will see awaken round him, in passionate burning all-defiant loyalty, the heart of England, and such a 'support' as no Division-List or Parliamentary Majority was ever yet known to yield a man! Here as there, now as then, he who can and dare trust the heavenly Immensities, all earthly Localities are subject to him. We will pray for such a Man and First-Lord;—yes, and far better, we will strive and incessantly make ready, each of us, to be worthy to serve and second such a First-Lord! We shall then be as good as sure of his arriving; sure of many things, let him arrive or not.

Who can despair of Governments that passes a Soldier's Guard-house, or meets a redcoated man on the streets! That a body of men could be got together to kill other men when you bade them: this, *a priori*, does it not seem one of the impossiblest things? Yet look, behold it: in the stolidest of Donothing Governments, that impossibility is a thing done. See it there, with buff belts, red coats on its back; walking sentry at guardhouses, brushing white breeches in barracks; an indisputable palpable fact. Out of grey Antiquity, amid all finance-difficulties, *scaccarium*-tallies, ship-monies, coat-and-conduct moneys,* and vicissitudes of Chance and Time, there, down to the present blessed hour, it is.

Often, in these painfully decadent and painfully nascent Times, with their distresses, inarticulate gaspings and 'impossibilities;' meeting a tall Lifeguardsman in his snow-white trousers, or seeing those two statuesque Lifeguardsmen in their frowning bearskins, pipe-clayed buckskins, on their coal-black sleek-fiery quadrupeds, riding sentry at the Horse-Guards,*—it strikes one with a kind of mournful interest, how, in such universal down-rushing and wrecked impotence of almost all old institutions, this oldest Fighting Institution is still so young! Fresh-complexioned, firm-limbed, six feet by the standard,* this fighting-man has verily been got up, and can fight. While so much has not yet got into being; while so much has gone gradually out of it, and become an empty Semblance or Clothes-suit; and highest king's-cloaks, mere chimeras parading under them so long, are getting unsightly to the earnest eye, unsightly, almost offensive, like a costlier kind of scarecrow's-blanket,—here still is a reality!

The man in horsehair wig advances, promising that he will get me 'justice:' he takes me into Chancery Law-Courts, into decades, half-centuries of hubbub, of distracted jargon; and does *get* me— disappointment, almost desperation; and one refuge: that of dismissing him and his 'justice' altogether out of my head. For I have work to do; I cannot spend my decades in mere arguing with other men about the exact wages of my work: I will work cheerfully with no wages, sooner than with a ten-years gangrene or Chancery Lawsuit in my heart!* He of the horsehair wig is a sort of failure; no substance, but a fond imagination of the mind. He of the shovel-hat, again, who comes forward professing that he will save my soul—O ye Eternities, of him in this place be absolute silence!—But he of the red coat, I say, is a success and no failure! He will veritably, if he get orders, draw out a long sword and kill me. No mistake there. He is a fact and not a shadow. Alive in this Year Forty-three,* able and willing to do *his* work. In dim old centuries, with William Rufus, William of Ipres,* or far earlier, he began; and has come down safe so far. Catapult has given place to cannon, pike has given place to musket, iron mail-shirt to coat of red cloth, saltpetre ropematch to percussion cap; equipments, circumstances have all changed, and again changed: but the human battle-engine in the inside of any or of each of these, ready still to do battle, stands there, six feet in standard size. There are Pay-Offices, Woolwich Arsenals, there is a Horse-Guards, War-Office, Captain-General; persuasive Sergeants, with tap of drum, recruit in market-towns and villages;—and, on the whole, I say, here is your actual drilled fighting-man; here are your actual Ninety-thousand of such,* ready to go into any quarter of the world and fight!

Strange, interesting, and yet most mournful to reflect on. Was this, then, of all the things mankind had some talent for, the one thing important to learn well, and bring to perfection; this of successfully killing one another? Truly you have learned it well, and carried the business to a high perfection. It is incalculable what, by arranging, commanding and regimenting, you can make of men. These thousand straight-standing firm-set individuals, who shoulder arms, who march, wheel, advance, retreat; and are, for your behoof, a magazine charged with fiery death, in the most perfect condition of potential activity: few months ago, till the persuasive sergeant came, what were they?

Multiform ragged losels,* runaway apprentices, starved weavers, thievish valets; an entirely broken population, fast tending towards the treadmill. But the persuasive sergeant came; by tap of drum enlisted, or formed lists of them, took heartily to drilling them;—and he and you have made them this! Most potent, effectual for all work whatsoever, is wise planning, firm combining and commanding among men. Let no man despair of Governments who looks on these two sentries at the Horse-Guards and our United-Service Clubs!* I could conceive an Emigration Service, a Teaching Service,* considerable varieties of United and Separate Services, of the due thousands strong, all effective as this Fighting Service is; all doing *their* work, like it;—which work, much more than fighting, is henceforth the necessity of these New Ages we are got into! Much lies among us, convulsively, nigh desperately *struggling to be born*.

But mean Governments, as mean-limited individuals do, have stood by the physically indispensable; have realised that and nothing more. The Soldier is perhaps one of the most difficult things to realise; but Governments, had they not realised him, could not have existed: accordingly he is here. O Heavens, if we saw an army ninety-thousand strong, maintained and fully equipt, in continual real action and battle against Human Starvation, against Chaos, Necessity, Stupidity, and our real 'natural enemies,' what a business were it! Fighting and molesting not 'the French,' who, poor men, have a hard enough battle of their own in the like kind, and need no additional molesting from us; but fighting and incessantly spearing down and destroying Falsehood, Nescience,* Delusion, Disorder, and the Devil and his Angels! Thou thyself, cultivated reader, hast done something in that alone true warfare; but, alas, under what circumstances was it? Thee no beneficent drill-sergeant, with any effectiveness, would rank in line beside thy fellows; train, like a true didactic artist, by the wit of all past experience, to do thy soldiering; encourage thee when right, punish thee when wrong, and everywhere with wise word-of-command say, Forward on this hand, Forward on that! Ah, no: thou hadst to learn thy small-sword and platoon exercise where and how thou couldst; to all mortals but thyself it was indifferent whether thou shouldst ever learn it. And the rations, and shilling a day, were they provided thee,—reduced as I have known brave Jean-Pauls, learning their exercise, to live on 'water *without* the bread?'* The rations; or any furtherance of promotion to corporalship, lance-corporalship, or due cat-o'-nine tails, with the slightest reference to thy deserts, were not provided. Forethought, even as of a pipe-clayed drill-sergeant, did not preside over thee. To corporalship, lance-corporalship, thou didst attain; alas, also to the halberts and cat:* but thy rewarder and punisher seemed blind as the Deluge: neither lance-corporalship, nor even drummer's cat, because both appeared delirious, brought thee due profit.

It was well, all this, we know;—and yet it was not well! Forty soldiers, I am told, will disperse the largest Spitalfields mob:* forty to ten-thousand, that is the proportion between drilled and undrilled. Much there is which cannot yet be organised in this world; but somewhat also which can, somewhat also which must. When one thinks, for example, what Books are become and becoming for us, what Operative Lancashires are become; what a Fourth Estate,* and innumerable Virtualities not yet got to be Actualities are become and becoming,—one sees Organisms enough in the dim huge Future; and 'United Services' quite other than the redcoat one; and much, even in these years, struggling to be born!

Of Time-Bill, Factory-Bill* and other such Bills the present Editor has no authority to speak. He knows not, it is for others than he to know, in what specific ways it may be feasible to interfere, with Legislation, between the Workers and the Master-Workers;—knows only and sees, what all men are beginning to see, that Legislative interference, and interferences not a few are indispensable;* that as a lawless anarchy of supply-and-demand, on market-wages alone, this province of things cannot longer be left. Nay interference has begun: there are already Factory Inspectors,—who seem to have no *lack* of work. Perhaps there might be Mine-Inspectors* too:—might there not be Furrowfield Inspectors withal, and ascertain for us how on seven and sixpence a week a human family does live!* Interference has begun; it must continue, must extensively enlarge itself, deepen and sharpen itself. Such things cannot longer be idly lapped in darkness, and suffered to go on unseen: the Heavens do see them; the curse, not the blessing of the Heavens is on an Earth that refuses to see them.

Again, are not Sanitary Regulations* possible for a Legislature? The old Romans had their Ædiles;* who would, I think, in direct contravention to supply-and-demand, have rigorously seen rammed up into total abolition many a foul cellar in our Southwarks, Saint-Gileses,* and dark poison-lanes; saying sternly, "Shall a Roman man dwell there?" The Legislature, at whatever cost of consequences, would have had to answer, "God forbid!"—The Legislature, even as it now is, could order all dingy Manufacturing Towns to cease from their soot and darkness; to let-in the blessed sunlight, the blue of Heaven, and become clear and clean; to burn their coal-smoke, namely, and make flame of it.* Baths, free air, a wholesome temperature, ceilings twenty feet high, might be ordained, by Act of Parliament, in all establishments licensed as Mills. There are such Mills already extant;*—honour to the builders of them! The Legislature can say to others: Go ye and do likewise;* better if you can.

Every toiling Manchester, its smoke and soot all burnt, ought it not, among so many world-wide conquests, to have a hundred acres or so of free greenfield, with trees on it, conquered, for its little children to disport in;* for its all-conquering workers to take a breath of twilight air in? You would say so! A willing Legislature could say so with effect. A willing Legislature could say very many things! And to whatsoever 'vested interest,' or such like, stood up, gainsaying merely, "I shall lose profits,"—the willing Legislature would answer, "Yes, but my sons and daughters will gain health, and life, and a soul."— "What is to become of our Cotton-trade?" cried certain Spinners, when the Factory-Bill was proposed; "What is to become of our invaluable Cotton-trade?" The Humanity of England answered steadfastly: "Deliver me these rickety perishing souls of infants, and let your Cotton-trade take its chance. God Himself commands the one thing; not God especially the other thing. We cannot have prosperous Cotton-trades at the expense of keeping the Devil a partner in them!"—

Bills enough, were the Corn-Law Abrogation Bill once passed, and a Legislature willing!* Nay this one Bill, which lies yet unenacted, a right Education Bill,* is not this of itself the sure parent of innumerable wise Bills,—wise regulations, practical methods and proposals, gradually ripening towards the state of Bills? To irradiate with intelligence, that is to say, with order, arrangement and all blessedness, the Chaotic, Unintelligent: how, except by educating, *can* you accomplish this? That thought, reflection, articulate utterance and understanding be awakened in these individual million heads, which are the atoms of your Chaos: there is no other way of illuminating any Chaos! The sum-total of intelligence that is found in it, determines the extent of order that is possible for your Chaos,—the feasibility and rationality of what your Chaos will dimly demand from you, and will gladly obey when proposed by you! It is an exact equation; the one accurately measures the other.—If the whole English People, during these 'twenty years of respite,'* be not educated, with at least schoolmaster's educating, a tremendous responsibility, before God and men, will rest somewhere! How dare any man, especially a man calling himself minister of God, stand up in any Parliament or place, under any pretext or delusion, and for a day or an hour forbid God's Light to come into the world, and bid the Devil's Darkness continue in it one hour more!* For all light and science, under all shapes, in all degrees of perfection, is of God; all darkness, nescience, is of the Enemy of God. 'The schoolmaster's creed is somewhat awry?'* Yes, I have found few creeds entirely correct; few light-beams shining *white*, pure of admixture: but of all creeds and religions now or ever before known, was not that of thoughtless thriftless Animalism, of Distilled Gin,* and Stupor and Despair, unspeakably the least orthodox? We will exchange *it* even with Paganism, with Fetishism; and, on the whole, must exchange it with something.

An effective 'Teaching Service' I do consider that there must be; some Education Secretary, Captain-General of Teachers,* who will actually contrive to get us *taught*. Then again, why should there not be an 'Emigration Service,'* and Secretary, with adjuncts, with funds, forces, idle Navy-ships, and ever-increasing apparatus;* in fine an *effective system* of Emigration; so that, at length, before our twenty years of respite ended, every honest willing Workman who found England too strait, and the 'Organisation of Labour' not yet sufficiently advanced, might find likewise a bridge built to carry him into new Western Lands,* there to 'organise' with more elbow-room some labour for himself? There to be a real blessing, raising new corn for us, purchasing new webs and hatchets from us; leaving us at least in peace;—instead of staying here to be a Physical-Force Chartist, unblessed and no blessing! Is it not scandalous to consider that a Prime Minister could raise within the year, as I have seen it done, a Hundred and Twenty Millions Sterling to shoot the French;* and we are stopt short for want of the hundredth part of that to keep the English living? The bodies of the English living, and the souls of the English living:— these two 'Services,' an Education Service and an Emigration Service, these with others will actually have to be organised!

A free bridge for Emigrants:* why, we should then be on a par with America itself, the most favoured of all lands that have no government; and we should have, besides, so many traditions and mementos of priceless things which America has cast away. We could proceed deliberately to 'organise Labour,' not doomed to perish unless we effected it within year and day;—every willing Worker that proved superfluous, finding a bridge ready for him. This verily will have to be done; the Time is big with this. Our little Isle is grown too narrow for us; but the world is wide enough yet for another Six Thousand Years. England's sure markets will be among new Colonies of Englishmen in all quarters of the Globe. All men trade with all men, when mutually convenient; and are even bound to do it by the Maker of men. Our friends of China, who guiltily refused to trade, in these circumstances,—had we not to argue with them, in cannon-shot at last, and convince them that they ought to trade!* 'Hostile Tariffs' will arise, to shut us out;* and then again will fall, to let us in: but the Sons of England, speakers of the English language were it nothing more, will in all times have the ineradicable predisposition to trade with England. Mycale was the *Pan-Ionian*, rendezvous of all the Tribes of Ion, for old Greece:* why should not London long continue the *All-Saxon-home*, rendezvous of all the 'Children of the Harz-Rock,'* arriving, in select samples, from the Antipodes and elsewhere, by steam and otherwise, to the 'season' here!—What a Future; wide as the world, if we have the heart and heroism for it,—which, by Heaven's blessing, we shall:

> 'Keep not standing fixed and rooted,
> Briskly venture, briskly roam;
> Head and hand, where'er thou foot it,
> And stout heart are still at home.
>
> In what land the sun does visit,
> Brisk are we, whate'er betide:
> To give space for wandering is it
> That the world was made so wide.'[1]*

Fourteen hundred years ago, it was by a considerable 'Emigration Service,'* never doubt it, by much enlistment, discussion and apparatus,

---

[1] Goethe, *Wilhelm Meister*.

that we ourselves arrived in this remarkable Island,—and got into our present difficulties among others!

It is true the English Legislature, like the English People, is of slow temper; essentially conservative. In our wildest periods of reform, in the Long Parliament itself, you notice always the invincible instinct to hold fast by the Old; to admit the *minimum* of New;* to expand, if it be possible, some old habit or method, already found fruitful, into new growth for the new need. It is an instinct worthy of all honour; akin to all strength and all wisdom. The Future hereby is not dissevered from the Past, but based continuously on it; grows with all the vitalities of the Past, and is rooted down deep into the beginnings of us. The English Legislature is entirely repugnant to believe in 'new epochs.'* The English Legislature does not occupy itself with epochs; has, indeed, other business to do than looking at the Time-Horologe and hearing it tick! Nevertheless new epochs do actually come; and with them new imperious peremptory necessities; so that even an English Legislature has to look up, and admit, though with reluctance, that the hour has struck. The hour having struck, let us not say 'impossible:'—it will have to be possible! 'Contrary to the habits of Parliament, the habits of Government?' Yes: but did any Parliament or Government ever sit in a Year Forty-three before? One of the most original, unexampled years and epochs; in several important respects totally unlike any other! For Time, all-edacious and all-feracious, does run on: and the Seven Sleepers, awakening hungry after a hundred years,* find that it is not their old nurses who can now give them suck!

For the rest, let not any Parliament, Aristocracy, Millocracy, or Member of the Governing Class, condemn with much triumph this small specimen of 'remedial measures;'* or ask again, with the least anger, of this Editor, What is to be done, How that alarming problem of the Working Classes is to be managed? Editors are not here, foremost of all, to say How. A certain Editor thanks the gods that nobody pays him three hundred thousand pounds a year, two hundred thousand, twenty thousand, or any similar sum of cash for saying How;—that his wages are very different, his work somewhat fitter for him. An Editor's stipulated work is to apprise *thee* that it must be done. The 'way to do it,' is to try it, knowing that thou shalt die if it be not done. There is the bare back, there is the web of cloth; thou shalt cut me a coat to cover the bare back, thou whose trade it is.

'Impossible?' Hapless Fraction, dost thou discern Fate there, half unveiling herself in the gloom of the future, with her gibbet-cords, her steelwhips, and very authentic Tailor's Hell;* waiting to see whether it is 'possible?' Out with thy scissors, and cut that cloth or thy own windpipe!

CHAPTER IV.

CAPTAINS OF INDUSTRY.*

IF I believed that Mammonism with its adjuncts was to continue henceforth the one serious principle of our existence, I should reckon it idle to solicit remedial measures from any Government, the disease being insusceptible of remedy. Government can do much, but it can in no wise do all. Government, as the most conspicuous object in Society, is called upon to give signal of what shall be done; and, in many ways, to preside over, further, and command the doing of it. But the Government cannot do, by all its signalling and commanding, what the Society is radically indisposed to do. In the long-run every Government is the exact symbol of its People, with their wisdom and unwisdom; we have to say, Like People like Government.—The main substance of this immense Problem of Organising Labour, and first of all of Managing the Working Classes, will, it is very clear, have to be solved by those who stand practically in the middle of it; by those who themselves work and preside over work. Of all that can be enacted by any Parliament in regard to it, the germs must already lie potentially extant in those two Classes, who are to obey such enactment. A Human Chaos *in* which there is no light, you vainly attempt to irradiate by light shed *on* it: order never can arise there.

But it is my firm conviction that the 'Hell of England' will *cease* to be that of 'not making money;' that we shall get a nobler Hell and a nobler Heaven! I anticipate light *in* the Human Chaos, glimmering, shining more and more; under manifold true signals from without That light shall shine. Our deity no longer being Mammon,—O Heavens, each man will then say to himself: "Why such deadly haste to make money? I shall not go to Hell, even if I do not make money! There is another Hell, I am told!" Competition, at railway-speed,* in all branches of commerce and work will then abate:—good felt-hats for the head, in every sense, instead of seven-feet lath-and-plaster hats on wheels, will then be discoverable! Bubble-periods, with their panics and commercial crises,* will again become infrequent; steady modest industry will take the place of gambling speculation. To be a noble Master, among noble Workers, will again be the first ambition with some few; to be a rich Master only the second. How the Inventive Genius of England, with the whirr of its bobbins and billy-rollers shoved somewhat into the backgrounds of the brain, will contrive and devise, not cheaper produce exclusively, but fairer distribution of the produce at its present cheapness! By degrees, we shall again have a Society with something of Heroism in it, something of Heaven's Blessing on it; we shall again have, as my German friend asserts, 'instead of Mammon-Feudalism with unsold cotton-shirts and Preservation of the Game, noble just Industrialism and Government by the Wisest!'

It is with the hope of awakening here and there a British man to know himself for a man and divine soul, that a few words of parting admonition, to all persons to whom the Heavenly Powers have lent power of any kind in this land, may now be addressed. And first to those same Master-Workers, Leaders of Industry; who stand nearest and in fact powerfulest, though not most prominent, being as yet in too many senses a Virtuality rather than an Actuality.

The Leaders of Industry, if Industry is ever to be led, are virtually the Captains of the World; if there be no nobleness in them, there will never be an Aristocracy more. But let the Captains of Industry consider: once again, are they born of other clay than the old Captains of Slaughter; doomed forever to be no Chivalry, but a mere gold-plated *Doggery*,*—what the French well name *Canaille*, 'Doggery' with more or less gold carrion at its disposal? Captains of Industry are the true Fighters, henceforth recognisable as the only true ones: Fighters against Chaos, Necessity and the Devils and Jötuns;* and lead on Mankind in that great, and alone true, and universal warfare; the stars in their courses fighting for them,* and all Heaven and all Earth saying audibly, Well-done! Let the Captains of Industry retire into their own hearts, and ask solemnly, If there is nothing but vulturous hunger, for fine wines, valet reputation and gilt carriages, discoverable there? Of hearts made by the Almighty God I will not believe such a thing. Deep-hidden under wretchedest godforgetting Cants, Epicurisms, Dead-Sea Apisms; forgotten as under foulest fat Lethe mud and weeds, there is yet, in all hearts born into this God's-World, a spark of the Godlike slumbering. Awake, O nightmare sleepers; awake, arise, or be forever fallen!* This is not playhouse poetry; it is sober fact. Our England, our world cannot live as it is. It will connect itself with a God again, or go down with nameless throes and fire-consummation to the Devils. Thou who feelest aught of such a Godlike stirring in thee, any faintest intimation of it as through heavy-laden dreams, follow *it*, I conjure thee. Arise, save thyself, be one of those that save thy country.

Bucaniers, Chactaw Indians,* whose supreme aim in fighting is that they may get the scalps, the money, that they may amass scalps and money: out of such came no Chivalry, and never will! Out of such came only gore and wreck, infernal rage and misery; desperation quenched in annihilation. Behold it, I bid thee, behold there, and consider! What is it that thou have a hundred thousand-pound bills laid-up in thy strong-room, a hundred scalps hung-up in thy wigwam? I value not them or thee. Thy scalps and thy thousand-pound bills are as yet nothing, if no nobleness from within irradiate them; if no Chivalry, in action, or in embryo ever struggling towards birth and action, be there.

Love of men cannot be bought by cash-payment; and without love men cannot endure to be together. You cannot lead a Fighting World without having it regimented, chivalried: the thing, in a day, becomes impossible; all men in it, the highest at first, the very lowest at last, discern consciously, or by a noble instinct, this necessity. And can you any more continue to lead a Working World unregimented, anarchic? I answer, and the Heavens and Earth are now answering, No! The thing becomes not 'in a day' impossible; but in some two generations it does. Yes, when fathers and mothers, in Stockport hunger-cellars, begin to eat their children,* and Irish widows have to prove their relationship by dying of typhus-fever; and amid Governing 'Corporations of the Best and Bravest,'* busy to preserve their game by 'bushing,' dark millions of God's human creatures start up in mad Chartisms, impracticable Sacred-Months, and Manchester Insurrections;*—and there is a virtual Industrial Aristocracy as yet only half-alive, spell-bound amid money-bags and ledgers; and an actual Idle Aristocracy seemingly near dead in somnolent delusions, in trespasses and double-barrels; 'sliding,' as on inclined-planes,* which every new year they *soap* with new Hansard's-jargon under God's sky, and so are 'sliding,' ever faster, towards a 'scale' and balance-scale whereon is written *Thou art found Wanting:*—in such days, after a generation or two, I say, it does become, even to the low and simple, very palpably impossible! No Working World, any more than a Fighting World, can be led on without a noble Chivalry of Work, and laws and fixed rules which follow out of that,—far nobler than any Chivalry of Fighting was. As an anarchic multitude on mere Supply-and-demand, it is becoming inevitable that we dwindle in horrid suicidal convulsion and self-abrasion, frightful to the imagination, into *Chactaw* Workers. With wigwam and scalps,—with palaces and thousand-pound bills; with savagery, depopulation, chaotic desolation! Good Heavens, will not one French Revolution and Reign of Terror suffice us, but must there be two? There will be two if needed; there will be twenty if needed; there will be precisely as many as are needed. The Laws of Nature will have themselves fulfilled. That is a thing certain to me.

Your gallant battle-hosts and work-hosts, as the others did, will need to be made loyally yours; they must and will be regulated, methodically secured in their just share of conquest under you;—joined with you in veritable brotherhood, sonhood, by quite other and deeper ties than those of temporary day's wages! How would mere redcoated regiments, to say nothing of chivalries, fight for you, if you could discharge them on the evening of the battle, on payment of the stipulated shillings,—and they discharge you on the morning of it! Chelsea Hospitals,* pensions, promotions, rigorous lasting covenant on the one side and on the other, are indispensable even for a hired fighter. The Feudal Baron, much more,—how could he subsist with mere temporary mercenaries round him, at sixpence a day; ready to go over to the other side, if sevenpence were offered? He could not have subsisted;—and his noble instinct saved him from the necessity of even trying! The Feudal Baron had a Man's Soul in him; to which anarchy, mutiny, and the other fruits of temporary mercenaries, were intolerable: he had never been a Baron otherwise, but had continued a Chactaw and Bucanier. He felt it precious, and at last it became habitual, and his fruitful enlarged existence included it as a necessity, to have men round him who in heart loved him; whose life he watched over with rigour yet with love; who were prepared to give their life for him, if need came. It was beautiful; it was human! Man lives not otherwise, nor can live contented, anywhere or any-when. Isolation is the sum-total of wretchedness to man. To be cut off, to be left solitary: to have a world alien, not your world; all a hostile camp for you; not a home at all, of hearts and faces who are yours, whose you are! It is the frightfulest

enchantment; too truly a work of the Evil One. To have neither superior, nor inferior, nor equal, united manlike to you. Without father,
without child, without brother. Man knows no sadder destiny. 'How
is each of us,' exclaims Jean Paul, 'so lonely in the wide bosom of the
All!'* Encased each as in his transparent 'ice-palace;' our brother visible in his, making signals and gesticulations to us;—visible, but forever unattainable: on his bosom we shall never rest, nor he on ours. It
was not a God that did this; no!

Awake, ye noble Workers, warriors in the one true war: all this must
be remedied. It is you who are already half-alive, whom I will welcome
into life; whom I will conjure, in God's name, to shake off your
enchanted sleep, and live wholly! Cease to count scalps, gold-purses;
not in these lies your or our salvation. Even these, if you count only
these, will not long be left. Let bucaniering be put far from you; alter,
speedily abrogate all laws of the bucaniers, if you would gain any victory that shall endure. Let God's justice, let pity, nobleness and manly
valour, with more gold-purses or with fewer, testify themselves in this
your brief Life-transit to all the Eternities, the Gods and Silences. It
is to you I call; for ye are not dead, ye are already half-alive: there is in
you a sleepless dauntless energy, the prime-matter of all nobleness in
man. Honour to you in your kind. It is to you I call: ye know at least
this, That the mandate of God to His creature man is: Work! The
future Epic of the World rests not with those that are near dead, but
with those that are alive, and those that are coming into life.

Look around you. Your world-hosts are all in mutiny, in confusion,
destitution; on the eve of fiery wreck and madness! They will not
march farther for you, on the sixpence a day and supply-and-demand
principle: they will not; nor ought they, nor can they. Ye shall reduce
them to order, begin reducing them. To order, to just subordination;
noble loyalty in return for noble guidance. Their souls are driven nigh
mad; let yours be sane and ever saner. Not as a bewildered bewildering mob; but as a firm regimented mass, with real captains over
them, will these men march any more. All human interests, combined
human endeavours, and social growths in this world, have, at a certain stage of their development, required organising: and Work, the
grandest of human interests, does now require it.

God knows, the task will be hard: but no noble task was ever easy.
This task will wear away your lives, and the lives of your sons and
grandsons: but for what purpose, if not for tasks like this, were lives

given to men? Ye shall cease to count your thousand-pound scalps, the noble of you shall cease! Nay the very scalps, as I say, will not long be left if you count only these. Ye shall cease wholly to be barbarous vulturous Chactaws, and become noble European Nineteenth-Century Men. Ye shall know that Mammon, in never such gigs and flunkey 'respectabilities,'* is not the alone God; that of himself he is but a Devil, and even a Brute-god.

Difficult? Yes, it will be difficult. The short-fibre cotton; that too was difficult. The waste cotton-shrub, long useless, disobedient, as the thistle by the wayside,*—have ye not conquered it; made it into beautiful bandana webs; white woven shirts for men; bright-tinted air-garments wherein flit goddesses? Ye have shivered mountains asunder, made the hard iron pliant to you as soft putty: the Forest-giants, Marsh-jötuns bear sheaves of golden grain; Ægir the Sea-demon* himself stretches his back for a sleek highway to you, and on Firehorses and Windhorses ye career.* Ye are most strong. Thor red-bearded, with his blue sun-eyes, with his cheery heart and strong thunder-hammer,* he and you have prevailed. Ye are most strong, ye Sons of the icy North, of the far East,—far marching from your rugged Eastern Wildernesses, hitherward from the grey Dawn of Time! Ye are Sons of the *Jötun*-land; the land of Difficulties Conquered. Difficult? You must try this thing. Once try it with the understanding that it will and shall have to be done. Try it as ye try the paltrier thing, making of money! I will bet on you once more, against all Jötuns, Tailor-gods, Double-barrelled Law-wards, and Denizens of Chaos whatsoever!

CHAPTER V.

PERMANENCE.

STANDING on the threshold, nay as yet outside the threshold, of a 'Chivalry of Labour,' and an immeasurable Future which it is to fill with fruitfulness and verdant shade; where so much has not yet come even to the rudimental state, and all speech of positive enactments were hazardous in those who know this business only by the eye,—let us here hint at simply one widest universal principle, as the basis from which all organisation hitherto has grown up among men, and all henceforth will have to grow: The principle of Permanent Contract instead of Temporary.

Permanent not Temporary:—you do not hire the mere redcoated fighter by the day, but by the score of years! Permanence, persistence is the first condition of all fruitfulness in the ways of men. The 'tendency to persevere,'* to persist in spite of hindrances, discouragements and 'impossibilities:' it is this that in all things distinguishes the strong soul from the weak; the civilised burgher from the nomadic savage,—the Species Man from the Genus Ape! The Nomad has his very house set on wheels; the Nomad, and in a still higher degree the Ape, are all for 'liberty;' the privilege to flit continually is indispensable for them. Alas, in how many ways, does our humour, in this swift-rolling, self-abrading Time, shew itself nomadic, apelike; mournful enough to him that looks on it with eyes! This humour will have to abate; it is the first element of all fertility in human things, that such 'liberty' of apes and nomads do by freewill or constraint abridge itself, give place to a better. The civilised man lives not in wheeled houses.* He builds stone castles, plants lands, makes lifelong marriage-contracts;—has long-dated hundred-fold possessions, not to be valued in the money-market; has pedigrees, libraries, law-codes; has memories and hopes, even for this Earth, that reach over thousands of years. Lifelong marriage-contracts: how much preferable were year-long or month-long—to the nomad or ape!

Month-long contracts please me little, in any province where there can by possibility be found virtue enough for more. Month-long contracts do not answer well even with your house-servants;* the liberty on both sides to change every month is growing very apelike, nomadic;—and I hear philosophers predict that it will alter, or that strange results will follow: that wise men, pestered with nomads, with unattached ever-shifting spies and enemies rather than friends and servants, will gradually, weighing substance against semblance, with indignation, dismiss such, down almost to the very shoeblack, and say, "Begone; I will serve myself rather, and have peace!" Gurth was hired for life to Cedric, and Cedric to Gurth. O Anti-Slavery Convention, loud-sounding long-eared Exeter-Hall*—But in thee too is a kind of instinct towards justice, and I will complain of nothing. Only black Quashee* over the seas being once sufficiently attended to, wilt thou not perhaps open thy dull sodden eyes to the 'sixty-thousand valets in London itself who are yearly dismissed to the streets,* to be what they can, when the season ends;'—or to the hungerstricken, pallid, *yellow*-coloured 'Free Labourers' in Lancashire, Yorkshire, Buckinghamshire, and all other shires!* These Yellow-coloured, for the present, absorb all my sympathies:* if I had a Twenty Millions, with Model-Farms and Niger Expeditions, it is to these that I would give it!* Quashee has already victuals, clothing; Quashee is not dying of such despair as the yellow-coloured pale man's.* Quashee, it must be owned, is hitherto a kind of blockhead. The Haiti Duke of Marmalade, educated now for almost half a century, seems to have next to no sense in him.* Why, in one of those Lancashire Weavers, dying of hunger, there is more thought and heart, a greater arithmetical amount of misery and desperation, than in whole gangs of Quashees. It must be owned, thy eyes are of the sodden sort; and with thy emancipations, and thy twenty-millionings and long-eared clamourings, thou, like Robespierre with his pasteboard *Être Suprême*, threatenest to become a bore to us: *Avec ton Être Suprême tu commences m'embêter!*—*

In a Printed Sheet of the assiduous, much-abused, and truly useful Mr. Chadwick's, containing queries and responses from far and near as to this great question, 'What is the effect of education on workingmen, in respect of their value as mere workers?' the present Editor, reading with satisfaction a decisive unanimous verdict as to Education, reads with inexpressible interest this special remark, put in by way of marginal incidental note, from a practical manufacturing Quaker, whom, as he is anonymous, we will call Friend Prudence. Prudence keeps a thousand workmen; has striven in all ways to attach them to him; has provided conversational soirées; play-grounds, bands of music for the young ones; went even 'the length of buying them a drum:' all which has turned out to be an excellent investment. For a certain person, marked here by a black stroke, whom we shall name Blank, living over the way,—he also keeps somewhere about a thousand men; but has done none of these things for them, nor any other thing, except due payment of the wages by supply-and-demand. Blank's workers are perpetually getting into mutiny, into broils and coils: every six months, we suppose, Blank has a strike; every one month, every day and every hour, they are fretting and obstructing the shortsighted Blank; pilfering from him, wasting and idling for him, omitting and committing for him. "I would not," says Friend Prudence, "exchange my workers for his *with seven thousand pounds to boot*."[1]*

Right, O honourable Prudence; thou art wholly in the right: Seven thousand pounds even as a matter of profit for this world, nay for the mere cash-market of this world! And as a matter of profit not for this world only, but for the other world and all worlds, it outweighs the Bank of England!—Can the sagacious reader descry here, as it were the outmost inconsiderable rock-ledge of a universal rock-foundation, deep once more as the Centre of the World, emerging so, in the experience of this good Quaker, through the Stygian mud-vortexes and general Mother of Dead Dogs,* whereon, for the present, all swags and insecurely hovers, as if ready to be swallowed?

Some Permanence of Contract is already almost possible; the principle of Permanence, year by year, better seen into and elaborated, may enlarge itself, expand gradually on every side into a system. This once secured, the basis of all good results were laid. Once permanent, you do not quarrel with the first difficulty on your path, and quit it in weak disgust; you reflect that it cannot be quitted, that it must be conquered, a wise arrangement fallen on with regard to it. Ye foolish Wedded Two, who have quarrelled, between whom the Evil Spirit has stirred up transient strife and bitterness, so that 'incompatibility' seems almost nigh, ye are nevertheless the Two who, by long habit, were it by nothing more, do best of all others suit each other: it is expedient for your own two foolish selves, to say nothing of the infants, pedigrees and public in general, that ye agree again; that ye put away the Evil Spirit, and wisely on both hands struggle for the guidance of a Good Spirit!

The very horse that is permanent, how much kindlier do his rider and he work, than the temporary one, hired on any hack principle yet known! I am for permanence in all things, at the earliest possible moment, and to the latest possible. Blessed is he that continueth where he is. Here let us rest, and lay out seedfields; here let us learn to dwell. Here, even here, the orchards that we plant will yield us fruit; the acorns will be wood and pleasant umbrage, if we wait. How much grows everywhere, if we do but wait! Through the swamps we

---

[1] Report on the Training of Pauper Children (1841), p. 18.

will shape causeways, force purifying drains; we will learn to thread the rocky inaccessibilities; and beaten tracks, worn smooth by mere travelling of human feet, will form themselves. Not a difficulty but can transfigure itself into a triumph; not even a deformity but, if our own soul have imprinted worth on it, will grow dear to us. The sunny plains and deep indigo transparent skies of Italy are all indifferent to the great sick heart of a Sir Walter Scott: on the back of the Apennines, in wild spring weather, the sight of bleak Scotch firs, and snow-spotted heath and desolation, brings tears into his eyes.[1]*

O unwise mortals that forever change and shift, and say, Yonder, not Here! Wealth richer than both the Indies lies everywhere for man, if he will endure. Not his oaks only and his fruit-trees, his very heart roots itself wherever he will abide;—roots itself, draws nourishment from the deep fountains of Universal Being! Vagrant Sam-Slicks,* who rove over the Earth doing 'strokes of trade,' what wealth have they? Horseloads, shiploads of white or yellow metal: in very sooth, what *are* these? Slick rests nowhere, he is homeless. He can build stone or marble houses; but to continue in them is denied him. The wealth of a man is the number of things which he loves and blesses, which he is loved and blessed by! The herdsman in his poor clay shealing, where his very cow and dog are friends to him, and not a cataract but carries memories for him, and not a mountain-top but nods old recognition: his life, all encircled as in blessed mother's-arms, is it poorer than Slick's with the ass-loads of yellow metal on his back? Unhappy Slick! Alas, there has so much grown nomadic, ape-like, with us: so much will have, with whatever pain, repugnance and 'impossibility,' to alter itself, to fix itself again,—in some wise way, in any not delirious way!

A question arises here: Whether, in some ulterior, perhaps some not far-distant stage of this 'Chivalry of Labour,' your Master-Worker may not find it possible, and needful, to grant his Workers permanent *interest* in his enterprise and theirs?* So that it become, in practical result, what in essential fact and justice it ever is, a joint enterprise; all men, from the Chief Master down to the lowest Overseer and Operative, economically as well as loyally concerned for it?—Which question I do not answer. The answer, near or else far, is perhaps,

---

[1] Lockhart's *Life of Scott.*

Yes;—and yet one knows the difficulties. Despotism is essential in most enterprises; I am told, they do not tolerate 'freedom of debate' on board a Seventy-four!* Republican senate and *plebiscita** would not answer well in Cotton-Mills. And yet observe there too: Freedom, not nomad's or ape's Freedom, but man's Freedom; this is indispensable. We must have it, and will have it! To reconcile Despotism with Freedom:*—well, is that such a mystery? Do you not already know the way? It is to make your Despotism *just*. Rigorous as Destiny; but just too, as Destiny and its Laws. The Laws of God: all men obey these, and have no 'Freedom' at all but in obeying them. The way is already known, part of the way;—and courage and some qualities are needed for walking on it!

CHAPTER VI.

THE LANDED.

A MAN with fifty, with five hundred, with a thousand pounds a day, given him freely, without condition at all,—on condition, as it now runs, that he will sit with his hands in his pockets and do no mischief, pass no Corn-Laws or the like,—he too, you would say, is or might be a rather strong Worker! He is a Worker with such tools as no man in this world ever before had. But in practice, very astonishing, very ominous to look at, he proves not a strong Worker;—you are too happy if he will prove but a No-worker, do nothing, and not be a Wrong-worker.

You ask him, at the year's end: "Where is your three-hundred thousand pound; what have you realised to us with that?" He answers, in indignant surprise: "Done with it? Who are you that ask? I have eaten it; I and my flunkeys, and parasites, and slaves two-footed and four-footed, in an ornamental manner; and I am here alive by it; *I* am realised by it to you!"—It is, as we have often said, such an answer as was never before given under this Sun. An answer that fills me with boding apprehension, with foreshadows of despair. O stolid Use-and-wont of an atheistic Half-century, O Ignavia,* Tailor-godhood, soul-killing Cant, to what passes art thou bringing us!—Out of the loud-piping whirlwind,* audibly to him that has ears, the Highest God is again announcing in these days: "Idleness shall not be." God has said it, man cannot gainsay.

Ah, how happy were it, if he this Aristocrat Worker would, in like manner, see *his* work and do it! It is frightful seeking another to do it for him. Guillotines, Meudon Tanneries, and half-a-million men shot dead,* have already been expended in that business; and it is yet far from done. This man too is something; nay he is a great thing. Look on him there: a man of manful aspect; something of the 'cheerfulness of pride' still lingering in him. A free air of graceful stoicism, of easy silent dignity sits well on him; in his heart, could we reach it, lie elements of generosity, self-sacrificing justice, true human valour. Why should he, with such appliances, stand an incumbrance in the Present; perish disastrously out of the Future! From no section of the Future would we lose these noble courtesies, impalpable yet all-controlling; these dignified reticences, these kingly simplicities;—lose aught of what the fruitful Past still gives us token of, memento of, in this man. Can we not save him:—can he not help us to save him! A brave man, he too; had not undivine Ignavia, Hearsay, Speech without meaning,—had not Cant, thousandfold Cant within him and around him, enveloping him like choke-damp, like thick Egyptian darkness,* thrown his soul into asphyxia, as it were extinguished his soul; so that he sees not, hears not, and Moses and all the Prophets address him in vain.

Will he awaken, be alive again, and have a soul; or is this death-fit very 'death? It is a question of questions, for himself and for us all! Alas, is there no noble work for this man too? Has not he thickheaded ignorant boors; lazy, enslaved farmers, weedy lands? Lands! Has not he weary heavy-laden ploughers of land; immortal souls of men, ploughing, ditching, day-drudging; bare of back, empty of stomach, nigh desperate of heart; and none peaceably to help them but he, under Heaven? Does he find, with his three-hundred thousand pounds, no noble thing trodden down in the thoroughfares, which it were godlike to help up? Can he do nothing for his Burns but make a Gauger of him;* lionise him, bedinner him, for a foolish while; then whistle him down the wind, to desperation and bitter death?—His work too is difficult, in these modern, far-dislocated ages. But it may be done; it may be tried;—it must be done.

A modern Duke of Weimar, not a god he either, but a human duke, levied, as I reckon, in rents and taxes and all incomings whatsoever, less than several of our English Dukes do in rent alone. The Duke of Weimar, with these incomings, had to govern, judge, defend, everyway

administer *his* Dukedom.* He does all this as few others did: and he
improves lands besides all this, makes river-embankments, maintains
not soldiers only but Universities and Institutions;*—and in his
Court were these four men: Wieland, Herder, Schiller, Goethe.* Not
as parasites, which was impossible; not as table-wits and poetic
Katerfeltoes; but as noble Spiritual Men working under a noble
Practical Man.* Shielded by him from many miseries; perhaps from
many shortcomings, destructive aberrations. Heaven had sent, once
more, heavenly Light into the world; and this man's honour was that
he gave it welcome. A new noble kind of Clergy, under an old but still
noble kind of King! I reckon that this one Duke of Weimar did more
for the Culture of his Nation than all the English Dukes and *Duces*
now extant, or that were extant since Henry the Eighth gave them the
Church Lands to eat, have done for theirs!—I am ashamed, I am
alarmed for my English Dukes: what word have I to say?

If our Actual Aristocracy, appointed 'Best-and-Bravest,' will be
wise, how inexpressibly happy for us! If not,—the voice of God
from the whirlwind is very audible to me. Nay, I will thank the Great
God, that He has said, in whatever fearful ways, and just wrath
against us, "Idleness shall be no more!" Idleness? The awakened
soul of man, all but the asphyxied soul of man, turns from it as from
worse than death. It is the life-in-death of Poet Coleridge.* That
fable of the Dead-Sea Apes ceases to be a fable. The poor Worker
starved to death is not the saddest of sights. He lies there, dead on
his shield; fallen down into the bosom of his old Mother; with haggard pale face, sorrow-worn, but stilled now into divine peace,
silently appeals to the Eternal God and all the Universe,—the most
silent, the most eloquent of men.

   Exceptions,—ah yes, thank Heaven, we know there are exceptions.
Our case were too hard, were there not exceptions, and partial exceptions not a few, whom we know, and whom we do not know. Honour
to the name of Ashley,*—honour to this and the other valiant Abdiel,*
found faithful still; who would fain, by work and by word, admonish
their Order not to rush upon destruction! These are they who will, if
not save their Order, postpone the wreck of it;—by whom, under
blessing of the Upper Powers, 'a quiet euthanasia spread over generations, instead of a swift torture-death concentred into years,'* may
be brought about for many things. All honour and success to these.
The noble man can still strive nobly to save and serve his Order;—at

lowest, he can remember the precept of the Prophet: "Come out of her, my people; come out of her!"*

To sit idle aloft, like living statues, like absurd Epicurus'-gods,* in pampered isolation, in exclusion from the glorious fateful battlefield of this God's-World: it is a poor life for a man, when all Upholsterers and French-Cooks have done their utmost for it!—Nay what a shallow delusion is this we have all got into, That any man should or can keep himself apart from men, have 'no business' with them, except a cash-account 'business!' It is the silliest tale a distressed generation of men ever took to telling one another. Men cannot live isolated: we *are* all bound together, for mutual good or else for mutual misery, as living nerves in the same body. No highest man can disunite himself from any lowest. Consider it. Your poor 'Werter blowing out his distracted existence because Charlotte will not have the keeping thereof:'* this is no peculiar phasis; it is simply the highest expression of a phasis traceable wherever one human creature meets another! Let the meanest crookbacked Thersites teach the supremest Agamemnon that he actually does not reverence him, the supremest Agamemnon's eyes flash fire responsive; a real pain, and partial insanity has seized Agamemnon. Strange enough: a many-counselled Ulysses is set in motion by a scoundrel-blockhead; plays tunes, like a barrel-organ, at the scoundrel-blockhead's touch,—has to snatch, namely, his sceptre-cudgel, and weal the crooked back with bumps and thumps!* Let a chief of men reflect well on it. Not in having 'no business' with men, but in having no unjust business with them, and in *having* all manner of true and just business, can either his or their blessedness be found possible, and this waste world become, for both parties, a home and peopled garden.

Men do reverence men. Men do worship in that 'one temple of the world,' as Novalis calls it, the Presence of a Man!* Hero-worship, true and blessed, or else mistaken, false and accursed, goes on everywhere and everywhen. In this world there is one godlike thing, the essence of all that was or ever will be of godlike in this world: the veneration done to Human Worth by the hearts of men. Hero-worship, in the souls of the heroic, of the clear and wise,—it is the perpetual presence of Heaven in our poor Earth: when it is not there, Heaven is veiled from us; and all is under Heaven's ban and interdict, and there is no worship, or worth-ship, or worth or blessedness in the Earth any more!—

Independence, 'lord of the lion-heart and eagle-eye,'*—alas, yes, he is one we have got acquainted with in these late times: a very indispensable one, for spurning-off with due energy innumerable sham-superiors, Tailor-made: honour to him, entire success to him! Entire success is sure to him. But he must not stop there, at that small success, with his eagle-eye. He has now a second far greater success to gain: to seek out his real superiors, whom not the Tailor but the Almighty God has made superior to him, and see a little what he will do with these! Rebel against these also? Pass by with minatory eagle-glance, with calm-sniffing mockery, or even without any mockery or sniff, when these present themselves? The lion-hearted will never dream of such a thing. Forever far be it from him! His minatory eagle-glance will veil itself in softness of the dove: his lion-heart will become a lamb's; all its just indignation changed into just reverence, dissolved in blessed floods of noble humble love, how much heavenlier than any pride, nay, if you will, how much prouder! I know him, this lion-hearted, eagle-eyed one; have met him, rushing on, 'with bosom bare,' in a very distracted dishevelled manner,* the times being hard;—and can say, and guarantee on my life, That in him is no rebellion; that in him is the reverse of rebellion, the needful preparation for obedience. For if you do mean to obey God-made superiors, your first step is to sweep out the Tailor-made ones; order them, under penalties, to vanish, to make ready for vanishing!

Nay, what is best of all, he cannot rebel, if he would. Superiors whom God has made for us we cannot order to withdraw! Not in the least. No Grand-Turk himself, thickest-quilted tailor-made Brother of the Sun and Moon can do it: but an Arab Man, in cloak of his own clouting; with black beaming eyes, with flaming sovereign-heart direct from the centre of the Universe; and also, I am told, with terrible 'horse-shoe vein' of swelling wrath in his brow,* and lightning (if you will not have it as light) tingling through every vein of him,—he rises; says authoritatively: "Thickest-quilted Grand-Turk, tailor-made Brother of the Sun and Moon, No:—*I* withdraw not;* thou shalt obey me or withdraw!" And so accordingly it is: thickest-quilted Grand-Turks and all their progeny, to this hour, obey that man in the remarkablest manner; preferring *not* to withdraw.

O brother, it is an endless consolation to me, in this disorganic, as yet so quack-ridden, what you may well call hag-ridden and hell-ridden world, to find that disobedience to the Heavens, when they send any messenger whatever, is and remains impossible. It cannot be done; no Turk grand or small can do it. 'Shew the dullest clodpole,' says my invaluable German friend, 'shew the haughtiest featherhead, that a soul higher than himself is here; were his knees stiffened into brass, he must down and worship.'*

CHAPTER VII.

THE GIFTED.

YES, in what tumultuous huge anarchy soever a Noble human Principle may dwell and strive, such tumult is in the way of being calmed into a fruitful sovereignty. It is inevitable. No Chaos can continue chaotic with a soul in it. Besouled with earnest human Nobleness, did not slaughter, violence and fire-eyed fury, grow into a Chivalry; into a blessed Loyalty of Governor and Governed? And in Work, which is of itself noble, and the only true fighting, there shall be no such possibility? Believe it not; it is incredible; the whole Universe contradicts it. Here too the Chactaw Principle will be subordinated; the Man Principle will, by degrees, become superior, become supreme.

I know Mammon too; Banks-of-England, Credit-Systems, world-wide possibilities of work and traffic; and applaud and admire them. Mammon is like Fire; the usefulest of all servants, if the frightfulest of all masters! The Cliffords, Fitzadelms* and Chivalry Fighters 'wished to gain victory,' never doubt it: but victory, unless gained in a certain spirit, was no victory; defeat, sustained in a certain spirit, was itself victory. I say again and again, had they counted the scalps alone, they had continued Chactaws, and no Chivalry or lasting victory had been. And in Industrial Fighters and Captains is there no nobleness discoverable? To them, alone of men, there shall forever be no blessedness but in swollen coffers? To see beauty, order, gratitude, loyal human hearts around them, shall be of no moment; to see fuliginous deformity, mutiny, hatred and despair, with the addition of half-a-million guineas, shall be better? Heaven's blessedness not there; Hell's cursedness, and your half-million bits of metal, a substitute for that! Is there no profit in diffusing Heaven's blessedness, but only in gaining gold?—If so, I apprise the Mill-owner and Millionaire, that he too must prepare for vanishing; that neither is *he* born to be of the sovereigns of this world; that he will have to be trampled and chained down in whatever terrible ways, and brass-collared safe, among the born thralls of this world! We cannot have *Canailles* and Doggeries* that will not make some Chivalry of themselves: our noble Planet is impatient of such; in the end, totally intolerant of such!

For the Heavens, unwearying in their bounty, do send other souls into this world, to whom yet, as to their forerunners, in Old Roman, in Old Hebrew and all noble times, the omnipotent guinea is, on the whole, an impotent guinea. Has your half-dead avaricious Corn-Law Lord, your half-alive avaricious Cotton-Law Lord, never seen one such? Such are, not one, but several; are, and will be, unless the gods have doomed this world to swift dire ruin. These are they, the elect of the world; the born champions, strong men, and liberatory Samsons of this poor world: whom the poor Delilah-world will not always shear of their strength and eyesight, and set to grind in darkness at *its* poor gin-wheel!* Such souls are, in these days, getting somewhat out of humour with the world. Your very Byron, in these days, is at least driven mad; flatly refuses fealty to the world. The world with its injustices, its golden brutalities, and dull yellow guineas, is a disgust to such souls: the ray of Heaven that is in them does at least predoom them to be very miserable here. Yes:—and yet all misery is faculty misdirected, strength that has not yet found its way. The black whirl-wind is mother of the lightning. No *smoke*, in any sense, but can become flame and radiance! Such soul, once graduated in Heaven's stern University, steps out superior to your guinea.

Dost thou know, O sumptuous Corn-Lord, Cotton-Lord, O mutinous Trades-Unionist, gin-vanquished, undeliverable; O much-enslaved World,—this man is not a slave with thee! None of thy promotions is necessary for him. His place is with the stars of Heaven: to thee it may be momentous, to thee it may be life or death, to him it is indifferent, whether thou place him in the lowest hut, or forty feet higher at the top of thy stupendous high tower, while here on Earth. The joys of Earth that are precious, they depend not on thee and thy promotions. Food and raiment, and, round a social hearth, souls who love him, whom he loves: these are already his. He wants none of thy rewards; behold also, he fears none of thy penalties. Thou canst not answer even by killing him: the case of Anaxarchus thou canst kill; but the self of Anaxarchus, the word or act of Anaxarchus, in no wise whatever.* To this man death is not a bugbear; to this man life is already as earnest and awful, and beautiful and terrible, as death.

Not a May-game is this man's life;* but a battle and a march, a warfare with principalities and powers.* No idle promenade through fragrant orange-groves and green flowery spaces, waited on by the choral Muses and the rosy Hours:* it is a stern pilgrimage through burning sandy solitudes, through regions of thick-ribbed ice. He walks among men; loves men, with inexpressible soft pity,—as they *cannot* love him: but his soul dwells in solitude, in the uttermost parts of Creation. In green oases by the palm-tree wells, he rests a space; but anon he has to journey forward, escorted by the Terrors and the Splendours, the Archdemons and Archangels. All Heaven, all Pandemonium are his escort. The stars keen-glancing, from the Immensities, send tidings to him; the graves, silent with their dead, from the Eternities. Deep calls for him unto Deep.*

Thou, O World, how wilt thou secure thyself against this man? Thou canst not hire him by thy guineas; nor by thy gibbets and law-penalties restrain him. He eludes thee like a Spirit. Thou canst not forward him, thou canst not hinder him. Thy penalties, thy poverties, neglects, contumelies: behold, all these are good for him. Come to him as an enemy; turn from him as an unfriend; only do not this one thing,—infect him not with thy own delusion: the benign Genius, were it by very death, shall guard him against this!*—What wilt thou do with him? He is above thee, like a god. Thou, in thy stupendous three-inch pattens,* art under him. He is thy born king, thy conqueror and supreme lawgiver: not all the guineas and cannons, and leather and prunella,* under the sky can save thee from him. Hardest thickskinned Mammon-world, ruggedest Caliban shall obey him, or become not Caliban but a cramp.* Oh, if in this man, whose eyes can flash Heaven's lightning, and make all Calibans into a cramp, there dwelt not, as the essence of his very being, a God's justice, human Nobleness, Veracity and Mercy,—I should tremble for the world. But his strength, let us rejoice to understand, is even this: The quantity of Justice, of Valour and Pity that is in him. To hypocrites and tailored quacks in high places, his eyes are lightning; but they melt in dewy pity softer than a mother's to the downpressed, maltreated; in his heart, in his great thought, is a sanctuary for all the wretched. This world's improvement is forever sure.

'Man of Genius?'* Thou hast small notion, meseems, O Mecænas
Twiddledee, of what a Man of Genius is. Read in thy New Testament
and elsewhere,—if, with floods of mealymouthed inanity; with mis-
erable froth-vortices of Cant now several centuries old, thy New
Testament is not all bedimmed for thee. *Canst* thou read in thy New
Testament at all? The Highest Man of Genius, knowest thou him;
Godlike and a God to this hour? His crown a Crown of Thorns? Thou
fool, with *thy* empty Godhoods, Apotheoses *edgegilt*; the Crown of
Thorns made into a poor jewel-room crown, fit for the head of blockheads; the bearing of the Cross changed to a riding in the Long-Acre
Gig! Pause in thy mass-chantings, in thy litanyings, and Calmuck
prayings by machinery; and pray, if noisily, at least in a more human
manner. How with thy rubrics and dalmatics,* and clothwebs and
cobwebs, and with thy stupidities and grovelling baseheartedness,
hast thou hidden the Holiest into all but invisibility!—

'Man of Genius:' O Mecænas Twiddledee, hast thou any notion
what a Man of Genius is? Genius is 'the inspired gift of God.'* It is
the clearer presence of God Most High in a man. Dim, potential in all
men; in this man it has become clear, actual. So says John Milton,*
who ought to be a judge; so answer him the Voices of all Ages and all
Worlds. Wouldst thou commune with such a one,—*be* his real peer,
then: does that lie in thee? Know thyself and thy real and thy apparent
place, and know him and his real and his apparent place, and act
in some noble conformity therewith. What! The star-fire of the
Empyrean shall eclipse itself, and illuminate magic-lanterns to amuse
grown children? He, the god-inspired, is to twang harps for thee, and
blow through scrannel-pipes,* soothe thy sated soul with visions
of new, still wider Eldorados, Houri Paradises,* richer Lands of
Cockaigne?* Brother, this is not he; this is a counterfeit, this twan-
gling, jangling, vain, acrid, scrannel-piping man. Thou dost well to
say with sick Saul, 'It is naught, such harping!'*—and in sudden
rage, grasp thy spear, and try if thou canst pin such a one to the
wall. King Saul was mistaken in his man, but thou art right in thine.
It is the due of such a one: nail him to the wall, and leave him there.
So ought copper shillings to be nailed on counters;* copper geniuses
on walls, and left there for a sign!—

I conclude that the Men of Letters too may become a 'Chivalry,' an
actual instead of a virtual Priesthood, with result immeasurable,—so
soon as there is nobleness in themselves for that. And, to a certainty,

not sooner! Of intrinsic Valetisms you cannot, with whole Parliaments to help you, make a Heroism. Doggeries* never so gold-plated, Doggeries never so escutcheoned, Doggeries never so diplomaed, bepuffed, gas-lighted, continue Doggeries, and must take the fate of such.

CHAPTER VIII.

THE DIDACTIC.

CERTAINLY it were a fond imagination to expect that any preaching of mine could abate Mammonism; that Bobus of Houndsditch will love his guineas less, or his poor soul more, for any preaching of mine! But there is one Preacher who does preach with effect, and gradually persuade all persons: his name is Destiny, is Divine Providence, and his Sermon the inflexible Course of Things. Experience does take dreadfully high school-wages; but he teaches like no other!

I revert to Friend Prudence the good Quaker's refusal of 'seven thousand pounds to boot.'* Friend Prudence's practical conclusion will, by degrees, become that of all rational practical men whatsoever. On the present scheme and principle, Work cannot continue. Trades' Strikes, Trades' Unions, Chartisms; mutiny, squalor, rage and desperate revolt, growing ever more desperate, will go on their way. As dark misery settles down on us, and our refuges of lies fall in pieces one after one, the hearts of men, now at last serious, will turn to refuges of truth. The eternal stars shine out again, so soon as it is dark *enough*.

Begirt with desperate Trades' Unionism and Anarchic Mutiny, many an Industrial *Law-ward*, by and by, who has neglected to make laws and keep them, will be heard saying to himself: "Why have I realised five hundred thousand pounds? I rose early and sat late, I toiled and moiled, and in the sweat of my brow and of my soul I strove to gain this money, that I might become conspicuous, and have some honour among my fellow-creatures. I wanted them to honour me, to love me. The money is here, earned with my best lifeblood: but the honour? I am encircled with squalor, with hunger, rage, and sooty desperation. Not honoured, hardly even envied; only fools and the flunkey-species so much as envy me. I am conspicuous,—as a mark for curses and brickbats. What good is it? My five hundred scalps hang here in my wigwam: would to Heaven I had sought something else than the scalps; would to Heaven I had been a Christian Fighter, not a Chactaw one! To have ruled and fought not in a Mammonish but in a Godlike spirit; to have had the hearts of the people bless me, as a true ruler and captain of my people; to have felt my own heart bless me, and that God above instead of Mammon below was blessing me,—this had been something. Out of my sight, ye beggarly five hundred scalps of banker's-thousands: I will try for something other, or account my life a tragical futility!"

Friend Prudence's 'rock-ledge,' as we called it, will gradually disclose itself to many a man; to all men. Gradually, assaulted from beneath and from above, the Stygian mud-deluge of Laissez-faire, Supply-and-demand, Cash-payment the one Duty, will abate on all hands; and the everlasting mountain-tops, and secure rock-foundations that reach to the centre of the world, and rest on Nature's self, will again emerge, to found on, and to build on. When Mammon-worshippers here and there begin to be God-worshippers, and bipeds-of-prey become men, and there is a Soul felt once more in the huge-pulsing elephantine mechanic Animalism of this Earth, it will be again a blessed Earth.

"Men cease to regard money?" cries Bobus of Houndsditch: "What else do all men strive for? The very Bishop informs me that Christianity cannot get on without a minimum of Four thousand five hundred in its pocket.* Cease to regard money? That will be at Doomsday in the afternoon!"—O Bobus, my opinion is somewhat different. My opinion is, that the Upper Powers have not yet determined on destroying this Lower World. A respectable, ever-increasing minority, who do strive for something higher than money, I with confidence anticipate; ever-increasing, till there be a sprinkling of them found in all quarters, as salt of the Earth once more.* The Christianity that cannot get on without a minimum of Four thousand five hundred, will give place to something better that can. Thou wilt not join our small minority, thou? Not till Doomsday in the afternoon? Well; *then*, at least, thou wilt join it, thou and the majority in mass!

But truly it is beautiful to see the brutish empire of Mammon cracking everywhere; giving sure promise of dying, or of being changed. A strange, chill, almost ghastly dayspring strikes up in Yankeeland itself: my Transcendental friends announce there, in a distinct, though somewhat lankhaired, ungainly manner, that the Demiurgus Dollar is dethroned;*

that new unheard-of Demiurgusships, Priesthoods, Aristocracies, Growths and Destructions, are already visible in the grey of coming Time. Chronos is dethroned by Jove;* Odin by St. Olaf:* the Dollar cannot rule in Heaven forever. No; I reckon, not. Socinian Preachers quit their pulpits in Yankeeland, saying, "Friends, this is all gone to a coloured cobweb, we regret to say!"—and retire into the fields to cultivate onion-beds, and live frugally on vegetables.* It is very notable. Old godlike Calvinism declares that its old body is now fallen to tatters, and done; and its mournful ghost, disembodied, seeking new embodiment, pipes again in the winds;—a ghost and spirit as yet, but heralding new Spirit-worlds, and better Dynasties than the Dollar one.*

Yes, here as there, light is coming into the world; men love not darkness, they do love light. A deep feeling of the eternal nature of Justice looks out among us everywhere,—even through the dull eyes of Exeter Hall; an unspeakable religiousness struggles, in the most helpless manner, to speak itself, in Puseyisms and the like. Of our Cant, all condemnable, how much is not condemnable without pity; we had almost said, without respect! The *in*articulate worth and truth that is in England goes down yet to the Foundations.

Some 'Chivalry of Labour,' some noble Humanity and practical Divineness of Labour, will yet be realised on this Earth. Or why *will*; why do we pray to Heaven, without setting our own shoulder to the wheel?* The Present, if it will have the Future accomplish, shall itself commence. Thou who prophesiest, who believest, begin thou to fulfil. Here or nowhere, now equally as at any time! That outcast help-needing thing or person, trampled down under vulgar feet or hoofs, no help 'possible' for it, no prize offered for the saving of it,—canst not thou save it, then, without prize? Put forth thy hand, in God's name; know that 'impossible,' where Truth and Mercy and the everlasting Voice of Nature order, has no place in the brave man's dictionary. That when all men have said "Impossible," and tumbled noisily elsewhither, and thou alone art left, then first thy time and possibility have come. It is for thee now: do thou that, and ask no man's counsel, but thy own only, and God's. Brother, thou hast possibility in thee for much: the possibility of writing on the eternal skies the record of a heroic life. That noble downfallen or yet unborn 'Impossibility,' thou canst lift it up, thou canst, by thy soul's travail, bring it into clear being. That loud inane Actuality, with millions in its pocket, too 'possible' that, which rolls along there, with quilted trumpeters blaring round it, and all the world escorting it as mute or vocal flunkey,—escort it not thou; say to it, either nothing, or else deeply in thy heart: "Loud-blaring Nonentity, no force of trumpets, cash, Long-acre art, or universal flunkeyhood of men, makes thee an Entity; thou art a *Non*entity, and deceptive Simulacrum, more accursed than thou seemest. Pass on in the Devil's name, unworshipped by at least one man, and leave the thoroughfare clear!"

Not on Ilion's or Latium's plains;* on far other plains and places henceforth can noble deeds be now done. Not on Ilion's plains; how much less in Mayfair's drawingrooms! Not in victory over poor brother French or Phrygians;* but in victory over Frost-jötuns, Marsh-giants, over demons of Discord, Idleness, Injustice, Unreason, and Chaos come again.* None of the old Epics is longer possible. The Epic of French and Phrygians was comparatively a small Epic: but that of Flirts and Fribbles, what is that? A thing that vanishes at cock-crowing,—that already begins to scent the morning air!* Game-preserving Aristocracies, let them 'bush' never so effectually, cannot escape the Subtle Fowler.* Game seasons will be excellent, and again will be indifferent, and by and by they will not be at all. The Last Partridge of England, of an England where millions of men can get no corn to eat, will be shot and ended. Aristocracies with beards on their chins will find other work to do than amuse themselves with trundling-hoops.

But it is to you, ye Workers, who do already work, and are as grown men, noble and honourable in a sort, that the whole world calls for new work and nobleness. Subdue mutiny, discord, wide-spread despair, by manfulness, justice, mercy and wisdom. Chaos is dark, deep as Hell; let light be, and there is instead a green flowery World.* O, it is great, and there is no other greatness. To make some nook of God's Creation a little fruitfuller, better, more worthy of God; to make some human hearts a little wiser, manfuler, happier,—more blessed, less accursed! It is work for a God. Sooty Hell of mutiny and savagery and despair can, by man's energy, be made a kind of Heaven; cleared of its soot, of its mutiny, of its need to mutiny; the everlasting arch of Heaven's azure overspanning *it* too, and its cunning mechanisms and tall chimney-steeples, as a birth of Heaven; God and all men looking on it well pleased.

Unstained by wasteful deformities, by wasted tears or heart's-blood of men, or any defacement of the Pit, noble fruitful Labour, growing ever nobler, will come forth,—the grand sole miracle of Man; whereby Man has risen from the low places of this Earth, very literally, into divine Heavens. Ploughers, Spinners, Builders; Prophets, Poets, Kings; Brindleys and Goethes, Odins and Arkwrights; all martyrs, and noble men, and gods are of one grand Host; immeasurable; marching ever forward since the Beginnings of the World. The enormous, all-conquering, flame-crowned Host, noble every soldier in it; sacred, and alone noble. Let him who is not of it hide himself; let him tremble for himself. Stars at every button cannot make him noble; sheaves of Bath-garters, nor bushels of Georges;* nor any other contrivance but manfully enlisting in it, valiantly taking place and step in it. O Heavens, will he not bethink himself; he too is so needed in the Host! It were so blessed, thrice-blessed, for himself and for us all! In hope of the Last Partridge, and some Duke of Weimar among our English Dukes, we will be patient yet a while.

> 'The Future hides in it
> Good hap and sorrow;
> We press still thorow,
> Nought that abides in it
> Daunting us,—onward.'*

THE END.

EXPLANATORY NOTES

ABBREVIATIONS

TC   Thomas Carlyle

JWC   Jane Welsh Carlyle

Altick   TC, *Past and Present*, ed. Richard Altick (New York: New York University Press, 1965)

Baker   William Baker, *The Early History of the London Library* (Lampeter: Mellen, 1992)

Butler   *The Chronicle of Jocelin of Brakelond*, ed. H. E. Butler (London: Nelson, 1949)

Calder   Grace Calder, *The Writing of* Past and Present: *A Study of Carlyle's Manuscripts* (New Haven: Yale University Press, 1949)

Chronicle   Jocelin of Brakelond, *Chronicle of the Abbey of Bury St Edmunds*, trans. Diana Greenway and Jane Sayers (Oxford: Oxford World's Classics, 2008)

CL   *The Collected Letters of Thomas and Jane Welsh Carlyle*, ed. Ian Campbell, Aileen Christianson, David R. Sorensen, Jane Roberts, Liz Sutherland, Katherine Inglis, and Brent E. Kinser, Duke-Edinburgh Edition, 49 vols. (Durham, NC: Duke University Press, 1970–)

CME i–v   TC, *Critical and Miscellaneous Essays*, vols. xxvi–xxx of *Works*, ed. H. D. Traill

Cromwell, vi–ix TC, *Oliver Cromwell's Letters and Speeches*, in *Works*, vols. vi–ix, ed. H. D. Traill

Engels, *Condition* Friedrich Engels, *The Condition of the Working Class in England*, ed. David McLellan (Oxford: Oxford World's Classics, 1999)

EOL   TC, *Essays on Literature*, ed. Fleming McClelland, Brent E. Kinser, and Chris R. Vanden Bossche, Strouse Edition (Berkeley and Los Angeles: University of California Press, 2020)

Forster Collection TC's MS Notes, Forster Collection, National Art Library, Victoria and Albert Museum (48.E.36)

FR   TC, *The French Revolution: A History in Three Volumes* [1837], ed. Mark Cumming, David R. Sorensen, Mark Engel, and Brent E. Kinser, Oxford Scholarly Edition, 3 vols. (Oxford: Oxford University Press, 2020)

Heroes   TC, *On Heroes, Hero-Worship, & the Heroic in History* [1840], ed. Michael K. Goldberg, Joel J. Brattin, and Mark Engel, Strouse Edition (Berkeley and Los Angeles: University of California Press, 1993)

Historical Essays   TC, *Historical Essays*, ed. Chris R. Vanden Bossche, Strouse Edition (Berkeley and Los Angeles: University of California Press, 2002)

Historical Sketches TC, *Historical Sketches of Notable Persons and Events in the Reigns of James I. and Charles I.*, ed. Alexander Carlyle (London: Chapman and Hall, 1898)

Hughes   TC, *Past and Present*, ed. A. M. D. Hughes (Oxford: Clarendon Press, 1921).

Lectures   TC, *Lectures on the History of Literature . . . Delivered in 1838*, ed. R. P. Karkaria (Bombay Curwen and Kane; London: Johnson, 1892).

LLC 1842   *Catalogue of the London Library* (London: M'Gowan, 1842)

LLC 1856   *Catalogue of the London Library* (London: Taylor, 1856)

OE   Old English

OED   *Oxford English Dictionary*

P&P Strouse   TC, *Past and Present* [1843], ed. Chris R. Vanden Bossche, Joel J. Brattin, and D. J. Trela, Strouse Edition (Berkeley and Los Angeles: University of California Press, 2005)

Rem.   TC, *Reminiscences* [1881], ed. K. J. Fielding and Ian Campbell (Oxford: Oxford World's Classics, 1997)

Rokewode   *Chronica Jocelini de Brakelonda, de rebus gestis Samsonis Abbatis Monasterii Sancti Edmundi: nunc primum typis mandata, curante Johanne Gage Rokewode* (London: Camden Society, 1840)

Sartor   TC, *Sartor Resartus* [1833–4; 1836], ed. Rodger L. Tarr, Strouse Edition (Berkeley and Los Angeles: University of California Press, 2000)

Tarr, 'TC Libraries'   Rodger L. Tarr, 'Thomas Carlyle's Libraries at Chelsea and Ecclefechan', *Studies in Bibliography* 27 (1974), 249–65

Works   TC, *The Collected Works of Thomas Carlyle*, ed. H. D. Traill, Centenary Edition, 30 vols. (London: Chapman and Hall, 1896–9)

WORKS which do not appear in the Abbreviations list are usually cited by surname of author, short title, and (at first mention) date; full details appear in the Select Bibliography.

Translations from foreign texts are our own unless otherwise indicated. All references to the Bible are to the King James Version (1611). Shakespearian references are to *The Riverside Shakepeare*, ed. G. Blakemore Evans (Boston: Houghton Mifflin, 1974).

BOOK I. PROEM

17 *MIDAS* : King of Phrygia; see note to p. 21.

THE condition of England: TC addressed the 'Condition of England Question' in his pamphlet *Chartism* (1839): 'What means this bitter discontent of the Working Classes? Whence comes it, whither goes it? Above all, at what price, on what terms, will it probably consent to depart from us and die into rest? These are questions' (*CME* iv. 119).

Workhouses, Poor-law Prisons; . . . 'out-door relief': the New Poor Law Amendment Act of 1834, which replaced the Elizabethan Poor Law of 1601, was passed by the Whig government of Lord Grey. Drafted by Edwin Chadwick and Nassau William Senior, the legislation was influenced by the theories of Jeremy Bentham and Thomas Malthus. It aimed to reduce welfare costs by eliminating the practice of outdoor relief and replacing it with the option of workhouses for those driven by 'extreme necessity . . . to accept the comfort which must be obtained by the surrender of their free agency, and the sacrifice of their accustomed habits and gratifications' (*Poor Law Commissioners' Report of 1834*, 1905 edn., 271). Because the number of 'paupers' vastly exceeded the available accommodation in workhouses, outdoor relief remained the chief means of support for the unemployed throughout the 1840s.

workhouse Bastille being filled to bursting: opponents of the New Poor Law frequently compared the workhouse to the Paris prison-fortress, the siege of which by crowds on 14 July 1789 ignited the French Revolution. See G. R. Wythen Baxter, *The Book of the Bastiles* (1841), p. iv: 'Had there been no *lettre de cachet*, the revolutionary *Marseillaise* would never have been tuned in retribution. . . . Had there been no New Poor-Law, the name of Chartism would never have been heard.'

Official Report: TC's source, which he cites inaccurately, was the *Ninth Annual Report of the Poor Law Commissioners* (1843), 9: '1842 Quarters ending Lady-day . . . In-door Paupers, 221, 954 . . . Out-door Paupers, 1, 207, 402' [Total: 1, 429, 356]'. From 1840, the increase in In-door Paupers was '52,722' and in Out-door Paupers, '177, 105'.

18 *picturesque Tourist*: this is TC himself. He first used the term in 1828 in 'Burns' (*EOL*, 63). In a letter to Ralph Waldo Emerson, 25 June 1841, TC scorned the 'whole gang of picturesque Tourists . . . who penetrate now by steam, in shoals every autum [*sic*], into the very centre of the Scotch Highlands' (*CL* xiii. 162). Many of them consulted *Black's Picturesque Tourist of Scotland . . . with . . . map; engraved charts . . . and a copious itinerary* (1838), a popular guidebook published in Edinburgh by Adam and Charles Black that 'incorporated a large amount of Traditionary, Historical, and Literary illustration, by which it is conceived a recollection of the scenery will be more permanently fixed in the memory of the tourist' (p. v). It was reissued in numerous editions throughout the century.

Workhouse of St. Ives in Huntingdonshire: the St Ives Union Workhouse, in the parish of Hemingford Grey, Huntingdon, near St Ives, was built between 1836 and 1838 at a cost of £4,000 and designed in the courtyard style by William Thomas Nash of Royston. The 1841 census listed eighty-eight inmates; by 1851, this number had increased to 320. TC visited the Union Workhouse on Wednesday, 7 September 1842.

18 *It is impossible, they tell us!*: echoing Mirabeau; see *FR* ii. 105 and n., quoted in Dumont, *Souvenirs sur Mirabeau* (1832), 311–12: 'Impossible! . . . *ne me dites jamais ce bête de mot.*'

Dr. Alison, who speaks what he knows: in *Observations on the Management of the Poor in Scotland* . . . (1840), Dr William Pultenay Alison cited the observations of 'an Assistant Commissioner' of the Handloom Inquiry, which had been established in 1837: 'The wynds [side-alleys] comprise a fluctuating population of from 15,000 to 30,000 persons. This quarter consists of a labyrinth of lanes, out of which numberless entrances lead into small square courts, each with a dunghill reeking in the centre. . . . In some of these lodging-rooms (visited at night) we found a whole lair of human beings being littered along the floor, sometimes fifteen and twenty, some clothed and some naked; men, women, and children huddled promiscuously together' (pp. 13–14).

19 *Scotland too . . . must have a Poor-law*: in Scotland the old Poor Law (1574–1845) assigned responsibility for the sick, elderly, insane, and orphans to local parishes funded by landowners and church courts. On 4 August 1845, the system was centralized under a Board of Supervision appointed by the Crown, which regulated the operation of the 880 parish parochial boards.

metal of Potosi: the immensely rich silver mine and byword for untold wealth located in Potosi, Bolivia.

Factory Inquiries, Agricultural Inquiries, by Revenue Returns, by Mining-Labourer Committees: the Factory Bill of 1833 prohibited children under the age of 9 from working, and limited children aged 9–13 to a nine-hour working day, and children aged 13–18 to a twelve-hour working day. The *Report from the Select Committee on Agriculture* (1833) concluded that 'the Stocks of home-grown Wheat in the hands of the Farmer and of the Dealer at the time of Harvest have gradually diminished; that the Produce of Great Britain is in the average of years unequal to the Consumption; that the increased Supply from Ireland does not cover the deficiency; and that in the present state of Agriculture, the United Kingdom is in years of ordinary production partially dependent on the supply of Wheat from Foreign Countries' (p. v). Subsequent agriculture reports were issued in 1836 and 1837. In February 1842 the Child's Employment Commission published its *First Report* 'for inquiring into the employment and condition of children in mines and manufactories' (p. iii), which prompted legislation introducing a minimum age of 10 for boys working underground and forbidding the employment of women.

At Stockport Assizes . . . a Mother and a Father are arraigned: *The Examiner* (1 Nov. 1840) reported this 'most extraordinary case'. Robert and Ann Sandys, together with Robert's brother George and sister-in-law Honor Sandys, were taken into custody. They were suspected of poisoning their three children with arsenic 'for the sake of the burial fees of of 3l. 8s. 6d. on each, recoverable from a society to which they belonged' (p. 701).

you had better not probe farther into that department of things: see Introduction, pp. 24–5.

This is in the autumn of 1841: the destitution of the working-class population in Stockport was widely reported in the London newspapers between September and November 1841. *The Examiner* (16 Oct. 1841) published excerpts from a letter written by a resident: 'During the last six years thirty thousand have left the town, and there are seven thousand starving in the streets. . . . The streets are crowded with groups of starving carpenters, painters, bricklayers, shoemakers, and tailors, who are parading them from morning to night' (p. 669). The same paper reported (20 Nov. 1841), 'At Stockport, the distress of the working classes, instead of diminishing, is on the increase. . . . Scores of families are literally starving. The streets are crowded with men, women, and children seeking relief' (p. 749).

'Brutal savages, degraded Irish': a prejudice that TC partially endorsed. In an editorial, *The West Kent Guardian* (22 May 1841) warned that the Corn Laws would cause the English peasantry to 'people by the thousands, the workhouse and the jail, or wander like the degraded Irish, over the face of the land, the curse and the dread of all' (p. 5). During the election campaign of 1841, won by Robert Peel and the Conservatives, the campaign of Irish nationalists for the repeal of the 1801 Act of Union provoked further antagonism. In a letter to the 'People of Ireland' (*The Morning Chronicle*, 9 June 1841), the movement's leader Daniel O'Connell denounced the stereotype of the Irish as ' "brutal savages" . . . and a "filthy and ferocious rabble" ' (p. 6). See also TC in *Chartism*: 'The Irish National character is degraded, disordered; till this recover itself, nothing is yet recovered.' But he adds that 'England is guilty towards Ireland; and reaps at last, in full measure, the fruit of fifteen generations of wrong-doing. . . . The condition of the lower multitude of English labourers approximates more and more to that of the Irish, competing with them in all the markets' (*CME* iv. 137–8, 141). Engels comments on TC's analysis: 'If we except his exaggerated and one-sided condemnation of the Irish national character, Carlyle is perfectly right. Thwese Irishmen who migrate for 4*d*. to England on the deck of a steamship on which they are packed like cattle, insinuate themselves everywhere. . . . With such a competitor the English working man has to struggle, with a competitor upon the lowest plane possible in a civilized country, who for this very reason requires less wages than any other. Nothing else is therefore possible than that, as Carlyle says, the wages of the English working man should be forced down further and further in every branch in which the Irish compete with him' (Engels, *Condition*, 102, 104). For TC and Ireland, see Edwards, 'Victorian Historical Consciousness' (2013) and 'True Thomas": Carlyle and the Legacy of Millenialism' (2004); Morrow, 'Condition of Ireland' (2008); and Fielding, 'Ireland, John Mitchel and His "Sarcastic Friend" Thomas Carlyle' (1992).

sunk here, in our dark cellar: see Alison, *Observations*, 12, quoting Dr Lee, minister of the Old Church, Edinburgh, 18 February 1836: 'I may mention the case of two Scotch families, living in a miserable kind of cellar, who had come from the country within a few months, in search of work. Since they came they had had two dead, and another apparently dying. In the place they inhabit, it is impossible at noonday to distinguish the features of the human face without artificial light.'

19 *in the Ugolino Hunger-tower, . . . Gaddo fallen dead on his Father's knees*: see Dante, *Inferno*, xxxiii. 1–90, describing the death by starvation of the Count Ugolino and his two sons, Gadda and Anselm.

20 *inquiry of ways and means*: TC mockingly uses the parliamentary terminology for raising revenue in the form of taxes in order to meet national expenditures.

'sodden their own children': Lam. 4:10.

How come these things?: Jer. 13:22.

Glasgow lanes: slum district in Glasgow, Scotland, also known as 'the wynds' (see note to p. 18). In the *Report from the Select Committee on the Health of Towns* (1840), the barrister Jelinger Cookson Symons testified on 30 March 1840 that 'I have seen human degradation in some of its worst phases, both in England and abroad, but I can advisedly say that I did not believe, until I visited the wynds of Glasgow, that so large an amount of filth, crime, misery, and disease existed in one spot in any civilized country'. He described 'the dense and motley community who inhabit the low districts of Glasgow, consisting chiefly of the alleys leading out of the High-street, the lanes in the Calton, but particularly the closes and wynds, which lie between the Tron-gate and the Bridge-gate, the Salt-market and Maxwell-street. These districts contain a motley population, consisting almost in all the lower branches of occupation, but chiefly of a community whose sole means of subsistence consists in plunder and prostitution' (p. 61).

Are they even what they call 'happier?': the goal of Benthamite theorists and legislators, defined by Jeremy Bentham in *A Fragment on Government* (1776), to promote 'the greatest happiness of the greatest number'. See TC to Macvey Napier, 20 January 1831: 'Bentham is a Denyer, he *denies* with a loud and universally convincing voice: his fault is that he can *affirm* nothing, except that money is pleasant in the purse and food in the stomach, and that by this simplest of all Beliefs he can reorganise Society. He can shatter it in pieces; no thanks to him, for its old fastenings are quite rotten: but he cannot reorganise it; this is a work for quite others than he' (*CL* v. 212). For TC and Benthamite reform, see Blake, *Pleasures of Benthamism* (2009), 82–110.

'to buy where he finds it cheapest, to sell where he finds it dearest': see Adam Smith, *An Inquiry into the Nature and Causes of the Wealth of Nations* (1776): 'The interest of a nation in its commercial relations to foreign nations is, like that of a merchant with regard to the different people with whom he deals, to buy as cheap and to sell as dear as possible' (1835, 9th edn., iii. 125–6). In his 1831 reminiscence of his father, TC recalled the book's importance to James Carlyle: 'Adam Smith's *Wealth of Nations*,

greatly as it lay out of his course, he had also fallen in with; and admired, and understood *and remembered*—so far as he had any business with it' (*Rem.*, 8–9). For TC's copy of the 1835–9 edition, see Tarr, 'TC's Libraries', 258.

21 *with awful eye*: see Milton, 'Hymn on the Morning of Christ's Nativity' (1645), l. 63.

Coercing fifty-pound tenants: the Reform Bill of 1832 extended voting rights to all ratepayers occupying premises of £10 or more, as well as to tenants who paid an annual rent of £50 or more.

doing what he likes with his own: echoing Henry Pelham Fiennes Pelham-Clinton, fourth duke of Newcastle, an opponent of parliamentary reform who in the House of Lords on 3 December 1830 defended his right to evict tenants who refused to vote for his candidate: 'Is it not lawful for me to do what I please with my own[?]' (*Hansard*, i. 752).

half-consciousness that his excellent Corn-law is indefensible: TC supported the repeal of the Corn Laws, protectionist tariffs first levied in 1815 to shield landowners against the import of cheap grain. In raising the price of food and restricting its supply, TC alleged, these tariffs demonstrated the intractability of the '*Divine Right of Squires*' ('Baillie the Covenanter' (1841), in *CME* iv. 259). But he refused to join the Anti-Corn Law League, founded in 1838 by Richard Cobden and John Bright, which advocated free trade as a prescription for greater prosperity, freedom, and social mobility. On the contrary, TC argued, the laissez-faire formulas of the 'Manchester School' reinforced the divisive 'Mammon-Gospel' of the middle classes. Writing to his brother Alexander on 28 December 1842, he proclaimed: 'I am already engaged for a far bigger LEAGUE (that of the oppressed Poor against the idle Rich; that of God against the Devil' (*CL* xv. 254). In early January 1843, while writing *Past and Present*, TC was invited to a series of meetings in Manchester hosted by the council of the National Anti-Corn Law League. On 10 January he replied to the chairman of the League, George Wilson. In his letter, published in *The Leeds Times* (21 Jan. 1843), TC apologized for being unable to attend, but delivered a blistering condemnation of the tariffs: 'For these ten years, I have heard no argument or shadow of an argument in behalf of [the Corn Laws], that was not of a kind (too literally!) "to make the angels weep." I consider that if there is a pernicious, portentous, practical solecism, threatening huge ruin under the sun at present, it is that of Corn Laws in such an England as ours of the year 1843. I consider that the Corn Laws lie on the threshold of all and of every improvement in our anomalous distressed and distressing condition of society; that they fatally block up all possibility of the innumerable improvements, which are fast becoming indispensable if England is to continue to exist; That it is the duty of all English citizens to do whatsoever is practicable for the removal of these laws; That they will have to be removed, unless this universe and *its* eternal laws are a chimera; That God declares against them, audibly to all just hearts; and that man is now fast declaring—that all men cannot too soon declare. How much lies behind the Corn Laws, desperately calling for revision, for reformation, among us? And till the Corn Laws are removed, the problem cannot so much as begin' (p. 2).

21 *the people perish*: Prov. 29:18.

Fatal paralysis spreading inwards . . . in Stockport cellars: TC borrowed William Cooke Taylor's *Notes of a Tour in the Manufacturing Districts of Lancashire* (1842) from the London Library on 23 September 1842 (Baker, 118). In his account of the plight of the Stockport operatives, Taylor notes: '[They] have become a broken-spirited and a broken-hearted population; their despair has assumed the form of listlessness and apathy; words of hope are received with a shake of the head and a melancholy smile. "All that remains for me is to lay me down and die" was the expression of a fine though faded young woman, when I expressed a hope that times would yet mend' (*Notes of a Tour*, 186).

Midas longed for gold, and insulted the Olympians: TC weaves details from two myths in Ovid's *Metamorphoses* about Midas, both of which suggest 'horrid enchantment'. In the first, Midas requests from Dionysius that everything he touches be turned to gold (xi. 85–145). In the second, Apollo punishes Midas for choosing Pan over himself in a musical contest by giving the king the ears of an ass (xi. 146–93).

Fable of the Sphinx: the Sphinx was a monster, with the body of a lion and the face and breasts of a woman, who sat on a rock by Thebes hurling to their death passers-by who failed to answer a riddle that had been posed to her by the Muses. Oedipus, king of Thebes, responded correctly, whereupon the Sphinx destroyed herself.

22 *grand unnameable Fact in the midst of which we live and struggle*: i.e. time. See *Heroes*, 9: 'That great mystery of TIME . . . is forever very literally a miracle; a thing to strike us dumb,—for we have no word to speak about it.'

her victorious bridegroom: in the Norse epic the *Nibelungen Lied* (*c*.1200), Brunhild, queen of 'Isenland' (Iceland) pledges to marry any man who triumphs over her in hurling a spear, throwing a stone, and leaping. Siegfried disguises himself as Gunther and meets her challenge, obliging her to wed him. See TC, 'The Nibelungen Lied' (1831): '[Siegfried] gains a decided victory and the lovely Amazon must own with surprise and shame that she is fairly won' (*CME* ii. 246).

rede the riddle of Destiny: See *Sartor*, 42: 'The secret of Man's Being is still like the Sphinx's secret: a riddle that he cannot rede.'

united twenty-seven million heads: the UK census of 1841 was the first to be administered by a national registrar general. On 6 June it enumerated the occupants of every household in England, Wales, Scotland, and Ireland, the total of which was 26,730,929.

23 *centre of the world-whirlwind*: Job 38:1 and Ezek. 1:4.

Mahometans, old Pagan Romans, Jews, Scythians and heathen Greeks: distinctive religions that share a common belief in divine justice. The Scythians were a nomadic tribe dominant in central Asia whose deities and rituals were described by the Greek historian Herodotus.

'redtape' strangled the inner life of thee: 'Excessive bureaucracy' (*OED*). See *The Examiner* (11 Dec. 1841), 785, quoting the *Morning Chronicle*: 'If useful reforms are to be staved off, or mimicked, or marred in the making by any of the shallow shuffling of the red-tape school, we shall have the satisfaction of aiding in that demonstration of public feeling which will speedily show our new masters that England will not be governed on Tory principles.'

Tarpeian Rock: a cliff on the Capitoline Hill in Rome over which criminals and traitors were thrown.

Longacre vehicle: Longacre, Covent Garden, was a luxury coach and carriage-building district.

Courts of Westminster: the courts of Common Pleas, the King's Bench, and the Exchequer of Pleas sat at Westminster Hall from the early thirteenth century until 1825, when they were moved to adjacent buildings.

'Adamant Tablet': TC's metaphor for the vehicle of divine truth. In the ancient world, laws and oracles were engraved on tablets of bronze in order to make them indelible.

24 *learned-sergeant*: or sergeant at law, 'a member of a superior order of barristers (abolished in 1880), from which, until 1873, the Common Law judges were always chosen' (*OED*).

reclaimer: TC uses the word to mean 'protester', from its Latin root, *reclamator* (*OED*).

three readings, royal assents: parliamentary protocol, requiring that a bill be given three readings by the House of Commons and Lords before being submitted for royal assent.

25 *the fool hath said in his heart*: Ps. 14:1.

artillery of Woolwich: the Royal Arsenal, in Woolwich, SE London.

a noble Conservatism as well as an ignoble: the election of Peel and the Tories to a second term on 22 July 1841 provoked a debate in the British press about the future of Conservatism. *The Times* (24 July 1841) predicted that the government would adopt a pragmatic approach to reconciling the interests of the urban commercial classes with those of its traditional supporters, the landed aristocracy and rural tenantry. The paper attributed this change to the Reform Bill of 1832, which by extending the parliamentary franchise 'destroyed Toryism, but . . . gave birth to the Conservative Party' (p. 4). *The Examiner* (31 July 1841) responded sceptically to this 'New Conservatism': 'It pretends that it differs from old Toryism, . . . but in what single instance has it signalised its possession of this new faculty, every change effected within the last ten years having been extorted from it after strenuous opposition' (p. 481). Revisiting the debate after Peel's first year in office, *The Examiner* (13 Aug. 1842) responded cautiously: 'Though . . . enough has not been done to give effect to sound doctrines, yet the important step has been gained of breaking down the false ones. Free trade is not adopted; but monopoly, though it is left standing, is left standing without defences' (p. 513). TC wrote to Richard Monckton Milnes, 2 December 1841, that he expected Peel would 'perhaps try to *abrogate* these insane Corn-Laws' and '*be* in verity a Governor to this country which is fast falling mad and moribund for want of being governed!'. Tory paternalism, however 'blind and lazy', did at least 'embody most of the religion, of the loyalty, humanity, and available worth that exists among us' (*CL* xiii. 311). Yet, as TC reported to Thomas Story Spedding, 13 February 1842, the government's failure to reduce unemployment and poverty suggested that Peel was a 'Windbag' and 'pitifullest pettifogging Quack', and that 'Conservatism so far as one can see it in Parliament is rushing swiftly to its ruin' (*CL* xiv. 42).

26 *His right and his might*: see *Chartism*: 'Might and right, so frightfully discrepant at first, are ever in the long-run one and the same' (*CME* iv. 147).

A heroic Wallace . . . cannot hinder that his Scotland become . . . a part of England: William Wallace, patriot and guardian of Scotland, was executed and quartered by Edward I. The Acts of Union, which took effect on 1 May 1707, combined the Scottish and English legislatures into the United Kingdom of Great Britain.

Valhalla and Temple of the Brave: the Valhalla or 'Hall of Odin', the Norse king, where the Valkyrs or 'Choosers of the Slain' transported the spirits of slain warriors to do battle and die, after which they were restored to life and invited to feast. See *Heroes*, 28: 'These *Choosers* lead the brave to a heavenly *Hall of Odin*; only the base and slavish being thrust elsewhither, into the realms of Hela the Death-goddess: I take this to have been the soul of the whole Norse Belief.'

semblant: 'Seeming, apparent, counterfeit' (*OED*, citing TC).

Scotland is not Ireland: TC in *Heroes* identified Scotland's redemption with the rise of the religious reformer John Knox, of whom Wallace was a spiritual forefather. Before the 'Reformation by Knox', Scotland was 'a poor barren country, full of continual broils, dissensions, massacrings; a people in the last state of rudeness and destitution, little better perhaps than Ireland at this day'. It was Knox, a 'god-created soul' who brought the nation 'a resurrection as from death' by kindling its 'internal life'. He defined 'a cause . . . high as Heaven, yet attainable from Earth;—whereby the meanest man becomes not a Citizen only, but a Member of Christ's visible Church; a veritable Hero, if he prove a true man!' (*Heroes*, 123–4).

Heptarchies: 'The seven kingdoms reckoned to have been established by the Angles and Saxons in Britain' (*OED*) were Northumberland, East Anglia, Essex, Mercia, Wessex, Sussex, and Kent.

waste-bickering: TC's term for fruitless quarrelling.

27 *What is Truth?*: see Bacon, 'Of Truth', *Essays* (1597): 'What is Truth; said jesting Pilate; And would not stay for an Answer' (1908 edn., 6). See also Pilate's questioning of Jesus, John 18:37–8.

amaurosis: 'Partial or total loss of sight arising from disease of the optic nerve' (*OED*, citing TC).

Westminister Hall: see note to p. 23.

tipstaves: or tipstaffs, 'a staff with tip or cap of metal, carried as a badge by certain officials' (*OED*).

Hansard Debatings: the Journals of the House of Commons first printed by Luke Hansard, and continued by his eldest son Thomas Curson Hansard in 1809.

bursts of Parliamentary eloquence: TC's expression for parliamentary bluster.

MANCHESTER INSURRECTION: a strike among miners for higher wages began in Hanley, Staffordshire, on 18 July 1842 and quickly spread across the region, with Chartists joining workers, women, and children in a 'Great National turn-out'. On 9 August, 20,000 people marched through Manchester, and strike committees were formed to coordinate a political response. Processions of workers shut down factories in the region by drawing plugs from boilers, and they resorted to more extreme vandalism if owners resisted their efforts. A delegate's conference was organized for 16 August, the twenty-third anniversary of the Peterloo massacre of 1819, when eleven people were killed and over 500 injured in a confrontation between yeomanry and demonstrators in St Peter's Fields, Manchester. The threat of a national strike grew as the National Charter Association endorsed the campaign of the delegates. Over the next several days, troops sent from London by the Home Secretary Sir James Graham fired on strikers in several cities, but in general the workers respected private property and exercised restraint. TC closely followed reports of the 'disturbances' in *The Examiner*, and wrote to JWC on 16 August: 'It seems to be the strangest insurrection in the world: no violence, all collision with Authority *avoided*; only "we will work no more till we see a fair day's wages for a fair days work,—till we see *the Charter*, which alone can secure us that!"' (*CL* xv. 22). By September, many of the leaders of the movement had been arrested, and factories gradually began to reopen. Summarizing the upheaval, *The Examiner* (27 Aug. 1842) commented, 'The grand *cause* of the insurrection was, in one word, *distress*; which, operating upon trade in all its branches, not only forced down wages, but also threw multitudes altogether out of employment. Then *political discontent*, arising out of a desire for the Charter or Universal Suffrage, availed itself of the widespread suffering of the labourers, and turned their minds in that direction for relief' (p. 555). Jenkins, *The General Strike of 1842* (1980), notes that 'at its height the General Strike of 1842 involved up to half-a-million workers and covered an area which stretched from Dundee and the Scottish coalfields to South Wales and Cornwall' (p. 21).

27 BLUSTEROWSKI, *Colacorde, and other Editorial prophets*: fictitious European revolutionaries ('Colacorde' suggests Fr. *col à la corde* = 'neck in a noose') modelled on Polish, French, German, Italian, and Irish radicals living in London since the 1830s. 'Blusterowski' may be a variation of Adam Gurowski, the Polish rebel and follower of Saint-Simon and Fourier, who participated in the armed rebellion against Russia in 1830. *P&P* Strouse notes that in the First Draft of *Past and Present*, 325, TC also refers to 'Tartarino' (It. *Tartaliere* = 'stammer' or 'tartar') and 'Schnaubhock' (Ger. *schnaub* = 'snort' or 'puff', *hoch* = 'high'). For the exiles and their political influence, see Pellegrino Sutcliffe, *Victorian Radicals and Latin Democrats* (2014); Lattek, *Revolutionary Refugees* (2006); Prothero, *Radical Artisans* (1997); and Brock, 'Polish Democrats and English Radicals' (1953). In this period TC met Godefroi Cavaignac, Charles Gavan Duffy, Joseph Lhotsky, and Giuseppe Mazzini. See Morrow, 'Condition of Ireland' (2008); Edwards, 'Carlyle and the Legacy of Millennialism' (2004); Kutolawski, 'Victorian Historians on Poland' (2004); Fielding, 'Ireland, John Mitchel and Carlyle' (1992); and Hilles, 'The Hero as Revolutionary' (1976). Another 'editorial prophet' was Engels, who lived in Manchester for the majority of the time that he spent in England between November 1842 and August 1844. He commented on the chaotic aspect of the upheaval in *Rheinische Zeitung* 344 (10 Dec. 1842): 'The whole affair was unprepared, unorganised and without leadership. The strikers had no definite aim, still less were they united on the nature and method of the action to be taken. Hence, at the slightest resistance on the part of the authorities they became irresolute and unable to overcome their respect for the law. When the Chartists took over the leadership and proclaimed the People's Charter to the assembled crowds, it was already too late. The only guiding idea vaguely present in the minds of the workers . . . was that of revolution by legal means . . . in their efforts to achieve which, they failed' (Marx and Engels, *Collected Works* (1975–2004), ii. 373–4). More generally, members of the 'Continental Democratic Movement' expressed surprise at how quickly and effortlessly the authorities quelled the revolt. The French republican journalist John Lemoinne similarly observed in 'De la législation anglaise sur les céréales', *Revue des deux mondes* 32 (1 Oct. 1842), 97: 'For a whole month we have seen England shaken by general commotion. The manufacturing districts were in the midst of an insurrection; the ardent hotbeds of industry poured out revolt and anarchy; bands of twenty to thirty thousand men roamed the towns and the principal roads . . . the mines threw waves of their subterranean population into the public places, and these men, strangers to the sun, appeared like barbarians in the midst of the astonished towns. And yet, even in the midst of this tumult, the depths of the country remained calm and fearless. . . . The government allowed anarchy to take possession of the great towns for several weeks, and when at last it gauged that public safety was seriously threatened, it launched on the railways some of the guns of Woolwich, of which only one apparition was sufficient to restore all appearances of order.'

to vilipend: 'To speak of with disparagement or contempt' (*OED*).

28 *to suppress this million-headed hydra*: the second of Hercules' twelve labours was to kill the Lernaean Hydra, a many-headed serpentine snake that grew two heads for every one removed. TC was not alone in comparing the strikers to the monster. In an editorial, *The Sun* (15 Aug. 1842) observed: 'Check the ebullition of popular feeling in Manchester, and it will instantly break out in Glasgow. Crush it in England, and it will bid defiance to you in Scotland. Lop off one of the heads of the Hydra, and a hundred others will sprout up to alarm and confound you' (p. 3). Similarly, *The Cambridge Independent Press* (27 Aug. 1842) predicted: 'The disturbances in the North of England, which had commenced with such fearful violence, may now be looked upon as crushed. . . . It seems, however . . . that the snake is only scotched, not killed, and that, sooner or later, from the heads already crushed of the hydra, others will yet arise' (p. 2).

revolts in Lyons, in Warsaw, . . . Paris City past or present: for the revolt of the *canuts* (Fr., 'silk-work artisans') at Lyons in 1831 and 1834 that sought higher wages and the right of association, see Rude, *La Révolte des Canuts* (1982); and Bezucha, *The Lyons Uprising of 1834* (1974). For the November 1830 armed uprising against Russia led by Polish cadets in Warsaw, see Davies, *God's Playground* (1982), ii. 306–33; and Hordynski, *History of the Late Polish Revolution* (1832). In the reference to Paris, 'past' relates to the July Revolution in 1830, which led to the overthrow of the Bourbon monarch King Charles X and the accession of his Orléanist cousin Louis-Philippe; see Pilbeam, *The 1830 Revolution in France* (1991). By 1841, dissatisfaction with Louis-Philippe had become widespread. *The Times* reported (15 Sept.) that an *émeute* had occurred on 9 Sept. in Clermont Ferraud, S of Paris, where 'several soldiers were killed and wounded' and 'a large number of the rebels fell in defence of the barricades they had erected'. On 11 September, 'about 300 individuals . . . assembled on the Place du Chatelet. . . . The band . . . directed by chiefs wearing blouses and caps, ascended the Rue St. Denis, singing the "Marseillaise," and crying "Down with Louis Philippe—the Republic for ever! Blood! We must have blood!"' The next day at the Hospice St Antoine, an assassin fired at the duke of Orléans, missing his target and wounding a nearby horse. *The Times* concluded the article by quoting the opinion of the *National* newspaper that 'the Government neglects no opportunity of bringing the army into collision with the citizens, and of habituating the troops to shed the blood of the people' (15 Sept., p. 4).

Our enemies are we know not who or what; our friends are we know not where!: TC refers to the various social and political aims of the Manchester insurrectionists, whose ranks included trade unionists, Owenite socialists, Chartists, and Anti-Corn Law League supporters.

Hyrcanian tiger: powerful cat once inhabiting region SE of the Caspian Sea. See *Macbeth*, III. iv. 101 and *Hamlet*, II. ii. 481.

Behemoth of Chaos: Job 40:15–24.

Woolwich grapeshot will sweep clear all streets: see note to p. 25.

29 *Nox and Chaos*: darkness and disorder; see *Paradise Lost* (1667), ii. 960–2.

Peterloo . . . very countable: see note to p. 27. On 15 February 1842, TC asked Thomas Ballantyne about the exact number of people killed at Peterloo; see *CL* xvi. 50, 67.

30 *O'Connor*: Feargus O'Connor, the charismatic Chartist leader and editor of *The Northern Star*, who tactically supported the threat of physical force in order to realize the goals of the movement. He arrived in Manchester on 16 August 1842, but cautioned workers against using violence. In a letter published in *The Northern Star* (20 Aug. 1842), he accused the Anti-Corn Law League of conspiring to 'originate a revolution' in order to discredit the strike, provoke a brutal counter-reaction, and advance the commercial interests of the factory owners. He urged his followers: '*Let no blood be shed. Let no life be destroyed. Let no property be consumed*. Let us, in God's name, set an example to the world of what moral power is capable of effecting' (p. 8). O'Connor was arrested on 30 September 1842 and prosecuted for sedition, but escaped conviction on 11 March 1843 as the result of a procedural error.

fish-oil transparencies: fish-oil refers to whale oil lamps; a transparency is 'a picture, print, inscription, or device on some translucent substance, made visible by means of a light behind' (*OED*).

no dayspring from on high: Luke 1:78.

'*A fair day's-wages for a fair day's-work*': the slogan of the Manchester strikers. See *The Examiner* (20 Aug. 1842), 536: 'The "mills" all being stopped at Stalybridge they all came in a body to Ashton; stopped every mill there; called a meeting between Ashton and Stalybridge. Resolution passed to the following effect:—"That no mill should be allowed to work until they got a fair day's wages for a day's work".'

31 *it is as just a demand as Governed men ever made of Governing*: TC broadly agreed with the Corn Law repealers about the destructiveness of the tariffs, but ridiculed their commitments to the extension of the ballot and laissez-faire policies. In an editorial, the Anti-Corn Law League paper *The Sun* (27 Aug. 1842) offered a similar defence of the workers' 'just demands': 'When it is borne in mind that these poor men underwent the severest privations before turning out, in the hope of obtaining "a fair day's wages for a fair day's work"—that they excited universal surprise by the extent to which they respected property—they were hardly guilty of a single outrage not provoked by the wanton intermeddling of the police, it will be difficult to discover any rational ground for setting aside the ordinary forms of law in bringing them to trial. There was nothing whatever treasonable—hardly anything seditious in the turn out of the operatives. . . . They sought nothing which the Constitution of this country, either in the letter or spirit, denies to all classes of British subjects' (p. 3).

Dilettantisms . . . Mammonisms: dilettantism is 'applied more or less depreciatively to one who interests himself in an art or science merely as a pastime and without serious aim or study'; mammonism is 'devotion to the pursuit of riches' (both definitions from *OED*, citing TC).

the all-victorious Light element, is . . . an all-victorious Fire-element: see *Heroes*, 35: 'There is to be a new Heaven and a new Earth; a higher supreme God, and Justice to reign among men. . . . All death is but a Phœnix fire-death, and new-birth into the Greater and the Better!'

The day's-wages of John Milton's day's-work, . . . escape from death on the gallows: in a contract dated 27 April 1667, Milton's printer Samuel Simmons (or Symmons) agreed to pay the author of *Paradise Lost* £5, with the promise of a second instalment for the same amount after 1,300 copies of the book had been sold. In exchange, Milton transferred the copyright and profits of the book to Simmons. For the manuscript of the contract, see British Library Add. MS 18861. In October 1660, with the Stuarts restored to the throne, Milton was arrested and imprisoned for his Republican sympathies, and copies of his works were burnt. Through the intervention of friends such as the poet Andrew Marvell, who also had served as Milton's assistant as Latin secretary to Cromwell's Council of State, he avoided possible execution and was released on 15 December.

Oliver Cromwell quitted his farming; undertook a Hercules' Labour: a member of the landed gentry, Cromwell entered Parliament in 1628, the first step in his journey to becoming Lord Protector.

shovel-hatted quack-heads: TC's derisive term for respectable Anglican clergymen, who wore 'a stiff broad-brimmed hat, turned up at the sides and projecting with a shovel-like curve in front and behind' (*OED*, citing TC).

32 *gallows-tree near Tyburn Turnpike, with his head on the gable of Westminster Hall*: Tyburn gallows is a 'triple tree' at the corner of Edgware Rd and Bayswater Rd. See *Cromwelliana* (1810), 186, entry for 30 January 1660: 'Jan. 30 . . . was doubly observed, not only by a solemn fast . . . for the precious blood of our late pious Sovereign *King Charles the First*, . . . but also by public dragging those odious carcasses of *Oliver Cromwell*, *Henry Ireton*, and *John Bradshaw* to *Tyburn*. To-day [the carcasses] were drawn upon sledges to *Tyburn*; all the way . . . the universal outcry and curses of the people went along with them. When these three carcasses were at *Tyburn*, they were pulled out of their coffins, and hanged at the several angles of that triple tree, where they hung till the sun was set; after which, they were taken down, their heads cut off, and their loathsome trunks thrown into a deep hole under the gallows. The heads of those three notorious regicides . . . are set upon poles on the top of *Westminster Hall*, by the common hangman.'

two centuries now of mixed cursing and ridicule: TC's campaign to rehabilitate Cromwell's reputation, begun in *Heroes*, had been anticipated by the Whig historians William Godwin and Catherine Macaulay, and the Nonconformists Benjamin Brook and William Orme; see Worden, 'The Victorians and Oliver Cromwell' (2000), 116–18. What was distinct about TC's emphasis was his endorsement of Cromwell's Puritan radicalism, which previous historians had equated with his religious 'fanaticism'; see Worden, 'Thomas Carlyle and Oliver Cromwell' (2000), 139–40.

32 *with the Tenpound Franchisers; in Open Vestry, or with any Sanhedrim of considerable standing*: ten-pound franchisers were radicals and reformers who sought to expand the suffrage; a vestry is 'an assembly or meeting of the parishioners [including all rate-paying householders, i.e. 'open'] or a certain number of these [limited to a select number of property holders, i.e. 'closed'], held originally in the vestry of the parish church, for the purpose of deliberating or legislating upon the affairs of the parish or upon certain temporal matters connected with the church' (*OED*). TC refers to a continuing dispute arising from the New Poor Law Amendment Act of 1834 about the most efficient method of distributing funds through local parishes. See Edward Smedley et al., *Encyclopædia Metropolitana* (1845), xxiii. 486: 'All rate-payers have a common interest in seeing the funds collected for the Poor are properly applied and economically administered; but it is found that where the management rests with the great Body of rate-payers, as in what are called Open Vestries, the Parish affairs are generally very ill conducted. In other Parishes, where affairs are best managed, the rate-payers place the powers intrusted to them in the hands of a small Body, chosen by them from their own number, called sometimes the Select Vestry, and sometimes the Guardians of the Poor.' Sanhedrin is the 'Name applied to the highest court of justice and supreme council at Jerusalem' (*OED*, citing TC).

high gibbets and treadmills: a high gibbet signifies 'an upright post with projecting arm from which the bodies of criminals were hung in chains or irons after execution' (*OED*); a treadmill was a machine invented in 1818 for workhouses, walked on by inmates to create power for grinding corn.

God's will is done on Earth even as it is in Heaven: from the Lord's Prayer. See Matt. 6:9–13.

33 *a dumb, altogether unconscious want*: see TC, *Chartism*: 'How inexpressibly useful were true insight into . . . these wild inarticulate souls, struggling there, with inarticulate uproar, like dumb creatures in pain, unable to speak what is in them!' (*CME* iv. 122).

Wealth of Nations, Supply-and-demand and such like: see Smith, *Wealth of Nations*, i. 145–6: 'The quantity of every commodity brought to market naturally suits itself to the effectual demand. It is the interest of all those who employ their land, labour, or stock, in bringing any commodity to market, that the quantity never should exceed the effectual demand; and it is the interest of all other people that it never should fall short of that demand.'

34 *Gurth, a mere swineherd, born thrall of Cedric the Saxon . . . did get some parings of the pork*: see Scott, *Ivanhoe* (1819), ch. 1, where Wamba explains to Gurth, a 'swine-herd' and 'born thrall of Cedric of Rotherwood', that 'pork is . . . good Norman French; and so when the brute lives, and is in charge of a Saxon slave, she goes by her Saxon name [swine]; but becomes

a Norman, and is called pork, when she is carried to the Castle-hall to feast among the nobles'.

There is not a horse in England, able and willing to work, but has due food and lodging: a favourite allusion of TC's, possibly indebted to book iv of Swift's *Gulliver's Travels* (1726), where the rational and communal Houyhnhnms rule over the degenerate and anarchic Yahoos. See TC, 'Occasional Discourse' (1849), in *CME* iv. 370; *Latter-Day Pamphlets* (1850), in *Works* xx. 26–7; and Sorensen, 'Carlyle, John Mitchel, and the Political Legacy of Swift' (2008).

Platitude: TC uses 'platitude' as a synonym for absurdity.

Jötuns . . . Brute-gods of the Beginning: see *Heroes*, 16: 'Giants, huge shaggy beings of a demonic character. Frost, Fire, Sea-tempest; these are Jötuns.'

MORRISON'S PILL: the 'quack-remedies' of James Morison, successful entrepreneur and self-styled 'Hygeist' who manufactured and marketed a variety of vegetable-based pills for the cure of different maladies. He claimed that 'the numerous cures [the pills] have effected in all kinds of diseases, surgical cases, and mental derangements, have gained them the name of Universal Medicine' (quoted in Helfand, 'James Morison and His Pills' (1974), 106). TC remarked to his sister Jean Carlyle Aitken, 29 October 1842, 'People expect that some kind of *Morrison's Pill* could be devised, some Act of Parl*t* or the like, by which the whole rotten dying System of Society could be made whole again, and then all go well' (*CL* xv. 151).

WHAT is to be done, what would you have us do?: see e.g. 'Carlyle's Chartism', *Tait's Edinburgh Magazine* 7 (Feb. 1840), 119: 'Though Mr Carlyle is clear that a great deal might be both done and undone, he never commits himself to details. It would have been something to have indicated one safe preliminary step, were it but one; and we are left in doubt whether he does not consider even extension of the suffrage a wild illusion, from the manner in which it is alluded. . . . In education . . . he appears to have some faith, and, like others, little present hope: but, on this head, as on others, when *things* come to be grappled with, Mr Carlyle rather seeks to evade handgrips and a throw, and quaintly gives us to perceive that much may be said on both sides.'

35 *some Act of Parliament, 'remedial measure' or the like*: see the Anti-Corn Law League's address 'To the People of the United Kingdom', *The Examiner* (27 Aug. 1842), 554: 'With the opening of the session of 1842, 700 delegates commenced their sittings in the metropolis. . . . They published an appalling statement of facts, proving the dreadful sufferings of the great mass of the population, and the intimate connexion between those sufferings and the working of the Corn Law. The Ministry proposed, and the Legislature sanctioned, a partial change in the law, worthless as a remedial measure, and tantamount to an utter denial of the just claims of the people.'

Life-fountain within you once again set flowing: see *Heroes*, 3: 'We cannot look, however imperfectly, upon a great man, without gaining something by him. He is the living light-fountain, which it is good and pleasant to be near.'

35 *Not Emigration, Education, Corn-Law Abrogation, Sanitary Regulation, Land Property-Tax*: TC refers to specific political reforms being debated in Parliament in 1842–3. Plans announced in *The Examiner* (15 Jan. 1842), 34 for a 'grand scheme of Emigration and Colonization' were never drafted but the paper reported (2 Apr. 1842) that the 'trying position of the operatives had led to the forming of "Emigration Clubs," to enable parties to leave England' (p. 221). There was a bill proposed by Sir James Graham in March 1843 to place district schools 'for the education of pauper children in the metropolis and large towns under the superintendence of the clergy of the established church, with provision for the instruction of children of dissenters by ministers of their own persuasion' (*The Examiner*, 4 Mar. 1843, 133). For Corn Law abrogation, see note to p. 234. Chadwick's proposals for improving the habitations of the poor were included in his *Inquiry into the Sanitary Condition of the Labouring Population of Great Britain* (1842), a copy of which TC received on 1 August: 'Glancing hastily thro' it, I am struck . . . by the frightful difference of the duration of workman life in Manchester and in Rutland. . . . The Gov*t* will actually have to attend to all that shortly, or prepare itself for being kicked to the Devil. We *cannot* go on in that way, and will not!' (*CL* xv. 3). On 19 April 1842 the Conservative Government published its income tax bill, announcing tariff reductions for manufacturers and reimposing land value taxes that had been repealed in 1816. In an editorial, *The Examiner* (29 Oct. 1842) denounced the measures as insignificant: 'The country gentlemen find that there is no danger of their being ruined, or of the people being fed—two events which they are always pleased to suppose in inseparable connexion' (p. 689). See also TC, *Chartism*: 'Two things, great things, dwell, for the last ten years, in all thinking heads in England. . . . Universal Education is the first . . . ; general Emigration is the second' (*CME* iv. 192).

Hustings: platforms for nominating parliamentary candidates.

36 *when the brains are out, an absurdity will die!*: *Macbeth*, III. iv. 78.

the very jackasses weep: *Measure for Measure*, II. ii. 122.

to have a millstone tied round your neck, and be cast into the sea: Matt. 18:6, Mark 9:42, and Luke 17:2.

no Reform Bill, Ballot-box, Five-point Charter: the Reform Bill of 1832 created uniform voting qualifications based on property ownership, increasing the electorate to 18 per cent of adult males. By the early 1840s, demands for expanding the franchise were growing more emphatic. *The Times* (23 Jan. 1841) reported details of a Chartist meeting held at Holbeck-Moor in Leeds with 8,000 people in attendance. At the meeting, the Radical MP Joseph Hume proposed the following resolution: 'That the great experiment made by means of the Reform Bill to improve the condition of the country has failed to attain the end desired by the people, and a further reform having therefore become necessary, it is the opinion of this meeting that the united efforts of all Reformers ought to be directed to obtain such a further enlargement of the franchise as should make the interests of the representatives identical with those of the whole country, and by this means secure a just government for all classes of people' (p. 5). The secret ballot was discarded from the original 1832 Reform Bill draft, and later became the sixth point of the Charter. The other five points in the Charter were universal male suffrage, annual elections, salaries for MPs, abolition of the property qualification for MPs, and electoral constituencies of equal size. Electoral reform did not occur again until 1867.

'Given a world of Knaves to produce an Honesty from their united action!': see *Heroes*, 195.

alembic after alembic: 'An early apparatus used for distilling, consisting of two connected vessels, a typically gourd-shaped cucurbit containing the substance to be distilled, and a receiver or flask in which the condensed product is collected' (*OED*).

'While we ourselves continue valets ... hero govern us?': see *Heroes*, 157: 'No man is a hero to his valet-de-chambre.'

37 *our dead hearts of stone for living hearts of flesh*: Ezek. 11:19 and 2 Cor. 3:3.

edge-gilt vacuity in man's shape: see *OED*, 'gilt-edged': 'Decorated with a gold edge or rim', and citing TC: 'Designating people or things of great wealth, quality, [and] luxury'.

Sorcerer's Sabbaths: on the eve of *Walpurgisnacht* (Walpurgis night), 30 April, when witches congregated on the Harz mountains to worship Satan; see Goethe, *Faust*, pt. i.

39 *Ye have forgotten God, ye have quitted the ways of God, or ye would not have been unhappy*: Is. 17:10, Jer. 3:21, and 13:25.

two-legged animal without feathers: attributed to Plato by Diogenes Laertius; see *Sartor*, 18.

Chimera: mythological monster with a lion's head, goat's body, and dragon's tail.

Sauerteig: (Ger.) 'sour dough' and 'leaven'; TC's fictional mouthpiece.

an old eight-day clock, made many thousand years ago, and still ticking, ... which the Maker ... sat looking at: a metaphor used by eighteenth-century deists. See Samuel Clarke to Gottfried Wilhelm von Leibniz, November 1715: 'The Notion of the World's being a great *Machine*, going on *without the Interposition of God*, as a Clock continues to go without the Assistance of a Clockmaker; is the Notion of *Materialism* and *Fate*, and tends ... to exclude *Providence* and *God's Government* in Reality out of the World' (Clarke, *Works* (1738), iv. 590).

Benthamee Radicalism, the gospel of 'Enlightened Selfishness': Bentham's Utilitarian argument that 'self-preference' enhances understanding of mutual social obligations and provides a secure basis 'for every practical purpose, in the character of a ground for all political arrangements' (*Constitutional Code* (1827, 1830), in Bentham, *Works* (1841), ix. 6). In a review of Chadwick's *Inquiry into the Sanitary Condition of the Labouring Population*, *The Examiner* (20 Aug. 1842) debated whether self-interest might encourage factory and housing reform: 'The existing factories are, speaking generally, extremely unhealthy; but that they are so only for want of proper ventilation and other important requisites, which, if the enlightened self-interest of the owners fail to supply, the law could and ought to enforce; and that in all instances in which, either from that enlightened self-interest or from benevolence, such improved arrangements have been carried into effect, and especially where the improvement of the private dwelling-places of the work-people has been included in the plan, its authors have been rewarded by seeing around them a healthy, thriving, and well-conducted factory population attached to them' (p. 531).

39 *Church-extension*: a proposal to increase the number of clergymen and churches in manufacturing districts was raised by Sir Robert Inglis in the House of Commons on 28 July 1842. Peel was sympathetic to the argument, but delayed acting upon it. *The Examiner* (11 Feb. 1843) commented, '[Peel] seems to think that the tranquillity of the manufacturing districts can be effected by new Churches. The first pacificator needed is bread, and let it not be said that instead of it he gives a stone' (p. 83).

Sliding-scale: introduced by the Duke of Wellington in 1828, allowing foreign corn to be imported free of duty when the domestic price rose to 73s. per quarter. In his 1842 budget speech, delivered on 11 March 1842, Peel proposed a reduced sliding scale on corn as well as a decrease in tariffs for raw materials and foreign manufactured goods. The result was the passage of a bill in July 1842 for a reformed sliding scale, which reduced the duty on corn from 34s. 8d. to 20s. per quarter (8 bushels) if the domestic price fell to 51s. or less per quarter. TC wrote to his brother Jamie on 30 November 1842, 'It is surmised by many that Peel will have to make some new change in his Law of *Sliding*, this very year. Whatever he may do, it seems very certain the Corn-Laws have not now long to last' (*CL* xv. 211).

40 *double-barrelled Aristocracies*: the double-barrelled shotgun, an innovation introduced by the gunsmith Joseph Manton and widely used in aristocratic hunts. Hughes, 281 also suggests an allusion to those with 'double surnames'.

our young friend of the Houndsditch Indicator: see John Stow, *A Survey of London* (1603), i. 128: 'From Aldgate Northwest to Bishopsgate, lieth the ditch of the Cittie, called Houndes ditch, for that in olde time when the same lay open, much filth (conveyed forth of the Citie) especially dead Dogges were there layd or cast: wherefore of latter time a mudde wall was made inclosing the ditch, to keepe out the laying of such filth as had beene accustomed.' In *London Labour and the London Poor* (1861–2), Henry Mayhew noted that the area was populated by 'street Jews, engaged in the purchase of second-hand clothes' (ii. 119). The allusion links TC's 'young friend' to Diogenes Teufelsdröckh in *Sartor*, 178, who sets out to 'pace and repace, in austerest thought, the pavement of Monmouth Street', where he derives inspiration for his 'Clothes-Philosophy' (p. 211). TC may have based the *Houndsditch Indicator* on *The Western Vindicator* (Feb.–Dec. 1839), a Radical paper edited and composed by Henry Vincent.

The Government shut it down on 16 December, following the armed uprising in Newport, Wales, on 4 November 1839, when troops killed twenty-two protesters. The upheaval was covered extensively in *The Examiner* and *The Times*. Vincent had been arrested on 9 May, but he continued to publish the paper. *The Times* (12 Nov. 1839) included several excerpts from *The Western Vindicator*, and described it as a paper 'circulated widely in the hills, inflaming the minds of the deluded people, and exciting them to rebellion'. In one provocative passage, Vincent declared: 'When we reflect upon the state of the country, and consider how our friends have been cast into dungeons, there to die of starvation, we are not at all surprised at what has taken place near our borders. We warned our rulers of it, they heeded not the warning. They persisted in their own unhallowed line of conduct, and now we witness the consequence thereof—a fearful and bloody revolution!' (p. 5).

"Aristocracy of Talent": the expression was first used by Peter Freeland Aiken, an Edinburgh advocate, in a lecture he delivered in 1842 comparing the British and American constitutions. Aiken was the grandson of Robert Aiken, patron of Robert Burns, and the father of Andrew Hunter Aiken, the recipient of Burns's 'Epistle to a Young Friend'. See Aiken, *A Comparative View of the Constitutions of Great Britain and the United States* (1842), 87: 'In England, what agitates the people, affects indeed the hereditary, and also the natural aristocracy of the country; namely the aristocracy of wealth, talent, and learning: but all are not agitated in the same manner and to the same extent. In America, the nation is all people. In England it consists of various orders united, sympathizing, yet not identical. . . . Those that rule are accustomed also to obey. The highest is not above the laws, whose just and humane arrangements afford protection and provision for the poorest. There is neither the arbitrary master nor the abject slave.'

41 *Bobus Higgins*: in addition to a Latinized form of the word 'booby', *bobus* in Latin is the dative case of the word *bos* ('cow' or 'bull'), suggesting the bovine or herd-like quality of Bobus as TC's fictional personification of middle-class 'mammon-worship'. See TC, *Latter-Day Pamphlets*, *Works*, *xx*. 270.

larders dropping fatness: Ps. 65:11.

Collective Wisdom: Cobbett's name for the House of Commons in its 'collective capacity' (*Collective Commentaries* [11 July 1822], 265).

Like people like priest: Hos. 4:9.

Bobissimus: 'greatest of boobies'.

42 *divine right*: see note to p. 191.

the life-tree everywhere is made a upas-tree: a legendary Javanese tree exuding poisonous fumes fatal to all animal and vegetable life, and thereby destroying the 'Tree Igdrasil', the 'Ash-tree of Existence' (*Heroes*, 19). See also Nixon, 'Thomas Carlyle's Igdrasil' (2009).

42 *Rhadamanthus, Æacus and Minos*: judges of the shades entering Hades.

wash Thames mud, by improved methods . . . to find more gold in it: TC refers to 'mudlarkers' scavenging the Thames at low tide for valuables; see Mayhew, 'Narrative of a Mudlark', *London Labour*, iv. 370–3.

like unto it: Matt. 22:39 and Mark 12:31.

heavy-wet: malt liquor and the title of a well-known ballad composed after the Beerhouse Act of 1830, which liberalized licensing laws governing the brewing and sale of beer. See George Cruickshank, 'Heavy Wet', *The Gallery of 140 Comicalities* (1831), no. 87, an etching under which appears a poem that begins: 'King William and Reform, I say, | In such a case who can be neuter? | Just let me blow the froth away, | And see how soon I'll drain the pewter' (ll. 1–4). See also Altick, 'Topicality as Technique' (1976), 123.

To him that hath shall be given . . . from him that hath not, shall be taken away even that which he hath: Matt. 13:12, Mark 4:25, and Luke 8:18.

43 *'Cash-payment for the sole nexus'*: see TC, *Chartism*: 'In these complicated times, with Cash Payment as the sole nexus between man and man, the toiling Classes of mankind declare, in their confused but most emphatic way, to the Untoiling, that they will be governed' (*CME* iv. 168).

The resuscitating of a soul . . . gone to asphyxia is . . . a long and terrible one: the metaphor may have been suggested to TC by a speech of the Anti-Corn Law League activist Thomas Perronet Thompson, reported in *The Examiner* (12 Feb. 1842): 'The existing national distress was stated [by Sir Robert Peel] to arise from a concurrence of various causes. There was a rope about the neck of the patient, but the doctor comes in and says that it was a concurrence of causes that was killing him. . . . The poor patient . . . had a flow of blood to the head. . . . A tendency to suffocation. . . . Say not a word of the rope—look for the cause to a concurrence of circumstances to account for the extravasation. . . . Did not this meeting see that if anything like patriotism was left in the country, it must consist in ousting these men from power (Tremendous cheering, renewed and continued for several minutes)' (p. 107).

true worships: (obsolete) 'a worthy person' (*OED*, citing TC).

44 *Burns an Exciseman . . . Byron a Literary Lion*: see 'Burns', where TC contrasts the 'theatrical, false, affected' poetry of Byron with Burns's 'honest' verse. Burns's language reflects his impoverished circumstances: to survive, he must 'go drudge as an Exciseman'. It also suggests his visceral opposition to the 'respectable' and artificial standards of the literary establishment (*EOL*, 37, 72).

Odin a God . . . Mahomet a Prophet of God: Odin, king of the Norse gods; Muhammad, founder and prophet of Islam. See *Heroes*, lectures 1 and 2.

Mammon's galvanic accursed one: referring to electricity developed by chemical action. For the figurative use of 'galvanic', see *OED*, citing TC, 'with allusion to the effects of the application of galvanism'.

45 *'Je demande l'arrestation des coquins et des lâches'*: see *FR* iii. 234, where TC quotes *Le Moniteur*, 245 (24 May 1795), 989.

Apage Satanas: (Lat.) 'Be gone Satan'. See Matt. 4:10 and Mark 8:33.

there lies the port and . . . stormtost seas: Tennyson, 'Ulysses' (1842), ll. 44–5.

College of Health: 'The British College of Health', 33 Euston Rd, opened by James Morison in 1828 to serve as an outlet for his pills.

46 *Saint-John's corrosive mixture . . . a little blistery fiction on the back*: John St John Long, who invented a corrosive liniment that claimed to cure consumption, gout, measles, smallpox, and insanity by extracting 'acrid fluids' from the body. In *Fraser's Magazine* 1 (1830), TC's brother Dr John Aitken Carlyle suspected that this 'mysteriously powerful nostrum . . . seems to be nothing else . . . than some cunningly disguised composition of emetic tartar' (p. 456).

ill-boding Cassandras in Sieges of Troy: daughter of Priam, legendary king of Troy during the Trojan War. She prophesied the fall of Troy, but was fated to be ignored.

Loadstar: 'A star that shows the way' (*OED*).

though wide seas . . . bloom the Happy Isles: Tennyson, 'Ulysses', ll. 60–3.

'There dwells the great Achilles whom we knew': Tennyson, 'Ulysses', l. 64.

'The choking Nightmare . . . has already fled': see TC, 'Jean Paul Friedrich Richter Again' (1830): 'Evil . . . is like a nightmare; the instant you begin to strive with it, to bestir yourself, it has already ended' (*CME* ii. 118).

Trismegistus: (Gr.) 'thrice-greatest'; Hermes Trismegistus is the name given to the Egyptian god Thoth, inventor of writing, art, science, and religion, and purported author of the 'Hermetica', a series of texts on occult, theological, and philosophical subjects.

47 *present laws of copyright*: on 28 February 1839, TC wrote a petition to the House of Commons in support of the Copyright Act sponsored by Sir Thomas Noon Talfourd. The aim was to allow dependants of authors to profit from the sales of their writings after their deaths. As TC argued, 'those dear to him will still be in need of [money]' (*CL* xi. 67). Talfourd's Act became law in 1842, when it was reintroduced by Philip Henry Stanhope, viscount Mahon. Under its provisions, the term of copyright in a book was to be forty-two years, or the life of the author and seven years, whichever of these two spans was longer. In his petition, published in *The Examiner* (7 Apr. 1839), 214–15, TC requested that the 'Honourable House . . . forbid . . . extraneous persons, entirely unconcerned in this adventure of his, to steal from him his small winnings, for a space of sixty years at shortest. After sixty years, unless your Honourable House provide otherwise, they may begin to steal' (*Works*, xxix. 206–7).

confused Paper-Masses now intrusted to him: TC assumes the daunting task of his fictional editor in *Sartor*, 59 to make sense of Teufelsdröckh's 'miscellaneous masses of Sheets'. On this occasion TC sifts through research material on the abbey of Bury St Edmunds that he himself has collected.

47 *the LIFE-TREE IGDRASIL*: see *Heroes*, 19: 'At the foot of [the Tree Igdrasil], in the Death-kingdom, sit Three *Nornas*, Fates,—the Past, Present, Future; watering its roots from the Sacred Well. Its "boughs," with their buddings and disleafings,—events, things suffered, things done, catastrophes,—stretch through all lands and times. Is not every leaf of it a biography, every fibre there an act or word? Its boughs are Histories of Nations. . . . It is the past, the present, and the future; what was done, what is doing, what will be done.'

BOOK II. THE ANCIENT MONK

49 *JOCELIN OF BRAKELOND*: Benedictine monk and biographer born in Bury St Edmunds, Suffolk. He served his novitiate under Abbot Samson, who appointed him chaplain in 1182.

confused Papers, printed and others: TC's notes, as well as the various sources that he consulted.

wig and black triangle: black caps were worn by judges to cover their wigs when delivering a death sentence.

le genre ennuyeux: see Voltaire, preface to *L'Enfant prodigue* (1736): 'Encore une fois, tous les genres sont bons, hors le genre ennuyeux' (Once again, all genres are good except the boring genre) (*Œuvres complètes*, x. 234).

50 *an extremely foreign Book*: as TC documents in the footnote, this is '*Chronica JOCELINI DE BRAKELONDA* . . . (Camden Society, London, 1840)', TC's primary source for Book II, which he borrowed from the London Library on 12 October 1842 (Baker, 119). In his MS Notes in the Forster Collection, TC expands further: 'The Camden Society Books do not in one sense come under the category of Foreign Literature; yet in another, in many others, they are mostly Foreign enough. The present book, for example, the private chronicle of an old St. Edmundsbury monk, now seven centuries old, is very far removed from us in many ways. It is in a language not only foreign, but dead; monk-Latin lies across not the British channel, but beyond the flood of Lethe, the vinefields of Styx, the one knows not where' (fo. 56r). The first major review of Rokewode, 'The Chronicle of Jocelin de Brakelond', was published in the *British and Foreign Review; or European Quarterly Journal* 29 (Apr. 1843), 54–79.

the labours of the Camden Society have brought to light in these days: the Camden Society, named after the antiquary William Camden, was founded in London in April 1838. *The Examiner* (29 Apr. 1838), 265 reported that 'A new literary club, under the title of the Camden Society, has just been formed . . . which promises to be of more general utility than any other association of the kind. It is not intended that the works printed under its auspices shall be exclusively confined to its members, . . . but will have claims upon the notice of all persons interested in the literary and histor- ical remains of this country. The object is to make the society as exten- sively useful as possible, by printing works which it would not answer the purpose of a bookseller to publish with a view to pecuniary profit, but which will merit to be rescued from oblivion, and to be put into a shape both convenient and permanent.' *The Bolton Chronicle* (28 Mar. 1840), announced that the 'Council of the Camden Society have resolved upon the publication of . . . "The Chronicle of Josceline de Brakelond, Monk of St. Edmundsbury, from A.D. 1157 to 1211," to be edited by Mr. J. G. Rokewode'.' John Gage Rokewode, a Suffolk historian, was director of the Society of Antiquities, 1829–42, and fellow of the Royal Society, 1824. He died suddenly on 14 October 1842.

the 'Chronicle,' or private Boswellean Notebook: TC compares Jocelin to James Boswell, biographer of Dr. Samuel Johnson. In 'Boswell's Life of Johnson' (1832), TC asserts that Boswell's biography ranks as an 'English *Odyssey*' that yields 'more real insight into the *History of England* during those days than twenty other Books, falsely entitled "Histories," which take to themselves that special aim' (*EOL*, 162, 158).

ninefold Stygian Marshes, Stream of Lethe: Styx, river of hate, over which the dead passed into Hades, had nine bends running through a great marsh; see *Aeneid*, vi. 439; Lethe is the river of forgetfulness, from which the dead drank in Hades.

Elysian Fields of Memory: the resting place of heroes in Greek mythology.

covered deeper than Pompeii: city S of Naples buried under lava in AD 79. The subject was popularized by Bulwer-Lytton in his novel *The Last Days of Pompeii* (1834), and featured in Victorian theatre, songs, opera, pantomime, and illustrations; see St Clair and Bautz, 'Imperial Decadence' (2012).

One other of those vanished Existences: see TC's MS Notes, Forster Collection, fo. 56r: 'One of those vanished Existences, utterly grown dark, whose footprints or works nevertheless are still clear to our eyes when we think of them.'

The builders of Stonehenge: prehistoric monument in Wiltshire, 2 miles (3.2 km) W of Amesbury, the origins of which were widely debated by Victorian antiquarians and scholars. See John Britton and Edward Wedlake Brayley, *The Beauties of England and Wales* (1801–15), xv. 357: 'Though the precise era of [Stonehenge's] erection cannot be demonstrated, nor the peculiar rites, ceremonies, and customs of the people who raised it clearly defined, yet we are disposed to believe that its history is less fabulous than has been generally represented. It is true, we know nothing of the rude mechanic, or architect, who designed it; and it is equally true, that we are not much better informed of the private life and character of the immortal Shakespear: as our knowledge, therefore, is so limited respecting the great dramatist of the sixteenth century, we ought not to be surprised at our ignorance of the former.' TC consulted this work in 1842 for his Cromwell research (Baker, 116).

Universal Review and Homer's Iliad: *The Universal Review; or, Chronicle of the Literature of all Nations* was published March 1824–January 1825 by George Byrom Whittaker; the *Iliad* is an ancient Greek epic poem recounting the Trojan War by a possibly mythical poet known as Homer.

50 *Brakelond being the known old name of a street or quarter in that venerable Town*: see Rokewode, p. v and n.: 'The Long Braklond, leading from the North Gate to the Market Place, and the Little Braklond, are ancient streets of St. Edmundsbury.'

'obedientia': see Rokewode, 2; *Chronicle*, 4. See also Gasquet, *English Monastic Life* (1904), 58: 'But as usually understood, by the word obedientiaries was signified the other officials, and not the prior and the sub-prior, who assisted in the general government of the monastery.'

chaplain to my Lord Abbot: Rokewode, 19; *Chronicle*, 24.

living beside him night and day for the space of six years: Rokewode, 27; *Chronicle*, 33–4.

51 *Johnsons are rare . . . Boswells perhaps still rarer*: see TC, 'Boswell's Life of Johnson': 'All Johnson's own Writings, laborious and in their kind genuine above most, stand on a quite inferior level to [Boswell's *Life*]; . . . and for some future generation may be valuable chiefly as Prolegomena and expository Scholia to this *Johnsoniad* of Boswell' (*EOL*, 156).

Veracity . . . the prime essence of all genius whatsoever!: Goethe, *Sprüche in Prosa: Maximen und Reflexionen* (1827): 'Das erste und letzte, was vom Genie gefordert wird, ist Wahrheitsliebe' (The first and last thing required of genius is the love of truth) (1908 edn., 48).

his Virgilius, his Flaccus, Ovidius Naso: Virgil, Horace, and Ovid, to whom Jocelin alludes frequently in his chronicle.

Breviaries: (Lat.) 'summary'; books listing the daily offices to be recited by ordained members of the monastery.

'eximiæ religionis, potens sermone et opere': (Lat.) 'excellent in religion and powerful in speech and work'. Rokewode, 50; *Chronicle*, 61.

a kind of Monk or Dog-Latin: see Rokewode, p. vii: 'The style of the work is easy, mixed, but not offensively, with the language of writers sacred and profane, according to the custom of the monastic historians of the age. The story is told throughout with a pleasing naïveté, and sometimes humour; the characters are drawn with spirit, and the whole seems written with truth.'

Liber Albus of St. Edmundsbury: see Rokewode, p. ix: 'The present Chronicle is edited from the Liber Albus Monasterii S. Edmundi, MS. 1005, in the Harleian Collection, which MS. belonged to the family of Bacon of Redgrave, and afterward to Dr. Stillingfleet, Bishop of Worcester; whence Bishop Tanner refers to it under the title "Registrum de Bury, MS. Stillingfleet".' The British Library catalogue entry reads: 'Bury St Edmunds customary ('Liber albus') / Harley MS 1005: Early 12th century–Early 15th century'.

Henry the Eighth, Putney Cromwell, the Dissolution of Monasteries: Henry VIII, king of England, 1509–47, promoted the notorious policy of the Dissolution of the Monasteries, which was administered in 1535–6 by Thomas Cromwell, born in Putney, Surrey.

Harleian Collection: collection of charters, manuscripts, tracts, and rolls bequeathed by Edward Harley, first earl of Oxford to his widow Henrietta Cavendish Harley. In 1753, she and her daughter Margaret Cavendish Bentinck sold the archive to the nation, which was subsequently housed in the newly established British Museum. On the same day that he borrowed *Chronica Jocelini* from the London Library, TC also borrowed a volume of William Oldys and Thomas Park's edition of *The Harleian Miscellany* (1808–13), an anthology of sixteenth- and seventeenth-century documents from the second earl of Oxford's collection (see *P&P Strouse*, 358 and *LLC 1856*). See *Cromwell*, vi. 214 and viii. 70, 95. Vol. i of the *Miscellany* includes James Heath's controversial study, *Flagellum, or, The Life, Death, Birth and Burial of Oliver Cromwell* (1663).

52 *what the correction of them ought to be*: see Rokewode, p. x: 'In publishing this Chronicle for the first time, we have thought it best to adhere to the orthography of the MS., at the same time freeing the text from the contractions. Occasionally, at the foot of our pages, we have noted errors of the scribe, or attempted to supply defects; adding often the references to the scriptural or classical allusions of the text.'

one wishes it had been a trifle larger: see the review of *Chronica* in *Gentleman's Magazine* 15 (1841), 175: 'The [Glossary], perhaps, might have been somewhat fuller, as for instance, in one of the extracts we have made, are the words *horologium, tabula*, and *aurea majestas*.' See also Calder, 28–9.

Spelman and Ducange at your elbow: the references are to Sir Henry Spelman, *Archaeologus in Modum Glossarii* (1626) and Charles du Fresne, seigneur du Cange, *Glossarium ad Scriptores Mediæ et Infamæ Latinitatis* (1678) and *Glossarium ad Scriptores Mediæ et Infamæ Græcitatis* (1688).

he who runs ... may read: Hab. 2:2.

Muratori Annals to Radcliffe Romances: Ludovico Antonio Muratori wrote *Rerum Italicarum Scriptores ab anno æræ Christianæ 500 ad annum 1500* (1723–51); Anne Radcliffe was a popular Gothic novelist, author of *A Sicilian Romance* (1790), *The Mysteries of Udolpho* (1794), and *The Italian* (1797).

hair-cilices: penitential hair-shirts.

magical speculum: a speculum is 'a metallic mirror forming part of a reflecting telescope' (*OED*). For the object as a symbol of TC's historical method, see Hill, 'The "Magical Speculum" ' (2004).

camera lucida: (Lat.) 'light chamber'; a photographic instrument for projecting the image of a distant object onto paper so that it can be traced.

Gospel of Richard Arkwright once promulgated: Richard Arkwright's mechanistic innovations in cotton-spinning machinery and manufacture, which according to TC made the monks' methods obsolete.

53 *Mastodon ... Megatherion ... Ichthyosauros*: a mastodon is a mammal resembling an elephant; a megatherion, a large sloth; an ichthyosauros, a marine animal with huge head and extended tail. TC's interest in these extinct species coincided with a visit that he paid on 28 August 1842 to

Richard Owen, curator at the Hunterian Museum at the Royal College of Surgeons, who gave him a tour of the collection (*CL* xv. 51). For the significance of Owen's skeletal archetypes to TC's conception of history, see Ulrich, 'Thomas Carlyle, Richard Owen' (2006).

53 *Rymer's Fœdera*: *Foedera* (1704–35) is a twenty-volume compilation of England's conventions with foreign powers, the first sixteen of which were edited by Thomas Rymer; the work was reissued by the Commission on Public Records, 1816–69.

Doctrines of the Constitution: TC refers to recently published works, including George Bowyer, *The English Constitution: A Popular Commentary on the Constitutional Law of England* (1841) and Henry Hallam, *Constitutional History of England*, 4th edn. (1842). TC borrowed this edition of Hallam from the London Library on 11 August 1842 (*P&P Strouse*, 361 and *LLC 1856*, 178).

Cœur-de-Lion was not a theatrical popinjay with greaves and steel-cap on it: TC may be referring to a revival of the Belgian composer André Gréty's comic opera *Richard Cœur de Lion* (1784), which opened at Covent Garden on 10 October 1842. The piece had been popular among royalists during the French Revolution, who had adopted its aria 'Ô Richard, ô mon Roi' as an anthem (see *FR* i. 188–91 and n.). Reviewing the performance, *The Times* (11 Oct. 1842) commended 'Mr. Travers' in the role of Richard for his performance: 'He sings with a great deal of feeling and earnestness. His only fault is one which arises from want of experience, and that is, that he has not yet learned to conceal his art, and gives a studied effect to his gestures and to his expression' (p. 5). Greaves are 'armour for the leg below the knee' (*OED*).

Peel's Tariff: see note to p. 35.

'Feretrum': (Lat.) 'bier': 'a portable or stationary shrine, often made of or adorned with costly materials, in which were deposited the remains or relics of saints' (*OED*).

ransom him out of the Danube Jail: Rokewode, 34; *Chronicle*, 42. In 1193 the emperor Henry V demanded a ransom of 150,000 marks of silver for the release of Richard I, king of England 1189–99, who was captured while returning from the Third Crusade. As part of a tax demanded to secure his release, religious houses were required to donate their sacred relics.

54 *These clear eyes of neighbour Jocelin looked on . . . King John . . . John Sansterre . . . who signed Magna Charta afterwards in Runnymead*: see Rokewode, 85–6; *Chronicle*, 102–3. John, king of England, 1199–1216, was known in the early 1180s as Lackland (from Fr. 'Sansterre'). He 'signed' Magna Carta with a royal seal at Runnymede, near Windsor, on 15 June 1215.

As through a glass darkly: 1 Cor. 13:12.

cramoisy: archaic word for 'crimson' (*OED*, citing TC).

rack and manger: 'Surrounded by abundance or plenty, wanting for nothing' (*OED*, citing TC).

gave us 'thirteen sterlingii': see Rokewode, 85, and *Chronicle*, 103: 'We naturally thought that he would make a sizeable donation, but he gave only a silk cloth which his servants had on loan from our sacrist—and still they have not paid for it. Although he had accepted St Edmund's most generous hospitality, when [King John] left he contributed nothing at all honourable or beneficial to the Saint, except the 13*d*. which he gave at Mass on the day he left us.'

Egyptian night again: see Exod. 10:22.

the grand peculiarity: see TC, 'Biography' (1832): 'Meanwhile, quitting these airy regions, let anyone bethink him how impressive the smallest historical *fact* may become, as contrasted with the grandest *fictitious event*; what an incalculable force lies for us in this consideration' (*EOL*, 138).

55 *the Minerva*: publishing firm specializing in Gothic and sentimental fiction established by William Lane, 33 Leadenhall St., 1790–*c*.1820.

THE Burg, Bury, or 'Berry' . . . of St. Edmund: see Edmund Gillingwater, *An Historical and Descriptive Account of St. Edmund's Bury in the County of Suffolk* (1804), 9: 'BURGH originally signifies a fortified place, or a place of defence, and is pronounced differently in different parts; in the southern parts, Bury, in others Burgh and Brough, and often Berry and Barrow.'

twenty or fifteen thousand busy souls: see *Abstract of the Population Census of 1841* (1845), 14: 'Bury St. Edmunds, Suff. 12,538'.

towards the rising sun . . . a range of monastic ruins: see Gillingwater, *Account*, 214–15: 'The approach to the Town and Abbey from the East, is both grand and interesting. Passing over the Lark, . . . the eye is at first struck with the rude and awful ruins of the great conventual church, the churches of St. Mary and St. James, all situated in the same yard; part of the ancient pillars and cemetery of the Abbey, are prominent and commanding objects, yielding only to the pre-eminence of the great gate of the Monastery. . . . Beyond these venerable relics of antiquity, appear, uprising on the western ridge, the houses and public edifices of the town, ancient and modern, and the picture at length terminates in a rich horizon of hill and dale, of wood and corn fields.' Gillingwater, *Account*, 62–3 cites John Leland's description from his *Itinerary* (*c*.1535–43): 'A Monastery more noble, whether one considers the endowments, largeness, or unparalleled magnificence, the sun never saw. One might even think the monastery alone a City; it has three grand gates for entrances, . . . many towers, high walls, and a church, than which nothing can be more magnificent.' See also Richard Yates, *History and Antiquities of the Abbey of St. Edmund's Bury*, 2nd edn. (1843), pt. ii., 12: 'The ascents to Guildhall-street and Abbey-gate-street, formerly Cook Row, must have been very considerable; and the view of the Abbey façade, comprising the two fine churches of St. Mary and St. James, the noble Tower Gatehouse, and the magnificent Abbey Gateway, connected, as they all were, by a high embattled wall, must have been unrivalled by any collection of ecclesiastical buildings in the kingdom, if not in Europe.'

55 *payment of one shilling*: see John Deck, *A Guide to the Town, Abbey and Antiquities of Bury St. Edmunds*, 2nd edn. (1836), 91: 'The subscription to the garden is £2.2s. per annum; . . . visitors are admitted by paying 1s. each.'

a botanic garden: the abbey gardens were designed in 1821 by Nathaniel Shirley Harness Hodson and expanded in 1831. See Deck, *Guide* (1836), 90: 'Few gardens in the kingdom can boast of a situation possessing so many advantages: on passing under the splendid arches of the abbey-gate the view extends over the garden to the plantations on St. Edmund's Hill, with the Vine-fields, to the abbey bridge; the river, whose gentle stream meanders along the valley, terminates the grounds of this once far-famed monastic establishment.'

the ancient massive Gateway: the Abbey Gate. See Deck, *Guide* (1836), 43: 'The architecture is of the best period of that style which is generally termed Gothic. The composition is judicious and harmonious: in the western front richness of design predominates; in the eastern, an elegant simplicity. . . . The height of this gate, which was built in the reign of Richard the Second, 1377, and which now forms the entrance to the Botanic Garden, is about sixty-two feet, its length fifty, and its breadth forty-one. The western front is divided into two horizontal compartments by an elegant embattled ornamented band, and perpendicular into three compartments, a centre, and two turriated projecting wings. The whole is superbly ornamented with carved devices and niches for statues.'

that other ancient Gateway, now about to tumble: the Norman Tower, built in the abbacy of Anselm, 1122–48. See Deck, *Guide* (1836), 83–4: 'It is eighty feet in height, of a quadrangular figure, and remarkable for the simple plainness and solidity of its construction. . . . It is to be regretted that time has made considerable ravages on this venerable edifice. In various parts, especially on the side next to the churchyard, wide fissures are conspicuous; and on the other side it is said to be twelve inches out of the perpendicular.' *The Bury and Norwich Post* (17 Aug. 1842), 2 reported that the 'Norman Tower' (also called the 'St James Tower') was 'under the survey of Mr. Cottingham, with the view, we trust, to its entire restoration'. Lewis Nockalls Cottingham, a leading Gothic Revival architect, had previously performed restoration work at Rochester Cathedral, Magdalen College, Oxford, St Alban's Abbey, Armagh Cathedral, and Hereford Cathedral. *The Bury and Norwich Post* (24 Aug. 1842) announced in a lengthy article, excerpts of which were published in the September issue of *Gentleman's Magazine*, that Cottingham 'has now completed his survey of this tower. . . . We are enabled to state that [he] views the injuries of the building in the most serious light. . . . Of the manner in which the arches in the upper stories of the tower have been, not bolstered *up*, but bolstered *out*, by past "repairs," it will give some idea to state that Mr. Cottingham has removed not less than 100 tons of brick, stone, and rubbish, which . . . tended materially to press [the building] more and more out of its balance.' The *Post* concluded that 'Cottingham is confident that the Tower may be restored to its former strength; and the bells may be vocal once more to the feelings of joy or woe, provided that they be properly supported below' (p. 2). In a separate history of the building, the *Post* referred to Rokewode's recent edition of the *Chronica*, and reminded readers that the Tower had once served as the ceremonial entrance to the abbey, where the monks received Abbot Samson after his election on Palm Sunday, 11 March 1182. It was 'converted into a belfry' (Rokewode, 112) for the adjacent parish church of St James around the time of the dissolution of the monastery. In 1785, ten bells were hung in the tower by Thomas Osborn of the Downham Market Foundry in Norfolk (Raven, *The Bells of England* (1906), 222). Subsequent alterations included the removal of a segmental tympanum from the west arch in 1789 to 'let hay-carts through' (Drewett and Stuart, 'Excavations' (1975), 242), the construction of a 'modern and wretchedly barbarous' cupola on the top in 1811, and the addition to the facade of 'a large copper dial plate' in 1824, both of which were removed by Cottingham (Yates, *Antiquities* (1843), pt. ii., 17–18).

subscribe money to cramp it and prop it: the *Bury and Norwich Post* (14 Dec. 1842), published Cottingham's architectural survey of the Norman Tower. He estimated that the cost for the restoration of 'this noble specimen of pure Norman architecture' would be '2,370l' (p. 2). The *Post* (1 Feb. 1843) reported that following a meeting of St James churchwardens held on 5 January 1843, a plan was devised to seek voluntary increases to the church rate as well as to establish 'a general subscription, with a view to carry out the thorough restoration of the structure' (p. 2).

That this was a very great Abbey: see Sir William Dugdale, *Monasticon Anglicanum* (1655, 1661, 1673), iii. 102: 'The statement of the property of St. Edmund's Bury abbey in Domesday is voluminous.' TC used the six-volume edition of 1817–30 (Calder, 37 and n.).

King Canute . . . gave St. Edmund his own gold crown: see Dugdale, *Monasticon Anglicanum*, iii. 99: 'In addition to his grants, K. Canute also honoured the church with his personal devotions. He offered his own crown at the tomb of the martyr.' For the cult of St. Edmund and royal patronage, see Webster, 'The Cult of St. Edmund, King and Martyr' (2020).

such and such a genus, such and such a number: see Dugdale: 'A Convict of Benedictine monks' and 'the establishment of this time appears to have consisted of eighty monks' (*Monasticon Anglicanum*, iii. 99, 117).

carucates: a carucate is 'a measure of land . . . being as much as could be tilled with one plough' (*OED*). See Dugdale, *Monasticon Anglicanum*, iii. 102, 141–53.

56 *large Tower or Belfry . . . smaller Belfry*: structures not to be confused with the Abbey Gate and Norman Tower; see Dugdale, *Monasticon Anglicanum*, iii. 163. Rokewode, 111 claims that the 'great bell tower, and the lateral towers, of the west end of the monastic church [were] begun by Abbot Baldwin, or his successor Robert; ruins of some portion of which are yet to be seen'. But Greenway and Sayers point out that 'it is not clear that there were western towers in Baldwin's church' (*Chronicle*, 129 and n.). See also note to p. 109.

56 *Philosophy of History*: the title of Voltaire's *La Philosophie de l'histoire, par feu l'abbé Bazin* (1765), an attack against intolerance and superstition ('*l'Infâme*') in the cause of science and enlightenment. TC identified the expression with 'modern Narrations, of the Philosophic kind', especially those written by Edward Gibbon, David Hume, and William Robertson, who upheld the 'dignity of history' by ironically exposing the distortions of irrational 'enthusiasm' ('Biography', in *EOL*, 133). For TC and the eighteenth century, see Young, *The Victorian Eighteenth Century* (2007) and O'Gorman and Turner, *The Victorians and the Eighteenth Century* (2004).

Titans: giants of Greek myth.

DRY RUBBISH SHOT HERE!: TC's favourite expression for the clutter of evidence 'dug up' by 'assiduous Pedantry'. Writing to John Sterling on 6 November 1842, TC lamented, 'I am sunk under a thousand fathoms of shot rubbish; and feel for most part as if I should have the life choked clean out of me there' (*CL* xv. 161). The *OED* cites TC in its definition of 'shot' as 'to be rid of'.

Golgotha: place where Jesus was crucified; see Matt. 27:33.

'*save us . . . the expense of salt*': see Ben Jonson, *Bartholomew Fair*, IV. ii. 54–6 and *The Devil is an Asse*, I. vi. 88–90.

57 *a brokened blackened shin-bone of the old dead Ages*: in September 1842, Edward Fitzgerald unearthed artefacts and human remains at the site of the Battle of Naseby (1643). These included a 'shin-bone', which he sent to TC (FitzGerald, *Letters* (1980), i. 360, and *CL* xv. 106). For a photograph and discussion of the artefacts, two of which are now housed in the Library of the University of California, Santa Cruz, see Fielding, 'Carlyle and Cromwell' (1985), 44, 52–3, 63.

twenty generations: from the founding of the monastery in 1020 to its dissolution in 1539.

of many humours: 'In ancient and medieval physiology and medicine: any of four fluids of the body (blood, phlegm, choler, and so-called melancholy or black bile) believed to determine . . . the state of health and the temperament of a person or animal' (*OED*)

World-Dramaturgist: 'A composer of a drama; a playwright' (*OED*, citing TC).

parchment Chartularies: collections of records.

Dryasdust: Dr Jonas Dryasdust, Walter Scott's fictitious pedant.

58 *Beodric's-worth*: see Rokewode, 75; *Chronicle*, 90: 'The manor-house of Beodric, lord of this town in ancient days, after whom the town used to be called "Beodricsworth."' For the etymology, see Dugdale, *Monasticon Anglicanum*, iii. 98.

Fornham St. Genevieve: village N of Bury St Edmunds, where on the banks of the River Lark, 11 October 1173, Flemish mercenaries led by

Robert de Beaumont, third earl of Leicester, in support of the rebellion of 'The Young King' Prince Henry against his father Henry II, were defeated by forces loyal to the king. See Rokewode, 1, 105–6; *Chronicle*, 3, 124. For the battle of Fornham, see Hosler, 'Chivalric Carnage?' (2017).

De Montfort breed: the Leicester title was carried on through the Franco-Norman family of Montfort as a result of the marriage of Amice, daughter of Robert de Beaumont and Petronilla de Grandmesnil, to Simon de Montfort, lord of Montfort-en-Yvelines, Île-de-France. She was the mother of Simon de Montfort, fifth earl of Leicester, military commander in the Albigensian Crusade.

peoþð . . . Estate: (OE) '*peoþð*', or 'worth, value, amount, price, ransom'. TC's etymology is inaccurate.

the Saxon peoþðn . . . to grow, to become: (OE) *peoþðn*, or 'to become, get, be done, be made, happen, arise, take place'.

'Wo worth the hour': Ezek. 30:2.

Threadneedle-street: location of the Bank of England since 1734.

59 *Fornham Church*: Fornham St Genevieve church, on the grounds of Fornham Park, destroyed by fire in 1782.

posse comitatus: (Lat.) 'the power of a country'; group of men available to the sheriff for the suppression of rebellion or disorder.

pleasure-ground to his Grace of Newcastle: 'Newcastle' was changed in later editions to 'Northumberland'. The allusion is to the park of Fornham Hall, purchased in 1789 by Bernard Edward Howard, twelfth duke of Norfolk. He died on 16 March 1842.

Copper pennies of Henry II.: see Rokewode, 106: 'This is a faithful description of the place, and human bones, fragments of weapons, and other relics of war, besides pennies of King Henry II. have been occasionally found upon the spot.'

into that same Lark River or ditch: for the anecdote, see George Lyttelton, *The History of Henry II*, 3rd edn. (1769–73), v. 172: 'The countess, seeing all lost, and coming in her flight to a river, threw into it a ring, with a jewel of great value, which she had on her finger, to prevent its being taken (as she immediately was herself) by those who pursued her.' TC borrowed vols. i and ii of the six-volume third edition of Lyttelton (1769–73) from the London Library on 10 December 1842, and vols. iii–vi on 19 December (*P&P Strouse*, 369; *LLC 1842*, 77). Rokewode also refers the countess of Leicester's ring: 'In the bed of the river, in the adjoining parish of Fornham St. Martin, was . . . found. . . a gold ring with a ruby, late in the possession of Charles Blomfield, Esq. [Charles James Blomfield., bishop of London, 1828–56], which is conjectured by some to be the ring that the Countess of Leicester is related . . . to have thrown away in her flight' (p. 106).

'a circular mound of skeletons wonderfully complete': see Rokewode, 106: 'In felling, in 1826, an ancient pollard ash that stood upon a low mound of earth, about fifteen feet in diameter, near the Church of Fornham St. Genevieve,

... a heap of skeletons, not less than forty, was discovered, in good preservation, piled in order, tier above tier, with their faces upward, and their feet pointing to the centre. Several of the skulls exhibited evident marks of violence, as if they had been pierced with arrows, or cleft with the sword.' The discovery was reported in *The Bury and Norwich Post* (27 Dec. 1826), 1.

59 *admired this ancient Landlord to a quite astonishing degree*: see Yates, *An Illustration of the Monastic Life and Antiquities of the Town and Abbey of St. Edmunds Bury* (1805), 32: 'Having seated Edmund on the throne of East Anglia, his biographers and historians proceed, in a strain of panegyric, to extol the excellence of his government, and the virtuous conduct of his life. . . . He is styled the enemy of flatterers; the protector of the widow and orphan; the father of his people; and a model for all Princes.'

60 *femoralia*: 'A pair of breeches' (*OED*).

preserved his game . . . by 'bushing' or how: 'To protect (land or game) from net-poachers by placing bushes or branches at intervals in the preserved ground, so as to interrupt the sweep of a net' (*OED*, citing TC).

Farmer's Friend: epithet echoing Cobbett's pamphlet, *The Farmer's Friend* (1822), applied ironically by Corn Law opponents to aristocrats. Their particular target was Richard Plantagenet Temple Nugent Brydges Chandos Grenville, second duke of Buckingham and Chandos, who resigned as Lord Privy Seal from the cabinet on 31 January 1842 in protest against Peel's sliding scale duties. See *The Examiner* (5 Mar. 1842), 153: 'The farmer's best friend has . . . the worst farmed estate in England, and . . . has done a thousand times more to injure English agriculture than any man living.'

one does not know: see Yates, *Antiquities* (1805), 33: 'This profusion of encomium, however, is not substantiated by evidence; no fact is stated to illustrate and establish it. We do not find recorded any instance of [St Edmund's] exertion to promote the safety and confirm the happiness of the people.'

'humbly with God': Mic. 6:8.

Howel and James: Howell, James & Co., silk merchants and linen drapers, 9 Regent St. (*The Small Edition of the Post Office London Directory 1843*).

61 *Physical-Force Ultra-Chartists, 'Danes' as they were then called*: TC likens the Danish invaders led by the semi-legendary Ivarr Ragnarsson ('Ivan the Boneless', or Hinguar) in the ninth century to 'Ultra Radical' Chartist proponents of 'physical force', such as Feargus O'Connor.

My life, I think, is my own to do what I like with!: see Richard Baker, *A Chronicle of the Kings of England* (1643), 7: 'The fifteenth king was *Edmund*, who assaulted by the *Danes* for his Possessions, was more assaulted for his Profession; for continuing constant in his Christian Faith, those Pagans first beat him with Bats, then scourged him with Whips, and lastly bound him to a Stake, and with their Arrows shot him to death.' For TC's copy of the 1684 edition of Baker, see Tarr, 'TC's Libraries', 251. See also Yates, *Antiquities* (1805), 40, quoting from Abbo of Fleury's *Passio Sancti Eadmundi*: 'This frail carcase you may break as an earthern vessel, but the freedom of the mind you can never for a moment constrain. . . . For me, to die is glory—to live contumacious bondage.' For the Latin text and English translation of St Edmund's declaration, see Hervey, *Corolla Sancti Eadmundi* (1907), 29–33.

And he died, under barbarous tortures, refusing to the last breath: see Dugdale, *Monasticon Anglicanum*, iii. 99; Paul de Rapin de Thoyras, *The History of England* (1732–3), i. 89; and Yates, *Antiquities* (1805), 41. For TC's copy of Rapin de Thoyras, *History*, see Tarr, 'TC's Libraries', 257.

Another version is, that Edmund . . . stood by his order: see Yates, *Antiquities* (1843), pt. 1, 45: 'Whether King Edmund, as some few writers suppose, lost his life, valiantly defending his country on the plains of Thetford; or, according to far the greater number, was basely murdered in the woods of Eglesdene; his body appears to have been interred in an obscure wooden chapel in a village now called Hoxne.'

Sons of Belial: Deut. 13:13.

washed its wounds with fast-flowing universal tears: Calder, 44 suggests the *Passio Sancti Eadmundi* as TC's source. See Hervey, *Corolla*, 42–3: 'Lifting up . . . with concordant devotion the pearl of inestimable price which they had discovered, and shedding floods of tears for joy, they brought back the head to its body.' See also Yates, *Antiquities* (1805), 42–3.

62 *the Temple of the Highest*: see 2 Chr. 6:18, Matt. 12:6, and Acts 17:23–4.

'Schnüspel the distinguished Novelist': Charles Dickens, who was welcomed by crowds of admirers on his tour of the USA, from 22 January to 7 June 1842. 'Schnüspel', from (Ger.) *Schnipsel* = 'scrap, snippet or thread'. Pratt, 'Carlyle and Dickens' (1983) suggests 'littleness' and quotes JWC: 'Dickens writes for "the greatest happiness of the greatest number" (of cockneys)' (pp. 236–7). TC originally wrote in the Printer's Copy, 'good Pickwick' (*P&P* Strouse, 771).

'all men, especially all women, are born worshippers': see TC, 'Goethe's Works' (1832), in *CME* ii. 396.

Lord Mayors' Shews: from 1751 to 1959, a parade held on 9 November to celebrate the installation of the Lord Mayor of the City of London.

These be thy gods, O Israel: Exod. 32:4.

seek out the severed head, and reverently reunite the same: see Rapin de Thoyras, *History of England*, i. 89: '*Edmund's* Head being found some time after, was interred with his Body at St. *Edmund's-Bury*, so called from him. Whilst the *Roman Catholick* Religion flourished in *England*, great Numbers of Miracles were said to be wrought at his Tomb.' See also Dugdale, *Monasticon Anglicanum*, iii. 99; Gillingwater, *Account*, 34–6; and Yates, *Antiquities* (1805), 42–3.

the very Pope and Cardinals at Rome were forced to hear of it: see Calder, 44: 'Carlyle scarcely could think without supplying concrete details; here he probably went beyond his authority in suggesting canonization by Rome.'

62 *Advocatus-Diaboli*: Devil's advocate.

full assent of 'private judgment': the right of private judgement and the rejection of papal authority were essential tenets of post-Reformation Protestantism denied by the Roman Catholic Church. Edmund retained his status as an Anglican saint after Henry VIII proclaimed the Church of England's separation from Rome in 1534.

loculus: 'A small chamber or cell in an ancient tomb for the reception of a body or an urn' (*OED*, citing TC).

63 *a wooden chapel, a stone temple*: the wooden church, built in 1032, replaced by the stone church in 1095. See Yates, *Antiquities* (1805), 78: 'The Sacrists . . . demolished the church which had been lately erected; and as that had been constructed of wood, . . . another structure was erected of hewn stone, in which "the precious, undefiled, uncorrupted Body of the most Glorious King and Martyr, St. Edmund," was translated.'

Ocean-tide would not be forbidden to wet: see Rapin de Thoyras, *History of England*, i. 126–7; Baker, *A Chronicle* 16; and Robert Henry, *The History of Great Britain*, 2nd edn. (1789–94), ii. 83. For TC's copy of the 1789–94 edition of Henry, *History*, see Tarr, 'TC's Libraries', 255.

Beodric's-worth has become St. Edmund's Bury: see Yates, *Antiquities* (1805), 51: '*Betricheswyrth* was discontinued; and the town began about this period to be called *St. Edmund's Bury*.'

present respectable Mayor of Bury may be said, like a Fakeer . . . to have his dwelling in the extensive, many-sculptured Tombstone of St. Edmund; in one of the brick niches thereof: John Greene, mayor of Bury St Edmunds, 9 November 1841 to 19 November 1842, lived at 1 The Churchyard, Abbey Ruins. See Introduction, p. xii. A fakeer (or fakir) is defined as 'Properly an indigent person, but especially applied to a Mahommedan religious mendicant, and then loosely, and inaccurately, to Hindu devotees and naked ascetics' (*OED*). TC's arguments against 'Dilettante' restoration resurfaced in the late 1980s, with the decision of the local authorities to restore the houses built in the niches rather than conduct further architectural investigation of the medieval west transept. See McAleer, 'The West-Facade Complex' (1998), 145–6: 'As the interiors of the infilling houses possessed no architectural qualities of any merit or interest, . . . the houses were more a matter of curiosity than of significance. Since by the late 1980s the structures were in such dilapidated condition as to be in many places unsafe and verging on collapse, their "restoration" has become a matter of complete new building,—therefore, in fact, not restoration at all. These intrusive structures could and should have been removed, except perhaps for their façade walls filling the large arches of the giant recesses, which are of minor interest and mild aesthetic impact. To rebuild these derelict structures, at the expense of further archaeological investigation of the west front, and indeed, to make such investigations nearly impossible, . . . reflects a very topsy-turvy set of values. Lamentably, a monument of outstanding historical importance is thereby reduced to a merely picturesque framework for a mundane function.'

pyramid or 'flame-mountain': see Hughes, 296–7: 'πυρ = fire, the Greek form being πυραμίς; which is an old explanation. The word is, however, of Egyptian origin.'

Cheops Pyramids or Sakhara clay ones: the references are to the tomb of King Cheops at Giza, 'the Great Pyramid', built of stone, and to the pyramids at Saqqara, built of bricks.

cattle, says my erudite friend!: see Du Cange, *Glossarium . . . Latinitatis* (1678), 882: '*Catallum* is the same as *capitale*, and denotes *cattle*.'

64 *ABBOT HUGO*: Hugh, abbot of Bury St Edmunds in 1157.

Bird-of-Paradise . . . with outspread wings: legendary floating bird living on scent or dew. See Tennyson, 'Day-Dreams' (1842), Epilogue: 'Like long-tailed birds of Paradise | That float through Heaven, and cannot light?' (ll. 7–8).

Drury-lane Theatre: Theatre Royal, Drury Lane, managed between 1841 and 1843 by the Carlyles' friend, William Charles Macready.

aliquantulum caligaverunt oculi ejus: Rokewode, 1; *Chronicle*, 3.

Dominus Abbas: (Lat.) 'Lord Abbot'.

65 *His one worldly care was to raise ready money*: Rokewode, 2; *Chronicle*, 3.

sufficient for the day is the evil thereof: Matt. 6:34.

usurious insatiable Jews: from the reign of Henry I, Jews were granted special protections and privileges as a result of their wealth and fiscal expertise. This policy was maintained by King Henry II and Richard I, but was challenged by figures such as Abbot Samson, who feared that the authority of the monasteries was being eroded by the influence of 'Hebrew' financiers. Frequent attempts by these monarchs to impose higher taxes on their creditors forced Jewish lenders to demand repayment of loans or increase interest rates, which in turn provoked popular antagonism towards them.

fresh horseleech: TC's term for a usurer, 'a rapacious, insatiable person' (*OED*).

crying continually, Give, Give!: Prov. 30:15.

William the Sacristan: a monk managing the abbey's buildings and furnishings, including the storehouse (*camera*). His cordial relations with the Jewish community angered Abbot Samson.

Benedict the Jew: he and his brother Jurnet were major financiers of the Crown.

Cellerarius or any public officer: (Lat.) *cellarius* = cellarer, the obedientiary placed in charge of an abbey's food and wine pantry, or *cellarium*.

Benedict's Twenty-seven pounds grew rapidly at compound-interest: Rokewode, 2; *Chronicle*, 4.

'Twelve hundred pounds besides interest': Rokewode, 2–3; *Chronicle*, 4.

65 *beleaguered Jews who hanged themselves in York Castle shortly afterwards*:
TC's source for the York massacres is Rapin de Thoyras, *History of England*
(see i. 245 and n.). On 16 March 1190, Palm Sunday weekend, the Jewish
community of York sought royal protection in Clifford's Tower after being
attacked by a violent mob. Many committed suicide, cutting the throats of
their wives and children rather than surrendering to the besiegers. Those
who tried to escape were slaughtered. Three days later on 18 March, the
townspeople of Bury St Edmunds massacred fifty-seven Jews. In October,
Abbot Samson sought and received King Richard I's permission to expel
the Jewish community from Bury on the pretext that it posed a threat to the
legal jurisdiction of the monastery. See Rokewode, 33; *Chronicle*, 42–3. For
the background and history of the Jewish persecution in York and Bury, see
Rees Jones and Watson, *Christians and Jews in Angevin England* (2013);
Widner, 'Samson's Touch and a Thin Red Line' (2012); and Bale, 'Anti-
Semitism and Hagiography in Medieval Suffolk' (2002).

usances . . . quittances . . . summarily set fire to!: a usance is 'a document
acknowledging a loan of money' (*OED*, citing TC); a quittance is 'a release
or discharge from a debt, obligation, etc'. (*OED*). In the First Draft, TC
deletes 'the Shylock, Jew that Shaksp drew!' after 'horseleech papers summarily consumed by fire' (Calder, 61–3).

66 *grinder-teeth successively pulled out of their head*: the original source for the
story is Matthew Paris, *Historia Anglorum* (*c.*1250–5); see Frederic
Madden, *Mattæi Parisiensis* (1866–9), ii. 121. In 1210, King John forcibly
expropriated the assets of the Jewish community to fund his army in
a campaign against the pope. TC's source is Rapin de Thoyras, *History of
England*, i. 270 and n.: 'The *Jews* of both Sexes were seized all over
England, and cruelly treated, till they would ransom themselves, according
to the King's Pleasure. Among the rest, a *Jew* at *Bristol*, though cruelly tormented, refusing to ransom himself, the King ordered that his Tormentors
should every Day pull out one of his Cheek Teeth, till he would pay down
ten thousand Marks. Accordingly they pulled out seven as in many Days,
but on the eighth Day he relented, and so with the Loss of seven Teeth,
parted with the ten thousand Marks to save the rest.' TC remembered the
anecdote. On 11 June 1861, Dickens reported in a letter to Macready that
'Carlyle has greatly intensified his aversion to Jews, and is greatly enraged
by beholding the gradual rise of of a mansion that [Lionel] Rothschild is
building next the Duke of Wellington's. He was with us the other day,
representing your old friend King John as an enlightened sovereign in
respect of drawing the teeth of Jews, to make them shed their money; and
was comforting himself with an imaginary picture of Rothschild haled to
the court of Queen Victoria, and having several double teeth pulled out'
(*Dickens Letters*, ix. 425). For TC's anti-Semitism in *Past and Present*, see
Park, 'Thomas Carlyle and the Jews' (1990), 2–3. TC's Chartist disciple
Isaac Ironside (see Introduction, p. xl), who regarded *Past and Present* as
a political manifesto, was evidently inspired by his mentor's anti-Semitism.
At a meeting of the Sheffield Town Council on 12 January 1848, he attacked

Lord John Russell's civil disabilities bill, claiming that the 'measure would place the government of this country in the hands of the Jews . . . who never do any work but live by the industry of the people' (*Sheffield and Rotheram Independent*, 22 Jan. 1848, 6).

Eadmer's Anselm: Eadmer of Canterbury wrote a two-part biography of St Anselm, archbishop of Canterbury, chronicling his public life in *Historia Novorum* (*c.*1124) and private life in *Vita S. Anselmi* (*c.*1124). TC borrowed John Selden's edition of *Eadmeri Monachi Cantuariensis Historiæ Nouorum, siue, sæculi libri VI* (1623) from the London Library on 7 October 1842 (*P&P Strouse*, 376; *LLC 1842*, 108). In his Journal TC recorded: 'Eadmer (by Selden, well edited, incorrectly printed) is also a monk-chronicle, worth its paper and ink' (*CL* xv. 131 and n.).

'personal religion': Methodism; see the next note.

have as yet nothing of 'Methodism': TC equates John Wesley's movement with idle introspection. See Robert Southey, *The Life of Wesley* (1820), i. 54–5: '[Methodists] drew up a scheme of self-examination, to assist themselves, by means of prayer and meditation, in attaining simplicity and the love of God. Except that it speaks of obeying the laws of the Church of England, it might fitly be appended to the spiritual exercises of St. Ignatius Loyola. Its obvious faults were, that such self-examination would leave little time for anything else; that the habits of life which it requires and pre-supposes would be as burthensome as the rules of the monastic orders; and that the proposed simplicity would generally end in producing the worst of artificial characters; for where it made one out of a thousand a saint, it would make the rest inevitably formalists and hypocrites.'

67 *Pharoah's lean kine*: Gen. 41:17–31.

assembles us in Chapter: the chapterhouse, adjoining the church; see Rokewode, 2; *Chronicle*, 5.

'If there is any complaint?': Rokewode, 3; *Chronicle*, 5.

'Fili mi': (Lat.) 'My son'.

Hinghams, Hugo and Robert: Rokewode, 3; *Chronicle*, 5. Rokewode identifies them as the brothers Hugh and Roger of Ingham.

what could poor old Abbot Hugo do?: Rokewode, 5–6; *Chronicle*, 7–8.

to St. Thomas of Canterbury: to the shrine of Thomas à Becket, archbishop of Canterbury.

One thing we cannot mention without a due thrill of horror: Rokewode, 6; *Chronicle*, 8.

68 *Ranulf de Glanvill Justiciarius of England for him*: the justiciar was 'the chief political and judicial officer . . . who represented the king in all relations of state, acting as regent in his absence and as royal deputy in his presence' (*OED*). See Rokewode, 20; *Chronicle*, 25.

St. Edmundsbury Town paying yearly Forty pounds for that express end: Rokewode, 53; *Chronicle*, 65.

68 *We have Processions . . . Mysteries . . . at which latter the Townsfolk sometimes quarrel*: medieval mystery or miracle plays based on biblical stories or the lives of saints, performed at Easter and Christmas. See Rokewode, 68–70; *Chronicle*, 82–3.

Friar Bacon's Brass Head: a brass head that speaks through the power of Satanic magic in Robert Greene's play *Friar Bacon and Friar Bungay* (1594). As one of the head's inventors Roger Bacon sleeps, it speaks three times, saying 'Time Was', 'Time Is', and 'Time's Past', and then shatters on the floor. See *FR* i. 153.

We are such stuff as Dreams are made of!: *Tempest*, IV. i. 156–7.

69 *Fullones, 'Fullers'*: see Rokewode, 76; *Chronicle*, 91. Cloth-makers who used the fuller 'to give (linen) a crimped or wavy edge' (*OED*).

We have Fairs too, Nundinæ: Rokewode, 55–6; *Chronicle*, 67.

Londoners . . . pretending that they . . . are exempt from toll: from the reign of Henry 1, Londoners were entitled to this exemption by royal charter. Samson challenged the edict and argued that 'before the Norman Conquest, St Edward [the Confessor] had granted and confirmed' to the Monastery 'toll and team and all regalian rights' (*Chronicle*, 67).

'dungheaps' lying quiet at most doors (ante foras . . .), for the Town has yet no improved police: Rokewode, 76; *Chronicle*, 92; *ante foras* (Lat.) 'before the doors'.

claim wager of battle: see Hughes, 300: 'The right of invoking the ordeal of battle, both in criminal and civil suits was introduced by William I.'

'Ketel the thief,' took this course; and it did nothing for him: Rokewode, 75; *Chronicle*, 89.

our Cellerarius to collect the repselver: Rokewode, 73; *Chronicle*, 88.

'vetulæ exibant cum colis suis,' says Jocelin, 'minantes et exprobrantes': see Rokewode, 73; *Chronicle*, 88: 'little old women came out with their distaffs threatening and reproaching him and his officers'.

to shriek, and rush out with your distaffs: 'A cleft staff . . . on which wool or flax was wound. . . . Hence symbolically, for the female sex, female authority or dominion' (*OED*, citing TC). 'There are Female Patriots . . . who have changed the distaff for the dagger' (*FR* iii. 116).

become Female Chartists, and . . . demand some Five-point Charter: *The Examiner* (22 Oct. 1842) reported that on 18 October 1842, a meeting organized by the activist Susanna Inge was held at the National Charter Association Hall, 55 Old Bailey, 'for the purpose of forming a "Female Chartist Association," to co-operate with the Male Association; and for other objects connected with the interests of "the People's Charter" '. The paper quoted remarks made at the meeting by Mary Ann Walker, who defended the role of women in the movement, and declared that the 'events which were at that moment taking place in the north, where their sisters and brothers were . . . demanding bread to appease their hunger and save themselves from dying of starvation . . . , were unfortunately of a nature to drag women from her retirement, and call upon her to lift up her voice against such deeds' (p. 682). In an editorial, *The Times* (22 Oct. 1842) mocked the meeting of the 'hen Chartists' and compared the speech of Walker unfavourably to that of the 'Lady-speaker' quoted by TC in his essay 'Parliamentary History of the French Revolution' (1837): 'MR. CARLYLE, in his miscellanies, has translated from the French *Histoire Parlementaire*, an account of a somewhat analogous proceeding in the Hall of the Jacobins, which we cannot help suggesting to the she-Chartists as a model for future proceedings. On the 18th of December, 1791, a deputation of ladies, "accustomed to honour the galleries with their presence," appeared there to hang up the flags of the English, French, and American nations, and to present a "pledge of their enthusiasm" to a "constitutional Whig," the bearer of congratulations to the National Assembly from the birds of his feather in England. Hark to the speech of the French *Citoyenne*, MISS MARY ANNE! . . . How different the sensibility of your prototype, from your "womanly scorn" and "contemptible scoundrel", MISS MARY ANN WALKER.' Quoting further excerpts from TC's essay, *The Times* continues: 'Let us stop to point out the superiority in effect of this tol-de-rol chorus of Jacobins to the "Hear, Hear," "Order, Order," and "Bravo, Miss WALKER," with which the speeches of our countrywomen are garnished. . . . When will Old Bailey get up anything like this? This would be worth doing. Let Miss SUSANNAH and MARY ANN read, learn, take courage, and try to imitate next time' (p. 4).

70 *Jerusalem was taken by the Crusaders, and again lost by them*: seized by the Crusaders under Godfroy de Bouillon in July 1099, and retaken by Saladin in October 1187.

Richard Cœur-de-Lion 'veiled his face': see Jean, Sire de Joinville, *Mémoires* (1819) in Claude Petitot et al. (eds.), *Collection complète des mémoires* (1819–29), ii. 358–9: 'And as they were discussing these sayings, one of the adjutants of the King of England cried out and said to him, Sir, Sir, come here and I will show you Jerusalem. And he covered his eyes with his coat of arms while weeping, and said to our Lord in a loud voice, Ha! Sire God, I pray you that you do not see your holy city of Jerusalem; then so be it, that I cannot deliver it from the hands of your enemies'. For TC and Petitot et al.'s collection, see *CL* vi. 331 and n.; vii. 91 and n.; and *LLC 1842*, 67.

trouble with the Lakenheath eels: Rokewode, 75–6; *Chronicle*, 91.

King Knut . . . or rather his Queen: see Rokewode, 150–1: 'Ælfgivu, Queen of Canute, gave to the Monastery yearly four thousand eels.'

vix dexem denarios et obolum: (Lat.) 'scarcely half the money'. See Rokewode, 75; *Chronicle*, 91.

aver-pennies . . . avragiums . . . fodercorns: aver-pennies are 'money paid in lieu of "average"'; avragium is 'some kind of service due by tenants to the feudal superior'; a fodercorn is 'a supply of fodder (or its monetary equivalent) provided to a feudal lord or other authority' (*OED*).

70   *under such conditions and averages as it can*: Rokewode, 21; *Chronicle*, 27.

Gurth born thrall of Cedric: see note to p. 34.

a Robert Hood, a William Scarlet and others have . . . taken to living, in some universal-suffrage manner: in 1795 the antiquary and French Revolutionary sympathizer Joseph Ritson published *Robin Hood: A Collection of All the Ancient Poems, Songs, and Ballads Now Extant Related to that Celebrated English Outlaw*. He portrayed Hood as a Jacobin precursor who pursued justice by 'transferring the superfluities of the rich to the necessities of the poor' (vol. i, p. xl). For Ritson and radicalism, see Barczewski, *Myth and National Identity in Nineteenth Century Britain* (2000), 43–4. See also Augustin Thierry, *Histoire de la conquête de l'Angleterre par les Normands* (1825), who locates Robin Hood in the years 1189–94, during the period of Richard I's captivity in Germany (see note to p. 53): 'Around the time when the hero of the Norman aristocracy visited Sherwood Forest, there lived in this same forest a man who was the hero of the poor, of the serfs, and of the Anglo-Saxon race.' Thierry refers to 'Robert, or more commonly, Robin Hood' and his cohorts, 'Little John', 'Scath Loke', and 'Brother Tuck' (*Histoire*, iii. 233, 236). *LLC 1842*, 117 lists the 1835 four-volume fifth edition of *Histoire de la conquête*.

under the greenwood tree!: *As You Like It*, II. v. 3–9.

71   *Willelmus Conquestor burnt the Country*: William I's campaign in 1069 to vanquish Danish invaders and their English allies. See Rapin de Thoyras, *History of England*, i. 172: 'As soon as the Siege [of York] was over, and the King found it in his Power to be revenged of the *Northumbrians*, he ravaged their Country in so merciless a manner, that for sixty Miles together, between *York* and *Durham*, he did not leave a single House standing. . . . It is impossible . . . to describe the Miseries of the northern Countries. The Lands lying untilled, and the Houses being destroyed, People died in heaps, after having endeavoured to prolong a wretched Life by eating of the most unclean Animals, and sometimes even human Flesh.'

The Ribble and the Aire roll down, as yet unpolluted by dyers' chemistry: the Ribble and the Aire are rivers in Yorkshire. In *Suggestions for the Improvement of our Towns and Houses* (1843), Thomas John Maslen described the condition of 'the river Aire, which runs through Leeds. Instead of being an ornament to the town, and a minister of pleasures to its citizens, by boating, swimming, and fishing, its banks are crowded and shut up with buildings, and its waters are like a reservoir of poison . . . . In that part of the river, extending from Armley mills to the King's mills, it is charged with the drainage and contents of about two hundred water-closets, cesspools, and privies, a great number of common drains, . . . chemical soap, gas, drug, dye-houses, and manufactures, spent blue and black dye, . . . with all sorts of dead animal and vegetable substances, and now and then a decomposed human body' (pp. 98–9).

Saint Mungo rules in Glasgow: St Kentigern, or St Mungo, was a seventeenth-century missionary identified with a cult based in Glasgow and the kingdom of Strathcylde.

James Watt: Scottish inventor of the steam engine, and herald of the machine age in the late eighteenth century.

Lither-pool: see Hughes, 301, quoting Henry Bradley: 'Liverpool is older than Litherpool, though the corruption is of quite early date. . . . The original name was Welsh *llifair* = overflow, "pool" being added afterwards.'

Tempus ferax, tempus edax rerum: (Lat.) 'Time the bearer, Time the devourer of things'; see Ovid, *Metamorphoses*, xv. 234.

Joe-Mantons!: see note to p. 40.

72 *a shadow of realities eternal*: see *Sartor*, 195: 'These limbs . . . are dust and shadow; a Shadow-system gathered around our ME; wherein, through some moments or years, the Divine Essence is to be revealed in the flesh.'

'pleasure of virtue': Bentham's argument that actions are virtuous that promote 'the greatest happiness of the greatest number'. See note to p. 20.

copperas banker's ink: 'Applied to green copperas, the proto-sulphate of iron or ferrous sulphate, also called green vitriol, used in dying, tanning, and making ink' (*OED*). See TC, *Chartism*, in *CME* iv. 144.

Mammon is not a god at all; but a devil: compare William Blake, *Laocoön* (1820): 'Money, which is the Great Satan or Reason | the Root of Good & Evil | In the Accusation of Sin'. For Blake, TC, and 'mammon-worship', see John, *Supreme Fictions* (1974), 96–101.

reflect, with Ben Jonson, that soul is indispensable: see note to p. 56.

and lodge them gratis: Rokewode, 7; *Chronicle*, 9.

into our Pitanceria; where they abide safe, with due pittances: Rokewode, 8; *Chronicle*, 10. From (Fr.) *pitancerie*, *pittancer*, 'officer in a religious house having the duty of distributing and accounting for pittances' of food (*OED*).

73 *Some of us can preach, in English-Saxon, in Norman-French, and even in Monk-Latin*: TC invents these words, based on details in Rokewode, 30; *Chronicle*, 37.

'frequentes bibationes et quædam tacenda': (Lat.) 'a lot of drinking and some things not to be uttered'. See Rokewode, 23; *Chronicle*, 28: 'The abbot even ordered the sacrist's house in the cemetery to be completely demolished, as if it were not fit to stand upon the earth, on account of the frequent drinking sessions and other unmentionable activities of which he had been made painfully aware as subsacrist.'

'tempora minutionis': (Lat.) 'times of decline'. Rokewode, 11; *Chronicle*, 14.

we can by rule amass to the extent of 'two shillings': Rokewode, 28; *Chronicle*, 35.

a certain Canterbury Monk . . . 'slipping, clanculo from his sleeve': for the anecdote, see Eadmer, *Historiæ Nouorum*, 8. *Clanculo* (Lat.) 'secretly, privately'.

73 *Lanfranc the noble Archishop*: Norman monk who served as archbishop of Canterbury, 1070–89.

'Fili mi, a burnt child shuns the fire': Rokewode, 3; *Chronicle*, 5.

'Norfolk Barrator,' or litigious person: Rokewode, 31; *Chronicle*, 39.

getting slightly streaked with grey: Rokewode, 29; *Chronicle*, 36.

from Tottington in Norfolk: Rokewode, 121.

74 *That once in his ninth year he had an alarming dream*: Rokewode, 27; *Chronicle*, 34.

has studied at Paris: Rokewode, 32; *Chronicle*, 40.

has taught in the Town Schools here: Rokewode, 25; *Chronicle*, 31.

like Dr. Caius, 'has had losses': TC confuses Caius, the French physician in Shakespeare's *The Merry Wives of Windsor*, with Dogberry in *Much Ado about Nothing*, 'who hath had losses' (IV. ii. 90).

in the time of the Antipopes: the antipope Victor IV (Cardinal Octavian), candidate of the Holy Roman Emperor Frederick Barbarossa, was installed on 7 September 1159, the same day as Alexander III was elected by a majority of the cardinals. Following the death of Victor IV in 1164, three more schismatic popes succeeded him, all appointed by the emperor.

as yet not grown chimerical: TC refers to Gregory XVI, pope from 1831 to 1846, an ultramontanist who aligned the papacy with the conservative views of the Austrian minister of foreign affairs Prince Metternich, and who 'pursued a policy in reaction against "innovators," meaning political liberalism and the French Revolution and all it stood for' (Chadwick, *History of the Popes* (1998), 1).

75 *I, however, pretended to be Scotch*: see Calder, 98–9: 'The vivacious story of Samson's journey to Rome, already referred to as a narrative developed in more than one stage in the First Draft . . . , comes to a climax in a translation. Attracted more and more by concrete details, perhaps by the humor of the monk's impersonating a Scotchman, Carlyle begins by telling the episode in one sentence and ends by indicating a full translation of Samson's "personal narrative".'

Ride, ride Rome; turne Cantwereberei: see Greenway and Sayers in *Chronicle*, 136 and n.: 'I am riding to Rome and have nothing to do with Canterbury'.

76 *Geoffry Ridell*: royal clerk who acquired the church of Woolpit in Suffolk in 1161, succeeded Thomas à Becket as acting chancellor in 1162, and became archdeacon in 1163. He was elected bishop of Ely in 1173.

'You know what trouble I had for that Church of Woolpit . . . except by stealth': Rokewode, 35–6; *Chronicle*, 43–4. Greenway and Sayers suggest that Alexander III ruled in favour of Bury on 12 January 1162, possibly confirming the bull Samson had obtained earlier (*Chronicle*, 136 and n.).

Such resting and welcoming found Brother Samson . . . clap 'foot-gyves on him' . . . '. . . and there I had to stay long': TC embellishes Samson's narrative;

see Rokewode 36; *Chronicle* 44–5. For the 'foot-gyves', or shackles, see Rokewode, 13; *Chronicle*, 33.

Our Lord Abbot next tried Samson with promotions . . . made him Librarian: For the Lord Abbot and promotions, see Rokewode, 5; *Chronicle*, 7; for Samson's ambition to be a librarian, see Rokewode, 27; *Chronicle*, 33.

Se nunquam vidisse: (Lat.) 'he had never seen himself'. Rokewode, 5; *Chronicle*, 7.

77 *In this way, not without troubles . . . practice on the Nurse's part will not be necessary!*: Rokewode, 7–8; *Chronicle*, 9–10. *Warinus monachus noster* (Lat.) 'Warren, our monk'.

Samson again obeys in silence: Rokewode, 8; *Chronicle*, 10–11.

come great news to St. Edmundsbury: Rokewode, 12; *Chronicle*, 15.

'one and twenty penitential Psalms, on our knees in the Choir': Rokewode, 8; *Chronicle*, 11: 'Three times a week after coming out of chapter, we prostrated ourselves in choir to sing the seven penitential Psalms.'

Dionysius' Ear: Dionysius the elder, tyrant of Syracuse, said to have made a subterranean cave, known as Dionysius' Ear, from which he could hear what was said by the prisoners confined there. See *Sartor*, 178.

Virgil's Horn-Gate of Dreams: see *Aeneid*, vi. 893, where Virgil describes the two gates of sleep from which dreams emanate: the true, from a gate of horn, and the false, from a gate of ivory.

Even gossip, seven centuries off, has significance: TC likens Jocelin to Boswell, who breached the conventions of the 'dignity of history' by giving priority to 'Gossip, Egotism, Personal Narrative . . . , Scandal, Raillery, Slander, and such like; the sum-total of which . . . constitutes that other grand phenomenon still called "Conversation"' ('Biography', in *EOL*, 132).

78 *'Dixit quidam de quodam...' . . . he never after looked at me with the same face again!*: Rokewode, 9–11; *Chronicle*, 11–14.

Candlemas season of the year 1182: the feast of the purification of the blessed Virgin Mary, 2 February.

Who shall be Abbot?: Rokewode, 15; *Chronicle*, 19: 'This one, and that one, and so-and-so have been chosen, and one of them is going to be abbot.'

79 *The sochemanni speak of it*: see John Harland, *Mamecestre: Being Chapters from the Early Recorded History of the Barony* (1861–2), i. 19 and n.: '*Freemen* or freeholders were those who held by free or military tenure, as distinguished from those who held by base or servile tenure. *Socmen* (from *Soca*, a soke, privilege, liberty or immunity) the occupiers of lands free from certain named services and other burdens.'

get ready 'Twelve Monks,' and set off with them to his Majesty at Waltham: Rokewode, 15; *Chronicle*, 19. Bishop's Waltham, Hampshire, 10 miles (16.1 km) SE of Winchester, residence of Richard of Ilchester, bishop of Winchester.

79 *Given the men a People choose . . . A heroic people chooses heroes, and is happy*:
in a review of *Past and Present*, *The Examiner* (29 Apr. 1843), 260 commented upon this passage: '[Mr Carlyle] sees no hope but in a kind of
radical universal alteration of our ways of life and regimen, whereby we
shall begin to know ourselves healthier . . . when in the work of self-reform
the veil drops off from quackery, and we find ourselves suddenly ashamed
of the worship of sham heroes'.

*how the St. Edmundsbury mountain manages its midwifery; and what mouse
or man the outcome is*: see Horace, *Ars poetica*, 139.

80 *ACCORDINGLY our Prior assembles us in Chapter; . . . under penalty of . . .
limbo . . . we struggle to ascertain what its virtual aim is, and succeed better or
worse*: Rokewode, 12; *Chronicle*, 15–16. Limbo is 'a region supposed to
exist on the border of Hell as the abode of the just who died before Christ's
coming, and of unbaptized infants' (*OED*).

Will the Dominus Rex allow us to choose freely?: see Rokewode, 12–13;
Chronicle, 16. *Dominus Rex* (Lat.) 'Lord King', i.e. Henry II.

*What if the Thirteen should not themselves be able to agree? . . . Six of our
venerablest elders . . . with their eye on the Sacrosancta . . . agree on Three . . .
that no man's secret bring him into trouble*: see Rokewode, 13; *Chronicle*,
16–17. *Sacrosancta* (Lat.) 'most holy', referring to the shrine of St Edmund
and its relics.

81 *So Samson advises, . . . 'Verba Mea, Give ear unto my words, O Lord, My
meditation weigh,' . . . and his Twelve will be ready to get under way*:
Rokewode, 13; *Chronicle*, 17. Ps. 5:1.

electoral winnowing-machine they have at St. Edmundsbury: see John Sproule,
A Treatise on Agriculture Suited to the Soil and Climate of Ireland (1839), 80:
'The objects accomplished by the winnowing machine are the removal of
the husks or chaff of the corn from the grain, and the separation of the
impurities and loose refuse intermixed.'

salt itself will not save us!: see Matt. 5:13. TC may also be alluding to the
invigorating effect of salt in soil, as well as to its presence in the composition of manure. See Sproule, *Treatise*, 44: '[Salt] has . . . been extensively
used as a manure. . . . Soils abounding in salt . . . have been found to produce herbage very nutritive and wholesome.' See also note to p. 56.

'his frock-skirt, looped over his elbows': Rokewode, 14; *Chronicle*, 18.

*across your Fleam-dike and Devil's-dike, no longer useful as a Mercian East-
Anglian boundary or bulwark*: earthen barriers, serving in the seventh cen-
tury as East Anglian fortifications against the warring Mercians, with the
Devil's Ditch following the boundary of St Edmund's Abbey, and the
Fleam running between Fulborn and Balsham in East Cambridgeshire, of
Bury St Edmunds.

82 *and he will rage among you like a wolf, sæviet ut lupus*: Rokewode, 14;
Chronicle, 18: 'You shall have one of your own, but he will rage among you
like a wolf.' Samson himself refers to the dream: 'I would do better to

remember the dream that was narrated about me before I was made abbot that I would rage like a wolf' (Rokewode, 27; *Chronicle*, 34). See also Butler, 19: 'You shall have one of your own, but he shall raven among you like a wolf.' Georgianna, 'Carlyle and Jocelin of Brakelond' (1980) contrasts Jocelin's deepening scepticism about Samson's 'ravening' in the *Chronicle* and TC's consistent 'hero-worship' of the abbot. Of this passage she remarks, 'When Carlyle first reports the dream, he simply changes the prophet's message, draining from it all possible ambiguity by substituting an innocuous "and" for Jocelin's "but"' (p. 109). Gerrard, 'Jocelin of Brakelond' (2014) comments that the image, derived from Matt. 7:15, was traditionally ambiguous: 'On the one hand, we retain the sense of monastic restraint on an innate ferocity. On the other, we have the idea that the convent's misbehaviour could make it Samson's *duty* to be wrathful' (p. 9).

alb and pallium, and with the attitude of one about to fight: for alb and pallium, see Altick, 83 and n.: 'Surplice and woollen vestment, the latter worn by archbishops'. TC combines details from the dreams of two monks, William of Hastings and Edmund; see Rokewode, 15; *Chronicle*, 18–19.

But now . . . at Waltham . . . the 22d day of February, year 1182 . . . The Winchester Manorhouse has fled bodily . . . Why there . . . peep through the blankets of the old Night . . . in what hangings or costume soever?: see Rokewode, 14–15; *Chronicle*, 19–20. Rokewode dates the meeting 21 February. Bishop's Waltham Palace was built in 1136 as a castle by Henry de Blois, bishop of Winchester, and restored in the 1160s, possibly by Richard of Ilchester. See Prossner, 'The Ruins of South Waltham Palace', *Antiquities of Hampshire* (1842), n.p.: 'In 1182 the King held "apud Waltham Episcopi Winton," a great council of the nobles of the realm, who granted him supplies for the carrying on of the Crusades, amounting to 42,000 marks of silver, and 500 of gold. The council was doubtless held at the palace, and the immediate scene of it was probably the great hall.' The palace was destroyed in 1644 after a siege by parliamentary forces. Cf. *Macbeth* I. v. 53.

83 *The Dominus Rex, benignantly receiving our Thirteen . . . commands by . . . Galfridus Cancellarius, Henry's and the Fair Rosamond's authentic Son . . . the names . . . of Hugo Tertius-Prior*: Rokewode, 15–16; *Chronicle*, 19–20. Galfridus Cancellarius is Geoffrey, the illegitimate son of Henry II, and rumoured by early authorities to be the offspring of the king's mistress, Rosamund Clifford; he was appointed royal chancellor in 1181, and elected archbishop of York in 1189.

The higher dignitaries . . . Tickle me Toby . . . Deus est cum eis . . . Pares and Episcopi, Lords or 'Law-wards' . . . The Monks wait silent in an outer room: Rokewode, 16; *Chronicle*, 19–20. 'Tickle me Toby,' a popular proverb, i.e. 'tickle me, and I will tickle you'. *Deus est cum eis* (Lat.) 'God is with them'. *Pares and Episcopi* (Lat.) 'peers and bishops'. 'Law-wards,' TC's etymology; see Hughes, 334: 'From Old English *hláford*, *hláfweard*, "keeper of the loaf"'.

In short while, they are next ordered . . . two only, Samson Subsacrista and the Prior: Rokewode, 16; *Chronicle*, 20–1.

84 '*Which of the two do you want?*' . . . *orders that Samson be brought in with the other Twelve*: Rokewode, 16–17; *Chronicle*, 21–2.

The King's Majesty . . . '*Miserere mei Deus, After thy loving-kindness, Lord, Have mercy upon me;*' . . . '*By God's eyes . . . govern the Abbey well*' . . . *may the Lord have mercy on him as Abbot!*: Rokewode, 17; *Chronicle*, 21–2. TC quoting Jocelin, begins Ps. 50.1 of the Vulgate (Rokewode, 17 n. 3) in Latin, *miserere mei Deus*, 'Have mercy on me, O God', but then shifts to the translation of Ps. 51.1 (following the English Protestant and Hebrew numbering system), from the Scottish Metrical Psalter of 1650. 'By God's eyes...': TC changes the emphasis of the King's comment; see *Chronicle*, 22: 'By God's eyes, this man considers himself worthy to take charge of the abbey'.

85 '*we shall not know the hero when we see him*': see *Heroes*, 186.

Speciosity: 'Specious actions, promises' (*OED*, citing TC).

'*change the figure of your Quack*': see *Heroes*, 186.

86 *So then the bells of St. Edmundsbury* . . . *plus quam mille comedentibus in gaudio magno*: (Lat.) 'more than a thousand eating in great joy'. Rokewode, 18–19; *Chronicle*, 23–4.

'*Fifty Knights under him*': Rokewode, 20; *Chronicle*, 25.

a change greater than Napoleon's: see *Heroes*, 205–6.

Chandos day-drudges: see note to p. 60.

enlarged, as in the solar microscope: a solar microscope, consisting of 'a set of lenses designed to project microscope slides onto screen using the brilliant light of the sun' (Kennedy, 'The Oxy-Hydrogen Microscope' [2019], 3), had been used in public lectures since the 1730s; see also Wells, 'Fleas the Size of Elephants' (2017) and Roberts, 'Philip Carpenter' (2017). In 1827, Philip Carpenter sought to extend the hours of his 'Microcosm exhibition' at his optical shop at 24 Regent St. by using 'hydrogen-oxygen' gas illumination. As the technology developed and projection and magnification increased, operators featured 'spectacular, even grotesque' subjects, including Thames water, which caused a panic in 1838 (Kennedy, 'The Oxy-Hydrogen Microscope', 93, 95). On 13 December 1842, the Royal Polytechnic Institution announced in *The Sun* newspaper a demonstration of John Cary's 'NEW OXY-HYDROGEN MICROSCOPE, of enormous power, exhibiting the HUMAN HAIR EIGHTEEN INCHES in diameter, being magnified seventy-four millions of times', as well as new 'DISSOLVING VIEWS, including a View of GHUZNEE and the BOLAN PASS in AFFGHANISTAN' (p. 1). TC may also be alluding here to the work of the photographer William Henry Fox Talbot, who since 1835 had been experimenting with photomicrography, using a solar microscope to project images of minuscule objects onto a large screen. He then photographed the projections, which had been exposed to sensitized paper. In 1839–40, he produced notable photomicrographs of light transmitted through crystals, insect wings, and a cross-section of plants. TC later remarked in his

Life of Sterling (1851), that Fox Talbot was 'known for photogenic and other scientific plans of extracting sunbeams from cucumbers' (*Works*, xi. 214). See Richards, 'William Fox Talbot and Thomas Carlyle: Connections' (2015–16).

87 *taxes on knowledge!*: an expression first used by Edwin Chadwick in 1830 (Finer, *Life and Times of Chadwick* [1952], 37), and adopted by working-class radicals and their middle-class supporters in opposition to the stamp duty levied on newspapers. In 1836 Thomas Spring Rice, chancellor of the exchequer, reduced the rate from 4*d*. to 1*d*., but the campaign against the tax continued. It was not abolished until 1855.

Such telescopes, such enlightenment: in late April and early May 1842, there were numerous press reports about the construction of the 'Leviathan of Parsontown', a 72-inch (1.8-m) telescope being built at Birr Castle, Parsontown, Co. Offaly, Ireland by William Parsons, third earl of Rosse. In a front-page letter published in the *Supplement to The Times* (27 Apr. 1842), the astronomer James South provided a detailed account of the preparations and concluded, 'The speculum will have a reflecting surface of 4,071 square inches, whilst that of the telescope made by the immortal [William] Herschel, under the auspices of George III, had but 1, 811.'

Mr. Sale informs me, the old Arab Tribes would gather in liveliest gaudeamus: see George Sale (trans.), *The Koran* (1734), i. 27: 'An excellent poet reflected an honour on his tribe, so that as soon as anyone began to be admired for his performances, . . . the other tribes sent publickly to congratulate them on the occasion, and themselves made entertainments, at which the women assisted, drest in their nuptial ornaments, singing to the sound of timbrels the happiness of their tribe'. For TC and Sale, see Sorensen and Kinser, *On Heroes* (2013), 212–14. *LLC 1842*, 70 lists the 1801 edition of Sale's translation of *The Koran*. Gaudeamus igitur (Lat.) 'So let us rejoice'.

set to gauge ale-barrels in the Burgh of Dumfries: see note to p. 44 and *Heroes*, 165: 'That a Europe, with its French Revolution breaking out, finds no need of a Burns except for gauging beer,—is a thing, I for one, cannot *rejoice* at!'

'patronage of genius': TC echoes critics who condemned the Scottish aristocracy for its neglect of Burns, but broadens the attack to include 'We English'. The Liverpool historian and patron of the arts William Roscoe anticipated TC's argument in a letter of 1796: '[Burns's] example has fixed the value of high poetical attainments in Scotland, and they amount to the place of an exciseman, with a salary of fifty pounds per annum. Such has been the munificence of the Scotch peerage and the Scotch gentry to a man who has done more honour to his country than all the throat-cutters it ever had. May they never have another opportunity of insulting genius with paltry and insidious rewards' Roscoe, *Life* (1833), i. 234). For Burns and Scottish patronage, see Andrews, *Genius of Scotland*, 124–7. TC read and admired Roscoe's *Life of Lorenzo di Medici* (1795); see *CL* i. 150.

88 *George the Third is Defender of . . . 'the Faith'*: Fidei defensor or *defensatrix*, Latin title of English, Scottish, and later British sovereigns used since 1507 when given by the pope to James IV of Scotland.

an Iliad in a nutshell: see Pliny, *Naturalis Historia*, vii. 21: 'Cicero records that a parchment copy of Homer's poem *The Iliad* was enclosed in a nutshell'.

cloth-worship and quack-worship: entirely confirmed Valethood: see *Heroes*, 157: 'The Valet does not know a Hero when he sees him! Alas, no: it requires a *Hero* to do that;—and one of the world's wants, in *this* as in other senses, is for most part want of such.'

Willelmus Sacrista sits drinking nightly . . . Jew Harpies . . . May the Lord have mercy on thee!: Rokewode, 23–4; *Chronicle*, 28–9. In Greek myth, harpies are monsters with the face of a woman and the body of a vulture; TC's anti-Semitic use of the term denotes 'a rapacious, plundering, or grasping person; one that preys upon others' (*OED*).

89 *vadium or plegium*: see Altick, 91 and n.: 'The terms mean, respectively, security in the form of property or money and the person who stands security for another.' See also Rokewode, 18; *Chronicle*, 22–3.

he will cut out every lawyer of us!: Rokewode, 25; *Chronicle*, 31.

division-lists: recording how each MP votes.

90 *a Duke of Logwood, now rolling sumptuously to his place in the Collective Wisdom*: Altick, 'Past and Present: Topicality as Technique' (1976), 118 and n. suggests a reference to 'quack-like adulteration', from the *OED* definition of logwood as the 'extract of logwood used for colouring or dyeing'.

seven-and-sixpence a week: *The Examiner* (31 Dec. 1842) referred to the case of an agricultural labourer in Dorsetshire 'who has a wife and five children. None of his children employed. He wishes he could get something for them to do. Two of them might work at many things on a farm. Work not plentiful. Has always enough to do himself. Knows many who have not. Has seven shillings a week. Had eight last year. Works to a farmer. Is a thresher. The owners of the farm are the trustees of the University of Oxford. Goes many a day with an hungry belly. Says he should like to know how he be to fill it, and how his children be to have anything but hungry bellies, out of seven shillings a week' (p. 839).

'First catch your hare!': proverbial misquotation of Hannah Glasse, who in her popular *The Art of Cookery Made Plain and Easy* (1747), merely instructs, 'TAKE your Hare when it is cas'd and make a Pudding' (p. 6). She does, however, begin her recipe for 'Portuguese rabbits' with the instruction to catch them first: 'Get some Rabbits, truss them Chicken fashion, the Head must be cut off' (p. 51).

list-shoes: shoes made from the 'selvage, border, or edge of a cloth, usually of different material from the body of the cloth' (*OED*).

elevating him to mastership, will you make a conflagration: i.e. the 'Quack'. See *Heroes*, 170: 'This is the history of all rebellions, French Revolutions, social explosions in ancient or modern times. . . . Unable Simulacrum of

Ability, *quack*, in a word, must adjust himself with quack, in all manner of administration of human things.'

91 *Fifty rough Milites (Feudal Knights), with his lazy Farmers, remiss refractory Monks, with Pope's Legates*: *i.* Rokewode, 20–1; *Chronicle*, 26. *ii.* Rokewode, 22–3; *Chronicle*, 27. *iii.* Rokewode, 39; *Chronicle*, 49.

Paterfamilias: 'A male head of a family or household' (*OED*).

92 *On the morrow after his instalment, he brings in a load of money-bonds . . . the Abbot only . . . shall seal any bond*: TC conflates three passages from Jocelin's *Chronicle*: *i.* Rokewode, 19; *Chronicle*, 24: 'a new seal should be made'; *ii.* Rokewode, 22; *Chronicle*, 28 'a bag full of cancelled charters'; *iii.* Rokewode, 28; *Chronicle*, 35: 'anyone who possessed a seal of his own should surrender it to him'.

'the eye of the master': see Aristotle, *Oeconomica*, 1. vi. 4.

Fiat lux: (Lat.) 'Let there be light' (Gen. 1:3).

'affairs and dues, res ac redditus': Rokewode, 21; *Chronicle*, 27.

Lakenheath eels: see note to p. 70.

penny of reap-silver to explode into the streets the Female Chartism of St. Edmundsbury: see note to p. 69.

Man is the Missionary of Order: see *Heroes*, 175: 'Man is the missionary of Order. Is not all work of man in this world a *making of Order*?'

"was not our Dream true!": in Jocelin's *Chronicle*, Samson, rather than the monks, refers to the dream; see Rokewode, 27; *Chronicle*, 34.

'To repress and hold-in such sudden anger he was continually careful,' and succeeded well: Rokewode, 27–8; *Chronicle*, 34.

"and gradually learn to walk": Rokewode, 19; *Chronicle*, 24.

93 *the harpy Jews not only settled with, but banished, bag and baggage*: TC embellishes. See *Chronicle*, 27, 41: 'Everything was written down, so that within four years of his election [i.e. 1186], no one could cheat him of a penny of the abbacy rents.'; 'The abbot asked the king [in 1190] for written permission to expel the Jews from St Edmund's town.'

Bannaleuca (Liberties, Banlieue): see Rokewode, 33: '*Bannamleucam*'. In his 'Glossarium', Rokewode defines 'Banna-leuca' as '*Locus jurisdictionis in cicuiti monasterii*' (p. 156). (Lat.) 'A place of jurisdiction in the circuit of a monastery'. '*Banlieue*' (Fr.) 'suburb'.

sentence of excommunication: Rokewode, 33; *Chronicle*, 42.

neither does he pause to rest: see Goethe, *Zahme Xenien* II (1796), 'Ohne hast, | Aber ohne rast' (*Werke* (1828–33), iii. 259). For TC's translation, see 'Goethe's Works': 'That maketh not haste, | That taketh not rest' (*CME* ii. 432).

Willelmus Sacrista, and his bibations and tacenda are . . . put an end to: Rokewode, 22–3; Chronicle, 27–8.

93 *'on its place grow rows of beans'*: Rokewode, 23; *Chronicle*, 28–9.

teetotalism was his only true course: referring to teetotalism in his time, TC contrasts the unrealistic 'speculations' of American abolitionists with the practical reforms of Temperance activists in London. He reported to his mother, 12 September 1840: 'We have great work with *Temperance* here: . . . reformed-drunkards . . . speaking to great crowds about it on the Sundays, who listen very considerably. I understand it is making real progress. The very Irish, poor wretches, are abjuring drink by the million. . . . It is the is the *first beginning of emancipation* to them' (*CL* xii. 254).

Sævit ut lupus: see note to p. 82.

Ranulf de Glanvill . . . took umbrage at him: Rokewode, 20; *Chronicle*, 25.

94 *shewed no extraordinary favour to the Monks who had been his familiars of old . . . a Norfolk barrator and paltenerius*: Rokewode, 31; *Chronicle*, 39: '*eum hominem iracundum, non socialem, paltenerium et baratorem de Norfolch*'; 'an irascible, unsociable, arrogant, Norfolk trickster'. In his Glossarium, Rokewode translates 'Barator' as '*Litigator*' and 'Paltenerius' as '*Pautener*', or in TC's usage 'paltener' (see p. 99), which is 'a rascal, a villain' (*OED*, citing TC).

except it were for idonei, 'fit men': Rokewode, 31; *Chronicle*, 39: 'unless they were also right for the job'.

supported with food and clothes to the end of his days at Abbot Samson's expense: Rokewode, 32; *Chronicle*, 40.

clapping 'conflagrations' on the public: see note to p. 94.

95 *He was right willing to remember friends, when it could be done . . . ". . . will wholly remit the said sum"*: Rokewode, 32–3; *Chronicle*, 40–1.

lodged Angels unawares: Heb. 13: 2.

'An eloquent man he was . . . he had caused a Pulpit to be erected in our church both for ornament of the same, and for the use of his audiences': Rokewode, 30; *Chronicle*, 37.

Itinerant Judges: circuit judges whose tasks were codified by Henry II in 1176.

"neither gold nor silver can help me to confound my enemy!": Rokewode, 25; *Chronicle*, 31.

96 *'A kinless loon,' as the Scotch said of Cromwell's new judges*: see *Cromwell*, vii. 336.

'talent of silence!': see *Sartor*, 39.

'"Deus, Deus," said the Lord Abbot . . . ". . . yet patiently stood it "': Rokewode, 27–8; *Chronicle*, 34–5.

He had this way, too . . . that . . . he never or hardly ever shewed a countenance of love: Rokewode, 31; *Chronicle*, 39.

"Many sons I have; it is not fit that I should smile on them": Cf. Ecclus. 7:24, which refers to daughters, not sons. Rokewode, 26; *Chronicle*, 33: 'You

should know what Solomon says, "Thou hast many daughters. Show not thy face cheerful towards them".'

He would suffer faults, damage from his servants: Rokewode, 31; *Chronicle*, 39.

"Let none . . . come to me secretly . . . you have free access to me, to speak . . . when you will": Rokewode, 28; *Chronicle*, 35.

'Mendaces, ebriosi, verbosi' . . . indifferent to all such things: Rokewode 29; *Chronicle*, 36–7.

97 *'Sweet milk, honey, and other naturally sweet kinds of food . . . he was angry at, and rebuked me for'*: Rokewode, 29–30; *Chronicle*, 36–7.

'For the first seven years he had commonly four sorts of dishes . . . and so got rid of such superfluous individuals': Rokewode, 31; *Chronicle*, 38–9.

As to his parks . . . 'he had laid out several . . . but he himself never meddled with hunting, that I saw': Rokewode, 21; *Chronicle*, 26: 'If any important guest was being entertained, the abbot would sit with his monks in a woodland clearing to watch the hounds giving chase, but I never saw him eat the meat of hunted animals.'

Dryasdust advances several absurd hypotheses as to the insensible but almost total disappearance of these woods: see George Chalmers, *Caledonia* (1807), 791–2: 'The many mosses of Scotland were once so many woods; as we may learn from the number of trees, which are constantly dug from the forests, that have lain for ages below the surface. During the twelfth, and thirteenth centuries, not only the kings, but the bishops, the barons, and abbots, had their forests, in every district of North-Britain, in which they reared infinite herds of cattle, horses, and swine. It will scarcely be credited, that many bleak moors, which now disfigure the face of the country, and produce only barren heath, were formerly clothed with woods, that furnished useful timber, and excellent pasturage; yet, is the fact clearly proved, by the positive evidence of record.' Chalmers attributes the disappearance of the woods to the 'devastation of . . . wars, the destruction of time, and chance, of neglect and idleness'. For the history of the St. Edmundsbury Abbey woods, see Rackham, 'The Abbey Woods' (1998).

98 *Why will men destroy noble Forests . . . turning loose . . . Henry-the-Eighths into them!*: the success of Henry VIII's efforts to expand the navy after he ascended the throne in 1509 resulted in a chronic shortage of native timber for ship-building, which led to the Act for the Preservation of Woods (1543).

The fifth part of our English soil: see Anthony Harmer [Henry Wharton], *A Specimen of Some Errors and Defects in the History of the Reformation of the Church of England* (1693), 40–1: 'The end of the eighth Century was the Year of our Lord 800, at which times very few Monasteries had been yet founded; nor had the Monks then in all appearance gained Possession of the hundredth part of the Riches of the Nation. Afterwards indeed they increased exceedingly in Numbers, Riches, and Possessions, especially in the tenth, eleventh, and twelfth Centuries; but after all, upon a just Account, they will not be found even in Title to have possessed above a fifth part of the Nation.' Wharton was responding to Gilbert Burnet's claim in the first part of *The History of the Reformation of the Church of England* (1679) that 'about the end of the eighth Century, the Monks had possessed themselves of the greatest part of the Riches of the Nation' (p. 187).

98 *better or worse*: see Harmer, *A Specimen*, 41: 'Then for that other Charge, that the best part of the Soil of the Nation being in such ill hands, it was in the Interest of the Nation to have it put to better uses, it is altogether Erroneous. From the beginning to the end, none ever improved their Lands and Possessions to better advantages, by Building, Cultivation, and all other methods, than the Monks did, while they kept them in their own hands.'

Gentle shepherd, tell me what!: misquoted by Macaulay, 'The Earl of Chatham', *The Edinburgh Review* 80 (Oct. 1844), 557; based on a song by Samuel Howard, published in *The Lyre* (1824), iii. 37. See also *CL* xiii. 303.

Double, double, toil and trouble: *Macbeth*, IV. i. 10.

'till we get out of debt, cor meum cruciatum est': Rokewode, 23; *Chronicle*, 29.

will appoint an officer of his own to see our Cellerarius keep them: Rokewode, 65; *Chronicle*, 78–9.

99 *subsannatio et derisio sumus, we have become a laughing stock to mankind*: in Rokewode, 66, Jocelin quotes the Vulgate, Ps. 78:4: *'facti sumus obprobrium vicinis nostris subsannatio et derisio his qui in circuitu nostro sunt'* (we have become a reproach to our neighbours, a scorn and derision to them that are around us). TC instead uses the translation of Ps. 79:4 (following the English Protestant and Hebrew numbering system) from the Scottish Metrical Psalter of 1650: 'Unto our neighbours a reproach most base become are we; | A scorn and laughingstock to them that round about us be.'

raging and gnashing teeth, fremens and frendens . . . a strength of 'subdued rage': Rokewode, 27–8; *Chronicle*, 34: 'I force myself not to rage in what I say or do, and my "suppressed grief chokes me and seethes within me"' (Ovid, *Tristia*, v. i. 63).

Murmurs from the Monks . . . Monastery seems near catching fire!: Rokewode, 87–8; *Chronicle*, 104–5.

100 *Abbot Samson returns. . . . '. . . "I would have taken revenge on thee had I not been angry". . . 'He wept; we all wept'*: Rokewode, 87–8; *Chronicle*, 104–5. Compare Cicero, *Tuscalanæ Disputationes*, IV. xxxvi. 78.

Those Jews . . . had 'visibly emaciated him': Rokewode, 23; *Chronicle*, 29: 'Both Jews and Christians rushed to meet him, demanding payment of debts, and they so worried him that he lost sleep and grew pale and thin.'

'In twelve years . . . had grown wholly white as snow, totus efficitur albus sicut nix': Rokewode, 29; *Chronicle*, 36: 'But within fourteen years of his election he had turned as white as snow.'

'Once my Lord Abbot and I' . . . determines to leave that Harlow manor yet unmeddled with, for a while: Rokewode, 24; *Chronicle*, 29–30.

101 *The Fifty feudal Knights . . . ten knights' fees . . . he watched his time*: Rokewode, 20–1; *Chronicle*, 26. A knight's fee under the Feudal System is 'The amount of land for which the services of an armed knight were due to the sovereign' (*OED*).

my Lord of Clare: Richard of Clare, earl of Hertford, lord of Clare.

a Rowland for his Oliver: Roland, legendary nephew of Charlemagne and reckless protagonist of *La Chanson de Roland*, and Oliver, his wise and reasonable companion. In the *Chanson*, both die heroically at the Battle of Roncevaux Pass.

'The Earl, crowded round (constipatus) with many barons' . . . Earl Alberic . . . Alfric son of Wisgar . . . Domesday Book . . . Banner of St Edmund: Rokewode, 41–2; *Chronicle*, 51–2. Aubrey de Vere, count of Guînes and earl of Oxford, was a magnate who 'held 5 ½ knights' fees of the abbot' (Greenway and Sayers in *Chronicle*, 139 and n.); Ælfric Modercope, son of Wihtgar, was an East Anglian magnate and steward to Queen Emma, mother of Edward the Confessor. The *Domesday Book* is the manuscript record of William I's survey of England, 1086. The banner of St Edmund was represented by John Lydgate, a monk of the abbey of Bury St Edmunds, in a miniature prefaced to his poem, 'The Lives of Sts. Edmund and Fremund' (1434). Lydgate presented the volume to King Henry VI, who stayed at Bury from Christmas 1433 to Easter 1434. In his edition of the *Chronicle* (1907), p. xi, Sir Ernest Clarke notes: 'The Standard depicts Adam and Eve on either side of the Tree of Knowledge, the devil (with a human face and a serpent's body) being curled round the tree. Above is a lamb and cross, with crescents in the background. (The counterseal of Abbot Samson also displayed the lamb bearing a cross.) In the original vellum manuscript this picture is highly coloured. The background is of a vivid red; the three figures and the lamb are in silver; the tree of life is gold with silver fruit; the ground on which Adam and Eve stand is green; and the stars and the crescents are in gold.' For the volume, see British Library, Harley MS 2278, fo. 9.

To which the Abbot: . . . Roger Earl Bigot . . . the Earl of Leicester and his Flemings were beaten at Fornham . . . Thomas de Mendham . . . undecided to the end of the world: Rokewode, 42; *Chronicle*, 51–2. Roger Bigod, second earl of Norfolk, was a magnate who 'held 3 knights' fees' of the abbot (*Chronicle*, 140 and n.). For the earl of Leicester, his Flemings, and the battle of Fornham, see note to p. 58. For Mendham, see Greenway and Sayers in *Chronicle*, 140 and n.: 'Mendham was one of Samson's senior advisers and he appears as one of the abbot's four constables shortly after 1200.'

102 *'One time, during my chaplaincy . . .' 'Who can believe such things?'*: Rokewode, 26–7; *Chronicle*, 33.

103 *our brave Abbot took helmet himself . . . and led his men in person to the siege of Windleshora . . . where Lackland had entrenched himself . . . 'the magnanimous*

Abbot': Rokewode, 40; *Chronicle*, 49. In his copy of Rapin de Thoyras, *History of England*, TC notes in the margin where the author describes the first siege of Windsor Castle in 1193, 'Abbot Samson too' (i. 253). Following the capture of Richard I by Leopold I, Holy Roman Emperor, near Vienna in December 1192, his younger brother Prince John (known as Lackland) seized Windsor Castle in March, but was forced to surrender four months later and flee to France.

103 *He also attended duly in his place in Parliament . . . de arduis regni . . . 'he acquired great praise for himself'*: Rokewode, 39; *Chronicle*, 48–9. *de arduis regni* (Lat.) 'to deal with the kingdom's troubles'.

  'with rich gifts to the King in Germany': Rokewode, 40; *Chronicle*, 49.

  Justiciarii ad Scaccarium: judges of the Court of the Exchequer, responsible for managing royal revenues.

104 *St. Edmund's Shrine . . . was still untouched . . . words which created a sensation around the woolsack . . . 'the Shrine was not meddled with, nor any ransom levied for it'*: Rokewode, 71–2; *Chronicle*, 86. A woolsack is 'A seat made of a bag of wool for the use of judges when summoned to attend the House of Lords' (*OED*).

  'force of public opinion': see TC, 'Voltaire' (1829): 'With regard to this . . . Force of Public Opinion, it is a force well known to all of us, . . . but nowise recognised as a final or divine force. . . . Without some celestial guidance, . . . it appears to us that the Force of Public Opinion would . . . become an extremely unprofitable one' (*EOL*, 125–6).

  OF St. Edmund's fearful avengements . . . too significant to be omitted . . . ambitious rhetorical Latin . . . Read it here; with ancient yet with modern eyes: Rokewode, 50; *Chronicle*, 61. See Rokewode, p. viii: 'Incorporated into our Chronicle is an episode, headed "De Henrico de Essexia," being an account of the duel between Henry de Essex and Robert de Montford. . . . This episode has certain pretensions to classical Latin, and forms a contrast to the easy colloquial style of Jocelin'.

  Henry Earl of Essex . . . had high places and emoluments: Rokewode, 51; *Chronicle*, 61. Of the section that begins here, Calder, 99, observes: 'In his own free style, Carlyle paraphrases or summarizes all the story except the last portion; he characterizes the eminent Henry, explains the sins of his youth, describes his cowardice as standard-bearer to Henry Second, and explains the duel precipitated by one Robert of Montford. Then, at this point, he offers the following translation, close to the original in meaning and often in phrasing.'

  He cast Gilbert into prison; and . . . wore the life out of him there: Rokewode, 52; *Chronicle*, 63.

105 *Potiphar's Wife*: see Gen. 39:7–20.

  While others in the Eastern Counties were adorning . . . the unjust Standard-bearer . . . has a most morbid lamentable flaw in the texture of him: Rokewode, 51; *Chronicle*, 61–2.

106 *In the year 1157, he went with his Standard to attend King Henry ... struggling to retreat Parthian-like ... Robert de Montfort ... into fruits of eternal Felicity'*: Rokewode, 51–2; *Chronicle*, 62–3. For Parthians, see Altick, 111 and n.: 'The Parthians were noted for the vigor of their rear-guard actions.' Robert de Montfort accused Henry of Essex of cowardice and treason; they duelled on 31 March 1163 at Fry's Island in the Thames, near Reading.

like light through coloured glass: see *Heroes*, 23: 'The colours and forms of your light will be those of the *cut-glass* it has to shine through.' See also Shelley, 'Adonais' (1821), ll. 463–4: 'Life, like a dome of many-coloured glass, | Stains the white radiance of eternity.'

107 *'on the rim of the horizon'*: Rokewode, 52; *Chronicle*, 63: 'at the water's edge'.

'sense of the Infinite nature of Duty': see *Heroes*, 64–5: 'What is all this but a rude shadow, in the rude Bedouin imagination, of that grand spiritual Fact, and Beginning of Facts, which it is ill for us too if we do not all know and feel: the Infinite Nature of Duty? That man's actions here are of *infinite* moment to him, and never die or end at all; that man, with his little life, reaches upwards high as Heaven, downwards low as Hell.'

PRACTICAL-DEVOTIONAL: Calder, 92 writes, 'Except for jottings and two or three fragments, [chapter xv] does not exist in the First Draft but is complete in the Printer's Copy. The alterations in the latter bring the wording ever closer to the source, thus showing that in composing the second manuscript Carlyle returned to the *Chronicle* for further borrowings or corrections.'

108 *a liberty of tourneying ... 'a gentle and free passage of arms'*: Rokewode, 40; *Chronicle*, 49–50.

there came to the same spot four-and-twenty young men ... morrow was the Vigil of the Apostles Peter and Paul .. young scamps, in the dandy state ... they gradually came in for repentance: Rokewode, 40–1; *Chronicle*, 50: 'Some time later, eighty fully armed young men ... came to this town afterwards to find lodgings.' The feast day for Peter and Paul was 28 June 1195. For 'dandy state', see *Sartor*, 200–10 (bk III, ch. x, 'The Dandiacal Body').

109 *'cuttings and the effusion of blood ... with bell, book and candle ... prostrate themselves at the Church door'*: Rokewode, 68–9; *Chronicle*, 82–3. The ritual of excommunication involved the ringing of a bell, closing of a book, and extinguishing of a candle.

Geoffrey Riddell Bishop of Ely ... our true nemus ... great tower we are building there! must seek wood for Glemsford edifice in some other nemus than this: Rokewode, 52–3; *Chronicle*, 63–4. See Calder, 92: 'The ... anecdote of the Bishop of Ely and the trees of Elmset is a paraphrase typical of the many that compose Chapters XI–XV'. *Nemus* (Lat.) 'grove, glade, or wood'. For the tower, see note to p. 56. In a footnote, Rokewode, 111 corroborates Jocelin's view (*Chronicle*, 19) that Samson completed 'the church towers that had been begun a hundred years earlier'. Rokewode refers to his own article on 'The Great Bell Tower' (1831), in which he explains that 'Samson, as subsacrist and master of the works, had collected a large quantity of material for building the great tower of the church, and after his accession to the abbacy, he was enabled, by the pecuniary assistance of some of the burgesses, to accomplish the structure' (p. 328). In his edition of the Chronicle, Rokewode adds that according to the Benedictine monk and chronicler John de Taxster, 'Samson's tower was blown down the year before his death' (p. 111).

110 *Herbert the Dean, who in a too thrifty manner has erected a wind-mill . . . glebe-lands . . . brevi manu . . . the ground already clear of it*: Rokewode, 42–3; *Chronicle*, 53–4. Glebe is 'a portion of land assigned to a clergyman as part of his benefice' (*OED*); *brevi manu* (Lat.) 'without delay'.

111 *Adam de Cokefield, one of the chief feudatories . . . died, leaving large possessions . . . "I will patiently endure"*: Rokewode, 72–3; *Chronicle*, 86–7. A feudatory is 'one who holds his lands by feudal tenure; a feudal vassal' (*OED*).

'Satan with outspread wings': Rokewode, 27; *Chronicle*, 34; see also Milton, *Paradise Lost*, i. 20.

Richard swore tornado oaths, worse than our armies in Flanders: Sterne, *Tristram Shandy* (1759): 'Our armies swore terribly in Flanders, cried my uncle Toby,—but nothing like this' (Oxford World's Classics edn., 139).

Richard replied by the present of a ring, which Pope Innocent the Third had given him: Rokewode, 72–3; *Chronicle*, 87.

it might seem, from Jocelin's Narrative, as if he had his eye all but exclusively directed on terrestrial matters: Rokewode, 30; *Chronicle*, 37.

'he sat down at the foot of St. Edmund's shrine': Rokewode, 36; *Chronicle*, 44: 'I took refuge under St. Edmund's shrine'.

112 *the zealous interest our Abbot took in the Crusades . . . the King himself indeed never went*: Rokewode, 39; *Chronicle*, 48.

'At the retaking of Jerusalem by the Pagans, Abbot Samson . . . abstained also from flesh and flesh-meats . . . to the end of his life': Rokewode, 29; *Chronicle*, 36.

The 'imaginative faculties?' 'Rude poetic ages?' The 'primeval poetic element?': TC may be referring to Macaulay's argument in his essay 'John Dryden' that poetry degenerates as civilization advances: 'In a barbarous age the imagination exercises a despotic power. So strong is the perception of what is unreal, that it often overpowers the passions of the mind, and all the sensations of the body. . . . The first works of imagination are . . . poor and rude, not from the want of genius, but from want of the materials' (*The Edinburgh Review* (Jan. 1828), 10–11). TC observed, 'Macaulay has been writing of Dryden lately; but of *true* Poetry . . . the man has no glimpse or forecast' (*CL* iv. 362). For TC and Macaulay, see Edwards, 'Carlyle versus Macaulay' (2011).

The garment of it only is dead: see *Heroes*, 49: 'That God is great; and that there is nothing else great! He is the Reality. . . . He is real. He made us at first, sustains us yet; we and all things are but the shadow of Him; a transitory garment veiling the Eternal Splendour.'

'The Unconscious is the alone Complete': see *Heroes*, 92: 'Shakspeare's Art is not Artifice; the noblest worth of it is not there by plan or precontrivance. . . . Such a man's works . . . grow up withal *un*consciously, from the unknown deeps in him; . . . with a symmetry grounded on Nature's own laws, conformable to all Truth whatsoever.'

113 *Methodism, with its eye forever turned on its own navel*: see *Sartor*, 202 and n.

Acheron: 'In Greek mythology: one of the rivers of Hades over which the souls of the dead had to pass' (*OED*, citing TC).

Memnon's music: one of the two statues of Pharoah Amenhotep III, on the left bank of the Nile, near Luxor. It was associated with Memnon, in Greek myth the son of Tithonos and Eos (the dawn). According to legend, the statue emitted musical sounds when touched by the first rays of the sun. See *Sartor*, 109 and *FR* i. 102.

Puseyism: named after the Church of England theologian Edward Bouverie Pusey, who wrote seven of the ninety *Tracts for the Times* (1833–41). His signature attached to *Tract XVIII* (1833) publicly identified him with the aims of the Oxford Movement, and the British press thereafter used the term 'Puseyism' as a synonym for 'Popery', the Catholic revival, and 'Tractarianism'. In an editorial, *The Sun* (27 Dec. 1842), commented, 'Puseyism . . . has its origin mainly in the recognised disability of the Church to satisfy the religious feelings of the people, and render them contented with the State. The early Christian Church and the Romish Church had such effects, and hence the idea that the Church can now only be made efficient as an ally of the State, and as the teacher of religion, by becoming what the early Church, or the Romish Church, was. Hence, too, we find the Puseyites recommending the abolition of pews, the revival of imposing ceremonies, and the re-establishment of numerous festivals and holidays, as they still prevail in Spain and Italy' (p. 2).

Was thy small Nine-and-thirty Articles?: TC remarked in a letter to Alexander John Scott, 27 January 1843 that he was 'writing a kind of "Tract for the Times," of some extent, *not* in the Pusey vein. . . . | The Maker of the Universe was wise, | He plann'd all Souls, all Systems, worlds and Particles; | The great Groundplan he used from end to end | Was the Rev*d* Newman's Nine-and-thirty Articles!' (*CL* xvi. 37). In *Tract XC*, the final of the series published on 25 January 1841, Newman argued that the Thirty-Nine Articles of Religion of the Anglican Church were in harmony with the basic tenets of the Roman Catholic faith.

114 *ABBOT SAMSON built many useful, many pious edifices*: Rokewode, 21; *Chronicle*, 26.

'the Hospital of Babwell': Rokewode, 33; *Chronicle*, 41.

'fit houses for the St. Edmundsbury Schools': Rokewode, 33; *Chronicle*, 41.

114 *'caused to be covered with tiles;' or . . . 'with lead'*: Rokewode, 70–1; *Chronicle*, 85.

'great tower of St. Edmund's': Rokewode, 53; *Chronicle*, 64.

One of the things he could not in any wise but rebuild was the great Altar: Rokewode, 78–9; *Chronicle*, 94–5.

"A Dream one of us had that he saw St. Edmund naked and in lamentable plight . . . with hunger and thirst!": Rokewode, 80–1; *Chronicle*, 97.

"It is we that are the naked and famished limbs of the Martyr": Rokewode, 81; *Chronicle*, 97.

115 *Clearly enough . . . the Altar . . . for which it is to serve as pediment*: Rokewode, 82; *Chronicle*, 98.

Nay farther . . . he enjoys . . . a glimpse of the glorious Martyr's very Body . . . as Te Deum is sung: Rokewode, 83–5; *Chronicle*, 100–2.

The Patriot Hampden, best beatified man we have, had lain in like manner some two centuries . . . when certain dignitaries of us, 'and twelve grave-diggers with pulleys,' raised him also up: John Hampden's arrest by Charles I on 4 January 1642, with four others, was one of the leading causes of the English Civil War. Hampden died of wounds received in a skirmish at Chalgrove, near Oxford on 24 June 1643, and was buried at Great Hampden. *The Annual Register* 70 (July 1828) reported that on 21 July 1828 his body was exhumed by a group of gravediggers led by George Nugent Grenville, who wished to 'ascertain . . . by what sort of wound he had been killed. . . . The coffin was extremely heavy, but, by elevating one end with a crow-bar, two strong ropes were adjusted under either end, and thus drawn up by twelve men in the most careful manner possible' (pp. 93–4). See also *Gentleman's Magazine* 98 (Aug. 1828), 125–7.

117 *'The Festival of St. Edmund now approaching . . . looking through, clearly saw all these things'*: Rokewode, 82–4; *Chronicle*, 98–101.

118 *reverence the right man, all is well*: see *Heroes*, 170: 'Find in any country the Ablest Man that exists there; raise *him* to the supreme place, and loyally reverence him; you have a perfect government for that country.'

Bare-back-ism, Sansculottism so-called!: the Sansculottes ('men without knee breeches'), urban labourers whom TC regarded as the generating force of the French Revolution.

119 *But however this may be, St. Edmund's Loculus . . . has the veils of silk and linen reverently replaced . . . and hastened to toll the bells in the Choir*: Rokewode, 84–6; *Chronicle*, 101–2.

'We touch Heaven when we lay our hand on a human Body': from Novalis's *Pollen* (*Fragments*, 1798); see TC, 'Novalis' (1829), in *CME* ii. 39.

Supernaturalism brought home to the very dullest: see *Sartor*, 187–95 (bk. III, ch. viii): 'Natural Supernaturalism'.

"A Chancery Lawsuit; justice, nay justice in mere money, denied a man, for all his pleading, till twenty, till forty years of his Life are gone seeking it": between

1840 and 1842, there was widespread press criticism of delays in the Court of Chancery, which exercised jurisdiction over matters related to property, wills, mortgages, and other disputes not addressed in courts of Common Law. According to *The Examiner* (30 Apr. 1842) it functioned with 'the *minimum* of progress and the *maximum* of expense' (p. 274). In *Bell's Weekly Messenger* (28 Mar. 1841) a plaintiff described the case of Wedderburn v. Wedderburn, which was filed in the court of Chancery in 1828: 'Three out of seven of the original defendants, and one out of four of the plaintiffs, have died since the bill was filed. The plaintiffs have been kept out of the property in dispute since May, 1801. . . . This Chancery suit may be taken as a sample of the majority of such suits, where large sums are in dispute. . . . The expense incurred by the delays, although a serious evil, is but a secondary evil to that caused by the plaintiffs being kept out of their money during the greater part if not the whole of their lives by the practical working of the court' (p. 3). There were other notorious examples, including Day v. Day and the Jennens inheritance case, which Dickens may have loosely used as the basis for Jarndyce and Jarndyce in *Bleak House* (1853); see Polden, (2003), pts. 1 and 2, and Dunstan, 'The Real Jarndyce versus Jarndyce' (1997).

"a Cockney Funeral": a cockney is 'a working-class person from the East End of London' (*OED*). In testimony published in the *Report from the Select Committee of the House of Commons on Improvement of Health in Towns (Interment of Bodies)*, dated 5 May 1842, Charles James Blomfield, bishop of London, recommended that 'a provision ought to be made . . . for the funerals of the poor; as it is, they are much too expensive for poor people. . . . There is, however, no expense so little thought of by the poor as the expense of a funeral. I have known repeated instances where they would deprive themselves of the necessaries of life for the sake of paying respect to the bodies of their departed friends' (pp. 185–6). In his *Inquiry into the Practice of Interment in Towns* (1843), Chadwick listed typical needs in a chart under the heading 'EXAMPLES OF ORDINARY UNDERTAKERS' BILLS IN THE METROPOLIS': 'Elm coffin, lined, ruffled, mattress, sheet, pillow . . . Outside case, brass engraved plate . . . 2 porters, scarfs, staves, covers, bands, & gloves . . . Six coach cloaks, bands, and gloves . . . truncheons & wands, Eighteen pages and bearers, silks bands, and gloves' (p. 267). For Dickens's account of a 'pauper funeral', see *Oliver Twist* (serialized 1837–9; published 1838), ch. v; for a 'respectable' funeral, see *Martin Chuzzlewit* (serialized 1842–4; published 1844), ch. xix.

"Death reverenced by hatchments": 'A diamond-shaped or (occasionally) square panel or canvas with a deceased person's armorial bearings, affixed to his or her house during mourning and often afterwards placed in a church' (*OED*). See the testimony of 'Mr. Wild the undertaker', in Chadwick's *Inquiry into the Practice of Interment in Towns*: 'Are you aware that the array of funerals, commonly made by undertakers, is strictly the heraldic array of a baronial funeral, the two men who stand at the doors being supposed to be the two porters of the castle, with their staves, in

black; the man who heads the procession, wearing a scarf, being a representative of the herald-at-arms; the man who carries a plume of feathers on his head being an esquire, who bears the shield and casque . . . ; the pall-bearers, with batons, being representative of knights-companions-at-arms; the men walking with their wands being supposed to represent gentlemen-ushers . . . :—are you aware that this is said to be the origin and type of the common array usually provided by those who undertake to perform funerals?—No; I am not aware of it' (p. 49).

119 *He had to run into France . . . and with great labour got it done*: Rokewode, 63–4; *Chronicle*, 76–7.

   He had to decide on the dilapidated Coventry Monks . . . in the City of Peeping Tom!: Rokewode, 69–70; *Chronicle*, 83–4.

   He had, not without labour, to controvert the intrusive Bishop of Ely: Rokewode, 98–100; *Chronicle*, 117–20.

   the intrusive abbot of Cluny: Rokewode, 92; *Chronicle*, 110.

120 *He is sent for again over sea to advise King Richard . . . departs . . . And Jocelin's Boswellean Narrative, suddenly shorn through by the scissors of Destiny, ends*: Rokewode, 100; *Chronicle*, 119–20. Samson was summoned by King John in 1202. Rokewode, p. vii, notes that 'the Chronicle . . . breaks off abruptly some years before the death of Abbot Samson'. The scissors of Destiny is a reference to Atropos, in Greek myth, one of the three Fates, who cut the thread of life.

   Time-Curtains: see *Sartor*, 192: 'The curtains of Yesterday drop down, the curtains of To-morrow roll up; but Yesterday and To-morrow both *are*.'

   real-phantasmagory: variant of 'phantasmagoria' (*OED*, citing TC), 'an exhibition of optical illusions produced chiefly by the use of a magic lantern, first exhibited in London in 1801, . . . *esp.* one in which preternatural phenomena are represented using artificial light' (*OED*). For TC and 'real-phantasmagoria', see 'The Diamond Necklace' (1837), in *Historical Essays*, 88, and *FR* i. 146: 'Such vision (spectral yet real) thou, O Thuriot, as from thy Mount of Vision, beholdest in this moment: prophetic of what other Phantasmagories, and loud-gibbering Spectral Realities, which thou yet beholdest not, but shalt!' In the same work (*FR* ii. 191), TC also refers to 'new quick-changing Phantasms, which shift like magic-lantern figures; more spectral than ever!' In 'Narrative and Explanations of the Appearance of Phantoms and Other Figures in the Exhibition of the Phantasmagoria' (1802), the chemist and inventor William Nicholson described the visual impact of the phantasmagoria: 'After a very short time of exhibiting the first figure, it was seen to contract gradually in all its dimensions, until it became extremely small and then vanished. . . . The mind is irresistibly led to consider the figures as if they were receding to an immense distance' (p. 148). The displays were enhanced in the Victorian period with the replacement of candles with lime ball, hydrogen, and magnesium gaslight, and the introduction of 'dissolving views', enabled by a metallic shutter 'which, by closing upon one projected image and opening on another, made it unnecessary for the audience to see one scene being pushed from the screen by the next' (Altick, *Shows of London* [1978], 219). See also Castle, 'Phantasmagoria' (1988). Sacred themes were particularly popular. On 6 August 1842 (*The Birmingham Journal*, p. 1), the Society of Arts in Birmingham announced the arrival of a major London exhibit of 'Moving Panoramic and Dissolving Views of the Holy Land', promoting 'quick perceptions of the sacred associations with the Holy Writ, and acquaintance with the sublime localities of landscape and architectural antiquities, in whose mouldering forms they are enshrined'.

vanish like Mirza's Vision: see Joseph Addison, 'The Vision of Mirza', *The Spectator* 159 (1 Sept. 1711), 317–18.

Formulas become dead: see *The French Revolution*: 'Man's Existence had for long generations rested on mere formulas which were grown hollow by course of time; and it seemed as if no Reality any longer existed but only Phantasm of realities, and God's Universe were the work of the Tailor and Upholsterer mainly' (*FR* i. 164).

121　*Ubi homines sunt modi sunt*: (Lat.) 'where there are men, there are manners'. See TC's translation of *Wilhelm Meister's Travels* (1827): 'Where men combine in society, the way and manner in which they like to be and to continue together is established' (*Works*, xxiv. 338). In a letter to John Stuart Mill, 20 January 1834, TC remarked that Goethe's maxim 'grows with me in significance the longer I meditate it; modifying innumerable things in my Philosophy' (*CL* vii. 71–2).

Habit is our primal, fundamental law: Calder refers to this sentence as one of the 'largest revisions in the whole book' from the Printer's Copy to the First Edition. The former reads, 'Habit is the deepest law; Habit and Imitation there is nothing deeper than these two' (Calder, 153).

122　*humour that thy mother gave thee*: see note to p. 57.

African Mandingo: sub-Saharan African ethnic group, based primarily in W Africa.

London-Tavern Meeting: a public house at 123 Bishopsgate; see *CL* vii. 339–49.

the genus Dandy?: see note to p. 108.

123　*Long-Acre cabs with white-breeched tiger*: 'A smartly-liveried boy acting as groom or footman; formerly often provided with standing-room on a small platform behind the carriage, and a strap to hold on by' (*OED*). For Long-Acre, see note to p. 23.

pococurantisms: marked by 'the character or style of a pococurante; indifference, carelessness, nonchalance' (*OED*).

out of the depths of Bedlam: 'The Hospital of St. Mary of Bethlehem, used as an asylum for the reception and treatment of the mentally ill; originally situated in Bishopsgate, in 1676 rebuilt near London Wall, and in 1815 transferred to Lambeth' (*OED*).

123 _Plantagenet_: 'A member of the English royal dynasty which held the throne from the accession of Henry II in 1154 to the death of Richard III in 1485' (_OED_).

lived before Agamemnon!: see Horace, _Odes_, IV. ix. 25–6; Agamemnon was king of Mycenae and leader of the Greek forces in the Trojan War.

Life-tree Igdrasil: see note to p. 47.

124 _Dan Chaucer_: 'Dan' or 'Dominus' (master); see Spenser's reference to Chaucer, _The Faerie Queene_, IV. ii. 32.

'_Thy very_ ATTENTION _does it not mean an attentio, a_ STRETCHING-TO?': see _OED_, etymology, 'to stretch to (still in Old French)'. See also _Sartor_, 56.

'_Select Beauties_': frequently used in titles of poetic anthologies in the eighteenth and nineteenth centuries. See e.g. _Lyra Britannica, or Select Beauties of Modern English Poetry_ (1830), ed. Revd John Wesley Thomas, who notes in his preface: 'Care has been taken to exclude from this selection, every sentiment and expression of an immoral or irreligious tendency' (p. x).

Œcumenic Councils . . . Useful-Knowledge Societies: Altick, 132 and n. suggests an ironic reference to Newman, _Tract XC_, in which he discusses 'the fallibility of the Church's ecumenic (universal) councils'. The Society for the Diffusion of Useful Knowledge was founded in 1826 by Henry Brougham to instruct a mass reading audience through the publication of cheap periodicals, books, and encyclopaedias covering a wide range of scientific and practical subjects. At a meeting of the society at the Freemason's Tavern on 17 May 1828, Brougham asserted that the 'society was so constituted, that no individual difference of opinion could interfere with the mode in which they should unite to advance education and knowledge' (_The Times_ (19 May 1828), 3).

forever UNNAMEABLE: on 22 October 1842, TC replied to a letter from Hensleigh Wedgwood, who had resigned a fellowship at Cambridge in 1830 because of his refusal to accept the Thirty-Nine Articles. TC outlined his resistance to religious dogma: 'Daily stronger too [grows] my impatience with all dogmatism on insoluble problems, on inconceivable objects; my deep manifold feeling that _this_ is verily the UNNAMEABLE, — which a man has to speak forth in his life and acts, not by any words (completely) that he can use at present. My impatience with most forms of words, and forms of jargons—especially when they get into the shrill or cackling condition,—is now and then very intense, it must be owned!' (_CL_ xv. 140).

Litanias, or Leitourgias: (Lat.) 'litanies' or 'liturgies'.

125 _What a poet he! . . . from whom as from a Nile-source all Forms of Worship flow_: TC may be echoing Thomas De Quincey, who in an article on 'Homer and the Homeridæ' in _Blackwood's Edinburgh Magazine_ 50 (Oct. 1841) compared the Greek epic poet to the Nile: 'Not the fountains of the Nile have been so diffusive, or so creative, as those of Homer. . . . A great

poet appearing in early ages, and a great river, bear something of the same relation to human civility and culture. In this view, with a peculiar sublimity, the Hindoos consider a mighty fertilizing river . . . as in some special meaning "the Son of God." . . . Hence arose the profound interest about the Nile . . . . Hence arose the corresponding interest about Homer; for Greece and the Grecian isles were in many moral respects as much the creation of Homer as the Egypt of the Nile' (p. 412).

Rotatory Calabash: written prayers that the Buddhist Kalmucks, a Mongolian nomadic people, insert into a revolving calabash and spin to produce perpetual worship. See TC's translation of Jean Paul Friedrich Richter's *Life of Quintus Fixlein*, in *German Romance* (1827), in *Works*, xxii. 220.

Archbishop Laud at St. Catherine Creed's: William Laud's ceremonial consecration of St Katharine (or Catherine) Kree, Leadenhall St., London, on 16 January 1631, was used as evidence against him during his trial for treason in 1644. See *Heroes*, 177 and *Cromwell*, vi. 43.

The Iliad Poem, and indeed most other poetic, especially epic things, have risen as the Liturgy did: see *Lectures*, 20–1: 'With these two qualities, Music and Belief, [Homer] places his mind in a most beautiful brotherhood, in a sincere contact with his own characters; there are no reticences.'

The great Iliad in Greece, and the small Robin Hood's Garland in England: in the seventeenth and eighteenth centuries numerous versions were published of *Robin Hood's Garland*, collections of ballads in booklet form that were originally intended for singing, but were later marketed to a more affluent reading audience; see Basdeo, 'Reading *Robin Hood's Garland*' (2018). Thierry recounted the history of the garlands in *Histoire de la conquête*, iii. 242–3: 'Throughout the seventeenth century, the old ballads of Robin Hood, printed in Gothic letters (a type of which the lower English people were especially fond) circulated in the villages, where they were peddled by sellers who sang and taught them to buyers. Several complete collections were compiled for the use of urban readers, and one of these bore the elegant title of Robin Hood's garland; today these collections are rare.'

the Wrath of a Divine Achilles, the Prowess of a Will Scarlet or Wakefield Pinder: see TC's MS Notes, Forster Collection, fo. 99r: 'Our English genius is not apt for Mythics,—least of all when only hatred and terror inspire it. Alas, instead of Homer's Iliad, our poor Homeridae have managed but a Robin Hood's Garland: for Ajax and Diomed we have Little John and Scarlet, for Hector the Pindar of Wakefield, for pious Aeneas a Castal Friar—happy enough that we have that. Blessing on thee, poor Robin; a little green islet with yellow fuzz blossoms and living men in the hazy uninhabitable sand wilderness of what they call the History of the Past. . . . The Homeridae were loquacious melodious Greeks; the Robin Hoodists were taciturn timbertoned English. The former sang also to Kings in royal Palaces; the latter in village alehouses to poor clowns for a copper coin or cup of mean liquor.' Will Scarlet and the 'Jolly Pinder of Wakefield' were companions of Robin Hood.

125 *De Tallagio non concedendo*: (Lat.) 'of not allowing taillage': a statute restricting the power of the king to levy taxes ('tailliage'), cited in the Petition of Right, 1628.

Statute-Book and Four Courts: Statue Book is 'a document or book containing written statutes or Acts of Parliament' (*OED*, citing TC); the Four Courts are the English judiciary, comprised of the Courts of Chancery, Exchequer, King's Bench, and Common Pleas.

Coke upon Lyttleton and Three Estates of Parliament: in *Institutes of the Lawes of England* (1628), vol. i, Sir Edward Coke revised and expanded Sir Thomas Littleton's *Treatise on Tenures* (1481). Coke entitled the volume *Coke on Littleton*, possibly implying a link between himself and Justinian, codifier of Roman law. See TC's MS Notes, Forster Collection, fo. 1: 'Coke upon Lyttleton, Sergeant Noy or some other must stretch the Temporary Laws. I always observe the art of Coke: whatever the old Parliaments had done when they are all Lords and Barons with armed England at their back, and not be gainsayed at all,—this our learned friend asserts to be competent to "Parliament" still now when we are poor commons paid by our boroughs.' See also *Historical Sketches*, 168–9. The Three Estates of Parliament consists of the Commons, in the House of Commons; the nobility (Lords Temporal) in the House of Lords; and the clergy (Lords Spiritual), also in the House of Lords.

Cain's slaying Abel: see Gen. 4:8.

slow heart-break for forty years: see note to p. 119.

Justice herself began by Wild-Justice: see Bacon, 'Of Revenge', in *Essays*: 'Revenge is a kind of wild justice' (1908 edn., 15); see also *FR* i. 159.

assiduously sowing tares!: see Matt. 13:24–30, 36–43.

Dryden's Head in the Battle of the Books: see Swift, *Battle of the Books* (1704), in which Dryden wore a helmet 'nine times too large for the head'.

126 *past the Nore*: sandbank at the mouth of the Thames Estuary, where the river meets the North Sea; figuratively, gone out to sea.

Wren built St. Paul's: Sir Christopher Wren, architect of St Paul's Cathedral, built 1673–1713.

Satanic-School, Cockney-School: Satanic-School is Southey's epithet in the preface (p. xxi) to his poem *A Vision of Judgment* (1821) for Byron and his imitators; Cockney-School is John Gibson Lockhart's epithet for Leigh Hunt, John Keats, William Hazlitt, and their imitators, in 'On the Cockney School of Poetry', *Blackwood's Edinburgh Magazine* 2 (Oct. 1817), 38–41.

Arachne started with forefinger and thumb, and had not even a distaff: the mythological Arachne challenged Athena to a weaving contest and was transformed into a spider by the infuriated goddess because her tapestry was flawless; see Ovid, *Metamorphoses*, vi. 1–145.

127 *Sir Jabesh Windbag*: Richard Monckton Milnes identified 'Windbag' as Robert Peel, who angered TC for failing to repeal the Corn Laws in

December 1841 and for introducing the sliding scale duties in March 1842 (see notes to pp. 25 and 39; see also Wemyss Reid, *Life* [1891], i. 293). For TC's later admiration of Peel, see Seigel, 'Carlyle and Peel' (1983) and Morrow, 'Paradox of Peel as Carlylean Hero' (1997).

to recollect a Shakspeare or so: Charles Knight published *The Pictorial Edition of the Works of Shakespere* between 1838 and 1841 in fifty-six monthly parts, comprising comedies, histories, and tragedies, and supplemented with background essays and notes, and woodcut illustrations. He also published the collection in an eight-volume edition (1838–43), which included 'doubtful plays' and a biography of 'Shakespere'.

onwards to the birth of Theuth: see *Lectures*, 112: 'The account given of [the German] form of worship by Tacitus, evinces a very superior species of Paganism, indicative of a deep nature; they worshipped the earth—Thorth or Teuth—from whom they themselves claimed to be descended.' TC repeated this description in *Chartism*, in *CME* iv. 170. For Tacitus, see *Germania*, i. 2. See also *The Popular Encyclopedia* (1835–41), vi. 690: 'TUISCON. According to Tacitus, the Germans, in their songs, gave this name to the founder of their nation. *Thuisco* or *Tuisco* is probably the adjective of *Theut* or *Teut*; hence *theutisch, teutsch*. . . . *Theut* signifies something original, independent, e.g. earth, nation, father and lord.'

Hengst's Invasion: Hengist, joint founder with his brother Horsa of the English kingdom of Kent. According to the *Anglo-Saxon Chronicle*, they arrived in 449 at Ebbsfleet in the parish of Minster in the Isle of Thanet.

Teutonic Languages, Teutonic Practices, Existences all came of their own accord: see *Lectures*, 112: 'The thought of the [German] people was forming its deep words long before they came out into speech.'

Wodan: Odin; see note to p. 44.

'small still voices': 1 Kgs. 19:12.

128 *'Heard are the Voices . . . "Choose well . . . despair not"'*: Goethe, 'Symbolum' (1817), in *Werke*, iii. 69–70. For TC's translation of the poem, 25 December 1842, see *CL* v. 252–3.

BOOK III. THE MODERN WORKER.

129 *'on the rim of the sky'*: see note to p. 107.

Moral Philosophies, sanctioned by . . . weak considerations of Pleasures of Virtue and the Moral Sublime: see note to p. 20. The term 'Moral Sublime' is especially relevant to the Scottish philosopher David Hume, who in *A Treatise of Human Nature* (1739–40) discusses the part played by envy and admiration in hero worship: 'Heroism or military glory is much admir'd by the generality of mankind. . . . Men of cool reflexion are not so sanguine in praises of it. The infinite confusions and disorder, which it has caus'd in the world, diminish much of its merit in their eyes. . . . But when we fix our view on the person himself, . . . there is something so dazling in his character, the mere contemplation of it so elevates the mind, that we cannot refuse it our admiration. The pain, which we receive from its tendency to the prejudice of society, is over-power'd by a stronger and more immediate sympathy' (pp. 600–1). See also Neill, 'Hume's Moral Sublime' (1997).

129 *we 'have forgotten God'*: see note to p. 39.

a great unintelligible PERHAPS: as in the last words of Rabelais: '*Je m'en vais chercher un grand peut-être*' (I'm going to search for a great perhaps); see TC, 'Burns', in *CME* i. 313 and *FR* ii. 115.

Greatest-Happiness Principle: see note to p. 20.

Herschel-telescopes: see note to p. 87.

man has lost the soul out of him: see note to p. 43.

This is verily the plague-spot; centre of the universal Social Gangrene: The *London Evening Standard* (16 Aug. 1842), 3 quoted *The Morning Herald*, which employed the same metaphor: 'The investigation . . . that we desire to have immediately commenced should not be confined to these [Lancashire] riots and disturbances . . . —but it is . . . unsafe to hesitate in ascertaining the state of society which exists in these districts—their political sentiments, organisation, and designs . . . and their educational and spiritual destitution. Good wages . . . do not constitute the only desideratum of Lancashire: there must be other removals besides those of unnecessary restrictions on trade and industry, if the seat of our manufacturing glory is not to become a permanent gangrene, a perpetually bursting ulcer.'

upas-boughs: see note to p. 42.

130 *frightful nosology of diseases*: 'A list or catalogue of known diseases' (*OED*, citing TC).

elephantine leprosy: elephantiasis, 'a tubercular disease, often identified with Eastern leprosy' (*OED*).

'Elle a trois cents ans dans le ventre . . . c'est pourquoi je la respecte!': (Fr.) 'She has three hundred years in the belly; that is why I respect her!' The dissident Saint-Simonian philosopher Pierre Leroux attributed the quotation to Victor Cousin, philosopher, professor, and educational reformer, whom he accused of misrepresenting the ideas of Théodore Simon Jouffroy. See Leroux, *De la Mutilation d'un écrit posthume de . . . Jouffroy* (1843), 35: "Quant à moi, reprit M. Cousin, je crois que le Catholicisme en a encore pour trois cents ans dans le ventre. . . . En conséquence, je tire humblement mon chapeau au Catholicisme, et je continue la Philosophie' (As for myself, resumed M. Cousin, I believe that Catholicism has another three hundred years in its womb. . . . As a consequence, I humbly take my hat off to Catholicism and I continue with Philosophy).

The old Pope of Rome . . . they cart him through the streets . . . on Corpus Christi Day: Gregory XVI, pope 1831–46. See Jeremiah Donovan's description of the procession of Corpus Christi in *Rome, Ancient and*

Modern (1842–4), i. 182: 'The Pope, although apparently kneeling, is really seated in a sort of Curule chair, and is borne on the shoulders of his Palafrenieri, dressed in liveries of scarlet silk.' TC's vignette of the 'stuffed' pope recalls his account of the Sansculottes burning the effigy of Pius VI, 'made of lath and combustible gum', on 4 May 1791. See *FR* ii. 116. For a discussion of the passage, see Rosenberg, *Carlyle and the Burden of History* (1985), 130.

131 *Chaos first shivered, and 'sneezed,' at the Arabs say*: Hughes, 317, cites the evidence of David Samuel Margoliouth, Laudian professor of Arabic at Oxford, from *Die verwandlungen des Ebu Seid von Serug; oder Die Makamen des Hariri* (*The Metamorphoses of Ebu Seid by Serug, or the Makamen of Hariri*) (1826), trans. Friedrich Rückert: 'Die Lieblichkeit der Nachtgespräche sprießte—bis daß der Morgen nieste' (The loveliness of the nocturnal conversations blossomed until the morning sneezed) (p. 346). Hariri, or Al-Hariri, Arab poet, scholar, and administrator, was the author of *Maqamat*. Friedrich Rückert was a German poet, translator, and professor of Oriental languages. See TC to John Sterling, 8 June 1837: 'I have met with an excellent Arabian thing the other day: Hariri's *Ebu Seid* translated into German by Rückert . . . . A genuine living soul; fiery-vital in its kind; shining thro' a most exotic Arab vesture' (*CL* ix. 228).

His poor Jesuits, in the late Italian Cholera . . . shone as luminous fixed stars, when all else had gone out in chaotic night: TC refers to the outbreak of cholera in Italy in June and July 1837. *The Times* (15 Sept. 1837) reported, 'Many of the Roman physicians having refused to attend cholera patients, the Government has issued a notice that all medical men withholding their assistance on the present occasion will be disqualified from practising hereafter. The Jesuits and Capuchins appear to be the most zealous of all the monks in their attendance on the sick' (p. 6). See also TC to his mother Margaret Aitken Carlyle, 9 November 1837: 'The poorer sets of Priests had uniformly behaved with courage, with heroism, in the business; . . . the old Pope and the other Cardinals, these with the upper classes generally had shewn the greatest cowardice' (*CL* ix. 345).

Resurgam: (Lat.) 'I will rise again'.

'Divine Humility,' or other 'Highest form of Valour': see *Heroes*, 102–3: 'Odinism was *Valour*; Christianity was *Humility*, a nobler kind of Valour. No thought that ever dwelt honestly as true in the heart of man but *was* an honest insight into God's truth on man's part.'

Jacobinism: the Jacobin Club, first founded by anti-Royalist deputies from Brittany in 1789, became the most powerful political group of the French Revolution and led the government from mid-1793 to mid-1794: 'All Clubs . . . fail, one after another, as shallow fountains: Jacobinism alone has gone down to the deep subterranean lake of waters; and may, unless *filled in*, flow there, copious, continual, like an Artesian well' (*FR* ii. 83).

Orcus . . . 'Groby Pool': Orcus (Lat.) is the personification of Death; for Groby Pool, see Scott, *The Heart of Midlothian*, ch. 29.

132 *Squallacci marching-music*: TC combines 'squall' with the pejorative Italian suffix '-acci' to mean 'wretched squall'. See 'On the Sinking of the Vengeur' (1839), where he refers to the operatic music at Covent Garden as 'the usual *squallacci* melody, natural to the place' (*FR* iii. 631).

Calabash of the Calmucks: see note to p. 125.

fast growing bankrupt too: the insurrections in the Papal States beginning in 1831–2 caused severe financial stress to the Vatican finances, but Pope Gregory XVI ignored the advice of the European powers to implement administrative reforms. From 1833 to 1846, no budgets or balance sheets were published. The *Evening Chronicle* (4 Oct. 1843) reported, 'The Papal finances are in a wretched state; even the current expenses obliged to be met by loans and anticipations, as is the case in Spain; and another Austrian occupation would weigh so heavily upon Papal resources, that the remedy thus applied to revolution would be almost as fatal as the disease' (p. 2). On the succession of Pope Pius IX in 1846, the total debt of the papacy exceeded 200 million francs. For the Vatican's finances in this period, see Cameron, 'Papal Finance and the Temporal Power, 1815–1871' (1957), 132–3 and Pollard, *Money and the Rise of the Modern Papacy* (2005), 27–8.

the 'three hundred': see note to p. 130.

to make his pot boil!: (proverbial) in a state of poverty.

Aristocracy has become Phantasm-Aristocracy: see TC's MS Notes, Forster Collection, fo. 95v: 'That obsolete Lords, not doing their trade or any trade, are still extant, nay abundant more than ever, and jostle you in all thoroughfares, makes nothing to the matter. Do not Phantasms abound at all times on earth, and outnumber Substances for most part there?'

In hydra-wrestle, giant 'Millo-cracy' so-called: for hydra, see note to p. 28. Millocracy is 'The rule of mill-owners; the body of mill owners regarded as a dominant or ruling class' (*OED*, citing TC). In a letter of 7 December 1841 to James Garth Marshall, the Leeds industrialist, TC declared that 'we must have industrial *barons*, of a quite new suitable sort; workers *loyally* related to their taskmasters,—related in God (as we may well say); not related in Mammon alone! This will be the real aristocracy, in place of the sham one; a thing far from us, alas; but infallibly arriving for us;—infallibly, as I think, unless we are to go to wreck altogether' (*CL* xiii. 317).

The Champion of England . . . 'being lifted into his saddle with little assistance': a medieval rite, last performed at the coronation of George IV on 19 July 1821, in which the king's champion challenged anyone to contest the right of the new monarch to reign. The role of champion belonged to the Dymoke family, and at the royal banquet held in Westminster Hall, it was performed by Sir Henry Dymoke. *The Times* (13 July 1821) reported details of the rehearsal of the ceremony: 'The Champion is a fine young man, about 5 feet 10 inches in height, and . . . has made great progress towards giving *eclat* to his character at the coronation. The armour weighs upwards of 70 lb. The Champion, on being dressed, mounted his charger with very little assistance, and immediately rode across the stage, bowing to the ladies' (p. 3).

133 *You will walk in no public thoroughfare or remotest byway of English Existence but you will meet a man . . . that has given up hope in the Everlasting, True*: TC echoes a passage from James Garth Marshall's letter of 5 February 1841 to Charles Wentworth, third earl of Fitzwilliam, reprinted from *The Leeds Times* (6 Feb. 1841) in *The Times* (12 Feb. 1841), 2: 'Look, again, at the crowded streets of our great manufacturing towns—peruse the various statistic accounts by impartial observers, of the terrible destitution, the fearful want, disease, degradation, misery, physical and moral, in every shape, that reigns there. Look at the wan and haggard faces of the workpeople that come into our courts of justice, that attend our public meetings. See how the very race of Englishmen is dwindling down and degenerating under the effects of the unremitting labour, the insufficient and wholesome food that their country's laws allow them to enjoy.' Marshall sent a copy of the letter to TC, who acknowledged receipt, 7 December 1841 (*CL* xiii. 316).

The Honourable Member complains unmusically that there is 'devil's-dust' in Yorkshire cloth: in a debate in the House of Commons, 7 May 1842, William Busfeild Ferrand, MP for Knaresborough, quoted a manufacturer who accused 'Yorkshire people' of using 'shoddy' or 'devil's dust' in the cloth they supplied to the Navy Board for uniforms (*Hansard*, lxi. 149). *The Chester Courant* (22 Mar. 1842) reported that 'one of the leading houses in our city has presented us with a piece of shoddy, *alias* devil's dust cloth, and a very neat specimen it affords of what the millocrats are capable, in pursuit of the mammon they worship' (p. 3). See Engels, *Condition*, 79: 'If a working man once buys himself a woollen coat for Sunday, he must get it from one of the cheap shops where he finds bad, so-called "Devil's Dust" cloth, manufactured for sale and not for use, and liable to tear or grow threadbare in a fortnight.'

the very Paper I now write on is made, it seems, partly of plaster-lime well-smoothed, and obstructs my writing!: see TC to his sister, Jean Carlyle Aitken, 24 October 1842: 'I can now get no paper here anywhere on which a man *can* write otherwise than abominably. It is not made of true rags, it is made of lime and size. An emblem of too many things and persons,—fast breaking down into one huge mass of ruin in these times' (*CL* xv. 145).

that great Hat seven-feet high, which now perambulates London Streets: see Charles Knight, *London* (1841), v. 38: 'The first attempt at something finer than the lumbering machines alluded to was a colossal hat, mounted upon springs like a gig (that badge of the "respectable") which may still be remembered—perhaps still be seen—dashing down Regent Street at the heels of a spirited horse, with the hatmaker's name in large letters on the outside.' For Sauerteig, see note to p. 39.

English Puffery: 'Extravagant or undeserved praise, esp. for advertising or promotional purposes' (*OED*, citing TC).

133 *deranged eightday clock*: see note to p. 39.

134 *burden of the misery*: compare Wordsworth, 'Lines Composed a Few Miles Above Tintern Abbey' (1798): 'the burthen of the mystery' (l. 38).

the broad way: see Matt. 7:13.

Cocker's Arithmetic: *Cocker's Arithmetick, being a Plain and Familiar Method* (1678), a popular textbook written by Edward Cocker.

135 *'consuming the way'*: Gen. 41:30.

it is frightful, when a whole Nation . . . has 'forgotten God': TC echoes Richard Oastler, the factory reformer and Tory Radical, who had been imprisoned for debt on 7 December 1840 and wrote a weekly newspaper, the *Fleet Papers*, from his prison cell. In the issue of 29 May 1841, Oastler attacked free-traders for destroying the quality of manufactured goods in the country: 'They think it no dishonour to buy of sinking men as cheap as they can, knowing full well that they are thus robbing their creditors, and are "greedily gaining of their neighbours by extortion, having forgotten God and his Commandment,—to do unto others as we would they should do unto us;" entirely forgetting that "He will smite His hand at their dishonest gain." . . . The manufacturer is then driven to make deceptive goods;—hence the reason why *now* it is next to impossible to buy any article, even down to a skein of silk or thread, which is worth using' (*Fleet Papers* (1841–4), i. 174).

136 *sound signifying little*: *Macbeth*, v. v. 25–7.

'No Lake of Sicilian or other sulphur burns now anywhere in these ages': as in the lake of fire and brimstone (another word for sulphur that means 'burning stone') in Rev. 20:10. In the nineteenth century, Sicily produced approximately three-quarters of the world's supply of sulphur.

Animalism: 'Animal-like response and behaviour; unmoderated brutality or sensuality' (*OED*, citing TC).

Pluto: in Roman mythology, the god of the underworld and dead.

137 *The terror of "Not succeeding"*: see TC to Thomas Story Spedding, 31 July 1842: 'A man speaks of "Hell" &c: but what is the actual thing he is infinitely afraid of, and struggles with the whole soul of him to avoid? It is what he calls "not succeeding," which, being interpreted, means—what we know. . . . This is verily not the fact of God's universe; God did *not* make his universe so' (*CL* xiv. 248).

'Tremble intensely,' as our friend the Emperor of China says: the Tao-Kuang, emperor of China, 1821–50. *The Examiner* (15 Mar. 1840) quoted from one of his edicts warning Britain not to violate Chinese law or encroach upon its territorial waters: 'The proclamation closes with a threat of the "Celestial Terrors." The "heaven derived-firmness" of the "Great Emperor" . . . invariably "forms its own resolves," and "what his will determines, that surely shall be done." It is quite a common thing to find these proclamations wound up with a piece of polite advice after the following fashion. "*Tremble at this, tremble intensely, intensely!*"' (p. 163). The

trade conflict between the two countries resulted in the First Opium War of 1840–2. The recent 'friendship' to which TC refers was established by the Treaty of Nanking, signed on 29 August 1842, which opened five port cities to British merchants and ceded Hong Kong to the British Empire. For the war and its aftermath, see Ward Fay, *The Opium War, 1840–1842* (1997), and Le Pichon (ed.), *China Trade and Empire* (2006).

Cash-payment is not the sole relation of human beings: see Engels, *Condition*, 282: '[The manufacturer] cannot comprehend that he holds any other relation to the operatives than that of purchase and sale; he sees in them not human beings, but hands, as he constantly calls them to their faces; he insists, as Carlyle says, that "Cash Payment is the only nexus between man and man"'.

'Am I my brother's keeper?': Gen. 4:9. See TC to Thomas Story Spedding, 31 July 1842: 'The Englishman believes that he has *done* with his fellow creature, when he has paid him his money wages; he asks Cain-like, Am I my brother's keeper? and thinks it much if he subscribe to some soup-kitchen' (*CL* xiv. 247–8).

'the very look of him . . . promises so much': see *Sartor*, 181: 'The finer nervous circulation, by which all things, the minutest that [man] does, minutely influence all men, and the very look of his face blesses or curses whomso it lights on, and so generates ever new blessing or new cursing.'

138 *Courts of Requests*: local and metropolitan tribunals established for the recovery of small debts.

last two centuries of Atheistic Government: TC argues here that the restoration of monarchy in 1660 marked the end of true government in England, and the beginning of 'sham-kingship' with the reign of Charles II. See *Cromwell*, vi. 1. 'We have wandered far away from the ideas which guided us in [the Seventeenth] Century, and indeed which had guided us in all preceding Centuries . . . : we have wandered very far; and must endeavour to return, and connect ourselves therewith again! . . . The last glimpse of the Godlike vanishing from this England; conviction and veracity giving place to hollow cant and formulism,—antique "Reign of God," which all true men in their several dialects and modes have always striven for, giving place to modern Reign of No-God, whom men name Devil: this, in its multitudinous meanings and results, is a sight to create reflections in the earnest man!'

Bridgewater Bequests: in 1830 Davies Gilbert, president of the Royal Society, with the assistance of William Howley, archbishop of Canterbury, and Charles James Blomfield, bishop of London, selected eight scientists to write and publish *The Bridgewater Treatises on the Power, Wisdom, and Goodness of God, as Manifested in his Creation* (1833–40). The awards were funded through a bequest of Francis Henry Egerton, eighth earl of Bridgewater.

no man is a Hero, or ever was a Hero, but all men are Valets and Varlets: see *Heroes*, 186: 'Not a Hero only is needed, but a world fit for him; a world not of *Valets*;—the Hero comes almost in vain to it otherwise!'

139 *yet will I despise him*: Job 13:15.

Gehenna and the Pool: 'The place of future torment; hell' (*OED*); see Matt. 5:22, 29.

'seventeen other persons' died of fever there in consequence: see Alison, *Observations*, 192 and n.: 'An Irish widow with four young children, who have been four or five years in Edinburgh, was refused relief from the Charity-Workhouse; and the managers, no doubt, thought they did a service to the city, by keeping this burden from the inhabitants. But mark the consequence. She and her children had lived for some time in extreme destitution, in a close cellar, in a small but crowded close. There one of the children took fever, the others soon sickened, the disease spread to the neighbours, fifteen cases occurred within a very limited space in a few weeks; some of which became a very heavy burden on the Infirmary; one young woman who supported her aged mother died, and the mother became a burden on the city.'

140 *old Spartans . . . compendiously shoot to death this poor Irish Widow*: see *Plutarch's Lives*, i. 153–4: 'It was not left to the father to rear what children he pleased, but he was obliged to carry the child to a place called *Lesche*, to be examined by the most ancient men of the tribe, who were assembled there. If it was strong and well-proportioned, they gave orders for its education, and assigned it one of the nine thousand shares of land; but if it was weakly and deformed, they ordered it to be thrown into the place called *Apothetæ*, which is in a deep cavern near the mountain Taygetus; concluding that its life could be no advantage either to itself or to the public, since nature had not given it at first any strength or goodness of continuation.' *LLC 1842*, 96, lists the 1823 six-volume edition of *Lives*, trans. John and William Langhorne. See also *Sartor*, 169.

Pâté de foie gras, much prized by some!: see *The Examiner* (8 Mar. 1840), 147, quoting from Alexandre Balthazar Laurent Grimod de la Reynière's *Almanach des Gourmands* (1803–12): 'Every one knows the description of the goose in training for the *pâté de foie gras*, in one of the profound French works on the culinary art.— "Placed before a great fire (says the author) and deprived of drink, the condition of the poor bird would, it must be confessed, be painful enough; but when he reflects that his liver, aggrandized to a size immensely exceeding that of all other geese, will be renowned throughout the world as the celebrated *pâté de foie gras*, he resigns himself to his fate without shedding a tear!" '

Gospel of Dilettantism: in *Ainsworth's Magazine* (May 1842), the author of 'The Diary of a Dilettante' argued that 'Diletttanti are "nothing if not critical;" and that their *dicta* are never oracular, but originate more in an enthusiastic love for, than from, any over-pedantic profundity in the mysteries of science and art. In short, Dilettanti are too enthusiastic to be wilfully biassed, and too superficial to be dull' (pp. 229–30).

'Go gracefully idle in Mayfair': Mayfair is a district in the West End of London associated with opulence and luxury.

141 *Man himself is definable in Philosophy as an 'Incarnate Word'*: see *FR* iii. 246.

the brains are quite out!: see note to p. 36.

'the knaves and dastards': see note to p. 45.

there is no serious conversation: see Boswell, *Life of Samuel Johnson* (1791), 756, entry for May 1776: 'Sir, there seldom is any such conversation'.

Moses and the Dwellers by the Dead Sea: TC's loosely paraphrases. See Sale (trans.), *The Koran*, ii. 9 and n.: 'In the days of *David* some *Israelites* dwelt at *Ailah* . . . on the *Red* sea, where on the night of the sabbath the fish used to come in great numbers to the shore, and stay there all the sabbath, to tempt them. At length, some of the inhabitants neglecting GOD's command, catched fish on the sabbath and dressed and ate them. . . . The other part of the inhabitants, who strictly observed the sabbath, used both persuasion and force to stop this impiety, but to no purpose . . . ; whereupon *David* cursed the sabbath-breakers, and GOD transformed them into apes. It is said, that one going to see a friend of his that was among them, found him in the shape of an ape, moving his eyes about wildly; and asking him whether he was not such a one? . . . They add, that these unhappy people remained three days in this condition, and were afterwards destroyed by a wind which swept them all into the sea.' See also *Historical Sketches*, 41: 'Man has fallen into eclipse; . . . he remains a mass of darkness, greediness, baseness; with the figure still of a man, but unhappier than most animals and apes,—than all apes except those that sit on Sabbath by the Shores of the Dead Sea!'

Asphaltic Lake: the Dead Sea; see Pliny, *Naturalis Historia*, cvi. 226: 'Asphaltite Iudeae lacu'.

142 *for commentary thereon, here and there an unmusical chatter or mew:—truest, tragicalest Humbug conceivable by the mind of man or ape!*: their behaviour may have reminded TC of the members of his friend Edward Irving's 'Catholic Apostolic Church'. See TC to his mother, 20 October 1831: 'Irving is pleased to . . . *janner* [talk foolishly] about at great length, as making *his* Church the peculiarly blessed of Heaven, and equal to or greater than the primitive one at Corinth! . . . Last Sabbath, it burst out publickly in the open Church; for one of the "Prophetesses" (a woman on the verge of derangement) started up in the time of worship, and began to "speak with tongues"; and as the thing was encouraged by Irving, there were some three or four fresh hands who started up in the evening sermon, and began their ragings; whereupon the whole congregation got into foul uproar, some groaning, some laughing, some shrieking, not a few falling into swoons: more like a Bedlam than a Christian Church' (*CL* vi. 24–5).

143 *'Worship of Sorrow'*: see TC, *Wilhelm Meister's Travels*, in *Works*, xxiv. 275 and *Sartor*, 143 and n.

Crown of Thorns: see Matt. 27:31.

whipster: 'A slight, insignificant, or contemptible person' (*OED*).

143 *synonymous with Stomach*: see TC, 'Schiller' (1831), in *CME* ii. 189.

may have cheaper New-Orleans bacon: both *The Sun* (5 Oct. 1842) and *The Examiner* (14 Oct. 1842) commented on the recent arrival of large quantities of American ham, bacon, and pork following Peel's reduction of duties on the import of foreign meat. *The Sun* predicted that 'JOHN BULL will now be able to get his ham and bacon cheaper than he has yet done' and hoped that government would realize that 'the more free trade is encouraged, the better it will be for all classes of the community' (evening edn., 5 Oct. 1842, p. 2). See also Taylor, who refers to a 'large . . . stock of pork, beef, and other provisions' that was delivered to New Orleans the previous year and left to rot on the quays because of high British tariffs. As a result, the 'putrescent mass tainted the air and greatly increased the mortality of the yellow fever which annually visits that city.' Taylor condemned an economic policy that produced 'pestilence on one side of the Atlantic and famine on the other;—nakedness in America and starvation in England' (*Notes of a Tour*, 154–5).

144 *A gifted Byron rises in his wrath*: for TC, the poet George Gordon, Lord Byron was representative of modern despair, the necessary spiritual preparation for hope, symbolized by Goethe: 'Close thy *Byron*; open thy *Goethe*' (*Sartor*, 143 and n.).

'it isn't of the slightest consequence': see TC's note to JWC's letter of 26 June 1844: 'A patient in the York Asylum (country attorney, I was told), a small shrivelled, elderly man, sat dining among others, being perfectly harmless, at the governor's table. He ate pretty fairly; but every minute or two inconsolably flung down his knife and fork, stretched out his palms, and twisting his poor countenance into utter woe, gave a low pathetic howl: "I've la-ast mi happetayte!" The wretchedest scarecrow of humanity I almost ever saw, who had found *his* "immeasurable of misery" in that particular "loss"! Date would be autumn 1819; my first visit to England—not farther south than York as yet' (*CL* xviii. 87 and n.). TC visited Yorkshire in October 1820; see *CL* i. 281–3.

"Once I was hap-hap-happy, but now I'm mees-erable!": an expression that TC and JWC converted into coterie speech soon after the publication of *Past and Present*; see TC to JWC, 23 July 1843 (*CL* xvi. 307*)*.

Rest, rest, perturbed spirit: *Hamlet*, i. v. 183.

144–5 *rusty Meat-jack*: 'A machine for turning the spit in roasting meet' (*OED*, citing TC).

145 *goes about pothering*: 'To fluster; worry; to perplex, confuse' (*OED*).

'Happiness our being's end and aim': Pope, *Essay on Man*, iv. 1.

wherein no man can work: John 9:4.

eupeptic Curtis: Sir William Curtis, Lord Mayor of London, 1795–6, and a frequent target of Whig and Radical cartoonists for his corpulent figure and flamboyant taste.

the fattest pig of Epicurus: see Horace, *Epistles*, 1. iv. 15–16; Epicurus was a Greek philosopher who 'taught (i) that pleasure is the only intrinsically valuable thing, though a tranquil life of moderation is the best way to secure it, and (ii) that the gods are not to be feared since they do not concern themselves at all with human affairs' (*OED*).

Job with potsherds: see Job 2:8.

Byron with Giaours: see Byron, *The Giaour* (1813).

146 *The English are a dumb people*: see TC's MS Notes, Forster Collection, fo. 93: 'For withal I honour thee old England for that grand thickheaded and obstinate nature of thine. Thy very stupidity is beautiful to me. Thou canst do greater works than thou canst logically understand, grammatically speak of! Unhappy he with whom it is not <u>even</u> so. I love thee so; are the great and true are so. Thou comest like Oliver Cromwell, a truculent stoical sorrow in thy looks: no wonder. There are things within thee, which no word has yet been coined to speak. Art thou not often lost in the infinite? Stupider of speech, wiser of act, I have known no people.'

Raphael... Reynolds... Mozart... Mr. Bishop: Raffaello Sanzio di Urbino, painter; Sir Joshua Reynolds, painter; Wolfgang Amadeus Mozart, and Sir Henry Rowley Bishop, composers.

Goethe spoke of the Horse: see Goethe, *Annalen oder Tag-und Jahreshefte* (1801): 'Das Pferd steht als Thier sehr hoch, doch seine bedeutende weitreichende Intelligenz wird auf eine wundersame Weise durch gebundene Extremitäten beschränkt' (The horse stands very high as an animal, yet his considerable far-reaching Intelligence is miraculously limited by his bound expression) (*Werke*, xxxi. 97–8).

neck clothed with thunder: Job 39:19.

the silent Russians . . . ever-gesticulating French: see TC to Karl August Varnhagen von Ense, 16 May 1841: 'The French are a speaking people, and persuade numbers of *men* that they are great. . . . Russia again, is not that a great thing, still speechless? From Petersburg to Kamtchatka, the Earth answers—, "Yes" I love the English too, and all the Teutons, for their silence. Th[ey] *can* speak too,—by a Shakspeare, by a Goethe, when the time comes. So[me] assiduous whisking "dog of knowledge" seems to itself a far cleverer creature than the great quiet elephant or noble horse;—but it is far mistaken!' (*CL* xiii. 135–6).

147 *Nature finds a bill against you*: a legal case presented for hearing, which becomes a 'true bill' if the evidence justifies its being heard by judge and jury.

The rugged Brindley: James Brindley, civil engineer who designed plans for building canals to link the river estuaries of the Mersey, Trent, Thames, and Severn. See Andrew Kippis (ed.), *Biographica Brittannica*, 2nd edn. (1778–93), ii. 603: 'When any extraordinary difficulty occurred to Mr. Brindley, in the execution of his works, having little or no assistance from books, or the labours of other men, his resources lay within himself. In order, therefore, to be quiet and uninterrupted, whilst he was in search of the necessary expedients, he generally retired to his bed; and he has been known to lie there, one, two, or three days, till he had attained the object in view.' For TC's copy, see Tarr, 'TC's Libraries', 252, and *Cromwell* vi. 32.

148 *his full-bent bow*: see *Hamlet*, II. ii. 29–31.

Mr. Bull: John Bull.

profound melancholy (as some have said) the basis of thy being: in *Aus Meinem Leben: Dichtung und Wehrheit* (1811–33), Goethe explains the literary origins of the melancholy that he described in *Die Leiden des jungen Werthers* (1774). See TC, 'Goethe': 'Such a cause existed for us in the Literature, especially, the Poetical Literature, of England, the great qualities of which are accompanied by a certain earnest melancholy, which it imparts to every one that occupies himself with it' (*CME* i. 221–2).

vis inertiæ: (Lat.) the power to resist external sensation.

Indian Empires, Americas, New-Hollands: British colonies in India, Canada, and Australia.

149 *Roman thews*: 'The bodily powers or forces of a man (Latin *vires*), might, strength, vigour' (*OED*).

hexameter Iliad: a line consisting of six feet, featuring a different combination of syllables, was a dominant metrical form in classical Greek and Roman literature.

College Philosophies: Hughes, 324 suggests 'academic philosophers like Adam Smith and Dugald Stewart'.

150 *'Art of Speech'*: logic, derived from the Greek *logos*. See Henry George Liddell and Robert Scott, *English–Greek Lexicon* (1893), 901: '(A) logos, the word, or outward form, by which the inward thought is expressed; (B) the inward thought itself, so that logos comprehends both the Latin *ratio* and *oratio*.'

'total stagnation of trade': a phrase employed frequently in the British press between 1840 and 1842. *The Examiner* (21 May 1842) reported widespread distress among the manufacturing districts of the north, including Sheffield, Leeds, and Birmingham: 'With respect to Birmingham, we learn from the [*Birmingham*] *Journal* that there is not so much a diminished flow, as an absolute stagnation, of all business. "Our best and busiest streets wear an appearance of desertion. The number of shops abandoned, and the still greater number that bear the marks of approaching abandonment, give to us the air of a city afflicted by some terrible epidemic, which the prudent householders have quitted, or are preparing to quit, until the calamity has departed. With capitalists, many ruined, and almost all reckless, and a working population, half employed, and half fed, at the best, and a greater number of them in a state approaching to starvation, there are mingled other symptoms of a general breaking up, which judging from history, cannot be looked upon as less fallible"' (p. 332).

All great Peoples are conservative: see TC's MS Notes, Forster Collection, fo. 155: 'Man is a born Conservative from the skin inwards, from the heart outwards. A man that has lost this quality,—let him reflect well,—he is become altogether a morbid, unfertile man!'

Customs . . . in all civilised countries, are accounted final: see *Sartor*, 190: 'What is Philosophy throughout but a continual battle against Custom[?]'

151 *Baconian Inductions*: the method of Francis Bacon, to arrive at the truth based on the facts of experience, rather than proceeding deductively from postulates.

Ready-Reckoner is a Solecism in Eastcheap: *Ready Reckoner; or, Trader's Sure Guide* (1788); for TC and JWC's copy, see Tarr, 'TC's Libraries', 257. A solecism is 'an error, incongruity, inconsistency, or impropriety of any kind' (*OED*, citing TC). Eastcheap is a street in London's financial district.

to be wholly a Reforming People: the *OED* cites the passage to define 'conservatism' as a principle that 'conserves, or favours the conservation of, an existing structure or system; (now esp.) designating a person, movement, outlook, etc., averse to change or innovation and holding traditional ideas and values, esp. with regard to social and political issues'. For TC and the debate between 'Old' and 'New Conservatism', see note to p. 25.

Berserkir-rage: 'A wild Norse warrior of great strength and ferocious courage, who fought on the battle-field with a frenzied fury known as the "berserker rage"' (*OED*, citing TC). Snorri Sturleson used the word 'Bersærker' in book i of *Heimskringla* (*c*.1220), which TC read in a Swedish, Latin, and Icelandic translation by J. Peringskiöld, published in 1697 (see *CL* xii. 32–3). See Sturleson, *The Heimskringla*, trans. Laing (1844), i. 221: 'Odin could make his enemies in battle blind, or deaf, or terror-struck, and their weapons so blunt that they could no more cut than a willow twig; on the other hand, his men rushed forward without armour, were as mad as dogs or wolves, bit their shields, and were as strong as bears or wild bulls, and killed people at a blow, and neither fire nor iron told upon them. These were called Bersærkers.' See also *Lectures*, 112–13: 'The Berserkir was one who despised danger and fear, rushed forth fiercely to battle, and, though without armour, trod down hosts of foes like shells under his feet. Hence his name, Berserkir, "Bare Shirt".' For the disputed etymology between 'bareshirt' and 'bearshirt', see Liberman, 'Berserks in History and Legend' (2005), 410–11.

Pyms and Bradshaws: John Pym was a prominent parliamentary opponent of Charles I; John Bradshaw was a lawyer, politician, and regicide.

Teutsch Fathers in Agrippa's days: for Teutsch Fathers, see note to p. 127; Marcus Vipsanius Agrippa was a Roman military commander who campaigned against the Germans in 38 BC.

'*in whom there is a rage unconquerable by the immortal Gods!*': see Edward Gibbon, *The Decline and Fall of the Roman Empire* (1776–89), I. ix. 215–16: 'But the influence of religion was far more powerful to inflame than to moderate the fierce passions of the Germans. . . . The consecrated standards, long revered in the groves of superstition, were placed in the front of the battle; and the hostile army was devoted with dire execrations to the gods of war and thunder. In the faith of soldiers (and such were the

Germans) cowardice is the most unpardonable of sins. . . . All agreed that a life spent in arms, and a glorious death in battle, were the best preparations for a happy futurity either in this or in another world.' See Sorensen, 'Carlyle, Gibbon, and the "Miraculous Thing" of History' (1991).

152 *Potosi and Golconda*: for Potosi, see note to p. 19. Golconda is a city in Hyderabad, India; a trading centre identified with its nearby diamond mines.

153 *five millions, as is insolently said, 'rejoice in potatoes'*: see Introduction, pp. xxviii–xxix.

'Healing Parliament': see Rapin de Thoyras, *History of England*, ii. 622, citing Charles II's address to the House of Commons and Lords, 29 December 1660: 'Many former Parliaments have had particular denominations from what they have done: they have been stiled Learned and Unlearned, and sometimes have had worse Epithets: I pray let us all resolve, that this be for ever called the HEALING, and the BLESSED PARLIAMENT.'

universal acclamations from the four corners of the British Dominions: see Rapin de Thoyras, *History of England*, ii. 618: 'Every one rejoiced to see at last a calm after so long a storm., and expected to enjoy a tranquillity, fought in vain for so many years. . . . It is not therefore strange that the whole Kingdom should resound with joyful transports, and unite in receiving with loud acclamations a King, who, according to the general expectation, was to restore the public tranquillity and happiness, and put all things in their natural order.'

govern only by so much of God's Christian Law as—as may prove quiet and convenient for us: see *Historical Sketches*, 40–1: 'Once hide this his celestial destiny from poor man; persuade him, by enchantment of whatever sort, that he has nothing to do with Heaven or the Infinitudes, except to cant about them on ceremonial occasions, and for making assurance doubly sure, pray by machinery to them,—alas! Has the thinking soul any sadder spectacle in this world?'

Nell-Gwyns: Eleanor Gwyn, actress and mistress of Charles II.

154 *Oliver Cromwell's body hung on the Tyburn-gallows*: see note to p. 32.

Four Pleas of the Crown: 'All criminal as opposed to civil proceedings, being regarded as conduct committed against the Crown (in Scotland historically limited to proceedings concerned with murder, rape, robbery, and arson)' (*OED*).

High-Church, Low-Church, Church-Extension, Church-in-Danger: High Church is 'a division or tradition within the Anglican communion emphasizing ritual, priestly authority, the Sacraments, and historical continuity with Catholicism' (*OED*); Low Church is 'a division or tradition within the Anglican communion which gives relatively little emphasis to rituals, sacraments, and authority of the clergy' (*OED*); for Church-Extension, see note to p. 39; 'Church in Danger' is a phrase used in debates about Catholic Emancipation Act of 1829 and, later, Church disestablishment.

'Church' of Hurd and Warburton: Richard Hurd, bishop of Worcester and William Warburton, bishop of Gloucester were religious moderates sympathetic to deism.

Anti-Church of Hume and Paine: David Hume, philosopher, historian, and religious sceptic; Thomas Paine, revolutionary activist, author, and deist accused of atheism.

sunk into the sere and yellow leaf: Macbeth, v. iii. 22–3.

'things well let alone': see *Sartor*, 172: '*Laissez-faire*; Leave us alone of *your* guidance, such light is darker than darkness; eat you your wages, and sleep!'

155 *from the inner Heart of Man, from the great Heart of Nature*: see TC, 'State of German Literature' (1827): 'Poetic beauty, in its pure essence, is not by [German] theory, as by all our theories . . . derived from anything external, or of merely intellectual origin. . . . It dwells and is born in the inmost Spirit of Man, united to all love of Virtue, to all true belief in God' (*CME* i. 55–6).

Philips: Ambrose Philips, whose *Pastorals* (1709) were attacked by Alexander Pope in 1713.

The Oracles have been dumb: Milton, 'Hymn on the Morning of Christ's Nativity', l. 173.

156 *an indictment of 'Over-production!'*: in their defence of the Corn Law tariffs, leading Conservatives argued that distress in the northern industrial districts had been caused by overproduction, which had been stimulated by cheap bank loans to manufacturers. The argument was given prominence by the physician George Calvert Holland, who wrote seven letters on the topic to James Garth Marshall that were published in *The Leeds Intelligencer* between 20 February and 5 June 1841. Six were included in Holland's book, *The Millocrat* (1841). *The Times* (13 Mar. 1841) welcomed the first letter as a 'seasonable and pungent dose administered to Mr. J. G. Marshall', and urged that 'every workman in the kingdom ought to read it' (p. 5). In a seventh and final letter to Marshall, published in *The Leeds Intelligencer* on 5 June 1841, Holland reiterated his claim that economic stagnation and poverty in the country were due to '*over-production and reckless speculation*': 'This diminished expenditure, or consumption of productions is alluded to by the repealers *as evidence of the value of the export trade, when it is a measure only of the evils occasioned by the reckless creation of production beyond the legitimate demands*' (p. 6). Marshall forwarded this final letter to TC, who replied on 21 December 1841, 'Pray do not send me any more; I am sick of the unmusical braying, and must dismiss it' (*CL* xiii. 325). Liberals and Radicals were divided in their response to the issue of overproduction. Liberals blamed the phenomenon on the economic imbalance caused by high tariffs. *The Examiner* (11 Dec. 1841) insisted that it is 'manifest that over-production is an untenable charge. It is absurd to suppose that a country of varied and ramified industry can produce too much of everything; it is evident, then, that where the charge

is made, some one industry is more productive than another. This is virtually admitted of the manufacturing industry, when the landlords complain
of the multiplying powers of machinery. Does this productive power harm
the landlords? No; but it injures the people, who make use of it' (p. 786).
Radicals viewed overproduction as a symptom of economic inequality.
The Northern Star (30 July 1842) declared that it is '*possible* TO
PREVENT OVER-PRODUCTION, and yet allow of the illimitable increase
of wealth! Other principles . . . to those adopted by our present *Commercial
men* must be brought into play. . . . The benefits and blessings of every
improvement in mechanics must be secured to all. . . . *Then*, no want; no
fear of want! Then, no "OVER-PRODUCTION"! . . . We have learned how
to *produce* wealth: we have not yet learned how to DISTRIBUTE the wealth
we produce' (p. 4). Influenced by his early reading of Sismondi and the
Saint-Simonians, TC regarded overproduction as a recurrent feature of
a laissez-faire economy organized on the basis of mechanization, competition, the division of labour, and low wages.

156 *fustian . . . cassimere . . . jane . . . nankeen*: fustian, 'a kind of coarse cloth
made of cotton and flax' (cotton and flax' (OED). See Engels, *Condition*,
78–9: 'Fustian has become the proverbial costume of the working man,
who are called "fustian jackets." When Feargus O'Connor . . . came to
Manchester during the insurrection of 1842, he appeared, amidst the
deafening applause of the working man, in a fustian suit of clothing.'
Cassimere is 'a thin fine twilled woollen cloth used for men's clothes'
(*OED*, citing TC); jane is 'a twilled cotton cloth; a kind of fustian' (*OED*);
nankeen is 'a kind of pale yellowish cloth . . . manufactured from ordinary
cotton which is then dyed' (*OED*).

157 *Commercial Bazaar*: the first commercial bazaar in London, the Soho
Bazaar (1815–89), was established by the army contractor and retailer
John Trotter between Soho Sq. and Oxford St. for the sale of fancy goods.
Schiell, *Fundraising, Flirtation and Fancywork* (2012) remarks that by
1816, 'there were at least sixteen additional commercial bazaars' (p. 19).

Howel-and-Jameses: see note to p. 60.

You have produced, produced . . . let him look around: see *Sartor*, 146. Inscribed
in Latin on a marble tablet in the crypt of St Paul's Cathedral, near
Sir Christopher Wren's tomb: 'Beneath is laid the builder of this church
and city, Christopher Wren, who lived above ninety years, not for himself,
but the public good. Reader, if you seek his monument, look around.'

*Millions of shirts, and empty pairs of breeches, hang there in judgment against
you*: there were frequent references in newspapers to the impoverished
condition of the workers and the 'glut' of material goods that they had
produced. *The Sun* (8 July 1842) reported the speech of R. R. Moore,
a delegate from Manchester at the Anti-Corn Law League conference
held at the Crown and Anchor, Arundel St, Strand, London on 6 July
1842: '[The people] were told that the great mischief which they were
suffering under was caused by this—too much clothes for the people to

wear—too much manufactures. . . . Was it to be wondered at that the warehouses were full in this country. How could the people buy shirts; how could the poor man do it? All his earnings went to buy bread. America was not allowed to give the people food for the shirtings they made. The law-makers were not obliged to go ragged. They sold bread, and would as long as there were people to buy. They rolled in purple and fine linen, while the people were starving' (p. 2). *The Examiner* (30 July 1842) quoted another delegate at the same conference who 'might observe of his own neighbourhood—the distress of which it was sometimes alleged had come from over-production—that there were families supported by the weaving of shirtings, who themselves were shirtless' (p. 489).

Two million shirtless or ill-shirted workers sit enchanted in Workhouse Bastilles: see TC's footnote on p. 17 where the total number of paupers listed as '1,429,089'. The *Ninth Annual Report of the Poor Law Commissioners* (1843) specified that 'in the parochial years 1840, 1841, and 1842, there has been a progressive increase in the number of persons relieved, both in and out of the workhouse' (p. 8). *The Examiner* (15 Oct. 1842) conjectured that 'every year the difficulty of producing corn from our own soil . . . augments. There is more than a million added to our population every *four* years, and this million consumes a quarter of wheat. The crop, therefore, that was enough to feed the nation in 1836 leaves, in 1840, a *million* without food; in 1844 *two* millions; and at the period of the next census there will be a population equal to that of the entire kingdom of Belgium' (p. 657).

five million more (according to some) in Ugolino Hunger-cellars: for the figure, according to Dr Robert Bullock Marsham, see Introduction, p. xxviii. For Ugolino, see note to p. 19.

'Raise our Rents!': *The Examiner* (15 Oct. 1842) argued, 'The prosperity of our manufactures and commerce, by increasing wealth and population, have made rents what they are. From the invention of improved machinery to 1814, . . . the rent of land in the United Kingdom was generally increased *four*-fold. It had been nearly stationary in the sixty preceding years' (p. 657).

on the Shores of the Dead Sea: see note to p. 141.

158 *fox-brushes nailed . . . at Melton Mowbray*: fox-brushes, 'The tail of a fox used *similatively*' (*OED*); Melton Mowbray is a fox-hunting centre in Leicestershire.

'consume,' and make away with!: TC implies 'to use up (esp. a commodity or resource), exhaust', as well as 'to purchase or use (goods or services); to be a consumer of' (*OED*).

filthy mills built on these fields of ours: TC parodies Holland's comments about 'rural scenes' in the first letter he sent to James Garth Marshall: 'Had the wealth spent in the building of factories in 1835 and 6 been spent in the gratification of your taste in rural scenes, you would have been better men, would have had larger souls, would have embraced a greater portion of humanity, and the artisan would have experienced none of the misery of the last four years. Take to field-sports, they may perhaps awaken some touch of humanity. You have lived among men until they present themselves to you as machines' (*The Leeds Intelligencer* (20 Feb. 1841), 7).

158 *Cannot we do what we like with our own?*: see note to p. 21.

melt Gneiss Rock: see G. F. Richardson, *Geology for Beginners* (1842), 169: 'Gneiss may be termed stratified, or slaty granite. . . . As regards geological position, it reposes on granite, and is succeeded by the other primary strata, frequently alternating in large masses with one or other of these. In Great Britain this rock occurs in the Western Islands, and North West Highlands of Scotland.'

Doggerbank: 'A large bank or shoal in the North Sea between England and Denmark' (*OED*).

159 *'retire three days to its bed'*: see note to p. 147.

'Land is the right basis of an Aristocracy': see Alexis de Tocqueville, *Democracy in America* (1835), i. 21: 'Land is the basis of an aristocracy, which clings to the soil that supports it; for it is not by privileges alone, nor by birth, but by landed property handed down from generation to generation, that an aristocracy is constituted. A nation may present immense fortunes and extreme wretchedness, but unless those fortunes are territorial there is no aristocracy, but simply the class of the rich and that of the poor.' Tocqueville observed that in the United States, 'Laws were made to establish a gradation of ranks; but it was soon found that the soil . . . was opposed to a territorial aristocracy. To bring that refractory land into cultivation, the constant and interested exertions of the owner himself were necessary; and when the ground was prepared, its produce was found to be insufficient to enrich a master and a farmer at the same time.' TC informed his brother John A. Carlyle on 26 December 1838 that he was reading *De la Démocratie en Amerique* (*CL* x. 252; see Introduction, p. xxx). He also read John Stuart Mill's review of the third and fourth volumes of Henry Reeve's translation, published in *The Edinburgh Review* 72 (Oct. 1840), 1–47. For TC and Henry Reeve, see *CL* vi. 90. See also Innes, Philp, and Saunders, 'The Rise of Democratic Discourse in the Reform Era' (2013).

160 *The soil . . . is properly worth nothing, except 'the labour bestowed on it'*: Hughes, pp. xxxviii–ix, notes similar arguments in the socialist writings of William Godwin, Thomas Spence, William Thompson, and Robert Owen. See Thompson, *An Inquiry into the Principles of the Distribution of Wealth* (1824), 13: 'No matter whether the land be rich or poor, let the desire of making it, or any thing attached to it, tributary to enjoyment, be once produced, and let labor be in consequence applied, the value of the land will necessarily depend on the quantity of labor guided by ordinary skill and judgment bestowed upon it.'

161 *soil . . . is the gift of God*: compare Ps. 24:1: 'The earth is the Lord's, and the fullness thereof; the world, and they that dwell therein.'

seventy millions or upwards: see John Ramsay McCulloch, *A Dictionary, Geographical, Statistical and Historical* (1846), who noted that in 1815 the total annual rent for England and Scotland was £39,405,704. He then cited a less 'authentic' source, an 'Account showing the Total Annual Value of the Real Property Tax in Great Britain [which includes England and Scotland] in 1842–3', which totals '£95, 284, 497' (i. 456).

Ye are as Gods: Gen. 3:5.

guidance and governance to England: see TC, *Chartism*: 'The old Aristocracy were the governors of the Lower Classes' (*CME* iv. 162).

St. Stephen's: St Stephen's Chapel, Westminster Palace, seat of the House of Commons before it burned on 16 October 1834. For TC's description of the fire, see *CL* vii. 319.

162 *"Why am I here?"*:: Liberal and Utilitarian critics voiced similar arguments against the notion of aristocracy. See James Mill (father of John Stuart Mill), 'Aristocracy', *London and Westminster Review* 30 (Jan. 1836), 294: 'A man is elevated above others, only by making others lower than him. But if I am made lower than another man without reason, that is an injury to me: it is injustice and oppression. If another man's pocket is filled out of mine, all the world acknowledges the oppression; but my dignity is dearer to me than my wealth. If then my dignity is lessened to augment the dignity of another man, I am injured in a most precious part.' *The Examiner* (31 Jan. 1836) cited the passage and denounced the author's 'revolutionary . . . justification' (p. 66).

Anti-Corn-Law League: political and economic pressure group comprised of Liberals, manufacturers, and free-trade advocates formed on 20 March 1839 after the House of Commons rejected a motion to reconsider the Corn Laws, which had been imposed in 1815. Members of the league argued that the tariffs threatened manufacturing prosperity by raising the price of grain and thereby reducing exports, increasing wages, and hindering free trade.

Ark of Deliverance: see Exod. 36–8.

163 *Working Aristocracy, admonished by Trades-unions, Chartist conflagrations*: from the inception of the Chartist movement in 1838, members were sceptical of the middle-class Anti-Corn Law League and its free-trade platform. *The Examiner* (9 Dec. 1838) complained that the 'Chartists will not hear of any agitation for the repeal of the Corn Laws. They would rather hunger for dear bread, and have their scope for their industry circumscribed, than take the benefit of the repeal of the Corn Laws by any other means than Universal Suffrage. . . . Like the saints of old, they propose to obtain the paradise of their wishes by starving and scourging themselves, and self-mortification in every form' (p. 769). On 16 February 1842, a petition urging the adoption of the Charter and the repeal of the Corn Laws was signed in Manchester between liberals and Chartists, but the violent agitation and strikes in the northern manufacturing districts in July and August, and the workers' demand for 'a fair day's wages' fractured the alliance. See Thompson, *The Chartists* (1984): 'For the Chartists free trade was not an absolute, but an aspect of economic policy which must

always be under political control. For many of the middle-class free traders, on the other hand, the question had the absolute quality of a religious belief' (2013 edn., 193).

163 *Hippocratic look*: 'An appearance of the face often seen in a person close to death after prolonged or severe illness . . . characterized by pinched features with sunken eyes, hollow cheeks, and a bluish pallor' (*OED*).

Bribery-Elections: following the Conservative election victory in 1841, *The Times* (26 Aug. 1841) endorsed the view of Lord Brougham that 'there never was a House of Commons in the election of which bribery was so universal. The greater part of the electors—the whole, in truth, of the electoral body created by the boasted Parliamentary Reform—consider the elective franchise as the mere means of serving themselves and their families—as an article for sale, to be obtained by the highest bidder' (p. 5). TC agreed. In a letter to his friend Richard Monckton Milnes on 19 July 1841, he predicted, 'Sir [Robert] Peel is a great man; can bribe, coerce, palaver, gain a majority of 70; but Sir Peel cannot make water run permanently upwards' (*CL* xiii. 194).

Kentish-fire: 'A prolonged and ordered salvo or volley of applause, or demonstration of impatience or dissent (said to have originated in reference to meetings held in Kent in 1828–9, in opposition to the Catholic Relief Bill' (*OED*).

MENE, MENE: mysterious words that appear on the wall at the feast of the exiled Babylonian king, Belshazzar. The prophet Daniel is called, and interprets MENE as 'God has numbered thy kingdom and finished it' (Dan. 5:26).

Tanneries of Meudon: see *FR* iii. 187 and n.

164 *Game-Laws*: see Engels, *Condition*, 271: 'One especially barbaric cruelty against the working class is embodied in the Game Laws, which are more stringent than in any other country, while the game is plentiful beyond all conception.' The Game Act of 1671 prohibited most people from hunting game except those who possessed freeholds worth at least £100 annually or leaseholds worth £150 a year. The next major legislative acts involved a ban on the selling of game (1755), and prohibitions against night poaching (1773 and 1817). The Game Act of 1831 'democratized' the hunting of game by the establishment of a close season when birds could not be legally taken, the appointment of gamekeepers, and the introduction of game licences. For the history of English game laws, see Munsche, *Gentlemen and Poachers* (1981).

Chandos-Clauses: introduced by the duke of Chandos (see note to p. 60.) during the committee stage of the 1832 Reform Act to negate the impact of a clause that enfranchised all freeholders of property worth 40s. a year, the bulk of which were urban tenants. The Chandos clause enfranchised tenants paying rents of £50 annually. Landowners inflated these numbers by including relatives in order to give themselves and the rural counties an electoral advantage.

Eldorados: 'The name of a fictitious country . . . abounding in gold, believed by the Spanish and by Sir Walter Raleigh to exist upon the Amazon within the jurisdiction of the governor of Guiana (now Guyana)' (*OED*). See *The Spectator*, 752 (26 Nov. 1842), 1139: 'There may be a feverish hopefulness, lavish credit, busy factories, banks, and joint-stock companies springing up like mushrooms, dreams of an Eldorado millennium, and then a crash, spreading bankruptcy, desolation, and despair over the land.'

'Cannot I do what I like with my own?': see note to p. 21.

Hercules . . . had slain Nemean Lions, cleansed Augean Stables: the first and fifth Labours of Hercules.

165 *Il faut payer de sa vie*: French proverb; 'One must pay with one's life.'

learn what wretches feel: *King Lear*, III. iv. 33–4.

The Czar of Russia . . . worked with his axe in the Docks of Saardam: Peter the Great, tsar of Russia, 1682–1725. See Voltaire, *Histoire de l'empire de Russie sous Pierre le Grand* (1759–63), i. 153–4: 'The tsar began by buying a boat, and with his own hands repaired its broken mast; he then worked on all aspects of constructing a vessel, living the same life as the artisans of Sardam, dressing and eating like them, working in the forges, rope factories, and mills that border the village in numbers, and in which they cut fir and timber, extract oil, make paper, and spin ductile metals. . . . As he wielded the compass and axe at Sardam, the news of the division of Poland was conveyed to him.' *LLC 1842*, 122 lists the forty-one-volume 1818 edition of *Œuvres de Voltaire* (1818), which includes vol. xv, *Histoire de l'empire de Russie sous Pierre le Grand*.

'living chaos of Ignorance and Hunger': *FR* i. 38.

Piepowder earthly Court: 'A summary court formerly held at fairs and markets to administer justice among itinerant dealers and others temporarily resident' (*OED*).

an apparitor: 'An officer of a civil court' (*OED*).

grinder-tooth . . . goes out of their jaw: see note to p. 66.

anatomist-subject: i.e. one worthy of dissection.

Land-Tax Bill, Property-Tax Bill: see note to p. 35.

no Chapter on the Corn-Laws: see Introduction, pp. xxvii–xxviii.

166 *When the brains are out*: see note to p. 36.

Anti-Corn-Law Lecturer: *The Morning Advertiser* (25 Feb. 1840) reported that at a meeting of the Metropolitan Anti-Corn Law Association on 24 February 1840, attended by the influential Liberal MPs John Arthur Roebuck and Charles Pelham Villiers, the delegates 'resolved that . . . lectures on the evils and enormities of the corn laws should be given in every part of London' (p. 2). In a letter to his brother Alexander on 27 December 1842, TC reported that on the previous day, Villiers, MP for Wolverhampton, had 'called here, and left his address, while I was out' in order to 'engage *me* too in the service of the "the League"; to "lecture" for him, or the like. I am already engaged for a far bigger LEAGUE' (*CL* xv. 244).

166 *'hundred thousand pounds an hour'*: see p. 152.

'strangled in the partridge-nets of an Unworking Dilettantism': see p. 130.

to cut us out of this market and then out of that!: in *Reports from Commissioners: Condition of the Hand-Loom Weavers* (1841), published on 19 February, a parliamentary committee led by Nassau William Senior cited the assessment of Dr John Bowring, editor of the *Westminster Review* (1824) and a member of the Committee on Manufactures and Trade (1833), on the impact of foreign competition on unemployment in the profession: 'Our legislation prohibiting the export of machinery has wholly failed in its object. It has not prevented the exportation of machines from England, for such machines are to be found in every continental establishment: but it has led to the introduction of many machine-making establishments on the continent, and to the emigration of large numbers of our most intelligent artisans. In fact, our prohibitions have only had the effect of transferring to the continent the trade in the manufacture of machinery, of which we might long have kept the monopoly; so that the prohibitions have injured nobody but ourselves' (*Reports from Commissioners*, 30). In the same month a parliamentary select committee was appointed to investigate the operation of laws affecting the exportation of machinery. For TC's correspondence with Bowring, see *CL* v. 227–8 and 300–1.

167 *Fill your lungs with cotton fuz*: in his article, 'Observations and Experiments Concerning Molecular Irritation of the Lungs' (1831), Dr James Phillips Kay Shuttleworth revealed the harmful impact of breathing 'cotton-fuzz' on the health of the factory workers: 'Entrance into the atmosphere of the mill immediately occasions a dry cough, which harasses him considerably in the day, but ceases immediately after he leaves the mill and inspires an atmosphere free from foreign molecules' (p. 359). See TC to his brother Alexander Carlyle, 26 March 1833: 'When one reads of the Lancashire Factories and little children labouring for sixteen hours a day, inhaling at every breath a quantity of cotton *fuz*, falling asleep over their wheels, and roused again by the lash of thongs over their backs, or the slap of "billy-rollers" over their little crowns . . . one pauses with a kind of amazed horror, to ask if this be Earth the place of Hope, or Tophet where hope never comes!' (*CL* vi. 372).

copperas-fumes: 'Ferrous sulphate . . . also called green vitriol, used in dyeing, tanning, and making ink' (*OED*, citing TC).

slaves of the lamp: as Aladdin's lamp in the *Arabian Nights*.

168 *straps and billy-rollers*: spinning implements, as well as instruments of punishment. TC's source for child labour in the Lancashire factories was probably the Paisley-born author and journalist John Wilson, whose article 'The Factory System' was published in the April 1833 issue of *Blackwood's Edinburgh Magazine*: 'A billy-roller is a heavy rod, from two to three yards long, and of two inches diameter, with an iron pivot at each

end. Its primary and proper function is to run on the top of the cording over the feeding cloth. Its secondary and improper function is to rap little children "on the head, making their heads crack, so that you may hear the blow at a distance of six or eight yards, in spite of the din and rolling of the machinery." . . . Suffice it to say, the billy-roller is in active employment in many factories—that black strap is in frequent work in them all' (p. 441).

Man is a Patent-Digester: TC's ironic reference to Dennis Papin's steam digester, forerunner of the steam engine and pressure cooker. See *Sartor*, 155.

Law of Nature must end, in 'over-population': Thomas Malthus's argument in *An Essay on the Principle of Population* (1798) that the growth of population would exceed the food supply and create 'positive checks' such as 'the want of proper and sufficient food' and 'hard labour and unwholesome habitations'. To these 'checks' Malthus also included 'vicious customs with respect to women, great cities, unwholesome manufactures, luxury, pestilence, and war' (p. 31). For TC's criticism of Malthus, see *Sartor*, 167–70, *Chartism*, in *CME* iv. 200–1; see also Jordan, 'Carlyle and Political Economy' (2017), 297–300.

169 *Trade in twenty years . . . could double itself*: see Malthus, *Essay* (1798), 7: 'The population of the Island is computed to be about seven millions, and we will suppose the present produce equal to the support of such a number. In the first twenty-five years the population would be fourteen millions, and the food being also doubled, the means of subsistence would be equal to this increase. In the next twenty-five years the population would be twenty-eight millions, and the means of subsistence only equal to the support of twenty-one millions. In the next period, the population would be fifty-six millions, and the means of subsistence just sufficient for half that number.'

man of Macedonia . . . 'Come and help us': Acts 16:9.

'minimum of Four thousand five hundred a year': see *First Report of the Church Commission*, 17 March 1835, appointed 'to consider the state of the Established Church, with reference to ecclesiastical duties and revenues'. The commission concluded that 'where the annual income of a Bishop amounts to 4,500*l.*, it is not necessary to make any addition; nor would we recommend any diminution, unless it exceed 5,500*l*' (n.p.). As a comparison, in his article, 'Statistics of the Present Depression Trade at Bolton' (1842), Henry Ashworth recorded that weavers and cotton hands earned in 1836 an average wage of £2. 14s. 2*d* per month (p. 79).

170 *Manchester Chamber of Commerce*: founded as a 'Commercial Society' in 1794, the Manchester Chamber of Commerce was initially guided by protectionist policies, but in 'the first twenty years of the present century . . . it became deeply imbued with the doctrine of Free Trade, which supplied the seed-bed in which the Manchester School was propagated and reared' (Helm, *Chapters in the History of the Manchester Chamber of Commerce* [1902], 4–5).

170 *Mahometan Paradises*: see Sale (trans.), *The Koran*, i. 96: 'The orthodox say [Paradise] is situate above the seven heavens (or in the seventh heaven) and next under the throne of GOD; and to express the amenity of the place, tell us that the earth of it is of the finest wheat flower, or of the purest musk, or, as others will have it, of saffron; that its stones are pearls and jacinths, the walls of its buildings enriched with gold and silver, and that the trunks of all its trees are of gold'.

adventurous Sindbads: 'Sindbad the Sailor' in the *Arabian Nights*, recounting the mariner's seven voyages in search of wealth.

Chandos Farm-labourers: see note to p. 60.

"nous avons changé tout cela!": (Fr.) 'we have changed all that!' In Molière's *Le Médecin malgré lui* (1666), the sham doctor Sganarelle's responds to Géronte's objection 'that the heart is on the right side, and the liver on the left side': 'Yes, that used to be so; but we changed all that, and now we are doing medicine in a whole new way' (II. iv).

Sinai Thunder: see Exod. 19:16.

Spinning-Mule: machine invented by Samuel Crompton in 1779 to enable the mass production of thread for the textile industry.

Mayfair Clothes-Horse: 'A person whose main function is or appears to be to wear or show off clothes' (*OED*, citing TC). For Mayfair, see note to p. 140.

171 *'wine-and-walnuts philosophy'*: Tennyson, 'The Miller's Daughter', ll. 31–2, published in *Poems* (1842), i. 102–14.

"Soul, take thy ease": Luke 12:19.

Castle-Rackrent: referring to 'a very high, excessive, or extortionate rent; *spec.* a rent equal . . . the value of the land' (*OED*); see also Maria Edgeworth, *Castle Rackrent* (1800).

Plugson, Hunks and Company, in St. Dolly Undershot: '*Plugson* means the son of (*Pflock* [*wooden peg* or *plug*] or *Stöpfel* [*stuffing*]), and is merely intended to indicate a coarse stupid Manchester man; *Undershot* is the name used by manufacturers for a mill-wheel supplied with water from below; as *overshot* is the name for one supplied from above. *Plugson of Undershot* may be said to be emblematic of *Manchester Commercial Philosophy*' (Mary Aitken Carlyle to Friedrich Althaus, 12 February 1869, in *CL* xlvi. 11). A hunk is 'a large piece cut off (e.g. from a loaf, cheese, etc.); a thick or clumsy piece; a lump; a hunch' (*OED*). Dolly is 'a black doll hanging outside . . . [a shop] often serving as a low or illegal pawn-shop' (*OED*).

Book-keeping by double entry: 'The method of bookkeeping in which every item entered to the credit of one account in the ledger is entered to the debit of another, and vice versa' (*OED*).

'written on the iron leaf': see TC, 'German Playwrights' (1829), in *CME* i. 384, and 'Boswell's Life of Johnson', in *EOL*, 162. See also Sale (trans.), *The Koran*, ii. 431: 'Every thing which they do *is recorded* in the books *kept*

by the guardian angels: and every *action*, *both* small and great, is written down in the *preserved table.*'

172 *a 'glorious Chivalry,' much besung down to the present day*: see William Robertson, *The History of the Reign of Charles V* (1769), i. 70–1: 'THIS singular institution [chivalry], in which valour, gallantry, and religion, were so strangely blended, was wonderfully adapted to the taste and genius of martial nobles; and the effects were soon visible in their manners. War was carried on with less ferocity, when humanity came to be deemed the ornament of knighthood no less than courage. . . . Violence and oppression decreased, when it was reckoned meritorious to check and to punish them. . . . The political and permanent effects of the spirit of chivalry have been less observed. . . . The sentiments which chivalry inspired, had a wonderful influence on manners and conduct during the twelfth, thirteenth, fourteenth, and fifteenth centuries. They were so deeply rooted, that they continued to operate after the vigour and reputation of the institution itself began to decline.' The *LLC 1842*, 102, lists the twelve-volume 1817 edition of Robertson's *Works*, which includes vols. iv–vii, *Charles V.* For TC and Robertson, see *CL* iii. 39, 42, and 58. See also Thomas Chalmers, *On Political Economy in Connexion with the Moral State and Moral Prospects of Society*, 2nd edn. (1832), 369: 'It is not for the sake of its ornaments and its chivalry alone . . . that we want the the high rank and fortune of our aristocracy to be upholden. . . . Where there are nobles, the common people are not so ignoble.' *LLC 1842*, 22 lists the twenty-one-volume 1840–1 edition of Chalmers's *Complete Works*, which includes vols. xix–xx, *On Political Economy.* For TC and Chalmers, see *Rem.*, 246–52.

173 *Mights . . . mean Rights*: 'I suppose, as usual, Might and Right will have to make themselves synonymous in some way. CANST and SHALT if they are *very* well understood, mean the same thing under this Sun of ours' (TC to Emerson, 5 November 1836, in *CL* ix. 84).

godless Bucanier and Chactaw Indian: see Sir Walter Scott, preface to his poem *Rokeby* (1813), p. x: 'When the Buccaneers carried on their depredations at sea, they boarded, without respect to disparity of number, every Spanish vessel that came in their way; and, demeaning themselves, both in the battle and after the conquest more like dæmons than human beings, they succeeded in impressing their enemies with a sort of superstitious terror. . . . From piracy at sea, they advanced to making predatory descents on the Spanish territories, in which they displayed the same furious and irresistible valour, the same thirst of spoil, and the same brutal inhumanity to their captives. The large treasures which they acquired in their adventures, they dissipated by the most unbounded licentiousness in gaming, women, wine, and debauchery of every species.' The Chatah are a Native American people who occupied what is today SE United States; see James Adair, *The History of the American Indians* (1775), 284–5: 'The Choktah quite deform their face, and give themselves an appearance, which is disagreeable to any but those of their own likeness. Their features and mind, indeed, exactly correspond together; for, except the intense love they bear to their native country, and their utter contempt of any kind of danger, in defence of it, I know no other virtue they are possessed of: the general observation of the traders among them is just, who affirm them to be divested of every property of a human being, except shape and language.' *LLC 1842*, 1 lists the 1775 edition of Adair.

173 *the rudest Caliban of a body*: Caliban, son of the witch Sycorax, 'not honor'd with | A human shape' (*The Tempest*, 1. ii. 283–4).

Fiat-Lux: see note to p. 92.

garments rolled in blood: Is. 9:5.

Howel Davies: Welsh pirate ambushed and killed while seeking to plunder the Portuguese island of Principe, 19 June 1719; his history is recounted in Captain Charles Johnson's popular *A General History of the Pyrates* (1724), 174–207.

174 *Napoleon is flung out, at last, to St. Helena*: after the French defeat at Waterloo, Napoleon was banished to the island in the South Atlantic, where he arrived on 15 October 1815.

Hence these tears: Terrence, *Andria*, i. 125.

175 *William the Norman Bastard*: William the Conqueror, illegitimate son of Robert II, duke of Normandy and Herleva.

Taillefers, Ironcutters: Taillefer (Fr.) 'Ironcutter', Norman troubadour who died while heroically leading William the Conqueror's troops into battle at Hastings in 1066. See *FR* i. 8 and n.

what we will call Law-ward: see note to p. 83. See also TC's MS Notes, Forster Collection, in the voice of Oliver Cromwell: 'My poor beloved countrymen,—alas, Priests have become chimerical, and your Lords (Law-wards) do stick the stubble ground with dry bushes in preservation of their partridges, and are become to the simplest what in my time they were becoming to the wisest, an incarnate solecism' (fo. 54v).

176 *Westminster*: see note to p. 157.

'A man by the very look of him promises so much': see note to p. 137.

'Organisation of Labour;'—which must be taken out of the hands of absurd windy persons: TC supported many of the social and economic objectives advocated by Henri, comte de Saint-Simon in *Nouveau Christianisme* (1825), which he translated in 1830 (*CL* v. 203). In particular, TC endorsed the Saint-Simonian model of a society governed by a meritocratic elite and guided by the motto, 'To each according to his capacity, to each capacity according to its works' (*CL* v. 278). But he rejected the democratic socialist revisions to Saint-Simon's hierarchical model that Louis Blanc outlined in a series of articles that he wrote in the periodical *Revue du progrès* in 1839 and published as *Organisation du travail* (1841). In the book Blanc declared, 'In the Saint-Simonian doctrine, hierarchy is established by election from above. In our project, on the contrary, the hierarchy is established mainly by election from below. In the Saint-Simonian doctrine, the action of society is entirely concealed behind the action of power.

In our project, society receives the impulse of power, but once this is received, she remains subject only to supervision. In the Saint-Simonian doctrine, the problem of the distribution of benefits is solved by this famous formula: *to each according to his capacity, to each capacity according to its works*. In our project, the inequality of ability is assigned as a basis for the difference in wages only temporarily and with significant restrictions' (p. 117). In 1849 TC wrote to Blanc to commend him for his 'denunciation of . . . the actual figure of Society'. Nonetheless, TC explained, he preferred the expression 'just *government*' to what Blanc called 'association'. In an earlier letter to Jelinger Cookson Symons in 1848, TC was more explicit, insisting that the 'Organization of Labour' was 'an actual inevitability in every country', but 'must be taken up not à la Louis Blanc but in precisely the opposite manner (by military *command* namely, and death-penalty needful)' (*CL* xxiii. 261, 163). For TC and the 'Organization of Labour', see Fielding, 'Carlyle and the Saint Simonians' (1976) and Jordan, 'Noble Just Industrialism' (2015), 217–310. For TC and Blanc, see Heyrendt-Sherman, 'From Social Reformer to Political Conservative' (2021–2).

177 *Know thy work and do it*: see *Sartor*, 123: 'Know what thou canst work at'. In 'Corn Law Rhymes' (1832), TC emphasizes the pedagogical value of work: 'To work! What incalculable sources of cultivation lie in that process, in that attempt; how it lays hold of the whole man, not of a small theoretical calculating fraction of him, but of the whole practical, doing and daring and enduring man; thereby to awaken dormant faculties, root out old errors, at every step! He that has done nothing has known nothing. Vain is it to sit scheming and plausibly discoursing: up and be doing! If thy knowledge be real, put it forth from thee: grapple with real Nature; try thy theories there, and see how they hold out' (*EOL*, 204). For the 'Gospel of Work' and the significance of the essay, see Waithe, 'The Pen and the Hammer' (2013). See also TC's advice to a young student, 14 March 1843: 'A man perfects himself by work much more than by reading. They are a growing kind of men that can wisely combine the two things . . . and prepare themselves withal for doing other wider things' (*CL* xvi. 83). For the political implications of TC's 'gospel of work', see Breton 'Utopia and Thomas Carlyle's "Ancient Monk"', (2013) and *Gospels and Grit* (2005), 38–40; Spencer, *Political Economy of Work* (2009), 32–46; Ulrich, *Signs of Their Times* (2002), '"A Labor of Death and A Labor Against Death"' (1995), and 'The Reinscription of Labor' (1995); and Himmelfarb, *Idea of Poverty* (1984), 204–5. Bell, *The End of Ideology* (1959) credits TC with reviving the traditional Protestant notion of *homo faber* that 'all work was endowed with virtue' (pp. 261–2).

fair seedfields: see TC, *Wilhelm Meister's Travels*: 'My inheritance, how wide and fair! | Time is my estate; to Time I'm heir' (*Works*, xxiv. 192). See also 'Characteristics' (1831), in *CME* vi. 43.

178 *A formless Chaos, once set it revolving . . . by mere force of gravity, into strata, spherical courses*: in *Mécanique céleste* (1805), the mathematical physicist

and astronomer Pierre-Simon Laplace extended Immanuel Kant's theory that the solar system began as a cloud of dispersed particles, the mutual gravitation of which eventually led to the formation of planets. See *Sartor*, 3: 'Our Theory of Gravitation is as good as perfect. . . . Laplace . . . even guesses that it could not have been made on any other scheme.' For TC and Laplace, see *Rem.*, 310.

178 *Potter's wheel . . . old as the Prophet Ezechiel*: TC confuses Ezekiel with Jeremiah; see Jer. 18:2–3.

179 *'Doubt, of whatever kind, can be ended by Action alone'*: see TC, *Wilhelm Meister's Apprenticeship* (1824): 'Doubt of any kind can be removed by nothing but activity' (*Works*, xxiii. 386).

All these things and persons are there not for Christopher's sake and his Cathedral's; they are there for their own sake mainly!: see 'Sir Christopher Wren', in *Lives of Eminent Persons* (1833), 23: 'Many improper persons were joined with [Wren] in the commission; and they, having private interests to serve, and selfish feelings to indulge, were thwarted by the inflexibility of Wren, who exposed at once their meanness and their ignorance. This, it may be supposed, was neither forgotten nor forgiven; and they joined in a cabal, persecuting him with every species of bitter malevolence.' *LLC 1842*, 75 lists the 1833 edition of *Lives*.

The pious munificence of England lies far-scattered, distant, unable to speak, and say, "I am here": see 'Sir Christopher Wren', 19: 'Thus was this splendid edifice, admitted to be the second for grandeur in Europe, completed in thirty-five years by one architect, under one bishop of London, costing only 736,000l., which was raised by a small impost on coals brought to London; whilst St. Peter's, the work of twelve architects, took one hundred and forty-five years to build, during the pontificate of nineteen popes.'

the last topstone of that Paul's Edifice: see 'Sir Christopher Wren', 19: 'In thirty-five years from the commencement of the building, the highest and last stone was laid by Christopher, the son of the architect.'

the stamp 'Great Man' impressed very legibly on Portland-stone there!: see 'Sir Christopher Wren', 19: 'But whilst Bramante, for the erection of St. Peter's, had the quarries of Tivoli at his command, which yielded blocks of nine feet in diameter, . . . Wren had only the quarries of Portland, and from them he could not reckon on blocks greater than four feet in diameter, nor were even these readily procured.'

179–80 *Like Gideon thou shalt spread out thy fleece at the door of thy tent*: Judg. 6:36–40.

180 *'It is so,' says Goethe, 'with all things that man undertakes in this world'*: see TC, *Wilhelm Meister's Travels*: '"We look upon our scholars," said the Overseer, "as so many swimmers, who, in the element which threatened to swallow them, feel with astonishment that they are lighter, that it bears and carries them forward: and so it is with everything that man undertakes"' (*Works*, xxiv. 321).

Norse Sea-king: see Washington Irving, 'Voyages of the Scandinavians', in *A History of the Life and Voyages of Christopher Columbus* (1828), iv. 213: 'It has been asserted that the Norwegians, as early as the ninth century, discovered a great tract of land to the west of Iceland, which they called Grand Iceland. . . . The most plausible account is one given by Snorro Sturleson, in his Saga or Chronicle of king Olaus.' *LLC 1842*, 61 lists the 1828 edition of Irving's *Columbus*. For TC and Irving, see *CL* ii. 134, 137. See also TC, 'Early Kings of Norway' (1875): 'These were the times of Norse colonisation; proud Norsemen flying into other lands, to freer scenes,—to Iceland, to the Faröe Islands, which were quite vacant' (*CME* v. 205).

it is no friendly environment this of thine, in the waste deep waters: see Irving, *History of Columbus*, i. 3: 'At the beginning of the fifteenth century, when the most intelligent minds were seeking in every direction for the scattered lights of geographical knowledge, a profound ignorance prevailed among the learned as to the western regions of the Atlantic; its vast waters were regarded with awe and wonder, seeming to bound the world as with a chaos, into which conjecture could not penetrate, and enterprise feared to adventure.'

Brother, these wild water-mountains . . . are not entirely there on thy behalf!: see Irving, *History of Columbus*, i. 3–4, quoting the Muslim cartographer, Egyptologist, and geographer Muhammad al-Idrisi: 'No one has been able to verify anything concerning the [ocean], on account of its difficult and perilous navigation, its great obscurity, its profound depth, and frequent tempests. . . . There is no mariner who dares to enter into its deep waters. . . . The waves of this ocean, although they roll as high as mountains, yet maintain themselves without breaking; for if they broke, it would be impossible for ship to plough them.'

Ursa Major: (Lat.) 'Greater Bear'; constellation in the northern sky, in a contrary direction to 'the Tropics and Equators'.

shoulder-of-mutton sails in this cockle-skiff of thine!: shoulder-of-mutton is 'a triangular sail attached to a mast' (*OED*). TC uses the word 'cockle' in the Scottish sense, 'to move or rock unsteadily . . . to fall or overturn' (*OED*). A cockle-skiff is 'a small light boat of any kind' (*OED*). See Irving, *History of Columbus*, i. 181–2: 'The smallness of the vessels was considered an advantage by Columbus . . . enabling him to run close to the shores, and to enter shallow rivers and harbours. . . . But that such long and perilous expeditions into unknown seas, should be undertaken in vessels without decks, and that they should live through the violent tempests by which they were frequently assailed, remains among the singular circumstances of these daring voyages.'

thou art among immeasurable dumb monsters, tumbling, howling wide as the world here: see Irving, *History of Columbus*, i. 409–10: 'Many lamented their friends as lost, . . . picturing them as driven over wild and desert wastes of water without a shore, or as perishing amidst rocks and quicksands, and whirlpools; or a prey to those monsters of the deep, with which credulity, in those days, peopled every distant and unfrequented sea.'

180 *the favouring East*: see Irving, *History of Columbus*, i. 193: 'In his computations Columbus advanced [Japan] about a thousand leagues too much to the east; supposing it to lie in the situation of Florida, and at this island, he hoped first to arrive.'

Mutiny of men thou wilt sternly repress; weakness, despondency, thou wilt cheerily encourage: see Irving, *History of Columbus*, i. 228: 'Columbus endeavoured to pacify [his crew] by gentle words and promises of large rewards; but finding that they only increased in clamour, he assumed a decided tone.'

181 *Brahmins, Antinomians, Spinning Dervishes*: a Brahmin is 'a member of the highest or priestly caste among the Hindus'; an Antinomian is 'one who maintains that the moral law is not binding upon Christians. . . . One of a sect which appeared in Germany in 1535'; a dervish is 'a Muslim friar, who has taken vows of poverty and austere life. Of these there are various orders, some of whom are known from their fantastic practices as dancing or whirling' (*OED*). See *FR* iii. 5 and n.

'Laborare est Orare, Work is Worship': TC's version of 'Ora et labora' ('work and prayer'), commonly regarded as a motto of the Benedictines. See TC to Thomas Erskine, 22 October 1842: 'For myself, I feel daily more and more what a truth there is in that old saying of the monks, *Laborare est orare* [to work is to pray]. I find really that a man cannot make a pair of shoes rightly unless he do it in a *devout* manner; that no man is ever paid for his real work, or should *ever* expect or demand angrily to be paid; that all *work* properly so called is an appeal from the Seen to the *Unseen*—a devout calling upon Higher Powers; and unless *they* stand by us, it will not be a work, but a quackery' (*CL* xv. 138).

Talfourd–Mahon Copyrights: see note to p. 47.

if thou have ears to hear: Mark 4:9.

Sinai thunders: see note to p. 170.

182 *wherein no man can work*: see note to p. 145.

Kepler calculations, Newton meditations: Johann Kepler's discovery of a law in the movement of planets prepared the ground for Isaac Newton's discovery of the law of gravitation.

'Agony of bloody sweat': Luke 22:44.

'With it, my son, or upon it!': see Plutarch, *Moralia: Lacænarum Apophthegmata*, xvi.

folding of the hands to mere sleep: Prov. 6:10.

183 *'Much of my life has been trifled away!'*: see Boswell, *Life of Johnson* (1791), entry for 5 August 1763: 'I have been an idle fellow all my life' (Oxford World's Classics edn., p. 329). See also Johnson, *Prayers and Meditations*, 2nd edn. (1785), 139 (14 Apr. 1775): 'I find that so much of my life has stolen unprofitably away'.

'Fair day's-wages for a fair day's-work': see note to p. 31.

'to the extent of keeping your worker alive that he may work more': see Smith, *Wealth of Nations*, i. 178: 'But though in disputes with their workmen, masters must generally have the advantage, there is however a certain rate, below which it seems impossible to reduce, for any considerable time, the ordinary wages of even the lowest species of labour. A man must always live by his work, and his wages must at least be sufficient to maintain him. They must even upon most occasions be somewhat more; otherwise it would be impossible for him to bring up a family, and the race of such workmen could not last beyond the first generation.'

Owen's Labour-bank: the socialist mill owner Robert Owen inaugurated the National Equitable Labour Exchange at 277 Gray's Inn Rd on 17 September 1832. In this new 'bazaar', cooperative producers could circumvent profiteering intermediaries by trading their goods directly for labour notes based on the time employed to perform skilled work. In a letter to *The Times* (5 Oct. 1832), Owen explained that the purpose of the exchange was to 'enable all who have wealth which they wish to dispose of for other wealth, of equal value in the present estimation of society, to do so with the least loss or trouble, without moral degradation, and ultimately to effect all exchanges between the producers of wealth or of valuable services of any kind, in a manner the most beneficial for all parties' (p. 2).

184 *My brother, the brave man has to give his Life away*: see TC's MS Notes, Forster Collection, fo. 53: 'A brave men then as now has to give his life away. I will not have your gain. Give it, I say: (as for them, the brave have always done so, will always (Lord be thanked) do so). Thou dost not expect to sell thy life in an adequate manner? What price for example, would content thee? The just price of thy life to thee—the whole universe of Space and Eternity of time: that is the price that would content thee; that and thou wilt consider, nothing short of that. It is thy all; thou wouldst for it have all. Thou wilt never sell thy life (or any part of thy life) in an adequate manner. Give it, like a free hero heart; let the price be nothing: thou hast then in a certain sense, the only possible sense, got all things for it.'

'By Heaven, they shall either be invaluable or of no value; I do not need your guineas for them!': see Lockhart, *Life of Robert Burns* (1828), 380, quoting a letter from Burns to his publisher George Thomson, [16] September 1792: 'As to any remuneration, you may think my songs either above or below price; for they shall absolutely be one or the other. In the honest enthusiasm with which I embark in your undertaking, to talk of money, wages, fee, hire, &c. would be downright prostitution of soul.' TC reviewed Lockhart's biography in his essay 'Burns'.

bodies forth the form of Things Unseen: *Midsummer Night's Dream*, v. i. 14–17.

his poor Delf Platter: delftware, tin-glazed pottery, associated with Delft, Holland, and manufactured in England from the sixteenth century.

185 *the Manes*: 'The deified souls of dead ancestors . . . the spirit or shade of a dead person, considered as an object of homage or reverence or as demanding to be propitiated' (*OED*).

Lubberlands: 'An imaginary land of plenty without labour; a land of laziness' (*OED*).

noise of greedy Acheron: see note to p. 113.

Thy work, like Dante's, shall 'make thee lean for many years': see Dante, *Paradiso*, xxv. 1–4.

waste waves and their weedy gulf-streams: see Irving, *History of Columbus*, i. 212–13: 'The sea, as far as the eye could reach, was covered with weeds, a phenomenon often observed in this part of the ocean, which has sometimes the appearance of a vast inundated meadow. . . . These field of weeds were at first regarded with great satisfaction, but at length they became, in many places, so dense and matted, as in some degree to impede the sailing of the ships, which must have been under very little head-way.'

'Se tu segui tua stella!': (It.) 'If you follow your star'; Dante, *Inferno*, xv. 55 and *Heroes*, 77.

Green-eyed dragons watching you, three-headed Cerberuses . . . 'Eccovi l' uom ch'è stato all' Inferno': for green-eyed, see *Othello*, III. iii. 194. Cerberus is 'The watch-dog that guarded the entrance of the infernal regions, represented as having three heads' (*OED*). See Dante, *Inferno*, vi. *Eccovi . . . all' Inferno* (It.) = 'Behold, there is the man who has been in Hell.' See *Heroes*, 78, where TC reports this reaction of the people of Verona 'when they saw [Dante] on the streets'. The quotation is loosely based on an anecdote, probably apocryphal, recounted by Boccaccio in *Trattatello in laude di Dante* (1350–5) and included in Cesare Balbo, *Vita di Dante* (1839), ii. 345–6 (*LLC 1842*, 7, lists this edition).

as Poet Dryden says, you do walk hand in hand with sheer Madness, all the way: see Dryden, 'The Epistle Dedicatory', *The Spanish Fryar or, the Double Discovery* (1681): 'So little value there is to be given to the common cry, that nothing but Madness can please Mad-men, and a Poet must be of a piece with the Spectators, to gain a reputation with them'. *LLC 1842*, 36, lists the eighteen-volume 1808 edition of Dryden's *Works*, edited by Walter Scott.

Eurydice from Tartarus: in Greek myth, the musician Orpheus tried to retrieve Eurydice from the underworld (Tartarus), but lost her by violating the command of the gods not to look back at her before reaching the upper world.

186 *'Black or White Surplice' Controversies*: see 'Movements in the Church,' *Fraser's Magazine* 26 (Dec. 1842), for a summary of recent efforts by Tractarians (see note to p. 113) to promote changes to Anglican religious practice. In particular, the Tractarians criticized the Anglican habit of wearing the black 'Geneva' gown during sermons and recommended 'the

white surplice, as the proper clerical habit, as well in the pulpit as in the reading desk' (p. 717). *The Examiner* (15 Oct. 1842) earlier reported the speech of Charles James Blomfield, bishop of London, at the triennial visitation of his diocese at St Paul's Cathedral. He advised his audience that 'when there was only one officiating clergyman, that it was much better for him to ascend the pulpit immediately after leaving the communion table, and thus preach in his surplice. The gown was probably first worn by lecturers when there was no communion service. On the whole, he thought it wise if the clergy would preach in their surplices in the morning, and in their gowns in the afternoon' (p. 658). The *Fraser's* article predicted that such compromises would do 'little good either to [the Bishop] or the Church' (p. 728).

All men, if they work not as in a Great Taskmaster's eye, will work wrong: see Milton, 'How Soon Hath Time' (1632), ll. 13–14.

Antæus-like: in Greek myth, Antaeus was the giant wrestler and son of Poseidon and Gaia, invincible as long as he remained in contact with his mother, the Earth.

187 *Civil-List*: 'A list of items of expenditure for the civil administration of the state, the support of the monarch and royal household, and other official pensions and salaries; the recipients of payments on this list' (*OED*).

Goulburn–Baring Budget: Henry Goulburn, chancellor of the exchequer, 1828–30 and 1841–6; Sir Francis Thornhill Baring, chancellor of the exchequer, 1839–41.

"sinews of war": Cicero, *Philippics*, v. ii. 5.

'Arms and the Man' . . . *'Tools and the Man'*: see *Aeneid*, i. 1 and *Sartor*, 31: 'Nowhere do you find [Man] without Tools; without Tools he is nothing, with Tools he is all.' See also TC to James Garth Marshall, 1 February 1843: 'A *real* Aristocracy, in place of a false imaginary Aristocracy, is becoming and already become indispensable for English Society,—and the Captains of Industry, not the Captains of Idleness whatever array and honours they may for the present hold, are the men for that. Not "arms and the man" now our epic; no, it is "Tools and the man!" Not "arms and the man"; how much less "White waistcoats and the man!" I counsel you to go on, and *be* a real King, and guide, and just *Law-ward* (antique for "Lord") or Preserver of God's Law, among your people' (*CL* xvi. 39–40).

188 *villani, bordarii, sochemanni*: '*Villani*, villeins, were so called from *villa* a country farm, whereat they were were dependent to do service. They were unfree, registered as of the soil, and bound to till the lord's lands; holding by the base tenure called villenage. So servile was their condition that they were usually sold and transferred with the farm to which they belonged'; '*Bordarii* or bordars were a . . . class of small, customary, unfree, cottage tenants; bound to supply the lord with poultry and eggs, and other small provisions for his *board* or entertainment' (Harland, *Mamecestre*, 19, and n.). For sochemanni, see note to p. 79.

189 *'Eu Sachsen, nimith euer saches, You Saxons, out with your gully-knives,
     then!'*: see Nennius, *Historia Britonum*, ed. Stevenson (1838), 37. TC bor-
     rowed the book, together with Giles's 1841 translation of Gildas and
     Nennius, from the London Library on 7 October 1842 (*P&P Strouse*,
     457). See also TC's MS Notes, Forster Collection, fo. 100, where TC links
     Cromwell's first recorded speech in Parliament, '11th day of February
     1628–29' (*Cromwell*, vi. 65–5 to Nennius' words: ' "If these be the steps to
     promotion what are we to expect?" Floats on the whirlpool of tradition like
     that other speech written down one knows not where first or when first by
     the Phantasm Nennius: "Eu Saxons, nimith eure Saxes!" '

     Fire-Chariot of Pain: 2 Kgs. 2:11.

     to die slowly all our life long, imprisoned in a deaf, dead, Infinite Injustice: see
     Tocqueville, *Democracy in America*, vol. i, p. xxv: 'Men are not corrupted
     by the exercise of power or debased by the habit of obedience; but by the
     exercise of power which they believe to be illegal and by obedience to
     a rule which they consider to be usurped and oppressive.'

     as in the accursed iron belly of a Phalaris' Bull: Phalaris was a legendary
     Sicilian tyrant of the sixth century who roasted his victims alive in a hollow
     brass bull, and eventually roasted in it himself. See *FR* iii. 81 and n.

     Revolts of Three Days: the 1830 Revolution in Paris.

     infecting seventeen persons: see note to p. 139.

     'Hlaf-dig,' Benefactress, 'Loaf-giveress': see Hughes, 340: 'The true deriv-
     ation is from OE *hlæf-diȝe*, from *hláf* = loaf + root *díg*, to knead (cf. dough) =
     the "loaf-kneader." '

     Presbyter or 'Priest': 'An elder in the Christian Church' (*OED*).

     Dahomey: an influential W African kingdom in the eighteenth and nine-
     teenth centuries, located in present-day Benin, known for its efficient
     military and flourishing economy built on slavery, conquest, and inter-
     national trade.

190 *'Let us pity the poor white man . . . no sister to grind him corn!'*: see Mungo
     Park, *Travels in the Interior Districts of Africa* (1799), 198: 'They lightened
     their labour by songs, one of which was composed extempore; for I was
     myself the subject of it. It was sung by one of the young women, the rest
     joining a sort of chorus. The air was sweet and plaintive, and the words,
     literally translated, were these.—"The winds roared, and the rains
     fell.—The poor white man, faint and weary, came and sat under our
     tree.—He has no mother to bring him milk; no wife to grind his corn.
     Chorus. Let us pity the white man, no mother has he, &c. &c." ' *LLC 1842*,
     91 lists the two-volume 1815–16 edition of *Travels*.

     *Gurth had the inexpressible satisfaction of feeling himself related indissolubly,
     though in a rude brass-collar way, to his fellow-mortals in this Earth*: Engels
     contrasts the unfavourable 'condition of the free Englishman of 1845 with
     the Saxon serf under the lash of the Norman barons of 1145': 'The serf
     had a guarantee for the means of subsistence in the feudal order of society

in which every member had his own place. The free working man has no guarantee whatsoever, because he has a place in society only when the bourgeoisie can make use of him; in all other cases he is ignored, treated as non-existent. The serf sacrificed himself for his master in war, the factory operative in peace. The lord of serf was a barbarian who regarded his villein as a head of cattle; the employer of operatives is civilized and regards his "hand" as a machine. . . . Slaves they both are, with the single difference that the slavery of the one is undissembled, open, honest; that of the other cunning, sly, disguised, deceitfully concealed from himself and everyone else, a hypocritical servitude worse than the old' (Engels, *Condition*, 192–3).

190 *Gurth is now 'emancipated'*: see Scott, *Ivanhoe*, ch. xxxii: 'No longer a serf, but a freeman and a landholder, Gurth sprung upon his feet. . . . "A smith and a file to . . . do away the collar from the neck of a freeman!" '

Liberty, I am told, is a divine thing: see Tocqueville, *Democracy in America*, i. 46: 'Religion is no less the companion of liberty in all its battles and its triumphs; the cradle of its infancy, and the divine source of its claims. The safeguard of morality is religion, and morality is the best security of law, and the surest pledge of freedom.'

You do not allow a palpable madman to leap over precipices: compare Tocqueville, *Democracy in America*, quoting Cotton Mather, *Magnalia Christi Americana* (1702): 'There is a liberty of corrupt nature, which is affected both by men and beasts to do what they list; and this liberty is inconsistent with authority, impatient of all restraint. . . . But there is a civil, a moral, a federal liberty which is the proper end and object of authority; it is a liberty for that only which is just and good: for this liberty you are to stand with the hazard of your very lives, and whatsoever crosses it, is not an authority, but a distemper thereof. This liberty is maintained in a way of subjection to authority; and the authority set over you will, in all administrations for your good, be quietly submitted unto by all but such as have a disposition to shake off the yoke and lose their true liberty, by their murmuring at the honour and power of authority' (i. 43–4).

191 *being themselves very truly* ἄριστος *BRAVEST, BEST*: see *OED*, etymology for 'aristocracy': 'Latin *aristocratia*, Greek ἀριστοκρατία, < ἄριστος best + -κρατία rule'.

a William the Conqueror, a Tancred of Hauteville: for William the Conqueror, see note to p. 175; Tancred was a Norman lord of southern Italy, one of the leaders of the First Crusade.

Hereward and the Fen Countries, fate of Earl Waltheof; Yorkshire and the North reduced to ashes: 'Hereward the Wake' was a legendary Anglo-Saxon nobleman who in 1070 allied with invading Danish forces against Norman rule in the fenlands of East Anglia; see Lyttelton, *Henry the Second*, i. 418–20; Rapin de Thoyras, *History of England*, i. 173–4; and Thierry, *Histoire de la conquête*, ii. 150–63. Waltheof, earl of Northumbria, was a magnate who joined Danish forces in 1069 in an attack against king

William's castles in York, but was later pardoned; see Lyttelton, *Henry the Second*, i. 45–9; Henry, *History of Great Britain*, iii. 13–19; Thierry, *Histoire de la conquête* ii. 51–63; and André Du Chesne et al., *Historiæ Anglicanæ* (1807; *LLC 1842*, 81) 322–7. For Yorkshire and the North, see Rapin de Thoyras, *History of England*, i. 171–2: 'The *Norman* Garrison upon the approach of the *Danes*, resolved to hold out to the last Extremity, not doubting but the King would come to their Relief with all possible expedition. In this expectation they set Fire to the Suburbs at the foot of the Castle, that the Houses might not be of Service to the Besiegers. But the Fire spreading farther than was designed, a great part of [York] was reduced to ashes. . . . William was so provoked with the *Northumbrians*, that he was heard to swear by God's Splendour, he would not leave a Soul alive. As soon as he entered Yorkshire, he began to execute his Threats by terrible ravages.'

191 *'A child, in this William's reign, might have carried a purse of gold from end to end of England'*: see Lyttelton, *Henry the Second*, i. 73: 'How well [William] performed [the duty of a sovereign] we may learn even from the testimony of a contemporary Saxon historian, who says, that during his reign a man might have travelled in perfect security all over the kingdom with his bosom full of gold.'

192 *'Par la Splendeur de Dieu!'*: see note to p. 191.

193 *To what extent Democracy . . . advances irresistible with ominous, ever-increasing speed, he that will open his eyes on any province of human affairs may discern*: see Tocqueville, *Democracy in America*, vol. i, p. xxi: 'The whole book which is here offered to the public has been written under the impression of a kind of religious dread produced in the author's mind by the contemplation of so irresistible a revolution, which has advanced for centuries in spite of such amazing obstacles, and which is still proceeding in the midst of the ruins it has made. . . . If the men of our time were led by attentive observation, and by serious reflection, to acknowledge that the gradual and progressive development of social equality is at once the past and future of their history, this solitary truth would confer the sacred character of a Divine decree upon the change. To attempt to check democracy would be in that case to resist the will of God.' For a draft version of this passage from *Past and Present*, see TC's MS Notes, Forster Collection, fo. 50.

From the thunder of Napoleon battles, to the jabbering of Open-vestry in St. Mary Axe, all things announce Democracy: TC appears to confuse the parish of St Mary Axe in the City of London with St Marylebone in NW London. The governing body or 'vestry' of Marylebone was dominated by Nonconformists and Radicals. In 1839 *The Morning Herald* journalist James Williamson Brooke argued in *The Democrats of Marylebone* that the 'principle of government in operation in the parishes of St. Marylebone and St. Pancras . . . approaches so nearly to that of a pure Democracy, that [it] furnishes . . . a deeply instructive illustration of the operation and effects of the form of government upon a larger scale. . . . It furnishes, in a word, an indication not to be mistaken of what would be the fate of those institutions, were a purely Democratic form of government established in England' (pp. iii–iv). TC may be referring specifically to a 'very stormy meeting' of the Marylebone Vestry held in St Pancras and reported in *The Times* on 14 November 1842. The purpose of the session was to decide on the proposal of Joseph Hume, the Radical MP for Middlesex, 'to erect a monument to the "Scotch Reformers" of 1793–94'—Maurice Margarot, Thomas Muir, Joseph Gerrald, Thomas Fyshe Palmer, and William Skirving—who had been tried for sedition and transported. After 'stormy discussion', plans were approved to 'select the three most appropriate designs, and submit them to the vestry for their choice of the most suitable for erection' (p. 5). TC, who regarded Hume as a 'block-head', had attended his commemoration of the 'Scotch Martyrs' in 1837 at the Crown and Anchor, 9 Great Guildford St., London, and quipped to John Stuart Mill, 'Let me be forgotten forever rather than remembered in that manner' (22 Feb. 1837; *CL* ix. 156).

Wahngasse of Weissnichtwo: Wahngasse ('Illusion') Street, in Weissnichtwo ('Know not where'), 'private domicile' of Professor Diogenes Teufelsdröckh; see *Sartor*, 16.

Democracy, which means despair of finding any Heroes to govern you: see TC, *Chartism*: 'Across all democratic turbulence . . . is the wish and prayer of all human hearts, everywhere and at all times: "Give me a leader; a true leader, not a false sham-leader; a true leader that he may guide me on the true way" ' (*CME* iv. 159).

his Excellenz the Titular-Herr Ritter Kauderwälsch von Pferdefuss-Quacksalber: 'Sir Gibberish Clovenfoot Quack-Doctor' (Altick, 215 and n.); an allusion to Robert Peel.

Malines-lace: Malines is a lace-making centre in Belgium.

Sumptuary Laws: 'Designating a law or regulation which limits personal expenditure or consumption, esp. relating to particular items of clothing, food, or furniture, typically for the purpose of preventing extravagance or reinforcing social hierarchy' (*OED*).

The first Antique Cheruscan who, of felt-cloth or bear's-hide, with bone or metal needle, set about making himself a coat . . . it was soon visible that . . . sleeves . . . would be an improvement: an early Germanic tribe living between the Elbe and Weser rivers, the Cherusci defeated the Romans at the Battle of Teuttoberg Forest in AD 9. See Tacitus, *Germania*, xvii. 1–3: 'For clothing, [the German tribes] wear a cloak, fastened with a clasp, or, in its absence, a thorn. . . . They also wear the skins of wild beasts, the tribes adjoining the river bank in casual fashion, the further tribes with more attention, since they cannot depend on traders for finery. . . . The women have the same dress as the men . . . the upper part of this costume does not widen into sleeves: their arms and shoulders are therefore bare, as is the adjoining portion of the chest.'

194 *Stulz, with huge somerset, vaults from his high shop-board down to the depths of primal savagery*: John Stultz, Regency tailor, and director of the firm

Stultz, Housley and Stultz, whose fashionable customers included Beau Brummell. *The Examiner* (9 Dec. 1832) reported his death on 17 November: 'The great Mr. Stultz, tailor, in Clifford Street [No. 10 Clifford St., Bond St.], who retired to France a few years ago, and was created Baron Stultz, died . . . at his estate called Aires, in the South of France, after an illness of nine days. This estate cost him upwards of 100,000ℓ. . . . He had another large estate on Baden-on-the-Rhine. About a year ago the Baron sent the Emperor of Austria a present of 40,000ℓ., to do with what he pleased, for which present he received in return the Order of Maria Theresa, and the patent of Count Gothenberg. The Baron had great wealth in the Bank of Vienna (Rothschild's). His property, besides his estates, exceeded 400,000ℓ' (p. 797). TC may be referring indirectly to a report in *The Times* (1 Jan. 1830) of the execution at the Old Bailey of William Leslie and Stephen Sandford 'who were tried and found guilty of a burglary on the premises of Messrs. Shultz, the well-known tailors in Bond-street, and the latter was also convicted of attempting to shoot the watchman in endeavouring to make his escape' (p. 3).

194 *Sedan and Huddersfield*: cloth-making centres in NE France and W Yorkshire respectively.

like the Genius of Sleep or of Death: Sleep and Death were twin brethren in classical mythology; see *Aeneid*, xvi. 231. They were represented on Roman tombs either leaning or holding a torch reversed.

195 *'the liberty of not being oppressed by your fellow man'*: compare Tocqueville, *Democracy in America*, ii. 161: 'Under the absolute sway of an individual despot, the body was attacked in order to subdue the soul . . . but such is not the course adopted by tyranny in democratic republics; there the body is left free, and the soul is enslaved.'

Windsor Georges: St George, patron of the Order of the Garter, the insignia of which includes two jewels, the Great George and the Lesser George.

Pot of Heavy-wet: see note to p. 42.

Thou who walkest in a vain shew: Ps. 39:6.

'fill himself with the east wind': Job 15:2.

196 *twenty-thousandth part of a Talker in our National Palaver*: by estimates of the population, each MP represented 20,000 constituents. From Portuguese, *palavra*, 'speech or talk'; TC uses it to denote 'unnecessary, profuse, or idle talk; chatter' (*OED*). See *FR* ii. 21 and n.

Pococurantism: see note to p. 123.

Beau-Brummelism: referring to George Bryan 'Beau' Brummell, Regency dandy and socialite.

if you go back to 'the Dead Sea,' there is, say our Moslem friends, a very strange 'Sabbath-day' transacting itself there!: see note to p. 123.

197 *a thousand Moseses . . . whom they would 'invite to dinner,' be glad to meet with in lion-soirées*: TC may be reminded of Lockhart's description of Burns's predicament in respectable society: 'To play the lion under such

circumstances, must be difficult at best; but a delicate business indeed, when the jackals are presumptuous' (Lockhart, *Burns*, 225); see also *Heroes*, 66.

'Stuffed Clothes-suits created by the ninth-parts of men': proverbial, 'nine tailors make a man'; see *Sartor*, 213: 'And this is [the tailor], whom sitting downcast, on the hard basis of his Shop-board, the world treats with contumely, as the ninth part of a man!'

198   *succedanea for salt*: a succedaneum is 'a substitute' (*OED*, citing TC). See note to p. 56.

SIR JABESH WINDBAG : see note to p. 127.

wondrous successive 'Births of Providence': see Cromwell's speech of 22 January 1655: 'If this be of human structure and invention, and if it be an old Plotting and Contriving to bring things to this Issue, and that they are not the Births of Providence,—then they will tumble' (*Cromwell*, viii. 188). See also *Heroes*, 200.

199   *Oliver . . . the Ablest-Man of England, the King of England*: see TC, MS Notes, Forster Collection, fo. 95r: 'Oliver Cromwell the last (King) Koenning of England may, now at this date when there is a prospect of either other kings or else of national destruction, be a figure worth dwelling on (Ah, Ah!) —'.

Mr. Facing-both-ways, Viscount Mealymouth, Earl of Windlestraw: Mr Facing-both-ways, as in Janus, the Roman god with two faces (after whom January is named); see *FR* ii. 215 and n. Mealy-mouthed is 'ingratiating, unctuous; hypocritical' (*OED*). Windlestraw is 'A dry, thin withered stalk of grass'; figuratively, 'light, trifling, or flimsy . . . of feeble health or character' (*OED*); see *Sartor*, 48.

Cagliostro, Cagliostrino, Cagliostraccio: Cagliostro, 'little Cagliostro', and 'scoundrel Cagliostro', referring to Giuseppe Balsamo, the 'Arch-Quack' and swindler known as Count Alessandro di Cagliostro. For his life, see TC, 'Count Cagliostro: In Two Flights' and 'The Diamond Necklace', in *Historical Essays*, 23–83 and 85–151 respectively.

Windbag . . . strong only in the faith that Paragraphs and Plausibilities bring votes: in an article entitled 'Our Predictions', *The Examiner* (12 Nov. 1842) summarized its year-long campaign against Peel, 'the Deceiver-General', justifying its original view of him in June 1841 as a 'juggler' who through "the science of darkness," or the concealment of his intentions, [seeks to obtain] the suffrage of both agriculturalists and manufacturers'. The paper hoped that it had 'sufficiently well understood the juggles of [the Tories] tricky chief. The whole craft . . . resolves itself into political sharping or swindling, and is just as easy to explain what the trickster is about to do as it is to tell a countryman what is to happen to him when a benevolent gentleman, whom he has met in the streets, cautions him against the London rogues, and shows him how to take care of his money' (p. 723).

Locker of Davy Jones: 'In nautical slang . . . the grave of those who perish at sea' (*OED*).

199 *Oliver knew that his America lay THERE*: see TC, *Wilhelm Meister's Apprenticeship*, quoting Lothario: '*Here or nowhere is America!*' (*Works*, xxiii. 11).

prosper and get Paragraphs: get coverage in the newspapers.

199–200 *redemption nowhere in the Worlds or in the Times discoverable for him*: TC suggests that Peel was distrusted by both Liberals and Conservatives. *The World* (1826–33) was the influential organ of the Congregationalist Church, edited by Stephen Bourne, who was a close friend of the prominent Whig peer Henry Vassall-Fox, third baron Holland. *The World* promoted various liberal causes, including universal freedom of religion, abolitionism, and solidarity between Christians and Jews; see Monaco, *Rise of Modern Jewish Politics* (2013), 34–5. *The Times* was edited by John Thadeus Delane, who succeeded Thomas Barnes in May 1841. H. R. Fox Bourne observed in *English Newspapers* (1887) that the paper 'was inclined towards more Liberal action than old-fashioned Tories favoured. . . . "The Times," under Delane, while personally attacking [Peel], helped his cause considerably in such ways as seemed good to it, with much prejudice and more arrogance, but in ways that were too serviceable for him to take much umbrage at whatever was ungracious in their method or adverse in their details.' With respect to his 1842 budget proposals, the paper 'condemned the change in guarded terms, writing in the interests of the wealthy merchants and great landowners with whom it was nearly always in accord' (ii. 168–9).

200 *Thou appealest to Posterity, thou?*: on 11 March 1842, Peel presented his budget to the House of Commons, in which he introduced an income tax levied at sevenpence in the pound on those with incomes over £150 for three years. His aim was to reduce the growing budget deficit and to offset any revenues that might be reduced as a result of the 'sliding scale' of reductions in import tariffs (see note to p. 39.). In his speech, Peel referred to the economic perils that the country now faced, and compared these to previous challenges: 'There may be a natural tendency to overrate the magnitude of the crisis in which we live . . . but I think it is impossible to deny that the period in which our lot and the lot of our fathers has been cast—the period which has elapsed since the first outbreak of the French revolution—has been one of the most memorable periods that the history of the world will afford. The course which England has pursued during that period will attract for ages to come the contemplation, and I trust, the admiration of posterity.' Peel described the deficit as a 'mighty evil', and warned landowners that 'if you do permit [it] to continue, you must expect the severe but just judgment of a reflecting and retrospective posterity' (*Hansard*, lxi. 464–6). *The Examiner* (19 Mar. 1842) rejected Peel's 'prating' comparison to 'the sacrifices of our fathers', and disputed the relevance of his historical parallels: 'There is no Napoleon now threatening the destruction of our commerce, but instead of that enemy the more formidable landlords compassing the same end, not by clumsy Berlin and Milan decrees, but by the surer process of the Corn Law' (p. 177).

201 *They appealed to the Eternal God; not to Posterity at all!*: see *Historical Sketches*, 280: 'The vision of Eternity shall be all; and the vision of Time, except in reference to that, shall be nothing.'

O Advanced-Liberal, one cannot promise thee any 'New Religion,' for some time; to say truth, I do not think we have the smallest chance of any!: TC advocated the Saint-Simonian economic model of the 'organisation of labour' (see note to p. 176), but remained sceptical of the group's religious arguments. See TC to Gustave D'Eichthal, 17 May 1831: 'Were the Saint-Simonian Doctrine stated as a mere Scientific Doctrine, or held out as the *Prophecy of an Ultimate Perfection* towards which Society must more and more approximate,—I could with few reservations subscribe to it, and heartily agree with you that it was the duty of all men, by whatever best means they had, to forward such a consummation. Nevertheless, in one quarter, lies a mighty chasm, the darkness of which is still to me quite void. You call yourselves a *Church*, and founders of a new *Religion;* which Religion, permit me to confess, I hitherto seek for in vain' (*CL* v. 278).

Fanaticism, for any Fanum: Latin etymology of 'fanatic' is *fānum, meaning* temple (*OED*).

202 *I will as soon think of making Galaxies and Star-Systems to guide little herring-vessels by, as of preaching Religion that the Constable may continue possible*: see *FR* iii. 51: 'Not a Parish Constable, in the furthest hamlet, who has said *De par le Roi*, and shewn loyalty, but must retire, making way for a new improved Parish Constable who can say *De par la République*.'

this new second progress, of proceeding 'to invent God,' is a very strange one!: see Saint-Simon, *Nouveau Christianisme* (1825), 7–8: 'La première doctrine chrétienne n'a donné à la société qu'une organisation partielle et très incomplète. . . . La nouvelle organisation chrétienne déduira les institutions temporelles, ainsi que les institutions spirituelles, du principe que *tous les hommes doivent se conduire à l'égard les uns des autres comme des frères*' (The first Christian doctrine gave society a very partial and incomplete organization. . . . The new Christian doctrine will deduce temporal institutions, as well as spiritual institutions, based on the principle that all men should behave towards one another as brothers). See also Introduction, pp. xxxi–xxxii.

Jacobinism unfolded into Saint-Simonism: see note to p. 176.

the thing itself might draw tears from a Stoic!: Stoicism was an ancient Greek school of philosophy 'conformable to the principles of the Stoics; austerity, repression of feeling, fortitude' (*OED*). For TC's indebtedness to the philosophy, see Jordan, 'Thomas Carlyle and Stoicism' (2021).

some twelve or thirteen New Religions, heavy Packets, most of them unfranked, having arrived here from various parts of the world: TC discussed the theme of 'New Religions' with a variety of correspondents during the period in which he wrote *Past and Present*, including Emerson, 29 August 1842 (*CL* xv. 56–9) and 17 November (*CL* xv. 192–4); Bronson Alcott, 22 September 1842 (*CL*, xv. 100); Joseph Ormrod, 8 October 1842 (*CL* xv. 120–1);

Hensleigh Wedgwood, 22 October 1842 (*CL* xv. 139–40); an Unidentified Correspondent, 27 October 1842 (*CL* xv. 150); and John Sterling, 2 November 1842 (*CL* xv. 159–61). He may also be recalling the 'packet of books' sent to him in July 1830 by Gustave D'Eichthal and the '*Saint Simonian Society*' (9 Aug. 1830; *CL* v. 136–7). Unfranked packets refer to those that were not prepaid.

202 *if the charge exceed one penny*: as a result of bylaws established by the new penny post in 1840, the cost of packages that exceeded the prescribed weight was to be paid by the recipient.

'*near to Reading Abbey*': see note to p. 106.

'*on the rim of the horizon*': see note to p. 107.

Inner Light or Moral Conscience: the doctrine of the 'inner light' is based on the revelation described by George Fox, founder of the Quakers, in his *Journal* (1694), 8: 'And when all my hopes in [Priests], and in all Men was gone, so that I had nothing outwardly to help me, nor could tell what to do; Then, O! then I heard a Voice, which said, "*There is one, even Christ Jesus, that can speak to thy Condition*." . . . For though I read the *Scriptures* . . . yet I knew him not, but by *Revelation*. . . . And I had not Fellowship with any *Peoples*, *Priests*, nor *Professors*, nor any sort of *separated People*; but with *Christ*, who hath the *Key*, and opened the door of *Light* and *Life* unto me.' But TC's identification of this 'light' with 'moral conscience' did not accord with Quaker teaching. As Robert Barclay explained in *An Apology for the True Christian Divinity* (1678), 93, 'We do further rightly distinguish [this Divine and pure Light] from man's natural Conscience; for Conscience, being that in man, which ariseth from the natural faculties of man's Soul, may be defiled and corrupted.' *LLC 1842*, 7, lists the 1780 8th edition of Barclay. For TC and George Fox, see *Sartor*, 154 and n.; for TC's article on the Quakers in David Brewster's *Edinburgh Encyclopædia*, see G. B. Tennyson, 'Unnoted Encyclopaedia Articles by Carlyle' (1963).

Kircherean Visual-Spectra: the magic lantern, misattributed to the German Jesuit polymath Athanasius Kircher. For 'Phantasms', see note to p. 120.

'*All religion issues in due Practical Hero-worship*': see *Heroes*, 11.

though you rose from the dead to preach him one: Luke 16:31.

203 *Non extat*: (Lat.) 'It does not exist'.

Fetishism: the worship of a fetish, 'an inanimate object worshipped by pre-literate peoples on account of its supposed inherent magical powers, or as being animated by a spirit' (*OED*).

founding Cities by the Fountain of Juturna, on the Janiculum Mount: landmarks of ancient Rome.

Prophet Samuel and Psalmist David: Samuel, prophet and judge who helped to reunite the Israelites in Canaan under the rule of King David.

Salem: Jerusalem; see Ps. 76:2.

'*Solemn before us . . . Graves under us silent!*': Goethe, 'Symbolum', in *Werke*, iii. 69–70.

204 *Carlton Clubs*: club founded by the Conservative party in 1832.

He will say with Faust: 'Who dare name HIM?': Goethe, *Faust*, pt. 1, sc. xviii, in *Werke*, xii. 180.

the Eternal Temple: 1 Cor. 3:16 and 2 Cor. 6:16.

'Thy will be done': Matt. 6:10.

204–5 *"Behold I will shew thee worse things than these: women weeping to Thammuz"*: Ezek. 8:13–14; Tammuz is the Mesopotamian god of fertility.

205 *thirty-two azimuths*: all of the points of a compass.

'the Inspiration of the Almighty': Job 32:8.

Joe-Manton Dilettantisms: see note to p. 40.

Tanneries at Meudon: see note to p. 163.

But for that same preternatural quasi-infernal Portent, one could not know what to make of this wretched world, in these days, at all: see *Heroes*, 173.

Flebile Ludibrium: (Lat.) 'A farce to weep at'.

206 *"A whole Eternity I waited to be born; and now I have a whole Eternity waiting to see what I will do when born!"*: see 'The Diamond Necklace', in *Historical Essays*, 86.

we will leave this of 'Religion;' of which, to say truth, it is chiefly profitable in these unspeakable days to keep silence: see TC to Geraldine Jewsbury, 15 June 1840: 'To call the worship one follows (the inner light that keeps one living) by any *name*, at present, is to transform it into a wretched logical crotchet; no Faith any more, for most part, but a barren jangle in the argumentative *head*. . . . SILENCE, SILENCE: in a thousand senses I proclaim the indispensable worth of Silence, our only safe dwelling-place often' (*CL* xii. 164).

Norse Odin . . . did not he . . . teach us that for the Dastard there was, and could be . . . no harbour anywhere, save down with Hela, in the pool of Night!: see *Heroes*, 28; Hela, or Hel, is the goddess of the underworld in Norse mythology.

The resuscitation of old liturgies fallen dead: as proposed by the Tractarians; see note to p. 186.

206–7 *the manufacture of new liturgies that will never be alive*: such as those practised by TC's friend Edward Irving and members of his Catholic Apostolic Church; see note to p. 142. Though he was dismayed by the efforts of his friend Edward Irving and the members of his Catholic Apostolic Church to commune with the Holy Ghost through 'the gift of tongues', TC was intrigued by the notion as a historian. He too aspired 'to raise the dead' and 'speak' with figures from the past. In the MS Notes, Forster Collection, fo. 54v, he considers writing a drama using 'the Ghost of Oliver Cromwell', justifying his creation on the grounds that 'any shadow of the Dead, if it rise authentically in the Thought of the Living, men called it once a Ghost'. See Introduction, p. vii.

207 *Stylitisms*: St Simeon Stylites, canonized Syrian ascetic, lived for thirty-seven years on a series of tall pillars near Antioch, sometimes preaching to the crowds below on the benefits of abstinence and austerity. See TC to Emerson, 19 July 1842, on his conversations with Bronson Alcott: 'I do not want another Simon Stylites, however cunning his pillar may be. In short, I will speak no more with Alcot, about his vegetables . . . but question him on Emerson, New England, on a thousand things; on which his tidings are well worth hearing' (*CL* xiv. 231). See also Tennyson, 'St. Simeon Stylites', *Poems* (1842), ii. 53–63.

Sauerteig's Æsthetische Springwurzeln: see TC, 'Biography': 'The Professor and Doctor is not a man whom we can praise without reservation; neither shall we say that his *Springwürzel* (a sort of magical picklocks, as he affectedly names them) are adequate to "*start*" every *bolt* that locks up an aesthetic mystery' (*EOL*, 135 and n.).

208 *It remains a religious duty, from oldest times, in the East*: TC contrasts the purification rituals of ancient Eastern religions with the 'unwashed' condition of industrial operatives. For the importance of bathing in ancient religion, see John Gardner Wilkinson, *Manners and Customs of the Ancient Egyptians* (1837), i. 277–8: 'In their ablutions as in their diet, they were equally severe, and they maintained the strictest observance of numerous religious customs. They bathed twice a day and twice during the night; and some who pretended to a more rigid observance of religious duties, washed themselves with water which had been tasted by the ibis, supposed in consequence to bear an unquestionable evidence of its purity.' *LLC 1842*, 132 lists the three-volume 1840 and 1841 editions of Wilkinson. In his *Inquiry into the Sanitary Condition of the Labouring Population*, Chadwick cited several examples of 'personal uncleanliness amongst whole classes of workpeople': 'One labourer remembered that a particular event took place at Easter, "because it was then he washed his feet." The effects of these habits are seen at the workhouse on almost every one of the paupers admitted. When it is necessary to wash them on their admission, they usually manifest an extreme repugnance to the process. Their common feeling was expressed by one of them when he declared that he considered it "equal to robbing him of a great coat which he had had for some years"' (p. 253).

Herr Professor Strauss: David Friedrich Strauss, theologian and philosopher, author of *Das Leben Jesu* (1835–6), in which he controversially represented Christ as a historical figure and denied his miraculous aspect. *LLC 1842*, 114 lists the two-volume 1841 edition of Strauss. See TC to John Sterling, 14 July 1841: 'Of late years rapidly the conviction grows on me that all we have of *Anti*-Straussism is little other than a Cant,—properly a despicable trembling sort of unbelief that there is anything intrinsically true in men, anything true at all except shovel hats tithe-pigs and such like' (*CL* xiii. 185–6).

"Cleanliness is near of kin to Godliness": proverbial. In his *Inquiry into the Sanitary Condition of the Labouring Population*, Chadwick argued that 'the

removal of noxious physical circumstances, and the promotion of civic, household, and personal cleanliness, are necessary to the improvement of the moral condition of the population; for that sound morality and refinement in manners and health are not long found co-existant with filthy habits amongst any class of the community' (pp. 371–2).

Our new friend, the Emperor there, is Pontiff of three hundred million men: see note to p. 137. For TC and China, see Wang, 'Thomas Carlyle and Chinese Matters' (2015–16). See also John Francis Davis, *The Chinese: A General Description of the Empire of China* (1836), i. 204: 'A population, estimated commonly at 300,000,000'. *LLC 1842*, 32 lists the 1836 edition of Davis.

authentically patronised by Heaven: see Davis, *The Chinese*, i. 99: 'All countries that send tribute [to the Chinese emperor] . . . constitute a part of the empire, and their respective kings reign under the sanction of "the Son of heaven." This of course signifies little enough at a distance, but the effect is felt in China; for any remonstrance against oppression, on the part of a subject of one of these states, must be stopped by such an unanswerable argument, which proves at once his relative inferiority and worthlessness.'

This Emperor Pontiff . . . observes, with a religious rigour, his 'three thousand punctualities': for 'Emperor Pontiff', see Davis, *The Chinese*, ii. 61: 'The fourth and last portion of the ancient poetical canon is called *Soong*, that is, eulogies or panegyrics on the ancestors of the dynasty Chow. . . . They appear to have been a species of hymn, sung before the Emperor when he sacrificed as *pontifex maximus* . . . in the temples of Heaven and Earth, or in the hall of his ancestors.' For 'three thousand punctualities', see Davis, *The Fortunate Union: A Romance* (1829), a translation of the 'Haoukewchuen', a fictional work from the period of the Ming dynasty (AD 1368–1644). The phrase appears in verses included in the appendix: 'In the singleness of her purpose, she relied upon herself— | Unconscious of wrong, what need had she for distrust? | Were she called on to observe the three thousand punctualities, | The hero (the dragon) would have found no place of refuge from his enemies' (ii. 251). Though unlisted in *LLC 1842*, *P&P Strouse*, 471, notes that library records indicate that TC borrowed the book on 6 August 1842.

He . . . believes . . . with the old Monks, that 'Labour is Worship': see Davis, *The Chinese*, i. 207: 'It may be observed that we make great account of the circumstance of *cheerful* industry; because this characteristic, which is the first to strike all visitors of China, is the best proof in the world that the people possess their full share of the results of their own labour. Men do not toil either willingly or effectively for hard masters.'

His most public Act of Worship . . . is the drawing solemnly at a certain day, . . . a distinct red Furrow with the Plough: see Davis, *The Chinese*, i. 310: 'The Emperor . . . honours the profession of husbandry by going through the ceremony of holding the plough. Accompanied by some Princes of the blood . . . he proceeds to a field set apart for the purpose, in the enclosure which surrounds the Temple of the Earth, where everything has been duly prepared by regular husbandmen in attendance. . . . After certain sacrifices, . . . the Emperor ploughs a few furrows. . . . The "five sorts of grain" are then sown, and, when the Emperor has viewed the completion of the work by the husbandmen present, the field is committed to the charge of an officer, whose business is to collect and store the produce for sacrifices.'

209 *"Who made him? What is to become of him and us?"* . . . . . . *the 'Tsien':* see Davis, *The Chinese*, ii. 67–8: 'Of *Tien*, or Heaven, they sometimes speak of as a Supreme Being, pervading the universe and awarding moral retribution: it is the same sense that the Emperor is styled "the son of Heaven." . . . *Ty*, the earth is called by the Chinese *mother*, in the same way that *Tien*, heaven, is styled *father*, and between the two, all sublunary things are said to have been produced.'

He and his three hundred millions . . . visit yearly the Tombs of their Fathers; each man the Tomb of his Father and his Mother: see Davis, *The Chinese*, i. 296–7: 'Twice in every year, in the spring and autumn, are the periods fixed for performing the rites to the dead, but the first is the principal period, and the only one commonly attended to. . . . About that time [*i. e.* the 5th of April] . . . the whole population of the town is seen trooping out in parties to the hills, to repair and sweep the tombs, and make offerings, leaving behind them, on their return home, long streamers of red and white paper, to mark the fulfilment of the rites.' See TC to Geraldine Jewsbury, 21 October 1840: 'On the whole, I find I have great sympathy with the Chinese religion too; that *worship* of their Dead Fathers practiced there. This so far as one can see is probably the chief *worship* they have' (*CL* xii. 296). See also TC to John Sterling, 3 January 1842: 'I wonder how people can ring bells at this season: I could rather chaunt Litanies; or go, like the Chinese, "to the grave of my fathers," and sit *silent* there' (*CL* xiv. 5).

Our friend the Pontiff-Emperor permits cheerfully, though with contempt, all manner of Buddists, Bonzes, Talapoins . . . to worship with . . . chantings, paper-lanterns and tumultuous brayings: see Davis, *The Chinese*, ii. 78: 'Confucianism is the orthodoxy, or state religion of China; and the other two ['Budhism; and the sect of *Taou*, or "Rationalists" '], though tolerated as long as they do not come into competition with the first, have been rather discredited than encouraged by the government.' For Buddhists, see Davis, *The Chinese*, i. 312–13: 'On the first day of the seventh moon . . . Priests of the Budh sect are engaged to chant masses for the dead, offerings of food are presented, and large quantities of paper representing clothes are burned, in order that they may pass into the other world for the use of the departed. . . . These celebrations being calculated to bring large numbers together, appear to consist in great measure of feasting and entertainment.' Bonze is a Buddhist monk in E Asia; Talapoins are Buddhist monks of Burma and Thailand.

make night hideous: Hamlet, 1. iv. 54.

'Practical Hero-worship:' he does incessantly: see Davis, *The Chinese*, i. 213–14: 'Wealth alone . . . is looked upon with less respect, comparatively, than perhaps in any other country; and this *because* all distinction and rank arises almost entirely from educated talent. The choice of official persons, who form the real aristocracy of the country, is guided, with a very few exceptions, by the possession of those qualities, and the country is therefore as ably ruled as it could be under the circumstances.'

These three hundred millions actually make porcelain, souchong tea: see Davis, *The Chinese*, ii. 255 on porcelain: 'With regard to the *porcelain* of the Chinese, it is indisputably the original from which the similar manufactures of Europe were borrowed'; ii. 461 on tea: 'Souchong (*Seaou-choong*, "small or scarce sort") is the finest of the stronger black teas, with a leaf that is generally entire and curly, but more young than in the coarser kinds.'

Seven-Years Wars, Thirty-Years War: the Seven Years War was a European struggle (1756–63) with France, Austria, Saxony, Sweden, and Russia aligned against Prussia, Hanover, and Great Britain; the Thirty Years War was a devastating conflict (1618–48) fought on the territory of the Holy Roman Empire.

210 *Antique devoutness, Antique veracity and heroism, has again become possible*: see 'Goethe's Works': 'We can call Goethe . . . "a clear and universal man"; we can say that, in his universality, as thinker, as singer, as worker, he lived a life of antique nobleness under these new conditions; and, in so living, is alone in all Europe; the foremost, whom others are to learn from and follow. . . . The question, Can man still live in devoutness, yet without blindness or contraction; in unconquerable steadfastness for the right, yet without tumultuous exasperation against the wrong; as an antique worthy, yet with the expansion and increased endowment of a modern? is no longer a question, but has become a certainty, an ocularly-visible fact' (*CME* ii. 440).

the arrival in it of a new Wise Man: see *Heroes*, 20.

scrannel-pipings: Milton, 'Lycidas' (1638), ll. 123–4.

'well selected from and burnt': see Bk. II, 'disused and burnt' (p. 124).

Literature . . . is yet 'the Thought of Thinking Souls': see 'Sir Walter Scott' (1838), in *EOL*, 323.

210–11 *The Mason's Ways are . . . 'Choose well . . . Work, and despair not'*: Goethe, 'Symbolum', in *Werke*, iii. 69–70.

BOOK IV: HOROSCOPE

213 *HOROSCOPE*: astrological almanacs, which included the horoscopes of political figures, were popular with the Victorian reading public. See the *Morning Post* (28 Dec. 1842), which included an advertisement for *Raphael's Prophetic Messenger, Almanac, and Ephemeris for 1843* 'showing

the Events, Predictions, and the Weather that will occur during each Month in 1843, with Horoscopes of the Queen, Wellington, Peel, Louis Philippe &c. &c.; showing the influence of the Planets on their Lives and Actions in 1843' (p. 1). *Raphael's Prophetic Messenger*, launched by Robert Cross Smith in 1826, reached annual publication sales of 100,000 by 1850. See Curry, *A Confusion of Prophets* (1992), 47–60.

the Past, looked at through the medium of 'Philosophical History' in these times: see note to p. 56.

Your Norman Conquerors, true royal souls . . . were vulturous irrational tyrants: see David Hume, *History of England* (1754–62; 1778), 1983 edn., ii. 519: 'The period in which the people of Christendom were the lowest sunk in ignorance, and consequently in disorders of every kind, may justly be fixed at the eleventh century, about the age of William the Conqueror; and from that aera, the sun of science began to re-ascend, threw out many gleams of light, which preceded the full morning when letters were revived in the fifteenth century.' For TC's reading of Hume, see *CL* i. 112, 115, 121, 222. *LLC 1842*, 59 lists the 1789–1805 edition of Hume's *History*.

Becket was a noisy egoist and hypocrite: Thomas à Becket, archbishop of Canterbury, murdered in Canterbury Cathedral, 29 December 1170. See Lyttelton, *Henry the Second*, iv. 361–2: 'It cannot be denied that [Becket] was guilty of a wilful and premeditated perjury: that he opposed the necessary course of publick justice, and acted in defiance of the laws of his country. . . . On what motives he acted can be certainly judged by Him alone, *to whom all hearts are open*. He might be misled by the prejudices of a bigotted age, and think he was doing an acceptable service to God, in contending, even to death, for the utmost excess of ecclesiastical and papal authority. Yet the strength of his understanding . . . would make one suspect, as many did in the times wherein he lived, that he only became the champion of the church from an ambitious desire of sharing its power. . . . And this suspicion is encreased by the marks of cunning and falseness, which are evidently seen in his conduct on some occasions.' See also Hume, *History of England*, 1983 edn., i. 336–7: 'Two years after his death [Becket] was canonized by pope Alexander . . . and it was computed, that, in one year, above a hundred thousand pilgrims arrived in Canterbury, and paid their devotions at his tomb. It is indeed a mortifying reflection to those who are actuated by the love of fame . . . that the wisest legislator and most exalted genius, that ever reformed or enlightened the world, can never expect such tributes of praise, as are lavished on the memory of pretended saints, whose whole conduct was probably, to the last degree, odious or contemptible, and whose industry was entirely devoted to the pursuit of objects pernicious to mankind.'

"Enthusiasm," and even "honest Enthusiasm": see Lyttelton, *History of Henry the Second*, iv. 362–3: 'Neither is it impossible, that, when first [Becket] assumed his new character, he might act the part of zealot, merely or principally from motives of arrogance and ambition; yet, afterwards, being engaged, and inflamed by the contest, work himself up into real

enthusiasm . . . . He certainly shewed in the latter part of his life a spirit as fervent as the warmest enthusiast's; such a spirit indeed as constitutes *heroism*, when it exerts itself in a cause beneficial to mankind.'

'The Dog . . . bit the Man!': Oliver Goldsmith, 'Elegy on the Death of a Mad Dog' (1766): 'The dog, to gain some private ends, | Went mad, and bit the man' (ll. 19–20).

'what it brought with it the means of seeing': see *FR* i. 6.

Bastille Workhouses; Irish Widows: see notes to pp. 17 and 139.

214 *'Bible of Universal History'*: see *Sartor*, 144: 'One BIBLE I know, of whose Plenary Inspiration doubt is not so much as possible; nay with my own eyes I saw the God's-Hand writing in it: thereof all other Bibles are but Leaves,—say, in Picture-Writing to assist the weaker faculty.'

we whose ancestors were all hanged, why should we talk of ropes!: proverbial.

Alexandrian Library: the Great Library of Alexandria, Egypt, centre of learning in the ancient world, established during the reign of Ptolemy II Philadelphus, 283–246 BC.

to survive for a while with the Physiologists: TC refers ironically to 'the branch of science that deals with the normal functioning of human organisms and their systems and organs' (*OED*).

ghastly Doctrines, and death's-head Philosophies 'teaching by example': see Henry St John, Viscount Bolingbroke, *Letters on the Study and Use of History* (1752), i. 15, 20: 'What then is the true use of history? . . . I will answer by . . . quoting what I have read some where or other, in DIONYSIUS HALICARN [Dionysius of Halicarnassus, *Ars Rhetorica*, xi. 2]. I think, that history is philosophy teaching by examples. . . . The school of example . . . is the world: and the masters of this school are history and experience.' See TC to John Stuart Mill, 17 December 1833: 'There are a thousand purposes which History should serve beyond "teaching by Experience": it is an Address (literally out of Heaven, for did not God order it all) to our *whole* inner man' (*CL* vii. 52).

what to our Moslem friends their godless ages are, 'the Period of Ignorance': see Sale (trans.), *The Koran*, i.14: 'The religion of the *Arabs* before *Mohammed*, which they call the *state of ignorance*, in opposition to the knowledge of GOD'S true worship revealed to them by their prophet, was chiefly gross idolatry.'

215 *Bourbonisms with their corollary of Three Day*: see note to p. 28. Louis XVIII and Charles X were the two Bourbon monarchs restored to the throne after the fall of Napoleon and whose reigns heralded periods of political reaction.

Your Luther, your Knox, your Anselm: for Martin Luther, Protestant reformer, and John Knox, Scottish reformer, see *Heroes*, lecture iv, 'The Hero as Priest'. St Anselm, archbishop of Canterbury was an opponent of royal control over the Roman Catholic Church.

till the whole be rent asunder: Matt. 27:51.

217 *William Rufus or Redbeard, Stephen Curthose himself, much more Henry Beauclerc and our brave Plantagenet Henry*: William II, known as William Rufus, was third son of William I (the Conqueror) and Matilda, and king of England. Stephen of Blois, king of England is confused by TC with Robert Curthose, eldest son of William I and Matilda, and duke of Normandy. Curthose's attempt to claim the throne of England was thwarted by his brother Henry I in 1106. Henry I, fourth and youngest son of William I and Matilda, whose epithet 'Beauclerc' originated in the fourteenth century, was king of England (1100–35). Henry II, eldest son of Geoffrey Plantagenet and empress Matilda, was king of England (1154–89).

as we once said, 'the unrealities, beaten into dust, flew gradually off': see Bk. I, p. 26, 'The *dust* of controversy'.

'The Knaves and Dastards': see note to p. 45.

218 *Gurth did belong to Cedric*: see note to p. 34.

there is no King in Israel: Judg. 18:1.

every man is his own king: Judg. 17:6. See also *FR* iii. 31.

Jarls, what we now call Earls, were Strong-Ones: TC's etymology is inaccurate. Jarl is 'an old Norse or Danish chieftain or under-king' (*OED*). Earl, 'in Anglo-Saxon England; a man of noble birth or rank'; in OE, used figuratively for 'a warrior; . . . a man' (*OED*).

We raise Fifty-two millions . . . to get our Governing done . . . and the 'peculiar burden of the Land' is to pay . . . one twenty-fourth part of all this: see *The Finance Accounts I.–VIII. of the United Kingdom for the Year 1842, Ended Fifth January 1843* (1843): 'Constituting the Public Income of Great Britain and Ireland; for the Year ending 5th January 1843: Totals of the Public Income of the United Kingdom, exclusive of Money raised by creation of Stock: £52,648,742.' The 'Excess of Expenditure' for the same period was '£4,075,121'. In the same report, the gross receipts listed for 'Land Tax for Land and Tenements' was '£1,137,657', and the total amount for 'Land and Assessed Taxes, Property and Income Tax' was '£4,778,729' (pp. 8, 14, 52). *The Examiner* (19 Mar. 1842) noted that in response to Peel's budget proposal of 11 March 1842, the Liberal MP for Sheffield Henry George Ward introduced a motion 'relative to the alleged peculiar burdens borne by the land of this country'. Citing the contradictory evidence of political economists, Peel replied that 'it was an exceedingly difficult question to determine the special burdens imposed on land. There were some . . . who affirmed that the malt-tax levied ten millions on the landed interest. No doubt the consumer paid a large proportion of it; but would a committee of inquiry settle this and other disputed points?' The Anti-Corn Law League activist Richard Cobden argued that 'the land-tax [of 1692] was intended to have grown with the increasing value of the land, but no new assessment had taken place for a century and a half, and it was levied on an absurd and unequal system' (p. 181). Following the defeat of the motion and the enactment of Peel's tax increase, *The Examiner*

(26 Mar. 1842) commented, 'He finds a deficiency in the revenue; he refuses to repair it by sources of revenue arising from the abatement of the corn and sugar monopolies; but this is not all, he actually makes the deficiency greater in order that he may make the case for an Income Tax. Like a tinker making holes that he may have to stop them' (p. 193).

Our first Chartist Parliament: on 27 December 1842, the philanthropist and reformer Joseph Sturge, head of the middle-class Complete Suffrage Association, convened a meeting in Birmingham of 400 delegates, which included the prominent Chartist Radicals Thomas Cooper, Bronterre O'Brien, and Feargus O'Connor. Widely derided in the British press as a 'Chartist Parliament', the conference exposed sharp differences of opinion between moderate and radical factions in the movement. *The Sun* (28 Dec. 1842) reported that the 'Chartist Parliament, which is to relieve Sir Robert Peel and the rest of her Majesty's Ministers from the cares of Government, commenced their sittings this morning . . . and a certainly more incongruous and ill-sorted assembly has seldom met together to effect the regeneration of mankind—the very praiseworthy object which these pseudo legislators and philanthropists propose to themselves' (p. 2). *The Times* (28 Dec. 1842) condemned the association's proposal to introduce 'annual parliaments' for the people: 'We have no doubt that when we have carried out the genuine plan of universal suffrage, which would include also female suffrage, there would be no difficulty in reducing the existence of Parliament, *if needs be*, to a fortnight's duration, or, if another Cromwell should arise, in making it so short, that more time shall be consumed in its elections than in its sittings. Then will come the period at which we have already darkly hinted, when it will be practicable to assail even the representative system itself, and to propose that the people shall legislate, judge, and exercise every political authority themselves, as they did at Athens—a species of government . . . which must speedily terminate in complete convalescence—or in utter dissolution' (p. 5).

Redivivus: (Lat.) 'come back to life; reborn'.

219 *But truly a 'Splendour of God,' as in William Conqueror's rough oath*: see p. 191: 'he was heard to swear by God's Splendour'.

'on the rim of the horizon': see note to p. 107.

Pandarus Dogdraught: a pander is 'a person who assists the immoral urges or evil designs of others' (*OED*); dogdraught or dog-draw is 'the act of "drawing after" or tracking venison illegally killed or wounded, using a dog led by hand to follow the scent' (*OED*).

'peace, peace, where there is no peace': Jer. 6:14.

'men of genius': coterie speech of TC and JWC. See *Sartor*, 108.

travelling to make his appeal to Rome: William II's quest for royal control over both Church and State conflicted with Anselm's belief in the primacy of papal authority in ecclesiastical matters. This division led to bitter quarrels over a range of issues, including William's refusal to recognize Pope Urban II or the pallium the pope conferred on Anselm, his demand that Anselm fund royal military campaigns in Normandy and Wales, and his insistence that the monarch alone was responsible for appointments to the abbeys. In October 1097, William gave Anselm permission to travel to Rome and consult with the pope about his prerogatives. Anselm was effectively exiled for three years and returned to England only after the king died in a hunting accident on 2 August 1100.

219 *Jean-Jacques*: Jean-Jacques Rousseau, philosopher whom TC regarded as the 'new Political Evangel' of the French Revolution (*FR* i. 99 and n.). See also *Heroes*, 158–61.

as not even an American population now venerates a Schnüspel the distinguished Novelist: for *Schnüspel*, see note to p. 62. The publication of Dickens, *American Notes: For General Circulation* (1842) provoked controversy on both sides of the Atlantic. The novelist visited the United States between January and May 1842, and travelled from Boston and New York to Canada, and as far west as St Louis. In his account, he conveys a generally favourable impression of the United States, but is critical of its penal system, copyright laws, worship of money and 'trade', and tolerance of 'the wrongs and horrors' of slavery. At the conclusion of the book, Dickens anticipated a critical response: 'I have little reason to believe, from certain warnings that I have had, since I returned to England, that it will be tenderly or favourably received by the American people' (ii. 24, 305). The backlash against him was severe, with a New York newspaper referring to him as a 'contemptible Cockney'. For the American reception of the *Notes*, see McParland, *Dickens's American Audience* (2010), 56–67. In a long review of the book, *The Examiner* (22 Oct. 1842) concluded 'that amidst a great deal of candid and not very flattering criticism, some of the best and most valuable points of character are frankly and freely conceded to our Transatlantic brethren' (p. 679). Dickens sent TC a copy of *American Notes* in October, which TC 'read' without comment. In his journal he commented: 'Decidedly I rather liked poor Dickens; and thought with sympathy of the way in which he is tossed and tumbled in these mad times.' JWC reported her impressions of the book in a letter to Jeannie Welsh, 22 Oct. 1842: 'In the second volume [Dickens] gives up dancing on the crown of his head for halfpence . . . and becomes quietly entertaining— and entertainingly instructive' (*CL* xv. 135 and n., 141).

They crowded round . . . to see the light of his face: see Selden (ed.), *Historiae Nouorum*, 41–2.

But the notablest was a certain necessitous or covetous Duke of Burgundy: see Selden (ed.), *Historiae Nouorum*, 42.

220 *steelclad Russian Bear emerges*: *Macbeth*, III. iv. 98–100.

he bethinks him that probably this feeble, fearless, hoary Figure has in it something of the Most High God: see Selden (ed.), *Historiae Nouorum*, 42: '*Nec enim hominis sed vultus*, ait, *Angeli Dei fulget in eo*'.

Per os Dei: (Lat.) 'by God's mouth'; see Rokewode 43; *Chronicle* 53. See also Deut. 8:3.

your divine Pope Gregory: Pope Gregory VII, who deposed a crowned ruler, Henry IV, emperor of Germany, and affirmed the supremacy of the canon law in determining the election of the pope by the College of Cardinals.

Our Western World had all become a European Thibet, with one Grand Lama sitting at Rome: see Davis, *The Chinese*, ii. 81–3: 'The curious resemblance that exists between the observances of the Budhist priests of China and Tartary, and those of the Catholic church, has excited the surprise of missionaries of the latter; and the observations and surmises of Père Gerbillon, who was intimately acquainted with the subject, may by some be considered as worthy of attention. He questioned a well-informed Mongol, as to the time when his countrymen had first become devoted to the Lama of Thibet, who is a spiritual sovereign resembling the Pope. The reply was, that priests first came into the Mongol Tartary in the time of Koblai Khân, but that these were really persons of holy and irreproachable lives, unlike the present. The father supposes that they might have been religious Christians from Syria and Armenia, the communication with which countries subsequently cut off by the dismemberment of the Mongol empire, the Budhist priests mixed up their superstitions with the Catholic observances.'

221 *Bromwicham Iron-trades, American Commonwealths, Indian Empires*: Bromwicham is an alternative name for Birmingham: 'The name does appear in early documents as Brimigham and Brymecham, as well as Bermingham (Home of the Beormingas). Bromich, in Castle Bromich, a district of Birmingham, is the *wic* or place covered with broom' (Hughes, 351). *American Commonwealths*: Lord Durham's *Report on the Affairs of British North America* (1839) proposed joining Upper and Lower Canada into a single colony. The union occurred in 1841, but further recommendations in the report for 'responsible government' were not implemented until 1847. *Indian Empires*: TC may be referring to the disastrous British invasion of Afghanistan in April 1838. The government justified the incursion by arguing that it was trying to prevent an Afghan alliance with Russia, which it accused of having designs on India. On 6 January 1842, over 4,500 British troops and 12,000 civilians retreated from Kabul to Jalalabad, but were massacred at a mountain pass leading from the city. *The Examiner* (12 Feb. 1842) declared in an editorial: 'Blood, treasure, and reputation have been profusely squandered in our Afghan expedition, and as is now generally seen by every one, and as ought to have been foreseen on the spot from the first moment, they have been spent in contending against a bugbear—a Russian and Persian invasion of India, forsooth, that is, for a phantom the creation of our own fears or ambition, which for forty years at least, have haunted the imagination of Indian statesmen' (p. 98).

Saxon Becket spilt his life in Canterbury Cathedral, as Scottish Wallace did on Tower-Hill: TC repeated this detail about Becket's Saxon lineage from Thierry, who was influenced by Scott's *Ivanhoe* in representing English history as a perpetual racial struggle between Norman oppressors and Saxon rebels. Thierry argued that Becket was by nature and character born 'for the torment of the Norman race' (*Histoire de la conquête*, ii. 378). But TC follows neither Scott nor Thierry in *Past and Present*, and instead attributes a 'Teutonic' identity to both the Saxons and Normans, treating the latter as 'Saxons who had learned to speak French'; see Simmons (1990), 87–102, 117–23. For Carlyle and Scott, see Frye, 'Romancing the Past' (1996). Wallace (see note to p. 26) was executed at Smithfield, and his head was placed on London Bridge.

221 *Our Epic having now become Tools and the Man*: see note to p. 187.

'good hap and sorrow': Goethe, 'Symbolum'; see note to pp. 210–11.

Sufficient for the day is the evil thereof: see note to p. 65.

To shape the whole Future is not our problem: see TC, 'Signs of the Times' (1829): 'To reform a world, to reform a nation, no wise man will under-take; and all but foolish men know, that the only solid, though a far slower reformation, is what each begins and perfects on *himself*' (*CME* xxvii. 82).

Life-tree Igdrasil: see note to p. 47.

223 *How, in conjunction with inevitable Democracy, indispensable Sovereignty is to exist*: see Tocqueville, *Democracy in America*, i. 61–2: 'Now I know of only two methods of establishing equality in the political world; every citizen must be put in possession of his rights, or rights must be granted to no one. For nations which are arrived at the same stage of social existence as the Anglo-Americans, it is therefore very difficult to discover a medium between the sovereignty of all and the absolute power of one man: and it would be vain to deny that the social condition which I have been describing is equally liable to each of these consequences.'

imprisoned in 'Impossibility': see note to p. 18.

the case of the late Bribery Committee: on 9 May 1842 the House of Commons, influenced by the arguments of John Arthur Roebuck, Liberal MP for Bath, voted to appoint a select committee on 'election compromises' to review claims of bribery outlined in petitions presented from Bridport, Falmouth, Harwich, Nottingham, Reading, Lewes, and Penryn. *The Examiner* (23 July 1842) observed that the report was inconclusive because the members of the committee 'were not called upon to decide upon the legality or illegality of the proceedings of any party, or upon the guilt or innocence of the transactions' (p. 475). In a further commentary, the paper (30 July 1842) declared that 'it is . . . not just to say that in brib-ery the Liberals are as bad as the Tories, there being this difference, that the Tories have led the way in the offence, and left their adversaries no choice but to adopt the same bad arts or to be driven from the field. . . . The degrading fact is, that bribery is now so general that no odium attaches to the offence of the individual. We live in a foul air, the immedi-ate purification of which is impossible, but the safety lamp may be intro-duced in it in the Ballot' (p. 481).

Bribery could not be put down: TC echoes Roebuck's speech in the House of Commons, 28 July 1842: 'Don't let us talk of [bribery] being this thing or that; of its being the concentrated essence of sin; or use any other wild phraseology. . . . I want to know why we should quarrel about names, and not join together to put it down?' (*Hansard*, lxv. 774). In a letter to JWC on 9 April 1841, TC described Roebuck as 'lean, acrid, contentious and loquacious as ever. He flew at me, do what I would, some three or four times, like a kind of cockatrice,—had to be swept back again. . . . We parted as good friends,—with small wish on my part or his to meet again' (*CL* xiii. 88).

224 *the soundest practical minds in Parliament*: one of these was TC's former pupil, Charles Buller, Liberal MP for Liskeard, who played a prominent part in drafting Durham's report on British North America and campaigning against election bribery. See TC to his brother Alexander, 27 June 1834: 'If his health were good, which unfortunately it is not, I should prophecy of Buller that he would do more good in Parliament than any other man in it' (*CL* vii. 224). For TC and Buller, see Haury, *Origins of the Liberal Party* (1987), 42–9.

this new Downing-street Schedule A: Peel's income tax of 1842 (see note to p. 200), published on 5 April, included Schedule A, which 'enacts—That for all lands, tenements, and hereditaments or heritages in Great Britain, there shall be charged *sevenpence* for every twenty shillings' (*The Examiner* (23 Apr. 1842), 266). In his satirical proposal to establish levels of enfranchisement based upon the amount of money raised by bribery, TC also refers to an earlier Schedule A, which listed 'The Sixty Boroughs Proposed to be Disfranchised' in the Reform Bill of 1832 (*The Examiner* (6 Mar. 1831), 153). These were nomination or 'rotten' boroughs that lacked populations large enough to warrant representation in the House of Commons. As a result of the legislation, fifty-six of these seats were abolished.

225 *Unless Belial and Beelzebub have got possession of the throne of this Universe, such Parliament is preparing itself for new Reform-bills*: Belial is a Vulgate word for 'Satan', and in Hebrew, 'worthless'; one of Satan's lieutenants in Milton, *Paradise Lost*, i. 490–6. Beelzebub, 'lord of the flies', or 'chief of the devils' (Matt. 10:25, Mark 3:22, and Luke 11:15), is Satan's chief lieutenant in Milton's *Paradise Lost*, i. 78–81. In his speech in the House of Commons of 28 July 1842, Roebuck referred to the political 'fiends' who engaged in bribery: 'He who bribes is the great criminal. Down goes the rich man with his purse to some constituency; he finds a man pressed with want, having a family at home, earning by the sweat of his brow a small pittance, and to him comes a fiend in the shape of a candidate, and offers to sell him his conscience for a bribe, and the man accepts the base and corrupt offer' (*Hansard*, lxv. 771).

six hundred and fifty-eight Consulting Men: the membership of the House of Commons in 1842.

poor old Parliament, thousands of years old: the Anglo-Saxon Witenagemot (OE: 'meeting of wise men'), which loosely formed a basis for the thirteenth-century parliament, had itself originated in ancient German assemblies. TC opposed the Whig view of history, which traced the principles of liberty and representative democracy back to these assemblies, but he shared their enthusiasm for the 'Teutonic' character of English institutions. See Jann, 'Democratic Myths' (1980), 129–40.

225 *'Ye are no Parliament. In the name of God,—go!'*: see *Cromwell*, viii. 35.

"Money does not bring money's worth; Put money in your purse": the first part is proverbial; the second a repeated refrain from Iago in *Othello*, 1. iii. 345–60.

Carlton Clubs, Reform Clubs: for the Carlton Club, see note to p. 204; the Reform Club was founded in 1832 by Radicals and Whigs.

The Parliament should really either punish and put away Bribery, or legalise it by some Office in Downing-street: see Roebuck's speech in the House of Commons, 28 July 1842: 'Let us have an exalted morality, and we shall have a virtuous people; but let us refine away the difficulty, let us call it yielding to the necessary result of circumstances under which we are labouring, and say, that these people do not think it a sin; but if we are content to bribe, let us have no bribery laws—let us have no hypocrisy' (*Hansard*, lxv. 772).

226 *It is we that vote wrong, and teach the poor ragged Freemen of Boroughs to vote wrong*: see Roebuck's speech in the House of Commons, 28 July 1842: 'How can we expect morality in the people unless those who are in high places in this country have an exalted morality? And if those who represent learned bodies and dignified persons exhibit a corrupt morality, we shall have a corrupt people' (*Hansard*, lxv. 771).

the Hebrew Psalmist, 'shun to sit': Ps. 26:5.

Ages of Flunkeyism: 'A male servant in livery, *esp.* a footman, lackey; usually with implied contempt' (*OED*, citing TC).

Aristides Rigmarole Esq. of the Destructive, or the Hon. Alcides Dolittle of the Conservative Party: Aristides was an Athenian statesman and general, known as 'the Just'; rigmarole is 'An unduly protracted, involved, or diffuse piece of speech or writing; a story, explanation, etc., regarded as unintelligent or incoherent' (*OED*); Alcides is an alternative name for Hercules.

227 *England will verily have to put an end to briberies on her Election Hustings and elsewhere, at what cost soever*: see Roebuck's speech in the House of Commons, 28 July 1842: 'Things are now come to that crisis when they can go on so no longer' (*Hansard*, lxv. 777).

228 *'from ten to twenty years of new possibility to live and find wages'*: see TC to Thomas Ballantyne, 24 January 1840: 'Abolition of the Corn-Law will very probably, as I compute, enlarge to a great extent the field of manufacturing industry for England; create, we shall hope, an additional demand for labour; raise the *economic* condition of the labourer,—for a certain number of years. That surely, even for the labourer's sake, is most important; *during* that number of years, how much, by a Government, an Aristocracy, *aware* of its task, might be done for the labourer!' (*CL* xii. 23).

as the shadow on King Hezekiah's Dial: 2 Kgs. 20:8–11.

Ixion's-Wheel: Ixion was bound eternally to a fiery wheel in Hades for having tried to seduce Hera.

Kilkenny Cats: 'A pair of cats fabled to have fought until only their tails remained; *transferred*, of combatants who fight until they annihilate each other' (*OED*).

229 *Spinning-Dervishes*: see note to p. 181.

"I cannot move in thee, and be a man": cf. Acts 17:28: 'For in Him we live, and move, and have our being'.

Mother of Dead Dogs: referring to Fleet Street, London's publishing centre, from Alexander Pope, *The Dunciad* (1728), in which he describes the River Fleet, known as Fleet Ditch, sending a 'large tribute of dead dogs to Thames' (ii. 271–2). See also TC's 'Boswell's Life of Johnson', in *EOL*, 179, and *CL* vi. 87. In the *Report from the Select Committee on the Health of Towns*, the writer and physician Jordan Roche Lynch, a resident of Lincoln's-Inn's Fields, testified on 25 March 1840 that the 'Fleet Ditch', in the district of 'St. George's Rookery' was 'in a very filthy state occasionally; it may be considered an open sewer. . . . It is, to a very considerable extent [productive of fevers]; and in this neighbourhood, there are a number of slaughter-houses and so on' (p. 51).

'spread out his Gideon's Fleece': see note to pp. 179–80.

Parishes of Palace-yard: the area surrounding the New Palace Yard, an open space at the NW corner of the Houses of Parliament, bounded S by Westminster Abbey, W by the Guildhall, and N by Whitehall and Downing Street. On 9 July 1842, after a meeting with Robert Peel at his 10 Downing Street residence, delegates to the Anti-Corn Law League conference (5 July–1 August 1842) assembled at the Palace Yard.

230 *scaccarium-tallies, ship-moneys, coat-and-conduct moneys*: for scaccarium, see note to p. 103. A tally is '*a*. A stick or rod of wood, usually squared, marked on one side with transverse notches representing the amount of debt or payment; *b*. such a cloven rod, as the official receipt formerly given by the Exchequer for a tax, tallage, etc. paid, in acknowledgement of a loan to the sovereign' (*OED*). Until the mid-seventeenth century, ship money was a tax levied on coastal towns that did not require Parliamentary approval. Coat-and-conduct money was a tax levied for the upkeep of new soldiers.

Lifeguardsman . . . riding sentry at the Horse-Guards: the Lifeguardsmen and the Royal Horse Guards comprised the cavalry of the royal household.

Fresh-complexioned, firm-limbed, six feet by the standard: one of the qualifications for entry to the Lifesguardsmen and Royal Horse Guards was a minimum height of 6 feet.

231 *The man in horsehair wig advances, . . . Chancery Lawsuit in my heart!*: the Court of Chancery, presided over by the Lord Chancellor. See note to p. 119.

Alive in this Year Forty-three: see Brattin, 'New Manuscript Evidence' (1996), who cites an earlier version of this passage from MS 1798, fo. 45

(National Library of Scotland): 'Alive in this year '41, able | and willing to do his work' (pp. 15–16).

231 *William Rufus, William of Ipres*: for William Rufus, see note to p. 217; William of Ypres, self-styled Count of Flanders, was a leading supporter and military commander of King Stephen.

Ninety-thousand of such: the size of the 'standing force' announced in the House of Commons on 27 February 1843 was 97,000 (*Hansard*, lxvi. 1367).

232 *ragged losels*: 'A worthless person; a profligate, rake, scoundrel; in weaker sense, a ragamuffin, ne'er-do-well' (*OED*, citing TC).

United-Service Clubs: founded in 1815 for senior officers in the Royal Navy and British Army.

an Emigration Service, a Teaching Service: see TC, *Chartism*: 'Universal Education is the first great thing we mean; general Emigration is the second' (*CME* iv. 192). For TC and education, see Campbell, 'Carlyle and Education' (2010).

Nescience: 'Absence or lack of knowledge, ignorance; a form or instance of ignorance' (*OED*, citing TC).

brave Jean-Pauls, learning . . . to live on 'water without the bread': see TC, 'Jean Paul Friedrich Richter Again', in *CME* ii. 120.

233 *the halberts and cat*: a halbert is variously 'A weapon consisting of a spear and and battleaxe combined', 'a symbol of the rank of sergeant', and 'A method of corporal punishment in which a soldier is fastened to a number of halberds . . . and whipped' (*OED*). A cat in this context is 'A whip with nine knotted lashes; till 1881 an authorized instrument of punishment in the British navy and army' (*OED*). On 15 April 1842 the House of Commons undertook a third reading of the annual Mutiny Act, which governed and funded the British Army. An amendment proposing the abolition of flogging 'in times of peace' was rejected, with the majority heeding the advice of the Duke of Wellington that 'an army without discipline would be no army at all' (*Hansard*, lxii. 533, 537).

Forty soldiers . . . will disperse the largest Spitalfields mob: Spitalfields had been the centre of the silk-weaving industry since the seventeenth century, but economic liberalization and mechanization in the 1820s had led to a steep rise in unemployment, poverty, and destitution in the district. TC's reference to the 'largest Spitalfields mob' is ironic. In his *Inquiry into the Sanitary Condition of the Labouring Population*, Chadwick observed that 'the chances of life in the labouring classes of Spitalfields are amongst the lowest that I have met with, and there it is observed of weavers, though not originally a large race, that they have become still more diminutive under the noxious influences to which they are subject. . . . One witness well acquainted with the class states, "They are decayed in their bodies; the whole race of them is rapidly descending to the size of Liliputians. You could not raise a grenadier company amongst them all. The old men have better complexions than the young." ' Another witness noted that as a group, the Spitalfields weavers were ' "an enfeebled and diminutive race of men" ' (p. 186), the physical antithesis of the 'fresh complexioned, firm limbed, six feet by the standard' members of the Lifeguardsmen and Royal Horse Guards previously described by TC.

Fourth Estate: the newspaper press, now aligned with the other three estates of Church, Lords, and Commons. See Macaulay, 'Hallam's Constitutional History', *The Edinburgh Review* 48 (1828): 'The gallery in which the reporters sit has become a fourth estate of the realm' (p. 165). For TC's use of the expression, see 'Boswell's Life of Johnson', in *EOL*, 182 and *FR* i. 180.

Time-Bill, Factory-Bill: the Ten Hours Act (1833), proposed by Lord Ashley (Anthony Ashley-Cooper, seventh earl of Shaftesbury), sought to reduce the working day for all labourers to ten hours. It was rejected by the House of Commons in favour of the Factory Act of 1833, which calculated children's working hours on the basis of age and time. Children between 9 and 13 were prohibited from working more than eight consecutive hours without an hour-long lunch break. They were also to receive two hours of education each day, and could not work longer than forty-eight hours a week. Children between the ages of 14 and 18 were not allowed to work more than twelve hours without a meal break. No one under the age of 18 was permitted to work between 8.30 a.m. and 5.30 p.m. For Ashley's reforms, see Turnbull, *Shaftesbury: The Great Reformer* (2010), 74–92.

Legislative interference, and interferences not a few are indispensable: the phrase was used by Roebuck in the launch of his campaign in the House of Commons on 6 May 1842 for an inquiry into election bribery: 'I ask for an inquiry, such as will free hon. Members from the accusations made against them, or by justifying those accusations will lay a ground for further legislative interference. And what is the legislative interference I ask for? Why, something that shall enable this House to consider an election petition something more than a fight between A and B. At present, the return to a seat in this House is considered as a mere matter between A and B. If A gains, his party is pleased; and if B gains, his party is pleased. But the public and the great business of this empire are totally unconsidered in this matter; and we buy and sell the constituencies of this country as if they were flocks of sheep' (*Hansard*, lxiii. 227). *The Examiner* (14 May 1842) prefaced its editorial with the quotation (p. 305).

Factory Inspectors . . . Mine-Inspectors: the Factory Act of 1833 stipulated that a corps of inspectors under the jurisdiction of the Home Secretary and independent of local authorities would conduct regular safety reviews of factories. In 1840 a Royal Commission led by Lord Ashley was appointed to investigate 'the employment and condition of the children in mines and collieries', and in 1841 the inquiry was expanded to include 'adolescents'. Following publication of the Children's Employment Commission's *First Report . . . Mines*, Ashley introduced a bill in the House of Commons on 7 June 1842 'to prohibit the employment of women and girls in mines and collieries, to regulate the employment of boys, and to make provisions for the safety of persons, working therein' (*Hansard*, lxv. 5). As a result of this legislation, all women and girls, and all boys under the age of 10, were excluded from mines. In their report, the commissioners also recommended the establishment of an inspection system directed by the Home Secretary, but this proposal was not enacted into legislation until 1850.

233 *how on seven and sixpence a week a human family does live!*: see note to p. 90.

Sanitary Regulations: Chadwick's *Inquiry into the Sanitary Condition of the Labouring Population* formed the basis of Public Health Act of 1848, which established a Central Board of Health and a loan scheme for public health infrastructure.

Romans had their Ædiles: Roman magistrates responsible for superintending both public and private buildings, including baths, aqueducts, roads, bridges, and causeways.

234 *many a foul cellar in our Southwarks, Saint-Gileses*: Southwark in S London and St Giles in the West End were areas of high crime, destitution, impoverishment, and overcrowding, known as 'rookeries' or 'slums', and fictionalized by Dickens in *Oliver Twist* and *Bleak House*. In his *Inquiry into the Sanitary Condition of the Labouring Population*, Chadwick cited the testimony of a sanitary engineer who had recently inspected houses in St Giles: 'It was necessary that my survey should extend from the garrets to the cellars: upon visiting the latter, I found the whole area of the cellars of both houses were full of night-soil, to the depth of three feet, which had been permitted for years to accumulate from the overflow of the cesspools; upon being moved, the stench was intolerable, and no doubt the neighbourhood must have been infected by it. . . . My duties, as one of the surveyors to a fire-office, call me to all parts of the town, and I am constantly shocked almost beyond endurance at the filth and misery in which a large part of our population are permitted to drag on a diseased and miserable existence. I consider a large portion, if not the whole, of this accumulation of dirt and filth is caused by the bad and inefficient sewerage of the metropolis' (p. 45). For Dickens and the London slums, see Jackson, *Dirty Old London* (2014) and Flanders, *The Victorian City* (2012). For slums and the Victorian response, see Wise, *The Blackest Streets* (2013); Dyos and Wolf, *The Victorian City* (1973); and Thomas Beames, *The Rookeries of London* (1850).

to burn their coal-smoke, namely, and make flame of it: in his *Inquiry into the Sanitary Condition of the Labouring Population*, Chadwick commented on the medical impact of 'the chimneys of the furnaces which darken the atmospheres and pour out volumes of smoke and soot upon the inhabitants of populous towns'. He noted that 'the specific effects of an excess of smoke on the general health of a population has not been distinguished, but from the comparatively high average of mortality amongst the middle classes . . . there is strong reason to believe that the prejudicial effect is much more considerable than is commonly apprehended even by medical practitioners'. He concluded that 'the greater part, if not the whole, of the excess of smoke and unconsumed gas by which the metropolis and the neighbourhoods of manufactories are oppressed, is preventible by the exercise of care in the management of fires and furnaces' (pp. 296–7, 298). *The Scotsman* (13 Dec. 1843) reported that on 17 August 1843, a parliamentary select committee investigating the 'smoke nuisance' had concluded 'that smoke always arises from imperfect combustion; in other words, from part of the fuel being unconsumed; and as various methods of producing more perfect combustion are known, the nuisance of factory smoke may be prevented, or at least greatly diminished' (p. 2).

Baths, free air, a wholesome temperature, ceilings twenty feet high, might be ordained . . . There are such Mills already extant: Temple Works (or Temple Mill), Holbeck, Leeds, comprising an office building and flax-spinning mill was built by John Marshall between 1836 and 1840. A pamphlet entitled 'The Manufacture of Linen Yarn' (1842), republished in *The Useful Arts and Manufacture of Great Britain* (1848), offered a detailed description of the new building: 'The lightness and airiness, warmth and ventilation, of this room are beyond all praise. The light is derived from the roof, which is formed of brick groined arches, sixty-six in number, each thirty-six span; and supported by iron pillars to the height of twenty-one feet. In the centre of each arch is a conical skylight, about fourteen feet in diameter, and rising above 10 feet above the roof. From the points of these lights the used air of the room is allowed to escape. Beneath this room is an immense vaulted cellar, with brick pillars. This cellar is employed for a variety of useful purposes; one of which is to supply hot air to the room above. This is done by means of a small steam engine working a large fan, which forces air through a series of 364 pipes, contained in two large steam-chests, which heat the air before it ascends into the mill. The temperature can be regulated by the quantity of steam which is admitted into the chests, or by allowing a portion of cold air to pass by without traversing the pipes. Valves and doors in the flues permit any temperature which is desired to be obtained, or that degree of moisture which is essential in the process of flax-spinning. The cellar also contains the shafts for communicating motion to the immense assemblage of machines in the mill. These shafts are moved by a pair of steam engines of 100 horses' power. This cellar also contains the gas and water pipes; carpenter's shop and warehouses; and among its miscellaneous contents the writer was pleased to notice an arrangement for promoting the health and comfort of the work-people; namely, a set of baths, for both hot and cold water. The operatives are entitled to the use of them on exhibiting a ticket of good conduct from the over-looker. The cold baths are gratis, but for a warm bath one penny is charged. Each bath is contained in a separate room, which is lighted with gas; and the whole is under proper regulation and control' (pp. 30–1).

Go ye and do likewise: Luke 10:37.

234 *to have a hundred acres or so of free greenfield, with trees on it, conquered, for its little children to disport in*: the *Report from the Select Committee on the Health of Towns* concluded that 'the augmentation of buildings in the vicinities of these crowded cities seem to call for provisions to insure some open spaces being preserved, calculated for public walks, essential to the health and comfort of the poorer classes'. Joseph Fletcher, secretary of the Royal Commission on handloom weavers, testified to the committee on 30 March 1840 that 'the general observation of the want of such open spaces applies to almost all the large towns, or most of those that have so rapidly risen in our commercial progress. . . . Birmingham is entirely devoid of it, and Manchester and Macclesfield are without any such convenience' (pp. xx, 70). See also TC to the Hon. Secretaries of the Manchester Athenaeum, 26 January 1843: 'I have regretted much, in looking at your great Manchester, and its thousand-fold industries and conquests, that I could not find, in some quarter of it, a hundred acres of green ground with trees on it, for the summer holidays and evenings of your all-conquering industrious men' (*CL* xvi. 33).

were the Corn-Law Abrogation Bill once passed, and a Legislature willing!: from 1837 to 1845 in the House of Commons, Charles Pelham Villiers introduced annual bills to repeal the Corn Laws, but Peel voted against all of them. His own attempt at a compromise through the introduction of sliding scales in his 1842 budget (see note to p. 39) provoked widespread protests against the government and intensified the campaign for the total abolition of the tariffs. The Corn Laws were partially repealed in 1846, after which tariffs were periodically reduced and eventually eliminated in 1849.

this one Bill, which lies yet unenacted, a right Education Bill: on 7 March 1843, the Home Secretary Sir James Graham sponsored Lord Ashley's Factories Bill, which included a plan to 'establish a national scheme of instruction upon a large scale' (*Hansard*, lxvii. 423). On 24 March, Graham urged the country to support his initiative, and conjectured that 'if some years ago, we could have been so fortunate as to agree upon some such comprehensive scheme of education as that which is now proposed; if we could but have done only ten years ago, my firm belief is that the outrages which took place last autumn . . . would never have taken place' (*Hansard*, lxvii. 1440). But sharp disputes between Anglicans and Dissenters about the content and control of the curriculum obliged Graham to modify the central role played by the Church of England in the administration of the plan. On 1 May he offered an 'olive branch' (*Hansard*, lxviii. 1118) to his Nonconformist opponents, requiring the election of school trustees and a more prominent role for Dissenting clergymen in the instruction of children. A loose coalition of disaffected Anglicans, Dissenters, and Roman Catholics overwhelmingly rejected his concessions and inundated Parliament with petitions of protest. On 15 June, Graham announced that the government would scrap the education portion of the Bill. On 20 July, Peel moved the Factory Bill itself to a 'future session' (*Hansard*, lxx. 1281). For the education debate, see Smelser, *Social Paralysis and Social Change* (1991), 91–7; Finlayson, *Seventh Earl of Shaftesbury* (1981), 190–3; and Paz, *Politics of Working-Class Education* (1980), 136–40.

235 these 'twenty years of respite': see note to p. 228.

How dare any man ... forbid God's Light to come into the world, and bid the Devil's Darkness continue in it one hour more!: see Lord Ashley's speech in the House of Commons, 24 March 1843: 'What a figure shall we then cut among the nations of the earth, if, knowing what we know, seeing what we do see, and feeling what we profess to feel, we fail to remove the abominations and corruptions which are festering in the very heart of our population. Lastly and above all, I pray that we will not so signally fail in our solemn duty as a nation, and call down upon our heads the Divine vengeance, by obstinately persisting in a course of neglect, and in disregard of those sacred duties for which . . . have been intrusted to us wealth, power, greatness, and dominion' (*Hansard*, xlvii. 1469).

'The schoolmaster's creed is somewhat awry?': during the 1840s the rivalry between the British and Foreign School Society, a teacher-training institution founded in 1808 by Nonconformists, and the 'National Schools' of the Anglican Church, had thwarted schemes to establish a national system of education.

Distilled Gin: in the same letter that he wrote to the Hon. Secretaries of the Manchester Athenaeum, 26 January 1843, TC remarked that workers were in need during the 'winter-season and bad weather [of] quite another sort of social meeting-places than the Gin-shops offered!' (*CL* xvi. 33).

Education Secretary, Captain-General of Teachers: in 1843, James Phillips Kay Shuttleworth operated as the equivalent of an 'Education Secretary'. He was appointed the first permanent secretary of the Committee of Council on Education in 1839 and was instrumental in increasing state control of education until he stepped down in 1847. TC's vision for a national system of education was not fully realized until the council was converted to a National Board of Education in 1899.

why should there not be an 'Emigration Service': on 10 January 1840, the Whig Home Secretary Lord John Russell announced the formation of a Colonial Land and Emigration Board to supervise the settling of colonists, conduct the sale in Britain of waste land in the colonies, and use the proceeds of such sales to settle emigrants, collect statistics on emigration rates, and manage intercolonial emigration (Hitchens, *Colonial Land and Emigration Commission* [1931], 45–6). TC's friend Thomas Frederick Elliot was one of three commissioners appointed to head the new bureau. He served as chairman of the board of advice and management between 1840 and 1847. TC wrote to Elliot on 15 November to obtain a position for JWC's cousin John Welsh (*CL* xv. 181). TC's brother-in-law Robert Hanning emigrated to Canada in 1841, and his brother Alexander and his family followed in June 1843.

235 *Secretary, with adjuncts, with funds, forces, idle Navy-ships, and ever-increasing apparatus*: for the use of 'idle Navy-ships', see TC, *Chartism*, in *CME* iv. 203.

a bridge built to carry him into new Western Lands: see *Sartor*, 60, 154.

a Hundred and Twenty Millions Sterling to shoot the French: from the period of Napoleon's forced abdication to Elba in April 1814 to his final defeat at Waterloo in June 1815, the British military spent £122.47 million on 'War Services', mostly by incurring debt; see Silberling, 'Financial and Monetary Policy' (1924), 215, and Halévy, *History of the English People in 1815* (1924), 312–13.

236 *A free bridge for Emigrants*: the Colonial Land and Emigration Board faced pressure from Liberals and Radicals to address the growing unemployment crisis at home by paying the travel expenses of emigrants. On 20 June 1840, the House of Commons debated and rejected a motion by the Irish nationalist and MP for Limerick County, William Smith O'Brien, 'that, in several of the British colonies, the demand for labour is urgent, continuous, and increasing, and its remuneration is comparatively ample, whilst the the prosperity of these colonies is much retarded by its inadequate supply. . . . That under these circumstances, it is expedient that a free passage to those colonies which offer the greatest reward to industry should be provided for by the State for such of the labouring classes as are disposed to emigrate thither' (*Hansard*, liv. 867). Concerned about the budget deficit, Peel reacted cautiously to such demands. *The Examiner* (15 Jan. 1842) reported 'that the Tory Government has in view, for the relief of the national distress, a grand scheme of Emigration and Colonization', but predicted that, given the costs involved, 'Peel is clearly not the man to engage in this wild wholesale speculation. . . . Corn-law abolition is a far better game to pursue than this' (p. 34). Thirteen months later, *The Spectator*, 765 (25 Feb. 1843) commented that 'there is another large question—that of Emigration—to which [Peel] has as yet given no sign of having directed his attention. One of the great obstacles in the way of emigration as a regular outlet for redundant numbers, has hitherto been the prejudice entertained against it by the working-classes. That prejudice is giving away. From Glasgow, Paisley, and other places, come urgent solicitations on the part of the unemployed operatives to have the means of emigrating afforded to them. . . . Government has only to take into its own hands the disposal of all unappropriated lands in the Colonies; to dispose of them except at a sufficient price; and to apply the proceeds of the sales of land in each colony, exclusively, to provide free passages for labourers wishing to proceed to that colony. This plan has not been offered as a substitute for free trade. Either free trade or a good system of emigration would be a boon to the country; but united, the operation of both would be more fully and beneficially felt' (p. 180).

Our friends of China . . . had we not to argue with them . . . and convince them that they ought to trade!: see note to p. 208.

'Hostile Tariffs' will arise to shut us out: The Examiner (22 Oct. 1842) included an article from *The Leeds Mercury* listing 'Six *Hostile Tariffs*' imposed on England in the previous six months by Russia, Portugal, France, Belgium, the United States, and Germany: 'We state these facts for no party purpose whatever, but with the view of calling the Government, of Parliament, and of the country to events themselves, and to the considerations they suggest as to the future commercial policy of England' (p. 680).

Mycale was the Pan-Ionian, rendezvous of all the Tribes of Ion, for old Greece: Mycale, a mountain on the W coast of Anatolia in central Turkey, was the location of assemblies and festivals organized by 'all of the Ionians' (Pan-Ionians), an eastern division of the ancient Greeks.

the 'Children of the Harz-Rock': see Grimm (ed.), *Deutsche Sagen* (1818), i. 62: 'Nach einer alten Volfssage sind die Sachsen mit Aschanes (Askanius), ihrem ersten Könige, aus dem Harzfelfen mitten im grauen Wald bei einem fützen Springbrünnlein herausgewachsen' (According to an old folk legend, the Saxons with Aschanes (Askanius), their first king, grew out of the Harz rocks in the middle of the green forest near a sweet fountain). TC argues in *Past and Present* that both the Saxons and Normans sprang from 'Teutonic' stock.

'Keep not standing fixed and rooted . . . That the world was made so wide': see TC's translation, *Wilhelm Meister's Travels*, in *Works*, xxiv. 345.

by a considerable 'Emigration Service': a reference to the Anglo-Saxon invasion of England, led by Hengist and Horsa (see note to p. 127), part of what the German historian Johann Jacob Mascou (or Mascov) referred to in *History of the Ancient Germans* (1737) as 'that so Famous and Grand Transmigration of a Swarm of Nations' in the fifth century (trans. Lediard [1738], p. v). TC refers to 'Mascou' in *Lectures* (p. 133). His source for the notion of a Saxon 'emigration' was Milton, *History of Britain* (1670): 'The Saxons, consulting first their gods . . . furnish out three long gallies, or kyules, with a chosen company of warlike youth, under the conduct of two brothers Hengist and Horsa, descended in the fourth degree from Woden. . . . The British Nennius writes, that these brethren were driven into exile out of Germany. . . . For it was the custom in Old Saxony, when their numerous offspring overflowed the narrowness of their bounds, to send them out by lot into new dwellings wherever they found room, either vacant or to be forced' (iv. 96–7). *LLC 1842*, 83 lists the seven-volume 1806 edition of Milton's *Prose Works*, ed. Charles Symmons, which includes vol. iv, *History of Britain*; see also *P&P Strouse*, 494.

237 *In our wildest periods of reform, in the Long Parliament itself, you notice always the invincible instinct to hold fast by the Old, to admit the minimum of New*: the Long Parliament, summoned by Charles I on 3 November 1640, and its remnant, the Rump Parliament, dismissed by Cromwell, 20 April 1653. See *Historical Sketches*, 150–1, where TC discusses the predicament of a political body reluctant to 'hold fast by the Old': 'Parliaments in old

times had agreed well with kings; as realities do naturally with things real. Had the Captain of the English people . . . stood there to guide the march of England through the undiscovered deep . . . what need had he to quarrel with his Serjeants and Corporals? . . . But when your chief Captain took the Spanish Match, Antichrist and the Devil and all the putrid Past, which still had money in its pocket, to be the road . . . what could your poor Corporals, Serjeants, Drummers and the Host do? They had to . . . stretch their old Parliamentary Formulas; in some way or other contrive not to go Devil-ward!'

237 *The English Legislature is entirely repugnant to believe in 'new epochs'*: see *Heroes*, 101–2: 'No man whatever believes, or can believe, exactly what his grandfather believed: he enlarges somewhat, by fresh discovery, his view of the Universe, and consequently his Theorem of the Universe. . . . It is the history of every man; and in the history of Mankind we see it summed up into great historical amounts,—revolutions, new epochs.'

the Seven Sleepers, awakening hungry after a hundred years: in Christian and Islamic legend, the seven sleepers hid in a cave outside Ephesus in ancient Greece to escape Roman persecution and emerged 300 years later.

'remedial measures': see note to p. 35.

238 *Tailor's Hell*: 'A place in a tailor's shop into which shreds or offcuts of material are thrown' (*OED*). See Introduction, pp. xxii–xxiii.

CAPTAINS OF INDUSTRY: see note to p. 187. TC originally wrote in the Printer's Copy, '4. ~~The Virtual Aristocracy~~' (*P&P Strouse*, 818). See also TC, 'Count Cagliostro: In Two Flights', in *Historical Essays*, 42. For 'Captains of Industry' and class warfare, see Vanden Bossche, 'Chartism, Class Discourse, and the Captain of Industry' (2010).

at railway-speed: when the first passenger line opened in 1830, the Liverpool and Manchester Railway, the maximum speed of trains was 30 mph. This speed capability quickly increased, but was limited by grade and track conditions to approximately 40 mph for much of the Victorian period. In a letter to his brother John on 13 September 1839, TC described his journey from Preston to London 'as if some huge steam nightbird had flung you on its back, and were sweeping thro' unknown space with you' (*CL* xi. 182).

239 *Bubble-periods, with their panics and commercial crises*: bubble in this context means 'An unsustainable or exaggerated rise in the price of stock or commodity which is soon followed by a collapse in prices' (*OED*). The term was used in an anonymous pamphlet entitled *Commerce in Consternation: or, the Banking Bubble Burst!* (1826). TC refers to the two most recent economic crises: 1837, when defaults by American importers put pressure on Anglo-American banks that had accepted American bills, and 1839–42, when poor harvests strained England's balance of payments and weakened its bullion reserves. In a speech opposing Peel's sliding scale of tariffs to the House of Commons on 16 February 1842, Lord Palmerston described the disastrous repercussions of the domestic corn shortage: 'We

send to buy the corn of the foreigner, and offer him our manufactures in payment. But he declines to receive them; he has made arrangements with other people. . . . From us he will take nothing but bullion; and bullion, and nothing else, must we send him. But that bullion is drawn from the Bank; and this large and sudden drain compels the Bank to restrict its issues. Your currency is deranged; the money value of all things are altered; and then follow distress, panic, bankruptcy' (Palmerston, *Speech*, 16). For the financial panics of the 1830s and 1840s, and the contemporary response, see Dimsdale and Hotson (eds.), *British Financial Crises* (2015), 32–5 and Besoni, 'The Periodicity of Crises' (2010).

Doggery: 'The rabble, the mob' (*OED*, citing TC).

Jötuns: see *Heroes*, 16: 'The dark hostile Powers of Nature [the Norse] figure to themselves as "*Jötuns*", Giants, huge shaggy beings of a demonic character.'

the stars in their courses fighting for them: Judg. 5:20.

240 *awake, arise, or be forever fallen*: *Paradise Lost*, i. 330.

Chactaw Indians: see note to p. 173.

when fathers and mothers, in Stockport hunger-cellars, begin to eat their children: see note to p. 19. TC may have in mind Swift's *A Modest Proposal for preventing the Children of Poor People from being a Burthen to Their Parents or Country, and for making them Beneficial to the Publick* (1729), in which he recommends that parents eat their children in order to reduce poverty.

'Corporations of the Best and Bravest': see TC, *Chartism*: in *CME* iv. 160.

impractible Sacred-Months, and Manchester Insurrections: the 'National Holiday' or 'Sacred Month', a national four-week strike planned by Chartists at their Convention in Birmingham to begin on 12 August 1839. But the forceful repression by the authorities of the 'Bull Ring riots' in Birmingham on 4 July convinced many Chartists that in the words of Feargus O'Connor, 'the country is not for it; there is no state of adequate preparation; there is no proper organisation among the people; they are not able to act in concert with each other; they are not a tenth part of them in possession of the means of self-defence; they are not agreed in their opinions, either as to the practicability or the necessity of the measure' ('The Sacred Month: The Crisis', *The Northern Star* (3 Aug. 1839), 4). The Convention abandoned the plan on 5 August in favour of peaceful processions and meetings. *The Examiner* (25 Aug. 1839) claimed that 'in some places where the Chartists struck work on the 12th instant, with the view of keeping the "sacred month," they soon got sick of their idleness when they found that, without labour, they and their families must necessarily starve; particularly so, when they became satisfied that, even at the end of the "sacred month," they would be no nearer the accomplishment of their object than when it was commenced' (p. 537). In the wake of the Manchester insurrection of August 1842, the paper adopted a more measured tone. Commenting on the coincidence of the upheaval in the industrial districts falling on 12 August 1842, *The Examiner* (27 Aug. 1842) noted that the 'grand *cause* of the insurrection was, in one word, *distress*; which, operating upon trade in all its branches, not only forced down wages, but also threw multitudes altogether out of employment. Then political dis-*content*, arising out of a desire for the Charter or Universal Suffrage availed itself of the widespread suffering of the labourers, and turned their minds in that direction for relief. And lastly, the Chartist proposal of a "Sacred Month," made so far back as 1839, appearing to the ignorant a safe way of intimidating and coercing the Government, gave to the outbreak its par-ticular character of a *holiday-insurrection*' (p. 555). For the 'Sacred Month' of August 1839, see Chase, *Chartism* (2007), 75–87 and Thompson, *The Chartists* (2013 edn.), 39–51.

'sliding,' as on inclined-planes: for sliding, see note to p. 39; inclined planes were used to raise and lower boats in canals that were without locks.

balance-scale whereon is written Thou art found Wanting: Dan. 5:27.

241 *Chelsea Hospitals*: the Royal Chelsea Hospital was founded by King Charles II in 1682 as a hostel for British military veterans.

242 *'How is each of us,' exclaims Jean Paul, 'so lonely, in the wide bosom of the All!'*: TC paraphrases Jean Paul Richter's *Siebenkäs* (1796–7); see 'Jean Paul Friedrich Richter Again', in *CME* ii. 157.

243 *gigs and flunkey 'respectabilities'*: see 'New South Wales', *Quarterly Review* 37 (Jan., 1828), recounting an exchange from the trial of John Thurtell in January 1824 for the murder of William Weare: 'The question was . . . "What sort of person was Mr. Weare? *Answer.* Mr. Weare was respectable. *Counsel.* What do you mean by respectability? *Witness.* He kept a gig"' (p. 15 and note; see also 'Jean Paul Friedrich Richter', *CME* ii. 130 and n.).

thistle by the wayside: see Matt. 13:4–8.

Ægir the Sea-demon: see *Heroes*, 17: 'Of the other Gods or Jötuns I will mention only for etymology's sake, that Sea-tempest is the Jötun *Ægir*, a very dangerous Jötun.'

on Firehorses and Windhorses ye career: creatures from Norse mythology (see *Heroes*, 16–17). TC may be referring indirectly to the introduction of fire-powered and wind-driven ships. On 31 March 1838, the SS *Great Western*, the first steam-powered transatlantic passenger vessel, sailed from Bristol to New York, achieving a top speed of roughly 8.5 knots (15.7 km per hour). *The Sun* (2 Apr. 1838) reported that 'no occurrence for a long time past has created so stirring an interest in the scientific world' (p. 3). *The Morning Advertiser* (16 Aug. 1839) announced the arrival in London from Aberdeen of the 'Scottish Maid, Watson', a 'fine new fast-sailing vessel' that achieved speeds of 16 knots or 30 km per hour when fully rigged and taking advantage of winds (p. 4). By 1842, the 'clipper schooner' had become the dominant type of vessel for long-distance jour-neys, particularly to China.

Thor red-bearded, with his blue sun-eyes, with his cheery heart and strong thunder-hammer: see *Heroes*, 17: 'The thunder was his wrath . . . wrathful he "blows in his red beard;" that is the rustling stormblast before the thunder begin.'

244 *The 'tendency to persevere'*: see TC, 'Diderot' (1833): 'Among the dualisms of man's wholly dualistic nature, this we might fancy was an observable one: that along with his unceasing tendency to change, there is a no less ineradicable tendency to persevere' (*EOL*, 267).

The civilised man lives not in wheeled houses: see TC, 'Diderot': 'Were man only here to change, let him, far from marrying, cease even to hedge in fields, and plough them; before the autumn season, he may have lost the whim of reaping them. Let him return to the nomadic state, and set his house on wheels; nay there too a certain restraint must curb his love of change, or his cattle will perish by incessant driving, without grazing in the intervals' (*EOL*, 267). See also TC's MS Notes, Forster Collection, fo. 49: 'The fool and the barbarian only is nomadic, sets his house on wheels; lies in the pastoral stage, or call it the fishing state.'

Month-long contracts do not answer well even with your house-servants: the Carlyles' own maid Helen Mitchell threatened to seek employment else-where in December 1842, claiming that she could obtain better wages. Writing to her cousin Jeannie Welsh on 16 March 1843, JWC admitted, 'Carlyle as well as myself is out of all patience with her, and for a long while back, I have only kept her because I *have* kept her, because I have a horror of changes' (*CL* xv. 233, xvi. 86).

Anti-Slavery Convention . . . long-eared Exeter-Hall: on 25 April 1839, *The Globe* reported that the inaugural meeting of the British and Foreign Anti-Slavery Society was held in Exeter Hall in the Strand on 18 April, and was chaired by Joseph Sturge to advocate 'the universal extinction of Slavery and the Slave-trade, and the protection of the rights and interests of the enfranchised population in the British possessions, and of all persons cap-tured as Slaves' (p. 1). In 1840 three separate anti-slavery conferences were held in London: the Society for the Extinction of the Slave Trade in Africa, in Exeter Hall, 1 June, addressed by Prince Albert; the Convention for the Extinction of Slavery and the Slave Trade throughout the World, in the Great Hall of the Freemasons' Tavern, 12–23 June; and the first annual meeting of the British and Foreign Anti-Slavery Society, Exeter Hall, 24 June, also addressed by Prince Albert.

black Quashee: from Ashanti *Kwasi*, 'a name commonly given to a child born on Sunday. Carribbean (chiefly derogatory). A generic name for: a black person, esp. one considered as credulous or insignificant' (*OED*, citing JWC). TC may have borrowed the name from his friend George Moir's Swiftian satire against abolitionism, *Fragments from the History of John Bull* (1835), which had been serialized in *Blackwood's Edinburgh Magazine* between December 1831 and January 1835. In chapter 6, 'Quashee', a slave, is persuaded by a fraudulent minister 'Obadiah' to demand his liberty from his benevolent master 'Christopher Bamboo, Sugar Baker and Distiller'. Apprenticed to 'John Bull' through the unscrupulous intervention of the agent 'Buckram', 'Quashee' is allowed to work 'only two days in the week' for Bamboo, while devoting the other five to Bull. He soon discovers that his 'freedom' is more oppressive than his previous enslavement, and cannot 'make out the difference between a slave and an apprentice' (*Blackwoods*, 34 [Dec. 1833] 897–8). There are numerous echoes of Moir's satire in TC's notorious 'Occasional Discourse on the Negro Question' (1849). For TC and Moir, see Charles Neaves, 'The Late George Moir', *Blackwood's Edinburgh Magazine* 109 (Jan. 1871), 109–17, to which TC contributed details (see *CL* xlvii. 134).

245 *'sixty-thousand valets in London itself who are yearly dismissed to the streets'*: TC's source is untraced. Critics of Peel's income tax of 1842 (see note to p. 35) claimed that it had forced wealthy families to reduce their domestic staff. *The Globe* (3 Dec. 1842) reported that at a meeting of the Merchant Company of Edinburgh on 2 December 1842, one of the members complained that 'Peel . . . thought to relieve those who had one hundred and fifty pounds a-year, while, in fact, he had placed it on the lower or working classes. The rich cut down their establishments; the middle-classes save it by economy; every trader feels the effect of this, and the poor man servant or maid servant is turned adrift—they are the real sufferers' (p. 3). In an article on 'Domestic Servants', the Christian missionary *Journal of Civilization* (25 Sept. 1841) stated that 'there are *always* ten thousand servants out of place in London only. This is a fearful number, and it may well be asked, where and how do these unemployed servants live?' (p. 327).

'Free Labourers' in Lancashire, Yorkshire, Buckinghamshire, and all other shires!: comparisons were frequently made in Parliament and the press between the condition of English 'white slaves' in the distressed industrial regions of northern England and African slaves. In the *First Report . . . Mines*, the Scottish civil engineer, surveyor, and abolitionist Robert Bald commented that 'when the nature of this horrible labour is taken into consideration, its extreme severity, its regular duration of from 12 to 14 hours daily . . . a picture is presented of deadly physical oppression and systematic slavery, of which I conscientiously believe no one acquainted with such facts would credit the existence in the British dominions' (p. 94). See also Engels, *Condition*, 91–2: 'The only difference as compared with the old, outspoken slavery is this, that the worker of today seems to be free because he is not sold once for all, but by piecemeal by the day, the week, the year, and because no one owner sells him to another, but he is forced to sell himself in this way instead, being the slave of no particular person, but of the whole property-holding class. For him the matter is unchanged at bottom, and if this semblance of liberty necessarily gives him some real freedom on the one hand, it entails on the other the disadvantage that no one guarantees him a subsistence, he is in danger of being repudiated at any moment by his master, the bourgeoisie, and left to die of starvation, if the bourgeoisie ceases to have an interest in his employment, his existence.'

These Yellow-coloured, for the present, absorb all my sympathies: on 3 July 1842, a group of female abolitionists from Massachusetts and Pennsylvania visited TC to win his support for their cause. On 13 June *The Sun* reported that on the previous day they had been denied delegate status at the Convention for the Extinction of Slavery and the Slave Trade throughout the World, which was being held at the the Freemasons' Hall: 'The grand objection that had been taken was, that, if admitted, the ladies would be placed upon a footing of equality with [the male delegates], and that that equality would be contrary to usage, custom, and principle' (p. 3). The group was led by Lucretia Mott, founder in 1833 of the Philadelphia Female Anti-Slavery Society. TC reported to his mother on 12 September 1840 that Mott and 'three others her bottle-holders; rigid-looking elderly Quakeresses' were 'terribly disappointed that I would not crusade with them in favour of the black slaves, as the one thing needful; I told them, as usual, that the *green* and yellow slaves, grown green with sheer hunger in my own neighbourhood were far more interesting to me! I added moreover that I myself had been a slave all the days of my life; and had a hard battle to fight, at all moments, to get a portion of my own just will made good' (*CL* xii. 253–4).

if I had a Twenty Millions, with Model-Farms and Niger Expeditions, it is to these that I would give it!: at the 1 June 1840 conference in Exeter Hall of the Society for the Extinction of the Slave Trade in Africa, the delegates approved a plan conceived by the philanthropist Sir Thomas Fowell Buxton, supported by Prince Albert and funded by the Government, to launch a naval expedition up the River Niger in order to establish a 'pattern farm'. As Buxton explained in *The African Slave Trade and Its Remedy* (1840), the aims of the mission were to spread commerce and Christianity, provide local chieftains with an alternative to the income derived from the slave trade, and 'use all the means that experience may point out, for a profitable and successful employment of British skill and capital in the African continent' (p. 521). *The Examiner* (7 June 1840) reported that at the conclusion of the meeting on 1 June, Peel thanked Prince Albert for his support, but cautioned that 'there will be some difficulties in the undertaking, and I am not sanguine as to its early success; but I confess that I have . . . confidence in the righteousness of this cause' (p. 361). Three iron steamers with crew, missionaries, and scientific specialists left England on 8 August 1841 and arrived on the coast of Africa, 5 September. But on 22 January 1842, *The Examiner* reported that the mission had been abandoned, and 'that all the commanders and most of the crews had died [of malaria]; and that all further attempts to explore the Niger had . . . been given up' (p. 58). Of the 145 European travellers, thirty-nine died of fever. The same paper (26 Nov. 1842) published an extract from a letter of 26 September detailing the chaos that the captain of the *Wilberforce* encountered when he sought to retrieve settlers who had remained on the farm: 'The "Model Farm" [was] a very perfect model of disorganization. The blacks, who had been left at it, having plenty of cowries (a species of India shell used as money) and goods, voted themselves to be independent country gentlemen, and managed to get hold of a lot of natives, whom they very coolly made slaves of, and whom they compelled to work on the farm, each gentleman being provided with a *cat*, or slave driver's whip, the better to enforce obedience.' Of the expedition itself, the writer concluded, 'A more mismanaged piece of business from beginning to end is not, I will venture to say, to be found recorded in history' (p. 761). In a widely published commentary, *The Morning Herald* (7 May 1842) questioned the government's priorities in funding Britain's campaign to abolish slavery in its empire: 'How strange that 20,000.000ℓ of money should have been heaped upon the fetters of negro slaves in the West Indies in order to break them; and that not one indignant tongue should yet have been heard within the walls of Parliament to denounce a legalised or at least permitted system of physical degradation, of moral ruin, and bodily torture to women, of barbarous captivity and toil to children, for which the bondage of Egyptian taskmasters, the tyranny of European "over-seers," and the humiliations of Moorish slavery have supplied no parallel, and can suggest no type!' (p. 4).

245 *Quashee is not dying of such despair as the yellow-coloured pale man's*: TC may be recalling Charles Sheppard's observation in *An Historical Account of the Island of St. Vincent* (1831), which was reviewed in *Fraser's Magazine* in November 1831, that 'there is no public or private establishment for the relief of the aged or sick poor *white* and *free* inhabitants: while the slaves on estates in their old age are enjoying the comforts of a decent maintenance from the support of their masters, the *infirm or sick white or free person* has no resource but individual support and charity; and this in a country where so few ties of relationship exist, must necessarily be precarious' (p. 210; quoted in 'England and her Colonies in the West', *Fraser's* 4 (Nov. 1831), 444).

The Haiti Duke of Marmalade, educated now for almost half a century, seems to have next to no sense in him: Jean-Pierre Richard, duc de la Marmelade, an African-born member of the Haitian aristocracy who served as a general and governor of Cap Henry in the court of King Henri I (Henri Christophe), who had died a year earlier. On 23 February 1821, Richard launched a *coup d'état* against the government in the district of l'Artibonite. He was arrested on the charge of treason two days later, and transported to Port-au-Prince, where he was sentenced to death by a military tribunal. He was executed by a firing squad on 3 March. In the indictment that he drew up against Richard and the conspirators, the new president Jean-Pierre Boyer described them as 'proud slaves of Christophe, who . . . regarded with a kind of horror the happy change that abolished their titles, their privileges, and put an end to their feudal despotism' (Wallez, *Précis historique* [1826], 336–7). TC refers more broadly to the condition of Haiti since its liberation from France in a series of revolutions between 1791 and 1803, which culminated in the abolition of slavery and the attainment of political independence. In an article entitled 'Mackenzie's Haiti and Bayley's Four Years in the West Indies' (Aug., 1830), a reviewer in *Fraser's Magazine* argued 'that industry, temperance, fore-thought, and every quality essential to the present comfort and future prospects of the negro,

forsake him in his freedom. And this, because . . . he has not passed
through those previous stages of moral improvement, without which, liberty has ever been and will ever be, instead of a boon, the heaviest curse
that can befall a people' (p. 62). More recently, *The Examiner* (16 July
1842) reported the devastating effects of an earthquake in Haiti on 7 May
and noted that 'the present Governor, Boyer, is said to be falling into dis-
repute, in consequence of adopting arbitrary measures. Some time ago,
finding the majority of the Legislature opposed to his Government, he
placed a guard before the House of Assembly, giving the officer a list of the
names of about 30 members who were to be forcibly excluded. Those
political differences have been interrupted by the earthquake, which . . .
has been all-absorbing; but it seems certain that no more Presidents will be
elected for life' (p. 460). For TC and the Duke of Marmalade, see Vanden
Bossche, 'Cedric the Saxon' (2004), 137–50.

Avec ton Être Suprême tu commences m'embêter!: see *FR* iii. 203 and n.
where TC attributes the quotation to Jacques Nicolas Billaud-Varenne.
The source may be François-Xavier Lanthenas, who asserts in *Écrits et
discours composés pour la Convention nationale* (1793, 1795), ii. 6 that the
'Jacobins n'ont parlé de l'être suprême que pour de nouveau nous embêter'
(Jacobins only spoke of the supreme being to bore us again).

246 *"I would not . . . exchange my workers for his with seven thousand pounds to
boot"*: see Chadwick, *Report . . . on the Training of Pauper Children* (1841),
quoting 'A.B'.: ' "I would not as a pecuniary speculation consent to take
less than 7000*l.* for my set of workmen, upwards of eight hundred, in
exchange for the uneducated and uncultivated workmen of another manufacturer opposite. We find the steadiness of the men induces steadiness of
work, and comparative certainty in the quantity and quality of the produce." Speaking of the recreations which he had provided for the work-
people, he said, "Thou mayest think it strange for one of my persuasion
(he is one of the Society of Friends,) "but it is true, I have paid for a big
drum and some horns, to give them mirth after their hours of labour" '
(p. 18). Chadwick sent TC a copy of his report on 19 December 1841. Two
days later, TC wrote to James Garth Marshall: 'Chadwick the Poor-Law
Atropos [the Fate who cuts the threads of life], who nevertheless has good
in him, sent me these fractions of Pamphlets about education; apparently
some Appendix to some of his Poor-Law Reports. If you have not seen
them they will interest you. A passage at p. 15 [p. 18, as correctly cited by
TC in his note] (in some Quaker's evidence) is to me like a beam of light:
if it be really *true* that a man would not change his own set of workmen
against another man's "for £7,000,"—then I say we have the beginning of
a real Industrial *Baron*hood, the sure prophecy of such!' (*CL* xiii. 325).

Stygian mud-vortexes and general Mother of Dead Dogs: see notes to p. 50
and p. 229.

247 *Sir Walter Scott: on the back of the Apennines, . . . the sight of bleak Scotch
firs, and snow-spotted heath and desolation, brings tears into his eyes*: see
Lockhart, *Memoirs of the Life of Sir Walter Scott, Bart* (1837–8): 'On the

17th [April 1832], a cold and dreary day, they passed the Apennines, and dined on the top of the mountains. The snows and pines recalled Scotland, and [Scott] expressed pleasure at the sight of them' (vii. 379). TC reviewed the first six volumes of Lockhart's biography in December 1837 (see *EOL*, 277–327). The Apennines are a mountain range in Italy.

247 *Vagrant Sam-Slicks*: Sam Slick, the wily clock pedlar in Thomas Chandler's Haliburton's popular series of sketches, *The Clockmaker; or the Sayings and Doings of Samuel Slick of Slickville* (1836–43).

Whether . . . your Master-Worker may not find it possible, and needful, to grant his Workers permanent interest in his enterprise and theirs?: there were several experiments in profit sharing in the early nineteenth century that were influenced by the ideas of Robert Owen. These included cooperative agricultural schemes established by John Scott Vandaleur and Edward Thomas Craig at Ralahine, Co. Clare in 1831, and Lord Wallscourt at Ardfry, Galway in 1833 (see Cunningham, 'Lord Wallscourt of Ardfry', 2005). In *On the Economy of Machinery and Manufactures* (1832), Charles Babbage theorized about 'a new system of manufacturing' in which 'every person employed should derive advantage from the success of the whole; and that the profits of each individual should advance, as the factory itself produced profit, without the necessity of making any changes in the wages' (1835 edn, 250–1). *LLC 1842*, 6 lists the 1835 4th edition of Babbage's *Economy*. TC described a meeting with Babbage in a letter to his brother, 4 February 1839: 'Did you ever see him? A mixture of craven terror and venomous-looking vehemence' (*CL* xi. 19). For profit sharing in the Victorian period, see Roberts, *Paternalism* (1979) and Church, 'Profit Sharing' (1971). Though opposed to Louis Blanc's democratic socialism in *Organisation du Travail* (see note to p. 176), TC was sympathetic to his contention that profit sharing would strengthen the mutual obligations between capitalists and workers: 'Would you say that capital is not, in the work of production, a less indispensable element than labour itself? From the fact that capital and labour are two equally necessary elements for the creation of wealth, must we conclude that from the point of view of equity, the capitalist and the worker are two equally meritorious agents?' (p. 120).

248 *'freedom of debate' on board a Seventy-four*: there had been widespread complaints about the severity of discipline in the Royal Navy. See Christopher Biden, *Naval Discipline* (1830), p. vi: 'I do not pretend to deny that the reins of discipline have been too rigorously held at times; but, I fearlessly deny the right of any class of seamen presuming or daring to dictate to their commanders and officers'. A seventy-four is 'A warship carrying seventy-four guns' (*OED*).

plebiscita: plural of *plebiscitum*, 'A direct vote of all the members of an electorate to decide a question of public importance; (also) an expression of popular opinion' (*OED*).

To reconcile Despotism with Freedom: in an editorial on 'the present condition of Chartism', *The Examiner* (17 Sept. 1842) referred to the movement as 'a despotism of the most absolute dye. It would allow no one to speak but itself. . . . It would listen to no promise of redress save its own promise to redress its own wrongs. It would allow no evil to be cured while the remedy for its favourite evil was remote; and every removable grievance was to be borne, because another was irremovable. Tyranny and folly could hardly go farther.' In a separate commentary on 'The Question Between Masters and Men', the paper argued, 'Society in England is top-heavy, and to avoid an upset sooner or later, it is necessary that the balance should be redressed more in favour of the lower part of the frame. The great object should be to give the labouring population an interest in the tranquility of the country, and if the classes who have power and influence kept this object steadily in view . . . great results . . . would be easily brought about' (p. 593).

Ignavia: 'Sluggishness, slowness, sloth' (*OED*, citing TC).

Out of the loud-piping whirlwind: Job 40:6–7.

249 *Guillotines, Meudon Tanneries, half-a-million men shot dead*: see note to p. 205. Roughly 600,000 French were killed during the military campaigns of 1792–1815.

Egyptian darkness: see note to p. 54.

Can he do nothing for Burns but make a Gauger of him: see note to p. 87.

250 *The Duke of Weimar . . . had to govern, judge, defend, everyway administer his Dukedom*: see Sarah Austin's translation of Friedrich von Müller's 'Memoir of the Grand-Duke Karl-August', in *Characteristics of Goethe* (1833), iii. 130: 'The Duke amended and simplified the administration of justice; took further precautions for the security of the poor and the unprotected; . . . public instruction was elevated and extended; normal schools for the formation of a regular supply of school-masters were founded; a free school of design instituted; art and industry on all sides encouraged'. Thanking Austin for sending *Characteristics* on 18 July 1833, TC wrote, 'We have all read them, with pleasure, with eagerness; for me, I could not skip even what I knew in German already, but must have it taste for me a second time in your fine clear-flowing English' (*CL* ix. 396).

maintains not soldiers only but Universities and Institutions: see Müller, in Austin, *Characteristics*, iii. 144: 'By a judicious change of the portion of the population bearing arms, the Duke made nine-tenths of the soldiery available for agriculture and mechanical employments.'

Wieland, Herder, Schiller, Goethe: Karl-August, duke of Weimar was a patron of poets, dramatists, philosophers, and intellectuals including Christoph Martin Wieland, prose writer, poet, and translator; Johann Gottfried von Herder, philosopher; Friedrich Schiller, poet and dramatist; and Johann Wolfgang von Goethe, poet, critic, dramatist, scientist, diplomat, and director.

Not as parasites . . . not as table-wits and poetic Katerfeltoes; but as noble Spiritual Men working under a noble Practical Man: Gustavus Katterfelto was an itinerant popular lecturer and quack. See Müller, in Austin, *Characteristics*, iii. 134–5: 'This was the most flourishing period of the university of Jena. Its preeminence was not produced by wealth, nor by any artificial excitements; it was the observant, encouraging eye of the prince which animated and enhanced those glorious efforts; which stimulated those noble aspirations. It was the mild and genial atmosphere of mental freedom and tolerance of opinion, which made every one feel so perfectly at ease in this narrow space; and as in the great garden of nature trees and flowers of the most differing kinds unfold in full luxuriance side by side, so did we here see the most various, nay repugnant, spirits distinguish themselves undisturbed, each in his own province, secure and free under the shield of their highminded Patron.'

250 *life-in-death of Poet Coleridge*: see 'The Rime of the Ancient Mariner' (1797), ll. 193–4.

Honour to the name of Ashley: Lord Ashley, who played a leading role in the Factory Acts of 1833, 1844, and 1847, the Mines Act of 1842, and in the movement for a national system of state-funded education for the working classes; see notes to pp. 233–4. TC echoes Taylor in *Notes of a Tour*, perhaps ironically: 'All honour be to Lord Ashley! If he succeeds with his Bill [the Mines Act of 1842; see note to pp. 233–4] he will put a check to the sacrifice of health, morals, and life, which has been going on to an enormous extent beneath the surface of the earth' (pp. 252–3). But earlier Taylor had ridiculed Ashley for refusing to visit factories where children were employed: '"He wondered how such a thing could be proposed to him!"—A greater wonder is that he did not discover himself to be virtually asserting that the best qualifications for legislating on any subject is utter ignorance of the entire matter' (p. 246).

the other valiant Abdiel: Abdiel was a seraph loyal to God (see Milton, *Paradise Lost*, v. 805, 896); 'the other' is possibly the Home Secretary Sir James Graham (see note to p. 234), who sponsored Ashley's education bill.

'*a quiet euthanasia spread over generations, instead of a swift torture-death concentred into years*': see *FR* ii. 173: 'Had [the Emigrant Nobles] understood their place, and what to do in it, this French Revolution, which went forth explosively in years and months, might have spread itself over generations; and not a torture-death, but a quiet euthanasia have been provided for many things.' TC may have been familiar with Edward Everett's pamphlet, *The Prospect of Reform in Europe* (1831), which had first been published as a review of Sismondi's *L'Avenir* (1830) in the July 1831 issue of the *North American Review*. In his conclusion, Everett borrowed a phrase from David Hume's essay, 'Whether the British Government Inclines More to an Absolute Monarchy or a Republic' (1741): 'Hume has paradoxically said, that the English monarchy would find its Euthanasia in despotism. . . . But if despotism is to be its Euthanasia, we believe republicanism will be its resurrection. If it must die an absolute Government, it will revive a popular one' (Everett, *Prospect of Reform*, 54). For TC and the *North American Review*, see *CL* viii. 278, 337.

251 "*Come out of her, my people; come out of her!*": Jer. 51:45.

Epicurus'-gods: see note to p. 145.

'Werter blowing out his distracted existence because Charlotte will not have the keeping thereof': Goethe's Sturm and Drang epistolary novel, *Die Leiden des jungen Werther* (*The Sorrows of Young Werther*) (1744), in which the protagonist shoots himself out of love for Charlotte, who has married an older rival, Albert.

Let the meanest crookbacked Thersites teach the supremest Agamemnon . . . a many-counselled Ulysses is set in motion . . . and weal the crooked back with bumps and thumps!: Thersites, a deformed officer, is beaten by Ulysses for taunting Agamemnon; see the *Iliad*, ii. 211–83.

Men do worship in that 'one temple of the world,' as Novalis calls it, the Presence of a Man!: see TC, 'Novalis', quoting from his *Fragments*: 'There is but one Temple in the World; and that is the Body of Man' (*CME* ii. 39).

252 *Independence, 'lord of the lion-heart and eagle-eye'*: Smollett, 'Ode to Independence' (1773), ll. 1–4.

'with bosom bare,' in a very distracted dishevelled manner: see Shelley, 'The Dæmon of the World' (1817), ll. 277–8: 'A multitudinous throng, around him knelt, | With bosoms bared, and bowed heads'.

an Arab Man, in cloak of his own clouting; with black beaming eyes, with flaming sovereign-heart direct from the centre of the Universe; and . . . terrible 'horseshoe vein' of swelling wrath in his brow: see *Heroes*: 'No emperor with his tiaras was obeyed as this man in a cloak of his own clouting.' TC's source is Antoine Isaac Silvestre de Sacy's entry on 'Mahomet', *Biographie universelle* xxvi (1820), 206: 'Il ne rougissait pas . . . de raccommoder lui-même ses vêtemens et ses chaussures' (He was not embarrassed . . . to mend his clothes and his shoes himself). For TC and Sacy, see Sorensen, in 'A New Source for Carlyle's Essay on Mahomet' (2007) and in Sorensen and Kinser (eds.), *On Heroes* (2013), 209–21. For clouting: 'To mend with a clout or patch; to patch (with cloth, metal, leather, etc.)' (*OED*, citing TC). For his eyes, see *Heroes*, 46: 'his fine sagacious honest face, brown florid expression, beaming black eyes; . . . that vein on the brow, which swelled-up black when he was in anger'. See also Sacy, 206: 'Il avait la tête grosse, le teint basané, mais animé par de vives couleurs, les trait réguliers, et fortement prononcés; ses yeux étaient grands, noirs et pleins de feu' (He had a large head, a swarthy complexion, but animated by vivid colours, regular features, and strongly pronounced; his eyes were large, black and full of fire). For the horseshoe vein, see Sacy, 206: 'Il avait un petit signe noir à la lèvre inférieure, et entre les sourcils une veine qui s'enflait lorsqu'il se mettait en colère' (He had a little black mark on his lower lip, and between his eyebrows a vein that swelled when he became angry). In *Heroes*, TC likens the prophet's facial appearance to Walter Scott's protagonist in *Redgauntlet* (1824), who has 'the visible mark of a horse-shoe in his forehead, deep dinted, as if it had been stamped there' (*Heroes*, 46; *Redgauntlet*, i. 232).

"Thickest-quilted Grand-Turk, tailor-made Brother of the Sun and Moon, No:—I withdraw not": see *Heroes*, 51; Sacy, *Biographie universelle*, xxvi:

'Abou Thaleb crut devoir avertir sérieusement son neveu du danger qu'il courait, et auquel il exposait ses amis. Le prophète, incapable de crainte, dit à son oncle, que quand même on placerait le soleil à sa droite, et la lune à sa gauche, il ne renoncerait pas à son entreprise. . . . Son oncle, le rappelant avec douceur, le laissa maître de suivre sa volonté, et promis de ne jamais l'abandonner. It tint parole, et quoiqu'il n'eût point embrassé le doctrine de son neveu, il continua d'être son plus zélé défenseur' (Abou Thaleb thought it was his duty to warn his nephew seriously of the dangers he was running, and to which he was exposing his friends. The prophet, incapable of fear, told his uncle that even if the sun were placed on his right and the moon on his left, he would not give up his enterprise. . . . His uncle, gently calling him back, let him follow his will, and promised never to abandon him. He kept his word, and though he never embraced the doctrine of his nephew, he continued to be his most zealous defender) (p. 190).

253 *'Shew the dullest clodpole,' says my invaluable German friend . . . '. . . he must down and worship'*: the words of Teufelsdröckh in *Sartor*, 213.

Cliffords, Fitzadelms: by Cliffords, TC may be referring to Geoffrey, bishop-elect of Lincoln and archbishop of York, whom Lyttelton in *Henry the Second* claims to be the 'natural son' (vi. 238) of Henry II and Rosamund Clifford, daughter of the Anglo-Norman nobleman Walter Clifford, landowner and soldier; in 1172–3, Geoffrey led a successful campaign in northern England against his rebellious legitimate half-brothers. William FitzAldelm, a Norman nobleman and king's marshal, was appointed deputy of Ireland by Henry II in 1176 (Lyttelton, *Henry the Second*, vi. 32–3, 60, and 70). See note p. 406.

254 *Doggeries*: 'In the usage of Carlyle, the rabble, mob. *Obsolete*' (*OED*, citing TC).

Delilah-world will not always shear of their strength and eyesight, and set to grind in darkness at its poor gin-wheel: Judg. 16.

254–5 *the case of Anaxarchus thou canst kill; but the self of Anaxarchus . . . in no wise whatever*: in *Lives of Eminent Philosophers*, Diogenes Laertius recounts the story of Nicocreon, tyrant of Cyprus, who reacted to a satirical remark directed against him by the Greek philosopher Anaxarchus by ordering that he be pounded to death with iron pestles. The philosopher responded, 'Pound, Nicrocreon, as hard as you like; it is but a pouch. Pound on; Anaxarchus' self long since is housed with Zeus' (ix. 59–60).

255 *Not a May-game is this man's life*: 'A performance or entertainment which traditionally forms part of the celebrations of May (latterly *spec.* those held on May Day), or of springtime generally' (*OED*).

a warfare with principalities and powers: Eph. 6:12.

the choral Muses and the rosy Hours: the Nine Muses are goddesses of science, literature, and the arts; the Horae are goddesses of the seasons.

Pandemonium . . . Deep . . . unto Deep: Hell; see *Paradise Lost*, i. 756–7; Rev. 42:7.

the benign Genius, were it by very death, shall guard him against this!: in Roman mythology, the genius is appointed guardian spirit to every newborn.

three-inch pattens: 'A kind of overshoe worn to raise an ordinary shoe above wet or muddy ground, consisting (from the 17th cent.) of a thick wooden sole mounted on an oval iron ring or similar base, and secured to the foot by a leather loop passing around the instep' (*OED*).

leather and prunella: see Pope, 'Essay on Man', iv. 203–4.

become not Caliban but a cramp: see *The Tempest*, v. i. 286 and I. ii. 325.

256 *'Man of Genius?'*: see note to p. 219.

rubrics and dalmatics: a rubric is 'A direction in a liturgical book as to how a church service should be conducted, traditionally written or printed in red ink. Also *figurative*' (*OED*); a dalmatic is 'An ecclesiastical vestment, with a slit on each side of the skirt, and wide sleeves, and marked with two stripes, worn in the Western Church by deacons and bishops on certain occasions' (*OED*).

'the inspired gift of God': see TC to Jane Baillie Welsh (JWC), 17 June 1822: 'It is truly gratifying to me to contemplate you advancing so rapidly in the path of mental culture. . . . There are a thousand peculiar obstacles—a thousand peculiar miseries that attend upon a life devoted to the task of observing & feeling, and recording its observations & feelings—but any ray of genius however feeble is the "inspired gift of God"; and woe to him or her that hides the talent in a napkin!' (*CL* ii. 132)

So says John Milton: see Milton, *The Reason of Church-Government* (1642): 'These abilities, wheresoever they be found, are the inspired gift of God rarely bestowed, but yet to some . . . in every nation; and are of power, beside the office of a pulpit, to inbreed and cherish in a great people the seeds of virtue and public civility, to allay the perturbations of mind, and set the affections in right tune' (*Prose Works* (1806), i. 120–1).

blow through scrannel-pipes: see note to p. 210.

Houri Paradises: see Sale (trans.), *The Koran*, i. 96: 'But all these glories will be eclipsed by the resplendent and ravishing girls of paradise, called, from their large black eyes, *Hûr al oyûn*, the enjoyment of whose company will be a principal felicity of the faithful.'

Lands of Cockaigne: '(The name of) an imaginary land in medieval mythology and folklore where there is plenty of good food and drink as well as an abundance of other pleasurable things, but none of the hardships of life' (*OED*).

Thou dost well to say with sick Saul, 'It is nought, such harping!': I Sam. 18:10–11.

copper shillings to be nailed on counters: proverbial, signifying worthlessness. See *Encyclopædia Britannica* 2 (1823), 241: 'SHILLING, an English coin, equal to twelve pence, or the twentieth part of a pound. . . . The Danes have copper shillings worth about one-fourth of a farthing sterling.'

257 *Doggeries*: see note to p. 254.

I revert to Friend Prudence the good Quaker's refusal of 'seven thousand pounds to boot': see note to p. 245.

258 *Christianity cannot get on without a minimum of Four thousand five hundred in its pocket*: see note to p. 169.

salt of the Earth once more: Matt. 5:13.

in Yankeeland . . . my Transcendental friends announce . . . that the Demiurgus Dollar is dethroned: 'Transcendental friends' is a reference to Ralph Waldo Emerson, an early admirer of TC, whom he met and befriended in 1833. Emerson had been a minister at the Unitarian Second Church in Boston from 1829 to 1832, when he resigned after a theological dispute. He was an influential figure in the transcendentalist movement, which included Amos Bronson Alcott, Margaret Fuller, George Ripley, and Henry David Thoreau. In a preface that TC wrote to the first English edition of Emerson's *Essays* (1841), he stressed the author's prophetic role in inspiring others to resist the dominant materialism of American life: 'That an educated man of good gifts and opportunities, after looking at the public arena . . . should retire for long years into rustic obscurity; and, amid the all-pervading jingle of dollars and loud chaffering of ambitions and promotions, should quietly . . . sit down to spend *his* life not in Mammon-worship, or the hunt for reputation, influence, place or any outward advantage whatsoever: this, when we get notice of it, is a thing really worth noting' (*EOL*, 336). In a letter to Emerson of 8 May 1841, TC exhorted him to persevere as a writer and educator: 'Persist, persist; you have much to say and to do. . . . You are a new era, my man, in your new huge country: God give you strength, and speaking and silent faculty, to do such a work as seems possible now for you!' (*CL* xiii. 129).

259 *Chronos is dethroned by Jove*: in Greek mythology, the overthrow of Kronos, leader of the Titans, by his son Zeus (in Roman mythology, Jove) the supreme God.

Odin by St. Olaf: Olaf III Haraldsson, king of Norway, 1067–93, who introduced Christianity to the country and banished the worship of Norse divinities. See TC, *The Early Kings of Norway*: 'Many were the jangles Olaf had with the refractory Heathen Things and Ironbeards of a new generation: . . . . but the Thing discerning, . . . that the King was stronger in men, seemed to say unanimously to itself, "We have lost, then; baptise us, we must burn our old gods and conform" ' (*Works*, xxx. 261).

Socinian Preachers quit their pulpits in Yankeeland . . . and retire into the fields to cultivate onion-beds, and live frugally on vegetables: Socinian is TC's term for Unitarians who rejected the doctrine of the Trinity and viewed Christ as mortal by nature, but divine by mission; their ideas were derived from the thought of the Italian theologians Laelius Socinus and his nephew, Faustus Socinus. As Emerson had done in 1832, Ripley resigned from his Unitarian pulpit in 1840 and the next year founded Brook Farm, a utopian community based on the socialist theories of François Marie Charles Fourier. Alcott visited TC in July 1842 and described his scheme to launch an experimental vegetarian community, Fruitlands, which he subsequently opened in 1845 and closed a year later. In a letter to Thomas Story Spedding on 31 July 1842, TC referred to Alcott as 'one of the strangest Potatoe Quixotes I ever fell in with. An elderly long thin man, with small irritable chin, with grey worn temples, mild sorrowful intelligent eyes, and the completest faith in man's salvation by vegetables. . . . The young Socinian Ministry, he tells me, are all quitting their pulpits in New England taking to the fields and farms' (*CL* xiv. 247).

Old godlike Calvinism declares that its old body is now fallen to tatters, and done; . . . a ghost and spirit as yet, but heralding new Spirit-worlds, and better Dynasties than the Dollar one: Calvinism is a system of Protestant theology espoused by John Calvin, with its central tenets of predestination, God's absolute sovereignty, and human sinfulness. Under the leadership of John Knox, Calvinism became the moral and spiritual foundation of the Church of Scotland. It was also imported into the New World by the *Mayflower* Pilgrims in 1620. See TC's MS Notes, Forster Collection, fo. 54r: 'Perhaps in the History of the World, surely in the History of Protestant Europe, no nation has risen into a nobler attitude of free devotedness to its Ideal than our brethren of Scotland in those days. It was a simultaneous burst of energy, heart conviction of this nation's, that Calvinistic Christianity is the true spiritual passport of God's Universe and man's life; to that end did the Maker form his Universe and send his creature Man to dwell there.'

without setting our own shoulder to the wheel: see Samuel Croxall (trans.), 'Hercules and the Carter', in *Aesop's Fables* (1722): 'Hercules, looking down from a cloud, bid him not lie there, like an idle rascal as he was, but get up and whip his horses stoutly, and clap his shoulder to the wheel' (1843 edn., 83).

260 *Ilion's or Latium's plains*: scenes of epic battles at Troy (Ilion) and Rome (Latium), in Homer's *Iliad* and Virgil's *Aeneid*.

French or Phrygians: the Phrygian Cap of Liberty, first worn by emancipated slaves in ancient Rome as a sign of their liberty, and later adopted by the French Revolutionaries; see *FR* ii. 36 and n.

Chaos come again: *Othello*, III. iii. 92.

A thing that vanishes at cock-crowing,—that already begins to scent the morning air!: *Hamlet*, I. i. 139, I. ii. 218, and I. v. 58.

Game-preserving Aristocracies, let them 'bush' never so effectively, cannot escape the Subtle Fowler: Prov. 6:5.

let light be, and there is instead a green flowery World: Gen. 1: 3–4, 11. See also TC, *Chartism*, in *CME* iv. 144.

261 *sheaves of Bath-garters, nor bushels of Georges*: TC conflates the Order of Bath (1725) and the Order of the Garter (1348), awards for distinguished military or civilian service. For the 'Georges', see note to p. 195.

'The Future hides in it . . . Daunting us,—onward': Goethe, 'Symbolum', in *Werke*, iii. 69–70.

ANNOTATED INDEX